Corwin on the
Constitution

Corwin on the Constitution

VOLUME ONE

The Foundations of American Constitutional and Political Thought, the Powers of Congress, and the President's Power of Removal

Edited with an Introduction and an Epilogue by RICHARD LOSS

 Cornell University Press, *Ithaca and London*

Copyright © 1981 by Cornell University Press

First published 1981 by Cornell University Press.
Published in the United Kingdom by Cornell University Press Ltd.,
Ely House, 37 Dover Street, London W1X 4HQ.
Second printing, 1982.

International Standard Book Number 0-8014-1381-8
Library of Congress Catalog Card Number 80-69823
Printed in the United States of America
Librarians: Library of Congress cataloging information appears
on the last page of the book.

The paper in this book is acid-free, and meets the guidelines for permanence and durability, of the Committee on Production Guidelines for Book Longevity of the Council on Library Resources.

For Ceil Noone,
Charles Diehl Brennan,
Casimir Bartnik, and
Thomas Jaconetty

The question is *whether* and *what* history has learned from the experiences that it went through during the Third Reich. To me, it seems, there lies a certain parallel between historical scholarship and jurisprudence: as the latter, through the experience with the unjust state, has turned back from legal positivism to the norms of natural law, so will history have to orient itself not toward legitimizing what exists, but toward drawing normative distinctions, ultimately those of justice and injustice, of good and evil— distinctions, as Ranke has said in words that set a limit to all historicism, which are inscribed in the breast of men. The scholarly and the humane conscience go here together, or should do so.—Hans Rothfels

In the constitutional mode we can retain our concern for nature and reason and justice and order in our social cosmos without binding ourselves to an impossible quest for final and definitive solutions. Truth about political life then ceases to be a goal that the human mind can attain once and for all. It becomes that measure of prudence and judgment and wisdom that men deploy in the ever-changing process of seeking to maintain living and effective contact between the realm of justice and reason and nature and order on the one hand and the sphere of men's daily doing in an actual political society on the other, a continual rethinking of our belief about the one and a continual reforming of our doings in the other.—J. H. Hexter

Contents

Preface

In 1955 Clinton Rossiter, Edward S. Corwin's last doctoral student, gathered and introduced the essays comprising Corwin's " 'Higher Law' Background of American Constitutional Law." The teaching of Rossiter and of Herbert J. Storing at the University of Chicago underlined the importance of Corwin's thought and sometimes stimulated graduate students to seek Corwin's essays in out-of-the-way publications. This quest was an irritant that lodged in my mind.

In 1974 I wondered how the Watergate crimes and impeachment proceedings against the president would challenge the received academic opinions, then firmly in the saddle, which were promoting the dominant presidency and relegating the Constitution to obscurity as a habit or "background" factor. In "Dissolving Concepts of the Presidency," 4 *Political Science Reviewer* 133–168 (Fall 1974), I attempted to show the superiority of Corwin's *President: Office and Powers* to Rossiter's *American Presidency,* Richard E. Neustadt's *Presidential Power,* and Arthur M. Schlesinger's *Imperial Presidency.* Believing that Corwin's general understanding of the presidency was demonstrably superior to the reigning academic opinions, whether judged by an effectiveness in upholding limited constitutional government or by the ability to predict the long-range consequences of a dysfunctional presidency, I edited and introduced *Presidential Power and the Constitution: Essays by Edward S. Corwin,* published in 1976 by Cornell University Press. Further study, "Edward S. Corwin: The Constitution of the Dominant Presidency," 7 *Presidential Studies Quarterly* 53–65 (Winter 1977), persuaded me that Corwin's critique of the founders' intention was poorly reasoned and that Corwin himself, during the 1930s, had been in large measure responsible for the intellectual justification and defense of the dominant presidency. I realized that the modern presidency had become resistant to limitation partly because of changes in opinion about the Constitution, changes that Corwin wrought and other writers took for granted. Nothing that I have seen since 1976, however, has altered my belief that the Corwin of *President: Office and Powers* and *Presidential Power and the Constitution* is preferable to the ruling academic opinions. But I began to realize that the problems of the presidency, including the avoidance of a constitutional settlement of presidential power through an impeachment trial in 1974, could be disclosed and clarified by attending first to the meaning of the Constitution as a whole. The essays in *Corwin on the Constitution* advance and deepen the inquiry, extending it from the presidency to the American regime, the Constitution, and the powers of the national government. These essays remind us that the presidency cannot be perfectly understood in isolation from the American political and constitutional thought that elaborates the reasons why an American national government exists in the first place and examines the kind of political and moral character the regime is intended to produce.

Edward S. Corwin wrote from the premise that law without American political thought has no roots, and political thought without law has no fruits. The epigraphs of this volume are by Hans Rothfels (''Die Geschichtswissenschaft in den dreissiger Jahren,'' in *Deutsches Geistesleben und Nationalsozialismus* 106 A. Flitner ed. 1965), the distinguished historian of the German resistance against Hitler, and by J. H. Hexter, an eminent American historian (*The Vision of Politics on the Eve of the Reformation* 230, 1973). Their arguments raise questions concerning the proper relationship of constitutional inquiry, history, and law to political theory. Rothfels holds that the experience of extreme injustice under Hitler has turned German jurisprudence back from legal positivism to natural law, and concludes that history and by implication all social science will have to escape the nihilism of historicism and resort to the distinctions of justice and injustice, good and evil. This is an endeavor that could scarcely be undertaken without political theory. Hexter, on the other hand, implicitly characterizes political theory as ''an impossible quest for final and definitive solutions.'' Once the impossibility of political theory is understood, ''truth about political life then ceases to be a goal that the human mind can attain once and for all.'' Constitutional inquiry, Rothfels implies, must be carried out *with* the aid of political theory, because of the more or less permanent threat exemplified by legal positivism and historicism. According to Hexter, constitutional inquiry must be carried out *without* political theory, though he does not tell us what to do about legal positivism and historicism except, perhaps, to act as if they posed no threat to constitutional and political inquiry, not to mention to ''justice and reason and nature and order.'' These epigraphs are intended to ask and to help the reader decide, after studying Corwin's essays, whether Corwin himself went far enough in the realm of political theory to safeguard constitutional inquiry and make it genuinely fruitful. However the reader may answer this question, at the very least what distinguishes Corwin's thought from mainstream political science and constitutional inquiry is that Corwin intransigently points us in the direction of fundamentals.

My intention has been to include the essays that best delineate Corwin's argument in political thought and constitutional law. The editorial priorities follow from the cohesive theme of the origin, purpose, and changing health of the American Constitution and the American regime that the Constitution reflects. The collection strives to include essays of seminal quality, to avoid duplication within the collection, to be comprehensive and yet judiciously selective. I have chosen the essays after consulting the Corwin Papers at Princeton University, reviewing his bibliography, and carefully examining his publications. The possibility cannot be ruled out that some essays, published in widely scattered journals during a scholarly career of over forty years, may have escaped me in spite of a persistent search. Sufficient essays have been found to identify Corwin's argument and to reveal the essays as a masterwork of American political science.

For further understanding and appreciation of Corwin's work, the reader may consult the *American Political Science Review,* volumes 1920 through 1924, for Corwin's summaries of constitutional law decisions of the United States Supreme Court.

I am reprinting in this volume of *Corwin on the Constitution* "The President's Removal Power under the Constitution" rather than the original formulation of the essay, "Tenure of Office and the Removal Power under the Constitution," 27 *Col. L. Rev.* 353 (1927), because the revision is Corwin's last thought on the subject. The essay "The Debt of American Constitutional Law to Natural Law Concepts" has been included both in Volume I and in *Presidential Power and the Constitution,* because of its importance among his publications. Entitled elsewhere "The Natural Law and Constitutional Law," it is one of the few essays that Corwin allowed to be published under different titles. "The 'Higher Law' Background of American Constitutional Law," included here, is also published as a paperback by Cornell University Press.

The present and forthcoming volumes arrange the essays as follows. Volume I deals with the foundations of American political and constitutional thought, the powers of Congress, and the President's power of removal. Volume II discusses the judiciary: the origins and exercise of judicial review, the development of judicial supremacy, and appraisals of judicial review. Volume III focuses on federalism, liberty against government, constitutional amendment, and international law. The plan of organization is largely topical, according to the article of the Constitution discussed, and chronological. The arrangement of *Corwin on the Constitution* reflects Corwin's judgment of the importance of his work and its various parts.

As for editorial policy, I have made some minor changes in the essays for consistency and ease of reading. There was considerable variation in style among the essays, and some of the essays had been carelessly edited. I have standardized capitalization and punctuation (according to his most frequent use), titles of books, names of cases, possessive forms, inclusive page numbers, the form of the footnotes, and quotations from the *Federalist*. I have used the *Federalist* (Jacob Cooke ed. 1961), a collation of the first edition corrected by Hamilton, the Hopkins edition of 1802, authorized by Hamilton, and the Gideon edition of 1819, Madison's version; but semicolons replace dashes in the middle of a sentence, and Constitution for the national Constitution is always capitalized. When, as in Chapter 1, for example, Corwin's original notes were unnumbered, they have been given numbers. Editorial comments of mine in the text have been placed in braces to distinguish them from Corwin's brackets.

I have attempted to supply information lacking in Corwin's citations, to modernize the most obvious old spellings, and to identify a few historical figures. It is surprising, however, how rarely Corwin alludes to contemporaries and how detachable these allusions are from his thesis and argument. With rare exceptions individuals for Corwin are scaffolding from which to launch the analysis of ideas. His analysis applies a sort of intellectual vanishing cream to the scaffolding, leaving the ideas bold and clear in the reader's mind. It would be unfortunate if the historical identifications seem to corroborate the contention that Corwin wrote tracts for the times (for Franklin D. Roosevelt, against Alfred Landon) and that the partisan battles of the 1930s exhaust the meaning and richness of his scholarship; there is an influential school of opinion that teaches this interpretation. Corwin, however, is essentially a historian of ideas whose jurisprudence and interpretations of the Constitution transcend the partisanship of his times.

Finally, in an Epilogue I discuss Corwin's understanding of Alexander Hamilton and the President's removal power, an important topic involving not only presidential prerogative, but the comparative excellence and rank of the *Federalist* and the Pacificus letters.

Corwin on the Constitution would have been impossible without the generosity of the Earhart Foundation, which supported research and manuscript preparation for these volumes, and the assistance of James Twiggs, former social science editor of Cornell University Press. I am particularly indebted to him for his unusually broad view of cooperation during the formative stages. Melvin Urofsky gave me some sound advice, and the late Herbert Storing was a never-failing source of encouragement, both when I was inside and, as now, outside the academic bower. The librarians at the University of Chicago Law School, Northwestern University Law School, and Boalt Hall of the University of California at Berkeley extended me rare privileges. Norval Morris, formerly dean of the University of Chicago Law School, went out of his way to grant me copying facilities of excellent quality. Kansas State University gave me assistance in various forms. I also acknowledge with deepest gratitude the generous assistance of Thomas Jaconetty, a member of the Illinois Bar, in completing this volume.

The precedent and guidance of *American Constitutional History: Essays by Edward S. Corwin* (1964; Peter Smith reprint), edited by Alpheus Mason and Gerald Garvey, were invaluable. Gerald Garvey has been kind in not objecting to my use of the title *Corwin on the Constitution,* which is the title of his Ph.D. dissertation, *Corwin on the Constitution: The Content and Context of Modern American Constitutional Theory* (Princeton University 1962). Last but not least, the editors and staffs of the law reviews represented in these pages deserve special thanks for their cooperation.

RICHARD LOSS

Evanston, Illinois

Introduction

EDWARD S. CORWIN was born in 1878 near Plymouth, Michigan, and studied under Andrew C. McLaughlin, the distinguished constitutional historian, before graduation from the University of Michigan in 1900.[1] After study with the historian John Bach McMaster, Corwin received his doctorate in history from the University of Pennsylvania in 1905.[2] He was soon invited by Woodrow Wilson, then president of Princeton University, to become one of the original preceptors there, where he continued to teach until 1946. A prolific author, Corwin wrote eighteen books and numerous essays that appeared in legal and professional journals, in addition to editing the 1953 annotated *Constitution*. In 1935 he was constitutional adviser to the Public Works Administration, in 1936 special assistant and in 1937 constitutional consultant to the attorney general. A biography of Corwin, which he reviewed prior to publication, declared that "in politics he is an independent."

Before his death in 1963 Corwin's writings and lectures established him as a, perhaps the, foremost twentieth-century authority on the Constitution. The Su-

---

1. T. M. Cooley, *The General Principles of Constitutional Law in the United States of America* (A. C. McLaughlin ed. 3d ed. 1898); A. C. McLaughlin, "James Wilson and the Constitution," 12 *Pol. Sci. Q.* 1–20 (1897); McLaughlin, "Social Compact and Constitutional Construction," 5 *Am. Hist. Rev.* 467 (1900); McLaughlin, "Democracy and the Constitution," 22 *Pro. Am. Antiquarian Soc.* N.S. 293 (1912); McLaughlin, *The Foundations of American Constitutionalism* (1932) (1961); McLaughlin, *A Constitutional History of the United States* (1935); Corwin, Review of McLaughlin, *A Constitutional History of the United States* (1935), in 41 *Am. Hist. Rev.* 348–51 (January 1936); on the relationship of Corwin's studies to McLaughlin, see R. Loss, "Edward S. Corwin: The Constitution of the Dominant Presidency," 7 *Presidential Studies Quarterly* 53, at 54 (Winter 1977); Letter from McLaughlin to Corwin, January 14(?), 1936, Box 2, Folder 14, McLaughlin Papers, Regenstein Library, University of Chicago.

2. McMaster, "The Political Depravity of the Fathers," in McMaster, *With the Fathers* 71–86 (1902); McMaster, *A History of the People of the United States* (1883–1927). On McMaster and Corwin, see Alexander Leitch, *A Princeton Companion* 118 (1978). I am indebted for this reference to Alpheus Mason.

preme Court and scholars and teachers of constitutional law have recognized the quality of his thought. He was among the ten legal writers most often cited over a thirty-two-year period by the Supreme Court: he was the only nonlawyer among these sages whose work was recognized for excellence by the nation's highest court.[3] *Selected Essays in Constitutional Law,* a five-volume monument of scholarship published by the Association of American Law Schools, included more of his essays than those of any other writer except Thomas Reed Powell. This judicial and scholarly recognition parallels Corwin's usefulness to undergraduate teachers. According to Martin Shapiro, "the work done by the famous commentators on constitutional law starting with Corwin" is "the basic stuff out of which we teach undergraduates about the Supreme Court."

Corwin is known as a philosopher of the Constitution. His work enables his readers to replace opinion about the Constitution with knowledge. As a commentator, he explains doctrines, makes interpretations, systematizes and gives a key to understanding judicial decisions, discovers their logical relationships and provides the courts with thorough commentary to help them render just decisions.[4] His essays help the reader to confront the debate over the expansion of the size and power of government, a debate that had "significant political consequences" in the "anti-Washingtonism" of the 1976 Carter and Reagan nomination campaigns.[5] Corwin's writings themselves have become the subject of controversy. In brief the question is whether he was an exception to the New Deal scholarship that viewed the Constitution as a frustration of majority rule and an enemy to be overcome, or whether in fact he founded the New Deal school of thought advocating a presidency unrestrained by the Supreme Court or Congress.[6] However this controversy may be resolved, his essays present the two traditions of American thought, liberty as opposed to government restriction, and the welfare or service state dominated by the executive, which are still today the source of many of our assumptions about the purpose of government.

Corwin's appraisal of New Deal concepts and practices of government is pertinent to today's debate over the excess of presidential power, as exerted by Nixon in the 1970s, for example. According to political critic Mee:

> the ruins of our Republic lie about us, like shards of some other ancient dead civilization. . . .
> Dare we admit that we did not at first notice? That it died when no one was looking, and we scarcely missed it for days or, it may even be, for years? We only

3. C. Newland, "Legal Periodicals and the Supreme Court," 3 *Midwest J. Pol. Sci.* 58, 65 (1959).
4. I have adapted this from R. Pound, *The Formative Era of American Law* 138–67 (1938).
5. M. Judd Harmon, "Introduction," *Essays on the Constitution of the United States* 3, at 9 (M. Judd Harmon ed. 1978).
6. Harmon, "Introduction," *Essays on the Constitution of the United States* 5; M. Shapiro, "The Constitution and Economic Rights," in Harmon, *Essays on the Constitution of the United States* 74; 176 nn.1,2.

first noticed it, reluctantly, wishing not to see, when Nixon buggered the works, and then buggered those who went after him, a Bulgar holding out against the hordes until at last, unimpeachable, he was told he must step down—not by Congress and not by the courts but by four-star General Haig in a pinch play with Bad Kissinger, and then—oh, God, where is our sense of shame?—pardoned by his handpicked successor for crimes he protested he did not commit. We said it proved the Republic worked, but we knew that Republics are not saved when their constitutional usages are forgotten or avoided and salvation depends upon the accidents of a tape-recording machine and the wits of a four-star general. Machiavelli could not do justice to this theme. Shakespeare's Richard II could not weep copiously enough. We watched it play itself out, with the nerves of dead men in a dead Republic.[7]

Whether the crisis has culminated in a "dead republic," politically and intellectually, or whether a recovery is possible, Corwin's essays can assist the diagnosis of our constitutional health and illuminate those aspects of the Constitution that are likely to be of increasing interest. Owing to his breadth as a humanistic political scientist, his essays meet some of the postbehavioral needs of political science. They deal not only with questions of constitutionality, but with the common good.

A final consideration is the substance of the essays themselves. Although he never wrote the masterwork he had planned on the Constitution, the essays, in collected form, reveal the essential Corwin.[8] It is certainly plausible to argue that the essay, rather than the treatise, was Corwin's natural form of expression and the one in which he did much of his best work. Or alternatively, the essays may well be the best introduction to his thought. Corwin's essays elude the definition of an essay as a "composition of moderate length . . . originally implying want of finish, . . . but now said of a composition . . . limited in range."[9] The range of some of the essays, such as "The 'Higher Law' Background of American Constitutional Law," is broad, indeed. Nor do the essays fit the pejorative definition of a composition that is usually much shorter and less systematic than a dissertation or thesis and that usually discusses the subject from a limited and often personal point of view.[10] Some of the essays, such as the "President's Removal Power under the Constitution," are in effect short books distinguished by their systematic and objective treatment of the subject. In the essays the reader can find the evidence and argument relied upon in certain of his treatises, such as the *President: Office and Powers* and *Liberty against Government*. The present volume, *Corwin on the Constitution*, differs from the valuable sampler edited by Alpheus Mason and Gerald Garvey, *American Constitutional History: Essays by*

7. C. Mee, *A Visit to Haldeman and Other States of Mind* 18-19 (1977).

8. A. Mason, G. Garvey, "Introduction," in Corwin, *American Constitutional History: Essays by Edward S. Corwin* X (A. Mason, G. Garvey eds. 1964) refers to the masterwork.

9. 3 *Oxford English Dictionary* 293 (1933).

10. *Webster's Third International Dictionary Unabridged* 777 (1965)

Edward S. Corwin (1964; Peter Smith reprint); its subject matter covers more than the topic of judicial review, and its essays and notes are reprinted completely, thus enabling readers to judge Corwin's evidence for themselves.

In 1955 Clinton Rossiter closed his appreciation of Corwin as follows: "Suspecting, like that prince of scholars, Otto von Gierke, that 'it is not probable that for some time to come anyone will tread exactly the same road that I have trod in long years of fatiguing toil,' he {Corwin} has seen to it that those who retrace his steps will find the way straight and secure."[11] I hope that this collection of Corwin's essays, which were hitherto scattered among various journals, will help government officials, scholars, and citizens to retrace Corwin's steps and perhaps to reopen certain constitutional questions that for too long have been considered closed. The publication of these essays, many of which, as Rossiter said of Corwin's books, "changed the minds of men in the seats of power in Washington as in the seats of learning around the country," is an invitation to a constitutional dialogue.[12] "American constitutional law—not just the law taught by professors, but the law debated by senators and proclaimed by judges —has never been quite the same since he first took his incisive pen in hand."[13] As Alexander Hamilton remarked, "the time may ere long arrive when the minds of men will be prepared to make an offer to *recover* the Constitution. . . ."[14] Perhaps that time is arriving.

Let us turn from *Corwin on the Constitution* as a whole to an overview of the essays in this volume. The fundamental problems in the essays on constitutional and political thought concern the Constitution, democracy, and natural and higher law. The essays ascend from opinion about the Constitution to constitutional theory between 1776 and 1787 to the idea of higher law. An essay on political science appraises the democratic dogma in light of certain conclusions of the social sciences. After stating the lessons of the Constitutional Convention of 1787, Corwin takes up in another essay the relationship of the Constitution and New Deal democracy. An essay on evolution shows how this idea replaced the idea of natural law in American constitutional and political thought. Two remaining essays deal with the contribution of natural law to American constitutional law and with the thought of founder James Madison. I should like now to discuss these essays in somewhat more detail. My purpose is partly descriptive, partly critical.

The essays begin in an Aristotelian manner, with opinion about the Constitution. In "The Worship of the Constitution" Corwin traces twentieth-century

11. C. Rossiter, "Prefatory Note," in Corwin, *The 'Higher Law' Background of American Constitutional Law* vii–viii (1955); Corwin's essay is reprinted in this volume.
12. C. Rossiter, "Biographical Note," in Corwin, *The 'Higher Law' Background of American Constitutional Law* xii.
13. *Id.* xi.
14. Italics in the original. Letter of Alexander Hamilton to Gouverneur Morris, Feb. 29, 1802, in 25 Alexander Hamilton, *The Papers of Alexander Hamilton* 545 (H. Syrett ed. 1977).

opinion about the Constitution to the ending of "constitutional worship," which refers in part to what Woodrow Wilson called an "undiscriminating and almost blind worship" of the Constitution's principles and to the Constitution's "unquestioned prerogative to receive universal homage." Constitutional worship also refers to the sentiment of Gladstone's praise that the Constitution was the "most wonderful work ever struck off at a given time by the brain and purpose of man." This praise of the Constitution and of the founders, said Corwin, is "amply vindicated," yet "it is altogether evident that the sentiment which it expresses is one today rarely encountered. The worship of the Constitution is at an end!" The reverence for the original Constitution found in an early judicial opinion today seems "quaint enough." Lincoln, the "archiconoclast," ended constitutional worship with the announcement that if it was necessary to violate the Constitution in order to save the Union, he would do so. Behind this assertion was "Lincoln's vision—others had it before him—of a nation greater than any Constitution." Lincoln's test of constitutionality was not the founders' intentions, but the "serviceability" of a measure to popular need during a crisis.

Corwin seems undisturbed by the passing of constitutional worship understood as the statesman's veneration and practice of the founders' "political science." The "most fundamental article of faith of the 'fathers'" was "their belief in the availability for their purposes of an existing 'political science.'"[15] This political science, some of the principles of which are summarized in *Federalist*, no. 9, shaped the work of the Constitutional Convention in 1787; in practice it included the principle of separation of powers and institutionalizing the idea of legal restraints on government. The Constitution after Lincoln "might still be the embodiment of sound political theory and of a venerable legal tradition, but these things alone would not save it. Henceforth it was the people's law." In sum: constitutional worship is a critical term referring to an attitude toward the Constitution's principles, the founders, and their political science. Constitutional worship contrasts with twentieth-century opinion about the Constitution, which emphasizes the serviceability of a measure to popular need as distinguished from its agreement with the founders' intention. The ending of constitutional worship dates primarily from a war President acting as the chief interpreter of the Constitution. The demise of constitutional worship, Corwin implies, made opinion about the Constitution both more democratic and more realistic than the founders' political science. In the next two essays to be discussed Corwin turns from opinion about the Constitution to its theoretical foundation.

"The Progress of Constitutional Theory between the Declaration of Independence and the Meeting of the Philadelphia Convention" argues that although the problems addressed by the Convention were suggested by the delegates' experi-

15. Corwin, "The Worship of the Constitution," 4 *Constitutional Review* 3, at 7 (January 1920); reprinted in this volume.

ence, the Convention's solutions to these problems "not infrequently owed far more to the theoretical prepossessions of its members than they did to tested institutions."[16] The "most persistent problem of the American constitutional system" was the "bias in favor of local autonomy" in giving state legislatures "many of the most important powers of government over the individual."[17] For it was state governments that violated the rights of property and contract, and the central government that had no essential powers to protect the individual. The solution came from four ideas current before the Constitutional Convention: legislative power was exceeded when it interfered with judicial power in the courts; the finality of judicial interpretation extended to the interpretation of standing law, partly on the basis of judicial knowledge of a "higher law" superior to ordinary law;[18] the Articles of Confederation were increasingly understood as such a higher law in relation to the acts of the state legislatures; and the problem of securing private rights and ensuring adequate powers for a national government were the same, because a stronger national government could subdue the state legislatures. The Constitutional Convention applied this last idea through the institution of judicial review. The essay concludes that the notions of the finality of judicial interpretation over standing law and the notion of a higher law "yielded the initial form of the doctrine of judicial review."[19]

In this essay Corwin identifies the "true doctrine of judicial review" on both logical and historical grounds: the Constitution is supreme; it is law enforceable by the courts; and the courts' interpretations of standing law are final in the cases before them.[20] Perhaps it is helpful to bear in mind that this essay defends an interpretation of the Constitution based on studying the ideas of the founders as opposed to their motives or economic interests.[21] This approach leads Corwin to take up the problem of legal obligation. The Constitution's claim to be considered law and to be obeyed may rest on either of two ideas. Law may be understood as "an unfolding of the divine order of things or as an expression of human will—as an act of knowledge (or revelation) or an act of power."[22] The distinction between knowledge and revelation on the one hand and power and human will on the other anticipates the discussion in "The 'Higher Law' Background of American Constitutional Law."

The " 'Higher Law' Background," one of Corwin's most celebrated essays, identifies two alternative explanations of the Constitution's supremacy. The first,

---

16. E. S. Corwin, "The Progress of Constitutional Theory between the Declaration of Independence and the Meeting of the Philadelphia Convention," 30 *Am. Hist. Rev.* 511 (1925); reprinted in this volume.

17. *Id.* 535.

18. *Id.* 523, 536.

19. *Id.* 536.

20. *Id.* 522.

21. Id. 511–12; *cf.* Corwin, Review of Beard, *An Economic Interpretation of the Constitution of the United States,* 5 *History Teachers Magazine* 65 (February 1914).

22. Corwin, 30 *Am. Hist. Rev.* 511, at 522 (1925).

which is briefly described, is the Constitution's source in popular will. The popular-will explanation is related to the "positive" idea of law as the particular commands of a human lawgiver, a "series of acts of the human will." The people are the highest source of such commands because they are the highest embodiment of human will.[23] The "positive" idea of jurisprudence "traces all rights to government and regards them simply as implements of public policy."[24] The second explanation derives the Constitution's supremacy and claim to be worshipped from a "higher law" superior to the will of human rulers. The term "higher law" serves as Corwin's general description of Aristotle's natural justice, Cicero's natural law, medieval natural law, and Lockean natural rights. More specifically, higher law may rest on the distinction of later medieval writers between "higher" and "lower" natural law, "of which only the first is unchangeable."[25] If so, the problem of higher law is whether there are "unchangeable" standards to guide human legislators.[26] The natural rights version of higher law, found in the Ninth Amendment (the enumeration of certain rights in this Constitution shall not prejudice other rights not so enumerated), holds that rights exist prior to government and constitutions, which must recognize them.

The essay's explicit subject is the origins, survival, and transformation of the higher law idea and the means by which it entered America and was applied in American government. The thesis appears to be, first, that the higher law idea gained in influence as it lost altitude and found institutional expression: "invested with statutory form and implemented by judicial review, higher law {in America} entered upon one of the great periods of its history."[27] The essay also calls into question the notion of higher law as an eternal, imperishable truth. Corwin's essay, then, bolsters the above-mentioned popular will and positive law explanation of the Constitution's supremacy.

Corwin's method in the " 'Higher Law' Background" essay is to extract the antecedents of American constitutional law and theory from such thinkers as

23. E. S. Corwin, "The 'Higher Law' Background of American Constitutional Law," 42 *Harv. L. Rev.* 149, at 151 (1928); reprinted in this volume.

24. E. S. Corwin, "The 'Higher Law' Background of American Constitutional Law," 42 *Harv. L. Rev.* 365, at 389 (1929); reprinted in this volume.

25. Corwin, 42 *Harv. L. Rev.* 164, n. 54 (1928); see also at 154.

26. Corwin does not identify an American reference to the term higher law. See William H. Seward, "The Higher Law," Speech of March 11, 1850, in *Famous Speeches by Eminent American Statesmen* (F. Hicks ed. 1929). This speech urges the admission of California to the Union as a free or nonslave state. "But there is a higher law than the Constitution, which regulates our authority over the domain, and devotes it to the same noble purposes." At 28. Seward mentions the "Creator of the Universe"; "when we are legislating for states, especially when we are founding states, all these laws must be brought to the standard of the laws of God, and must be tried by that standard, and must stand or fall by it." At 18. Another reference to higher law is in Lord Acton, "The History of Freedom in Antiquity" (1877) in Acton, *Essays on Freedom and Power* 33 (G. Himmelfarb ed. 1948): "The example of the Hebrew nation laid down the parallel lines on which all freedom has been won—the doctrine of national tradition and the doctrine of the higher law...." See also W. Lippmann, "Journalism and the Higher Law," in Lippmann, *Liberty and the News* 3 (1920).

27. Corwin, 42 *Harv. L. Rev.* 365, at 409 (1929).

Aristotle, Cicero, Coke, Locke, and Blackstone. The essay discovers in Aristotle's natural justice and its identification of the rational with the general the "foundation of the American interpretation of the doctrine of the separation of powers and so of the entire American system of constitutional law."[28] The reference is to Aristotle's distinction between the passion of the ruler and the reason and generality of the law. Aristotle's natural justice is a set of standards for legislators. Both Plato and Aristotle understood the law as an "ideal code, the work of a sole legislator of almost superhuman wisdom.... In comparison should be recalled the virtues attributed to the framers of the Constitution of the United States, and one source of its worship."[29] But "Plato's and Aristotle's belief that human felicity was to be achieved mainly by political means had proved illusory."[30] Cicero, who is more important for Corwin than Plato and Aristotle, transformed natural law from an ethical idea into a legal and political one, and his "distinctive contribution" was to show that the obligation of civil law depended on its agreement with human nature. The essay refers to Cicero's contribution that there is "in the permanent elements of human nature itself a durable justice which transcends expediency, and the positive law must embody this if it is to claim the allegiance of human conscience."[31] Cicero also "foreshadowed . . . with greater or less distinctness" other aspects of the natural law doctrine entering into American constitutional theory, such as the ideas of popular sovereignty, a social contract and a contract between the rulers and the ruled.[32] Cicero's idea of equality prepared for the "translation of *natural law* into *natural rights.*"[33]

The "distinctive contribution of the Middle Ages to modern political science" was "the notion of all authority as intrinsically limited."[34] American constitutional theory received a "naive" theory of natural law as a "direct inheritance" from the Middle Ages.[35] Corwin accepts Holmes' criticism of a "brooding omnipresence in the sky" and remarks upon the "supposed precepts of a higher law" in medieval times.[36] The weakness of medieval natural law was that it "checked and delimited authority from without."[37] Corwin here attacks what he later calls "the characteristic medieval idea of all authority as deriving from the law and as, therefore, limited by it."[38] He praises the "classical conception of natural law," the purpose of which he says was to "account for a prevalent

28. Corwin, 42 *Harv. L. Rev.* 149, at 156 (1928).
29. *Id.* 155–56 n.16.
30. *Id.* 156–57.
31. *Id.* 158.
32. *Id.* 162.
33. *Id.* 162 n.44.
34. *Id.* 165.
35. *Id.* 168–69.
36. *Id.* 168, 166.
37. *Id.* 168.
38. *Id.* 172–73.

justice'' rather than to correct a prevalent injustice.[39] Classical natural law enlightened rather than circumscribed authority and "conferred its chief benefits by entering into the more deliberate acts of human authority.'[40] Corwin's criticism of the "naive" theory of natural law influencing American constitutional theory thus explicitly opposes the medieval idea of legal limitation on authority. He at least raises doubts concerning the medieval notion of all authority as intrinsically limited. The continental idea of higher law, he concludes, was in the Middle Ages "relatively vague and ineffective.'[41]

The "outstanding characteristic of English higher law,'' on the other hand, was that "before it was higher law it was positive law in the strictest sense of the term.'[42] This means that, in addition to having definite content, English higher law was enforced when the courts settled private controversies. Corwin finds in Coke's dictum in Dr. Bonham's Case, that the common law will control acts of Parliament and sometimes judge them to be invalid, the most important single source of the American doctrine of judicial review.[43] Coke contributed procedure and institutions, but "the conveyance of natural law ideas into American constitutional theory was the work pre-eminently—though by no means exclusively''—of Locke's *Second Treatise*.[44] Coke and Locke relied upon legislative supremacy, limited by annual elections, to maintain the higher law. Locke taught legislative supremacy within the law. Corwin finds the "dimensions'' which Locke assigns to executive prerogative "not a little astonishing'' and a means of "extrication from the trammels of a too rigid constitutionalism through a broad view of executive power.'[45] Here Corwin commends Locke for that aspect of his doctrine which has the least to do with the limitation of human authority in the name of higher law. "After the Bible, Locke was the principal authority relied on by the preachers'' in America.[46] Locke's influential ideas included those of natural rights, the social compact, a government limited by law, and the right to resist illegal measures.[47]

Blackstone's idea of legislative supremacy was an "essential contradiction'' of earlier elements of the higher law theory.[48] Legislative supremacy was checked in America by the identification of the written American Constitution with higher law and the implemention of the Constitution by judicial review. In short the higher law and secular positive law became the same. The Constitution was now understood in a new light as a "statute emanating from the sovereign

39. *Id.* 168.
40. *Id.* 168.
41. *Id.* 169.
42. *Id.* 169–70.
43. Corwin, 42 *Harv. L. Rev.* 365, at 379 (1929).
44. *Id.* 383.
45. *Id.* 393.
46. *Id.* 396.
47. *Id.* 396.
48. *Id.* 407.

people'' and was esteemed more because of its origin than the excellence of its principles. As Coke observed of Littleton's transformation of the Magna Carta, Corwin's essay transforms the American Constitution from a fundamental charter into a statute. The essay's conclusion contrasts with the alternative explanation of the Constitution's supremacy mentioned at the outset, the idea of higher law as distinct from positive law.

The '' 'Higher Law' Background,'' as Clinton Rossiter explains, has been ''one of the most universally admired and heavily used essays in constitutional law and American political thought.''[49] In spite of Corwin's following and the wide approval given to his essay it is necessary to examine more closely certain arguments that make the essay a somewhat confusing combination of a defense and a criticism of higher law.[50] The essay concludes that ''the arguments of the analytical school against higher law notions must be conceded to this extent: it is better to confine the term 'law' to rules enforced by the state. But that fact does not prove that the term should be applied to all such rules. In urging that it should be, the analytical thinkers endeavor to steal something—they try to transfer to unworthy rules supported by the state the prestige attaching to the word 'law' conceived of as the embodiment of justice.''[51] Corwin's rebuttal to the analytical school fails to establish the superiority of the idea of law, conceived of as the embodiment of justice, to the idea of law conceived of as rules enforced by the state. Corwin is also silent concerning the standard of ''unworthy'' rules. Hence, the essay's most explicit defense of higher law is inconclusive and lacking in evidence. In a later writing, moreover, he complained of ''that lack of clear distinction between the ethical and the strictly legal which a prevalence of 'higher law' concepts usually betokens.''[52] Thus Corwin adopts in 1934 the separation of the strictly legal from considerations of ethics or justice, a position he opposed in 1928. As we have seen, however, he failed to support his 1928 objection against the separation of what is legal from what is just. The '' 'Higher Law' Background'' neglects or avoids an opportunity to demonstrate or uphold Cicero's notion of the ''constancy of the distinctive attributes of human nature, those which supply the foundation of natural law.''[53] This omission is a serious one in light of the crucial importance of the idea of human nature for the higher law position.

Corwin's distance from the higher law position may also be judged by his acceptance of the idea of the dependence of thought on its historical milieu. He interprets Locke's *Second Treatise,* for example, ''as an apology for the Glori-

---

49. C. Rossiter, ''Prefatory Note,'' in Corwin, *The 'Higher Law' Background of American Constitutional Law* vi (1955).

50. For discussion along other lines, see C. B. Swisher, Review, 5 *J. Public Law* 227-31 (1956); C. M. Whelan, Review, 54 *Mich. L. Rev.* 726-30 (1955-56).

51. Corwin, 42 *Harv. L. Rev.* 365, at 409 (1929).

52. Corwin, *The Twilight of the Supreme Court* 56 (1934).

53. Corwin, 42 *Harv. L. Rev.* 149, at 162 (1928).

ous Revolution.'"[54] Higher law thinkers, however, understood contemplation as an autonomous activity and presented their argument as a timelessly true account. Corwin accepts the "commonplace that every age has its own peculiar categories of thought. . . . Nowadays intellectual discourse is apt to be cast in the mould of the evolutionary hypothesis. In the seventeenth and eighteenth centuries the doctrine of natural law, with its diverse corollaries, furnished the basic postulate of theoretical speculation.'"[55] This, clearly, is a denial of the autonomy of contemplation. Corwin holds that in each age contemplation is carried out with certain basic categories of thought. These must be adopted by those who would be understood by their age and then adapted to their purpose. But the adaptation of, say, the category of evolution can never transcend it and return to higher law. Nor would such a return be desirable, since Corwin understands the idea of evolution in the sense of progress. By denying the autonomy of contemplation, Corwin denies the possibility of timelessly true ideas, and therefore he attempts to understand higher law from an alien assumption. If human thought is inevitably contaminated by its genesis, time, place, and circumstances, then the idea of higher law is merely a temporary hypothesis, one available prejudice among several.

An alternative to Corwin's thesis of the dependence of ideas on their historical milieu is Ernst Troeltsch's conclusion that "not the 'how?' of their genesis but the 'that' of their objectively significant contents and of their logical connections is here decisive. This applies to all domains concerned with standards, and therefore to the moral domain also.'"[56] Corwin's submergence of higher law into the written Constitution and the institution of judicial review is vulnerable to Leo Strauss' criticism that "the appeal to a higher law, if that law is understood in terms of 'our' tradition as distinguished from 'nature,' is historicist in character, if not in intention.'"[57] At one point, though briefly, Corwin recognizes the distinction between natural law and national tradition. That is, he distinguished natural law from the institution and tradition of judicial review. He refers to Cicero's "assertion that natural law requires no interpreter other than the individual himself, a notion which is still sometimes reflected in the contention of courts and commentators that unconstitutional statutes are unconstitutional *per se,* and not because of any authority attaching to the court that so pronounces

54. Corwin, 42 *Harv. L. Rev.* 365, at 383 (1929).

55. *Id.* 380; for a later example: "Antirationalism has won out in the nineteenth and twentieth centuries for the same reason that rationalism trumphed in the two preceding ones, i.e., because of the sustenance it has drawn from the intellectual atmosphere of the period." Corwin, "The Democratic Dogma and the Future of Political Science," 23 *Am. Pol. Sci. Rev.* 569, at 579 (1929); reprinted in this volume.

56. E. Troeltsch, *Christian Thought: Its History and Application* 46 (1923). This is a translation of the more aptly titled *Der Historismus und seine Überwindung* (1924; 1966).

57. L. Strauss, "Preface to the 7th Impression," *Natural Right and History* vii (1971) (1953); for a definition of the position Corwin occupies in the " 'Higher Law' Background" essay, see P. Kecskemeti, "Introduction," in K. Mannheim, *Essays on the Sociology of Knowledge* 6 (1952).

them.''[58] In sum: Corwin's explicit defense of higher law against the criticisms of the analytical school is unsuccessful. His criticism of higher law flows from his acceptance of the positive idea of law, popular sovereignty, and the thesis that thought is historically dependent. A return to higher law, understood in contrast to positive law, is for Corwin neither possible nor desirable.[59]

In his 1948 work *Liberty against Government* Corwin reconsidered the problem of higher law, specifically the idea of a "higher law of liberty."[60] This work combines the interest of the "'Higher Law' Background" essay in political thought and judicial review with a criticism of certain ideas and Supreme Court decisions. *Liberty against Government* does not explicitly retract the criticisms of higher law that Corwin made in the "'Higher Law' Background," but instead concludes that "it is easy to imagine in the light shed by current ideologies that the demands upon the legislative power, national and state, might so multiply in behalf of 'the common man,' whose century this is said to be, that the notion of liberty against government and its implement, judicial review, would be gradually but inexorably crowded to the wall.''[61] If the "energies of the mass of men tend to a common level of achievement and of hoped-for security," "perhaps, indeed, that is what is meant when it is said that this is 'the century of the common man.' ''[62] "The great question is, can the 'common man,' unaided by the uncommon man, keep civilization going—will he wish to make the effort?'' After mentioning the possibility that the uncommon man will act less selfishly and more for the sake of "community advantage," Corwin concludes that increasing evidence supports Tocqueville's "prophetic vision" that nations can no longer prevent the equalization of conditions, but can only choose whether the principle of equality will lead to liberty or servitude. Just as the "'Higher Law' Background" essay showed the decline of higher law understood as justice and excellence, *Liberty against Government* concludes that the decline of the "higher law of liberty" is "nearly complete.''[63] *Liberty against Government* provokes the same question as the essay on "higher law": if higher law ideas are rejected, what is the ethical basis, if any, of political science and political action?

This question is addressed in the essay entitled "The Democratic Dogma and the Future of Political Science." In this essay, Corwin's central statement on the purpose of political science, he defines the democratic dogma as the belief that

58. Corwin, 42 *Harv. L. Rev.* 149, at 161 (1928).

59. In a later writing Corwin vigorously criticized the positive conception of law and its separation of law and morals. Corwin, Review, 37 *Cornell L. Q.* 345 (Winter 1952). I am not aware of his criticism of the thesis that thought is dependent on its historical milieu. For an alternative to Corwin's analysis, see L. Strauss, "The Three Waves of Modernity," in Strauss, *Political Philosophy: Six Essays* 81–98 (H. Gildin ed. 1975). This address was delivered as the Messenger Lecture at Cornell University.

60. Corwin, *Liberty against Government* 170 (1948).

61. *Id.* 182.

62. *Id.* 182–83.

63. *Id.* 1.

the people should rule because men act on reason. Modern normative political science springs from such Enlightenment ideas. The modern criticism of the democratic dogma has pointed to the "growing indifference of the voter" and the challenge to the assumption that the voter will act rationally. Behavioristic psychology has tended to confirm the "thesis of the essential irrationality of popular political thought and action."[64] But the essay denies that political science should aspire to be a natural science. Nor should behavioristic psychology be the pattern for making political science into a natural science. Corwin in particular criticizes the conception of social science represented by Watson's behaviorism:

> Human beings {said Watson} do not want to class themselves with other animals. They are willing to admit that they are animals but "something else in addition." It is this "something else" that causes the trouble. In this "something else" is bound up everything that is classed as religion, the life hereafter, morals, love of children, parents, country and the like. The raw fact that you, as a psychologist, if you are to remain scientific, must describe the behavior of man in no other terms than those you would use in describing the behavior of the ox you slaughter, drove and still drives many timid souls away from behaviorism.[65]

After attacking the "stifling soul cloud," that is, the idea of the soul, Watson argues that the "interest of the behaviorist in man's doings is more than the interest of the spectator—he wants to control man's reactions as physical scientists want to control and manipulate other natural phenomena."[66] Corwin finds that the "new political science" has made only modest gains in understanding group or individual attitudes with political implications. The primary lesson of political behaviorism appears to be the "indefinite educability, and even re-educability, of the masses."[67] Corwin asks somewhat facetiously, "Why should the political scientist spend his time measuring stereotypes planted in the public mind by other people when he could be planting some of his own?"[68]

The essay approves of the use of the scientific method within the commitment of political science to do "more expertly and more precisely what it has always done: {provide} criticism and education regarding the true ends of the state and how best they may be achieved." This conclusion implies a large role for political theory and for other branches of political science capable of being enriched by the wisdom and insight of political theory. Political science must retain its Aristotelian quality as a normative, telic science. Its goal is to "create consent." The ethical basis of this political science is perhaps a revision of the democratic dogma in which popular education will make the people somewhat more likely to act rationally. The "realistic" criticism of democracy in this essay, which seems to rest on Lippmann's *Public Opinion* (1922), should be

64. Corwin, "The Democratic Dogma," 23 *Am. Pol. Sci. Rev.* 569, at 586.
65. J. Watson, "Introduction," *Behaviorism* v (rev. ed. 1966).
66. *Id.* at 3, 11.
67. Corwin, "The Democratic Dogma," 23 *Am. Pol. Sci. Rev.* 569, at 589.
68. *Id.* 590.

compared to the account in "The Constitution as Instrument and as Symbol."
Corwin rejects the definition of political science as either a field of "formal
description and legalistic philosophy" or a natural science.[69] The "Democratic
Dogma" does not explicitly answer the question of whether behavioristic psychology, in its criticism of nineteenth-century ideas of voter rationality, validates
the thesis of Aristotle, "the father of political science," on the inequality of men.
The essay leaves open the question of whether Aristotle's doctrine is preferable
to the Enlightenment basis of modern normative political science.

"Some Lessons from the Constitution of 1787," a lesser known example of
popular education, was delivered as a lecture at Yenching University. The essay
takes off from the observation that "a contemporary writer of some critical and
philosophical acumen finds that the fundamental religion of today is *"time
worship"*—either time is worshipped as a force making inevitably for progress,
or with equal ineluctability, for decay."[70] The "contemporary writer" is Wyndham Lewis, whose *Time and Western Man* (1927) set out to contradict and if
possible to defeat the time cult, that is, the opinion that "asks us to see everything *sub specie temporis.*"[71] Corwin continues that to the practitioners of time
worship, whether in its optimistic or pessimistic phase, it may be useless to
praise permanence, especially the permanent direction of affairs that results from
establishing a Constitution. The purpose of "Some Lessons from the Constitution of 1787" is to explain how the permanence of the American Constitution
results from its adaptability and to offer some advice to potential drafters of a
Chinese constitution. What, then, does Corwin find in the American Constitution
when it is seen in the "cold light of eternity?"

The American founders pursued a "limited remedial goal" by analyzing the
existing institutions in light of the needs of serviceable government and "more or
less speculative considerations." The Constitution established some "original
constructions" of government, the presidency, Senate, judicial review, and
"above all" the federal system. The addition of the national government to state
governments, however, is an example of the continuity between the Articles of
Confederation and the Constitution. The new system "did not suddenly foist an
impossible burden upon the political immaturity and inexperience of the American people." Corwin in effect warns his Chinese audience that the outstanding
lesson from the Constitution of 1787 is that the makers of a constitution must
accommodate what is desirable to the character of the governed. Democracy, he
adds, is possible only on the basis of widespread prosperity. The Chinese,
moreover, would have to modify the antipolitical tendency of their family institu-

---

69. Id. 586; see Corwin, Review, H. Lasswell, *World Politics and Personal Insecurity,* 181
Annals 188–89 (Sept. 1935).

70. "Some Lessons from the Constitution of 1787," in Corwin, *The Democratic Dogma and the
Future of Political Science and Other Essays* 67 (1930); reprinted in this volume.

71. Lewis, *Time and Western Man* xv (1927): Lewis is also the author of *Hitler* (1931) and *The
Hitler Cult* (1939).

tions. Much would depend on the presence of political genius in the founders of a Chinese constitution. The essay attributes the endurance of the American Constitution to its adaptability, reticence, and brevity, to the founders' "pragmatism" and self-restraint, and to the Constitution's support by political democracy and by property interests. The implication is that it will be difficult at best for other nations to equal the achievement of the American Constitution.

"The Constitution as Instrument and as Symbol," one of Corwin's better known essays, discusses the proper relationship of the Constitution and judicial review to New Deal democracy. The essay distinguishes the idea of the Constitution as a symbol protecting private interests against governmental power, from the idea of the Constitution as an "instrument of popular power... for the achievement of progress." Corwin's reference to the Ninth Amendment underlines the kinship between constitutional symbolism and the higher law theory of the Constitution.[72] Corwin prefers the instrumental interpretation which he also attributes to the founders. He criticizes the spokesmen for constitutional symbolism, such as Governor Landon and the American Liberty League, and the Supreme Court's implementation of constitutional symbolism, particularly in restricting congressional power in taxation and the regulation of interstate commerce.[73] The fundamental purpose of the Constitution was not, Corwin implies, to protect certain minority interests from popular majorities. In short, the Supreme Court should uphold the exercise of the New Deal's national legislative power over "'big business' and its methods." The essay calls for an adjustment of our constitutional symbolism to the instrumental idea of a people's government and a unified nation, that is, to majority rule led by a dominant President.

Corwin finds that constitutional limitations, judicially implemented, are compatible with popular government if the Supreme Court expands its ideas of legitimate governmental power to include, in effect, the power to regulate the economy. If the Court remolds its thought, Corwin implies, then it will decline to limit national legislative power in such an area. "'Most people have to take orders from some source or other, and ... therefore the problem of human liberty is not to be completely solved by the purely negative device of setting acts of Congress aside as contrary to the Constitution.'"[74] This essay is a frank statement of the sort of constitutional limitations that follow from the ideas of progress, an instrumental Constitution, majority rule, and the dominant presidency.[75] The essay points to the question of how the enlargement of national power is justified according to American political thought.

In one of his most provocative essays, "The Impact of the Idea of Evolution

---

72. E. S. Corwin, "The Constitution as Instrument and as Symbol," 30 *Am. Pol. Sci. Rev.* 1071, at 1072 (1936), reprinted in this volume; Corwin, 42 *Harv. L. Rev.* 149, at 152-53 (1928).
73. Corwin, 30 *Am. Pol. Sci. Rev.* 1071, at 1073, 1082 (1936).
74. *Id.* 1085.
75. See the *Twilight of the Supreme Court* xxvii, 140, 147, and R. Loss, note 1 above, for Corwin's interpretation of the dominant presidency.

on the American Political and Constitutional Tradition," Corwin measures the impact of evolutionary ideas, or the idea of "progress," on the "central" idea of classical American political thought: that man's reason enables him to discover "a natural law of final moral and political values."[76] Evolutionary ideas challenged natural law, the "cornerstone" of classical American political thought, and the related "original passive {that is, limited} conception of governmental function."[77] The Spencerian idea of evolution confirmed the American tradition of liberty against government by emphasizing competition among individuals. Later the Darwinian idea of evolution lent support to activist, reformist government by replacing competition among individuals with a struggle against the environment. Government was to be a means of improving the social environment and of equitably distributing the fruits of this struggle. This role required a great enlargement of governmental power. It is noteworthy that the idea of activist, reformist government may be found in certain of Corwin's own writings, those supporting the positive state and the dominant presidency.[78] The essay on evolution may be a landmark in Corwin's revision of his position. By contrasting the ideas of natural law, final moral and political values, limited government, and liberty with the ideas of evolution, the relativity of truth, the lack of ultimate moral and political values, the positive state, equality and welfare, the essay connects the erosion of the natural law cornerstone and the changes (which Corwin tends to see as evidence of a decline) in our national political institutions.

This essay is important for several reasons. It critically explores the basic alternative to higher and natural law, the evolutionary hypothesis, stated in "The 'Higher Law' Background of American Constitutional Law." Thus Corwin informs us that he understands natural law and evolution or progress as the major competing ideas of American political thought. The essay makes no demonstration of the truth or merits of natural law. Corwin finds that although the idea of evolution may have overthrown the idea of natural law, the idea of evolution and its consequences may endanger the supporting principles of limited constitutional government. Recourse to the idea of natural law is evidently impossible; recourse to the idea of evolution has harmful consequences. The reader may wish to pursue Corwin's hint, in his phrase "the American ideological tradition," of a decline or corruption of the American tradition of political thought.[79] Finally,

---

76. E. S. Corwin, "The Impact of the Idea of Evolution on the American Political and Constitutional Tradition," in *Evolutionary Thought in America* 182, 184, 195–96 (S. Persons ed. 1950); reprinted in this volume.

77. *Id.* 195–96.

78. Corwin, *The Twilight of the Supreme Court* (1934); E. S. Corwin, "Constitution v. Constitutional Theory," 19 *Am. Pol. Sci. Rev.* 290 (1925); "Congress' Power to Prohibit Commerce, a Crucial Constitutional Issue," 18 *Cornell L. Q.* 477 (1933), reprinted in this volume; "The Constitution as Instrument and as Symbol," 30 *Am. Pol. Sci. Rev.* 1071 (1936); "The Court Sees a New Light," 91 *New Republic* 354 (1937).

79. E. S. Corwin, "The Impact of the Idea of Evolution on the American Political and Constitutional Tradition," in *Evolutionary Thought in America* 186; see also at 194–95.

Corwin outlines the role of the Supreme Court under the ascendant presidency, where the power of review over congressional legislation survives as "little more than a superfluous pageant."[80] This is one of Corwin's most negative evaluations of the importance of judicial review after the New Deal. But one might argue today that he wrote a premature obituary for judicial review, that judicial review over legislation may be a useful, even a necessary, pageant, or that scandals such as Watergate have led the presidency to decline even more drastically than the Supreme Court. His essay on the idea of evolution reminds us of the historic importance of the idea of natural law for American constitutional and political thought.

The essay on "The Debt of American Constitutional Law to Natural Law Concepts" performs a similiar service for the understanding of constitutional law. This essay shows "how very large a part of its content American constitutional law has always owed, and still owes, to its natural law genesis." Corwin deals with two juristic connotations of natural law: first, that it is entitled by its excellence to override law resting solely on human authority; second, that human beings may appeal to natural law against injustices sanctioned by human authority. The essay focuses on the idea of natural law as a "challenge to the notion of unlimited human authority." The thesis of this essay concerns the effect of natural law ideas on the Constitution, the proper exercise of judicial review by the Supreme Court, and the soundness of the natural law idea today. Corwin traces the doctrines of judicial review, substantive due process, and the doctrine that the obligation-of-contracts clause protects public contracts—three of the "four great doctrines" developed before the Civil War—to the addition of "natural law, natural rights concepts" to the documentary Constitution.[81] Even the idea of popular sovereignty derives from the "natural right" of government by the consent of the governed.[82] Having traced the influence of natural law ideas before the Civil War, Corwin turns to the corruption of natural law and its judicial implementation. The Supreme Court's decisions in certain freedom-of-contract and First Amendment cases exemplify "mechanical jurisprudence." The Court's use of "patent formulas," such as the "clear and present danger" test, departs from the "characteristic judicial duty of adjusting the universal and eternal to the local and contingent, the here and now."[83] The essay concludes that American constitutional law is an attempt to implement the challenge of natural law to unlimited human authority: "The record is a somewhat mixed one,

---

80. *Id.* 197; *cf.* M. Shapiro, "The Constitution and Economic Rights," in Harmon, *Essays on the Constitution of the United States* 96 (M. J. Harmon ed. 1978).

81. E. S. Corwin, "The Debt of American Constitutional Law to Natural Law Concepts," 25 *Notre Dame Lawyer* 258, at 275 (1950); reprinted in this volume.

82. *Id.* 282; in the "'Higher Law' Background" Corwin treats popular sovereignty and higher law as alternatives. In making popular sovereignty derivative from the "natural right" of the consent of the governed (a species of higher law), the "Debt of American Constitutional Law to Natural Law Concepts" accomplishes a major revision of the "'Higher Law' Background."

83. E. S. Corwin, "The Debt of American Constitutional Law to Natural Law Concepts," 25 *Notre Dame Lawyer* 258, at 282 (1950).

but it is clear that in the judgment of the American people it has been on the whole a record of success. May it continue to be.''[84]

The essay defends the soundness of natural law in replying to Mr. Justice Holmes' criticism that the right to life ''is sacrificed without a scruple whenever the interest of society, that is, of the predominant power of the community, is thought to demand it.''[85] The right to life, Corwin replies, is ''also the right to spend life for worthwhile ends,'' and that as long as these ends are determined by the consent of the governed, the demands of natural law are met. But one may wonder whether Corwin has identified the most serious ''disturbing comment'' against natural law. Corwin's defense of natural law is limited to discussing Holmes' objection. This essay, however, marks a great departure from Corwin's earlier approval of Holmes: ''What are the qualities of mind that stand out in Justice Holmes' judicial opinions, besides learning and lucidity? They are, first, the completest sense of the relativity of things; and, secondly, an almost paradoxical strength of determination to prevent liberty from being strangulated by property. The latter makes him the champion of democracy; the former puts him entirely beyond democracy's comprehension. The two together have furnished him with a scale of values in the field of constitutional interpretation that, to the reviewer at least, rings true nine cases out of ten.''[86] For Holmes, ''all values were relative,'' and ''Holmes saw in *power* the central fact of society, even of democratic society.''[87] Corwin's early praise of Holmes' sense of the ''relativity of things'' gave way to a defense of natural law. In the postwar period Corwin also reconsidered the thought of James Madison.

''James Madison: Layman, Publicist, and Exegete,'' originally presented as an address to the James Madison Bicentennial, discusses Madison's lack of formal legal training and his interpretations of the nature and source of the Constitution and of the commerce clause. The essay traces the ''deterioration of Madison's nationalism'' from the opinion that the Constitution rests on an act of the people to the opinion that the Constitution resulted from a compact of states.[88] Then Corwin explains the influence and demise of Madison's mistaken thesis that Congress was granted less power over interstate than over foreign commerce. Perhaps a chief interest of this essay is Corwin's characterization of the thought of Madison and Hamilton.[89] Hamilton's ideas have proved more important and predictive of the future than Madison's, but the ''Hamiltonian gloss has about erased some of the most important features'' of the Constitution, particularly those provisions ''intended to delineate the respective fields of legislative and executive power.''[90] In short: the Madisonian gloss has deservedly

84. *Id.* 284.
85. *Id.* 283.
86. Corwin, Review, 24 *Am. Pol. Sci. Rev.* 780 (1930).
87. Corwin, Review, 52 *Harv. L. Rev.* 346, at 347 (1938–1939).
88. E. S. Corwin, ''James Madison: Layman, Publicist and Exegete,'' 27 *N.Y.U. Law Rev.* 277, at 289 (April 1952); reprinted in this volume.
89. *Id.* at 298; 285–86.
90. *Id.* at 298.

disappeared from the constitutional document, while the Hamiltonian gloss has been somewhat destructive of the Constitution's separation of powers. The essay leaves open the direction of future constitutional developments with the conclusion that "at the moment Hamilton appears to have won out." This essay on Madison's constitutional interpretation is a convenient transition to Corwin's own interpretation of the powers of Congress and the President's power of removal.

Corwin's earliest essay on the powers of Congress centers on foreign affairs. In "The Treaty-making Power: A Rejoinder" he concludes that although national power is limited, the reserved powers of the states are no part of the limitation. "The Power of Congress to Declare Peace" rests on its power to repeal previous acts. A duly passed declaration of peace with Germany would bind both the courts and the executive. Hence Corwin finds no sound constitutional reason why Congress should not extricate the United States from a condition of war declared in 1917. The student of Corwin's writings on Congress may wish to consult his letter to *The New York Times* of October 13, 1940, pp. 6–7, entitled "Fifty Destroyers versus the Constitution: A Criticism of the Attorney General's Opinion of August 28, 1940." The letter discusses Attorney General Robert Jackson's advice that President Roosevelt had the right, without securing the consent of either Congress or of the Senate, to exchange fifty destroyers of the Navy for a lease of certain British defense areas in the Atlantic. Was this advice "good law and good Constitution?" the letter asks, and Corwin replies that Attorney General Jackson's opinion is "an endorsement of unrestrained autocracy in the field of our foreign relations, neither more nor less. No such dangerous opinion was ever penned by an attorney general of the United States." Corwin finds, in brief, that the President may not extricate the United States from a congressionally imposed condition of neutrality without the approval of Congress.

The remaining essays on the powers of Congress deal with the spending power and the regulation of commerce. "The Spending Power of Congress, apropos the Maternity Act" principally discusses whether the act exceeds the power granted to Congress by Article I, section 8, clause 1, of the Constitution: "The Congress shall have the power to lay and collect taxes, duties, imposts, and excises, to pay the debts and provide for the common defense and general welfare of the United States." The essay studies in detail congressional and presidential opinion on the meaning of the "general welfare." Corwin concludes that the general welfare is what Congress finds it to be. "The Anti-Trust Acts and the Constitution" reviews the Supreme Court's decisions under the Sherman Anti-Trust Act of 1890 and determines the extent to which these decisions are still "good law today." "Congress' Power to Prohibit Commerce, a Crucial Constitutional Issue" assumes that the national government (Congress and the President) must take "a large hand" in social and economic reconstruction and sets forth the constitutional basis of such activity.

The essays in *Presidential Power and the Constitution* (in which are gathered most of Corwin's essays on the presidency), examine whether limited constitutional government is possible, or even conceivable under the ascendant presidency of this century.[91] In that book the essays begin with an explanation of the natural law doctrine that curbs the presidency and other branches short of plenary power. The middle essays of *Presidential Power and the Constitution* explain the contributions of Presidents Wilson, Roosevelt, and Truman to the constitutional revolution in presidential power. The concluding essays warn of the unhealthy impact of presidential dominance upon American constitutional law and suggest how to adjust the constitutional revolution in favor of democracy. Since it is impossible to reprint those essays here, I have included the "President's Removal Power under the Constitution," a criticism of the logic of Myers v. United States, 272 U.S. 52 (1926), that the President may remove at his pleasure executive officers of the United States government.

This decision concerned the constitutionality of section 6 of the act of July 12, 1876, which made first class postmasters removable by the President with the advice and consent of the Senate. Myers was relieved from office in 1920 without the consent of the Senate and apparently without being informed of the reasons. What was at stake, said Solicitor General James Beck, was a "vital prerogative of the President . . . his power to remove a postmaster for the good of the service and without accountability to the Senate."[92] The Senate itself was at first compliant with the President's decision. The chairman of the Senate Committee on Post Offices and Post Roads informed Myers that the "statute has been construed that . . . the President, through the postmaster general, removes for various statutory offenses, and Congress does not pass upon his decision in the matter."[93] Thus the chairman of the responsible Senate committee waived its right to advise and consent on Myers' removal. The Court of Claims refused to rule on the constitutionality of the act and dismissed the case. The Supreme Court, by a vote of 6–3, declared section 6 of the act, which denied the President an unrestricted power of removal of first class postmasters, unconstitutional. Chief Justice Taft's conclusion on the merits was that Article II of the Constitution grants the President the executive power of the government, that is, the general administrative control of those executing the laws, and appointment and removal of executive officers.[94]

"The President's Removal Power under the Constitution" is an example of one of Corwin's early criticisms of the aggrandizement of presidential power. The essay analyzes "one of the most significant decisions in American constitutional history."[95] The "main purpose" of the essay is to criticize Chief Justice

91. *Presidential Power and the Constitution: Essays by Edward S. Corwin* introd. xii–xiii (R. Loss ed. 1976).

92. Brief for the U.S. on Reargument, in *The Power of the President to Remove Federal Officers* Sen. Doc. 174 69th Cong. 2d Sess. 1926, at 107.

93. Transcript of Record, *id.*, at 15.

94. 272 U.S. 52, at 163–64 (1926).

95. A. T. Mason, *William Howard Taft: Chief Justice* 253 (1965).

Taft's argument that the congressional power to determine the tenure of officers may not limit the President's power of removal.[96] Among the essay's premises are Corwin's belief in the "natural primacy both in point of time and authority of legislative action."[97] Since the "need of the administrative expert is . . . in modern conditions, an ever increasing one," Corwin holds that the expert should enjoy a measure of independence from presidential removal.[98] The "positive thesis" of the essay is that the characteristic duties of an office define its nature, and the nature of the office should determine the scope of the President's removal power in relationship to Congress' power to determine the tenure of the office.[99] The "final conclusion" is that Chief Justice Taft's reasoning in Myers gives the President an unrestrainable power of removal, which Congress cannot limit by giving the removal power to others or by limiting its exercise to stated causes.[100] The essay does not fully address the manner or justice of Myers' removal, though it notes that the Myers decision puts "no legal obstacles in the way of the development by the removal power itself of self-restraining principles favoring official independence."[101] Corwin calls upon Congress to set down a procedure of removal to guarantee "fair play and publicity."[102] The essay closes with the criticism that the President's power of removal is a political question, and that it was "unfortunate" that the Supreme Court decisively ruled on an issue that it had succeeded in avoiding for over a century.[103]

The essay is divided into eight sections. Section I summarizes the decision and discusses the implications of certain statutes of the previous forty years. Section II describes the organization of the essay: first, it examines the chief justice's reasoning; second, it attempts to state propositions superior to those of the chief justice on the grounds of history and logic. Section III discusses what Corwin describes as the "main citadel" of Chief Justice Taft's opinion, the "decision of 1789," which concerns the President's power to remove the Secretary of State without Senate approval. Section IV considers whether Taft's interpretation of the decision of 1789 is supported by opinion before the Civil War and distinguishes the decision's meaning from its finality. Section V investigates the chief justice's other arguments, including those from Andrew Jackson's Protest message. In Section VI Corwin discusses the "supporting outposts" of Taft's opinion, such as separation of powers and the take-care clause. Section VII lists Corwin's propositions, which he says do not conflict with the Myers decision,

---

96. Corwin, *The President's Removal Power under the Constitution* vi (1927), reprinted in this volume.

97. *Id.* at 48.

98. *Id.* at xiii, 5.

99. *Id.* at viii.

100. *Id.* at 7.

101. *Id.* at xiv.

102. On President Wilson's loyalty removals, see Corwin, *The President: Office and Powers* 101, 383–84, n.100 (1957).

103. Corwin, *The President's Removal Power* 68.

including the assertion that the President's power of removal is "not an inherent executive power," but a specific power. The removal power "when it exists is an incident solely of the power of appointment."[104] Section VIII determines whether the Supreme Court may exercise judicial review against a congressional definition of tenure of office according to the necessary and proper clause.

Corwin's criticism of the Myers decision has itself been the object of criticism. According to Louis Fisher, "Corwin could not delineate with any precision the boundaries between executive-legislative prerogatives over the removal power. He asserted that Congress' power was not absolute, any more than the President's, for it was 'conditioned in each case by the nature of the office being dealt with as shown particularly by the source and nature of its powers.' But who describes the 'nature,' and using what criteria?"[105] However that may be, Corwin's essay criticizes judicial resort to the founders' intention where the Constitution is silent. The essay does not supply the incentive for seriously studying the founders' intention as a guide to constitutional understanding.

Corwin's discussion of Hamilton's statement in *Federalist*, no. 77, that Senatorial consent "would be necessary to displace" and to appoint, is less helpful than Solicitor General James Beck's. Corwin merely praises Hamilton's "eminent testimony," while Beck, as government counsel, argues that "Hamilton simply made an assertion as to what the Constitution provided, without showing that the Constitution warranted his assertion."[106] In short, Beck shows that the "eminent testimony" of *Federalist*, no. 77, is mere assertion.[107] Corwin's essay on the removal power also seems to misunderstand Chief Justice Taft and Hamilton (writing as Pacificus) on the "residence of the power of removal."[108] Taft, said Corwin, contends that Hamilton "changed his view" of the removal power between writing *Federalist*, no. 77, and the Pacificus letters. But Taft "adduces no evidence" to show that Hamilton had abandoned the position of *Federalist*, no. 77, that the "power of removal is incident to the power of appointment" and is shared with the Senate. Taft, however, does adduce such evidence in quoting Pacificus' conclusion that "with these exceptions [the participation of the Senate in the appointment of officers and in the making of treaties; the right of Congress to declare war and grant letters of marque and reprisal], the executive power of the United States is completely lodged in the President. This mode of construing the Constitution has indeed

---

104. *Id.* at 51–52.

105. L. Fisher, *The Constitution between Friends* 67 (1978); for the criticism that Corwin misunderstood the opinion, see J. Hart, *Tenure of Office under the Constitution* 200 (1930).

106. Brief for the United States on Reargument, in *The Power of the President to Remove Federal Officers*, at 85.

107. J. Marshall, 2 *The Life of George Washington* 189–191 (Walton Book Co. ed. 1930) omits any reference to the authority of *Federalist*, no. 77, in describing the decision of 1789.

108. Corwin, *The President's Removal Power* 25.

been recognized by Congress in formal acts upon full consideration and debate; *of which the power of removal from office is an important instance.*"[109] In *Federalist,* no. 77, then, Hamilton speculates that the President and Senate would share the removal power, while Pacificus, referring to the decision of 1789, holds that the removal power belongs to the President alone because of the grant of executive power in Article II. Thus, contrary to Corwin's criticism, Taft correctly concluded that Hamilton "changed his view" of the removal power after publication of the *Federalist.*[110] Corwin's quotation of the chief justice's excerpt from Pacificus unfortunately omits the instructive words on the removal power. Neither Taft nor Corwin explicitly discuss the comparative authority and excellence of the *Federalist,* nos. 67–77, and the Pacificus letters, but Taft clearly preferred the latter's discussion of the first sentence of Article II.

But to return to Corwin's essay: its discussion of the debate between Pacificus and Helvidius (Madison) over Washington's Proclamation of Impartiality of 1793 contrasts with the treatment and importance of this exchange in Corwin's other writings. In his *President's Control of Foreign Relations* long selections were reprinted from the letters of Pacificus and Helvidius; in arguing that the control of foreign relations is an "executive prerogative," Corwin adopted Pacificus' interpretation of Article II as a grant of power.[111] The essay on the removal power briefly refers to the letters of Pacificus and faults Taft for making "no reference to the answering *Letters of Helvidius,*" as though Helvidius' argument is superior to Pacificus'.[112] In *The President: Office and Powers* Corwin stressed the importance of the letters, remarking that the "principal issue" of the debate on the removal power in 1789 and the Pacificus-Helvidius letters "was the same . . . whether the opening clause of Article II was a grant of power or not."[113] He reserved judgment on the merits of the arguments of Pacificus and Helvidius by saying, "however the palm for argumentation be awarded in this famous disputation."[114] In sum: Corwin's preference for Pacificus in 1917 contrasts with his implied preference for Helvidius in the removal-power essay and with his later reservation of judgment. The removal-power essay may, in fact, be read as an attempt to reopen the debate between Pacificus and Helvidius in the guise of commenting upon the Myers decision. Without identifying this as the main issue, the essay combats at least three times the idea that the executive

109. Myers v. United States 272 U.S. 52, at 139 (1926); italics added.
110. Corwin later conceded that "in the *Federalist* Hamilton had stated explicitly that the Senate would be associated with the President in the removal of officers, although he seems later to have retracted this opinion." Corwin, "The President as Administrative Chief," reprinted in Corwin, *Presidential Power and the Constitution: Essays by Edward S. Corwin* 100 (R. Loss ed. 1976); the same sentence appears in Corwin, *The President: Office and Powers* 88 (1957 rev. ed.).
111. Corwin, *The President's Control of Foreign Relations* 28, 205 (1917).
112. Corwin, *The President's Removal Power* 26.
113. Corwin, *The President: Office and Powers* 17 (1957 rev. ed.).
114. *Id.* at 181; see, however, at 204.

power clause, Article II, was intended as a grant of power.[115] The interpretation of the executive power clause may be termed the grand issue of the essay.

Perhaps the essay fails to follow the implications of Corwin's theory of the President's removal power over Cabinet officers. He bases this power only on custom, and not on the President's inherent power, but custom can be changed to make senatorial consent a condition of removal.[116] However that may be, the essay refers to "a leading, and oft-cited case," Field v. People, in support of the thesis that "the power of removal when it exists is an incident of the power of appointment."[117] The essay continues that "in the constitutional law of the states especially has the doctrine that the power of removal inheres in 'executive power' found slight lodgment."[118] The Field decision denied that the governor of Illinois had the power to remove the Secretary of State. The Field decision, however, argued that "between the powers of the President and governor, and between the character, duties, and accountability of the officers whom the President may remove, and the secretary of this state, there is no similiarity, so far as regards the decision of this case."[119] The Field decision found that the power of removal was conceded to the President in 1789 in part "because of the general grant to him {by the Constitution} of executive power."[120] "From the discretionary powers with which the President is clothed, there is a necessity for his possessing the power of removal."[121] In short, while the Field decision denies the power of removal to the governor, as Corwin suggested, it affirms the President's power of removal on the grounds of inherent power, but without using this exact expression, except where offices are created by law. Hence the Field decision distinguishes between the removal powers of the governor and the President, and does not support Corwin's thesis that "the {President's} removal power when it exists is an incident of the power of appointment."

Two of Corwin's later writings tend to soften the criticisms he made in the essay on the President's removal power. "Some Lessons from the Constitution of 1787" describes the Myers decision as seeking, "though not with entire success," to ratify the results of political development, that is, presidential ascendancy over Congress.[122] The President: Office and Powers merely concludes that "it seems very questionable" whether the decision of 1789, giving

115. Corwin, *The President's Removal Power under the Constitution* 30–31, n.60; 43, n.77; 70, n.117; *cf.* Corwin, "Tenure of Office and the Removal Power under the Constitution," 27 *Col. L. Rev.* 353, at 375, n.60; 383, n.77. A. T. Mason, *Harlan Fiske Stone* 226 (1956), identified Taft's "basic premise—that the power of removal is an inherent part of the constitutional grant of executive power."

116. Corwin, *The President's Removal Power under the Constitution* 60.

117. *Id.* at 52, 53, n.92.

118. *Id.* at 52–53.

119. 3 Ill. 79, at 120 (1839).

120. *Id.* at 121.

121. *Id.* at 122.

122. Corwin, "Some Lessons from the Constitution of 1787," in *The Democratic Dogma and Other Essays* 74 (1930).

the President an unrestricted power of removal over the Secretary of State, is "capable of sustaining the sweeping conclusions" of Taft's opinion in Myers.[123]

In Humphrey's Executor v. United States, 295 U.S. 602 (1935), the Supreme Court decided that the Myers decision involved a narrow point, disapproved of dicta in Myers that may have included Taft's theoretical analysis of presidential power, and held that section 1 of the Federal Trade Commission Act limits removals to those for cause. The Court argued that the character of the office determines whether the President's power of removal will prevail over Congress' power to fix tenure and to specify the causes of removal.[124]

Scholarly opinion is divided over the condition of the Myers decision today. According to Philip Kurland, the Myers decision was "distinguished to death in Humphrey's Executor v. United States."[125] Yet Charles Miller, also writing after the Humphrey's Executor Case, concluded that "the decision in Myers is still law, but the expansive reasoning in support of it no longer has constitutional validity."[126] Whether the Myers decision is dead or alive, perhaps "the issues and values surrounding presidential control over executive officers are today not essentially different from those at the time of the founders."[127] The clarification of the theoretical problem of presidential power may be aided more by the sort of doctrinal analysis attempted in the Myers decision and Corwin's essay than by the flaccid formalism of the Humphrey's decision.

The argument and thesis of this introduction may be stated in briefest compass. Corwin's essays on the principles of American constitutional and political thought have displayed him as a critic of constitutional worship and higher law, as an advocate of popular sovereignty and an instrumental Constitution, and as a defender of natural law and judge of the respective claims of "these two great men," Madison and Hamilton. First in time Corwin criticized constitutional worship, his code phrase denoting popular veneration of the Constitution's principles and the statesman's use of the founders' political science, including separation of powers and the idea of institutionalizing legal restraints upon government. For Corwin, Lincoln ended constitutional worship and made opinion about the Constitution more democratic and realistic than the founders' political science. Turning to higher law, Corwin partly traced the finality of judicial interpretations of standing law to supposed judicial knowledge of a higher law superior to ordinary law. The problem of higher law was, in no small measure, whether

123. Corwin, *The President: Office and Powers* 87 (1957 rev. ed); L. Fisher, *The Constitution between Friends* 73-74 (1978) argues that Corwin's discussion of disloyalty exhumed the majority's opinion in Myers.

124. For a discussion of developments after the Myers decision, see P. Kurland, *Watergate and the Constitution* 95-103 (1978); in Elrod v. Burns, 427 U.S. 347, at 352 (1976), a case involving local patronage appointments, counsel for Mayor Daley of Chicago and the sheriff of Cook County unsuccessfully invoked the Myers decision in support of the argument that the local executive's faithful execution of the laws requires the power of appointment and removal at will.

125. Kurland, *Watergate and the Constitution* 95.

126. C. A. Miller, *The Supreme Court and the Uses of History* 55 n.9 (1969).

127. *Id.* at 61.

unchangeable standards, superior to the will of human rulers, existed to guide
human legislators. The " 'Higher Law' Background" essay intended to discourage the belief in higher law. The essay weakly defended higher law against the
analytical school's separation of what is legal from what is just, and Corwin
accepted the positive idea of law and the dependence of thought on its historical
setting. In effect, therefore, Corwin labored to show that higher law was an
illusion, because no unchangeable standards existed to guide human legislators.
Second, and complementing his criticism of constitutional worship and rejection
of higher law, Corwin advocated popular sovereignty and an instrumental Constitution. He filled the vacuum left by the founders' political science and higher
law with the idea of progress, an instrumental, as distinguished from a symbolic,
Constitution, majority rule, and a dominant presidency. It would be an oversimplification, but by no means misleading, to observe that today's dominant
presidency resulted from jettisoning the founders' political science and higher
law. By endorsing the enfeeblement of judicial review in "The Constitution as
Instrument and as Symbol," Corwin impaired judicially imposed constitutional
limitations.

Did Corwin's late defense of natural law supply a means of escape from his
criticism of the founders and higher law and his advocacy of instrumental constitutionalism? In order to assess Corwin's understanding of natural law, it is
necessary to compare his thought on the ideas of natural law and evolution. The
essays on principles identify natural law and evolution as the major competing
ideas of American political thought. For Corwin the Darwinian idea of evolution
bolsters activist, reformist government and so is hostile to the founders' idea of
limited constitutional government. But he saw natural law itself beset by objections based on the dependence of thought on its milieu, that is, historicism, legal
positivism, and egalitarianism. The shortcoming of Corwin's defense of classical
American natural law is that he defends it against Mr. Justice Holmes and the
legal positivists without replying adequately to the weightier objections of historicism and egalitarianism. Hence it is accurate to say that Corwin makes a
partial, limited, and flawed defense of natural law. His theoretical legacy is an
invitation and an opportunity for the present generation of scholars. His intention, to assist the recovery of classical American natural law, will be fulfilled if
his successors in the fields of political thought and constitutional law defend
natural law against historicism and egalitarianism.

His essays also charted the limits of congressional power in particular areas of
foreign and domestic policy and, taken together with the essay on the President's
removal power, these essays show Corwin more approving of congressional than
of presidential power. The removal-power essay overlooks crucial evidence of a
change in Hamilton's opinion that is found in the Pacificus letters. Contrary to
Corwin's criticism, the Pacificus letters tend to strengthen Chief Justice Taft's
opinion in the Myers Case. The idea of natural law and the removal-power essay,
I contend, illustrate two sides of what may be a fundamental problem in Corwin's

thought: its relationship to the founding and to the founders' intentions. Consequently, the essays on political thought and the removal power, far from ending debate, establish an agenda for his successors, namely, to grapple anew with the idea of natural law and the first sentence of Article II. Nor are these tasks entirely unrelated, for the return of the presidency to constitutional health may require no less than the recovery of natural law as a challenge to the notion of unlimited human authority.

I.

FOUNDATIONS OF AMERICAN CONSTITUTIONAL AND POLITICAL THOUGHT

1. The Worship of the Constitution

THE sine qua non of democratic government is a feeling of like-mindedness among the members of the community and the mutual confidence which this feeling engenders. The initial tendency, therefore, of an agricultural democracy, rooted to the soil and deficient in social experience as it inevitably is, will be toward localism. We see this fact illustrated today in the case of Russia, but it appears not less strikingly in our own early history as an independent community. Fortunately there existed in America a considerable group of men whose views and interests passed beyond local boundaries and who were able by a well-timed effort to arrest the dissolving tendency of the times. Their work was the Constitution.

Yet the formal ratification of the Constitution was only a commencement, and not an especially propitious one. It was brought about in the face of active opposition, which was supported by a widespread surly indifference. In the moderate words of John Adams, "the Constitution was extorted from the grinding necessity of a reluctant people." Hardly, however, had the Constitution gone into effect than the transforming miracle occurred. As Woodrow Wilson has written: "Even hostile criticism of its provisions . . . not only ceased, but gave place to an undiscriminating and almost blind worship of its principles. . . . The divine right of kings never ran a more prosperous course than did the unquestioned prerogative of the Constitution to receive universal homage."[1] Nor has this prerogative been seriously challenged till the other day. Other skepticisms have waxed and waned, but the worship of the Constitution has continued unabated. It is true that abolitionists denounced the Constitution as "an agreement with hell," but their shrill infidelity only stirred the great mass of Americans to a reaffirmation of the national faith. Even secession posed as loyalty to the *princi-*

From 4 *Constitutional Review* 3 (January 1920).
{1. W. Wilson, *Congressional Government* 17 (1967;1885).}

ples of the Constitution and a protest against their violation; and in form at least the Constitution of the southern Confederacy was, with a few minor discrepancies, a replica of the instrument of 1789. Walter Bagehot's appraisement of the English monarchy may, without exaggeration, be repeated of the Constitution, for by far the greater part of its history it has strengthened "{our} government with the strength of religion."[2]

Many theories have been offered at various times to account for the hold which the Constitution so early acquired upon the devotion of the American people and retained so long. On the floor of the Federal Convention, Hamilton, voicing the conviction of a generation which applied to all political institutions the rigorous test of utility, listed as the first of "the great essential principles necessary for the support of government" an "active and constant *interest* in supporting it." Pursuant to this principle, the Convention sought systematically to bring every great interest of the country, whether economic or political, within the sheltering fold of the new system, and at the same time, by the avoidance of a "too minutious wisdom," to render their work accessible to new forces as these should arise.

The theory of interest was, moreover, speedily vindicated by event. For the adoption of the Constitution was succeeded by a wave of prosperity, and it was this unquestionably which first launched the new instrument upon the affections of the great majority. Speaking on the floor of Congress four or five years later, Richard Bland Lee declared: "I will only mention the stimulus which agriculture has received. In travelling through various parts of the United States, I find fields a few years ago waste and uncultivated filled with inhabitants and covered with harvests, new habitations reared, contentment in every face, plenty on every board; confidence is restored and every man is safe under his own vine and fig tree, and there is none to make him afraid. To produce this effect was the intent of the Constitution, and it has succeeded." It is possible indeed that too much praise was lavished upon the Constitution on this score. "It has been usual with declamatory gentlemen," complained sour old Maclay, "in their praises of the present government, to paint the state of the country under the old Congress as if neither wood grew nor water ran in America before the happy adoption of the Constitution." And a few years later, when the European turmoil at once assisted, and by contrast advertised, our own blissful state, Josiah Quincy voiced a fear that "we have grown giddy with good fortune, attributing the greatness of our prosperity to our own wisdom, rather than to a course of events and a guidance over which we had no influence."[3]

But whether warranted by facts or not, the belief that the Constitution brought

{2. W. Bagehot, *The English Constitution* 94 (Dolphin Books ed. n.d.).}

3. For the references in this paragraph, I am indebted to an article by Mr. Frank I. Schechter entitled "The Early History of the Tradition of the Constitution," in 9 *Am. Pol. Sci. Rev.* 720–21 (1915). {William Maclay was U.S. Senator from Pennsylvania (1789–1791); Josiah Quincy was a public official and educator.}

prosperity in its wake accounts only for the *beginning* of the worship of the Constitution; it does not account for the *quality* of this worship, for its intensity, its continuance. I say that it accounts for its beginning; but it would be accurate to say that it accounts for the *transference* of worship to the Constitution, for in essential spirit this worship long antedated its idol. The aptitude of the English race to find in law an object of worship first evidenced itself in relation to the common law at the close of the Wars of the Roses. Writing of this time, Mr. Figgis, in his brilliant little volume on *The Divine Right of Kings,* says: "The common law is pictured invested with a halo of dignity peculiar to the embodiment of the deepest principles and to the highest expression of human reason and of the law of nature implanted by God in the heart of man. . . It is { . . . } the symbol of ordered life and disciplined activities, which are to replace the license and violence of the evil times now passed away. . . . It {*sic;* And the common law} is the perfect ideal of law {;} for it is natural reason developed and expounded by the collective wisdom of many generations."[4]

The connective link between the worship of the common law and worship of the Constitution is supplied by Coke's view of the Magna Carta as a "law fundamental," a view which he erected as a defense against the Stuart theory of divine right. Thence arose Cromwell's demand for a written instrument of government embodying "somewhat fundamental"; whence in turn derived Harrington's famous phrase, "an empire of laws and not of men"—a phrase which will be found repeated almost word for word in the Massachusetts constitution of 1780, and in substance in Marshall's famous opinion in Marbury v. Madison. And meantime Blackstone had incorporated in his *Commentaries* the lesson that it was the duty of every Englishman to understand and venerate the British constitution—a lesson which Burke presently improved upon by urging the duty to venerate whether with understanding or not.

It was to the British constitution, too, that our forefathers appealed against British tyranny, and when this appeal proved unavailing they determined to bulwark the rights of man in a constitutional system of their own. Thus the author of *Common Sense,* at the very moment of his electrifying proposal that America declare her independence, foreshadowed the basis upon which the new commonwealth was to rest. Urging in February 1776, a "continental conference," he wrote:

> The conferring members being met, let their business be to frame a continental charter or charter of the united colonies (answering to what is called the Magna Carta of England) fixing the number and manner of choosing members of Congress and members of assembly . . . and drawing the line of business and jurisdiction between them (always remembering that our strength is continental, not provincial) securing freedom and property to all men . . . with such other matter as it is necessary for a charter to contain. But where, say some, is the king of America? That we may not appear to be defective even in earthly honors, let a day be solemnly set

{4. J. Figgis, *The Divine Right of Kings* 228–29 (2d ed. 1914).}

apart for proclaiming the charter; let it be brought forth placed on the divine law, the word of God; let a crown be placed thereon, by which the world may know that so far we approve monarchy that in America the law is king.[5]

So the Constitution appeared from the beginning as the outgrowth of a racial tradition, of an ancient struggle for liberty. There are those, however, who would further insist that its connection with the past was one of tissue as well as of spirit, and that indeed its success has been due in great part to this fact. Thus when, some years ago, Mr. Gladstone pronounced the Constitution "the most wonderful work ever struck off at a given time by the brain and purpose of man," a storm of learned protest informed him that his kindly intention at compliment had missed its mark. Nor is the basis of this protest far to seek. Impressed by the continuity of the development of English institutions and influenced by the Darwinian theory of evolution by minute accretions, our historians have been naturally eager to emphasize the English and colonial antecedents of our governmental system. Nevertheless Gladstone's words do set forth very adequately the view of the Constitution whereby Americans themselves for generations explained their worship of it—a view which the framers themselves shared.

Furthermore, it must be owned, I think, that so far at least as the point of view of science and philosophy is concerned, Gladstone's dictum today occupies a much safer footing than when it was uttered. The eloquence of Bergson has made the idea of "creative evolution" common property; geology has long since ceased to scorn cataclysm as a causal agency; in the realm of biology Mendel and his disciples have pressed the Darwinian hypothesis behind restricted frontiers. Nor would a well-schooled political scientist be disposed nowadays to claim overmuch for the mere formal similarity of institutions divorced from their institutional environment and atmosphere. Thus a bicameral legislature composed, like Parliament, of an hereditary house and an elective house and possessed of legislative sovereignty, is one thing, and a legislature made up like Congress and subject to the double check of the executive and the courts quite another. In other words, in passing upon the question of originality, whether of governments or engines, it is to the *ensemble* rather than to the separate parts that attention should be directed. The most nearly unique invention ever contrived was simply an assemblage of two or more of five or six mechanical principles. And there are limits to possible variety in governments also, though your parlor bolshevist may not wish to admit it.

It must never be lost to sight that the first American constitutions, including the instrument of 1787, were the work of the greatest era of political reconstruc-

5. {1 T. Paine, *The Political Writings of Thomas Paine* 45–46 (1835).} It is to be noted that this suggestion of a constitutional convention antedates Hamilton's Duane letter of September 3, 1780 {2 A. Hamilton, *The Papers of Alexander Hamilton* 400 (H. Syrett ed. 1961)}, by more than three years, and also any state constitutional convention. It is curious that it should have dropped out of notice so entirely.

tion that the world has ever seen, and furthermore that they were framed very early in this period. The "fathers" wrought, accordingly, with the eyes of expectant mankind riveted upon them.

> If it is permissible in a political memoir [wrote a French advocate of his government's intervention in America early in 1777] to consider the subject philosophically, one can see with some interest a people forming itself into a national body. . . . This is not a collection of savages gradually emerging from barbarism, and which rather receives than gives to itself the constitution which circumstances impose upon it. This is a people already civilized by its understanding, and which, after having acquired its political independence, is about to choose for itself the legislature that is to establish its destiny for all time. The history of the world perhaps shows no spectacle more interesting, and the political stage have never, perhaps, presented an event the consequences of which are more important and more widespread in the general condition of the globe.[6]

The point of view which these words express has been too often missed by those who have written in an epoch of scientific determinism. But the attitude of nonresistance to natural causes was far from that of the period of the Declaration of Independence and the years following. For America, no less than France, it was an "age of rationalism," by which is meant not a blind ignoring of the lessons of experience, but confidence in the ability of reason, *working in the light of experience,* to divert the course of events into beneficial channels; and in no respect was man more the master of his destiny than in that of statecraft. The political philosophy of the period presented the free sovereign individual as the basis of all political arrangements; indeed, society itself was his deliberate contrivance. And if this was not the fact universally, yet at least it was in America, where revolution had wiped the political slate clean of the ancient usurpation of monarchy. Other characteristics of the period, too, were calculated to stir the imagination of the "fathers" and to enhance what may be termed their sense of mission. It was a cosmopolitan age, when the best minds of all nations were in constant touch with each other, with the result that the idea existed that all peoples were, politically speaking, in much the same case and in quest of very like utopias. Even Montesquieu surrendered himself to this point of view in his famous Book XI, which became the evangel of the "fathers," while the scientifically valuable part of his great work remained unread. Again, it was a period when economic change was all but imperceptible; and this fact, while it heightened the spectacle of political transformation, also supported the belief, derived from the pages of Plutarch and Harrington, in the feasibility of polities constructed out of hand.

We thus come upon the most fundamental article of faith of the "fathers," their belief in the availability for their purposes of an existing "political sci-

{6. Private Citizen, "Reflections . . . ," in Corwin, *French Policy and the American Alliance of 1788* 397–98 (1916).}

ence." Early legislators had been forced to work in comparative ignorance of the laws of political mechanics; but at last mankind was able to read and comprehend the lessons of their failures and successes, and to apply them.

> The citizens of America [wrote Washington in his Letter to the Governors of June 18 {sic; 8?}, 1783], placed in the most enviable condition, as the sole lords and proprietors of a vast tract of continent, . . . are, from this period, to be considered as the actors on a most conspicuous theater, which seems to be peculiarly designed {sic; designated?} by Providence for the display of human greatness and felicity; here they are not only surrounded with everything that can contribute to the completion of private and domestic enjoyment, but Heaven has crowned all its other blessings by giving a surer opportunity for political happiness than any other nation has been favored with. . . . The foundation of our empire was not laid in a gloomy age of ignorance and superstition, but at an epoch when the rights of mankind were better understood and more clearly defined than at any other period; researches of the human mind after social happiness have been carried to a great extent; the treasures of knowledge acquired by the labors of philosophers, sages, and legislators {sic; legislatures?}, through a long succession of years, are laid open to us {sic; for our use?}, and their collected wisdom may be happily applied in the establishment of our forms of government. . . . At this auspicious period the United States came into existence as a nation, and if their citizens should not be completely free and happy, the fault will be entirely their own.[7]

In his *Defense of the Constitutions,* written three years later, John Adams enumerates the principal "discoveries in the constitution of a free government since the institutions of Lycurgus." He then draws the following moral: "The people of America have now the best opportunity and the greatest trust in their hands that Providence ever committed to so small a number since the transgression of the first pair; if they betray their trust their fault will merit even greater punishment than other nations have suffered, and the indignation of Heaven."[8]

The first efforts of the fathers at constitution-making were, however, greatly hampered by the interruptions of war, and their work speedily disclosed many defects. But the outcome, far from weakening confidence in "political science," rather strengthened it, since it was precisely the failure to heed the lessons of "political science" that accounted for these defects.[9] Furthermore, the breakdown of "the political system of the United States," as Madison named it, before 1787 enhanced tremendously what I have called the sense of mission of the framers of the Constitution, since it was felt that, if adequate remedies could not be devised for the shortcomings of the existing system, not only the unity of America but republican government itself must disappear from the earth. "It was more than probable," Madison on the floor of the Convention declared, "we were now digesting a plan which in its operation would decide forever the fate of

---

{7. 26 Washington, *The Writings of George Washington* 484–85 (J. C. Fitzpatrick ed. 1938).}

{8. 4 J. Adams, *Life and Works* 284 {?} (C. F. Adams ed. 1851).}

9. In this connection, see the very instructive "Address to the People of the United States" by Dr. Benjamin Rush, in {H.} Niles' {*Centennial Offering. Republication of the*} *Principles and Acts of the Revolution in America* 234 (1876).

republican government,'' an observation in which Hamilton and others heartily concurred. The Convention felt indeed that it had not only the future of America in its hands but of all mankind. "When he considered,'' said {James} Wilson, ''the influence the government we are to form will have, not only on the present generation of our people and their multiplied posterity, but on the whole globe, he was lost in the magnitude of the subject.'' "Something must be done,'' added Gerry, ''or we shall disappoint not only America, but the whole world.'' And Gouverneur Morris spoke to like effect: "He came here as a representative of America: he flattered himself he came in some degree as a representative of the whole human race; for the whole human race will be affected by the proceedings of this Convention.''

Nor did the Convention forget its "political science.'' Hamilton wrote in the *Federalist:*

> The science of politics, { . . . } like most other sciences, has received great improvement. The efficacy of various principles is now well understood, which were either not known at all or imperfectly known to the ancients. The regular distribution of power into distinct departments; the introduction of legislative balances and checks; the institution of courts composed of judges, holding their offices during good behavior; the representation of the people in the legislature by deputies of their own election; these are wholly new discoveries or have made their principal progress toward perfection in modern times. They are means, and powerful means, by which the excellencies of republican government may be retained and its imperfections lessened or avoided. To this catalogue of circumstances, that tend to the amelioration of popular systems of civil government, I shall { . . . } add one more { . . . }; I mean the *enlargement* of the *orbit* within which such systems are to revolve.

He then quotes Montesquieu's words: "It is very probable that mankind would have been obliged, at length, to live constantly under the government of a single person, had they not contrived a kind of constitution that has all the internal advantages of a republican, together with the external force of a monarchical, government. I mean a confederate republic.''

In like spirit Madison, also writing in the *Federalist,* defended the Constitution against the criticism of novelty: "Had no important step,'' he declares, ''been taken by the leaders of the Revolution for which a precedent could not be discovered . . . the people of the United States might at that moment have been numbered among the melancholy victims of misguided councils, and must at best have been laboring under the weight of some of those forms which had crushed the liberties of the rest of mankind. Happily for America, happily, we trust, for the whole human race, they pursued a new and more noble course. They accomplished a revolution which has no parallel in the annals of human society. They reared the fabrics of governments which have no model on the face of the globe.''

But not only was the Constitution a work of original political construction; it was an act of free will, wherein again it stood out against the past. Said James

Wilson in the Pennsylvania ratifying convention: "The science of government seems yet to be almost in its state of infancy. Governments in general have been the result of force, of fraud, and accident. After a period of six thousand years has elapsed since the creation, the United States exhibits to the world the first instance of a nation assembling voluntarily, deliberating fully, and deciding calmly concerning that system of government under which they would wish they and their posterity should live." In the same spirit the act of ratification of the Massachusetts convention thanked "the Supreme Ruler of the Universe" for "affording the people of the United States" the opportunity "deliberately and peaceably, without fraud or surprise, of entering into an explicit and solemn compact with each other, by assenting to and ratifying a new Constitution."

It is, however, in the words of a foreign observer that the breach which the Constitution was thought contemporaneously to effect with the entire history of government in the past is brought out most strikingly. "All governments that now exist in the world," wrote the celebrated Dr. MacIntosh { sic; Mackintosh} in his *Defense of the French Revolution,* "have been fortuitously formed. They are the produce of chance, not the work of art. They have been altered, impaired, improved, and destroyed by accidental circumstances beyond the foresight or control of wisdom. Their parts, thrown up against present emergencies, formed no systematic whole." From this uncomplimentary description MacIntosh explicitly excepts "the United States of America."[10]

By its framers and by the generation which received it, the Constitution was regarded as marking the climax of a great though brief period of original political creation. And what, moreover, are the facts? In the words of Lord Acton, the Constitution of 1787 "resembled no other constitution, for it was contained in half a dozen intelligible articles"; indeed, outside of America, written constitutions did not yet exist. The idea of putting legal restraints upon government in the interest of private rights, though of respectable antiquity, had never before received institutional embodiment. The principle of the separation of powers was, even in America before the Massachusetts constitution of 1780 mere literary theory, but it furnishes the constructive principle of the Constitution of 1787. So, too, the derivative notion of checks and balances had hitherto failed as against legislative power; for only in Massachusetts and New Hampshire did the executive veto exist even in form, and though judicial review had been asserted in three or four dicta and one or two decisions, it was still, when the Federal Convention assembled, the rawest sort of raw idea. More noteworthy still, however, was the work of the Convention in adjusting the relations of the states and the nation. There had been confederacies before—history was strewn with the wrecks of them—but no earlier confederacy had possessed a central government which operated directly upon *individuals* rather than indirectly through the governments of its corporate members, and yet without sacrifice of the principle of local

{10. J. Mackintosh, *Vindiciae Gallicae: Defense of the French Revolution* (London 1791) ?}

autonomy. Lastly, the method by which the Constitution was adopted employed the principle of popular sovereignty on an unparalleled scale; for the first time did the right of revolution appear as the more positive right of the citizens of a great national community, acting through bodies chosen for the specific purpose, to remodel their political institutions.

Gladstone's dictum is amply vindicated; yet it is altogether evident that the sentiment which it expresses is one today rarely encountered. The worship of the Constitution is at an end! That reverence for the very document which, for instance, is displayed in the following passage from an early decision today seems quaint enough: "The most wonderful instrument ever drawn by the hand of man," wherein "is a comprehension and precision that is unparalleled," wherein "after a lifetime of study" we may "still daily find some new excellence."[11] Very different is the attitude that accounts for the Eighteenth Amendment!

The question is inevitably prompted, how did this great change come about? Undoubtedly the Civil War was greatly instrumental in it, when in the estimation of millions of Americans it affixed a certain interpretation to the Constitution by sheer force of arms. But the archiconoclast was Lincoln. If the demise of the Constitution's divinity is to be given a date, it ought to be that day on which Lincoln announced that if it was necessary to violate certain provisions of the Constitution in order to save the Union he would do that very thing. For back of this announcement was Lincoln's vision—others had had it before him—of a nation greater than any Constitution. Henceforth, accordingly, the Constitution must meet a new test—or rather, it must meet again the test which had primarily determined its fate when it was first set going and before the halo of divinity had yet descended upon it—the test of serviceability. It might still be the embodiment of sound political theory and of a venerable legal tradition, but these things alone would not save it. Henceforth it was the people's law, and must meet their need.

11. Justice William Johnson in Elkisin v. Deliesseline, 8 F. Cas. 493 (1823).

2. The Progress of Constitutional Theory between the Declaration of Independence and the Meeting of the Philadelphia Convention

CRITICS of Gladstone's famous aphorism on the Constitution seem often to assume that he supposed the members of the Philadelphia Convention to have emptied their minds of all experience upon their arrival in the convention city.[1] The assumption is an entirely gratuitous one. Unquestionably the problems before the Convention were suggested by the experience of its members and were not posed *ex thesi*. But the fact remains, nevertheless, that the solutions which the Convention supplied to those problems not infrequently owed far more to the theoretical prepossessions of its members than they did to tested institutions.

For Americans hardly less than for Frenchmen the period of the Constitution was "an age of rationalism," whereby is intended not a blind ignoring of the lessons of experience, but confidence in the ability of reason, working in the light of experience, to divert the unreflective course of events into beneficial channels; and in no respect was man more the master of his destiny than in that of statecraft. Surely if any man of the time may be regarded as representative of the sober, unimaginative intelligence of America, it was Washington, in whose "Circular Letter addressed to the Governors," of June 8, 1783, occurs the following passage:

> The foundation of our empire was not laid in the gloomy age of ignorance and superstition; but at an epocha when the rights of mankind were better understood

From 30 *American Historical Review* 511–536 (1925). Reprinted by permission.

1. See, e.g., R. L. Schuyler, *The Constitution of the United States* 5 (1923). Professor Schuyler voices the opinion (at 6) that "the Constitution is not to be regarded as in any true sense an original creative act of the Convention at Philadelphia, which framed it." It is interesting to oppose to this sentiment the following passage from Professor Roscoe Pound's *Interpretations of Legal History* 127 (1923): "Except as an act of omnipotence, creation does not mean the making of something out of nothing. Creative activity takes materials and gives them form so that they may be put to uses for which the materials unformed are not adapted." Professor Schuyler's sweeping statement would probably be quite as near the truth if the word "not" were omitted from it.

and more clearly defined, than at any other period. The researches of the human mind after social happiness have been carried to a great extent; the treasures of knowledge acquired by the labors of philosophers, sages, and legislators, through a long succession of years, are laid open for our use, and their collected wisdom may be happily applied in the establishment of our forms of government. . . . At this auspicious period, the United States came into existence as a nation: and, if their citizens should not be completely free and happy, the fault will be entirely their own.[2]

The same sense of command over the resources of political wisdom appears again and again in the debates of the Convention, in the pages of the *Federalist*, and in writings of contemporaries.[3]

Nor does the economic interpretation of history, of which one has heard much in late years, detract greatly from the significance of such facts. No one denies that the concern felt by the "fathers" for the rights of property and contract contributed immensely to impart to American constitutional law its strong bias in favor of these rights from the outset, but the concession only serves to throw certain still unanswered questions into a higher relief. For, what warrant had these men for translating any of their interests as *rights;* and why did they adopt the precise means which they did to advance their interests or secure their rights—in other words, why did they choose the precise system set up by the Constitution to do the work which they put upon it? Questions of this nature are altogether incapable of answer by any theory of human motive standing by itself. As Sir Henry Maine has phrased it: "Nothing in law springs entirely from a sense of convenience. There are always certain ideas existing antecedently on which the sense of convenience works, and of which it can do no more than form some new combination; and to find these ideas," he adds, "is exactly the problem."[4]

I.

A colloquy which occurred between Madison and Sherman of Connecticut in the early days of the Philadelphia Convention as to its purposes affords an excellent preface to the more particular intention of this paper. "The objects of the Union," Sherman had declared, "were few": defense, domestic good order, treaties, the regulation of foreign commerce, revenue. Though a conspicuous omission from this enumeration is of any mention of commerce among the states and its regulation, it was not this omission which drew Madison's fire:

2. 10 *Writings* 254, 256 (W. C. Ford ed. 1889–1893).
3. See 1 Farrand, *Records of the Federal Convention* 83–84, 134–35, 137, 139, 151–52, 161, 254, 285 ff., 304 ff., 317, 356, 398 ff., 426 ff., 437–38, 444–49, 451, etc. (1911). The lessons of the past, its successes and failures, are cited for the most part. The term "political science" is used by Mercer, *id.* 2 at 284, while "the science of politics" is Hamilton's expression in *Federalist*, no. 9 (H. C. Lodge ed. 1888). This, he says, "has undergone great improvement." The entire passage is worth perusal in this connection. See also Madison in *Federalist*, nos. 14 and 47, and Adams' preface to his *Defense* in 4 *Life and Works* 283–98 (C. F. Adams. ed. 1850–1856).
4. *Ancient Law* 226 (1888).

He differed from the member from Connecticut in thinking the objects mentioned to be all the principal ones that required a national government. Those were certainly important and necessary objects; but he combined with them the necessity of providing more effectually for the security of private rights, and the steady dispensation of justice. Interferences with these were evils which had more perhaps than any thing else, produced this Convention. Was it to be supposed that republican liberty could long exist under the abuses of it practiced in some of the states?[5]

These views were heartily chorused by other members: the faulty organization of government within the states, threatening as it did, not alone the Union, but republican government itself, furnished the Convention with a problem of transcendent, even world-wide importance.[6]

In short, the task before the Convention arose by no means exclusively from the inadequacies of the Articles of Confederation for "the exigencies of the Union"; of at least equal urgency were the questions which were thrust upon its attention by the shortcomings of the state governments for their purposes. Indeed, from the point of view of this particular study the latter phase of the Convention's task is, if anything, the more significant one, both because it brings us into contact at the outset with the most persistent problem of American constitutional law—that which has arisen from the existence of a multiplicity of local legislatures with indefinite powers; and also because it was to the solution of this phase of its problem that the Convention brought its "political science" most immediately to bear.

The singular juxtaposition in the revolutionary state constitutions of legislative supremacy and the doctrine of natural rights need not detain us here.[7] In the words of a contemporary critic of those constitutions: Although their authors "understood perfectly the principles of liberty," yet most of them "were ignorant of the forms and combinations of power in republics."[8] Madison's protest, on the other hand, against "interferences with the steady dispensation of justice" had reference to something more subtle—to what, in fact, was far less a structural than a functional defect in these early instruments of government. That the majority of the revolutionary constitutions recorded recognition of the principle of the separation of powers is, of course, well known.[9] What is not so generally understood is that the recognition was verbal merely, for the reason that the material terms in which it was couched still remained undefined; and that this was true in particular of "legislative power" in relation to "judicial power."

---

5. 1 Farrand, *Records* 133–34.

6. 1 *id.* 48, 255, 424, 525, 533; 2 at 285.

7. See W. C. Webster, "State Constitutions of the American Revolution," in 9 *Annals* 380 (1897).

8. H. Niles, {*Centennial Offering. Republication of the*} *Principles and Acts of the Revolution* 234 {(1876)} [hereinafter *Principles*]; from an address by Dr. Benjamin Rush delivered at Philadelphia on July 4, 1787, before members of the Convention and others. The address testifies throughout to the importance of the governmental situation in the states as a problem before the Convention.

9. See *Federalist*, no. 47.

It is pertinent in this connection to compare the statement by a modern authority of what is law today with actual practice contemporaneous with the framing of the Constitution of the United States. "The legislature," writes Sutherland in his work on {*Statutes and*} *Statutory Construction,*

> may prescribe rules of decision which will govern future cases. . . . But it has no power to administer judicial relief—it cannot decide cases nor direct how existing cases or controversies shall be decided by the courts; it cannot interfere by subsequent acts with final judgments of the courts. It cannot set aside, annul, or modify such judgments, nor grant or order new trials, nor direct what judgment shall be entered or relief given. No declaratory act, that is, one professing to enact what the law now is or was at any past time, can affect any existing rights or controversies.[10]

Turn now to the operation of the principle of the separation of powers in a typical instance in 1787. The New Hampshire constitution of 1784 contained the declaration that "in the government of this state, the three essential powers thereof, to wit, the legislative, executive, and judicial, ought to be kept as separate and independent of each other as the nature of a free government will admit or as is consistent with the chain of connection that binds the whole fabric of the constitution in one indissoluble bond of union or amity." Notwithstanding which the laws of New Hampshire for the years 1784–1792 are replete with entries showing that throughout this period the state legislature freely vacated judicial proceedings, suspended judicial actions, annulled or modified judgments, cancelled executions, reopened controversies, authorized appeals, granted exemptions from the standing law, expounded the law for pending cases, and even determined the merits of disputes.[11] Nor do such practices seem to have been more aggravated in New Hampshire than in several other states. Certainly they were widespread, and they were evidently possible in any of the states under the views then obtaining of "legislative power."[12]

Neither is the explanation of such views far to seek. Coke's fusion of what we should today distinguish as "legislative" and "judicial" powers in the case of the "High Court of Parliament" represented the teaching of the highest of all legal authorities before Blackstone appeared on the scene.[13] What is equally important, the Cokean doctrine corresponded exactly to the contemporary necessities of many of the colonies in the earlier days of their existence.[14] Thus, owing to the dearth not only of courts and lawyers, but even of a recognized code of

---

10. Sec. 11 (2d ed. J. Lewis ed. 1904).

11. See 5 *Laws of New Hampshire* (Batchellor ed. 1904–1922) *passim*. Some of the less usual items are those at 21, 66, 89, 90–91, 110–11, 125–26, 130–31, 167–68, 243, 320–21, 334–35, 363, 395–96, 400–401, 404–406, 411–12, 417–18, 455–56, 485, 499, 522. The volume is crowded with acts "restoring" a defeated or defaulting party "to his law," "any usage, custom, or law to the contrary notwithstanding."

12. See the references I have collected in my *Doctrine of Judicial Review* 69–71 (1914); also S. E. Baldwin, *The American Judiciary* ch. 2 (1905).

13. C. McIlwain, *The High Court of Parliament and Its Supremacy* ch. 3 (1910)

14. Baldwin, *American Judiciary* ch. 1.

law, bodies like the Massachusetts General Court had thrust upon them at first a far greater bulk of judicial and administrative work, in today's sense of these terms, than of lawmaking proper, while conversely such judges as existed in these early days performed administrative as well as judicial functions, very much as had been the case with the earliest itinerant judges in England. By the middle of the eighteenth century, it is true, a distinct improvement had taken place in these regards. Regularly organized systems of courts now existed in all the colonies. A bar trained in the common law was rapidly arising. Royal governors sometimes disallowed enactments interfering with the usual course of justice in the ordinary courts, on grounds anticipatory of modern doctrine.[15] Then, however, came the outbreak of the Revolution, and with it a reversion to more primitive practices and ideas, traceable in the first instance to the collapse of the royal judicial establishment, but later to the desire to take a short course with enemies of the new regime, against whom, first and last, every state in the Union appears to have enacted bills of pains and penalties of greater or less severity.[16] Furthermore, it should be observed that, owing to a popular prejudice, certain of the states—notably New York and Massachusetts—at first withheld equity powers from their courts altogether, while several others granted them but sparingly.[17] The result was fairly to compel the legislature to intervene in many instances with "special legislation," disallowing fraudulent transactions, curing defective titles, authorizing urgent sales of property, and the like.[18] Between legislation of this species and outright interferences with the remedial law itself there was often little to distinguish.

That, therefore, the vague doctrine of the separation of powers should at first have been interpreted and applied in the light of this history is not astonishing. This, as we have seen, left legislative power without definition on its side toward judicial power, except as the power of the supreme organ of the state, which meant, however, the withholding from judicial power of that which, to the modern way of thinking, is its highest attribute—to wit, power of deciding with finality. Nothing could be more instructive in this connection than some sentences from Jefferson's *Notes on Virginia,* dating from about 1781. Pointing out that the Virginia constitution of 1776 incorporated the principle of the separation of powers, Jefferson proceeds to expound this principle in a way which leaves it meaning little more than a caution against plurality of offices. "No person shall exercise the powers of more than one of them [the three departments] at the same time," are his words. But even more significant is the following passage:

> If [it runs] the legislature assumes executive and judiciary powers, no opposition is
> likely to be made; nor, if made, can it be effectual; because in that case they may

15. See, e.g., 1 *Messages from the Governors* (of New York) 55 (C. Z. Lincoln ed. 1909).

16. A good summary of legislative persecution of the Loyalists appears in C. H. Van Tyne, *American Revolution* 255 ff. (1905).

17. *Two Centuries' Growth of American Law* {*1701-1901*} 129-33 (1902).

18. T. Cooley, *Constitutional Limitations* ch. 5 {5th ed. 1883}.

put their proceedings into the form of an act of assembly, which will render them obligatory on the other branches. They have, accordingly, in many instances, decided rights which should have been left to judiciary controversy; and the direction of the executive, during the whole time of their session, is becoming habitual and familiar.[19]

The concept of legislative power here expressed is obviously a purely formal one: "legislative power" is any power which the legislative organ may choose to exercise by resort to the ordinary parliamentary processes.

And not less striking is the recital which Hamilton gives in *Federalist*, no. 81, of certain objections by opponents of the Constitution to the powers of the Supreme Court:

> The authority of the { . . . } Supreme Court of the United States, which is to be a separate and independent body, will be superior to that of the legislature. The power of construing the laws according to the *spirit* of the Constitution will enable that Court to mould them into whatever shape it may think proper; especially as its decisions will not be in any manner subject to the revision or correction of the legislative body. This is as unprecedented as it is dangerous. . . . The Parliament of Great Britain, and the legislatures of the several states, can at any time rectify, by law, the exceptionable decisions of their respective courts. But the errors and usurpations of the Supreme Court of the United States will be uncontrollable and remediless.

Hamilton's answer to all this was simply that "the theory neither of the British, nor the state constitutions, authorizes the revisal of a judicial sentence by a legislative act," that "the impropriety of the thing" even in the case of the United States Constitution rested not on any distinctive provision thereof, but "on the general principles of law and reason"; that a legislature could not, "without exceeding its province, ... reverse a determination once made in a particular case," though it might "prescribe a new rule for future cases"; and that this principle applied "in all its consequences, exactly in the same manner and extent, to the state governments as to the national government."[20] This answer, for which is cited only the authority of Montesquieu, is conclusive from the standpoint of modern constitutional doctrine; but its contradiction of the views and practices which were prevalent in 1787 is manifest.

II.

Finally, the structural and functional shortcomings of the early state constitutions played directly into the hands of both popular and doctrinal tendencies

---

19. 2 *Writings* 163–64 (Memorial ed. 1903). See to the same effect Chief Justice Pendleton's words in 4 Call 5, 17 (Va. 1782).

20. In *Federalist*, no. 47, Madison also declares that "the entire legislature [i.e., Parliament] can perform no judiciary act." This assertion is based on his reading of Montesquieu, but it is untrue even of Parliament today. 4 H. J. Stephen, *Commentaries* 283 (11th ed.); A. F. Pollard, *Evolution of Parliament* 239 (1920).

which distinctly menaced what Madison called "the security of private rights." Throughout the Revolution the Blackstonian doctrine of "legislative omnipotence" was in the ascendant. Marshall read Blackstone and so did Iredell—to what effect later developments were to make clear.[21] And even more radical doctrine was abroad. One Benjamin Hichborn's assertion, in a speech delivered in Boston in 1777, that civil liberty was "not a government by laws," but "a power existing in the people at large" "to alter or annihilate both the mode and essence of any former government" "for any cause or for no cause at all, but their own sovereign pleasure"[22] voiced an extension to the right of revolution hitherto unheard of outside the pages of Rousseau; and even so good a republican as John Adams was disturbed at manifestations of social ferment which he traced to a new spirit of equality.[23]

The sharp edge of "legislative omnipotence" did not pause with the Tories who, as enemies of the state, were perhaps beyond the pale of the Constitution. Everywhere legislative assemblies, energized by the reforming impulse of the period, were led to attempt results which, even when they lay within the proper field of lawmaking, we should today regard as requiring constitutional amendments to effect them. Virginia, as Bancroft writes, used her "right of original and complete legislation to abolish the privileges of primogeniture, cut off entails, forbid the slave trade, and establish the principle of freedom in religion as the inherent and inalienable possession of spiritual beings";[24] while elsewhere the liberal forces of the hour assailed the vested interest of negro slavery more directly. Vermont, Massachusetts, and New Hampshire ridded themselves of slavery by constitutional amendment or in consequence of judicial construction of the Constitution.[25] In Pennsylvania, Rhode Island, and Connecticut, on the other hand, gradual emancipation was brought about by ordinary legislative enactment.[26] Yet the cause of reform did not have it all its own way. When a similar measure was proposed in New Jersey, it drew forth a protest on constitutional grounds which is remarkable in its anticipation of later doctrines.[27]

But it was not reform, nor even special legislation, which early affixed to the

---

21. Iredell's perusal of Blackstone produced an entire change in his theory of the basis of judicial review. Compare 2 G. J. McRee, *Life and Correspondence of James Iredell* 172-73 (1857); and Calder v. Bull, 3 Dallas 386 at 398 (1798). One aspect of Marshall's thinking on the same matter is touched upon briefly in note 40, below.

22. Niles, *Principles* 47.

23. 6 *Life and Works* 94-97 (C. F. Adams ed. 1850-1856); A. E. Morse, *The Federalist Party in Massachusetts* 68-69 (1909).

24. 5 *History* 329 (1892).

25. A. B. Hart, *Slavery and Abolition* 153 (1906). See also G. H. Moore, *Slavery in Massachusetts* (1866).

26. Hart, *Slavery and Abolition* 154.

27. F. Moore, *Diary of the American Revolution* 362 (1875). See also 4 *Works of Alexander Hamilton* 232 (Constitutional ed. 1885-1886).

state legislature a stigma of which as an institution it has never even yet quite ridded itself.[28] The legislation just reviewed belonged for the most part to the period of the war and was the work of a society which, the Tory element apart, was politically unified and acknowledged an easily ascertainable leadership. Once, however, hostilities were past and the pressure alike of a common peril and a common enthusiasm removed, the republican lute began to show rifts. The most evident line of cleavage at first was that between seaboard and back country; but this presently became coincident to a large extent with a much more ominous division into creditors and debtors. That class of farmer-debtors which now began to align itself with the demagogues in the state legislatures, in opposition to the mercantile-creditor class, was experiencing the usual grievance of agriculturists after a war, that of shouldering the burden of the return to normalcy. But the point of view of the creditor class may not be justly ignored either. By their provincial policies with respect to commerce the state legislatures had already seriously impaired legitimate interests of this class,[29] and they now proceeded to attack what under the standing law were its unchallengeable rights. In each of the thirteen states a "rag money" party appeared, which in seven states triumphed outright, while in several others it came near doing so. Nor was payment even in paper currency always the creditor's lot, for besides rag-money measures and tender laws, or in lieu of them, statutes suspending all actions upon debts were enacted, payment of debts in kind was authorized, and even payment in land.[30]

It is a frequent maxim of policy that things must be permitted to grow worse before their betterment can be attempted to advantage. The paper-money craze at least proved serviceable in invigorating the criticism which had begun even earlier of the existing state governments. One such critic was Jefferson, who in his *Notes on Virginia* bitterly assailed the Virginia constitution of 1776 for having produced a concentration of power in the legislative assembly which answered to "precisely the definition of despotic government." Nor did it make any difference, he continued, that such powers were vested in a numerous body "chosen by ourselves"; "one hundred and seventy-three despots" were "as oppressive as one"; and "an elective despotism was not the government we fought for, but one which should not only be founded on free principles, but in which the powers of government should be so divided and balanced among several bodies of magistracy, as that no one could transcend their legal limits, without being effectually checked and restrained by the others."[31]

28. This seems to have been the origin of the American distrust of legislatures, upon which Bryce comments in his 1 *American Commonwealth* 427, 451 (2d ed. 1889).

29. D. W. Brown, *The Commercial Power of Congress* ch. 2 (1910); A. A. Giesecke, *American Commercial Legislation before 1789* (1910).

30. A. McLaughlin, *The Confederation and the Constitution* ch. 9 (1905).

31. 2 *Writings* 160 ff. (Memorial ed.).

And this was also the point of view of the Pennsylvania Council of Censors, in their celebrated report of 1784.[32] Extending through some thirty finely printed pages, this document listed many examples, "selected," we are told, "from a multitude" of legislative violations of the state constitution and bill of rights. Several of the measures so stigmatized were of a general nature, but those for which the censors reserved their severest strictures were acts involving the rights of named parties. Thus fines had been remitted, judicially established claims disallowed, verdicts of juries set aside, the property of one given to another, defective titles secured, marriages dissolved, particular persons held in execution of debt released—and all by a species of legislative activity which had been explicitly condemned both by "the illustrious Montesquieu" and "the great Locke."

Two years later came the early volumes of John Adams' *Defense of the Constitutions,* in answer to M. Turgot's criticism that the American constitutions represented "an unreasonable imitation of the usages of England." In reality the work was much less a "defense" than an exhortation to constitutional reform in other states along the lines which Massachusetts had already taken under Adams' own guidance. A new and significant note, however, appears in this work. In his earlier writings Adams had assumed with Montesquieu that the great source of danger to liberty lay in the selfishness and ambition of the governors themselves. But with the lesson of the paper-money agitation before him, he now gives warning of the danger to which republics, when they have become populous and overcrowded and the inevitable doom of poverty has appeared in their midst, are peculiarly exposed from the rise of parties. "Misarrangements now made," he writes, "will have great, extensive, and distant consequences; and we are now employed, how little soever we may think of it, in making establishments which will affect the happiness of a hundred millions of inhabitants at a time, in a period not very distant."[33]

Copies of the *Defense* reached the United States early in 1787, and were circulated among the members of the Philadelphia Convention, reviving and freshening belief in "political science" and particularly in the teachings of Montesquieu. Yet in one respect at least the idea of reform for which Adams' work stood and that which the Convention represented were poles apart. For while the former still illustrated the opinion that constitutional reform was a purely local problem, the Convention represented the triumph of the idea that reform to be effective must be national in scope and must embrace the entire American constitutional system in a single coherent program. That such a program could have been elaborated without the signal contribution to it of the effort for local reform is, on the other hand, altogether improbable.

32. *Proceedings Relative to the Calling of the Conventions of 1776 and 1790* 83ff. (Harrisburg, 1825). For a contemporary criticism of the report, see *Federalist,* no. 49.
33. 4 *Life and Works* 273 ff. The quotation is at 587.

III.

It was Walter Bagehot's opinion that Americans were prone to give credit to the Constitution which was more justly due themselves. "The men of Massachusetts," he declared, "could work *any* constitution."[34] What had evidently impressed him was the American habit of supplying shortcomings in the Constitution by construction rather than outright amendment. Yet for construction to do really effective work, it must have elbowroom and a handle to take hold of; and at least the merit of having afforded these cannot be denied the Constitution.

Nor were the early state constitutions entirely lacking in invitation to this American aptitude for documentary exegesis, which had its origin, one suspects, in an earlier taste for theological disquisition. The executive veto, which was the practical nub of all Adams' preachments, was brought about, to be sure, through specific provision being made for it in the written constitution, and to so good purpose that it is to be found today in nearly every constitution in the country.[35] The other suggested remedy of critics of "the legislative vortex," on the contrary, was introduced solely by the processes of interpretation and without the slightest textual alteration being made in the constitutions involved. This was judicial review. Thus while the executive veto and judicial review have a common explanation in the political necessity which they were devised to meet, the manner in which they were respectively articulated to the American constitutional system was widely and for us most significantly divergent. The executive veto was and remains mere matter of fact without the slightest further interest for us; judicial review is both a practice and a *doctrine,* and in the latter aspect especially is of immediate interest.

As a practice judicial review made its initial appearance in independent America in 1780, in the case of Holmes v. Walton,[36] in which the Supreme Court of New Jersey refused to carry out an act of the legislature providing for the trial of a designated class of offenders by a jury of six, whereas, the court held, the state constitution contemplated the common law jury of twelve. Although the opinion of the court apparently was never published, the force of the example may have been considerable. From this time on the notion crops up sporadically in other jurisdictions, at intervals of about two years, in a series of dicta and rulings which—thanks in no small part to popular misapprehension as to their precise bearing—brought the idea before the Philadelphia Convention.[37] And meantime the main premises of the *doctrine* of judicial review—the principles whereby it came to be annexed to the written constitution—had been worked out.

First and last, many and various arguments have been offered to prove that

---

34. *The English Constitution* 296 (1906).

35. F. J. Stimson, *Federal and State Constitutions* sec. 304 (1908).

36. Austin Scott, "Holmes v. Walton, the New Jersey Precedent," in 4 *Am. Hist. Rev.* 456 ff. (1899).

37. See generally my *Doctrine of Judicial Review* at 71–75 and references there given.

judicial review is implied in the very nature of a written constitution, some of them manifestly insufficient for the purpose; though that is not to say that they may not have assisted in securing general acceptance of the institution. "Superstitions believed are, in their effect, truths"; and it has accordingly happened more than once that the actual influence of an idea has been out of all proportion to its logical or scientific merits. These more or less spurious proofs of judicial review, however, we here pass by without further consideration, in order to come at once to what, on both historical and logical grounds, may be termed the true doctrine of judicial review. This embraces three propositions: first, that the Constitution is supreme; second, that it is law, in the sense of a rule enforceable by courts; and third, that judicial interpretations of the standing law are final, at least for the cases in the decision of which they are pronounced. Let us consider the two latter propositions somewhat further.

The claim of the Constitution to be considered *law* may rest on either one of two grounds, depending on whether "law" be regarded as an unfolding of the divine order of things or as an expression of human will—as an act of knowledge (or revelation) or an act of power.[38] Considered from the former point of view—which is that of Locke and other exponents of the law of nature—the claim of the Constitution to be obeyed is due simply to its content, to the principles which it incorporates because of their intrinsic sanctity; considered from the latter point of view—that of Hobbes and the "positive school of jurisprudence"—its claim to obedience is due to its source in a sovereign will—that of the people. Actually both views have been taken at different times, but that judicial review originally owed more to the former than to the latter conception seems fairly clear.

Of all the so-called "precedents" for judicial review antecedent to the Convention of 1787, the one which called forth the most elaborate argument on theoretical grounds and which produced the most evident impression on the membership of the Convention, was the Rhode Island case of Trevett v. Weeden,[39] which was decided early in 1786. The feature of the case which is of immediate pertinence is the argument which it evoked against the act on the part of the attorney for defendant, James Varnum. In developing the theory of a law superior to legislative enactments, Varnum appealed indifferently to the Rhode Island charter, "general principles," "invariable custom," "Magna Carta," "fundamental law," "the law of nature," "the law of God"; asserting with reference to the last, that "all men, judges included," were bound by it "in preference to any human laws." In short, Varnum, going directly back to the Cokean tradition, built his argument for judicial review on the loose connotation of the word "law" still obtaining in the eighteenth century, especially among American readers of Coke and Locke—to say nothing of the host of writers on

38. T. E. Holland, *Elements of Jurisprudence* 19–21, 32–34, 41–45 (13th ed. 1924).
39. See note 37, above; also Varnum's contemporary pamphlet on the case. The case was the first and last case of judicial review of the sort under the old charter.

the law of nations. Nor is the conduciveness of such an argument to judicial review open to conjecture. In the first place, it kept alive, even after the fires of revolution had cooled, the notion that the claim of law to obedience consists in its intrinsic excellence rather than its origin. Again, it made rational the notion of a hierarchy of laws in which the will of merely human legislators might on occasion be required to assume a subordinate place. Lastly, by the same token, it made rational the notion of judges pitting knowledge against sheer legislative self-assertion.

Contrariwise, the Blackstonian concept of legislative sovereignty was calculated to frustrate judicial review not only by attributing to the legislature an uncontrollable authority, but also by pressing forward the so-called "positive" conception of law and the differentiation of legal from moral obligation which this impels. Fortunately, in the notion of popular sovereignty the means of checkmating the notion of legislative sovereignty was available. For, once it became possible to attribute to the people at large a lawmaking, rather than a merely constituent, capacity, the Constitution exchanged its primary character as a statement of sacrosanct principles for that of the expressed will of the highest lawmaking power on earth.[40]

But to produce judicial review, the notion of the Constitution as law must be accompanied by the principle of the finality of judicial constructions of the law, which obviously rests upon a definition of the respective roles of "legislative" and "judicial" power in relation to the standing law. In other words, judicial review raised from the other side of the line the same problem as did "legislative interferences with the dispensation of justice"; and, in fact, it can be shown that the solution of the two problems proceeded in many jurisdictions *pari passu*.[41] The whole subject is one which demands rather ample consideration.

Although the functional differentiation of the three powers of government, first hinted in Aristotle's *Politics*,[42] necessarily preceded their organic distribution to some extent, it is not essential for our purposes to trace either process further back than to Coke's repeated insistence in his *Institutes* that "the king hath wholly left matters of judicature according to his laws to his judges."[43] In these words, it is not too much to say, the royal prerogative, which had long lain fallow in this respect, was thrust forever from the province of the courts. One of these same courts, on the other hand, was "the High Court of Parliament"; and

40. Compare in this connection Luther Martin's "Genuine Information," in 3 Farrand's *Records* 230, with Hamilton's argument for judicial review in *Federalist,* no. 78, and Marshall's opinion in Marbury v. Madison, 1 Cranch 129 (1803). The former regards political authority as a *cessio* from the people to the government which "never devolves back to them" except in events amounting to a dissolution of government. The latter regard it as a revocable *translatio* to agents by a principal who is by no means bound to act through agents.

41. See my "Basic Doctrine of American Constitutional Law," in 12 *Mich. L. Rev.* 256, 260 (1914).

42. Bk. IV, ch. 14.

43. 4 *Institutes* 70, 71; 12 *Reports* 63.

Coke nowhere suggests that "the power of judicature" which he attributes to Parliament is to be distinguished from the power which Parliament ordinarily exercised in "proceeding by bill."[44] Far different is the case of Locke. His declaration that "the legislative or supreme authority cannot assume to itself a power to rule by extemporary arbitrary decrees, but is bound to dispense justice and decide the rights of the subject by promulgated standing laws and known authorized judges" represents progress toward a "material" as against a merely "formal" definition of legislative power, both in the total exclusion which it effects of the legislative body from the business of judging and also in the ideal which it lays down of statute law.[45] Noteworthy, too, from the same point of view is Montesquieu's characterization of the judges as "but the mouthpieces of the law," accompanied, as it is, by the assertion that the mergence of "the judiciary power" with "the legislative" would render the judge "a legislator" vested with arbitrary power over the life and liberty of the subject.[46]

As usual, Blackstone's contribution is somewhat more difficult to assess. He adopts without qualification the views just quoted from Locke and Montesquieu, and he urges that "all laws should be made to commence *in futuro*." Yet the very illustration he furnishes of his definition of "municipal law" as "a rule . . . permanent, uniform, and universal" violates this precept radically, since it shows that in his estimation the *ex post facto* operation of a rule, however undesirable in itself, does not affect its title to be regarded as "law." Nor, in fact, does it occur to him, in assigning to Parliament power to "expound" the law, to distinguish those instances in which the exercise of this power would mark an intrusion upon judicial freedom of decision, while his sweeping attribution to Parliament of jurisdiction over "all mischiefs and grievances, operations and remedies that transcend the ordinary course of the laws"—a matter evidently to be judged of by Parliament itself—lands us again in the Cokean bog from which we set out.[47]

The differentiation of legislative and judicial power, upon which judicial review pivots, appears to have been immediately due, not to any definition of legislative *power*, but to a definition of judicial *duty* in relation to the standing law and especially to the law of decided cases. In the opening sentence of Bacon's "Essay on Judicature" one reads: "Judges ought to remember that their office is *'jus dicere'* and not *'jus dare'*; to interpret law, and not to make or give law"—words which have been reiterated many times as embodying the doctrine of *stare decisis*.[48] Coke employs different language, but his thought is not essentially different: "Judges discern by law what is just"; the law is "the

44. 4 *Institutes* 23, 26, 36.
45. *Second Treatise on Civil Government* ch. 11, sec. 136.
46. *Spirit of Laws* bk. 11, ch. 6 (Prichard tr. 1902).
47. 1 Bl. *Comm.* 44, 46, 58, 160–61, 267, 269.
48. H. Broom, *Maxims* 105 and citations (5th American ed. Philadelphia 1864); at 140–41 of the original edition.

golden metwand whereby all men's causes are justly and evenly measured.'' He also notes the artificiality of the law's ''reason and judgment,'' and pays full tribute to the burden of study and experience ''before that a man can attain to the cognizance of it.''[49] Judicial duty is thus matched with judicial aptitude—the judges are the experts of the law—or, in the words of Blackstone, its ''living oracles,'' sworn to determine, not according to their own private judgment, ''but according to the known laws and customs of the land; not delegated to pronounce a new law, but to maintain and expound the old one.''[50]

In brief, it is the duty of judges to conserve the law, not to change it, a task for which their learning pre-eminently fits them. Yet a mystery remains to clear up; for how came this *duty* of subordination to the law to be transmuted into a claim of exclusive *power* in relation to it—the power of interpreting it with final force and effect? By the doctrine of the separation of powers, the outstanding prerogatives of each department are no doubt its peculiar possession; but still that does not explain why in the final apportionment of territory between the legislative and judicial departments in the United States, the function of law interpretation fell to the latter. The fact is that we here confront *the* act of creation—or perhaps it would be better to say, act of prestidigitation—attending the elaboration of the doctrine of judicial review; and what is more, we know the authors of it—or some of them.

In his argument in the case of Trevett v. Weeden, Varnum put the question: ''Have the judges a power to repeal, to amend, to alter, or to make new laws?'' and then proceeded to answer it thus: ''God forbid! In that case they would be legislators. . . . But the judiciary have the sole power of judging of laws . . . and cannot admit any act of the legislatures as law against the Constitution.'' And to the same effect is the defense which James Iredell penned of the North Carolina Supreme Court's decision in Bayard v. Singleton,[51] while Davie, his associate in the case, was in attendance upon the Convention at Philadelphia.

> The duty of that [the judicial] department [he wrote] I conceive in all cases is to decide according to the laws of the state. It will not be denied, I suppose, that the constitution is a law of the state, as well as an act of assembly, with this difference only, that it is the *fundamental* law, and unalterable by the legislature, which derives all its power from it. . . . The judges, therefore, must take care at their peril, that every act of assembly they presume to enforce is warranted by the constitution, since if it is not, they act without lawful authority.

Nor is this a power which may be exercised by ministerial officers, ''for if the power of judging rests with the courts their decision is final.''[52]

Here are all the premises of the doctrine of judicial review either explicitly stated or clearly implied: the superiority of the Constitution to statute law—the

49. See note 43, above.
50. 1 Bl. *Comm.* 69–71.
51. 1 Martin 42.
52. 2 McRee, *Life and Correspondence of Iredell* 145–49.

case of the common law had still to be dealt with; its quality as law knowable by judges in their official capacity and applicable by them to cases; the exclusion of "legislative power" from the ancient field of parliamentary power in law interpretation, except in circumstances in which the law is subject to legislative amendment. The classical version of the doctrine of judicial review in *Federalist*, no. 78, improves upon the statement of these premises but adds nothing essential to them.

IV.

We turn now to that phase of the problem which confronted the Philadelphia Convention in consequence of the insufficiencies of the government established by the Articles of Confederation. And at the outset let it be remarked that with all their defects, and serious as these were, the Articles nonetheless performed two services of great moment: they kept the idea of union vital during the period when the feeling of national unity was at its lowest ebb; and they accorded formal recognition that the great powers of war and foreign relations were intrinsically national in character. Those two most dramatic and interesting functions belonged to the general government from the first and became the central magnet to which other powers necessarily gravitated.

The essential defect of the Articles of Confederation, as has been so often pointed out,[53] consisted in the fact that the government established by them operated not upon the individual citizens of the United States but upon the states in their corporate capacity—that, in brief, it was not a government at all, but rather the central agency of an alliance. As a consequence, on the one hand, even the powers theoretically belonging to the Congress of the Confederation were practically unenforceable; while, on the other hand, the theoretical scope of its authority was unduly narrow. Inasmuch as taxes are collectible from individuals, Congress could not levy them; inasmuch as commerce is an affair of individuals, Congress could not regulate it; and its treaties had not at first the force of laws, since to have given them that operation would again have been to impinge upon individuals directly and not through the mediation of the state legislatures. Furthermore, the powers withheld from Congress remained with the states—which is to say, *with their legislatures*. The evil thence resulting was thus a double one. Not only was a common policy impracticable in fields where it was most evidently necessary, but also the local legislatures had it in their power to embroil both the country as a whole with foreign nations and its constituent parts with each other. So the weakness of the Confederation played directly into the hands of the chief defect of government within the states themselves—an excessive concentration of power in the hands of the legislative department.

The endeavors which were made to render the Articles of Confederation a

---

53. See especially *Federalist*, no. 15.

workable instrument of government proceeded, naturally, along the two lines of amendment and construction. In theory the Articles were amendable; but owing to the requirement that amendments had to be ratified by all the states, in practice they were not so.[54] Recourse, therefore, had early to be had to the other method, and eventually with fruitful results.

Yet the possibilities of constitutional construction, too, were at the outset seriously curtailed by the transmutation of the Blackstonian teaching into the dogma of state sovereignty.[55] Fortunately, the notion of American nationality, which the early fervors of the Revolution had evoked into something like articulate expression, did not altogether lack a supporting interest. This consisted in the determination of the states with definite western boundaries to convert the territory between the Alleghenies and the Mississippi into a national domain. Their spokesman accordingly advanced the argument that the royal title to this region had devolved, in consequence of the Revolution, not upon the states with "sea-to-sea" charters, but upon the American people as a whole[56]—a premise of infinite possibilities, as soon appeared.

On the very last day of 1781 Congress passed the act incorporating the Bank of North America. Not only was there no clause of the Articles which authorized Congress to create corporations, but the second article specifically stipulated that "each state retains its sovereignty, freedom, and independence, and every power, jurisdiction, and right which is not by the Confederation expressly delegated to the United States in Congress assembled." Quite naturally, the validity of the charter was challenged, whereupon its defense was undertaken by James Wilson. The article just quoted Wilson swept aside at the outset as entirely irrelevant to the question. Inasmuch, said he, as no state could claim or exercise "any power or act of sovereignty extending over all the other states or any of them," it followed that the power to "incorporate a bank commensurate to the United States" was "not an act of sovereignty or a power . . . which by the second Article . . . must be expressly delegated to Congress in order to be possessed by that body." Congress' power, in fact, rested on other premises. "To many purposes," he continued, "the United States are to be considered as one undivided nation; and as possessed of all the rights and powers, and properties by the law of nations incident to such. Whenever an object occurs to the direction of which no particular state is competent, the management of it must of necessity belong to the United States in Congress assembled."[57] In short, from the very fact of its exercise on a national scale a power ceased to be one claimable by a state. The reflection is suggested that if the Articles of Confederation had con-

---

54. McLaughlin, *Confederation and Constitution* ch. 11.

55. Van Tyne, "Sovereignty in the American Revolution" in 12 *Am. Hist. Rev.* 529 ff. (1907).

56. 18 *Journals of the Continental Congress* 936–37 (Hunt ed. 1904–1937); 5 F. Wharton, *Revolutionary Diplomatic Correspondence* 88–89 (1888); New York Historical Society, Collections 138–39 (1878); J. C. Welling in 3 *Am. Hist. Assoc.*, Papers 167 ff. (1888).

57. 1 *Works of James Wilson* 558 ff (J. D. Andrews ed. 1896).

tinued subject to this canon of construction, they might easily have come to support an even greater structure of derived powers than the Constitution of the United States does at this moment.

The question, however, upon which the permanently fruitful efforts of constitutional construction were at this time brought to bear was that of treaty enforcement; and while the story is not a new one, its full significance seems not to have been altogether appreciated. The starting point is furnished by the complaints which the British government began lodging with Congress very shortly after the making of the peace treaty that the state legislatures were putting impediments in the way of British creditors and were renewing confiscations of Loyalist property contrary to Articles IV and VI, respectively, of the treaty.[58]

Now it should be observed that the immediate beneficiaries of these articles were certain classes of *private persons,* whose claims, moreover, were such as would ordinarily have to be asserted against other individuals *in court.* If, therefore, it could only be assured that the state courts would accord such claims proper recognition and enforcement, the obligation of the United States as a government, under the treaty, would be performed and the complaints of the other party to the treaty must thereupon cease. But how could this be assured? The answer was suggested by the current vague connotation of the word "law" and the current endeavor to find in "judicial power" a check upon legislative power in the states.

Nor can there be any doubt as to who first formulated this solution. It was Alexander Hamilton in his argument before a municipal court in New York City in the case of Rutgers v. Waddington in 1784, practically contemporaneously with the British protests above referred to.[59] The case involved a recent enactment of the state legislature creating a right of action for trespass against Tory occupants of premises in favor of owners who had fled the city during the British possession. In his capacity as Waddington's attorney, Hamilton assailed the act as contrary to principles of the law of nations, to the treaty of peace, which he asserted implied an amnesty, and the Articles of Confederation, and as, therefore, void. Only the manuscript notes of his argument are extant, but these sufficiently indicate its bearing for our purpose:

> Congress have made a treaty [they read in part]. A breach of that would be a breach of their constitutional authority. . . . as well a county may alter the laws of the state as the state those of the Confederation. . . . While Confed. exists its cons. autho. paramount. But how are judges to decide? Ans.: Cons. giving jud. power only in prize causes in all others judges of each state must of necessity be judges of United States. And the law of each state must adopt the laws of Congress. Though in relation to its own citizens local laws might govern, yet in relation to foreigners

58. W. MacDonald, *Documentary Source Book* 207–208 (1908).
59. See H. B. Dawson's pamphlet on the case; also Coxe's and Haines's well-known volumes. Hamilton had the year previous been a member of a committee of Congress which had the subject of violations of the treaty of peace under consideration. For the report of this committee, see 4 *Journals of the American Congress* 224–25 (Washington 1823).

those of United States must prevail. It must be conceded leg. of one state cannot repeal law of United States. All must be construed to stand together.[60]

There is a striking parallel between the cases of Rutgers v. Waddington and Trevett v. Weeden, and especially between the subsequent fate of Hamilton's argument in the one and Varnum's in the other. In each case the court concerned decided adversely to the party relying upon the statute before it, but did so on grounds which avoided its committing itself on the issue of judicial review. In each case, nevertheless, the exponents of Blackstonian absolutism raised loud protests in behalf of the threatened legislative authority, with the result of spreading the impression that the judges had met the issue squarely. Yet since what the judges had said hardly bore out this impression, interested attention was naturally directed in turn to the franker and more extensive claims of counsel; and while Varnum was spreading his argument broadcast as a pamphlet, Hamilton was reiterating his views in his *Letters from Phocion*.[61]

Of the various repercussions from Hamilton's argument in Rutgers v. Waddington the most important is the report which John Jay—a fellow New Yorker—rendered to Congress as Secretary for Foreign Affairs, in October 1786, on the subject of state violations of treaties. The salient passage of this document reads as follows:

> Your Secretary considers the thirteen independent sovereign states as having, by express delegation of power, formed and vested in Congress a perfect though limited sovereignty for the general and national purposes specified in the Confederation. In this sovereignty they cannot severally participate (except by their delegates) or have concurrent jurisdiction.... When therefore a treaty is constitutionally made, ratified and published by Congress, it immediately becomes binding on the whole nation, and superadded to the laws of the land, without the intervention, consent or fiat of state legislatures.

It was, therefore, Jay argued, the duty of the state judiciaries in cases between private individuals "respecting the meaning of a treaty," to give it full enforcement in harmony with "the rules and maxims established by the laws of nations for the interpretation of treaties." He accordingly recommended that Congress formally deny the right of the state legislatures to enact laws construing "a national treaty" or impeding its operation "in any manner," that it avow its opinion that all acts on the statute books repugnant to the treaty of peace should be at once repealed, and that it urge the repeal to be in general terms which would leave it with the local judiciaries to decide all cases arising under the treaty according to the intent thereof "anything in the said acts ... to the contrary notwithstanding."[62]

The following March, Congress adopted the resolutions which Jay had pro-

---

60. A. M. Hamilton, *The Intimate Life of Alexander Hamilton* 457, 460–61 (1911). "Our sovereignty began by a Federal act," he asserts (at 459).
61. See 4 *Works of Alexander Hamilton* 238–40 (Constitutional ed.).
62. 4 *Secret Journals of Congress* 185–287 (Boston 1821).

posed, without a dissenting vote, and in April, within a month of the date set for the assembling of the Philadelphia Convention, transmitted them to the state legislatures, by the majority of which they were promptly complied with.[63] Nor is the theory on which such repeals were based doubtful. We find it stated in the declaration of the North Carolina Supreme Court in the above-mentioned case of Bayard v. Singleton, which was decided the very month that the Convention came together, that "the Articles of Confederation are a part of the law of the land unrepealable by any act of the General Assembly."

From all this to Article VI of the Constitution is manifestly only a step, though an important one. The supremacy which Jay's plan assured the national treaties is in Article VI but part and parcel of national supremacy in all its phases; but this broader supremacy is still guaranteed by being brought to bear upon individuals, in contrast to states, through the intervention in the first instance often of the state courts. Thus the solution provided of the question of treaty enforcement, whereby the cause of national supremacy was linked with that of judicial review, clearly foreshadowed the ultimate character of the national government as a government acting upon individuals in the main rather than upon the states. Logically, national power operative through courts is a deduction from a government over individuals; chronologically, the order of ideas was the reverse.

V.

The theory that the Articles of Confederation were for some purposes law, directly cognizable by courts, entirely transformed the character of the Confederation so far forth, and must sooner or later have suggested the idea of its entire transformation into a real government. Nor was judicial review the only possible source of such a suggestion. As Madison points out in the *Federalist*, "in cases of capture, of piracy, of the post office, of coins, weights, and measures, of trade with the Indians, of claims under grants of land by different states, and, above all, in the case of trials by courts-martial in the army and navy," the government of the Confederation acted immediately on individuals from the first.[64] Again, proposals which were laid at various times before the states for conferring a customs revenue on Congress, though none was ever finally ratified, served to bring the same idea before the people, as also did the proposals which never reached the states from Congress to endow the latter with "the sole and exclusive" power over foreign and interstate trade.[65]

But even earlier the suggestion of a "continental conference" for the purpose of framing a "continental charter" akin to Magna Carta had been propounded in that famous issue of *Common Sense* in which the signal was given for indepen-

---

63. Jefferson's letter of May 29, 1792, to the British minister Hammond, gives all the facts. 16 *Writings* 183–277 (Memorial ed.).

64. *Federalist*, no. 40.

65. D. W. Brown, *Commercial Power of Congress* ch. 2.

dence itself. It would be the task of such a body, wrote Paine, to fix "the number and manner of choosing members of Congress and members of assembly," and to draw "the line of business and jurisdiction between them (always remembering that our strength is continental and not provincial)." Such a charter would also secure "freedom and property to all men," and indeed, would fill the place of monarchy itself in the new state. "That we may not appear to be defective even in earthly honors, let a day be solemnly set apart for proclaiming the charter; let it be brought forth placed on the divine law, the word of God; let a crown be placed thereon, by which the world may know that so far we approve monarchy that in America the law is king."[66]

In this singular mixture of sense and fantasy, so characteristic of its author, are adumbrated a national constitutional convention, the dual plan of our federal system, a national bill of rights, and "worship of the Constitution"; and this was some months before the earliest state constitution and nearly four years before Hamilton's proposal, in his letter to Duane of September 3, 1780, of "a solid, coercive Union."[67]

But the great essential precursor to the success of all such proposals was the consolidation of a sufficient interest transcending state lines, and this was slow in forming. It was eventually brought about in three ways: first, through the abuse by the states of their powers over commerce; secondly, through the rise of the question—in which Washington was especially interested—of opening up communications with the West; thirdly, on account of the sharp fear which was aroused among property owners everywhere by the Shays' Rebellion. The last was the really decisive factor. The call for a constitutional convention which had emanated from Annapolis in the autumn of 1786 was heeded by only three states, Virginia, New Jersey, Pennsylvania, and was ignored by Congress; but the call which Congress itself issued in the following February under the stimulus imparted by the uprising in Massachusetts was responded to by nine states in due course—New Hampshire being the last on account of the late date of the assembling of its legislature.[68] Testimony from private sources is to the same effect; it shows how the Massachusetts uprising completed the work of the paper-money craze in convincing men that constitutional reform had ceased to be a merely local problem.[69]

In this connection a paper prepared by Madison in April 1787, and entitled "Vices of the Political System of the United States,"[70] becomes of great interest both for its content and because of the leading part later taken by its author in the work of the Convention. The title itself is significant: "the Political System of

---

66. 1 *Political Writings of Thomas Paine* 45–46 (1835); {see F. von Gentz, *The Origin and Principles of the American Revolution, Compared with the Origin and Principles of the French Revolution* (John Quincy Adams tr. 1800 R. Loss ed. 1977)}.

67. 1 *Works of Alexander Hamilton* 213 (Constitutional ed.).

68. See the credentials, 1 Elliot's *Debates* 159 ff. (2d ed. 1836–1859).

69. 1 Beveridge, *Life of John Marshall* ch. 8 (1916–1919).

70. 2 *Writings of James Madison* 361 ff. (Hunt ed. 1900–1910).

the United States" is *one,* and therefore the problem of its reform in all its branches is a single problem; and the argument itself bears out this prognosis. The defects of the Confederation are first considered: the failure of the states to comply with the requisitions of Congress, their encroachments on the central authority, their violations of the treaties of the United States and the law of nations, their trespasses on the rights of each other, their want of concert in matters of common interest, the lack of a coercive power in the government of the Confederation, the lack of a popular ratification of the Articles—all these are noted. Then in the midst of this catalogue appears a hitherto unheard-of specification: "want of guaranty to the states of their constitutions and laws against internal violence"—an obvious deduction from the Shays' Rebellion.

It is, however, for the legislative evils which he finds within the states individually that Madison reserves his strongest words of condemnation. "As far as laws are necessary," he writes, "to mark with precision the duties of those who are to obey them, and to take from those who are to administer them a discretion which might be abused, their number is the price of liberty. As far as laws exceed this limit, they are a nuisance; a nuisance of the most pestilent kind." Yet "try the codes of the several states by this test, and what a luxuriancy of legislation do they present. The short period of independency has filled as many pages as the century which preceded it." Nor was this multiplicity of laws the greatest evil—worse was their mutability, a clear mark "of vicious legislation"; and worst of all their injustice, which brought "into question the fundamental principle of republican government, that the majority who rule in such governments are the safest guardians both of public good and private rights."

Indeed Madison proceeded to argue, in effect, that majority rule was more or less of a superstition. No doubt the evils just recounted were traceable in part to the individual selfishness of the representatives of the people; but their chief cause lay in a much more stubborn fact—the natural arrangement of society.

> All civilized societies [he wrote] are divided into different interests and factions, as they happen to be creditors or debtors—rich or poor—husbandmen, merchants or manufacturers—members of different religious sects—followers of different political leaders—inhabitants of different districts—owners of different kinds of property, etc., etc. In republican government the majority however composed, ultimately give the law. Whenever therefore an apparent interest or common passion unites a majority what is to restrain them from unjust violations of the rights and interests of the minority, or of individuals?

Merely moral or persuasive remedies Madison found to be useless when addressed to political selfishness—which itself never lacks a moral excuse—nor does he once refer to the teachings of Montesquieu, for the reason, it may be surmised, that the model constitution of the Union by this test had broken down at the very moment of crisis. One device, nevertheless, remained untried: the enlargement of the geographical sphere of government. For the advantage of a large republic over a small one, Madison insisted, was this: owing, on the one hand, to the greater variety of interests scattered through it, and, on the other, to the natural barrier of distance, a dangerous coalescence of factions became much more difficult. "As a limited monarchy tempers the evils of an absolute one; so an extensive republic meliorates the administration of a small republic."

And how precisely was this remedy to be applied in the case of the United States? In the paper before us, Madison seems to imply the belief that the states ought to surrender all their powers to the national government, but his letters make it plain that this was not his program. Rather, the powers of the central government should be greatly enlarged, and it should be converted into a real government, operative upon individuals and vested with all the coercive powers of government; then this enlarged and strengthened government, which on account of the territorial extent of its constituency would with difficulty fall a prey to faction, should be set as a check upon the exercise by the state governments of the considerable powers which must still remain with them. "The national government" must "have a negative in all cases whatsoever on the legislative acts of the states," he wrote, like that of the king in colonial days. This was "the least possible abridgment of the state sovereignties." "The happy effect" of such an arrangement would be "its control on the internal vicissitudes of state policy and the aggressions of interested majorities on the rights of minorities and individuals." Thus was the balance of power, which Montesquieu had borrowed from the stock teachings of the eighteenth-century diplomacy, to transform it into a maxim of free constitutions, projected into the midway field of federal government.

Every constitutional system gives rise, in relation to the interests of the people whom it is designed to serve, to certain characteristic and persistent problems. The most persistent problem of the American constitutional system arises from the fact that to a multitude of state legislatures are assigned many of the most important powers of government over the individual. Originally, indeed, the bias in favor of local autonomy so overweighted the American constitutional system in that direction that it broke down entirely, both within the states, where the basic rights of property and contract were seriously infringed, and throughout the nation at large, because from the central government essential powers had been withheld.

In the solution of the problems thence resulting, four important constructive ideas were successively brought forward in the years immediately preceding the Philadelphia Convention, all of them reflecting the doctrine of the separation of powers or the attendant notion of a check and balance in government. The abuses resulting from the hitherto undifferentiated character of "legislative power" were met by the idea that it was something intrinsically distinct from "judicial power," and that therefore it was exceeded when it interfered with the dispensation of justice through the ordinary courts. Then building upon this result, the finality of judicial determinations was represented as extending to the interpretation of the standing law, a proposition which, when brought into association with the notion of a higher law, yielded the initial form of the doctrine of judicial review. Meantime, the idea was being advanced that the Articles of Confederation were, in relation to acts of the local legislatures, just such a higher law, thus suggesting a sanction for the acts of the Confederation which in principle entirely transformed its character. Finally, from Madison, who from the first interested himself in every phase of the rising movement for constitutional reform both in his own state and the country at large, came the idea that the problem of providing adequate safeguards for private rights and adequate powers for a national government was one and the same problem, inasmuch as a strengthened national government could be made a make-weight against the swollen prerogatives of the state legislatures. It remained for the Constitutional Convention, however, while it accepted Madison's main idea, to apply it through the agency of judicial review. Nor can it be doubted that this determination was assisted by a growing comprehension in the Convention of the *doctrine* of judicial review.[71]

71. *Cf.* 2 Farrand, *Records* 73–80; and *Federalist*, no. 78.

3. The "Higher Law" Background of American Constitutional Law

Theory is the most important part of the dogma of the law, as the architect is the most important man who takes part in the building of a house.

—HOLMES, COLLECTED LEGAL PAPERS

THE Reformation superseded an infallible pope with an infallible Bible; the American Revolution replaced the sway of a king with that of a document. That such would be the outcome was not unforeseen from the first. In the same number of *Common Sense* which contained his electrifying proposal that American should declare her independence from Great Britain, Paine urged also a "continental conference," whose task he described as follows:

> The conferring members being met, let their business be to frame a continental charter, or charter of the united colonies (answering to what is called the Magna Carta of England) fixing the number and manner of choosing members of Congress and members of assembly . . . and drawing the line of business and jurisdiction between them (always remembering that our strength is continental, not provincial) securing freedom and property to all men . . . with such other matter as it is necessary for a charter to contain. . . . But where, say some, is the king of America? Yet that we may not appear to be defective even in earthly honors, let a day be set apart for proclaiming the charter; let it be brought forth placed in the divine law, the word of God; let a crown be placed thereon, by which the world may know that so far as we approve of monarchy that in America the law is king.[1]

This suggestion, which was to eventuate more than a decade later in the Philadelphia Convention, is not less interesting for its retrospection than it is for its prophecy.

In the words of the younger Adams, "the Constitution itself had been extorted from the grinding necessity of a reluctant nation";[2] yet hardly had it gone into operation than hostile criticism of its provisions not merely ceased but gave place

From 42 *Harvard Law Review* (sections I and II) 149–85 (1928), and (sections III, IV, and V) 365–409 (1929). Copyright 1928, 1929 by the Harvard Law Review Association. Reprinted by permission.

1. 1 Paine, *Political Writings* 45–46 (1835).
2. Adams, *Jubilee Discourse on the Constitution* 55 (1839).

to "an undiscriminating and almost blind worship of its principles"[3]—a worship which continued essentially unchallenged till the other day. Other creeds have waxed and waned, but "worship of the Constitution" has proceeded unabated.[4] It is true that the abolitionists were accustomed to stigmatize the Constitution as "an agreement with Hell," but their shrill heresy only stirred the mass of Americans to renewed assertion of the national faith. Even secession posed as loyalty to the *principles* of the Constitution and a protest against their violation, and in form at least the constitution of the southern Confederacy was, with a few minor departures, a studied reproduction of the instrument of 1787. For by far the greater reach of its history, Bagehot's appraisal of the British monarchy is directly applicable to the Constitution: "The English monarchy strengthens our government with the strength of religion."[5]

The fact that its adoption was followed by a wave of prosperity no doubt accounts for the initial launching of the Constitution upon the affections of the American people. Travelling through various parts of the United States at this time, Richard Bland Lee found "fields a few years ago waste and uncultivated filled with inhabitants and covered with harvests, new habitations reared, contentment in every face, plenty on every board. . . ." "To produce this effect," he continued, "was the intention of the Constitution, and it has succeeded." Indeed it is possible that rather too much praise was lavished upon the Constitution on this score. "It has been usual with declamatory gentlemen," complained the astringent Maclay, "in their praises of the present government, by way of contrast, to paint the state of the country under the old (Continental) Congress, as if neither wood grew nor water ran in America before the happy adoption of the new Constitution;" and a few years later, when the European turmoil at once assisted, and by contrast advertised, our own blissful state, Josiah Quincy voiced a fear that "we have grown giddy with good fortune, attributing the greatness of our prosperity to our own wisdom, rather than to a course of events and a guidance over which we had no influence."[6]

But while the belief that it drew prosperity in its wake may explain the beginning of the worship of the Constitution, it leaves a deeper question unanswered. It affords no explanation why this worship came to ascribe to the Constitution the precise virtues it did as an efficient cause of prosperity. To answer this question we must first of all project the Constitution against a background of doctrinal tradition which, widespread as European culture, was at the time of the founding of the English colonies especially strong in the mother country, though by the irony of history it had become a century and a half later the chief source of division between mother country and colonies.

---

3. W. Wilson, *Congressional Government* 4 (13th ed. 1898).

4. On the whole subject, see 1 Von Holst, *Constitutional History* ch. 2 (1877); Schechter, "Early History of the Tradition of the Constitution," 9 *Am. Pol. Sci. Rev.* 707 *et seq.* (1915).

5. Bagehot, *English Constitution* 39 (2d ed. 1925) "The monarchy by its religious sanction now confirms all our political order. . . . It gives . . . a vast strength to the entire constitution, by enlisting on its behalf the credulous obedience of enormous masses." *Id.* 43–44.

6. Schechter, 9 *Am. Pol. Sci. Rev.* 720–21.

It is customary nowadays to ascribe the *legality* as well as the *supremacy* of the Constitution—the one is, in truth, but the obverse of the other—exclusively to the fact that, in its own phraseology, it was "ordained" by "the people of the United States." Two ideas are thus brought into play. One is the so-called "positive" conception of law as a general expression merely for the particular commands of a human lawgiver, as a series of acts of human will;[7] the other is that the highest possible source of such commands, because the highest possible embodiment of human will, is "the people." The same two ideas occur in conjunction in the oft-quoted text of Justinian's *Institutes:* "Whatever has pleased the prince has the force of law, since the Roman people by the *lex regia* enacted concerning his *imperium,* have yielded up to him all their power and authority."[8] The sole difference between the Constitution of the United States and the imperial legislation justified in this famous text is that the former is assumed to have proceeded immediately from the people, while the latter proceeded from a like source only mediately.

The attribution of supremacy to the Constitution on the ground solely of its rootage in popular will represents, however, a comparatively late outgrowth of American constitutional theory. Earlier the supremacy accorded to constitutions was ascribed less to their putative source than to their supposed content, to their embodiment of essential and unchanging justice. The theory of law thus invoked stands in direct contrast to the one just reviewed. *There are,* it is predicated, *certain principles of right and justice which are entitled to prevail of their own intrinsic excellence, altogether regardless of the attitude of those who wield the physical resources of the community. Such principles were made by no human hands; indeed, if they did not antedate deity itself, they still so express its nature as to bind and control it. They are external to all will as such and interpenetrate all reason as such. They are eternal and immutable. In relation to such principles, human laws are, when entitled to obedience save as to matters indifferent, merely a record or transcript, and their enactment an act not of will or power but one of discovery and declaration.*[9] The Ninth Amendment of the Constitution of the United States, in its stipulation that "the enumeration of certain rights in this Constitution shall not prejudice other rights not so enumerated," illustrates this

---

7. Bentham, as quoted in Holland, *Elements of Jurisprudence* 14 (12th ed. 1916) {hereinafter Holland, *Elements*}: For further definitions of "positive law," see *id.* 22–23; Willoughby, *Fundamental Concepts of Public Law* ch. 10 (1924).

8. *Inst.* I, 2, 6: "Quod principi placuit, legis habet vigorem, cum lege regia quae de ejus imperio lata est, populus ei et in eum, omne imperium suum et potestatem concessit." The source is Ulpian, *Dig.* I, 4, 1. The Romans always regarded the people as the source of the legislative power. "Lex est, quod populus Romanus senatorie magistratu interrogante, veluti Consule, constituebat." *Inst.* I, 2, 4. During the Middle Ages the question was much debated whether the *lex regia* effected an absolute alienation (*translatio*) of the legislative power to the emperor, or was a revocable delegation (*cessio*). The champions of popular sovereignty at the end of this period, like Marsiglio of Padua in his *Defensor Pacis,* took the latter view. See Gierke, *Political Theories of the Middle Ages* 150, nn. 158, 159 (Maitland tr. 1922).

9. For definitions of law incorporating this point of view, see Holland, *Elements* 19–20, 32–36. Cf. 1 Bl. *Comm.* Intro.

theory perfectly, except that the principles of transcendental justice have been here translated into terms of personal and private rights. The relation of such rights, nevertheless, to governmental power is the same as that of the principles from which they spring and which they reflect. They owe nothing to their recognition in the Constitution—such recognition was necessary if the Constitution was to be regarded as complete.

Thus the *legality* of the Constitution, its *supremacy,* and its claim to be worshipped, alike find common standing ground on the belief in a law superior to the will of human governors. Certain questions arise: Whence came this idea of a "higher law"? How has it been enabled to survive, and in what transformations? What special forms of it are of particular interest for the history of American constitutional law and theory? By what agencies and as a result of what causes was it brought to America and wrought into the American system of government? It is to these questions that the ensuing pages of this article are primarily addressed.

I.

Words of Demosthenes attest the antiquity of the conception of law as a discovery: "Every law is a discovery, a gift of god—a precept of wise men."[10] Words of President Coolidge prove the persistence of the notion: "Men do not make laws. They do but discover them. . . . That state is most fortunate in its form of government which has the aptest instruments for the discovery of law."[11] But not every pronouncement of even the most exalted human authority is necessarily law in this sense. This, too, was early asserted. A century before De-

10. Holland, *Elements* at 44n. "If there be any primitive theory of the nature of law, it seems to be that laws are the utterance of some divine or heroic person who reveals . . . that which is absolutely right." 1 Pollock & Maitland, *History of English Law* xxviii (1895).

11. Coolidge. *Have Faith in Massachusetts* 4 (1919). John Dickinson, *Administrative Justice and the Supremacy of Law* 85–86 n. (1927), juxtaposes the above definitions, and also one from St. Augustine, *De Vera Religione* ch. 31 in 34 Migne, *Patrologia Latina* 147 (1845): "Aeternam . . . legem mundis animis fas est congnoscere, judicare non fas est." This notion of the possibility of the spontaneous recognition of higher law has its counterpart in American constitutional theory, as will be pointed out later. Bacon voiced the "discovery" theory of lawmaking in the following words: "Regula enim legem (ut acus nautica polos) indicat, non statuit." *De Justitia Universali,* Aphor. lxxxv, quoted in Lorimer, *Institutes of Law* 256 (2d ed. 1880). Burke also accepted the theory: "It would be hard to point out any error more truly subversive of all the order and beauty, of all the peace and happiness of human society, than the position that any body of men have a right to make what laws they please; or that laws can derive any authority whatever from their institution merely, and independent of the quality of their subject matter. . . . All human laws are, properly speaking, only declaratory. They may alter the mode and application, but have no power over the substance of original justice." Burke, *Tract on the Popery Laws* (c. 1780) ch. 3, pt. 1, 6 Burke, *Works* 322–23 (1867); Lorimer, *Institutes of Law* 256. To the same effect is James Otis' assertion: "The supreme power in a state, is *jus dicere* only: —*jus dare,* strictly speaking, belongs only to God." Otis, *The Rights of the British Colonies Asserted and Proved* 70 (1765). For a brilliant effort to effect a logical reconciliation of the "positive" and the "discovery" theories of lawmaking, in a modern terminology, see Del Vecchio, *The Formal Bases of Law* (Mod. Leg. Philos. Ser. 1914).

mosthenes, Antigone's appeal against Creon's edict to the "unwritten and stead-fast customs of the Gods" had already presented immemorial usage as superior to human rule-making.[12] A third stage in the argument is marked by Aristotle's advice to advocates in his *Rhetoric* that, when they had "no case according to the law of the land," they should "appeal to the law of nature," and, quoting the Antigone of Sophocles, argue that "an unjust law is not a law."[13] The term law is, in other words, ambiguous. It may refer to a law of higher or a law of lower content; and, furthermore, some recourse should be available on the basis of the former against the latter.

But as Aristotle's own words show, the identification of higher law with custom did not remain the final word on the subject. Before this idea could enter upon its universal career as one of the really great humanizing forces of history, the early conception of it had to undergo a development not dissimilar to that of the Hebrew conception of God, although, thanks to the Sophists and to their critic, Socrates, the process was immensely abbreviated. The discovery that custom was neither immutable nor invariable even among the Greek city states impelled the Sophists to the conclusion that justice was either merely "the interest of the strong," or at best a convention entered upon by men purely on considerations of expediency and terminable on like considerations.[14] Ulti-mately, indeed, the two ideas boil down to the same thing, since it is impossible to regard as convenient that which cannot maintain itself, while that which can do so will in the long run be shaped to the interests of its sustainers. Fortunately these were not the only possible solutions to the problem posed by the Sophists. Building on Socrates' analysis of Sophistic teaching and Plato's theory of Ideas, Aristotle advanced in his *Ethics* the concept of "natural justice." "Of political justice," he wrote, "part is natural, part legal—natural, that which everywhere has the same force and does not exist by people's thinking this or that; legal, that which is originally indifferent. . . ."[15] That is to say, the essential ingredient of the justice which is enforced by the state is not of the state's own contrivance; it is a discovery from nature and a transcript of its constancy.

But practically what is the test of the presence of this ingredient in human laws and constitutions? By his conception of natural justice as universal, Aristotle is unavoidably led to identify the rational with the general in human laws. Putting the question in his *Politics* whether the rule of law or the rule of an individual is

---

12. Holland, *Elements* at 32n; Sophocles, *Antigone* vv, 450 *et seq.* Creon typifies in Sophocles' drama the Greek tyrant, whose coming had disturbed the ancient customary regime of the Greek city state.

13. Ritchie, *Natural Rights* 30 (1903), citing Aristotle, *Rhetoric* I, 15, 1375a, 27 *et seq.*

14. Barker, *The Political Thought of Plato and Aristotle* 33-37 (1906) {hereinafter Barker, *Political Thought*}. "Right is the interest of the stronger," says Thrasymachus in Plato, *Republic* bk. I, sec. 338 (Jowett tr. 1875). "Justice is a contract neither to do nor to suffer wrong," says Glaucon, *id.* bk. II, sec. 359. See also Philus in Cicero, *De Republica* bk. III, 5.

15. Aristotle, *Nicomachean Ethics* v. 7, secs. 1-2 (Ross tr. 1925). See also Barker, *Political Thought* 328.

preferable, he answers his own inquiry in no uncertain terms. "To invest the law then with authority is, it seems, to invest God and reason only; to invest a man is to introduce a beast, as desire is something bestial, and even the best of men in authority are liable to be corrupted by passion. We may conclude then that the law is reason without passion and it is therefore preferable to any individual."[16] Nearly two thousand years after Aristotle, the sense of this passage, condensed into Harrington's famous phrase, "a government of laws and not of men,"[17] was to find its way successively into the Massachusetts constitution of 1780[18] and into Chief Justice Marshall's opinion in Marbury v. Madison.[19] The opposition which it discovers between the desire of the human governor and the reason of the law lies, indeed, at the foundation of the American interpretation of the doctrine of the separation of powers and so of the entire American system of constitutional law.

It has been said of Plato that "he found philosophy a city of brick and left it a city of gold."[20] The operation of the Stoic philosophy upon the concept of a higher law may be characterized similarly. While Aristotle's "natural justice" was conceived primarily as a norm and guide for lawmakers, the *jus naturale* of the Stoics was the way of happiness for all men. The supreme legislator was nature herself; nor was the natural order the merely material one which modern science exploits. The concept which Stoicism stressed was that of a moral order, wherein man through his divinely given capacity of reason was directly participant with the gods themselves. Nature, human nature, and reason were one.[21] The conception was, manifestly, an ethical, rather than a political or legal one, and for good cause. Stoicism arose on the ruins of the Greek city state. Plato's and Aristotle's belief that human felicity was to be achieved mainly by political

16. Aristotle, *Politics* bk. III, 15–16, especially at 154 (Welldon tr. 1905). I have departed slightly from the translation at one or two points. As Professor Barker points out, the Greek was apt to think of the law as an ideal code, the work of a sole legislator of almost superhuman wisdom, a Solon or a Lycurgus. Indeed, Plato and Aristotle look upon themselves as just such legislators. Barker, *Political Thought* 323. In comparison should be recalled the virtues attributed to the framers of the Constitution of the United States, and one source of its worship. On the equity of general laws enacted with deliberation and "without knowing on whom they were to operate," see Marshall, C. J., in *Ex parte* Bollman, 4 Cranch 75, 127 (U.S. 1807).

17. Harrington, *Oceana and Other Works* 37 (1747). "An empire of laws and not of men." *Id.* 45, 240; see also *id.* 49, 240, 257, 362, 369. Harrington ascribes the idea to Aristotle and Livy.

18. Declaration of Rights Article 30; see Thorpe, *American Charters, Constitutions, and Organic Laws* (1909).

19. 1 Cranch 137, 163 (U.S. 1803).

20. Joubert, *Pensées* xxiv (5th ed. 1869).

21. On the doctrines of the Stoics, see Diogenes Laertius, *Lives and Opinions of Eminent Philosophers* bk. vii, "Zeno," chs. 53, 55, 66, 70, 72–73 (Young tr. 1853). "Again, they say that justice exists by nature, and not because of any definition or principle; just as law does, or right reason." *Id.* ch. 66. "The Stoics . . . thought of nature or the universe as a living organism, of which the material world was the body, and of which the Deity or the universal reason was the pervading, animating, and governing soul; and natural law was the rule of conduct laid down by this universal reason for the direction of mankind." Salmond, *Jurisprudence* 27 (7th ed. 1924).

means had proved illusory; and thrown back on his own resources, the Greek developed a new outlook, at once individualistic and cosmopolitan.

The restoration of the idea of natural law, enlarged and enriched by Stoicism, to the world's stock of legal and political ideas was accomplished by Cicero. In a passage of his *De Republica* which has descended to us through the writings of another (the preservative quality of a good style has rarely been so strikingly exemplified), Cicero sets forth his conception of natural law:

> True law is right reason, harmonious with nature, diffused among all, constant, eternal; a law which calls to duty by its commands and restrains from evil by its prohibitions. . . . It is a sacred obligation not to attempt to legislate in contradiction to this law; nor may it be derogated from nor abrogated. Indeed by neither the Senate nor the people can we be released from this law; nor does it require any but ourself to be its expositor or interpreter. Nor is it one law at Rome and another at Athens; one now and another at a later time; but one eternal and unchangeable law binding all nations through all time. . . .[22]

It is, however, in his *De Legibus* that Cicero makes his distinctive contribution. Identifying "right reason" with those qualities of human nature whereby "man is associated with the gods,"[23] he there assigns the binding quality of the civil law itself to its being in harmony with such universal attributes of human nature. In the natural endowment of man, and especially his social traits, "is to be found the true source of laws and rights,"[24] he asserts, and later says: "We are born for justice, and right is not the mere arbitrary construction of opinion, but an institution of nature."[25] Hence justice is not, as the Epicureans claim, mere utility, for "that which is established on account of utility may for utility's

---

22. Lactantius, *Div. Inst.* vi, 8, 370 (Roberts & Donaldson tr. 1871); see also *id.* 24. It will be observed that Cicero does not overlook the imperative element of law. Bracton knew of the passage from the *De Republica*, and Grotius' indebtedness to Cicero is beyond peradventure. "Jus naturale est dictatum rectae rationis, . . ." I Grotius, *De Jure Belli ac Pacis* 10 (Whewell ed. 1853). See also note 24, below.

23. Cicero, *De Legibus* I, 7, 23 (Müller ed.): "Inter quos autem ratio, inter eosdem etiam recta ratio et communis est; quae cum sit lex, lege quoque consociati homines cum dis putandi sumus." *Id.* I, 8, 25. "Est igitur homini cum deo similitudo." See also *id.* I, 7, 22–23. The entire passage is the source of Shakespeare's famous apostrophe to man in Hamlet. It ought to be remembered that the classical conception of "nature" was of an active, creative force, so that the "nature" of a thing became an innate tendency toward the realization of a certain ideal of the thing. Both Cicero's conception of "human nature" and his conception of "natural law" rest on this basis. The former is an expression of the highest attributes of man; the latter is the perfect expression of the idea of law.

24. *Id.* I, 5, 16: "Nam sic habetote, nullo in genere disputando posse ita patefieri, quid sit homini a natura tributum, quantam vim rerum optimarum mens humana contineat, cujus muneris colendi efficiendique causa nati et in lucem editi simus, quae sit conjunctio hominum, quae naturalis societas inter ipsos; his enim explicatis fons legum et juris inveniri potest." This passage is especially significant for its emphasis upon certain qualities of human nature as the immediate source of natural law. The idea is not lacking in Stoic teaching, but it is subordinate. The same feature reappears in the continental natural law school of the seventeenth and eighteenth centuries. "Naturalis juris mater est ipsa humana natura," I Grotius, *De Jure Belli ac Pacis*, Proleg. 16, xlix. Puffendorf and Burlamaqui also illustrate the same point of view, which contrasts with the legalism of Hobbes and Locke.

25. Cicero, *De Legibus* I, 10, 28.

sake be overturned.''[26] There is, in short, discoverable in the permanent elements of human nature itself a durable justice which transcends expediency, and the positive law must embody this if it is to claim the allegiance of the human conscience.

Ordinarily, moreover, human authority fulfills this requirement—this Cicero unquestionably holds. Hence his statement that ''the laws are the foundation of the liberty which we enjoy; we all are the laws' slaves that we may be free.''[27] The reference is clearly to the civil law. And of like import is his assertion that ''nothing is more conformable to right and to the order of nature than authority [*imperium*],''[28] and the accompanying picture of the sway of law, in which the civil law becomes a part of the pattern of the entire fabric of universal order. That, nonetheless, the formal law, and especially enacted law, may at times part company with ''true law'' and thereby lose its title to be considered law at all, is, of course, implied by his entire position. We do have to rely upon implication. ''Not all things,'' he writes,'' are necessarily just which are established by the civil laws and institutions of nations''; nor is ''justice identical with obedience to the written laws.''[29] The vulgar, to be sure, are wont to apply the term ''law'' to whatever is ''written, forbidding certain things and commanding others''; but it is so only in a colloquial sense.[30] ''If it were possible to constitute right simply by the commands of the people, by the decrees of princes, by the adjudications of magistrates, then all that would be necessary in order to make robbery, adultery, or the falsification of wills right and just would be a vote of the multitude''; but ''the nature of things'' is not thus subject to ''the opinions and behests of the foolish.''[31] Despite which, ''many pernicious and harmful measures are constantly enacted among peoples which do not deserve the name law.''[32] True law is ''a rule of distinction between right and wrong according to nature''; and ''any other sort of law not only ought not to be regarded as law, it ought not to be called law.''[33]

But what, when that which wears the form of law is at variance with true law, is the remedy? Certain Roman procedural forms connected with the enactment of law suggested to Cicero, in answering this question, something strikingly like judicial review. It was a Roman practice to incorporate in statutes a saving clause to the effect that it was no purpose of the enactment to abrogate what was

26. *Id.* I, 15, 42.
27. *Pro A. Cluentio Oratio* ch. 53, sec. 146.
28. ''Nihil porro tam aptum est ad jus condicionemque naturae . . . quam imperium, sine quo nec domus ulla nec civitas nec gens nec hominum universum genus stare nec rerum natura omnis nec ipse mundus potest. . . .'' *De Legibus* III, 1, 2–3.
29. *Id.* I, 15, 42.
30. *Id.* I, 6, 19.
31. *Id.* I, 16, 43–44.
32. *Id.* II, 5, 13.
33. *Id.* II, 6, 13.

sacrosanct or *jus*.[34] In this way certain maxims, or *leges legum,* as Cicero styles them,[35] some of which governed the legislative process itself,[36] were erected into a species of written constitution binding on the legislative power. More than once we find Cicero, in reliance on such a clause, invoking *jus* against a statute. "What is it," he inquires on one such occasion, "that is not *jus! . . .* This saving clause [*adscriptio*] declares that it is something, otherwise it would not be provided against in all our laws. And I ask you, if the people had commanded that I should be your slave, or you mine, would that be validly enacted, fixed, established?"[37] On other occasions he points out that it was within the power both of the augurs and of the Senate to abrogate laws which had not been enacted *jure,* though here the reference may be to the procedure of legislation, and he mentions instances of the exercise of these purgative powers.[38] On one occasion, finally, in addressing the Senate, we find him appealing directly to "*recta ratio*" as against the "*lex scripta.*"[39]

Whether Cicero's adumbrations of judicial review ever actually came to the attention of the framers of the American constitutional system to any considerable extent seems extremely doubtful.[40] Taken, nonetheless, along with Aristo-

34. See Brissonius (Barnabé Brisson), *De Formulis et Solennibus Populi Romani Verbis* Lib. 2, ch. 19, 129–30 (Leipzig 1754). This admirable work first appeared in 1583. The Leipzig edition, for the loan of which I have to thank the authorities of the Elbert H. Gary Library of Law, is based on a revision and extension of the original work by one Franciscus Conradus, and contains a life of Brisson, who was {at} one time President of the Parlement of Paris. The customary form of the saving clause was, "Si quid sacri sanctique est, quod jus non sit rogari, ejus hac lege nihil rogatur." In his *Pro Caecina Oratio,* Cicero gives a somewhat different form, taken from an enactment of Sulla: "Si quid jus non esset rogari, ejus ea lege nihilum rogatum." *Id.* chs. 32–33. A variant on this form appears in his *Pro Domo Sua* ch. 40. See note 37, below. On these occasions Cicero is relying on the saving clause; but in his *Pro Balbo,* the shoe is on the other foot, and he there argues against the extension of such a clause to a certain treaty, that nothing can be "sacrosanctum—nisi quod populus plebesve sanxisset," whereas the treaty in question had been made by the Senate. *Id.* ch. 14. Cicero himself suffered from "a new and previously unheard of use" of the clause by his enemy Clodius, who endeavored by affixing it to the law exiling Cicero and confiscating his property, to render the latter irrepealable. For Cicero's argument against the possibility of thus clothing statutes with immortality, see *Epistolae* III, 22; Brissonius, above, at 130.

35. Cicero, *De Legibus* II, 7, 18. Here Cicero is dealing with the laws of religion. In book three he treats of the civil laws similarly.

36. "The *lex Caecilia et Didia* was a portion of the *jus legum* which prohibited the proposal of any law containing two or more matters not germane." Coxe, {*An Essay on*} *Judicial Power and Unconstitutional Legislation* iii (1893), citing Smith, *Dictionary of Greek and Roman Antiquities* art. *lex* (1842).

37. *Pro Caecina* ch. 33. *Cf. Pro Domo Sua* ch. 40. I must acknowledge the valuable assistance so kindly lent by my friend, Professor John Dickinson, in tracing down these anticipations by Cicero of judicial review.

38. Cicero, *De Legibus* II, 12, 31; *Pro Domo Sua* chs. 16, 26, 27.

39. *Phil.* XI, 12. Here Cicero invokes natural law in the public interest—an anticipation of one aspect of the doctrine of the police power.

40. There is, however, one apparent instance of this happening. In the notes for his argument in Rutgers v. Waddington, Mayor's Ct., New York City (1784), Hamilton included the following passage: "Si leges duae aut si plures aut quot quot erunt conservari non possunt quia discrepent inter se ea maxime conservanda sunt quae ad maximas res pertinere videatur," citing *De In:* L. 4,

tle's similar suggestion, they serve to show how immediate, if not inevitable, is the step from the notion of a higher law entering into the civil law to that of a regular recourse against the latter on the basis of the former. And if Cicero did not contribute to the establishment of judicial review directly, he at any rate did so indirectly through certain ideas of his which enter into the argumentative justification of that institution. The first of these is his assertion that natural law requires no interpreter other than the individual himself,[41] a notion which is still sometimes reflected in the contention of courts and commentators that unconstitutional statutes are unconstitutional *per se,* and not because of any authority attaching to the court that so pronounces them. The other consists in his description of the magistrate as "the law speaking [*magistratum legem esse loquentem, legem autem mutum magistratum*].'"[42] The sense of this passage from the *De Legibus* is reproduced in Coke's *Reports* in the words, "*Judex est lex loquens.*'"[43] The importance of both these ideas for the doctrine of judicial review will be indicated later.

Of the other features of the Ciceronian version of natural law, the outstanding one is his conception of human equality: "There is no one thing so like or so equal to one another as in every instance man is to man. And if the corruption of custom and the variation of opinion did not induce an imbecility of minds and turn them aside from the course of nature, no one would more resemble himself than all men would resemble all men. Therefore, whatever definition we give to man will be applicable to the entire human race.'"[44] Not only is this good Stoic teaching, it is the inescapable consequence of Cicero's notion of the constancy of

---

No. 145. See A. M. Hamilton, {*The Intimate Life of Alexander*} *Hamilton* 462 (1910). The passage is in fact from *De Inventione* II, 49. The context casts some doubt on whether it was intended by Cicero in quite the sense for which Hamilton appears to have employed it.

41. "Neque est quaerendus explanator, aut interpres ejus alius." *De Rep.* III, 22; Lactantius, *Div. Inst.* vi, 8. See also note II {11?}, above.

42. Cicero, *De Legibus* III, 1, 2-3.

43. Calvin's Case, 4 Co. I (1609). "Neither have judges power to judge according to that which they think to be fit, but that which out of the laws they know to be right and consonant to law. *Judex bonus nihil ex arbitrio suo faciat, nec proposito domesticae voluntatis, sed juxta leges et jura pronuntiet.*" *Id.* 27(a). See Chief Justice Marshall's rendition of the same idea in Osborn v. Bank of United States, 9 Wheat. 738, 866 (U.S. 1824): "Judicial power, as contradistinguished from the power of the laws, has no existence." The maxim which assigns to the judges the power of *jus dicere* but not that of *jus dare* is traceable to Bacon, "Judicature," *Essays* 365 (Reynold's ed. 1890). On the entire subject see my article, "The Progress of Constitutional Theory, 1776-1787," 30 *Am. Hist. Rev.* 511-36 (1924-25); see also notes 104 and 121, below.

44. Cicero, *De Legibus* I, 10, 12-28, 33. "There is no conception which is more fundamental to the Aristotelian theory of society than the notion of the natural inequality of human nature. . . . There is no change in political theory so startling in its completeness as the change from the theory of Aristotle to the later philosophical view represented by Cicero and Seneca. Over against Aristotle's view of the natural inequality of human nature we find set the theory of the natural equality of human nature. . . . There is only one possible definition for all mankind, reason is common to all." 1 Carlyle, *A History of Medieval Political Theory* 7-8 (1927) {hereinafter Carlyle, *History*}. The identification of *jus naturale* with *recta ratio*, the universal possession of mankind, leads to the doctrine of the equality of mankind, and this in turn paves the way for the translation of *natural law* into *natural rights.*

the distinctive attributes of human nature, those which supply the foundation of natural law.

With respect to certain other elements of the doctrine of natural law as it entered American constitutional theory, the allocation of credit cannot be so confidently made. The notion of popular sovereignty,[45] of a social contract,[46] and of a contract between governors and governed[47] are all foreshadowed by Cicero with greater or less distinctness. The notion of a state of nature, on the other hand, is missing, being supplied by Seneca and the early church fathers, the latter locating their primitive polity in the Garden of Eden before the fall.[48] It is Seneca also who corrects Cicero's obtuseness, later repeated by the signers of the Declaration of Independence, to the contradiction between the idea of the equality of man and the institution of slavery;[49] and his views were subsequently ratified by certain of the great Roman jurists. Ulpian, writing at the close of the second century, asserts unqualifiedly that "by the law of nature all men are born free," words which are repeated in the *Institutes* three hundred years later.[50] Natural law is already putting forth the stem of natural rights that is ultimately to dwarf and overshadow it.

The eloquence of Cicero's championship of *jus naturale* was matched by its timeliness. It brought the Stoic conception of a universal law into contact with Roman law at the moment when the administrators of the latter were becoming aware of the problem of adapting a rigid and antique code, burdened with tribal ceremoniousness and idiosyncrasy, to the needs of an empire which already

45. *De Rep.* I, 25. Editors also assign to the same chapter, preserved by St. Augustine, the following: "Quid est res publica nisi res populi? Res ergo communis, res utique civitatis." See St. Augustine, *Epistles* 138, 10, and *De Civitate Dei* v, 18. From what has been said already, it is evident that the notion of popular sovereignty cannot be attributed to Cicero in the sense of unlimited legislative power. See *De Rep.* III, 3. See also notes 8 and 37, above.

46. *De Rep.* I, 26, 32; *id.* III, 31. "Generale quippe pactum est societatis humanae oboedire regibus." St. Augustine, *Confessions* III, 8 (Gibb & Montgomery tr. 1908). "Est autem civitas coetus perfectus liberorum hominum juris fruendi et communis utilitatis causa sociatus." I Grotius, *De Jure Belli ac Pacis* I, 14. It should be recalled that *societas* in Roman private law meant partnership. The idea of the *civitas* as a deliberately formed association smacks of Epicurean and Sophistic ideas, rather than Stoic, but there is no necessary conflict between it and Stoic conceptions. That which is done with deliberation may still be done in response to natural impulse and necessity. The contribution of the Middle Ages to the social contract theory sprang from the nature of feudal society, and was a deepened sense of the obligation of contracts. See Gierke, *Political Theories of the Middle Ages* nn. 303, 306, and Gierke, *Althusius* 99 *et seq.* (Zur deutschen Staats u. Rechts Geschichte 1879-1880); also note 61, below.

47. *De Rep.* III, 13. This is an interesting forecast of the process of "commendation" by which feudalism actually did arise in parts of Europe.

48. 1 Carlyle, *History* 23-25, 117, 134, 144-46; Gierke, *Althusius* 92-94; Lactantius, *Div. Inst.* v, 5. *Cf.* Lucretius, *De Rerum Natura* v, II, 1105-60 (Merrill ed. 1907). Especially to be noted is Lucretius' phrase, "communia foedera pacis." *Id.* at 1155.

49. 1 Carlyle, *History* 7-8. Aristotle in his *Politics* is evidently dealing with an attack on slavery. Aristotle, *Politics* i, 4-7. A certain Alcidamas is reported to have said (4th century?): "God made all men free; nature made none a slave." Ritchie, *Natural Rights* 25.

50. *Dig.* I, 1, 4; *Inst.* I, 2, 2. Slavery is explained by Ulpian by reference to the *jus gentium*. "Quod ad jus naturale attinet, omnes aequales sunt." *Dig.* L, 17, 32; see 1 Carlyle, *History* 47.

overshadowed the Mediterranean world. In the efforts of the *praetor peregrinus* to meet the necessities of foreigners resorting to Rome, a beginning had early been made toward the building up of a code which, albeit without the conscious design of its authors, approximated in many ways to the Stoic ideal of simplicity and of correspondence with the fundamental characteristics of human relationship; but the clear presentation of the Stoic ideal to the Roman jurists may be imagined to have stimulated this development vastly. The outcome is to be seen in the concept of *jus gentium,* which is defined by Gaius and later in the *Institutes,* as "that law which natural reason established among all mankind" and "is observed equally by all peoples," whereas the *jus civile* of each people is peculiar to itself.[51] Recast in the light of this conception the Roman civil law became the universal code, and by the same token *jus naturale* took on the semblance of a law with definite content and guaranteed enforcement—in a word, that of "positive law."[52]

The conception of a higher law pervades the Middle Ages; it also becomes sharpened to that of a code distinctively for rulers. In the pages of the *Policraticus* of the Englishman, John of Salisbury, the first systematic writer on politics in the Middle Ages, one learns that "there are certain precepts of the law which have perpetual necessity, having the force of law among all nations and which absolutely cannot be broken."[53] This clear reflection of the Ciceronian conception of natural law had found its way to later centuries notably through the writings of Saint Isidore of Seville and the *Decretum* of Gratian.[54] But joined with the same conception, and clearly contributing to its survival over a critical period, was the identification of the higher law with scripture, with the teachings of the church, and with the corpus juris. As remarked by his translator, John was not confronted with the difficulty which has so often troubled later exponents of *jus naturale* "of identifying any specific rules or precepts as belonging to this law." He had them "in the form of clear-cut scripture texts" and in maxims of the Roman law.[55]

Of even greater importance is the fact that John addresses his counsels exclu-

---

51. *Inst.* I, 2, 1–2. Gaius, in contrast with Ulpian, regards the *jus gentium* as identical with *jus naturale.* 1 Carlyle, *History* 38; Bryce, *Studies in History and Jurisprudence* 581 (1901).

52. This work of revision fell to the great jurisconsults. As Dean Pound has pointed out: "The jurisconsult had no legislative power and no *imperium.* The authority of his *responsum . . .* was to be found in its intrinsic reasonableness; in the appeal which it made to the reason and sense of justice of the *judex . . .* it was law by nature." Pound, *Introduction to the Philosophy of Law* 29 (1922).

53. Dickinson, *The Statesman's Book of John of Salisbury* 33 (1927) {hereinafter Dickinson, *Statesman's Book*}.

54. Pollock, *Essays in the Law* 40 *et seq.* (1922); 2 Carlyle, *History* 29; 41, 94–109. Gratian discusses the question why it was that while the *jus naturale* is contained in the "law," some of the latter is variable. He concludes that not all law is natural law, even when it claims the support of God. *Id.* 109. Later medieval writers distinguish two varieties of the *jus naturale,* the higher and the lower, of which only the first is unchangeable. Gratian also passes on to us the phase *jus constitutionis,* signifying a system of written law, the first example being the legislation of Moses. *Id.* 115.

55. Dickinson, *Statesman's Book* xxxv.

sively to princes. There were two sets of reasons for this. On the one hand, yielding to the Christian dispensation with its "other world" outlook, *jus naturale* had lost all significance as a "way of life" the promised goal of which was earthly bliss. At the same time, the art of legislation, which Aristotle and Cicero always had pre-eminently in mind, had for the time being ceased to exist. On the other hand was the Teutonic conception of the ruler as simply soldier and judge. The business of the judge, however, is justice; yet justice by what standard? The answer that John returns to this question is in effect *jus naturale* furnished out with the content just described.

A not less significant feature of John's doctrine is his insistence upon the distinction between "a tyrant" as "one who oppresses the people by rulership based upon force" and "a prince" as "one who rules in accordance with the laws."[56] In these words John foreshadows the distinctive contribution of the Middle Ages to modern political science—the notion of all political authority as intrinsically limited. Proceeding from this point of view, John makes short work of those troublesome texts of Roman law which assert that the prince is "*legibus solutus*"[57] and that "what he has willed has the force of law."[58] It is not true, he answers, that the prince is absolved from the obligations of the law "in the sense that it is lawful for him to do unjust acts," but only in the sense that his character should guarantee his doing equity "not through fear of the penalties of the law but through love of justice"; and as to "the will of the prince," in respect of public matters, "he may not lawfully have any will of his own apart from that which the law or equity enjoins, or the calculation of the common interest requires."[59] Indeed the very title *rex* is derived from doing right, that is, acting in accordance with law (*recte*).[60]

The sweep and majesty of the medieval conception of a higher law as at once the basis and test for all rightful power is emphasized by the German historian, von Gierke. Natural law constrained the highest earthly powers. It held sway over pope and emperor, over ruler and sovereign people alike, indeed over the whole community of mortals. Neither statute (*Gesetz*) nor any act of authority, neither usage nor popular resolve could break through the limits which it imposed. Anything which conflicted with its eternal and indestructible principles was null and void and could bind nobody. Furthermore, while there was no sharp disseverance of natural law from morality, yet the limits thrown about the legiti-

56. *Id.* 335. The notion that the prince is subject to the law is, of course, much older than the *Policraticus*. Stobaeus credits Solon with saying that "that was the best government where the subjects obeyed their prince, and the prince the laws." Notice also Fortescue's quotation from Diodorus Siculus, that "the kings of Egypt originally did not live in such a licentious manner as other kings, whose will was their law: but were subject to the same law, in common with the subject, and esteemed themselves happy in such a conformity to the laws." Fortescue, *De Laudibus Legum Angliae* ch. XIII (Amos tr. 1825).

57. *Dig.* I, 3, 31.

58. See note 8, above.

59. Dickinson, *Statesman's Book* 7.

60. *Id.* 336. See also *id.* lxvii-iii, nn. 221-22, and Zane, *Story of Law* 214 (1927).

mate sphere of supreme power should by no means, von Gierke insists, be regarded as merely ethical principles. Not only were they designed to control external acts and not merely the ruler's internal freedom, but they were addressed also to judges and to all having anything to do with the application of the law, who were thereby bound to hold for naught not only any act of authority but even any statute which overstepped them. They morally exonerated the humblest citizen in defiance of the highest authority; they might even justify assassination.[61]

Read in the light of Austinian conceptions, these words may easily convey a somewhat exaggerated impression. Yet the outstanding fact is clear, that the supposed precepts of a higher law were, throughout the Middle Ages, being continually pitted against the claims of official authority and were being continually set to test the validity of such claims. At the same time was occurring throughout Western Europe the ever renewed contest between secular and ecclesiastical authority over the question of jurisdiction. The total result was to bring the conception of all authority as inherently conditional to a high pitch of expression.

Furthermore, the Middle Ages—which is to say certain writers of that period—must also be credited with at least a partial apprehension of the concept of natural rights. This is to be seen in the reference to *jus gentium* of the two most fundamental of modern legal institutions, private property and contracts. In the words of von Gierke: "property had its roots . . . in law {*sic;* therefore} which flowed out of the pure law of nature without the aid of the state and in law which was when as yet the state was not. Thence it followed that particular rights which had been acquired by virtue of this institution in no wise owed their existence exclusively to the state." Likewise, the binding force of contracts was traced from natural law, "so that the sovereign, though he could not bind himself or his successors by statute, could bind himself and his successors by contract." It followed thence "that every right which the state had conferred by way of contract was unassailable by the state," exception alone being made in the case of "interferences proceeding *ex justa causa.*"[62]

61. Gierke, *Political Theories of The Middle Ages* 75–76, 85; Gierke, *Althusius* 272, and n. 22, where Aquinas, Occam, Baldus, Alliacus, Cusanus, Gerson, and others are cited; *id.* 275–76 and nn. 30 and 31. The doctrine was stated that when the emperor acted against the law he did not act as emperor ("non facit ut imperator"). Bartolus and his followers attributed greater authority to statutes than to judicial judgments, but held nonetheless that even statutes contrary to natural law were void. Laws were binding, it was taught, so far as they concerned those matters "quae ad potestatem pertinent, non in iis quae ad tyrranidem"; nor was a superior entitled to obedience "quando egreditur fines sui officii." See also *id.* 142, n. 57, where Occam is cited for the expression "potestas limitata." See also 2 Carlyle, *History* 32, 78–79.

62. Gierke, *Political Theories of the Middle Ages* 80–81, and nn. 278, 279. To same effect is Gierke, *Althusius* 270–71, and nn. 18 and 19. "Deus ipse ex promissione obligatur," wrote Decius Constantinus. Writers of the Middle Ages, it might be explained, distinguished *jus naturale, jus divinum,* and *jus gentium.* The first was described as having been planted by God in natural reason for purely mundane ends; the second as having been communicated by a supernatural revelation for purely supramundane ends, the last as those rules which flowed from the pure *jus naturale* when due

In the writings which von Gierke thus summarizes, notably those of the glossators and their successors, the emphasis, it is true, is upon the sanctity of the two institutions of property and contract as such. Yet both of these are quickly resolvable into terms of individual interest. The strong initial bias of American constitutional law in favor of rights of property and contract has, therefore, its background in speculations of the Middle Ages.

Upon the observed uniformities of the human lot, classical antiquity erected the conception of a law of nature discoverable by human reason when uninfluenced by passion, and forming the ultimate source and explanation of the excellencies of positive law. *Jus naturale* was thus a code which challenged the skill and stirred the intuition of legislators, and in the corpus juris the triumph of Roman jurisprudence in its approximation to this noble goal is to be seen. The inauguration of the Middle Ages was marked by the reverse process. An almost complete paralysis of legislative activity characterized the outset of this period, and as this fact indicates, rulership had become personal, irresponsible, and unhampered by institutional control. Meeting the needs of the time, a new attitude toward higher law became predominant. Definite texts of Roman law, teachings of the church, and scriptural passages were projected upward, to become a mystic overlaw, "a brooding omnipresence in the sky."[63] The purpose of this naive construction, the very reverse of that which generally pervades antique conceptions, was not to account for a prevalent justice but rather to correct a prevalent injustice, not to enlighten authority but rather to circumscribe it. In other words, whereas the classical conception of natural law was that it conferred its chief benefits by entering into the more deliberate acts of human authority, the medieval conception was that it checked and delimited authority from without.[64] This conception, the direct inheritance of American constitutional theory from the Middle Ages, was confirmed by the current struggle between papacy and

---

account was taken of the human relationships which resulted from the fall of man, of which property and contract were instances. *Jus gentium* thus tended to take on a certain appearance of positive law, while the broader concept tended to be relegated to the sphere of ethics, lying midway between law proper and religion. Thus despite von Gierke's sweeping statement, which is substantially correct for the civilians, there would seem to have been considerable conflict of opinion among the canonists, deriving from the communism of the church fathers, whether property existed even mediately by *jus naturale*. 2 Carlyle, *History* 49 *et seq*. St. Germain, *Doctor and Student*, written early in the sixteenth century, reflects this doubt. See the Second Dialogue in *Doctor and Student* 99 (Muchall ed. 1787). Von Gierke also asserts that "medieval doctrine was already filled with the thought of the inborn and indestructible rights of the individual, the formulation and classification" of which, he admits, "belonged to a later stage in the growth of the theory of natural law." This and his sharp contrast between "the theories of antiquity" and the "thought revealed by Christianity and grasped in all its profundity by the Germanic spirit" bespeak perhaps the enthusiastic Teutonist rather than the critical historian. Gierke, *Political Theories of the Middle Ages* 81–82; Gierke, *Althusius* 274–75.

63. Compare Mr. Justice Holmes in Southern Pac. Ry. v. Jensen, 244 U.S. 205, 222 (1917).

64. In ancient theory *jus naturale* was a *terminus ad quem*—a goal toward which actual law inevitably tended; in medieval theory it was a *terminus a quo*—a standard from which human authority was always straying. Cicero's optimism regarding human nature offers a similar and not unrelated contrast to the Christian doctrine of original sin.

empire over the question of jurisdiction, as it has been confirmed in American constitutional theory by the existence of a similar issue between the nation and the states.

That, on the other hand, the practical importance of the higher law doctrine in actually frustrating political injustice during this era may be easily exaggerated is, so far as the Continent is concerned, clearly apparent. Lacking the institutional equipment to make good its claims except very haphazardly, lacking, too, a final authoritative interpretation except at times that of the papacy, the conception still remained, after all the confident asseverations of generations of writers, relatively vague and ineffective, and altogether incapable, as time revealed, of repelling despotism once the latter was furnished with an answering argument, as it was from the beginning of the sixteenth century. In England alone were these deficiencies supplied in appreciable measure, and in England alone were the pretensions of divine right defeated in the following century. So while we look to the Continent during the Middle Ages for ideas, we look to England during the same period for both ideas and institutions.

II.

The eve of the controversy over rights which preceded the American Revolution found John Adams, a briefless attorney of twenty-eight, paying the following tribute to the subject of his favorite studies:

> It has been my amusement for many years past, as far as I have had leisure, to examine the systems of all the legislators, ancient and modern, fantastical and real . . . , and the result . . . is a settled opinion that the liberty, the unalienable, indefeasible rights of men, the honor and dignity of human nature, the grandeur and glory of the public, and the universal happiness of individuals, were never so skillfully and successfully consulted as in that most excellent monument of human art, the common law of England.[65]

This passage conveys admirably the outstanding characteristic of English higher law. Before it was higher law it was positive law in the strictest sense of the term, a law regularly administered in the ordinary courts in the settlement of controversies between private individuals. Many of the rights which the Constitution of the United States protects at this moment against legislative power were first protected by the common law against one's neighbors. The problem we have hitherto been discussing takes on consequently an altered emphasis as we approach higher law concepts in medieval England. The question is no longer how certain principles that ought to be restrictive of political authority took on a legal character or of the extent to which they did so, but rather how certain principles of a legal character in their origin assumed the further quality of principles

---

65. Adams, *Life and Works* 440 (C. F. Adams ed. 1851); and see note 96, below.

entitled to control authority and to control it as law. In other words, the problem is not how the common law became *law*, but how it became *higher*, without at the same time ceasing to be enforceable through the ordinary courts even within the field of its more exalted jurisdiction.

The generation in which the Constitution was framed was wont to ascribe the transcendental quality of the common law above all to its vast antiquity.[66] Nor was this by any means the first appearance of the idea. The Conqueror professed to restore the laws of Edward the Confessor, and Stephen did the same in the century following. The idea was, obviously, a politically valuable one, since it proclaimed from the first the existence of a body of law owing nothing to royal authority and capable therefore of setting limits to that authority. That the substance of the common law as it was known in 1787 really antedated the Norman Conquest is, none the less, the veriest fiction, however important a one. As Sir Frederick Pollock has observed: "For most practical purposes the history of English law does not begin till after the Norman Conquest, and the earliest things which modern lawyers are strictly bound to know must be allowed to date only from the thirteenth century, and from the latter half of it rather than the former."[67] Indeed the so-called dooms which the constitutional fathers were wont to regard so worshipfully were, by modern standards, pretty poor affairs, being filled in large part "by minute catalogues of the fines and compositions payable for manslaughter, wounding, and other acts of violence"; while the most important of them in legend, the laws of Edward the Confessor, were, in the form in which they have come down to us, an antiquarian compilation in verse dating from the twelfth century.[68]

The true starting point in the history of the common law is the establishment by Henry II in the third quarter of the twelfth century of a system of circuit courts with a central appeal court. To this fact beyond all others is due one striking difference between English and continental higher law. The latter was not regarded as incorporating indigenous custom—rather it was an appeal from it—for the reason that on the Continent custom remained till the French Revolution

---

66. "Alfred . . . magnus juris Anglicani conditor . . . with the advice of his wise men, collected out of the laws of Ina, Offa, and Ethelbert such as were best, and made them to extend equally to the whole nation." Later kings, Edward the Elder, Edward the Confessor, William the Conqueror, and so on, continued the good work. "King John swore to restore them [the laws]; King Henry III confirmed them; Magna Carta was founded on them, and King Edward I in Parliament, confirmed them." 3 Adams, *Life and Works* 541–42. To like effect was Jefferson's quaint theory that the American constitutional system only restored to mankind the long lost polity of Anglo-Saxon England, along with which was broached the notion that the Tories of eighteenth-century England were the lineal descendants of the Normans and the Whigs of the Saxons. Jefferson to Cartwright, June 5, 1824, in 7 Jefferson, *Writings* 355 (Washington ed. 1854); Jefferson, *Common Place Book* 351–62 (Chinard ed. 1926).

67. 1 Pollock, *Select Essays in Anglo-American Legal History* 88 (1907).

68. *Id.* 97. See also "English Law before the Norman Conquest," in Pollock, *Expansion of the Common Law* 139 (1904).

purely local. The common law, on the contrary, was regarded from the first as based upon custom. In truth it was custom gradually rendered national, that is to say, common, through the judicial system just described. Yet it was not custom alone. For in their selection of what customs to recognize in order to give them national sway, and what to suppress, the judges employed the test of "reasonableness,"[69] a test derived in the first instance from Roman and continental ideas. Indeed, the notion that the common law embodied right reason furnished from the fourteenth century its chief claim to be regarded as higher law. But once again a sharp divergence must be noted from continental ideas. The right reason to which the maxims of higher law on the Continent were addressed was always the right reason invoked by Cicero: it was the right reason of all men. The right reason which lies at the basis of the common law, on the other hand, was from the beginning *judicial* right reason. Considered as an act of knowledge or discovery, the common law was the act of experts, and increasingly so, with the ever firmer establishment of the doctrine of *stare decisis*.

With certain nineteenth-century historians of the law in mind, Dean Pound voices the legitimate complaint that they will not "hear of an element of creative activity of men as lawyers, judges, writers of books, or legislators.... They think of the phenomena of legal development as events, as if men were not acting in the bringing about of every one of them. For the so-called events of legal history are in truth acts of definite men, or even of a definite man."[70] Certainly the history of the common law is far from being a mere anonymous tradition; and especially is this so of the story of its elevation to the position of a higher law binding upon supreme authority. The story of Magna Carta is an important chapter in this larger story, and for our purposes is sufficiently treated as an event. But it is otherwise with the labors of that series of judicial commentators on the common law which begins with Bracton and ends with Blackstone. The signal contribution of each to the final result still remains identifiable—their total contribution spans some five hundred years.

Bracton, Henry of Bratton, was a judge of the King's Bench in the reign of Henry III.[71] His great work, in preparation for which, in addition to his studies of Roman law, he collected some two thousand decisions, is entitled *De Legibus et Consuetudinibus Angliae*. For us the outstanding importance of the work consists in the fact that for the first time it brought the rising common law into direct contact with Roman and medieval continental ideas of a higher law. "The king himself," runs an oft-quoted passage of this treatise, "ought not to be subject to man, but subject to God and to the law, for the law makes the king. Let the king then attribute to the law what the law attributes to him, namely, dominion and

69. For illustrative cases see Allen, *Law in the Making* 359 *et seq.* (1927). *Cf. Co. Inst.* I, 113(a).

70. Pound, *Interpretations of Legal History* 118 (1923).

71. For an excellent sketch of Bracton's life see the Introduction in 1 Bracton, *Note Book* 13–25 (Maitland tr. 1887).

power, for there is no king where the will and not the law has dominion."[72] In these words we have again the characteristic medieval idea of all authority as deriving from the law and as, therefore, limited by it. Bracton's own words, it will be noted, are strongly reminiscent of John of Salisbury, and elsewhere the similarity becomes even more striking. The king's power, he writes, is the power of justice, not of injustice. So long as he does justice, the king is the vicar of God; but when he turns aside to injustice, he is the minister of the devil. Indeed, he is called king (*rex*) from ruling well (*regendo*), not from reigning (*regnando*). "Let him therefore, temper his power by law, which is the bridle of power . . . likewise is nothing so appropriate to empire as to live according to the laws, and to submit the princedom to law is greater than empire."[73]

What sharply distinguishes Bracton from his predecessors and contemporaries—men like John of Salisbury and Saint Thomas Aquinas—is his conception of law. Thanks to his study of the Roman law, and even more perhaps to his experience as judge, this is even by modern tests strikingly positivistic. He lets us know at the outset that the law (*lex*) which he has primarily in mind is the law which rests on "the common sanction of the body politic." It embraces various elements: customs (unwritten laws), decisions of prudent men, which in like cases should be treated as precedents—"It is good occasion to proceed from like to like"—and finally the law made by the king in council.[74] The question arises whether he considered the last category as subject to any limitation, and on this point Bracton is ambiguous. Discussing the maxim that "the pleasure of the prince has the force of law," he says that it applies not to "whatever is rashly presumed of the king's own will" but only to "that which has been rightly defined with the counsel of his magistrates, the king himself authorizing it, and deliberation and discussion having been had upon it."[75] The implication is that the requirements mentioned having been met in its expression, the will of the prince does have the force of law. And not less noteworthy is his attitude toward *jura naturalia;* these are said to be immutable because they cannot be repealed in their entirety; but in fact they can be and have been abrogated in part. Yet at the same time he asserts, in words harking back to Cicero, that not everything that passes as law (*lex*) necessarily is so. "Although in the broadest sense of the term everything which may be read is law, nevertheless, in a special sense it signifies a rightful warrant enjoining what is honest, forbidding the contrary."[76] The fact seems to be that Bracton is struggling to adjust the notion of legislative sovereignty, conveyed by the texts of Roman law, to his own desire to subordinate to

---

72. Bracton, *De Legibus et Consuetudinibus Angliae* f. 5b (Twiss ed. 1954) {hereinafter Bracton, *De Legibus*}.

73. *Id.* f. 107b. *Cf.* Dickinson, *Statesman's Book* lxviii, chs. 1, 2, 17, 22.

74. Bracton, *De Legibus* ff. I, Ib.

75. *Id.* f. 107b.

76. *Id.* f. 2; see note 22, above.

the law the royal power in its more usual aspects. Blackstone, five hundred years later, is troubled by a like dilemma.

But what sanction does Bracton supply to his law as against the king? In the printed text of the *De Legibus* there is a passage which declares that not only is the king below God, but that he has also his court, namely, counts and barons, and that "he who has an associate has a master, and, therefore, if the king be without a bridle, that is without law, they ought to put a bridle upon him."[77] These words have been sometimes set down, on the ground of conflict with other passages, as an interpolation, but they easily may be a reminiscence, evoked perhaps by De Montfort's rebellion against Henry III, of chapter sixty-one of Magna Carta. That the ordinary remedies are not available against royal injustice, Bracton makes clear. No writ will run against the king, the author of all writs.[78] Through his domination of his judges, he may even bring about unjust judgments.[79] And while the king is subject to the law, yet if he orders an official to do wrong, the official can plead the royal order.[80] Also the official shares the royal immunity from jurisdiction and may be complained against only to the king or to those appointed by the king for the purpose.[81] Bracton has, in brief, no idea of the modern concept of the "rule of law." In the last analysis, he intimates, the sole redress against tyranny is reliance on divine vengeance, though doubtless this might operate through human agency.[82] Thus the problem of providing an institutional control upon the acts of the king is left in the *De Legibus* exactly where it is left by the continental writings of the period. The measure of such control should be the law, and Bracton's conception of this is full and definite; but the institution capable of applying this test with regularity and precision has not yet disclosed itself.

From the *De Legibus* we turn to Magna Carta and in so doing from the legal tradition of higher law to the political. Coke was eventually to bring the two together in his presentation of Magna Carta as "a restoration and declaration of the ancient common law";[83] but before this notion could become plausible, Magna Carta had to become absorbed into the common law.

The constitutional fathers regarded Magna Carta as having been from the first a muniment of English liberties, but the view of it adopted by modern scholarship

77. *Id*. f. 34. See Maitland's comment in Bracton, *Note Book* 29-33.
78. "Sumoneri non potest per breve." *Id*. f. 382b. *Cf*. ff. 5b and 17lb. See also Ehrlich, *Proceedings against the Crown* 23, 26, 45, 54 (6 Oxford Studies in Leg. and Soc. Hist. 1921).
79. Bracton, *De Legibus* ff. 368b, 369.
80. Ehrlich, *Proceedings against the Crown* 129.
81. *Id*. III {*sic;* 111?}.
82. *De Legibus* f. 369. The origin of the maxim that "the king can do no wrong" has been assigned by some authorities to the minority of Henry III; but if the saying existed in Bracton's day, it meant nearly the opposite of what it does today. "If the king, or anybody else, said that the king 'could not' do something, that meant, not that the act would not, if done, be attributed to the king, but that the king was no more allowed to do it, than a subject was allowed to commit a trespass or a felony," Erlich, *Proceedings against the Crown* 127.
83. Co. *Inst*. I, 8; *id*. II, 81; *cf*. 2 Hansard, *Parliamentary History* 333 (1628).

is a decidedly different one. This is that Magna Carta was to begin with a royal grant to a limited class of beneficiaries, and more or less at the expense of the realm at large. The king promised his barons that henceforth he would not infringe their customary feudal privileges as he had done in the immediate past, even though many of these were by no means accordant with the best interests of the remainder of his subjects.[84]

The eventual role, indeed, of Magna Carta in the history of American constitutional theory is due immediately to its revival at the opening of the seventeenth century, largely by Sir Edward Coke. The tradition which Coke revived was, however, by no means his own invention; it referred back to and was to a great extent substantiated by an earlier period in the history of this famous document—famous especially because it was a *document* and so gave definite, tangible embodiment to the notion of higher law.

From the first, Magna Carta evinced elements of growth, and it was fortunately cast into a milieu favoring growth. For one thing, its original form was not that of an enactment, but of a compact. It is, therefore, significant that when John sought escape from his solemn promises, he turned to the pope; and while his suit was immediately successful, subsequent confirmation restored the impaired obligation in full force. Far more important is it that certain of the charter's clauses, like those of the Fourteenth Amendment six hundred and fifty years later, were drawn in terms that did not confine their application to the immediate issues in hand or to the interests therein involved; while to match this feature of the document itself came the early discovery by the baronage that the successful maintenance of the charter against the monarch demanded the cooperation of all classes and so the participation by all classes in its benefits. Then, toward the close of the thirteenth century, the king, no longer able to "live off his own," eked out by the customary feudal revenues, was forced to call Parliament into existence to relieve his financial necessities. Parliament's subventions, however, were not to be had for the asking, but were conditioned on, among other things, the monarch's pledge to maintain Magna Carta.[85] And all this took place, it must be again remembered, in an age whose thought was permeated with the idea of authority limited by law. Had Magna Carta been the source of this idea, or the sole expression of it, it must soon have disappeared. Its very different fate testifies to the fact that it not only supported but was also supported by the universal tradition.

For the history of American constitutional law and theory no part of Magna Carta can compare in importance with chapter twenty-nine.[86] Without embarrass-

---

84. Adams, *Origin of the English Constitution* ch. 5 (1912); McIlwain, *The High Court of Parliament and Its Supremacy* 54 *et seq.* (1910).

85. Adams, *Origin of the English Constitution*, particularly at 160n., 162 *et seq.*; McIlwain, "Magna Carta and Common Law," in *Magna Carta Commemoration Essays* 156–60 (Malden ed. 1917).

86. "Nullus liber homo capiatur vel imprisonetur aut disseisiatur de libero tenemento suo vel libertatibus vel liberis consuetudinibus suis aut utlagetur aut exuletur aut aliquo modo destruatur nec

ing later discussion, this may be translated as follows: "No free man shall be taken or imprisoned or deprived of his freehold or of his liberties or free customs, or outlawed, or exiled, or in any manner destroyed, nor shall we go upon him, nor shall we send upon him, except by a legal judgment of his peers or by the law of the land."

Our present interest in this famous text is confined to its opening phrase, *"nullus liber homo,"* a term evidently intended to indicate the beneficiaries of the clause, perhaps of the charter as a whole. Although the words *liber homo* may have designated at first few outside the vassal class,[87] in this as in other respects the charter early manifested its capacity for growth. The second issue of the charter in 1225 was contemporaneously described as conceding their liberties alike "to people and to populace (*tam populo quam plebi*)."[88] A quarter-century later we find the term "common liberties" being used to characterize the subject matter of the charter.[89] Even more striking is Bracton's term for it—*"constitutio libertatis"*[90]—a phrase which, wittingly or not, attributes to the charter the consolidation of all particular liberties into *one* liberty. Once again we encounter a form of words of greatest interest to the student of American constitutional law and theory. It is noted at the moment for the evidence it affords of the final and complete emergence of Magna Carta from its feudal chrysalis.

Nor did Magna Carta develop solely along one dimension. As the range of classes and interests brought under its protection widened, its quality as higher law binding in some sense upon government in all its phases steadily strengthened until it becomes possible to look upon it in the fourteenth century as something very like a written constitution in the modern understanding. By his *Confirmatio Cartarum* of 1297, Edward I ordered all "justices, sheriffs, mayors, and other ministers, which under us and by us have the laws of our land to guide," to treat the Great Charter as "common law," in all pleas before them. Furthermore, any judgment contrary to the Great Charter or the Charter of the Forest was to be "holden for nought"; and all archbishops and bishops were to pronounce "the sentence of great excommunication against all those that by deed, aid, or counsel" proceeded "contrary to the aforesaid charters" or in any point transgressed them.[91] The conception of Magna Carta as higher law reached

super eum ibimus nec super eum mittemus, nisi per legale judicium parium suorum vel per legem terrae." Compare the issue of 1225 and caption 39 of the original issue. It is the later issue which "became the Great Charter of English law." Adams, *Origin of the English Constitution* 282. It was also called "Magna Carta."

87. Adams, *Origin of the English Constitution* 265; McIlwain, in *Magna Carta Commemoration Essays* 80–81, 170.

88. McIlwain, in *Magna Carta Commemoration Essays* 171. In 1354 it was enacted (28 Edw. III, ch. 3) that *"no man of what estate or condition he may be* [nul homme, de quel estate ou condicion qil soit], shall be put out of land or tenement, nor taken, nor imprisoned, nor disinherited, nor put to death, without being brought to answer by due process of law." 1 Stat. Realm 345.

89. McIlwain, in *Magna Carta Commemoration Essays* 172.

90. Bracton, *De Legibus* f. 168b. He also terms it simply "Constitutio," *id.* 169b.

91. Adams and Stephens, *Select Documents of English History* 86–87 (1911).

its culmination in the reign of Edward III. Of the thirty-two royal confirmations of the charter noted by Coke, fifteen occurred in this reign,[92] while near the end of it, in 1368, to the normal form of confirmation the declaration was added by statute that any statute passed contrary to Magna Carta *"soit tenuz p'nul."*[93] The actual operation of such measures in curtailing royal action will be treated later.

The glorious epoch of Magna Carta is the century stretching from the confirmation of Edward I to the deposition of Richard II. Another hundred years and the charter is found rarely mentioned, while from then on the obscurity in which it is wrapped becomes ever denser, till the anti-Stuart revival of it at the opening of the seventeenth century. For the later and longer portion of this period the explanation is simply Tudor despotism. As the biographer of Henry VIII points out, Shakespeare's *King John* contains not an allusion to Magna Carta.[94] For the period antedating the Tudors the explanation is less simple, but in general it consists in the fact that almost from its appearance Magna Carta was in process of absorption into the general stream of the common law. Bracton regards Magna Carta as a statute, part and parcel of the entire body of law of which he is treating. Edward I, as we have seen, ordered his judges to give Magna Carta, in causes coming before them, the force and effect of common law. The circumstances of the Wars of the Roses aided the same development. The particular guardian of the integrity and identity of Magna Carta was Parliament; but with the extermination of the old nobility, Parliament ceased practically to exist till the Tudors recreated it out of their own adherents. On the other hand, at a time when people did not know from day to day whether Lancaster or York sat on the throne, the common law courts continued for the most part in the discharge of their proper business.[95] It resulted that, as Englishmen recognized in the daily practice of the courts an actual realization of most that Magna Carta had symbolized, they transferred to the common law as a whole the worship which they had so long reserved more especially for the charter.

Writing with this period particularly in mind, Father Figgis has remarked:

The common law is pictured invested with a halo of dignity peculiar to the embodiment of the deepest principles and to the highest expression of human reason and of the law of nature implanted by God in the heart of man. As yet men are not clear that an act of Parliament can do more than declare the common law. It is the

---

92. Of these later confirmations Adams writes: "They express not so much a desire that specific provisions of the charter should be reaffirmed . . . as a desire to get the king's acknowledgment in general that he was bound by the law." Adams, *Origin of the English Constitution* 289–90n.

93. 42 Edw. III ch. I (1368); 1 Stat. Realm 388 (1368); 3 Co. *Inst.* III; also 1 *id.* 81.

94. Pollard, *Henry VIII* 35 (1905). But, as Pollard notes, allusion was made to the charter in the proceedings against Wolsey for *Praemunire;* and a translation of Magna Carta by one George Ferrers was printed in London in 1541. *Id.* 35.

95. For some evidence of interruption by sporadic violence, consult the *Paston Letters passim* (Fenn ed. 1873). Magna Carta is "part of the common law and the ancient law of this kingdom," 2 Hansard, *Parliamentary History* 333. "The king cannot dispense with Magna Carta, which is incorporated into the common law." 6 Comyn, *Digest* 35 tit. *Praeogative,* D. 7 (Dublin ed. 1793), citing 2 Rol. 115.

common law which men set up as an object of worship. They regard it as the
symbol of ordered life and disciplined activities, which are to replace the license
and violence of the evil times now passed away. . . . The common law is the perfect
ideal of law; for it is natural reason developed and expounded by a collective
wisdom of many generations. . . . Based on long usage and almost supernatural
wisdom, its authority is above, rather than below that of acts of Parliament or royal
ordinances which owe their fleeting existence to the caprice of the king or to the
pleasure of councillors, which have a merely material sanction and may be repealed
at any moment.[96]

The spokesman *par excellence* of this attitude is Sir John Fortescue, Henry
VI's chief justice, who followed his king into exile and there prepared his famous
work. This is his *Praises of the Laws of England*,[97] the importance of which,
slight as is the toll {total?} of its pages, is abundantly attested by Coke's and Blackstone's repeated citations of it, not to mention the unqualified adoption by both these
writers of its estimate of English legal customs and institutions. The *De Laudibus*
is, however, no mere ratification of past pieties; it contributes elements of the
greatest importance to the development of Anglo-American constitutional
theory. Written in France, it stresses the contrast between French autocracy and
what Fortescue terms the "mixed political government" of England. The former
is treated as sheer usurpation. Inasmuch as the people submitted themselves in the
first place to royal authority only in order to preserve their properties and persons, he argues, it is clear that they could never have assented to absolute power
and yet "if not from them, the king could have no such power rightfully at all."[98]
Thus, as in Locke two centuries later, the notion of authority as limited is based
on the notion of its popular origin. The laws of England, consequently, do not
admit of the maxim, *quod principi placuit;* on the contrary, the king can neither
"change the laws thereof nor take from the people what is theirs against their
consent";[99] and these laws "in all cases, declare in favor of liberty, the gift of
God to man in his creation."[100]

    96. Figgis, *Divine Right of Kings* 228-30 (2d ed. 1914). "The common law is the absolute
perfection of reason." 2 Co. *Inst.* 179. The common law, "having a principle of growth and progress
in itself . . . is already . . . the most complete and admirable system of law—the most healthy and
vigorous in its principles, the most favorable to civil liberty, standing the nearest to the divine law,
and the best fitted to be the auxiliary and helper of religion itself in the government of individual men
and of human society—that has ever existed on earth." Barnard, *Discourse on the Life, Character,
and Public Services of Ambrose Spencer* 52 (1849) {hereinafter Barnard, *Discourse*}. See also
Adams, *Origin of the English Constitution, passim.*
    97. Fortescue, *De Laudibus Legum Angliae* (Amos ed. 1825). This edition follows Francis
Gregor's translation of 1775—sometimes too faithfully. At the close of chapter 34, at 128, Fortescue
is made by both editors to say: "It is not a restraint, but rather a liberty to govern a people by the just
regularity of a *political* government, or rather right reason." No equivalent of the last four words
appears in the Latin original. The page references here are to the 1825 Amos edition.
    98. Fortescue, *De Laudibus Legum Angliae* ch. 14, at 41. See also *id.* 26, 38, 126.
    99. *Id.* chs. 9, 13, 18, 34, 36, at 26-27, 38, 55, 125, 136. The expression "Representatives in
Parliament" occurs at 55.
    100. *Id.* ch. 42, at 157.

Nor was liberty the only fruit of English institutions, for to this in turn was English prosperity directly traceable. A quaint passage of the *De Laudibus* reads:

> Every inhabitant is at his liberty fully to use and enjoy whatever his farm produceth, the fruits of the earth, the increase of his flock, and the like: all the improvements he makes, whether by his own proper industry, or of those he retains in his service, are his own to use and enjoy without the let, interruption, or denial of any: if he be in any wise injured, or oppressed, he shall have his *amends* and satisfaction against the party offending: hence it is, that the inhabitants are rich in gold, silver, and in all the necessaries and conveniences of life. They drink no water, unless at certain times, upon a religious score, and by way of doing penance. They are fed, in great abundance, with all sorts of flesh and fish, of which they have plenty everywhere; they are clothed throughout in good woollens; their bedding and other furniture in their houses are of wool, and that in great store; they are also well provided with all other sorts of household goods and necessary implements for husbandry: every one, according to his rank, hath all things which conduce to make life easy and happy . . . they are treated with mercy and justice, according to the laws of the land; neither are they impleaded in point of property, or arraigned for any capital crime, how heinous soever, but before the king's judges, and according to the laws of the land. These are the advantages consequent from that *political mixed government* which obtains in *England. . . ."* [101]

And as English legal institutions supported English prosperity, so English prosperity supported them. In no other country in the world, Fortescue contends, would trial by a jury of the vicinage be feasible, for the simple reason that in no other country would there be a sufficient number of honest men of the neighborhood capable of undertaking the service. [102]

But the distinctive contribution of the *De Laudibus* has still to be mentioned, that feature of it which discriminates it sharply from all earlier eulogies of higher law. This is Fortescue's conception of the law as a professional mystery, as the peculiar science of bench and bar. Almost at the outset he asserts the identity of "perfect justice" with "legal justice." [103] Later, through the mouth of his chief interlocuter, the chancellor, he develops the same thought at length. [104] The laws of England, he says, involve two distinct constituents: first, customs, statutes, or acts of Parliament, and the law of nature, all of which correspond to Aristotle's "elements of natural things"; secondly, "maxims," "principles which do not admit of proof by reason and argument," but carry with them their own evidence, and which correspond to that same philosopher's "efficient causes." But

---

101. *Id.* ch. 36, at 136–38.

102. *Id.* chs. 25, 26, 29, especially at 91, 104–105. In chapter 27, at 93, occurs the famous sentiment that "one would much rather that twenty guilty persons should escape the punishment of death, than that one innocent person should be condemned, and suffer capitally." Fortescue's complacency with English institutions, as well as his contempt for French, is most amusingly illustrated by his comment on "modern French," that "it is not the same with that used by our lawyers in the *Courts of Law,* but is much altered and depraved by common use." *Id.* 78.

103. *Id.* ch. 4, at II.

104. *Id.* ch. 8, at 20.

the knowledge which men in general have of either of these categories of legal
learning is, and can be, but superficial, comparable with that which they have of
"faith, love, charity, the sacraments, and God's commandments," while leaving
"other mysteries in Divinity to those who preside in the church." Nor is the case
of the ruler himself different from that of the generality of his subjects in this
respect; wherefore the chancellor is made to say:

> My Prince, there will be no occasion for you to search into the arcana of our laws
> with such tedious application and study. . . . It will not be convenient by severe
> study, or at the expense of the best of your time, to pry into nice points of law: such
> matters may be left to your judges and counsel. . . ; furthermore, you will better
> pronounce judgment in the courts by others than in person, it being not customary
> for the kings of England to sit in court or pronounce judgment themselves. [*Proprio
> ore nullus regum Angliae judicium proferre usus est.*]
>
> I know very well the quickness of your apprehension and the forwardness of your
> parts; but for that expertness in the laws the which is requisite for judges the studies
> of twenty years [*viginti annorum lucubrationes*] barely suffice.[105]

The colloquy thus imagined by Fortescue was enacted in solemn earnest one
hundred and thirty years later. On Sunday morning, November 10, 1608, Coke
and "all the judges of England, and the barons of the Exchequer" faced James I
at Hampton Court to confute the notion which had been instilled in him by
Archbishop Bancroft that, inasmuch as the judges were but his delegates, he was
entitled to decide cases in his own person. "The judges informed the king,"
Coke records, "that no king after the Conquest assumed to himself to give any
judgment in any cause whatsoever, which concerned the administration of justice
within this realm, but these were solely determined in the courts of justice. . . ."
To this the king answered that "he thought the law was founded on reason, and
that he and others had reason, as well as the judges"; but Coke pointed out the
fallacy of this view in the following words:

> True it was, that God had endowed his Majesty with excellent science, and great
> endowments of nature; but his Majesty was not learned in the laws of his realm of
> England, and causes which concern the life, or inheritance, or goods, or fortunes of
> his subjects, are not to be decided by natural reason, but by the artificial reason and
> judgment of the law, which law is an act which requires long study and experience,
> before that a man can attain to the cognizance of it; and that the law was the golden
> metwand and measure to try the causes of the subjects; and which protected his
> Majesty in safety and peace.

"The king," the report continues, "was greatly offended," saying that, "then
he should be under the law, which was treason to affirm," to which Coke re-

---

105. *Id.* ch. 8. On this subject see an excellent note by Amos in Fortescue, *De Laudibus Legum
Angliae* 23–25; see also 2 Co. *Inst.* 56. Bodin recognized that the prince ought not to administer
justice in person. Bluntschli, *Theory of the State* 517 (1895). For Bracton's very different view, see
De Legibus f. 107. Edward III endeavored to make royal interference with the course of justice
impossible.

sponded in Bracton's words: *"Quod Rex non debet esse sub homine, sed sub Deo et lege."*[106]

We are thus brought back to a question raised earlier: By what methods was the supremacy of the common law maintained against the royal power? Or to phrase the same question somewhat differently: By what methods was "higher law" kept "positive"? In Bracton's day, as we have seen, there was no regular remedy available to a subject who deemed himself to have been wronged by the king or by the king's officials; but in this respect institutional improvement in the course of the century following was notable. In the first place, as to his lower officials Edward I began the policy of waiving their, that is *his,* immunity. By chapter thirteen of the statute of Westminster II, enacted in 1285, persons illegally imprisoned by sheriffs were given as complete recovery as if the authors of the wrong had no official capacity.[107] Still more important was the development during the same reign of the so-called petition of right.[108] Such a petition might be addressed to the king, his chancellor, or his council. On the granting of it, the issues raised were determined by the chancellor, the council, the Exchequer, or the King's Bench, and in accordance with the law;[109] since, when the king sued or consented to be sued, he was considered a party and nothing more.[110] The climax of this development was reached in 1346, when Edward III having instructed his justices that they should not, on account of any letters or orders purporting to come from him, "omit to do right," a proviso to that effect was inserted in the oath of the justices.[111] Hence, royal acts and royal claims were brought constantly to the test of the ordinary law, and often as administered by the ordinary courts.

Such a system was certainly not far from realizing the modern conception of the rule of law. There were, nevertheless, facts of a contrary tendency that must not be overlooked. For one thing, the king was recognized by the courts themselves to be in many instances above the law by virtue of his prerogative, and that for the common good.[112] Again, the judges who decided such matters were the

---

106. Prohibitions del Roy, 7 Co. 63–65 (1609). "Law was to an important extent conceived by both governors and governed as a subject of science, capable of being learnt by special study, but not capable of being altered by the mere arbitrary will of government, any more than the principles or conclusions of mathematics." Sidgwick, *Elements of Politics* 652–53 (2d ed. 1897), quoted in McIlwain, *High Court of Parliament* 47. "A portion, and a very large portion, of that justice which it belongs to God alone to dispense with exact and unerring equity, is committed to them [judges] to administer." Barnard, *Discourse* 52.

107. Ehrlich, *Proceedings against the Crown* III {sic. 111?}.

108. *Id.* 82–96, *passim; id.* 179–88. For an ancient fiction dating from the time of Edward I, supporting the courts on the ground of right and usage in the jursidiction acquired by petition, see *id.* 54.

109. *Id.* 107, 120.

110. *Id.* 108.

111. *Id.* 131.

112. *Id.* 17–19, 40–41, 51, 56–64, 131–41.

king's appointees and held their offices at his pleasure. Yet again, one of these prerogatives was a quite undefined power of rendering statutes ineffective, called the "dispensing power." Lastly, and most important of all, shortly after 1500 theories gained currency which claimed for the king, at least in his legislative capacity, complete independence from every legal restraint. It was the clash of facts and theories such as these with the notion of a higher law which filled English history in the seventeenth century, and it was forces emergent from this clash which projected the notion of higher law across the Atlantic into eighteenth-century America.

III.*

It was the happy strategy of the Tudors to convert Parliament from an outpost against the royal power into its active instrument. The result of this alliance for English constitutional ideas was momentous. Contemporaneously Bodin was attributing to the king of France the whole power of the state and describing that power as "perpetual and absolute," as "*legibus soluta.*"[1] Very different is the doctrine of Sir Thomas Smith in his *Commonwealth of England,* written near the middle of Elizabeth's reign: "The most high and absolute power of the realme of Englande, consisteth in the Parliament. . . . That which is doone by this consent is called firme, stable, and *sanctum,* and is taken for lawe. The Parliament abrogateth olde lawes, maketh newe . . . and hath the power of the whole realme, both the head and the body. For everie Englishman is entended to bee there present, either in person or by procuration and attornies."[2] In consequence of the Tudor reformation, the joint work of king and Parliament, the concept of sovereignty in the sense of *potestas legibus soluta* became confined to that branch of his power which the king customarily exercised "by and with the advice and consent" of Parliament.

Yet to begin with, this characteristically English compromise was assailed from both sides. The Stuarts, not enjoying the cooperation of Parliament, sought to put themselves beyond the need of it by appealing to the doctrine of the divine right of kings. In answer, their parliamentary opponents did not hesitate to challenge, in the name of the supremacy of the common law, the outstanding constitutional result of the Tudor reformation; and the foremost figure of this reaction was Sir Edward Coke.

---

* This is the concluding installment of Corwin, "The 'Higher Law' Background of American Constitutional Law," 42 *Harv. L. Rev.* 149-85 (1928) and 365-409 (1929). The original footnote numbering has been retained.

1. 2 Dunning, *History of Political Theories* 96 *et seq.* (1916).

2. Smith, *De Republica Anglorum* bk. ii, ch. 1 (Alston ed. 1906). Coke regards the bulk of the law of his time, both common and statute, as unalterable. 2 Co. *Inst.* 187. "The people of England, have both ancient fundamental rights, liberties, franchises, laws, and a fundamental government, which like the laws of the Medes and Persians, neither may nor ought to be altered." Prynne, *Good Old Fundamental Liberties* pt. I, 27 (1655).

Coke was best known to our ancestors as the commentator on Littleton's *Tenures*. "Coke's Lyttleton," wrote Jefferson many years afterward with reference to the prerevolutionary period, "was the universal lawbook of students, and a sounder Whig never wrote, nor of profounder learning in the orthodox doctrines of the British constitution, or in what was called British liberties."[3] Before he was a commentator on the law of England, however, Coke was successively law reporter, crown attorney, chief justice of the Common Pleas, chief justice of the King's Bench, and member of Parliament; and always he was Edward Coke, an outstanding, aggressive personality, with a fixed determination to make himself mightily felt in whatever place of authority he might occupy. That such a person, having occasion to express himself from the standpoint of such various capacities, should be altogether self-consistent, would be demanding too much. Medievalist and legalist, Coke's objective is sharply political—the curbing of the pretensions of royalty. So precedent and authority—the legalist's stock materials—must be bent to the selected end. Indeed, if occasion require, they may be embroidered upon somewhat, for Coke's outlook upon such procedures is not unlike that of a medieval chronicler of edifying intent. In another respect, too, Coke is thoroughly medieval; his method, even in his *Institutes,* is irritatingly fragmentary, with the result that his larger ideas have often to be dug out and pieced together from a heterogeneous mass. Nor should the student of Coke fail to reckon on the difficulty which arises from the sheer operation of time on the significance of the terms which he employs. Madison's warning centuries later against "those errors which have their source in the changed meaning of words and phrases," is singularly pertinent in this instance.[4]

While Coke as attorney general had shown himself conspicuously subservient to the royal interest, his clashes as judge with James I make a notable chapter in judicial history. His basic doctrine was "that the king hath no prerogative, but that which the law of the land allows,"[5] and that of this the judges and not the king were the authorized interpreters.[6] The circumstances of his admonition to James that he had no right to judge as between subject and subject save through

---

3. 12 Jefferson, *Writings* iv (Memorial ed. 1903). As a student himself, Jefferson entertained a very uncomplimentary opinion of Coke. 4 *id.* 3.

4. See especially MacKay, "Coke—Parliamentary Sovereignty or the Supremacy of the Law?," 22 *Mich. L. Rev.* 215–47 (1924); and 5 Holdsworth, *History of English Law* 423–93 (1924). Wallace, *Reporters* 112–42 (3d ed. 1855), makes a convincing defense of Coke's reliability as a reporter.

5. Proclamations, 12 Co. 74, 76 (1611).

6. Nicholas Fuller's Case, 12 Co. 41 (1608); Case of the King's Prerogative in Saltpetre, 12 Co. 12 (1607); Case of Non Obstante, or the Dispensing Power, 12 Co. 18 (c. 1607). In Commissions of Enquiry, 12 Co. 31 (1608), Coke, commenting on Bates' Case, 2 How. St. Tr. 371 (1606), sustains the king's power to exact retaliatory duties from foreign merchants, and also his power to exact benevolences. Exaction of Benevolence, 12 Co. 119, 120 (c. 1610). See also 2 Co. *Inst.* 63. Today the royal prerogative is subject absolutely to the legislative power of Parliament, and when a statute has directed the exercise of the prerogative in a certain way there is no "remnant prerogative." See Morgan, "Introduction," in Robinson, *Public Authorities and Legal Liability* xiv (1925). See Chitty, *Prerogatives of the Crown* 383 (1820), for statement of the older view.

the ordinary courts proceeding without royal interference were reviewed above. Later he had cause to inform James that the latter could not by proclamation "make a thing unlawful which was permitted by the law before."[7] On these occasions Coke had the support of his judicial brethren; but in the matter of the commendams they deserted him to a man. The question put the judges was whether, in a case pending before them which the king thought "to concern him either in power or profit," they could be required to stay proceedings till the king could consult with them. All but Coke answered yes. Coke's answer was "that when that case should be, he would do that which should be fit for a judge to do."[8] Shortly after he was removed from his chief justiceship.

For students of the origins of American constitutional law and theory, however, no judicial utterance of Coke's—few indeed in language—can surpass in interest and importance his so-called dictum in Dr. Bonham's Case, which was decided by the Court of Common Pleas in 1610.[9] Holding that the London College of Physicians was not entitled, under the act of Parliament which it invoked in justification, to punish Bonham for practicing medicine in the city without its license, Coke said: "And it appears in our books, that in many cases, the common law will controul acts of Parliament, and sometimes adjudge them to be utterly void: for when an act of Parliament is against common right and reason, or repugnant, or impossible to be performed, the common law will controul it and adjudge such act to be void."[10] In these words we have foreshadowed not merely the power which American courts today exercise in the disallowance of statutes on the ground of their conflict with the Constitution, but also that very test of "reasonableness" which is the ultimate flowering of this power. We must determine if we can to what extent Coke's own intention sanctions the modern application of his doctrine, and also to what extent the historical background of the dictum does so.

We may first dispose of a matter having only incidental reference to these questions. In employing the phrase "common right and reason," Coke is no doubt again alluding to "that artificial reason and judgment of the law" of which he regarded bench and bar as the especial custodians. What is pertinent to note here is that his employment of these terms is by no means the narrowly official and precisionist one that it would probably have been a hundred years before. Early in the sixteenth century the author of *Doctor and Student,* possibly voicing the suspicion of the Tudor epoch toward principles restrictive of governmental

7. Proclamations, 12 Co. 74, 75 (1611).
8. The Case of Commendams, Hobart 140–66 (1616); Hicks, *Men and Books* 67–70 (1921).
9. 8 Co. 107a (1610), 2 Brownl. 225 (1610).
10. 8 Co. 118a (1610). The best comment on the dictum is to be found in McIlwain, *High Court of Parliament and its Supremacy* ch. 4 (1910), and Plucknett, "Bonham's Case and Judicial Review," 40 *Harv. L. Rev.* 30 *et seq.* (1926). Coxe, {*An Essay on*} *Judicial Power and Unconstitutional Legislation* chs. 13–17 (1893) is of incidental value. Ellesmere's charge that Coke had the support of only one judge and that three others were against him seems to be refuted both by Coke's and by Brownlow's report of the case. Apparently only three judges participated, and all agreed with Coke's statement.

authority, had taken pains to explain that the term "law of nature" "is not used among them that be learned in the laws of England.'"[11] The attitude revealed by Coke and his associates contemporaneously with Bonham's Case is very different. Reporting Calvin's Case, which was decided the same year, following argument by the chief legal lights of England, Coke says, by way of summary: "1. That ligeance or obedience of the subject to the sovereign is due by the law of nature; 2. That this law of nature is part of the laws of England; 3. That the law of nature was before any judicial or minicipal law in the world; 4. That the law of nature is immutable, and cannot be changed.'"[12] He then recites in support of these propositions the following quaint argument:

The law of nature is that which God at the time of creation of the nature of man infused into his heart, for his preservation and direction; and this is *lex aeterna*, the moral law, called also the law of nature. And by this law, written with the finger of God in the heart of man, were the people of God a long time governed before the law was written by Moses, who was the first reporter or writer of law in the world. . . . And Aristotle, nature's secretary Lib. 5. Æthic. saith that *jus naturale est, quod a pud omnes homines eandem habet potentiam.* And herewith doth agree Bracton lib. I. cap. 5. and Fortescue cap. 8. 12. 13. and 16. *Doctor and Student,* cap. 2. and 4.[13]

The receptive and candid attitude thus evinced toward natural law ideas, a fresh influx of which from the Continent was already setting in, is a matter of profound importance. In the great constitutional struggle with the Stuarts it enabled Coke to build upon Fortescue, and it enabled Locke to build upon Coke. It made allies of sixteenth-century legalism and seventeenth-century rationalism, and the alliance then struck has always remained, now more, now less vital, in American constitutional law and theory.

11. St. Germain, *Doctor and Student* 12–13 (Muchall ed. 1787). Suspicion of ecclesiastical domination is given by Pollock as the reason for the reluctance of the sages of the common law before the Reformation to refer expressly to the laws of nature. Pollock, *Expansion of the Common Law* 112–13 (1904). Fortescue, however, evinced no such reluctance. Bryce notes that both Yelverton and Lord Chancellor Stillington, who held office under Edward IV, referred to the law of nature. Bryce, *Studies in History and Jurisprudence* 601 (1901). Pollock himself adds: "It is not credible that a doctrine which pervaded all political speculation in Europe, and was assumed as a common ground of authority by the opposing champions of the empire and the papacy, should have been without influence among learned men in England." Bryce, *Studies in History and Jurisprudence* 601. See also Pollock, "History of the Law of Nature," in his *Essays in the Law* 157 (1922); Lowell, *Government of England* 480–88 (1908). 4 Holdsworth, *History of English Law* 276, 279–82; 5 *id.* 216, points out the close connection between equity and the law of nature in the fifteenth and sixteenth centuries. Though equity never served the purposes of a higher law, restrictive of royal or Parliamentary authority, it may have helped to keep natural law ideas alive for that use in the seventeenth century. The adaptability of the common law was referred in the nineteenth century to its resting upon the law of nature. See argument of Alexander Hamilton in People v. Croswell, 3 Johns. 337 (N.Y. 1804); also Bernard, *Discourse on the Life, Character, and Public Services of Ambrose Spencer* 52 (1849). Thus the applied law changes through the progressive revelation to the judges of the immutable law.

12. 7 Co. 1, 4b (1610).

13. 7 Co. at 12a–12b. Bacon's argument in the case invoked the law of nature. 2 Bacon, *Works* 166, 176 (Montague ed. 1825).

The question of the significance which Coke attached to "common rights and reason" can, however, be answered in much more definite terms. Let the reader's mind revert in this connection to those "maxims" which, according to Fortescue, "do not admit of proof by reason and argument" but bear with them their own evidence, and which, according to the same authority, constituted the very substance of the peculiar science of the judges.[14] Coke yields very little to his predecessor in the reverence he pays to such "fundamental points of the common law."[15] It was, moreover, just such a maxim that Coke found to be involved in Bonham's Case. The College of Physicians had, under color of authority from an act of Parliament, amerced Bonham and taken half the fine for themselves. Coke's comment is as follows: "The censors cannot be judges, ministers, and parties; judges to give sentence or judgment; ministers to make summons; and parties to have the moiety of the forfeiture, quai aliquis non debet esse judex in propria causa; imo iniquum est aliquem suae rei esse judicem."[16] Thereupon follows the famous dictum.

"Common right and reason" is, in short, something fundamental, something permanent; it is higher law. And again it is relevant to note the ratification which Coke's doctrine received in American constitutional law and theory. With such axioms, traceable in many instances to the *Digest* and *Code* of Justinian, Coke's pages abound;[17] and from his work many of them early found their way into American judicial decisions, sometimes as interpretative of the written constitution, sometimes as supplementary of it. Such a postulate is the doctrine that "a statute should have prospective, not retrospective operation."[18] Another is the principle that "no one should be twice punished for the same offense."[19] Another is the maxim that "every man's house is his own castle."[20] Still another is the aphorism which has played so large a role in the history of the judicial

14. See p. 103 above. *Cf.* St. Germain, *Doctor and Student* 25-26.

15. "In truth they are the main pillars and supporters of the fabric of the Commonwealth." 1 Co. *Inst.* 74. He also issues a warning that "the alteration of any of these maxims of the common law is most dangerous." *Id.* 210; see also *id.* 97.

16. "Ne quis in sua causa judicet vel jus sibi dicat." (No man may be a judge in his own cause.) *Code* III, 5, 1; Woolf, *Bartolus* 159 (1913). Cf. Bracton, *De Legibus et Consuetudinibus Angliae* f. 119 (Twiss ed. 1854); Earl of Derby's Case, 12 Co. 114 (1614); Tumey v. Ohio, 273 U.S. 510 (1926); also cases cited in notes 35 and 37, below. {To "amerce" is to punish by a pecuniary penalty the amount of which is not fixed by law but is left to the discretion of the court.}

17. I have used Broom, *Legal Maxims* (5th Am. ed. 1870). There are earlier collections by Wingate and by Noy.

18. Broom, *Legal Maxims* 34-35. "Nova constitutio futuris formam imponere debet, non praeteritis." *Cf.* "Leges et constitutiones futuris certum est dare formam negotiis, non ad facta praeterita revocari; nisi nominatim etiam de praeterito tempore adhuc pendentibus negotiis cautum sit." *Code* I, 14, 7. In this, the original form, no suggestion of a restriction on the legislative power appears.

19. "Nemo debet bis puniri pro uno delicto. . . . Deus non agit bis in idipsum." Bonham's Case, 8 Co. 114 (1610). See also Wetherel v. Darly, 4 Co. 40 (1583); Hudson v. Lee, 4 Co. 43 (1589); and Broom, *Legal Maxims* 347.

20. Semayne's Case, 5 Co. 91 (1605); Broom, *Legal Maxims* 321: "Domus sua cuique est tutissimum refugium." *Cf.* "Nemo de domo sua extrahi debet." *Dig.* I, 17, 103.

concept of the police power, *"sic utere tuo ut alienum non laedas"*;[21] while another, almost equally famous in the history of constitutional litigation, is the axiom *"delegata potestas non potest delegari."*[22] Every one of these axioms is citable to the *Reports* or the *Institutes,* and each one was first taken thence, if not from intermediate derivative works, by early American lawyers and judges. Mention might also be made of the numerous rules for the construction of written instruments which were originally adapted from the same sources to the business of constitutional construction.[23]

We are thus brought to the question of Coke's meaning when he speaks of "controuling" an act of Parliament and "adjudging such act to be void." When the Supreme Court of the United States pronounces an act of Congress "void," it ordinarily means void *ab initio,* because beyond the power of Congress to enact, and it furthermore generally implies that it would similarly dispose of any future act of the same tenor. Was Coke laying claim to any such sweeping power for the ordinary courts as against acts of Parliament?

One thing seems to be assured at the outset—Coke was not asserting simply a rule of statutory construction which owed its force to the assumed intention of Parliament as it would today, although the statute involved in Bonham's Case was also construed from that point of view.[24] As we have already seen, Coke was enforcing a rule of higher law deemed by him to be binding on Parliament and the ordinary courts alike. This also appears from his treatment of the precedents he adduces. The most ancient of these is Tregor's Case, which occurred in the eighth year of Edward III's reign.[25] On that occasion Chief Justice Herle had used these words: "There are some statutes made which he himself who made them does not will to put into effect"; although just why this is so is not stated. In Coke's opinion these words become: "Some statutes are made against common law and right, which they that made them perceiving would not put into execution." In other words, the lawmaking body itself recognized the binding and invalidating force of principles external to the legislative act. Two other precedents Coke submits to similar elaboration.[26]

Furthermore, we should recall in this connection, Coke's repeated assertion that statutes made against Magna Carta were "void," a doctrine that Parliament

21. Aldred's Case, 9 Co. 57, 59 (1611); Broom, *Legal Maxims* 274. In these places the maxim is considered purely as rule of private conduct.

22. 2 Co. *Inst.* 597; Broom, *Legal Maxims* 665, where it is stated as a principle of the law of agency.

23. See, e.g., Broom, *Legal Maxims* 650, 682.

24. "An act of parliament . . . (as a will) is to be expounded according to the intention of the makers." 8 Co. 114, 119 (1610). This is said with reference to a comparison of certain clauses of the act before the court. *Cf.* 1 Bl. *Comm.* 91: "Where some collateral matter arises out of the general words, and happens to be unreasonable, there the judges are, in decency, to conclude that this consequence was not foreseen by the Parliament."

25. McIlwain, *High Court of Parliament* 286 *et seq.*

26. Plucknett, 40 *Harv. L. Rev.* 30 *et seq.* (1926). See also above note 11.

itself had confirmed more than once in annulling its own past enactments.[27] Nor may we overlook his words in the Case of *Non Obstante* or the Dispensing Power: "No act can bind the king from any prerogative which is sole and inseparable to his person, but that he may dispense with it by a *non obstante;* as a sovereign power to command any of his subjects to serve him for the public weal"; or the sovereign power of pardon, and he instances acts of Parliament itself which recognize this principle.[28] In Calvin's Case, decided the term before Bonham's Case, the same doctrine is repeated, with the exception that the royal prerogative is rested on the "law of nature.'"[29] Nor does such doctrine lose in impressiveness when we reflect that along with it, in Coke's mind, went the doctrine that the royal prerogative was subject to delimitation by the common law as applied by the ordinary courts.

At the very least, therefore, we can assert that in Bonham's Case Coke deemed himself to be enforcing a rule of construction of statutes of higher intrinsic validity than any act of Parliament as such. Does this, on the other hand, necessarily signify that he regarded the ordinary courts as the *final* authoritative interpreters of such rule of construction? A contemporaneous critic of the dictum in Bonham's Case was Lord Chancellor Ellesmere, whose objection was couched in the following significant terms: "He challenged not power for the judges of this Court [King's Bench] to correct all misdemeanors as well extrajudicial as judicial, nor to have power to judge statutes and acts of Parliament to be void, if they conceived them to be against common right and reason; but left to the king and Parliament to judge what was common right and reason. I speak not of impossibilities or direct repugnances."[30] The issue contemporaneously raised by the dictum, therefore, was not, as we should say today, between judicial power and legislative power; but between the law declaring power of the ordinary courts and the like power of "the High Court of Parliament."

There may have been a period when Coke, in view of the threatened deadlock between the king and the Houses, dreamed of giving the law to both through the mouths of the judges. Otherwise it is difficult to account for such criticisms as that voiced by Ellesmere, the accumulation of which was a material factor in forcing Coke's retirement from the bench six years later. And further confirming

---

27. 1 Co. *Inst.* 81; 2 *id.* 51; 3 *id.* III {111?}; Proclamations, 12 Co. 74, 76 (1611); Ehrlich, *Proceedings against the Crown* 114 (6 Oxford Studies in Leg. and Soc. Hist. 1921). In 1341 the chancellor and others protested that "they could not keep them [certain statutes] in case those statutes were contrary to the laws and customs of the realm, which they were sworn to keep." *Id.* 115. In other words, a statute merely as such is not necessarily law of the realm. *Cf.* Proclamations, 12 Co. 74, 76 (1611). The first recorded judicial application of the word "void" in relation to a statute seems to have been in the Annuity Case, in Fitzherbert, *Abridgment* (Pasch. 27 Hen. VI (1450), one of the precedents cited by Coke in support of the dictum. Its precise significance, however, in that connection seems to have been uncertain to Coke himself. Coxe, *Judicial Power and Unconstitutional Legislation* 153–60.

28. 12 Co. 18 (c. 1607).

29. 7 Co. la, 14a (1609).

30. McIlwain, *High Court of Parliament and its Supremacy* 293–94, citing Moore 828 (1663).

this suspicion is, on the one hand, the obviously gratuitous character of the dictum, the case having been adequately disposed of on other grounds, and, on the other hand, Coke's apparent effort later to effect a retreat from an untenable position. In Rowles v. Mason, decided in 1612, Coke stated that the common law "corrects, allows, and disallows, both *statute law, and custom,* for if there be repugnancy in *statute;* or unreasonablenesse in custom, the common law disallowes and rejects it, as appears by Doctor Bonham's Case.... "[31] This statement of the matter seems to bring his own theory into line with Ellesmere's. His later expressions in the *Institutes* are in the same tone. Indeed, at one point he asserts, on the authority of Chief Justice Herle, a judge in the reign of Edward III, that an award by the High Court of Parliament is "the highest law that could be."[32]

In brief, while Coke regarded the ordinary courts as peculiarly qualified to interpret and apply the law of reason, he also, finally at least, recognized the superior claims of the High Court of Parliament as a *law-declaring body.* Indeed, as we shall see in a moment, his last years were especially devoted to asserting the competence of Parliament in this respect. While the dictum uncovers one of the indispensable premises of the doctrine of judicial review, the other, that which rests on the principle of separation of powers, he still lacks. This, of course, is a matter to be treated later.

A word should be added regarding the reception and transmission of the dictum. Though there is no reference in Day v. Savadge[33] to Bonham's Case, Chief Justice Hobart's words in the later case are doubtless an echo: "Even an act of Parliament, made against natural equity, as to make a man judge in his own cause, is void in itself; for *jura naturae sunt immutabilia* and they are *leges legum.* "[34] Thus Bracton—and ultimately Cicero—is brought to Coke's support. In Captain Streater's Case,[35] decided in 1653, while the Barebones Parliament was in control, the dictum for the first time encountered the rising principle of legislative sovereignty. Streater, who had been arrested on an order by the Parliament, applied for a writ of *habeas corpus* on the ground that such an order

---

31. 2 Brownl. 192, 198 (1612). He adds that "statute law . . . corrects, abridges, and explains the common law." Notice also his expression in his "humble and direct answer" in explanation of a precedent used in Bonham's Case: "and, because that this is against common right and reason, the common law adjudges the said act of parliament *as to this point* void" (italics mine). 2 Bacon, *Works* 506.

32. 2 Co. *Inst.* 497–98. A still more decisive passage may be found in 4 *id.* 37; *cf.* 1 Bl. *Comm.* 91. See also Co. *Inst.* 272 (a)(b); *id.* 360(a), 381(b); 2 *id.* 148, 301; *cf.* 6 Bacon, *Abridgment* 383, 635, 643 (6th ed. 1807). I do not find however, that Coke anywhere in the *Institutes* says that a statute may be void in relation to "common right and reason," though he does say that statutes contrary to Magna Carta are, and that "words of an act of Parliament must be taken in lawful and rightful sense." 1 Co. *Inst.* 381(b). See also Coxe, *Judicial Power and Unconstitutional Legislation* 154–55.

33. Hobart 85 (1614).

34. *Id.* at 87a–87b.

35. 5 How. St. Tr. 365 (1653).

was not "law of the land" and so was void. He pleaded that "Parliaments ever made laws, but judges of the law judged by those laws." The court answered: "Mr. Streater, one must be above another, and the inferior must submit to the superior. . . . If the Parliament should do one thing, and we do the contrary here, things would run round. We must submit to the legislative power. . . ."[36]

Yet even as late as 1701, we find Chief Justice Holt reaffirming the dictum, in the case of City of London v. Wood,[37] but not without significant ambiguity. At one point in his opinion, Holt says that the difference between a municipal by-law and an act of Parliament is "that a by-law is liable to have its validity brought in question, but an act of Parliament is not." Yet he later adds: "And what my Lord Coke says in Dr. Bonham's Case in his 8 Coke is far from any extravagancy, for it is a very reasonable and true saying, That if an act of Parliament should ordain that the same person should be party and judge, or, which is the same thing, judge in his own cause, it would be a void act of Parliament; for it is impossible that one should be judge and party, for the judge is to determine between party and party. . . ."[38] What precisely does Holt mean by the word "impossible" here? Does he mean impossible without injustice; or does he mean impossible without logical absurdity—what Coke himself had termed "repugnancy"—and giving rise perhaps to something approaching physical impossibility? In the one case the restraint on the act of Parliament is still the higher law, in the other it is not. The question cannot be resolved further than to say that Holt, like Blackstone later, seems to be attempting to bridge the gap between two conflicting theories of law. As we shall see, these attempts furnished a useful prop to judicial review in its earlier American stages.[39]

From Holt's time, the dictum finds no place in important judicial opinion in England; but it does find its way into the *Digests* and *Abridgments* of the time, works which are apt to be comprehensive rather than critical. Through these works, as well as the *Reports,* it passed to America to join there the arsenal of weapons being accumulated against Parliament's claims to sovereignty.

In 1616 Coke, who had three years earlier been transferred from the Common Pleas to the King's Bench, was dismissed as judge altogether. Four years later he was elected to the House of Commons, and there at once assumed the leadership of the growing opposition to the Stuarts. In 1625 Charles succeeded James, and

---

36. *Id.* at 386. Meantime Finch, C. J., in his *Law* (1636), had surpassed the dictum in dogmatic assertion of the legal limits on Parliament's powers. "Therefore lawes positive, which are directly contrary to the former [the law of reason] lose their force, and are no lawes at all. As those which are contrary to the law of nature." Finch, *Law* bk. 1, ch. 6 (1636), quoted by Pound, "Common Law and Legislation" 21 *Harv. L. Rev.* 391–92 (1908). In the Ship-Money Case, Finch, C. J., advanced a similar doctrine in defense of the royal prerogative. "No act of Parliament can bar a king of his regality. . . . Therefore acts of Parliament to take away his royal power in defense of the kingdom are void." See Maitland, *Constitutional History* 299 (1909).

37. 12 Mod. 678 (1701).

38. *Id.* at 687.

39. Coxe, *Judicial Power and Unconstitutional Legislation* 176–78, and ch. 25.

in 1627 occurred the arbitrary arrest by royal order of the Five Knights, giving rise in Parliament to the great Inquest on the Liberties of the Subject, and eventually to the framing of the Petition of Right.[40] In all these proceedings the leading role fell to Coke, and their general tendency is made clear in the quaint words of Sir Benjamin Rudyard, who expressed his great gratification to see "that good, old, decrepit law of Magna Carta, which hath been so long kept in and lain bed-rid, as it were . . . walk abroad again.'"[41] Coke's main objective was still the curbing of the royal prerogative, but the terms in which he expressed himself also assert the existence of constitutional limits to Parliament's power as well. Especially significant are his remarks on the clause "saving the sovereign power" of the king which was at first attached to the Petition by the Lords. The question arising, "What is sovereign power?" a member quoted Bodin to the effect "that it is free from any conditions"; whereupon Coke arose and said: "This is *magnum in parvo*. . . . I know that prerogative is a part of the law, but 'sovereign power' is no parliamentary word. In my opinion it weakens Magna Carta, and all the statutes; for they are absolute without any saving of 'sovereign power'; and should we now add it, we shall weaken the foundation law, and then the building must needs fall. Take heed what we yield unto: Magna Carta is such a fellow, that he will have no 'sovereign.' "[42] The words of Wentworth and Pym during the same debate were to like effect. The former said, "these laws are not acquainted with 'sovereign power' "; while Pym added that, far from being able to accord the king sovereign power, Parliament itself was "never possessed of it.'"[43] Another noteworthy feature of the debate was the appearance in the course of it of the word "unconstitutional" in essentially its modern sense when used in political discussion.[44]

In his *Institutes,* Coke, still the embattled commoner, completes his restoration of Magna Carta as the great muniment of English liberties. It is called "Magna Carta, not for the length or largeness of it . . . but . . . in respect of the great weightiness and weighty greatness of the matter contained in it; in a few words, being the fountain of all the fundamental laws of the realm.'"[45] Declaratory of the common law, "this statute of Magna Carta hath been confirmed above thirty times.'"[46] Judgments and statutes against it "shall be void.'"[47] Its benefits extend to all, even villeins, they being freemen as to all save their own

40. 2 Hansard, *Parliamentary History* 262–366 (1628).
41. *Id.* 335.
42. *Id.* 356–57.
43. *Id.*
44. The occasion was Serjeant Ashley's expression of "divine right" sentiment. *Id.* 317. "The doctrine advanced by this gentleman seemed so unconstitutional that he was ordered into custody." *Id.* 328–29. Chalmers in his *Political Annals* notes that the word "unconstitutional" was applied in New England to certain acts of Parliament in 1691. 1 New York Historical Society Collections 81 (1868).
45. 1 Co. *Inst.* 81; 2 Hansard, *Parliamentary History* 327. See also 2 Co. *Inst.* 57.
46. 1 *id.* 36, 81.
47. See note 27, above; also 4 Bacon, *Abridgment* 638.

lords.[48] And what are these benefits? Especially they are the benefits of the historical procedure of the common law, the known processes of the ordinary courts, indictment by grand jury, trial by "law of the land," *habeas corpus,* security against monopoly, taxation by the consent of Parliament.[49] Thus the vague concept of "common right and reason" is replaced with a "law fundamental" of definite content and traceable back to one particular document of ancient and glorious origin.

And alongside Magna Carta in the pages of the *Institutes* stands "the High Court of Parliament," Coke's description of whose powers has been often interpreted as flatly contradicting his teachings regarding a "law fundamental." "Of the power and jurisdiction of Parliament," runs a famous passage, "for the making of laws in proceeding by bill, it is so transcendent and absolute, as it cannot be confined either for causes or persons within any bounds."[50] A century and a quarter later this same passage was to be quoted by Blackstone as expressing the notion of parliamentary sovereignty.[51] Actually in Coke's pages it has no such significance. As his own words indicate, he classifies Parliament as primarily a *court,* albeit a court which may make new law as well as declare the old; and what he is describing is not a power and jurisdiction which is entitled to override rights at will, though it is entitled to reach all "persons and causes."[52] Furthermore, the illustrations which he gives of Parliament's "transcendent power and jurisdiction" are not, by today's standards, instances of lawmaking at all, but of the exercise of a species of equity jurisdiction in individual cases which, while it may seem often to invade the rights of those most immediately affected, was apparently controlled by the motive of vindicating rights of others.

> Daughters and heirs apparent . . . may by act of Parliament inherit during the life of the ancestor. It may adjudge an infant or minor of full age. To attaint a man of treason after death. [To attaint a man during life was too ordinary a manifestation of parliamentary authority to deserve, in Coke's estimate, special mention.] To naturalize a mere alien, and make him a subject born. It may bastard a child that by law is legitimate, the father being a proved adulterer. To legitimize one that is illegitimate. . . .[53]

Clearly, what we have here exemplified is not legislative sovereignty, but rather entire absence of the modern distinction between legislation and adjudication.

That Coke generally regards the cause of Parliament and that of the law as identical is altogether evident. Magna Carta itself was of parliamentary origin,

---

48. 2 Co. *Inst.* 45.
49. *Id.* 2–77, furnishing a general commentary on the charter.
50. 4 *id.* 36.
51. 1 Bl. *Comm.* 160–61.
52. McIlwain, *High Court of Parliament* 141 *et seq.;* also *id.* 312n.; 2 Co. *Inst.* 497–98; 2 Hansard, *Parliamentary History* 271–312; Pease, *The Leveller Movement* 43–45 (1916). "These two judgments in Parliament by way of declaration of law, against which no man can speak." See the "Argument in Calvin's Case" in 2 Bacon, *Works* 179.
53. 4 Co. *Inst.* 36.

and Parliament had later forced more or less reluctant monarchs to confirm the charter no less than thirty-two times. "A Parliament," he writes, "brings judges, officers and all men into good order. . . . [Note the inclusion of judges in this list.] Parliament and the common law are the principal means to keep greatness in order and due subjection."[54]

Coke's contributions to the beginnings of American constitutional law may be briefly summarized. First, in his dictum in Bonham's Case he furnished a form of words which, treated apart from his other ideas, as it was destined to be by a series of judges, commentators, and attorneys, became the most important single source of the notion of judicial review. This is true even though we of the present day can see that, in view of the universal subordination of the common law as such to statute law, judicial review grounded simply on "common right and reason" could not have survived. But, as if in anticipation of this difficulty, Coke came forward with his second contribution, the doctrine of a law fundamental, binding Parliament and king alike, a law, moreover, embodied to great extent in a particular document and having a verifiable content in the customary procedure of everyday institutions. From his version of Magna Carta, through the English Declaration and Bill of Rights of 1688 and 1689, to the bills of rights of our early American constitutions the line of descent is direct; and if American constitutional law during the last half century has tended increasingly to minimize the importance of procedural niceties and to return to the vaguer tests of "common right and reason," the intervening stage of strict law was nevertheless necessary. Lastly, Coke contributed the notion of parliamentary supremacy *under* the law, which in time, with the differentiation of legislation and adjudication, became transmutable into the notion of *legislative* supremacy within a law subject to construction by the processes of adjudication.

IV.

It has become a commonplace that every age has its own peculiar categories of thought; its speculations are carried on in a vocabulary which those who would be understood by it must adopt, and then adapt to their own special purposes. Nowadays intellectual discourse is apt to be case in the mould of the evolutionary hypothesis. In the seventeenth and eighteenth centuries, the doctrine of natural law, with its diverse corollaries, furnished the basic postulates of theoretical speculation. For this there were several reasons; but our interest is naturally centered upon those which were especially operative in England.

The immense prestige of the natural law doctrine in the seventeenth and eighteenth centuries was due particularly to the work of two men, Grotius and Newton. In erecting the law of nations upon a natural law basis as a barrier

---

54. 2 *id.* 626; 2 Hansard, *Parliamentary History* 246. For quaint comparisons of Parliament with a clock and with an elephant, see 4 Co. *Inst.* 2-3.

against the current international anarchy, Grotius imparted to the latter a new solidity, as well as an immediate practicality such as it had never before been able to boast. Yet even more important was Grotius' revival of the Ciceronian idea of natural law, which served at one stroke to clear the concept from the theological implications which it had accumulated during the Middle Ages and from any suspicion of dependence on ecclesiastical and papal interpretation. Once again natural law is defined as right reason; and is described as at once a law of, and a law to, God. God himself, Grotius asserted, could not make twice two other than four; nor would his rational nature fail to guide man even though there were no God, or though God lacked interest in human affairs.[55] And at this point Newton enters the story.[56] While modern science employs the term "natural law" in a sense that is alien and even hostile to its juristic use, the vast preponderance of deduction over observation in Newton's discoveries at first concealed this opposition. His demonstration that the force which brings the apple to the ground is the same force that holds the planets in their orbits, stirred his contemporaries with the picture of a universe which is pervaded with the same reason which shines in man and its accessible in all its parts to exploration by man. Between a universe "lapt in law" and the human mind all barriers were cast down. Inscrutable deity became scrutable nature. On this basis arose English deism, which, it has been wittily remarked, "deified nature and denatured God."[57] And one section of nature is human nature and its institutions. With Newton's achievement at their back men turned confidently to the formulation of the inherently just and reasonable rules of social and political relationship. Entire systems were elaborated which purported to deduce with Euclidean precision the whole duty of man, both moral and legal, from a few agreed premises.[58] It was the discredit

55. I Grotius, *De Jure Belli ac Pacis* I, 5, 10; Grotius, *Proleg.* II (Whewell ed. 1853). Von Gierke finds a German precursor of Grotius in Gabriel Biel, who wrote in 1495: "Nam si per impossibile Deus non esset, qui est ratio divina, aut ratio illa divina esset errans: adhuc si quis ageret contra rectam rationem angelicam vel humanam aut aliam aliquam sit qua esset: peccaret." Gierke, *Althusius* 74, n. 45 (Zur. deutschen Staats u. Rechts Geschichte 1879–80). Related to this question is the medieval controversy whether *jus naturale* is divine will (*voluntas*) or divine reason (*ratio*), whether God is a lawgiver or a teacher working through the reason. Grotius, *Proleg.* 73, n. 44.

56. See Becker, *The Declaration of Independence* 40–53 (1922).

57. *Id.* 51. "The eighteenth century, conceiving of God as known only through his work, conceived of his work as itself a universal harmony, of which the material and the spiritual were but different aspects." *Id.* 52–53. Addison's famous Hymn is a fine expression of the deistic cosmology. It is Pope, however, who condensed the deistic philosophy of history into a line: "Whatever is, is right." *Essay on Man* Ep. i, 1. 294 (1732). The theological classic of deism is Butler's *Analogy,* where Christianity is presented as "a promulgation of the law of nature . . . with new light . . . adapted to the wants of mankind." 1 Butler, *Works* 162 (Gladstone ed. 1897). Note also Butler's contention that "miracles must not be compared to common natural events . . . but to the extraordinary phenomena of nature." *Id.* 181. The later and most extreme representatives of deism, for example Voltaire and Jefferson, scouted miracles altogether, which led to their being termed "atheists" and "infidels."

58. See an interesting note in Dickinson, *Administrative Justice and Supremacy of Law* 115–18 (1927). See also the same writer's reference to Domat, Dickinson 125n. Puffendorf took issue with

into which such systems ultimately fell that revealed the disparity between the two uses of the term "natural law" of which we today are aware—or should be.[59]

The revived Ciceronian conception of natural law, extended and deepened by Newtonian science, furnishes, therefore, the general background of credibility against which the contemporary political applications of natural law have to be projected. But these political applications also bring into requisition certain new elements—new, that is to say, in the combinations in which they now appear. For it is always a question when theoretical notions are under consideration whether the term "new" is in strict propriety admissible. Systems fall apart and new systems are assembled from the wreckage. Any serious turn of events is apt to produce a fresh coruscation of ideas, elevating some and suppressing others; but the contents of the kaleidoscope remain throughout much the same. And never was this observation better borne out than by the political speculations of the sixteenth, seventeenth, and eighteenth centuries. These speculations contributed immensely to the shattering of the existing foundations of authority and in transferring authority to an entirely new basis. The particular ideas in which they dealt were, nevertheless, for the most part, far from novel. Not a few of them are identifiable, in embryo at least, among the writings of the ancients; and nearly all of them had been stated with varying degrees of clarity before the Reformation.

The conveyance of natural law ideas into American constitutional theory was the work pre-eminently—though by no means exclusively—of John Locke's *Second Treatise on Civil Government*, which appeared in 1690 as an apology for the Glorious Revolution. The outstanding feature of Locke's treatment of natural law is the almost complete dissolution which this concept undergoes through his handling into the natural rights of the individual; or—to employ Locke's own

---

Grotius' contention that "there is not equal certainty to be met with in morals and mathematics." I Puffendorf, *Law of Nature and Nations* 2, 9 (Spavan ed. 1716). "Principles of civil knowledge, fairly deduced from the law of nature." Wise, *Vindication of the Government of New England Churches* 45 (1860).

59. "Natural law" in the sense of "the observed order of phenomena" has tended in recent years to crowd the earlier rationalistic conception to the wall, thus aiding the triumph of the idea of human and governmental law as an expression solely of will backed by force. The nineteenth century was no stranger to the idea that there are factors of human behavior which are obdurate to advantageous political control; only such factors are ordinarily represented as of a nonrational nature and *as having no necessary tendency to produce human justice*. Savigny's apotheosis of custom was an appeal to a natural law of this subrational or scientific type. So also were the confident pronouncements of the classical economists regarding the "laws of political economy." So again were the characteristic preachments of Herbert Spencer concerning the proper field of governmental intervention, wherein is linked up, with an altogether shameless illogic, the notion of an automatic industrial organism to a revived theory of natural rights. Professor Duguit would also have us regard his "social solidarity" as a scientific datum. In fact, all these theories are only endeavors to dragoon science into the service of some variety or other of utopianism. Professor Duguit's theory, for example, is only that of Locke stood on its head—nor is that to question but that twentieth-century conditions may demand this novel perspective.

phrase, borrowed from the debates between Stuart adherents and parliamentarians—into the rights of "life, liberty, and estate."[60] The dissolving agency by which Locke brings this transformation about is the doctrine of the social compact, with its corollary notion of a state of nature. Indeed, it is hardly an exaggeration to say that the only residuum which remains in the Lockean crucible from the original Ciceronian concept is the sanction which is claimed from natural law for the social compact, and at one point, he dispenses even with this. It thus becomes of interest to inquire whence Locke derived his intense preoccupation with rights, as well as the form in which he chose to express them.

A recent effort has been made to refer Locke's system to Calvinistic premises;[61] but if it is meant that the outstanding features of Locke's political thinking are traceable to Calvin himself, the thesis falls of its own weight. Calvin knows nothing of the social compact—he rests civil authority on the basis of divine right. Far from being an apologist for revolution, he in general teaches nonresistance. The doctrine of the sovereignty of God which looms so large in his pages bears not the faintest analogy to anything in Locke; and the doctrine of election with its undemocratic implications is entirely antithetical to Lockean optimism.[62] The founder of the Geneva theocracy, who burned Servetus at the stake, and the author of the *Letters on Toleration* have little in common.

It is evident that certain important distinctions have been overlooked. The entire Protestant movement with its emphasis on the priesthood of the individual believer was permeated with individualistic implications; but before these could come to effective political expression, they had to be released from the very medievalism which Calvinism seems at the outset to have been principally bent on restoring.[63] Fortunately for its ultimate reputation in the history of political

60. 2 Dunning, *History of Political Theories* 222, 346n (1923) {hereinafter Dunning, *History*}. "It is not a common principle that the law favoureth three things, life, liberty, and dower. . . . This because our law is grounded upon the law of nature. And these three things do flow from the law of nature. . . ." Bacon, "Argument in Calvin's Case" in 2 Bacon, *Works* 176. See also Hale, *History of the Common Law* sec. 13 (1779): "Of the Rights of the People or Subject," where it is said these are protected according to their "lives, their liberties, their estates."

61. Foster, "International Calvinism through John Locke and the Revolution of 1688," 32 *Am. Hist. Rev.* 475 (1927).

62. 2 Dunning, *History* 26 *et seq.*; 2 MacKinnon, *History of Modern Liberty* 147-53 (1906). "It is, however, the disciples of Calvin, rather than the master himself, who advanced the theory of resistance, and Calvin's attitude was more authoritarian than that of Luther. Luther's intolerance was merely that of an enthusiast, Calvin's was that of a strong ruler, who dislikes all obstacles in the way of a uniform system. Calvin's bigotry was that of a lawyer or an inquisitor, Luther's that of a preacher or a schoolboy." Figgis, *Gerson to Grotius* 138 (1916). Calvinism "certainly did not favor individual liberty; but it was opposed in theory to secular interference, and by its own methods to monarchical power. Hence in spite of itself Calvinism in France, in the Netherlands and Scotland became either in the world of thought or in that of practice the basis of modern liberty." *Id.* 155-56. Calvin's chief service to liberty, by way of theory, was shunting "sovereignty" off to heaven. This helped to keep the ground clear for popular sovereignty once the theocrats were disposed of. The Jesuits, operating from different premises, performed a similar service by emphasizing the secular character of political authority.

63. Figgis, *Gerson to Grotius* 21-22.

thought, Calvinism found itself much more frequently than not in the position of a religious minority subject to persecution. Its adherents were consequently forced either to adopt Calvin's own teaching of nonresistance, or to develop a type of political theory that countenanced resistance, and many of them took the latter route. That is to say, because of the actual situation of Calvinism, certain Calvinists developed doctrines of political liberalism, as for that matter did also certain Catholic writers of the same era.[64] As Dr. Figgis has put it, "political liberty is the residuary legatee of ecclesiastical animosities."[65]

Nor is this to disparage Locke's indebtedness to such forerunners, which was indeed immense. For taking up the thread of later medieval political thought at the point where it had been broken off by Machiavelli and Bodin, to say nothing of Luther and Calvin, they at once revived the postulates of popular sovereignty which underlay Roman law and institutions and supplemented these by principles adapted from the matured Roman law of private contract.[66] Yet, this concession made, it still remains true that the contact of Locke's system with the writers alluded to is indirect, and through a question which they left unsolved rather than through those they purported to answer. Sixteenth-century liberalism rested its case largely on the notion of an original compact between governors and governed, between rulers and the people.[67] The question inevitably emerged: Who are "the people," and how did they become an entity capable of contracting?

Locke's own answer to these questions springs from a threefold rootage. Its primary source was English legal tradition as illustrated in Fortescue and Coke, the entire emphasis of which has always been on rights of the individual rather than on rights of the people considered in the mass.[68] The latter, indeed, was sufficiently provided for in Parliament. A second source was English Independency, which was in turn the direct outgrowth of Luther's doctrine of the priesthood of the individual. For in a period in which religious and political controversy were so closely involved with each other as in seventeenth-century England, ideas developed in the one forum were easily and inevitably transferred to the other. Finally, Locke himself would have been the first to own his indebtedness to Grotius and Puffendorf[69] and so ultimately to Cicero; while his

---

64. 2 Dunning, *History* 67 *et seq.*, also ch. 4.

65. Figgis, *Gerson to Grotius* 118.

66. 2 Dunning, *History* ch. 2; Gooch, *English Democratic Ideas in the Seventeenth Century* Intro. and ch. 1 (1898). On the doctrine of popular sovereignty in the later Middle Ages, see Gierke, *Althusius* 69 and n.36; Gierke, *Political Theories of the Middle Ages* 37–40 (Maitland tr. 1922); Figgis, *Gerson to Grotius* ch. 2.

67. 2 Dunning, *History* 79.

68. See p. 102 above for Fortescue's anticipation of Locke.

69. "When a young Gentleman has pretty well-digested *Tully's Offices*, and added to it *Puffendorff de Officio Hominis & Civis*, it may be seasonable to set him upon *Grotius de Jure Belli & Pacis*; or, which perhaps is the better of the two, *Puffendorff de Jure naturali & Gentium*; wherein he will be instructed in the natural rights of man and the originals and foundations of society and duties resulting from thence. . . ." 3 Locke, *Works* 84 (1823), quoted in the introduction to Fortescue, *De Laudibus Legum Angliae* xx (Gregor ed. 1775).

citations of "the judicious Hooker," a still earlier apostle of the Ciceronian revival, outnumbered those to any other writer. The first and last of these sources need only to be cataloged. The second, however, demands some further comment.

The leader of the extreme sect of the Independents, called the Levellers, was John Lilburne, a veritable ragamuffin, in whose writings the concern of his highly respectable successor, Locke, for "property" is replaced by demands for the "natural rights" of freedom of conscience and expression, and to political equality[70]—demands which even in the deepest dungeons he seems never to have lacked pen and ink to indite. The political *chef d'oeuvre* of Independency was the famous Agreement of the People of 1647, which was an effort to give concrete realization to the principle of the social compact.[71]

In America the filiation of Independency with the social compact philosophy can be traced at a still earlier date in connection with the Pilgrim foundation of Plymouth. The expedition comprised John Robinson's Scrooby congregation, of which a contemporary critic wrote: "Do we not know the beginnings of his church? that there was first one stood up and made a covenant, and then another, and these two joyned together, and so a third, and these became a church, say they."[72] And the procedure which, under the sanction of God, was effective to produce a church, could also be availed of under the same sanction to produce a commonwealth, as was shown in the famous Mayflower Compact:

> In the name of God, Amen. We whose names are underwritten, the loyall subjects of our dread soveraigne lord, King James . . . doe by these presents solemnly and mutualy in the presence of God, and one of another, covenant and combine oursselves togeather into a civill body politick, for our better ordering and preservation . . . and by vertue hearof to enacte, constitute, and frame such just and equall lawes, ordinances, acts, constitutions, and offices, from time to time, as shall be thought most meete and convenient for the general good of the colonie, unto which we promise all due submission and obedience.[73]

Thus, more than two generations before Locke's *Second Treatise*, a social compact was conceived as supplying the second permanent government within what is now the United States. Whereas with Locke the ultimate basis of authority is supplied by natural law, here it is supplied by God. We shall observe presently how the rapprochement between the two positions was effected by eighteenth-century deism.

A generation later, though still more than a generation before the appearance of Locke's *Treatise*, we find another Independent, Thomas Hooker of Connecticut, proffering the theory of contract as explanatory of all human association.

70. 2 Dunning, *History* 234 *et seq.;* Gooch, {*English Democratic Ideas in the Seventeenth Century?*} 141–46, 200–03, 253–56; Pease, *The Leveller Movement passim.*

71. 2 Dunning, *History* 238. The agreement was greatly modified in 1648 and further so in 1649.

72. Davis, *John Robinson* 48 (1903).

73. MacDonald, *Documentary Source Book of American History* 19 (1920).

"Every spiritual or ecclesiastical corporation receives its being from a spiritual combination . . . there is no man constrained to enter into such a condition, unless he will; and he that will enter, must also willingly bind and engage himself to each member of that society to promote the good of the whole, or else a member actually he is not.''[74] Though Hooker is here speaking of "ecclesiastical corporations," the Fundamental Orders of Connecticut of 1639, whereby the inhabitants of the three towns did "assotiate and conjoyne" themselves "to be as one Publike State or Commonwelth," embodies his political application of the same thought.[75] Nor is this the only significance of the Fundamental Orders. Taken along with the Agreement of the People a decade later, it shows the powerful, ineluctable necessity felt by those who held the compact theory for placing governmental institutions on a documentary basis.

One other predecessor of Locke must be mentioned before turning more particularly to the *Second Treatise,* Thomas Hobbes, author of the *Leviathan*. It is usual to contrast these two writers, but they also have much in common, and in relation to American constitutional theory, their contributions are often complementary rather than contradictory. For if Locke shares with Coke the paternity of American constitutional limitations, Hobbes's emphasis upon the *salus populi* is a definite forerunner of the modern doctrine of the police power, as well as a clear prophecy of legal tendency even in a constitutional state when conditions of emergency menace public order. Hobbes is at the outset as thoroughly individualistic as Locke, and the prosecution by the individual of his own interest is as much his objective as it is Locke's. Both Hobbes and Locke also agree in dispensing with the governmental contract; but whereas a sovereign lawmaking body is the direct outcome of the social compact with Hobbes, with Locke it is the corporate majority, which then determines the form of government.

Where Hobbes and Locke part company is in their view of the state of nature, that is to say, in their view of human nature when not subjected to political control. Hobbes, a timid man who had been called upon to witness stern events, pictures the state of nature as one of "force and fraud," in which "every man is to every man a wolf.''[76] Locke, who was perhaps of a more robust type, and at any rate wrote amid happier surroundings, depicts the state of nature as in the main an era of "peace, good will, mutual assistance, and preservation," in which the "free, sovereign" individual is already in possession of all valuable rights, though from defect of "executive power" he is not always able to make them good or to determine them accurately in relation to the like rights of his fellows.[77] And from this difference flow all the others. With Hobbes a dissolution

---

74. Walker, *Life of Thomas Hooker* 124–25 (1891). I am indebted for this and the reference in note 72, to my friend, Professor W. S. Carpenter.

75. MacDonald, *Documentary Source Book of American History* 36–39.

76. Hobbes, *Leviathan* ch. 13 (1651).

77. Locke, *Second Treatise on Civil Government* ch. 2, 118 (Everyman's ed. 1924).

of government is substantially a dissolution of society; with Locke it is not, society having existed before government. With Hobbes natural law and civil law are coextensive; that is to say, "when a commonwealth is once settled, then are they [natural laws] actually laws, and not before."[78] With Locke, natural law approximates to positive law from the first, while even after the establishment of government, popular interpretation of natural law is the ultimate test of the validity of civil law. Thus Hobbes becomes, more or less in spite of himself, the founder of the positive school of jurisprudence, which traces all rights to government and regards them simply as implements of public policy. Locke, on the other hand, regards government as creative of no rights, but as strictly fiduciary in character, and as designed to make more secure and more readily available rights which antedate it and which would survive it.

The two features of the *Second Treatise* which have impressed themselves most definitely upon American constitutional law are the limitations which it lays down for legislative power and its emphasis on the property right. The legislature is the supreme organ of Locke's commonwealth, and it is upon this supremacy that he depends in the main for the safeguarding of the rights of the individual. But for this very reason legislative supremacy is supremacy within the law, not a power above the law. In fact, the word "sovereign" is never used by Locke in its descriptive sense except in reference to the "free, sovereign" individual in the state of nature. In detail, the limitations which Locke specifies to legislative power are the following:[79] First, it is not arbitrary power. Not even the majority which determines the form of the government can vest its agent with arbitrary power, for the reason that the majority right itself originates in a delegation by free sovereign individuals who had "in the state of nature no arbitrary power over the life, liberty, or possessions" of others, or even over their own. In this caveat against "arbitrary power," Locke definitely anticipates the modern latitudinarian concept of due process of law.

"Secondly, the legislative ... cannot assume to itself a power to rule by extemporary, arbitrary decrees, but is bound to dispense justice and decide the rights of the subject by promulgated standing laws, and known authorized judges"; nor may it vary the law in particular cases, but there must be one rule for rich and poor, for favorite and the plowman. In this pregnant passage, Locke

78. Hobbes, *Leviathan* ch. 26. " 'Civil law,' is to every subject, those rules, which the commonwealth hath commanded him, by word, writing, or other sufficient sign of the will, to make use of, for the distinction of right and wrong; that is to say, of what is contrary and what is not contrary to the rule." *Id.* ch. 26. In the face of this definition of "right," Hobbes, in order to base his commonwealth on contract, asserts that "when a covenant is made, then to break it is 'unjust'; and the definition of 'injustice' is no other than 'the nonperformance of covenant.' " *Id.* ch. 15. Nor does Locke escape a contradiction of a different sort. The *Second Treatise on Civil Government* is founded on conceptions not drawn from experience, whereas the object of the *Essay Concerning Human Understanding* is to discredit such ideas. 1 Stephen, *Horae Sabbaticae* 150 (1892) in Carpenter, "Introduction," to Locke, *Second Treatise* xvii.
79. "Of the Extent of the Legislative Power" in Locke, *Second Treatise* ch. 11, 183 *et seq.*

foreshadows some of the most fundamental propositions of American constitutional law: *Law must be general; it must afford equal protection to all; it may not validly operate retroactively; it must be enforced through the courts—legislative power does not include judicial power.*

Thirdly, as also follows from its fiduciary character, the legislature "cannot transfer the power of making laws to any other hands: for it being but a delegated power from the people, they who have it cannot pass it over to others." More briefly, *legislative power cannot be delegated.*

Finally, *legislative power is not the ultimate power of the commonwealth,* for "the community perpetually retains a supreme power of saving themselves from the attempts and designs of anybody, even their legislators, whenever they shall be so foolish or so wicked as to lay and carry on designs against the liberties and properties of the subject." So while legislative supremacy is the normal sanction of the rights of men, it is not the final sanction. The identical power which was exerted against James II would in like case be equally available against Parliament itself.[80]

Locke's bias in favor of property is best shown in the fifth chapter of the *Treatise,* where he brings the labor theory of value to the defense of inequality of possessions, and endeavors to show that the latter is harmonious with the social compact. His course of reasoning is as follows: All value, or almost all, is due to labor; and as there were different degrees of industry, so there were apt to be different degrees of possession. Yet most property, in those early days, was highly perishable, whence arose a natural limit to the accumulation of wealth, to wit, that no man must hoard up more than he could make use of, since that would be to waste nature's bounty. Nevertheless, "the exceeding of his just property" lay, Locke is careful to insist, not "in the largeness of his possession, but the perishing of anything uselessly in it." Accordingly, when mankind, by affixing value to gold, silver, and other imperishable but intrinsically valueless things for which perishable commodities might be traded, made exchanges possible, it thereby, as by deliberate consent, ratified unequal possessions; and the later social compact did not disturb this covenant.[81]

So, having transmuted the law of nature into the rights of men, Locke next converts these into the rights of ownership. The final result is to base his commonwealth upon the balanced and antithetical concepts of the rule of the majority and the security of property. Nor, thanks to the labor theory of value, is this the merely static conception that at first consideration it might seem to be. Taken up a century later by Adam Smith, the labor theory became the cornerstone of the

80. Locke, *Second Treatise* ch. 19, 224.

81. "Of Property," *id.* ch. 5, 129. Locke uses the term "property" with various degrees of precision. In Chapter 5 he is thinking of *things* with exchangeable value. In Chapter 7 he uses the word to cover "life, liberty, and estate." In *A Letter on Toleration* he says that the commonwealth exists to promote "civil interest," and "civil interest I call life, liberty, inviolability of body, and the possession of such outward things as money, lands, houses, furniture, and the like." 2 Locke, *Works* 239, quoted by Laski, *Grammar of Politics* 181 (1925).

doctrine of *laissez faire*.[82] It thus assisted to adapt a political theory conceived in the interest of a quiescent landed aristocracy to the uses of an aggressive industrial plutocracy. By the same token, it also assisted to adapt a theory conceived for a wealthy and civilized community to the exactly opposed conditions of life in a new and undeveloped country. In a frontier society engrossed in the conquest of nature and provided with but meager stimulation to artistic and intellectual achievement, the inevitable index of success was accumulation, and accumulation did, in fact, represent social service. What is more, the singular affinity which Calvinistic New England early discovered for Lockean rationalism is in some measure explicable on like grounds. The central pillar of Calvinism was the doctrine of election. It goes without saying that all who believed this dogma also believed themselves among the elect; yet of this what better, what more objective evidence than material success? Locke himself, it may be added, was a notable preacher of the gospel of industry and thrift.[83]

Two other features of Locke's thought deserve brief comment. The first is his insistence upon the "public good" as the object of legislation and of governmental action in general. It should not be supposed that this in any way contradicts the main trend of his thought. Rather he is laying down yet another limitation on legislative freedom of action.[84] That the public good might not always be compatible with the preservation of rights, and especially with the rights of property, never once occurs to him. A century later the possibility did occur to Adam Smith, and was waived aside by his "harmony of interests" theory. Also the dimensions which Locke assigns to executive perogative are, in view both of the immediate occasion for which he wrote and of his "constitutionalism," not a little astonishing. On this matter he writes:

> Where the legislative and executive power are in distinct hands (as they are in all moderated monarchies and well-framed governments), there the good of the society requires, that several things should be left to the discretion of him that has the executive power: for the legislators not being able to foresee, and provide by laws,

82. Carey, *Harmony of Interests, Agricultural, Manufacturing and Commercial* (1872). Henry C. Carey attempts an application of Smith's theory to American conditions in favor of a protective tariff.

83. Foster, 32 *Am. Hist. Rev.* 475, at 486. See also Robinson, *Case of Louis the Eleventh and Other Essays* (1928); Weber, "Protestantische Ethik u. der "Geist" des Kapitalismus," 30 *Archiv für Sozial-wissenschaft u. Sozial Politik* 1–54 (1904); 21 *id.* 1–110 (1905); Sombart, *Quintessence of Capitalism* 257–62 (1915); and Tawney, "Puritanism and Capitalism," 46 *New Republic* 348 (1926). Puritanism has been not inaptly characterized as "a religious sublimation of the virtues of the middle class." Puritan abhorrence of beauty and amusement necessarily led to concentration on the business of money-getting; and the belief of the Puritans that they were "chosen people" worked to the same end, for it turned their attention to the Old Testament, where the idea that prosperity is proof of moral worth is repeatedly presented. Nor is the New Testament devoid of such ideas. Compare the parable of the talents, Matthew xxv, 29; also Romans xii, 11; and see especially the texts from Baxter, *Christian Directory,* quoted by Robinson, above.

84. "Their [the legislature's] power, in the utmost bounds of it, is limited to the public good of the society." Locke, *Second Treatise* ch. 11, sec. 135; *cf.* secs. 89, 110, 134, 142, 158 with secs. 124, 131, 140.

for all that may be useful to the community, the executor of the laws, having the power in his hands, has by the common law of nature a right to make use of it for the good of the society, in many cases, where the municipal law has given no direction, till the legislative can conveniently be assembled to provide for it; many things there are, which the law can by no means provide for; and those must necessarily be left to the discretion of him that has the executive power in his hands, to be ordered by him as the public good and advantage shall require: nay, it is fit that the laws themselves should in some cases give way to the executive power, or rather to the fundamental law of nature and government—viz., that as much as may be, all the members of the society are to be preserved.[85]

Extrication from the trammels of a too rigid constitutionalism through a broad view of executive power is a device by no means unknown to American constitutional law and theory.

Locke's contribution is best estimated in relation to Coke's. Locke's version of natural law not only rescues Coke's version of the English constitution from a localized *patois,* restating it in the universal tongue of the age, it also supplements it in important respects. Coke's endeavor was to put forward the historical procedure of the common law as a permanent restraint on power, and especially on the power of the English crown. Locke, in the limitations which he imposes on legislative power, is looking rather to the security of the substantive rights of the individual—those rights which are implied in the basic arrangements of society at all times and in all places. While Coke rescued the notion of fundamental law from what must sooner or later have proved a fatal nebulosity, yet did so at the expense of archaism. Locke, on the other hand, in cutting loose in great measure from the historical method of reasoning, opened the way to the larger issues with which American constitutional law has been called upon to grapple in its latest maturity. Without the Lockean or some similar background, judicial review must have atrophied by 1890 in the very field in which it is today most active; nor is this to forget his emphasis on the property right. Locke's weakness is on the institutional side. While he contributed to the *doctrine* of judicial review, it was without intention; nor does he reveal any perception of the importance of giving imperative written form to the constitutional principles which he formulated. The hard-fisted Coke, writing with a civil war ahead of him instead of behind him, was more prescient.

V.

The influence of higher law doctrine associated with the names of Coke and Locke was at its height in England during the period when the American colonies were being most actively settled, which means that Coke had, to begin with, the advantage since he was first on the ground. The presence of Coke's doctrines in the colonies during the latter two-thirds of the seventeenth century is widely

85. "Of Prerogative" in Locke, *Second Treatise* ch. 14, sec. 159.

evidenced by the repeated efforts of colonial legislatures to secure for their constituencies the benefits of Magna Carta and particularly of the twenty-ninth chapter thereof. Because of the menace they were thought to spell for the prerogative, the majority of such measures incurred the royal veto.[86] In point of fact, since the "law of the land" clause of chapter twenty-nine was interpretable as contemplating only law which was enacted by the colonial legislature, the menace went even further. Clothed with this construction, chapter twenty-nine afforded affirmation not only of rights of the individual, but also of local legislative autonomy.[87] The frequently provoked discussion of such matters, moreover, served to fix terminology for the future moulding of thought. Magna Carta became a generic term for all documents of constitutional significance, and thereby a symbol and reminder of principles binding on government.[88]

But more specific evidence of Coke's influence also occurs during this period. One such instance is furnished by the opinion of a Massachusetts magistrate in 1657 holding void a tax by the town of Ipswich for the purpose of presenting the local minister with a dwelling house. Such a tax, said the magistrate, "to take from Peter and give it to Paul," is against fundamental law. "If noe kinge or Parliament can justly enact or cause that one man's estate, in whole or in part, may be taken from him and given to another without his owne consent, then surely the major part of a towne or other inferior powers cannot doe it.'"[89] An opinion of the attorney general of the Barbados, rendered sometime during the reign of Anne, which held void a paper-money act because it authorized summary process against debtors, is of like import. The entire argument is based on chapter twenty-nine of Magna Carta and "common right, or reason.'"[90] Evidence of the persistence of the dictum in Bonham's Case also crops up outside New England now and then, even before its notable revival by Otis in his argument in the Writs of Assistance Case.[91] As late as 1759 we find a New York man referring quite incidentally to "a judicial power of declaring them [laws] void.'"[92] The allusion is inexplicable unless it was to Coke's "dictum."

If the seventeenth century was Coke's, the early half of the eighteenth was Locke's, especially in New England. After the Glorious Revolution the migration to America of important English elements ceased. Immediate touch with political developments in the mother country was thus lost. The colonies were fain henceforth to be content for the most part with the stock of political ideas already on hand; and in fact these met their own necessities, which grew chiefly out of the quarrels between the governors and the assemblies, extremely well.

86. For details, see Hazeltine, *Magna Carta Commemoration Essays* 191–201 (1917). Mott, *Due Process of Law* chs. 1, 6 (1926), adds some further items.
87. Hazeltine, *Magna Carta Commemoration Essays* 195.
88. *Id.* 199–200.
89. 2 Hutchinson, *Papers* 1–25 (Prince Soc. Pubs. 1865).
90. 2 Chalmers, *Opinions of Eminent Lawyers* 27–38 (1814), especially at 30.
91. See Mott, *Due Process of Law* 91, n.19.
92. 2 New York Historical Society Collections 204 (1869).

And along with this comparative isolation from new currents of thought in the mother country went the general intellectual poverty of frontier life itself. There were few books, fewer newspapers, and little travel. But one source of intellectual stimulation for the adult there was, one point of contact with the world of ideas, and that was the sermon. Through their election sermons in particular and through controversial pamphlets, the New England clergy taught their flocks political theory, and almost always this was an elaboration upon the stock of ideas which had come from seventeenth-century England. The subject has been so admirably treated in a recent volume that it is here necessary only to record some of the outstanding facts.[93]

After the Bible, Locke was the principal authority relied on by the preachers to bolster up their political teachings, although Coke, Puffendorf, Sydney, and later on some others were also cited. The substance of the doctrine of these discourses is, except at two points, that of the *Second Treatise*. Natural rights and the social compact, government bounded by law and incapable of imparting legality to measures contrary to law, and the right of resistance to illegal measures all fall into their proper place. One frequent point of deviation from the Lockean model is the retention of the idea of a compact between governed and governors; that notion fitted in too well with the effort to utilize the colonial charters as muniments of local liberty to be discarded.[94] The other point of deviation from Locke is more apparent than real, for all these concepts are backed up by religious sanction. Yet to the modern reader the difference between the Puritan God of the eighteenth century and Locke's natural law often seems little more than nominal. "The voice of nature is the voice of God," asserts one preacher; "reason and the voice of God are one," is the language of another; "Christ confirms the law of nature," is the teaching of a third.[95] The point of view is thoroughly deistic; reason has usurped the place of revelation, and without affront to piety.

Nor should it be imagined that all this teaching and preaching on political topics took place *in vacuo*—in deliberate preparation, as it were, for a great emergency as yet descried only by the most perspicacious. Much of it was evoked by warm and bitter controversy among the New England congregations themselves.[96] One such controversy was that which arose in the second decade of the eighteenth century over the question whether the congregations should submit themselves to the governance of a synod. Even more heated was the quarrel which was produced by the great awakening consequent on the preaching of George Whitefield in 1740. Whitefield's doctrine was distinctly and disturbingly equalitarian. A spirit of criticism of superiors by inferiors, of elders by juniors

93. Baldwin, *The New England Clergy and the American Revolution* (1928).
94. The same fact may also account for John Wise's preference for Puffendorf over Locke, though this may be due to his having had a copy of the former and not of the latter.
95. Baldwin, *The New England Clergy and the American Revolution* 29n., 43, 73n. See also note 57, above.
96. *Id.* chs. 5–6.

ensued from it; while, at the same time the intellectual superiority of the clergy was menaced by the sudden appearance of a great crop of popular exhorters. Men turned again to Locke, Sydney, and others, but this time in order to discover the sanctions of authority rather than its limitations. Still some years later the outbreak of the French and Indian Wars inspired a series of sermons extolling English liberty and contrasting the balanced constitution of England with French tyranny, sermons in which the name of Montesquieu was now joined with that of Locke.[97]

This kind of preaching was not confined to New England, nor even to dissenting clergymen. Patrick Henry from his eleventh to his twenty-second year listened to an Anglican preacher who taught that the British constitution was but the "voluntary compact of sovereign and subject." Henry's own words later were "government is a conditional compact between king and people . . . violation of the covenant by either party discharges the other from obligation";[98] and more than half of the signers of the Declaration of Independence were members of the Church of England.[99] It is also an important circumstance that the famous Parson's Cause, in which Henry participated as the champion of local liberty, was pending in Virginia from 1752 to 1758, helping to bring the people of Virginia during the period face to face with fundamental constitutional questions.[100] "On a small scale, the whole episode illustrates the clash of political theories which lay back of the American Revolution."[101] And meantime the first generation of the American bar was coming to maturity—students of Coke, and equipped to bring his doctrines to the support of Locke should the need arise.[102]

The opening gun of the controversy leading to the Revolution was Otis' argument in 1761 in the Writs of Assistance Case,[103] which, through Bacon's and Viner's *Abridgments,* goes straight back to Bonham's Case. Adams' summary of it reads: "As to acts of Parliament. An act against the Constitution is void: an act against natural equity is void: and if an act of Parliament should be made, in the very words of the petition, it would be void. The executive courts must pass such acts into disuse.—8 Rep. 118, from Viner.'"[104] "Then and there" exclaims

97. *Id.* 88–89.

98. Van Tyne, "Influence of the Clergy on the American Revolution," 14 *Am. Hist. Rev.* 49 (1913).

99. Letter of G. MacLaren Brydon, *The New York Times,* May 30, 1927, citing Perry, *The Faith of the Signers of the Declaration of Independence* (1926). All the signers from the Southern colonies except one from Maryland (a Catholic) and one from Georgia were Anglicans.

100. Scott, "The Constitutional Aspects of the 'Parson's Cause,' " 31 *Pol. Sci. Q.* 558 *et seq.* (1916). The controversy evoked much talk of "void laws," though from the clerical party and with reference to acts of the Virginia Assembly.

101. *Id.* 577.

102. Warren, *History of the American Bar* chs. 2–8 (1911); Lecky, *American Revolution* 15–16 (Woodburn ed. 1922).

103. Quincy (Mass. 1761) 51–57, and appendices 395–552, of which 469–85 are especially relevant; also 2 Adams, *Life and Works* 521–25 (C. F. Adams ed. 1850), and 10 *id.* 232–362 *passim.*

104. Quincy 474 (Mass. 1761).

Adams, "the child Independence was born."[105] Today he must have added that then and there American constitutional law was born, for Otis' contention goes far beyond Coke's: an ordinary court may traverse the specifically enacted will of Parliament, and its condemnation is final.

The suggestion that the local courts might be thus pitted against an usurping Parliament in defense of "British rights," served to bring the idea of judicial review to the very threshold of the first American constitutions, albeit it was destined to wait there unattended for some years. Adams himself in a plea before the governor and council of Massachusetts, turned Otis' argument against the Stamp Act,[106] while a Virginia county court actually declared that measure void. "The judges were unanimously of the opinion," a report of the case reads, "that the law did not bind, affect, or concern the inhabitants of Virginia 'inasmuch as they conceived the said act to be unconstitutional.'"[107] As late as 1776, Chief Justice William Cushing of Massachusetts, who was later one of Washington's first appointees to the Supreme Court of the United States, was congratulated by Adams for telling a jury of the nullity of acts of Parliament.[108]

Nor did the controversy with Great Britain long rest purely on Coke's doctrines. Otis himself, declares Adams, "was also a great master of the law of nature and nations. He had read Puffendorf, Grotius, Barbeyrac, Burlamaqui, Vattel, Heineccius. . . . It was a maxim which he inculcated in his pupils . . . that a lawyer ought never to be without a volume of natural or public law, or moral philosophy, on his table or in his pocket."[109] Otis' own pamphlet, *The Rights of the British Colonies Asserted and Proved*, none the less was almost altogether of Lockean provenance. The colonists were entitled to "as ample rights, liberties, and privileges as the subjects of the mother country are and in some respects to more. . . . Should the charter privileges of the colonists be disregarded or revoked, there are natural, inherent, and inseparable rights as men and citizens that would remain."[110] And Adams argues the year following in his dissertation on

---

105. 10 Adams, *Life and Works* 248.

106. 2 *id.* 158–59; Memorial of Boston, Quincy 200–202 (Mass, 1765). Otis also spoke to the same effect. *Id.* at 205. Adams reiterated his argument in "Letters of Clarendon" in 3 Adams, *Life and Works* 469. An argument greatly stressed against the Stamp Act was its tendency to abolish trial by jury contrary to Magna Carta, through its extension of the jurisdiction of the admiralty courts, over penalties incurred under the act. *Id.* at 470. Governor Hutchinson wrote at this period: "The prevailing reason at this time is, that the act of Parliament is against Magna Carta, and the natural rights of Englishmen, and therefore, according to Lord Coke, null and void." Appendix, Quincy 527n. (Mass. 1769); and to same effect, *id.* at 441, 445.

107. 5 McMaster, *History of the American People* 394 (1920).

108. 9 Adams, *Life and Works* 390. Meanwhile, the dictum, with a strong Lockean infusion, had been invoked against domestic legislation. See George Mason's argument in Robin v. Hardaway, Jefferson 109–23 (Va. 1772), in which an act of the Virginia Assembly, passed in 1682, was declared void. Mason relied mainly on Coke and Hobart.

109. 10 Adams, *Life and Works* 275.

110. The date of the pamphlet is 1764. A summary of it in 10 Adams, *Life and Works* 293, is a summary of Locke's eleventh chapter. In Otis, *Vindication of the House of Representatives* (1762), Locke is characterized as "one of the most wise . . . most honest . . . most impartial men that ever lived . . . as great an ornament . . . the Church of England ever had to boast of."

The Canon and the Feudal Law for "rights antecedent to all earthly government—rights that cannot be repealed or restrained by human laws—rights derived from the great Legislator of the universe. . . . British liberties are not the grants of princes or Parliaments, but original rights, conditions of original contracts . . . coeval with government. . . . Many of our rights are inherent and essential, agreed on as maxims, and established as preliminaries, even before a Parliament existed."[111]

But it is the Massachusetts Circular Letter of 1768 that perfects the blend of Coke and Locke, while it also reformulates in striking terms, borrowed perhaps from Vattel, the medieval notion of authority as intrinsically conditioned. The outstanding paragraph of the letter is the following:

> The House have humbly represented to the ministry, their own sentiments, that his Majesty's high court of Parliament is the supreme legislative power over the whole empire; that in all free states the constitution is fixed, and as the supreme legislative derives its power and authority from the constitution, it cannot overleap the bounds of it, without destroying its own foundation; that the constitution ascertains and limits both sovereignty and allegiance, and, therefore, his Majesty's American subjects, who acknowledge themselves bound by the ties of allegiance, have an equitable claim to the full enjoyment of the fundamental rules of the British constitution; that it is an essential, unalterable right, in nature, engrafted into the British constitution, as a fundamental law, and ever held sacred and irrevocable by the subjects within the realm, that what a man has honestly acquired is absolutely his own, which he may freely give, but cannot be taken from him without his consent; that the American subjects may, therefore, exclusive of any consideration of charter rights, with a decent firmness, adopted to the character of free men and subjects, assert this natural and constitutional right.[112]

Notwithstanding all this, as late as the first Continental Congress there were still those who opposed any reliance whatsoever on natural rights. One of "the two points which we laboured most" John Adams records in his *Diary* was "whether we should recur to the law of nature, as well as to the British constitution, and our American charters and grants. Mr. Galloway and Mr. Duane were for excluding the law of nature. I was strenuous for retaining and insisting on it, as a recourse to which we might be driven by Parliament much sooner than we were aware."[113] The "Declaration and Resolves" of the Congress proves that Adams carried the day. The opening resolution asserts "that the inhabitants of the American colonies in North America," by the immutable laws of nature, the principles of the British constitution, and the several charters or compacts "are entitled to life, liberty, and property."[114]

111. 3 Adams, *Life and Works* 448–64, especially at 449, 463.

112. MacDonald, *Documentary Source Book* 146–50 (1768 {*sic;* 1920}). *Cf.* Vattel, *Law of Nations* bk. i, ch. 3, sec. 34 (London tr. 1797). The subordination of the legislative authority and that of the prince to the constitution is the gospel of this and the succeeding chapter. The work first appeared in 1758.

113. 2 Adams, *Life and Works* 374.

114. MacDonald, *Documentary Source Book* 162–66.

Nor did the corollary notion of a single community claiming common rights on the score of a common humanity, escape American spokesmen. It was in this same first Continental Congress that Patrick Henry made his famous deliverance: "Government is dissolved. . . . Where are your landmarks, your boundaries of colonies? We are in a state of nature, sir. . . . The distinctions between Virginians, Pennsylvanians, New Yorkers, and New Englanders, are no more. I am not a Virginian, but an American."[115] And the less casual evidence of everyday speech is to like effect: "the people of these united colonies," "your whole people," "the people of America," "the liberties of Americans," "the rights of Americans," "American rights," "Americans."[116] The constant recurrence of such phrases in contemporary documents bespeaks the conscious identity of Americans everywhere in possession of the rights of men. Natural rights were already on the way to become national rights.

At the same time it is necessary to recognize that the American Revolution was also a contest for local autonomy as well as one for individual liberty. The two motives were in fact less competitive than complementary. The logical deduction from the course of political history in the colonies, especially in the later decades of it, was that the best protection of the rights of the individual was to found in the maintenance of the hard-won prerogatives of the colonial legislatures against the royal governors; in other words, of what they locally termed their "Constitutions."[117] The final form of the American argument against British pretentions was, therefore, by no means a happy idea suggested by the stress of contention, but was soundly based on autochthonous institutional developments. As stated by Jefferson in his *Summary View,* published in 1774, it comprised the thesis that Parliament had no power whatsoever to legislate for the colonies, whether in harmony with the rights of men or no; that the colonies were mutually independent communities, equal partners in the British empire with England herself; that each part had its own Parliament which was the supreme lawmaking power within its territorial limits; that each was connected with the empire only through the person of a common monarch, who was "no more than the chief officer of the people, appointed by the laws . . . to assist in working the great machine of government erected for their use."[118] The Declaration of Independence, two

---

115. 2 Adams, *Life and Works* 366–67.

116. Baldwin, *View of the Origin and Nature of the Constitution of the United States* 15–16 (1837); Dillon, *Laws and Jurisprudence of England and America* 46–48 (1895). See also Niles, *Principles and Acts* 134–35, 148 (1876).

117. For this use of the term "Constitution," sometimes referring to the colonial charter, sometimes referring to the established mode of government of the colony, see 2 Journals of the House of Representatives of Massachusetts 370 (1720); 8 *id.* 279, 302, 318 (1728). In New Jersey, which had no charter after 1702, the term "constitution" referred altogether to the mode of government that had developed on the basis of the royal governor's instructions, but may have been suggested by the Fundamental Constitutions of 1683 of East Jersey. C. R. Erdman, *The New Jersey Constitution of 1776* (1929).

118. 11 Jefferson, *Writings* 258 (Memorial ed. 1903); *The Jeffersonian Cyclopedia* 963–68 (Foley ed. 1900). Jefferson characteristically claimed his to be the first formulation of this position. 9

years later from the same hand, proceeds on the same theory. It is addressed not to Parliament but to the king, since it was with the king alone that the bond about to be severed had subsisted; in it the American doctrine of the relation of government to individual rights finds its classic expression; these rights are vindicated by the assertion of the independence of the thirteen states.[119]

From the destructive phase of the Revolution we turn to its constructive phase. This time it was Virginia who led the way. The Virginia constitution of 1776 is preceded by a "Declaration of rights made by the representatives of the good people of Virginia . . . which rights do appertain to them and their posterity, as the basis and foundation of government."[120] In this document, antedating the Declaration of Independence by a month, are enumerated at length those rights which Americans, having laid claim to them first as British subjects and later as men, now intended as citizens to secure through governments of their own erection. For the first time in the history of the world the principles of revolution are made the basis of settled political institutions.

What was the nature of these governments? Again the Virginia constitution of 1776 may serve as a model.[121] Here the horn of the legislative department is mightily exalted, that of the executive correspondingly depressed. The early Virginia governors were chosen by the legislature annually and were assisted by a council of state also chosen by the legislature, and if that body so desired, from the legislature. The governor was without the veto power, or any other participation in the work of lawmaking, and his salary was entirely at the mercy of the assembly. The judges were in somewhat better case, holding their offices "during good behavior," yet they too were the legislature's appointees, and judicial review is nowhere hinted. Finally, both judges and governors were subject to impeachment, which as still defined by English precedents, amounted to a practically unrestricted inquest of office. The underlying assumption of the instrument, gatherable from its various provisions, is that the rights of the individual have nothing to fear from majority rule exercised through legislative assemblies

Jefferson, *Writings* 258. But in this he was seriously in error. Richard Bland, Stephen Hopkins, John Adams, James Wilson, Benjamin Franklin, Roger Sherman, James Iredell, and others all preceded him, Hopkins and Franklin by nearly ten years. Indeed, advocates had developed a similar doctrine in Ireland's behalf in the seventeenth century. On the whole subject see Adams, *Political Ideas of the American Revolution* chs. 3, 5 (1922); Becker, *The Declaration of Independence* ch. 3; McIlwain, *The American Revolution* (1923).

119. Jefferson's indebtedness to the Virginia Declaration of Rights of 1776 appears more striking when the Declaration of Independence is compared with the former as it came from the hands of George Mason. Niles, *Principles and Acts* 301–303. The phrase "pursuit of happiness" was probably suggested by Blackstone's statement that the law of nature boils down to "one paternal precept, "that man should pursue his own true and substantial happiness.' " 1 Bl. *Comm.* 41. Burlamaqui, *Principles of Natural and Political Law* (1859), an English translation of which appeared in 1763 (the work was first published in 1747), teaches the same doctrine at length. See e.g., 2 *id.* 18. The phrase "a long train of abuses," is Jefferson's recollection of Locke, *Second Treatise* sec. 225, ch. 19.

120. 7 Thorpe, *Federal and State Constitutions, Colonial Charters and other Organic Laws* 3812–14 (1909).

121. *Id.* 3814–19.

chosen for brief terms by a restricted, though on the whole democratic, elector- ate. In short, as in both Coke and Locke, the maintenance of higher law is entrusted to legislative supremacy, though qualified by annual elections. Fortu- nately or unfortunately, in 1776 the influence of Coke and Locke was no longer the predominant one that it had been. In the very process of controversy with the British Parliament, a new point of view had been brought to American attention, the ultimate consequences of which were as yet unforeseeable.[122]

Lord Acton has described the American Revolution as a contest between two ideas of legislative power. Even as late as the debate on the Declaratory Act of 1766, the American invocation of a constitution setting metes and bounds to Parliament did not fail of a certain response among the English themselves. Burke, it is true, brushed aside all questions of prescriptive rights and based his advocacy of the American cause on expediency only; but Camden, who pos- sessed the greatest legal reputation of the age, quoted both Coke and Locke in support of the proposition that Parliament's power was not an unlimited one; while Chatham, taking halfway ground, pretended to discover a fundamental distinction between the power of taxation and that of legislation, qualifying the former by the necessity of representation.[123] Camden and Chatham were, none the less, illustrious exceptions. The direction which the great weight of profes- sional opinion was now taking was shown when Mansfield, who a few years earlier had as solicitor general quoted the dictum in Bonham's Case with ap- proval, arose in the House of Lords to support the Declaratory Act.[124] The passage of that measure by an overwhelming majority committed Parliament substantially to Milton's conclusion of a century earlier that "Parliament was above all positive law, whether civil or common."[125]

The vehicle of the new doctrine to America was Blackstone's *Commentaries,* of which, before the Revolution, nearly 2500 copies had been sold on this side of

---

122. On the revolutionary state constitutions, see generally Nevins, *The American States during and after the Revolution* (1924); Morey, "First State Constitutions," 4 *Annals* 201–32 (1893); Webster, "Comparative Study of the State Constitutions of the American Revolution," 9 *id.* 380– 420 (1897).

123. See the debate on the Declaratory Bill, 16 Hansard, *Parliamentary History* 163–81, 193– 206 *passim* (1813). Camden was especially vehement: The bill is "illegal, absolutely illegal, con- trary to the fundamental laws of nature, contrary to the fundamental laws of this constitution." *Id.* 178. On the other hand, it was denied that Magna Carta was any proof "of our Constitution as it now is. The Constitution of this country has been always in a moving state, either gaining or losing something." *Id.* 197.

124. *Id.* 172–75.

125. McIlwain, *High Court of Parliament* 94. On the rise of the notion of parliamentary sover- eignty, see Holdsworth, *Some Lessons from Our Legal History* 112–41 (1928). The first to assert the supremacy of the king in Parliament over the king out of Parliament was James Whitlocke, in the debate on Impositions, in 1610. *Id.* 124. A division on the subject is shown in the debate on the Septennial Act of 1716. *Id.* 129; 7 Hansard, *Parliamentary History* 317, 334, 339, 348–49. The doctrine of the Declaratory Act evoked numerous protests outside of Parliament. Mott, *Due Process of Law* 63n. For a belated expression of the doctrine of limited parliamentary power, see *id.* 67n., citing various works of Toulmin Smith. Smith, however, was no advocate of judicial review, but warned his people against such an institution as the Supreme Court of the United States. *Id.* 68n.

the Atlantic,[126] while the spread of his influence in the later days of the prerevolutionary controversy is testified to by Jefferson in his reference to that "young brood of lawyers" who, seduced by the "honeyed Mansfieldism of Blackstone . . . began to slide into Toryism."[127] Nor is Blackstone's appeal to men of all parties difficult to understand. Eloquent, suave, undismayed in the presence of the palpable contradictions in his pages, adept in insinuating new points of view without unnecessarily disturbing old ones, he is the very exemplar and model of legalistic and judicial obscurantism.

While still a student, Blackstone had published an essay on *The Absolute Rights of British Subjects,* and chapter one of book one of his greater work bears a like caption. Here he appears at first glance to underwrite the whole of Locke's philosophy, but a closer examination discloses important divergences. "Natural liberty" he defines as "the power of acting as one thinks fit, without any restraint or control, unless by the law of nature." It is "inherent in us by birth," and is that gift of God which corresponds with "the faculty of free will." Yet every man, he continues, "when he enters into society, gives up a part of his natural liberty as the price of so valuable a purchase," receiving in return "civil liberty," which is natural liberty "so far restrained by human laws (and no farther) as is necessary and expedient for the general advantage of the public."[128] The divergence which this phraseology marks from the strictly Lockean position is twofold. Locke also, as we saw above, suggests public utility as one requirement of allowable restraints upon liberty, but by no means the sole requirement; nor is the lawmaking power with him, as with Blackstone, the final arbiter of the issue.

The divergence becomes even more evident when the latter turns to consider the positive basis of British liberties in Magna Carta and "the corroborating statutes." His language in this connection is peculiarly complacent. The rights declared in these documents, he asserts, comprise nothing less than

> either that residuum of natural liberty, which is not required by the laws of society to be sacrificed to public convenience, or else those civil privileges, which society hath engaged to provide in lieu of the natural liberties so given up by individuals. These, therefore, were formerly, either by inheritance or purchase, the rights of all mankind; but, in most other countries of the world, being now more or less debased and destroyed, they at present may be said to remain, in a peculiar and emphatical manner, the rights of the people of England.[129]

Yet when he comes to trace the limits of the "rights and liberties" so grandiloquently characterized, his invariable reference is simply to the state of the law in his own day—never to any more exalted standard.

126. The first volume appeared in 1765, the fourth in 1769. An American edition appeared in Philadelphia in 1771-1772, of the full work, 1,400 copies having been ordered in advance. Warren, *History of the American Bar* 178.
127. 11 Jefferson, *Writings* iv (Memorial ed. 1903). Jefferson had no high opinion of "Blackstone lawyers." He termed them "ephemeral insects of the law."
128. 1 Bl. *Comm*. 125-26.
129. *Id*. 127-29.

And so by phraseology drawn from Locke and Coke themselves, he paves the way to the entirely opposed position of Hobbes and Mansfield. In elaboration of this position he lays down the following propositions: First, "there is and must be in all of them [states] a supreme, irresistible, absolute, uncontrolled authority . . ."; secondly, this authority is the "natural, inherent right that belongs to the sovereignty of the state . . . of making and enforcing laws"; thirdly, to the lawmaking power "all other powers of the state" must conform "in the execution of their several functions or else the Constitution is at an end"; and, finally, the lawmaking power in Great Britian is Parliament, in which, therefore, the sovereignty resides.[130] It follows, of course, that neither judicial disallowance of acts of Parliament nor yet the right of revolution has either legal or constitutional basis. To be sure, "acts of Parliament that are impossible to be performed are of no validity"; yet this is so only in a truistic sense, for "there is no court that has power to defeat the intent of the legislature, when couched in . . . evident and express words."[131] As to the right of revolution—"So long . . . as the English constitution lasts, we may venture to affirm that the power of Parliament is absolute and without control."[132]

Nor does Blackstone at the end, despite his previous equivocations, flinch from the conclusion that the whole legal fabric of the realm was, by his view, at Parliament's disposal. Thus he writes:

> It hath sovereign and uncontrollable authority in the making, confirming, enlarging, restraining, abrogating, repealing, reviving, and expounding of laws . . . this being the place where that absolute, despotic power which must in all governments reside somewhere, is entrusted by the Constitution of these kingdoms. All mischiefs and grievances, operations and remedies that transcend the ordinary course of the laws, are within the reach of this extraordinary tribunal. . . . It can, in short, do everything that is not naturally impossible, and therefore some have not scrupled to call its power by a figure rather too bold, the omnipotence of Parliament. True it is, that what the Parliament doth no authority upon earth can undo.[133]

This absolute doctrine was summed up by De Lolme a little later in the oft-quoted aphorism that "Parliament can do anything except make a man a woman or a woman a man."

Thus was the notion of legislative sovereignty added to the stock of American political ideas.[134] Its essential contradiction of the elements of theory which had been contributed by earlier thinkers is manifest. What Coke and Locke give us is, for the most part, cautions and safeguards against power; in Blackstone, on the other hand, as in Hobbes, we find the claims of power exalted. This occurred,

130. *Id.* 49–51.
131. *Id.* 91.
132. *Id.* 161–62.
133. *Id.* 160–61.
134. Blackstone, however, was not the first to introduce the notion in the colonies. See some earlier pulpit utterances recorded in Baldwin, *The New England Clergy and the American Revolution* 42n. "The legislature is accountable to none. There is no authority above them. . . ."

moreover, at a moment when, as it happened, not merely the actual structure of government in the United States, but this strong trend of thought among the American people afforded the thesis of legislative sovereignty every promise of easy lodgement.

The formula laid down by the Declaration of Independence regarding the right of revolution is a most conservative one. The right is not to be exercised for ''light and transient causes,'' but only to arrest a settled and deliberate course of tyranny. Yet within a twelve month of the Declaration we find one Benjamin Hichborn of Boston proclaiming the following doctrine: ''I define civil liberty to be not a 'government by laws,' made agreeable to charters, bills of rights or compacts, but a power existing in the people at large, at any time, for any cause, or for no cause, but their own sovereign pleasure, to alter or annihilate both the mode and essence of any former government, and adopt a new one in its stead.''[135]

Ultimately the doctrine of popular sovereignty thus voiced was to be turned against both legislative sovereignty and at a critical moment against state particularism. But at the outset it aided both these ideas, because the state was conceived to stand nearer to the people than the Continental Congress, and because, within the state, the legislature was conceived to stand nearer to the people than the other departments.[136] Thus legislative sovereignty, a derivative from the notion of popular sovereignty in the famous text from Justinian which was quoted at the outset of this study, was recruited afresh from the parent stream, with the result that all the varied rights of man were threatened with submergence in a single right, that of belonging to a popular majority, or more accurately, of being represented by a legislative majority.[137]

Why, then, did not legislative sovereignty finally establish itself in our constitutional system? To answer at this point solely in terms of institutions, the reason is twofold. In the first place, in the American *written Constitution,* higher law at last attained a form which made possible the attribution to it of an entirely new sort of validity, the validity of a *statute emanating from the sovereign*

135. Niles, *Principles and Acts* 47.

136. On the growth of particularism, as shown by the proceedings in the Continental Congress, especially regarding the Articles of Confederation, see Adams, *Jubilee Discourse on the Constitution* 13 *et seq.* (1839).

137. ''The law of nature is not, as the English utilitarians in their ignorance of its history supposed, a synonym for arbitrary individual preferences, but on the contrary it is a living embodiment of the collective reason of civilized mankind. . . . But it has its limits. . . . Natural justice has no means . . . of choosing one practical solution out of two or more which are in themselves equally plausible. Positive law, whether enacted or customary, must come to our aid in such matters.'' Pollock, *Expansion of the Common Law* 128. The arguments of the analytical school against higher law notions must be conceded to this extent: it is better to confine the term ''law'' to rules enforced by the state. But that fact does not prove that the term should be applied to all such rules. In urging that it should be, the analytical thinkers endeavor to steal something—they try to transfer to unworthy rules supported by the state the prestige attaching to the word ''law'' conceived of as the embodiment of justice. The trouble with the analysts, in other words, is not that they define ''law'' too narrowly, but too broadly.

people. Once the binding force of higher law was transferred to this new basis, the notion of the sovereignty of the ordinary legislative organ disappeared automatically, since that cannot be a *sovereign* lawmaking body which is subordinate to another lawmaking body. But in the second place, even statutory form could hardly have saved the higher law as *a recourse for individuals* had it not been backed up by *judicial review*. Invested with statutory form and implemented by judicial review, higher law, as with renewed youth, entered upon one of the great periods of its history, and juristically the most fruitful one since the days of Justinian.

4. The Democratic Dogma and the Future of Political Science

Everyone has heard the gibe that the specialist is a man who knows more and more about less and less, while a sociologist is one who knows less and less about more and more. Another quip has it that while psychology is all data and no conclusions, sociology is all conclusions and no data. Political science itself has not escaped a certain amount of cheap disparagement from those who know little or nothing about it. Thus a political scientist has been described as one who among politicians is reckoned a scientist, and among scientists is reckoned a politician; or, indeed, as one who is called a political scientist because he is neither—an obvious paraphrase of Voltaire's famous sarcasm regarding the Holy Roman Empire. At any rate, the time has come when a certain group of political scientists have wearied of such gibes, to say nothing of that condescension which they think they detect in the attitude of laboratory scientists toward them; and they have registered a vow to convert political science from a "normative" or "telic" science, as it has been variously called, into a natural science, into a science which will hereafter be printed in lower case instead of in upper, and will, moreover (the height of ambition of all true sciences) be able to predict the future just as astronomy, physics, and chemistry are able to do—not to mention astrology, alchemy, and palmistry. Nor is this newly conceived ambition the product merely of discontent; it is rather more, perhaps, response to the beckoning of opportunity—the opportunity spelled by the rise of the behavioristic psychology, For if human behavior in general can be made the subject of scientific measurement leading to prediction, why cannot that particular portion of it which has political consequences? At this point another consideration enters.

From 23 *American Political Science Review* 569–592 (1929). Reprinted by permission. This paper was read last January {1929} before the Chinese Social and Political Science Association of Peking and the Friends of Political Science of Yenching and Tsing-hua Universities.

The father of political science based his work on the doctrine of the inequality of man and a defense of slavery. But certainly until recent years the connection of modern political science with Aristotle has been highly discontinuous, not to say casual. To the *Politics* are traceable the classification of governments into those of the one, the few, and the many; the doctrine of three intrinsically distinct functions of government; and the earliest formulation of the principle of a government of laws and not of men. But even for these ideas the indebtedness of American writers has usually been indirect, while on the other hand in England, where the *Politics* is still read in university courses, the term political science is an exotic; nor is there a single English periodical which bears this label. The fact of the matter is that modern political science—the normative, telic science—is a belated offspring of eighteenth-century rationalism, and has taken all its ideals from that source. It sprang from the same matrix as the democratic dogma, and it has heretofore fought in the same ranks and for the same causes as its older relative. So the question arises, what would the consequences be if political science, renouncing its role of crusader, became a mere laboratory science; and especially if it did so in alliance with behaviorism, which repudiates, if not with scorn and contumely, at any rate with scientific finality, the most fundamental assumption of the democratic dogma, the assumption that man is primarily a rational creature, and that his acts are governed by rational considerations?

I. The Intellectualist Fallacy

It becomes pertinent at this point to devote a word or two to the opening phrase in the title of this paper. "The democratic dogma" is, of course, the doctrine that the people should rule. But why should they? Not because they wield the physical forces of society, which in this modern machine-gun era they rarely do, but because they know their own good, and act upon their knowledge, and so know the most widely spread public good, which they will endeavor to bring to pass. The dogma involves, it will be noted, not a few questionable assumptions, but the only one of interest to us in this connection is the one already mentioned, that men act on reason.[1]

In his *Human Nature and Politics* Professor Graham Wallas has collected many interesting illustrations of what he terms "the intellectualist fallacy" as it has found utterance in the field of political thought. Contradicting the utilitarian idea that it was possible to produce a science of government from the principles of human nature. Macaulay, writing in 1829, himself accepted the major premise of utilitarianism. "What proposition," said he, "is there respecting human nature which is absolutely and universally true? We know of only one, and that is not only true but identical—that man always acts from self interest. . . . When we

1. Thus, I do not consider it necessary for my purpose to deal with the contention of the Groupist philosophers that men always seek the interest of some group less than the state.

see the actions of a man we know with certainty what he thinks his interest to be''[2] Burke's oft-quoted definition of ''party'' was from the same mint: ''A body of men united for promoting by their just endeavors the national interest upon some particular principle in which they are all agreed.''[3] However applicable this definition may be to new parties, third parties, and revolutionary parties, few parties that have once sampled the sweets of office would survive its acid test. Yet another aspect of the intellectualist outlook is revealed by the invocation in the Declaration of Independence of certain ''self-evident truths,'' and its con-comitant solicitation of ''the decent opinion of mankind.'' For in these words we perceive not only the Newtonian background of eighteenth-century political rationalism, but its assumption of the uniformity of human thought and the universal compulsion thereupon of the principles of correct political reasoning.

And the social product—or, speaking more accurately, the algebraic sum—of individual reasons was, in the rationalist cosmology, that which is termed ''public opinion.'' It is true that earlier (as also later), public opinion was regarded as connoting anything but intellectual processes; but in the period of which we are now speaking, when anyone used this term he was at once understood to mean the highest fruition of human mentality when its attention was directed to public questions, and to convey that the prompt enactment of its mandates into law was the be-all and end-all of political association, as well as the conclusive test of excellence in government.

Again we draw an illustration from Professor Wallas' pages. It is culled from the speech of James A. Garfield before the convention which nominated him for the presidency. Garfield was evidently somewhat troubled by certain things he had witnessed in the convention, things that did not fit very well into his rationalistic presuppositions; so we find him comforting himself and his auditors with the reflection that the final decision lay with a body of men whose spirit of reasonableness and rectitude of intention were not open to impeachment. ''I have seen,'' the passage runs, ''the sea lashed into fury and dashed into spray, and its grandeur moves the soul of the dullest man. But I remember that it is not the billows but the calm of the sea from which all heights and depths are mea-sured.... Not here in this brilliant circle where fifteen thousand men and women are gathered is the destiny of the Republic to be decreed for the next four years... but by four millions of Republican firesides where [are] thoughtful voters with wives and children about them, with the calm thoughts inspired by love of home and country, the history of the past, the hopes of the future, and the knowledge of the great men who have adorned and blessed our nation in the days gone by. There God prepares the verdict that shall determine the wisdom of our work tonight.''[4]

2. Quoted in G. Wallas, *Human Nature in Politics* 22 (1909).
3. *Id.* 83.
4. *Id.* 111.

To be sure, there are touches here—lapses into sentimentalism—which an eighteenth-century rationalist could only deplore. Would not wife and child be apt to disturb the cogged premises of intellectualist thought? What, moreover of the implication that only Republicans have "calm thoughts"—and this before the days of "keeping cool with Coolidge?" And, worst of all, what of the tactics of giving Deity a finger in the pie? That would have spoiled the picture entirely for an eighteenth-century deist. But at least we are assured that the final result will be all right. It will be *as if* "calm thoughts" alone determined it.

The *als ob* way out of difficulties is also the one taken by Bryce in his *American Commonwealth*. "In the ideal democracy," he wrote, "every citizen is intelligent, patriotic, disinterested, his sole wish is to discover the right side in each contested issue, and to fix upon the best man among competing candidates. His common sense, aided by a knowledge of the situation of his country, enables him to judge wisely between arguments submitted to him, while his own zeal is sufficient to carry him to the polling booth."[5] By "ideal democracy" Bryce evidently meant a realizable ideal, considering the facts of human nature. Certainly, as Graham Wallas comments, "no doctor would begin a medical treatise by saying 'the ideal man requires no food and is impervious to the action of bacteria, but this ideal is far removed from the actualities of any known population.' No modern treatise on pedagogy begins with the statement that 'the ideal boy knows things without being taught them, and his sole wish is the advancement of science, but no boys at all like this have ever existed.' "[6] No doubt, as Bryce himself owned, the American Commonwealth, regarded as the ideal democracy, had its limitations. "It is rather sentiment than thought," he wrote, "that the mass can contribute," and in the political beliefs of nineteen out of twenty there is "little solidity and substance."[7] And yet, for all that, the democratic regime in the United States was a regime of reason.

A subsequent chapter is entitled "How Public Opinion Rules in America";[8] and still later the statement is added: "There is no class or set of men whose special function it is to form and lead opinion. The politicians certainly do not; public opinion leads them."[9] Then, quoting Lincoln: " With public sentiment on its side, everything succeeds; with public sentiment against it, nothing succeeds." Thereupon, on his own account, Bryce proceeds: "Public opinion is a sort of atmosphere, fresh, keen, and full of sunlight, like that of the American cities, and this sunlight kills many of those noxious germs which are hatched where politicians congregate"; and, "it is the habit of breathing as well as helping to form public opinion that cultivates, develops, trains, the average

5. *Id.* 126.
6. *Id.* 127.
7. 2 *American Commonwealth* 254 (1910).
8. *Id.* ch. 78.
9. *Id.* 308.

American.''[10] The final sentences of Bryce's elaborate analysis read: "Public opinion grows more temperate, more mellow, and assuredly more tolerant. Its very strength disposes it to bear with opposition or remonstrance. It respects itself too much to wish to silence any voice.''[11]

This was written nearly fifty years before the campaign of 1928! In his last work, incorporating his final assessment of the world's great democracies, Bryce still recorded a favorable view of the quality of public opinion in America as compared with other democracies; but the complimentary verdict was seriously qualified by his discovery of the growing indifference of the masses the world over toward political questions. "The lapse of years," he says, "has given us a fuller knowledge. It is time to face facts and to be done with fancies. . . . The proportion of citizens who take a lively and constant interest in politics is so small, and likely to remain so small, that the direction of affairs inevitably passes into the hands of a few.''[12] In the end, he challenged Aristotle's classification of governments. There is, he found, only one kind of government, whatever the external forms, "the government of the few."

Two other expositions of public opinion from the rationalist point of view demand passing notice. Of Ostrogorski's *Democracy and the Organization of Political Parties,* which appeared in 1902 and represented the results of fifteen years' observation of the party system at work in America and England, I quote Professor Wallas' pertinent criticism: "The instances given in the book might have been used as the basis of a fairly full account of those facts in the human type which are of importance to the politician." Instead, they are "regretfully contrasted with 'free reason,' 'the general idea of liberty,' 'the sentiments which inspired the men of 1848'; and the book ends with a sketch of a proposed constitution in which the voters are to be required to vote for candidates known to them through declarations of policy 'from which all mention of party is rigorously excluded.' One seems to be reading a series of conscientious observations of the Copernican heavens by a loyal but saddened believer in the Ptolemaic astronomy.''[13]

The other work referred to is President Lowell's *Public Opinion and Popular Government.* The earlier pages of the book waft one back to the closing days of the eighteenth century as on a Whittall carpet endowed with magic. Public opinion must be both "public" and "opinion"; and while opinion "need not be entirely rational," it does denote two things: first, a process of reasoning, and secondly, knowledge of facts to furnish the basis of the reasoning. The writer then proceeds to show, and quite convincingly, how little likely these conditions are to be realized when the electorate at large attempts to legislate.

10. *Id.* 367.
11. *Id.* 376.
12. 2 *Modern Democracies* 549 (1902).
13. *Human Nature in Politics* 124–25.

II. The Lesson of Popular Indifference

As may have been discovered from what has already been said, modern attack on the democratic dogma has proceeded from a twofold basis: first, from the basis afforded by the phenomenon noticed by Bryce of the growing indifference of the voter; secondly, from the basis uncovered especially by Wallas in his challenge of the notion that the voter, when he does condescend to show an interest, will act on rational considerations. As to the former phenomenon, American experience is especially illuminating, and so may be briefly recounted at this point.

The progress of the democratic dogma in the United States was marked by a double process: first, the extension of the franchise, a development apparently brought to an end by the Nineteenth Amendment, though not certainly, since children still remain without votes, to say nothing of the parlor furniture; secondly, by the constant increase of the burden of the voter. Perhaps it was thought that as the electorate was enlarged it became proportionately capable of bearing a heavier load—an erroneous assumption, since to each voter the burden is cumulative. The first thing that happened along this line was the conversion in the second quarter of the last century of nearly all local and state offices into elective offices, with the result that it became impossible for the voter to inform himself, even if he were disposed to make the effort, as to the fitness of more than a small fraction of the candidates for office. What, however, the voter was unable or unwilling to do for himself, the professional politician was only too glad to do for him. The final outcome is stated graphically by Professor Kales in his witty brochure entitled *Unpopular Government in the United States.*

> The elector by being required to vote too much has been compelled to surrender to a large extent his right to vote at all. . . . Formerly people were disfranchised when they were given no opportunity to vote. Today they are disfranchised by being required to vote too much. Formerly the legal rulers of the disfranchised mass were selected for them by the few without equivocation. Today our legal rulers are selected for us by the few through the subterfuge of the mass casting ballots according to the direction of the few.

For aristocracy has been substituted politocracy.[14]

The only criticism that can be made of this statement of the situation is that it impliedly exaggerates the voter's interest. That political indifference in the United States is by no means due to the complexity of the task the voter is confronted with is shown by the fact that it operates most conspicuously in the presidential elections. In the election of 1924 less than fifty per cent of the eligible vote was cast, and in that of 1928 less than fifty-five per cent. No— American political indifference is due chiefly to circumstances as to which agitation for the "short ballot" is little apposite. It arises from the average American's

14. At 24–25.

sense of well-being and his consequent confidence in his governors, from the general homogeneousness of political sentiment as to fundamentals among the American population—at least in a period of prosperity—and, above all, from the fact that, with the incoming of radio, the movie, and cheap motor transportation, politics has largely lost its capacity to entertain and amuse.

This, however, political science, still blinded by its inherited intellectualism, has failed to appreciate; and while on the one hand it was launching campaigns for fewer elective offices, on the other hand it was lending aid and comfort to the movement for the initiative, referendum, and recall. "The cure for democracy is more democracy," was the sage shibboleth of the supporters of the I. and R., a teaching which has received justification in certain instances, e.g., Italy and Spain, where, applied as a vaccine, the democratic virus has at last produced an apparently complete immunity. In the United States, on the other hand, democracy had long since become the normal state of health of the body politic; so what possible pertinence could the therapeutics of prophylaxis have in such a case? Besides, *similia similibus curantur* never did mean—until the excellent Hahnemann happened to run across this tag-end of Latin somewhere—that an ailment was to be cured by taking more of it, but only that when a substantially similar disease to the one just cured is met with, like remedies should be employed. What a torrent of error from so slight a source; and how the *corpus humane* and the *corpus politicum* have suffered! In the ideal democracy the study of the classics will not be neglected! Meantime we may note for the consolation of the overworked voter (actually a sybaritic loafer) Bernard Shaw's conclusion that "government presents only one problem, the discovery of a trustworthy anthropometric measure." Give the intelligence tester time, and he will relieve the voter of both the ballot's burden and the political parasite.

III. The Lesson of Mass Suggestibility

The indifference of the masses toward their political rights and duties—an indifference which paradoxically increases with the importance of governmental intervention in daily life—forms a crucial test of the assumptions of eighteenth-century political thought. But the question remains, What is the quality of popular political response when it is forthcoming? What aptitudes does it reveal on the part of the political animal? In general, the answers to this question may be said to boil down to two: first, the political animal has a pronounced liking for nonrational inference, that is to say, for conclusions not drawn from premises that are statable in terms of public interest, or even, for that matter, of his own interest; secondly, he is a highly suggestible creature, with the result that it becomes a very simple matter for those who know the game, as the professional politician, advertising expert, and paid propagandist very well do, to plant in his mind (the word "mind" is used subject to withdrawal later on in deference to Dr. Watson) just those premises, prejudices, "stereotypes," which can be counted on to produce in such a mind the kind of inference that said politician, advertising expert, or propagandist wishes to have produced.

As every student of political history is aware, there never was a time when *credo* of democracy escaped challenge. There were reactionaries even in early days. One of these was Alexander Hamilton, who on one occasion asserted that while man is no doubt a reasoning being he is not a reasonable one; and on another refuted the slogan *"vox populi vox dei"* with the blunt assertion: "Your people, sir, is a great beast." A contemporary reactionary, equally distinguished, was Edmund Burke, although he is also quotable, as we have seen, on the other side of the question. "Politics," said Burke, "ought to be adjusted not to human reasoning, but to human nature; of which the reason is but a part, and by no means the greatest part."[15] The anti-intellectualist criticism has never been put more completely or more compactly. The French Revolution definitely fixed Burke's attitude.

Nowadays, anti-intellectualism has become a philosophy of life, and the disparagement of reason—as, for example, in the case of Bergson—a species of religion. This could never have come about solely on the warrant of a few political pessimists, however eminent, nor even from the support lent by the observed facts of human behavior. Antirationalism has won out in the nineteenth and twentieth centuries for the same reason that rationalism triumphed in the two preceding ones, that is, because of the sustenance it has drawn from the intellectual atmosphere of the period. For anti-intellectualism is itself highly intellectual. Political rationalism was a growth of the period when the conception of the Newtonian physics dominated human thought, a science which was preponderantly mathematical and deductive. The thesis of the essential irrationality of the political animal has been, I will not say supported, it has been rendered inevitable, by the Darwinian biology. This is so for several reasons. The Darwinian doctrine of evolution by the slow accumulation of slight differences is necessarily hostile to any suggestion of sudden or brilliant change due to the intervention of mind, whether human or divine. "You cannot add a cubit to your stature by taking thought" is its motto; and this is just what eighteenth-century political thought asserted could be done. There was from the first an irrepressible conflict between the two points of view. Again, the Darwinian biology has stimulated the study of institutional origins. It is the mother of the modern science of anthropology, and the confirmation which anthropology lends to the assumption of man's rationality is, to say the least, not impressive. The study of taboo, totemism, primitive marriage customs, and the like, does show, it is true, a sort of innate tendency on the part of the human mind toward rationalization— but such rationalization! Fear, superstition, unalloyed silliness, are its ingredients. Finally, the Darwinian biology is also the mother of the modern science of psychology, which in the effort to justify its parentage has been driven increas-

15. *Present State of the Nation.* 1 Burke, *Works* 280.

ingly to the necessity of corralling its subject matter in the laboratory—in short, of reducing mind to matter.

But even before there was psychology there were psychologists, and especially political psychologists. One of the very greatest of these was Walter Bagehot, whose *English Constitution,* in its penetrating analysis of the political mentality of the English masses of that period (1860), anticipates most that has since been merely put into scientific jargon regarding nonrational inference and mass suggestibility. Sparks thrown off from Bagehot's wheel, both in this work and in his *Physics and Politics,* were fanned into a brisk flame by the Frenchman, Tarde, in his *Lois de l'Imitation,* and the latter's compatriot, Le Bon, in his famous *Psychologie des Foules* and his later *Psychologie Politique.* Tarde argued, in effect, that nothing creative comes from the people, that popular movements, fashions, vogues, all take their origin with the conspicuous few, the brilliant, the successful. Mass thinking, in short, is essentially parasitic and imitative. Tarde was thinking of the dispersed mass; Le Bon's studies were, to begin with, of the crowd, the public meeting, the mob. Its outstanding trait is its gullibility, its mysticism, its irresponsibility, its capacity for autointoxication by the exuberance of its own violent sentimentalism, generous at times as this may be. Instead of resulting in intellectual clarification, the assemblage of large numbers for political purposes is inevitably productive of obfuscation; as by an inherent gravitation, the mood of such aggregations strikes for the lowest common denominator of human behavior in the emotions. Nor is this true solely of crowds gathered in a single spot at a definite time; long-sustained efforts to maintain mass alignments, like a war or a revolution (or a political campaign), produce all the symptoms of crowd psychology—its irrationality, its alarmism, its instability. Politics Le Bon sums up as "a struggle of phantoms," and leadership as "genius in utilizing these."[16]

It was, however, in 1909, in Graham Wallas' *Human Nature in Politics,* that the cornerstone of "the new political science" was laid. In this work, based upon the personal political experiences and first-hand observations of its author, interpreted in the light of wide reading, the intellectualist preconceptions of the nineteenth-century democracy are squarely challenged for the first time; and the promise is held out that, emulating political economy, which had long since cast aside "the economic man" of the "classical school," and so proceeding with a truer view of human nature, political science could hope to avail itself of quantitative methods and become a real science.[17] Both the professional and personal vanity of the political scientist were thereby ministered to at one stroke. He foresaw a term to the condescension of honest-to-goodness laboratory scientists, and he foresaw himself elevated as never before to the post of professional adviser of the masses in matters political. Instead of being merely the heir of all

16. *Psychologie politique* 61–63 (1910). See also his *Psychology of the Great War* (1916).
17. *Human Nature in Politics* 167.

the ages along with the rest of Western mankind, he would be trustee of this vast estate and the guardian of a populace destined to an indefinite nonage.

Wallas' approach to his problem is furnished by the Darwinian notion of struggle for existence, and by the old associationist psychology of the British school. By the struggle for existence human nature has been grooved with certain instincts, which are immensely more important in determining conduct than rational considerations; and the art of the politician consists simply in trading on the fact that one mental state can be relied on to call up another, a desired one, "because the two have been associated together in the history of the individual, or because a connection between the two has proved useful in the history of the race."[18] Sometimes the appeal to the instinct of the voter is direct, as by the politician who cultivates a pleasant smile, a hearty manner, and a not too discriminating taste in babies. More often it is indirect, through the use of words bearing a symbolic value, such as liberty, justice, loyalty, country, party, and so on. For the mass of men do their so-called thinking in such terms, or "entities," which they seem to assume have always the same validity whatever the facts of the particular case being dealt with, and response to which is, therefore, quite automatic.[19] Affection and interest, in other words, may be, and by the professional politician systematically are, "directed toward political entities which are very different from those facts in the world around us which we can discover by deliberate observation and analysis."[20] Furthermore, it is too much to hope—certainly this is the implication—that the thinking of men in the mass can ever be entirely purged of its inherited puerility. But well-intentioned men can be trained to beat the politician at his own game, while officialdom, with whom the future of society rests more and more, can be brought under the domination "of interest and variety, of public spirit and the craftsman's delight in his skill." Wallas' utopia is a time when what we today call politics shall have been superseded by a professional public service with professional ideals and scientific methods.[21]

The importance of this book in supplying political science with a new outlook would be hard to overestimate, and the appreciation of its contribution is apt to increase rather than diminish for some years to come. Time may be when *Human Nature in Politics* will be grouped with *The Prince* for its union of realistic outlook with a constructive intention. It is nonetheless necessary to recognize that the work has one important deficiency. Placing the reliance he did on "instincts" as the product of an assumed struggle for existence, Wallas was led into a twofold error. In the first place, while dismissing with deserved opprobrium the intellectualist eighteenth-century version of the political animal, he underestimated the plasticity of the human mental constitution; and he consequently, in the second place, permitted himself to be diverted from the most interesting

18. *Id.* 101.
19. *Id.* 84.
20. *Id.* 98.
21. *Id.* 268.

single problem suggested by his book, namely that of the source of the "political entities" of which he makes so much. These he apparently regards as relatively fixed data,[22] if indeed they are not inherited along with the instincts of which they are categories or antennae, so to speak. We of today, however, with the lessons of the Great War and its propaganda, to say nothing of modern advertising, whereby the steady purchase of Listerine has been rendered a social duty taking precedence even over forbearance from homicide, know better.

Nor are these the only developments that stand between us—I am thinking particularly of the United States—and the publication of *Human Nature in Politics*. Since then the regimentation of labor in the service of great industry has proceeded apace; since then the model of popular education has been nationalized as never before; since then the automobile has put everybody on the highways on Sunday ("all the automobiles in the United States, placed end to end, make a Sunday afternoon"); since then radio has come to aspire to an almost nightly "hook-up" of thirty million listeners in; since then Andy Gump and Barney Google have become national figures. Subjected to this uniform, protracted, million-atmosphere pressure, the human mentality simply must take shape from it; wherefore the primary interest of the political scientist of today is significantly different from that of Graham Wallas. His interest was in the methods whereby the professional politician succeeded in eliciting the desired responses from certain fixed instincts; ours is in the method by which the professional politician and his imitators proceed in the first place to plant in the minds of people the responses which they know they shall want subsequently to elicit. And we are also interested in the political possibilities of a popular mentality resembling nothing so much as a conjuror's hat. We are thus brought face to face with behaviorism.

IV. The Gospel of Behaviorism

For our purposes, no passage in the entire range of behavioristic literature can possibly be more intriguing than the following from Dr. John Watson's volume entitled *Behaviorism:*

> In 1912 the behaviorists reached the conclusion that they could no longer be content to work with intangibles and unapproachables. They decided to give up psychology or else {to} make it a natural science. They saw their brother scientists making progress in medicine, in chemistry, in physics. Every new discovery in those fields was of prime importance; every new element isolated in one laboratory could be isolated in some other laboratory; each new element was immediately taken up in the warp and woof of science as a whole. May I call your attention to the wireless, to radium, to insulin, to thyroxin, and hundreds of others? Elements so isolated and methods so formulated immediately began to function in human achievement.
>
> In his efforts to get uniformity in subject-matter and in methods the behaviorist

22. *Id.* 61.

began his own formulation of the problem of psychology by sweeping aside all medieval conceptions. He dropped from his scientific vocabulary all subjective terms, such as sensation, perception, image, desire, purpose, and even thinking and emotion as they were subjectively defined.

The behaviorist asks: Why don't we make what we can *observe* the real field of psychology? Let us limit ourselves to things that can be observed, and formulate laws concerning only those things. Well, we can observe *behavior—what an organism does or says.* And let me make this fundamental point at once, that *saying* is doing, that is, *behaving.* Speaking overtly or to ourselves (thinking) [Here the benign doctor seems to be trying to "slip one over;" but see below] is just as objective a type of behavior as baseball.[23]

The writer of these words is today the psychological expert of a large advertising concern, and is said to draw a salary of fifty thousand dollars a year. Can there be any question that this new method has enabled psychologists "to function in human achievement''; and if psychology, why not political science?

The central concept of behaviorism is the *response,* that is, the reaction of the human organism to external stimulus. Some responses, like breathing, are automatic and unconditional, but "conditional" responses are much more numerous, and the basis, or rather the content, of the individual's mental life. The behaviorist seems to admit—Watson, at least, does—that human beings have an innate capacity for fear, rage, and love, although the matrix of each of these emotions is, of course, held to be purely biological. Provided with this simple behavior pattern, the responses of infants to a given stimulus are fairly uniform, and soon become habitual. Thus man is a creature of education, and "personality" is only the sum of the habits foisted on him by his education. But suppose a man's habits fail to bring him happiness? In that case he should be provided with a new set of habits, which can be done by furnishing him with a new education, that is, a new environment, a new set of stimuli. Yet while continuously plastic, the human mental (or nervous) constitution is most plastic in early childhood. Indeed, when it comes to the question of child training, Dr. Watson far outbids the Jesuits. They wanted a child for his first six years; Dr. Watson promises to head him for the scaffold or the throne within his first six months. What Dr. Johnson said of the Scot, Dr. Watson holds applicable to the human individual wherever found—"much may be made of him if you catch him early enough."[24]

Some other concepts of behaviorism according to the gospel of Watson may be dismissed more briefly. Memory—the term itself is taboo—is a dormant habit capable of reasserting itself when presented with the proper stimulus. Dr. Watson himself proved this to be so by experimenting with rats. Mind and consciousness are, on the same authority, "passing concepts"; language a collection of verbal

23. *Behaviorism* 6 (1925).
24. See *Behaviorism* ch. 5. The behaviorist position, though anti-intellectualist, is extremely egalitarian. It is a revival of Helvetius' contention that "intelligence, genius, and virtue are the products of education," and that differences of intelligence spring solely from this source. See Aldous Huxley, *Proper Studies* 11 (1928).

objects; and thinking only talking to one's self, a process in which "your whole body is as busy as though you were cracking rocks, although your laryngeal mechanisms are setting the pace, . . . are dominant."[25]

A question obtrudes itself: thinking is a kind of muscular response—let it be granted—but response to what sort of stimulus? For, no stimulus, no response. Dealing with this question at one point, Dr. Watson says that he gave a certain lecture because he was offered fifty dollars to do so. The answer seems inadequate. It may explain why Dr. Watson gave *a* lecture, but not that *particular* lecture—which may not have been worth fifty dollars. Elsewhere Dr. Watson returns to the same question in these words: "How do we ever get new verbal creations such as a poem or a brilliant essay? The answer is that we get them by manipulating words, shifting them about until a new pattern is hit upon."[26] That is to say, creative thinking is a game of anagrams. Nevertheless, the question still remains as to any particular poem or essay—why, that particular "new pattern" having been "hit upon," thinking thereupon ceased. Dr. Watson's apparent answer is that the mere satisfaction of achieving a *new* pattern—the "equivalent" he says "of getting food"—brought stimulation to an end; in other words, there was adjustment to the stimulating environment. So, in addition to fear, rage, and love, man would seem also to have an instinct which is satisfied only by achievement of novelty.

But such speculations are, after all, somewhat afield from our purpose. Our interest in behaviorism, apart from the confirmation which it lends to the thesis of the essential irrationality of popular political thought and action, is twofold; first, for the hope which, as earlier mentioned, it has stirred in certain bosoms of converting political science into a real science; secondly, for the role which it indicates for education in a democracy. Let us consider these matters in turn.

V. The "Is" Versus the "Ought-to-Be"

Taking the position that "government itself is behavior," one distinguished political scientist contends that it becomes "possible for political scientists to cease considering their field as one of formal description and legalistic philosophy, and to regard it as a *natural science;* and furthermore, when so regarded, political science and behavioristic psychology become one and the same thing. There will, of course, be a difference of opinion as to whether the political scientist should accept a complete merging of his field with that of the psychologist. Many believe, and perhaps justly, in the existence of political facts *per se,* and in an order of reality cast in terms of social and political structures. Perhaps they are right. . . . Some persons, however, will desire to discard the structural view as descriptively possible but as barren of promise for scientific understand-

25. *Behaviorism* 197.
26. *Id.* 198.

ing and control. These persons will see in the relation between political science and psychology not an overlapping but an identity."[27]

It would be gratuitous to comment on this passage from the point of view of one who, without the advantages of training in a psychological laboratory, has to make his daily living by teaching political science—so-called. Let me say, nevertheless, that even the psychologically trained political scientist should not be too complacent about his prospects. For in a later article this same writer gives us reason to think that possibly behaviorism is no better than it ought to be when regarded as a real science. Let me quote again.

> He [the behavioristic psychologist] *begins*[28] to interpret behavior through the generalizations which can be given him by the neurologist and the general physiologist. The physiologist, in his turn, describes the action of nerve and muscle fibres and then analyzes the cells of which they are composed, either actually or conceptually (*sic*), into their organic, and finally into their inorganic, components. By the aid of generalizations in the fields of organic chemistry and physics, the nerve impulse and muscle contractions are interpreted in the simpler and more universal terms of chemical dissociation, electrical polarization, and the like. The physical chemist, in his turn, peers into such phenomena as electromagnetism and "ether conduction," seeking to identify a still more elementary plane upon which even broader generalizations can be discovered.[29]

Is it not apparent that political science will not be a *real* science until the relation between it and chemistry has become "not an overlapping but an identity?" This consummation doubtless waits upon further knowledge regarding the nature and the function of the endocrine glands.

Meantime, the great obstacle in the way of making political science a natural science lies, of course, in the difficulty attending experimentation in this field; and that is threefold. Scientific experimentation is describable with fair accuracy as the planning of a series of situations of which the recognizable factors will all remain constant except one, the importance of which will then be registered in the result. But while the chemist can plan an indefinite number of situations, the political scientist must usually wait for his situations to develop of themselves, and, what is more, when they do develop it is almost never in consequence of the alteration of a single factor, but rather of a multiplicity of factors. Lastly, and worst of all, whereas the natural scientist, being in a position to measure and control all the factors of a given situation, can select for variation the one that he thinks is of greatest importance for work needing to be accomplished, the political scientist is only too happy if he can isolate any factor at all, and without regard to its promise for future accomplishment.

Let us consider in this connection the achievement to date of "the new political science." For the most part, it comprises statistical studies in what one of its

27. F. H. Allport, in Ogburn & Goldenweiser, *The Social Sciences and Their Interrelations* 277 (1927).

28. The present writer's italics.

29. 22 *Publications of the American Sociological Society* 85 (1927).

exponents terms "political behavioristic psychology"—in other words, of group or individual attitudes having political implications, with an effort to determine the factors of these. It would be quite impossible to exaggerate the impression left by the studies of this nature which the writer has seen, as to the competence of their authors; but as to the results obtained, the expression of enthusiasm may reasonably be more restrained. There was always an immense unlimbering of apparatus, an immense polishing of a technique already spotless; but it was all apparently for the sake of the game itself. The problems set were of no great evident moment, and the solutions provided either were inconclusive or merely substantiated what must have been the off-hand verdict of any rather intelligent and well-read observer. Nor is this to say that profitable experimentation is out of the question in the field of governmental activity—that is, experimentation of a sort. The student of municipal government is especially fortunate in this respect, for every municipality is a potential laboratory. Still, the question remains, What should be the objective of such experimentation? Should it be a compiling of statistics and a plotting of curves explanatory of why La Follette was not elected president, or to prove that most people are prone to classify a heavily bewhiskered person as a bolshevist rather than a banker; or should it be the ascertainment of the value, from the point of view of widely agreed tests of public welfare, of suggested governmental programs and expedients?

What, let it be asked therefore, is the outstanding lesson of political behaviorism—a lesson supplemented by that of war propaganda, of modern advertising methods, of the thing called vogue, and in a dozen other ways? Is it not the lesson of the indefinite educability, and even re-educability, of the masses? Is it not the lesson that if those who are best qualified by good will, lack of bias, trained minds, and precise methods to do this work as it should be done, and for proper ends, do not do it, others will—indeed are doing it at this moment—and for selfish ends?[30] Is it not, in short, that the real rulers of the race are those who educate it—who, in the words of Mr. Lippmann, "create consent"?[31]

Consider the matter of vogue alone, and its dictators. Says Mr. Wyndham Lewis in his too little appreciated volume, *The Art of Being Ruled:*

> Were these rulers world rulers . . . they would have the power to impose any orthodoxy they chose from China to Peru. They would be able to make a matron in Yokohama and Dublin simultaneously appear in a dress of lotus leaves, a vest of mail, a ballet dancer's skirt, or a crinoline; to shave her head or dangle her hair in a plait; to see that she had seven lovers or to see that she confined herself to her husband . . . that . . . she was a confirmed vegetarian one week, and a hearty beefeater the next. . . . And she would be quite happy. All these things in any case can be observed around us in an imperfect, primitive form today.[32]

30. *Par example,* the "power trust."
31. *Public Opinion* 248 (1922).
32. *The Art of Being Ruled* 44.

There may be a slight strain of exaggeration about this, but the moral which Mr. Lewis deduces from it loses none of its manifest cogency on that account.

Again quoting from the same volume:

> The harsh and ominous words, *ruler* and *ruled,* although they must be used, are in practice infinitely tempered to the shorn lamb in our educationalist era. Education plays, and will continue to play, a much more important part than physical and exterior force. Force is a passing and precarious thing; whereas to get inside a person's mind and change his very personality is an effective way of reducing him and making him yours. Merely to chain him up like a dog or a slave is the act of an unimaginative tyrant. To kill him is equally meaningless. It is by taking him when he is young and educating him that you can secure him to yourself. The physical part of power, like the bloody part of revolution, should not be insisted upon.[33]

Again a trifle of exaggeration possibly. Even so, is political science to be deterred by a touch of hyperbole from accepting an invitation to ascend the seats of the mighty? We have already seen the alternative that solicits; but, to be perfectly fair, let it be restated in the words of an exponent: "Social scientists have frequently attempted the impossible task of eating their cake and keeping it too. They have sought to retain scientific status for themselves and their subjects at the same time that they have sought to become arbiters of social goals and values."[34] The answer is, Why should the political scientist spend his time measuring stereotypes planted in the public mind by other people when he could be planting some of his own? The issue, indeed, is not whether the political scientist can have his cake and eat it too, but whether he shall trade his cake for a mass of pottage. And why should society be barred from having a few arbiters of social values who know what scholarly method is, as well as so many of the other sort? There is certainly nothing about being an arbiter that inhibits one's using scientific, statistical, or any other device of intellectual precision.

That the primary task of political science is today one of popular education, and that therefore it must still retain its character as a "normative," a "telic," science, is then, my thesis. Why, indeed, should there be another natural science anyway? The general obtuseness of the laboratory sciences to social values is boasted by their would-be imitators, and is as notorious as it is infantile. With modern physics and chemistry brandishing sticks of dynamite with the insouciance of a four-year old, what could be more preposterous than to induct political science into the same nursery of urchins?

One objection remains to be disposed of, namely, the suggestion that possibly the people will not want to accept the guidance which political science has to proffer. The objection should not be taken too seriously; with the success of contemporary biologists and psychologists before him in persuading the public

---

33. *Id.* 98. See also at 112.

34. S. Rice, *Quantitative Methods in Political Science* {*sic; Quantitative Methods in Politics*} 157 (1928).

that their pronouncements on any topic whatever are scientific, the political scientist should not be downcast. As an acute foreign observer has recently remarked, Americans, in "their sanctimonious way, are always ready to accept a theory" if "they think it is scientific."[35] Perhaps, indeed, this is just where "the new political science" will come in handy; it may not make political science more scientific, but it will make it *appear* to be so. So, all in all, there is no reason why political science should not become again what Aristotle thought it to be, the most important of all sciences—*the basic science;* and this even though it must still leave the reading of the future to physics, chemistry, and astronomy, not to mention astrology, alchemy, and palmistry.

A closing reference to behaviorism: modern democratic theory begins with a psychological theory, and it ends with one, and superficially they are one and the same theory; actually the *tabula rasa* of the late John Locke and that of the extant John Watson are two very different things. The former is a photographic film which builds up its picture by a process of absorption; the other is an enticing white wall inviting human impudence to do its worst. Yet is there any reason why effrontery and self-interest alone should wield the pencil? And is there any reason why good will, scientific method, and intellectual independence should not? The real destiny of political science is to do more expertly and more precisely what it has always done; its task is criticism and education regarding the true ends of the state and how best they may be achieved. So far as it contributes to this end, the more of scientific method the better.

35. A. Siegfried, *America Comes of Age* 114 (1928).

5. Some Lessons from the Constitution of 1787

A contemporary writer of some critical and philosophical acumen finds that the fundamental religion of today is *"time worship"*—either time is worshipped as a force making inevitably for progress, or with equal ineluctability, for decay.[1] To such a state of belief, whether existing in its optimistic or pessimistic phase, it may seem a waste of breath to praise permanence. Yet there are certain human undertakings that of their very nature assume the possibility of giving affairs a more or less durable direction and mould, and one of these is the establishment of a Constitution. As the great Chief Justice Marshall pointed out, such a task requires an extraordinary exertion of society at large which is not apt to be successfully repeated except at rare intervals. On the other hand, it is also true that one of the fundamental conditions of permanence in a world of change is adaptability. Now, the Constitution of the United States from the point of view just suggested, whatever else may be said regarding it, seems to be singularly successful. Today, with one exception, the constitution of Massachusetts, one of the states of the American Union, it is the oldest written constitution in the world, and unquestionably, it has furnished in greater or less measure a model for its successors. Made for an agricultural community with a population of three and a half millions, it is today the basic law of the most highly industrialized community in the world, supporting a population of one hundred and twenty millions. Made for a strip of country bordering on the Atlantic seaboard, it survives for an empire that stretches from the Atlantic to the Pacific. Made for the age of the ox-cart and the sailing vessel, it still functions in an era of airplanes, the Ford car,

From "Some Lessons from the Constitution of 1787," in Edward S. Corwin, *The Democratic Dogma and the Future of Political Science and Other Essays* 67–84 (1930). Corwin wrote this essay on the "lessons of American political experience" during his voyage to China, where he was a visiting professor at Yenching University in 1928–1929. The reader should compare this argument for a Chinese audience with Corwin's writings for American historians and political scientists.
1. W. Lewis, *Time and Western Man* (1927).

the movie, and the radio. This is certainly indicative of qualities of survival which should interest all students of political structure, and especially those who will presently be called upon to participate in the framing of governmental institutions for the greatest population on the globe, one with whose welfare that of the entire world of the future is inescapably involved.

I.

The first and most obvious fact about the Constitution of the United States is that it is a document. It was formerly the custom of writers on these subjects to classify constitutions into written and unwritten. The latter type comprehended a more or less heterogeneous mass of established governmental practices, decisions of courts, and formal acts or statutes from divergent sources, dating often from a remote past. Such a "constitution," so-called, had certain evident advantages, but its successful working presupposed an aristocratic society—indeed its arcana were the secrets of a comparatively small group. Today only one such constitution survives, that of Great Britain, and it is a notable fact that the rising commonwealths of the British empire have one and all evidenced their preference for the other type—a document capable of being passed on by the people at large, and understood by them in its chief essentials. In short, constitutional law has passed from the stage of aristocratic custom to that of the popular code. And in this connection a further advantage of a written constitution for democracies may be noted in passing—the facility with which such an instrument lends itself to popular worship. In the absence of a monarchy it is the sign and symbol of the continuity of the national political life, and the rallying point of all parties and creeds, whose animosities and conflicts are thus given a curb that minimizes their menace for the public order. So, at least, the Constitution of the United States has operated. To use Bagehot's phrase, it has furnished government in the United States with its dignified, its ceremonial, elements. And to quote the same writer further, what he says of the British crown applies to the Constitution with emphasized force: "It has strengthened {our} government with the strength of religion." To be sure, it may be contended this result has been due to a certain intellectual aptitude of the American people rather than to the form of the Constitution—in other words, to American talent for legalistic discussion. Thus Bryce informs us that the literature of commentary which has grown up about the clauses of the Constitution of the United States is the greatest literature of that nature in the history of the world, if exception be made of the Pentateuch, and the Koran. But Bryce is inaccurate on this point. A still more extensive literature of commentary has sprung from the Confucian classics. The American talent for legalistic disquisition is matched by a similar talent of the Chinese, which furnished with the right sort of constitutional document as text, should be capable of developing an elaborate constitutional jurisprudence.

The question is hence provoked: What has been the tendency of constitutional jurisprudence in the United States? Has it been of service or disservice to the Constitution, and to the state? In answer to this question a second feature of the Constitution of 1787 comes into notice; not only is it a document, but it is an exceedingly compact one, uniting qualities of brevity and comprehensiveness to an almost unexampled extent. With its amendments it contains about 3,500 words, and can be easily read through in twenty minutes. It will illuminate further discussion to survey briefly its contents. The Constitution falls naturally into certain major divisions; first, comes the framework of the national government, comprising Articles I–III. This framework is furnished by the doctrine of the separation of powers. In Article I legislative power is called into existence and bestowed upon Congress. The central characteristic of this article is that the legislative power is a limited, delegated power, extending only to certain designated subject matter, and so leaving the great bulk of legislative power to the states of the Union. Article II provides for the national executive power, which is bestowed upon one person, the President of the United States. The executive power is thus both unified and autonomous, that is, it springs directly from the Constitution, and is in no sense a delegation from Congress. And the judicial power provided by Article III is similarly autonomous. The next major division of the Constitution comprehends Articles IV, V, and VI, which define the relations between the national government and the states in certain essentials. Article V provides for their joint participation in the process of amending the Constitution, and Article VI lays down the fundamental rule that while the national government is one of limited powers, with its assigned sphere, the national power is always supreme over conflicting state power.

The third division of the Constitution comprises its amendments, which fall into two groups, It is the main purpose of the first section, called the Bill of Rights, to protect certain rights of the individual as against the national government; and it is the purpose of the first section of Amendment XIV, the great fruit, along with Amendment XIII which abolishes slavery, of the Civil War, to extend a like safeguard to private rights as against the states. Thus while the Constitution divides governmental authority into two fields, the national and the local, it also sets aside a realm of individual rights upon which no governmental power may intrude, at least without the strongest justification from the social point of view.

II.

Such is the ground covered by the Constitution, and with a precision and concision of phrase that has repeatedly won the warmest encomiums from jurists, both American and foreign. And that this quality of the Constitution has contributed to its survival, is an important source of its vitality, can hardly be gainsaid, for the reason that it in turn results from the care of the framers of the instrument to confine themselves to fundamentals and to leave the rest to the future and to change. How adaptability and flexibility resulted from this prophetic self-restraint, I shall now proceed to show briefly.

The powers of the national government are, as I have pointed out, confined to a limited field, but where given, they are given in flexible terms. The stock example is "the commerce clause," which gives Congress the right to regulate commerce among the several states, and with foreign nations. To come within the national field commerce must involve more than one state, but all commerce which does involve more states than one falls absolutely under national control without any exception as to subject matter, and without any qualification upon the regulatory power. Furthermore "commerce" here does not mean simply that which was commerce in 1787; it covers every transaction that falls within that designation today. As Chief Justice Marshall early pointed out, inasmuch as the Constitution was designed "for ages to come," its terms "must be adapted to the various crises of human affairs." And he elsewhere added: "We cannot comprehend that train of reasoning which would maintain that the extent of power granted by the people is to be ascertained, not by the nature and terms of the grant, but by its data." And not only have the powers of government been subjected to this liberalizing construction, the rights of the individual have been similarly treated, with the result of producing what so far has proved to be a thoroughly workable compromise between social convenience and individual security. In this connection the most important clauses are those which forbid the national government and the states alike from "depriving persons of life, liberty, or property without due process of law." Originally "due process of law" had the strictly historical significance of the procedure of the old English common law, especially trial by jury. This construction, however, interposed an insurmountable obstacle in the way of the improvement of the adjective law,[2] and today it has been abandoned. Due process of law today means "reasonable law" or "upon reasonable justification"—a matter finally determined by the Supreme Court of the United States. In other words, for a fixed and rigid limitation upon governmental power, protective for the most part only of the interests of persons accused in court, has been substituted a pervasive supervising function over all legislative power, which is exercised by the most conservative organ of government in the United States—the Supreme Court of the United States. It is true that this function of the Supreme Court—called judicial review—is not without its disadvantages. However that its extension has contributed substantially to the maintenance of the Constitution in its present form, and essentially without amendment, would not, I believe, be denied by its most convinced critic.

But the brevity of the Constitution has also contributed to its adaptability in yet

{2. Adjective law has been defined as "the aggregate of rules of procedure or practice . . . according to which the substantive law is administered. *Black's Law Dictionary* 62 (4th rev. ed. 1968).}

another way; for another consequence is the discreet silence of the Constitution on a great number of most interesting and important matters, with the result that in the determination of these the political forces of the country, reflecting its social and economic development, have had full sway, so that in this respect the Constitution of 1787 has manifested most of the virtues that have been usually claimed for the unwritten (i.e., the British) constitution. However, before I pass to an illustration of this point I am bound in candor to admit that not all of the reticences of the Constitution have been beneficial. One of them indeed proved tragic, and that was its silence on the question of the so-called right of secession. Were the states of the Union free to leave the Union if they desired to do so? The Constitution did not say; and it took the greatest civil war in history (excepting your own Taiping Rebellion) to determine the question in the negative. Why, then, did the framers of the Constitution avoid so important an issue? The answer is to be found in their essential pragmatism—in their conviction that in the long run the written instrument must bend to persistent social and political forces, and that the permanence or impermanence of the Union rested with these, and could not be guaranteed by any written text, however excellent abstractly. What the framers of the Constitution did not foresee was the divisive power of slavery. Had they done so, they might at least have incorporated into the Constitution provisions that would have prevented it from being warped into a thesis for its own destruction.

At other points the pragmatism of the framers of the Constitution wrought more happily, and particularly was this so on certain questions of the relation of the three departments. For instance, may be taken the question of the control of the power of removal. With the first Congress of the United States the problem came up for discussion and action. Three divergent views were urged with almost equal cogency. By one view the power ought to belong to the President and the Senate; by another it ought to belong to the President alone; by a third, it ought to be at the disposal of Congress. In effect, Congress accepted the second view, and two years ago—137 years after the debate just referred to—we were informed by the Supreme Court that this was the view contemplated by the Constitution from the outset. In so speaking the Court sought, though not with entire success, to ratify the results of political development. Somewhat similar has been the outcome of the struggle, renewed from time to time between Congress and the President, or between the President and the Senate, over the right to direct American foreign relations. In this field, too, notwithstanding some conspicuous reversals (e.g., that of President Wilson in 1919) the net result has been the aggrandizement of presidential authority; and this result too had been anticipated from an early date. For as a {*sic;* the?} *Federalist* remarks, secrecy, knowledge, and dispatch are essential to the successful conduct of diplomacy, and these qualities are to be found in the executive branch to a far greater extent than in the others. At the same time, both the Senate and Congress as an entirety, possess powers in the exercise of which they are often able to influence the course of foreign policy very materially. An even more remarkable example of self-denial on the part of the framers of the Constitution in deference to the preferences of posterity is afforded in the matter of judicial review, or the power of the courts, and ultimately of the Supreme Court of the United States, to pass upon the constitutionality of acts of the Congress. On general principle, the framers were of opinion for the most part that the Supreme Court would have this power, yet they did not incorporate any clause in the Constitution for the precise purpose of putting the matter beyond debate. The question was settled by decision of the Court itself, and by the acquiescence of public opinion. Today the Supreme Court sets aside acts of Congress which collide with its interpretation of the Constitution, without ever provoking pause-worthy criticism of its right to do so, even though its view of the Constitution may be sharply assailed. On the other hand, since the size of the Supreme Court is a matter for Congress to determine, the latter body is able at any time to "swamp" an adverse majority of the Court; that it has never exercised this power except on one doubtful occasion, seems again to prove that the development which the Constitution has taken in this most important matter was in response to prevalent and persistent forces. And to the same effect is the evidence afforded by state constitutional history. Since judicial review was established in the national constitution by judicial decision, scores of state constitutions have been enacted, and {there is?} not one of them that has not incorporated judicial review for state purposes.

III.

The Convention that framed the Constitution of the United States in 1787 was not enamoured of "democracy." Indeed, one of the sentiments most frequently voiced on the floor of the Convention was that the country was suffering from "excesses of democracy" in states, and that unless some remedy could be found for these, the republican form of government must soon disappear from America, and so be lost to the world. "Make democracy safe for the world" was the motto of this famous body, presided over by George Washington, and attended by Benjamin Franklin. In the face of all this, the hospitality manifested by the Constitution to the rising forces of democracy becomes very striking, and is perhaps the best proof we have of the disinclination of the Convention to mortgage the future. In the first place, the state governments were still left in the possession of vast powers; in the second place, they were wrought directly into the new structure at various points—most conspicuously in the choice of senators and presidential electors; again the Convention voted down every motion looking to the imposing of property qualifications for the suffrage or for officeholding. The question of suffrage, in fact, was relegated to the states themselves. Anyone who had the right to vote under the state laws was also to have the right to vote for members of Congress. The development of democracy in the new system was thus made dependent on its advancement in the states. The attitude assumed toward the rising West was similarly liberal. Some members were for putting the new states which it was foreseen would soon be admitted into the Union from this region at a disadvantage in relation to the original members of the Union, but all such efforts were rejected in favor of the principle of equal treatment. The Constitution was to be the home roof of all the commonwealths new and old, Western and Eastern alike—there were to be no Cinderellas at that hearthstone.

Yet democracy and its attendant localism did not go altogether unchecked. The Constitution, as Woodrow Wilson has put it, was the work of "men whose interests transcended state lines." But the great mass of the people were small farmers, tied to the soil, and without social experience. The state governments under their control had shown themselves hostile to an effective national government, to the developing interstate commerce, to national good faith toward other nations, and to all property rights but those of the small farmers. This narrow localism in fact was the cause of the Convention, and furnished it with its major problem. Consequently, the Constitution not only enlarged the powers of the national government, but it laid corresponding restraints on the state governments. It also, by the creation of a national executive and a national judicial system, rendered the national government independent of the state governments for administrative purposes. A new type of federal system was thus brought into existence—one directly operative for its assigned purposes upon all persons and things within its territorial limits—in short, a true government. Lastly, restraints were laid upon the state governments in favor of the rights of property and contract, and these were greatly enlarged in 1868 by the adoption of the Fourteenth Amendment. So without checking in any way the development of political democracy, the Constitution brought within its protecting folds the great developing private interests of credit and commerce, with the result that at one stroke it captured the support of wealth. And in the long run democracy itself has benefited, for democracy cannot function effectively except on the basis of a widespread material prosperity.

Another cause, therefore, for the success of the Constitution as evinced by its survival is its success in affording shelter to so many and such important social forces and interests, and especially its success in balancing the often temporarily opposed interests of numbers and property. The Convention recognized that whether for good or ill, democracy had become the political faith of the American people, and so avoided the fatal error of attempting to stem the unopposable rising tide. But they did contrive sluiceways for it; henceforth not every casual surge was to overwhelm the painfully earned rights of economic respectability. So by one and the same device, democracy was given a new and vastly enlarged theater in which to operate, and the elements of society which most distrusted democracy, and with most justification, were given assurance against its excesses.

It is for this reason above all others that the Constitution became the rallying point of all classes and interests from the beginning.

IV.

The durability and adaptability of the Constitution have been often assigned to its supposed utilization of institutions of more ancient date—institutions tested by the practice of the race and adapted to its habits and aptitudes. When Mr. Gladstone many years ago characterized the Constitution as "the most wonderful instrument ever struck off at a given time by the brain and purpose of man," his complimentary attribution of spontaneous creative power to the America of 1787 evolved a veritable storm of adverse criticism, especially on the part of students of history. Whole volumes were written showing in detail how every feature of the Constitution was borrowed from some or other source, either English or colonial. The very merit of the Constitution, it was contended, was its *lack of* originality; the very merit of its framers their assiduity as copyists of what actual practice had shown to be workable. There was an important truth back of such criticism, but it was badly formulated, and was carried to an extreme. There are very few totally original things under the sun, as Solomon, and others since (and by hypothesis, before him, too) have frequently remarked. In the field of mechanics there are said to be but five (or is it seven) "principles," of one or more of which every machine must be a combination or application; in the field of politics it is perhaps somewhat the same. So as things go in this imitative world, in which even history repeats itself, the so-called "new" must almost inevitably consist of recognizable elements. As Dean Pound has put it, "save as an act of Omnipotence, creation does not mean making something out of nothing, but rather the reshaping of existing materials to new uses." Regarded from this point of view the outstanding features of the government established by the Constitution of 1787 were original constructions embodying ideas as yet untested in the political practice of the American people, though juxtaposed upon institutions that had been so tested. I would instance particularly in this connection the presidency, the Senate, judicial review, and above all the federal system itself. Nor would the framers have resented the charge of innovation. These men were eighteenth-century rationalists and participants in the greatest age of political innovation that the world has ever witnessed. They believed that reason and knowledge could often be applied to the improvement of institutions, and they believed that for the first time in human history men possessed a real political science which was susceptible of such application. The point of view of Mr. Gladstone's critics was very different. They were students of Darwin and the classical political economy. They believed in improvement, it is true, but an improvement in which human effort could play little part. "Evolution" by the slow accumulation of slight increments and laissez-faire submission to "economic laws'' comprehended their cosmogony, and they were highly distrustful of anything like cataclysm, miracle, or special creation. Furnished with this outlook, they regarded the British constitution as embodying a superlative political wisdom because, forsooth, it embodied no wisdom at all, being a "growth"; and they thought it a patriotic service, nothing less, to follow Sir Henry Maine in regarding the American Constitution as simply "the British constitution reduced to written form; but with monarchy left out."

But while their Darwinian prepossessions blinded them to its true nature, Mr. Gladstone's critics did have a case, and it is important in connection with our present subject to discover what this was. Mr. Gladstone spoke of the Constitution as "being struck off at a given time." The mental image called up is of a committee engaged in a literary composition and under compulsion to take account of nothing but their own ideas of the fitness of things. In fact the Constitution of the United States was very slowly elaborated after weeks of debate, in which the sharp clash of opposed interests evoked compromise after compromise; a debate, which, moreover, was constantly conducted under the shadow of the menace that if the impracticable was attempted, all the work done would be for nought. The fact of the matter is that the Convention of 1787 had no yearning for a utopia. They regarded the country as suffering rather from too much of that sort of thing. Their objective was a limited remedial one. The existing system centering in the state constitutions had proved defective, and so must be corrected. But there was little suggestion that the existing system should be scrapped—rather it must be amended and supplemented. So the national government was *added to the state governments, but did not supersede them;* on the contrary, at various points, as we have seen, it directly utilized them. And as the continuity between the old system and the new was not seriously interrupted, the latter did not suddenly foist an impossible burden upon the political immaturity and inexperience of the American people. Here, indeed, we discover the essential truth adumbrated by Mr. Gladstone's Darwinian critics.

V.

The reasons for the success or failure of a constitution will be apt to involve factors extrinsic to such constitution, factors over which its framers had, from the nature of the case, no control. Contemporaneously with the United States, Poland established a new constitution. Its very merits so alarmed Poland's neighbors that she was crushed, and blotted for the time being from the map of nations. But while misfortunes from without, may, with a propitious Heaven, be avoided, those arising from the intrinsic defects of an institution cannot be. So far as the success and survival of the Constitution of 1787 are ascribable to its own merits, they may be set down as due to the qualities I have mentioned. The objectives of the Convention of 1787 were not dictated by an abstract utopianism, but by a careful analysis of the causes of the deficiencies of existing institutions when judged by the obvious requirements of serviceable government. Its methods of meeting these objectives *were* in a measure dictated by more or less speculative considerations, in the application of which, nonetheless, concrete interests and existing conditions were correlated at every turn. The Constitution is an exceedingly brief document, and is couched in terms of great plasticity. It has consequently proved readily adaptable to changing conditions. Furthermore, the Convention did not put all its money on one horse, or all its eggs in one basket. It was a body in which a wide range of conflicting interests were represented, and the Constitution, in consequence, gives shelter to a wide range of interests finding a common advantage in the maintenance of the peace thus established. But the outstanding success of the Constitution was twofold; first, its utilization of existing and familiar institutions even while improving them; secondly, its quite paradoxical success in enlarging the field of operation of political democracy, while curbing its excesses, in favor of property, commerce, and business—in other words, individual enterprise.

The Constitution has survived by the support of the interests which it supports, and especially those of political democracy and of property.

It may seem to some a futile proceeding to suggest a comparison between the task confronting China today, and that which confronted the American people in 1787. But along with the obvious differences between the two situations, there are also some pause-worthy similarities. Let me point out some of these. Both countries had just overthrown a detested foreign domination; both were essentially democratic in social structure; both had a largely homogeneous population, largely agricultural in character and undivided by religious differences; both had a national literature, and (to a great extent) a national language; both were large territorial states and without adequate transportational facilities; both had a powerful tradition of local self-government; and both were faced by the exigent task of unification to escape foreign control. Regarded as contemporaries, the great difference between America in 1787 and China in 1929 is the predominance of family institutions in the latter, and the supporting system of ethics. Chinese political construction will be successful in proportion as it is successful in building on the family, and at the same time modifying its antipolitical characteristics. This will not be the achievement of a day. For the rest, the difference between the China of 1929 and the United States of 1787 is largely the product of modern science, is, in other words, the product of the years since 1787.

There is therefore, no extravagance in drawing your attention to some features of the Constitution of 1787 and its development. I only ask pardon for the tone of encomium that I may seem to have adopted in this paper. That was forced upon me from the very nature of my subject. I wished to call attention to the causes of the survival of the Constitution of 1787—not to defects *despite* which it has survived. Cubits cannot be added to the political stature of a nation by some of its members taking thought of the morrow—many morrows must be thought of and lived through before desire can be attained. And furthermore, if new cubits are to count, they must be *added* to the existing stature. The Constitution of the United States embodied novel features, but it built upon existing institutions to a great extent; and it did not make any strikingly novel requirements of existing political experience.

6. The Constitution as Instrument and as Symbol

On an early page of his celebrated *Constitutional Limitations*, Judge Cooley defines "constitution" in the following curt terms: "That body of rules and maxims in accordance with which the powers of sovereignty are habitually exercised." Returning later to the subject, he quotes with approval a more elaborate conception, couched in these words.

> What is a constitution, and what are its objects? It is easier to tell what it is not than what it is. *It is not the beginning of a community, nor the origin of private rights; it is not the fountain of law, nor the incipient state of government; it is not the cause, but consequence, of personal and political freedom; it grants no rights to the people,* but is the creature of their power, the instrument of their convenience. *Designed for their protection in the enjoyment of the rights and powers which they possessed before the constitution was made, it is* but the framework of the political government, and *necessarily based upon the pre-existing condition of laws, rights, habits, and modes of thought. There is nothing primitive in it, it is all derived from a known source. It presupposes an organized society, law, order, property, personal freedom,* a love of political liberty, and enough of cultivated intelligence to know how to guard it against the encroachments of tyranny. *A written constitution is in every instance a limitation upon the powers of government in the hands of agents;* for there never was a written republican constitution which delegated to functionaries all the latent powers which lie dormant in every nation, and are boundless in extent, and incapable of definition."[1]

The first of these definitions answers to what I mean in this paper by the term "constitutional instrument"; the second approximates, particularly in the pas-

From 30 *American Political Science Review* 1071–1085 (1936). Reprinted by permission.
This paper was read at the Tercentenary Conference of Arts and Sciences at Harvard University, September 1936.

1. Cooley, *Constitutional Limitations* 2, 38 (2d ed. 1871).

sages which I have stressed, what I have in mind when I speak of "constitutional symbol."

To the modern mind, confident in the outlook afforded by science and its achievements, the word "instrument" connotes the future and things needing to be done in the future. It assumes that man is the master of his fate, able to impart a desired shape to things and events. And regarded from this point of view a constitution is *an instrument of popular power—sovereignty,* if you will—*for the achievement of progress.*

American constitutional symbolism looks, on the other hand, to the past and links hands with conceptions which long antedate the rise of science and its belief in a predictable, manageable causation. Its consecration of an *already established order of things* harks back to primitive man's terror of a chaotic universe, and his struggle toward security and significance behind a slowly erected barrier of custom, magic, fetish, tabu. While, therefore, the constitutional instrument exists to energize and canalize *public power,* it is the function of the constitutional symbol to protect and tranquilize *private interest or advantage as against public power,* which is envisaged as inherently suspect, however necessary it may be. What has been the relation of these two conceptions in the case of the Constitution of the United States? To answer this question is the main purpose of this paper.

The aspect of the Constitution of the United States as an instrument of popular government for the achievement of the great ends of government is stamped on its opening words: "We, the people of the United States, in order to form a more perfect union, establish justice, insure domestic tranquillity, provide for the common defense, promote the general welfare, and secure the blessings of liberty to ourselves and our posterity, do ordain and establish this Constitution for the United States of America."

The aspect of the Constitution as symbol and bulwark of a previously achieved order of human rights appears most evidently in the ninth article of the Bill of Rights: "The enumeration in the Constitution of certain rights shall not be construed to deny or disparage others retained by the people." The same idea was expressed by Webster in the following words: "Written constitutions sanctify and confirm great principles, but the latter are prior in existence to the former." Or as Governor Landon put the same idea recently: "The Constitution was not framed to give us anything, but to protect inherent rights already possessed."[2]

That the attitude of the members of the Federal Convention toward their task was predominantly instrumentalist and practical is clear at a glance. They had not gone to Philadelphia merely to ratify the past, Governor Landon to the contrary

2. Speech at Topeka, Kansas, Jan. 29, 1936. {Alfred M. Landon was the unsuccessful Republican candidate for President in 1936.}

notwithstanding, but with *reform* in mind, and specifically the creation of *a strong, effective national government*. Theirs, it must be remembered, was one of the great creative periods in the history of political institutions, and they were thoroughly imbued with the faith of their epoch in the ability of the human reason, working in the light of experience, to divert the unreflective course of events into beneficial channels; and in no respect did they deem man more evidently the master of his destiny than in that of statecraft. Furthermore, most of these men had been reared in the mercantilist tradition, and accordingly regarded governmental intervention in the field of economic activity as one of the chief reasons for the existence of government, while the importance to government in turn of engaging the self-interest of groups and individuals by its active policies was a thing constantly present to their minds. The atmosphere of the Convention was, in fact, almost scandalously secular. Despite the social pre-eminence of the cloth in 1787, not a clergyman was listed among its fifty-five members; and when Franklin suggested that one be recruited to open the meetings with prayer, the proposal was shelved by his obviously embarrassed associates with almost comical celerity. Nor did the Constitution as it came from their hands contain a bill of rights.

And naturally the party which brought the Constitution into existence continued to regard their work pragmatically while they elaborated a working government under it. "You have made a good Constitution," a friend remarked to Gouverneur Morris shortly following the Convention. "That," Morris replied, "depends on how it is construed"; and in his characterization of the Constitution as "an experiment," Hamilton voiced the same pragmatic point of view. The new ship of state was quickly crowded with all the canvas of powers "implied," "resultant," "inherent," that its slender, vibrant phrasing would carry; and it is a significant fact that the constitutional validity of not a single item of the Hamiltonian program was challenged judicially, even in principle, until a generation later.

The constitutional instrument was the work of a limited class, comprising those whose "interests and outlook," as Woodrow Wilson put it, "transcended state lines." The constitutional symbol, on the other hand, *being a symbol,* was the work of the many, a creation of the *mass mind.* Indeed, prevision of the symbolic role of the Constitution is older than the Constitution itself. In the same number of *Common Sense* in which he urged independence, in February 1776, Thomas Paine also urged "a continental conference." He said:

> The conferring members being met, let their business be to frame a continental charter or charter of the united colonies (answering to what is called the Magna Carta of England), fixing the number and manner of choosing members of Congress and members of assembly . . . and drawing the line of business and jurisdiction between them (always remembering that our strength is continental, not provincial) securing freedom and property to all men . . . with such other matters as it is necessary for a charter to contain. But where, say some, is the king of America?

That we may not appear to be defective even in earthly honors, let a day be solemnly set apart for proclaiming the charter; let it be brought forth placed on the divine law, the word of God; let a crown be placed thereon, by which the world may know that so far we approve monarchy that in America the law is king.[3]

That so able a propagandist as Paine proved himself to be should have sensed the popular need for a symbol, as well as the fact, of authority is perhaps not to be wondered at. At any rate, the Constitution had not long been in operation before his prediction was fulfilled most amazingly. The outbreak of the wars of the French Revolution, by enlarging British and continental demand for American products, brought a hazardous prosperity which minds unaccustomed to looking so far afield for causes attributed to the Constitution. Speaking on the floor of the Congress in 1794, Richard Bland Lee declared:

I will only mention the stimulus which agriculture has received. In travelling through various parts of the United States, I find fields a few years ago waste and uncultivated filled with inhabitants and covered with harvests, new habitations reared, contentment in every face, plenty on every board; confidence is restored and every man is safe under his own vine and fig tree, and there is none to make him afraid. To produce this effect was the intent of the Constitution, and it has succeeded.[4]

To be sure, there were skeptics. "It has been usual with declamatory gentlemen," complained sour old Maclay, "in their praises of the present government, to paint the state of the country under the old Congress as if neither wood grew nor water ran in America before the happy adoption of the Constitution."

Such disparagement, discreetly confided to the pages of a private journal, did not stem the course of opinion. Hardly has Holy Writ itself been more eulogized than the constitutional symbol presently came to be. "In the Constitution of the United States," wrote Justice William Johnson in 1823, "—the most wonderful instrument ever drawn by the hand of man—there is a comprehension and precision that is unparalleled; and I can truly say that after spending my life in studying it, I still daily find in it some new excellence."[5] And inevitably the virtues of the framers were imputed to their handiwork, as were its virtues to them. Jefferson, ordinarily no reverent spirit, at first described the Convention as an assemblage of "demigods," though he later reconsidered this appraisal. On the other hand, while Hamilton's cold evaluation of the Constitution as "an experiment" was repeated by Washington in his farewell address eight years later, Jackson in his farewell address in 1837 demurred to this description as no longer suitable. Even in the midst of civil war, when the "experiment" seemed to have failed, it was apostrophized as embodying much more than "calm wisdom

3. 1 Paine, *Political Writings* 45–46 (1837).

4. For this and the quotation in the next paragraph, see Schechter, "The Early History of the Tradition of the Constitution," in 9 *Am. Pol. Sci. Rev.* 707, 720 (1915).

5. Elkisin v. Deliesseline, 8 *Fed. Cas.* 493 (1823).

and lofty patriotism,'' as "providential,'' "God's saving gift,'' "His creative
fiat over a weltering chaos: 'Let a nation be born in a day.' "[6]

But when one says that the Constitution had become "a symbol," one has not
advanced very far, for the question remains, *symbol of what?* Initially the symbol
was, it would seem, hardly more than decorative—the tribute which the American people rendered their own political sagacity for ordaining such a marvelous
Constitution. Yet this symbol of high political achievement became in time a
symbol of distrust of the political process—a symbol of democracy's fear of
democracy. How explain this seeming paradox, and what have been the results?

It is no contradiction of what has been said in preceding paragraphs to point
out that the *original* attitude of the American masses toward the document which
came from the Philadelphia Convention was very far from being one of worship.
The said masses were small farmers with slight social experience and vast social
suspicions, and the latter had been given by the agitation leading to the Revolution a decided antigovernment—and especially an *anticentral-government*—
set. Nor, in fact, was the Constitution, which its former opponents presently vied
with its former champions in praising, altogether the same Constitution as the
one over whose merits they had originally divided. Not only had it now a Bill of
Rights, but what was vastly more important, the authors of the Virginia and
Kentucky Resolutions, squaring the logical circle, had succeeded in affixing to
it, for those who chose to welcome the improvement, a gloss of the extremest
statesrightism. It is true, of course, that Marshall was still to propound from the
bench for more than a third of a century the original conception of the Constitution as the ever adaptable instrument of national needs; yet only, as it were,
academically, and in behalf of statutes for which the Congresses of the period
were enacting few counterparts. The national sovereignty had become in truth,
long before the end of Marshall's chief justiceship, a sovereignty *in vacuo,* in no
small measure.

But certain environmental factors have been, perhaps, even more potent than
intellectual currents in finally affixing to the constitutional symbol its distinctively negative quality. The presence to the eastward of the Atlantic Ocean, with
its fair assurance against hostile invasion, discredited from the outset any plea in
favor of strong government in the name of defense. The presence to the westward
of endless stretches of cheap lands opened to even the humblest members of
society an opportunity for self-assertion on a scale never before approached in the
history of mankind. Lastly, the presence throughout this richest of continents of
vast mineral and other natural resources which public policy, or rather the lack of
it, threw open to private pre-emption with little restriction vested the acquisition
of wealth with a moral and legal sanction of its own. People were content with
the answer that the country was being developed.

It is a commonplace that constitutionalism has worked in this country to

6. Quoted by F. M. Green in 22 *Pubs. of Emory Univ.*, No. 5, at 7 (1936).

impress upon the discussion of public measures a legalistic—not say theological—mould. By a terminology which treats *doctrines* as *facts,* the actualities which should control statesmanship have been too often kept at arm's length, while for the question of the beneficial *use* of the powers of government has been substituted the question of their *existence.* The tendency in question manifested itself at an early date. Said W. H. Crawford in a speech in the Senate in February 1811: "Upon the most thorough examination, I am induced to believe that many of the various constructions given to the Constitution are the result of the belief that it is absolutely perfect. It has become so extremely fashionable to eulogize the Constitution, whether the object of the eulogy is the extension or contraction of the powers of the government, that whenever its eulogium is pronounced, I feel an involuntary apprehension of mischief."[7]

Crawford's words carry the significant suggestion that there were those who looked upon the constitutionality of a measure as a positive quality, a reason by itself for the measure's enactment. Such an attitude is, in truth, a normal phase of the psychology of constitutionalism. What better reason can there be for doing a thing than the right to do it when that was challenged in the first instance? Speaking generally, nevertheless, constitutional debate proceeds characteristically from the point of view of *negation* and treats the constitutional symbol as a source of *tabu;* and the "great constitutional lawyer" is one who knows how to make two constitutional restrictions grow where one grew before. Indeed, it is astonishing the extent to which the taint of constitutional obliquity has always dogged the footsteps of the American people and their representatives. The Constitution itself was unconstitutional by an argument to which Madison felt it necessary to reply in the *Federalist.* Most of Hamilton's legislative program was unconstitutional in the opinion of half of Washington's cabinet. The Louisiana Purchase was unconstitutional in the opinion of the President who accomplished it. The most important measure by which the slavery question was kept in abeyance for years was unconstitutional in the opinion of large numbers of people, and finally in the opinion of the Supreme Court. The Civil War was brought to a successful issue by resorting to measures which two out of three Americans alive at that time would have voted to be unconstitutional; and according to the Democratic *Almanac* of 1866, the Thirteenth Amendment was unconstitutional. And the enumeration might easily be prolonged to include almost every measure of scope and of somewhat novel character that the Congress of the United States has enacted within the last half-century.

Despite all which, it may be remarked of constitutional negativism, as Lord Acton remarked of liberty, that it must have remained impermanent and ineffi-

---

7. 4 {T. H.} Benton, *Abridgment {of the Debates of Congress, from 1789 to 1865}* 266 (1857–1861). See also his further statement (*id.* at 308): "The gentlemen . . . still view it [the Constitution] as a model of perfection. They are certainly at liberty still to entertain that opinion. Every man has a right to erect his idol in this land of liberty, and to fall down and worship it according to the dictates of his conscience."

cient had it not found embodiment in an implementing institution. I refer, of course, to judicial review, and especially to the power of the Court to disallow acts of Congress on the ground of their being in conflict with the Constitution. Recently there has been a renewal of the old debate as to the intentions of the framers in this respect. Neither party, perhaps has quite all the truth on its side. That the framers anticipated some sort of judicial review of acts of Congress there can be little question. But it is equally without question that ideas generally current in 1787 were far from presaging the present vast role of the Court.

Thus, as we saw earlier, constitutional negativism exalts the Bill of Rights as the bulwark of achieved liberties. In the Virginia convention, on the other hand, which ratified the Constitution, Marshall declared of bills of rights that they were "merely recommendatory. Were it otherwise," he continued, ". . . many laws which are found convenient would be unconstitutional." The principle of the separation of powers, too, was originally thought to be "directory only," and hence as not affording a judicially applicable restriction upon legislative power. Again, the Constitution is today assumed to comprise *a closed, a completed system*. Indeed, this assumption is asserted by Cooley to be the underlying basis of judicial review. Yet in the debate on the location of the removal power in the first Congress to assemble under the Constitution the most strongly held theory was that the Constitution did not declare itself on the point, as obviously it does not, and that accordingly Congress was confronted with a *casus omissus* which under the necessary and proper clause it was entitled to supply. And no less paradoxical by modern standards is Chief Justice Marshall's suggestion early in 1805, while the Chase impeachment was pending, that the power of impeachment ought to be surrendered by Congress in return for power to reverse such "opinions" of the Court as Congress found objectionable. In a recent discussion of this episode in the Senate, it was confidently asserted that what Marshall had in mind was an amendment to the Constitution.[8] But quite clearly this was not the case. The situation was an urgent one; Marshall was trembling not only for the safety of the Court but for the safety of his own position. What he evidently had in mind was an *ad hoc* understanding between the two branches, one that would ripen in time into a fixed custom of the Constitution.

The opinion of our senatorial wise men confirms Professor Maitland's statement as to the tendency of the law (that is, of the lawyers) to "antedate the emergence of modern ideas," and it may be added that they sometimes antedate other things too. How account otherwise for that door panel of the new Supreme Court building which pictures—or at least was originally thought to do so—Chief Justice Marshall as handing to Justice Story the former's opinion in Marbury v. Madison, although this opinion was rendered some nine years prior to Story's appointment to the bench;[9] or for the occasionally encountered motif in court-

8. *Cong. Rec.* 10013 (daily ed. June 18, 1936).

9. See Mr. Benjamin Ginsburg's communication to the *Washington Evening Star*, Sept. 15, 1936; also *The New York Times* of July 5, 1936.

room murals of the *signing* of Magna Carta by King John, although John probably could not write, and at any rate the great seal, affixed by the Chancellor, was thought to serve such occasions very adequately. Nor is this to mention Senator Borah's speech last February 22, in which Washington is represented as delivering the farewell address in the new capital named for him some four years before said capital was open for business!

Judicial review of national legislation first disclosed its potentialities seventy years after the framing of the Constitution, in the Dred Scott Case, where it is placed squarely on a symbolic basis. The Constitution, Chief Justice Taney there declares, speaks always "not only with the same words, but with the same intent" as when it came from the framers. Thus is the miracle which is the Constitution of 1787 to be maintained and preserved by the mystery which is judicial power—its clairvoyance into the intentions of men long dead as to things which did not exist when they lived!

And by the same token, if judicial review has conserved the constitutional symbol, the constitutional symbol has conserved judicial review, by screening its operations behind the impersonal mask of the unbiased past. Even today, the notion of the judicial mouthpiece of a self-interpreting, self-enforcing law has its adherents. Listen, for instance, to this defense by a correspondent of *The New York Times* of the decision in the Rice Millers' Case, which awarded some 200 millions of dollars to people most of whom were probably not entitled to it: "For so long as the Constitution of the United States endures in its present form, it must operate with the infallibility of the laws of nature. Sound and fecund growths will be fortified by its influences. Its impact will always strip the fruit from any governmental tree which is too defective to maintain its own integrity. The office of the Supreme Court is simply to elucidate the process."[10]

Coming now to the heart of the problem here under discussion, I propose to point out briefly certain restrictions upon the national legislative power which the Court has from time to time ratified in favor, primarily, of certain minority interests, on the theory that such interests comprised an essential part of a prior order of things which it was a fundamental—*the* fundamental—purpose of the Constitution to put beyond the reach of popular majorities. Viewed from this angle, the constitutional symbol is seen to part company with the constitutional instrument very radically. *The symbol of the many becomes the instrument of the few, and all the better instrument for being such symbol.*

The two minority interests which have left the deepest imprint on our constitutional law, so far as national power is concerned, are slavery and that fairly coherent group of interests which are commonly lumped together as "big business." Slavery was awakened to its situation by the Tariff of 1828. But as no appeal could be taken to the Court with any hope of success so long as Marshall dominated it, Calhoun, reversing his constitutional creed almost overnight,

10. *The New York Times*, May 5, 1936.

fashioned a fantastic substitute from the Virginia and Kentucky Resolutions of thirty years previous; and by the aid of nullification the South was presently able to force a compromise with the adherents of the American system.

Twenty years later the question of slavery in the territories was to the fore, and meantime the menacing possibility had presented itself that the rising forces of antislavery in Congress would attempt to put a stop to the interstate slave trade. Whether by dint of foresighted management or by accident, the slaveholding states had now a majority on the Court, and the drive which culminated nine years later in the Dred Scott decision, to get a judicial determination of the territorial question was launched. But what line ought the Court to take in handling questions of national power affecting slavery? Should it treat slavery as constituting a special case, a sort of enclave, withdrawn by the intention of the framers from the constitutional powers of the national government; or should it construe these powers in such a way as to render them harmless for slavery considered simply as any proprietarian interest? In his opinion in the Passenger Cases, Justice Wayne of Georgia, the strongest nationalist on the Taney bench, suggested the former expedient, but without success. The consequence is that the two doctrines which have proved most restrictive of the powers of Congress in recent years are directly traceable to the Taney Court. The first of these is the doctrine that the Tenth Amendment segregates to the states certain "subjects," "fields," or "interests," and hence forbids Congress to exercise any of its powers, but especially its interstate commerce and taxing powers, with the effect or intention of governing such "subjects," "fields," or "interests." The second is that the due process clause of the Fifth Amendment authorizes the Court to invalidate any act of Congress which it finds to impair property rights "unreasonably." Furthermore, from the defenders of the Dred Scott decision came the doctrine of the "finality" of the Court's interpretations of the Constitution—a doctrine which Lincoln assailed in his first inaugural as transferring to the Court the people's right of self-government.

And it is on these bases, shaky as they are in both logic and history, that the Court has chosen to rest the most outstanding of its recent decisions. There is no need to review these holdings in any detail in order to show their bearing on our subject. The climax is reached when they are considered for their impairment of the constitutional instrument, in the A.A.A. Case {United States v. Butler, 297 U.S. 1 (1936)}, which, when evaluated in the light of Justice Roberts' opinion, appears to assert that Congress may not legitimately employ its granted powers in order to further on a *national* scale any end which the states may legitimately attempt on a *local* scale. Others of these decisions have suddenly thrust into prominence as a restrictive principle the heretofore innocuous and unused doctrine that a legislature may not delegate its power, but without giving that doctrine coherent or understandable form. Still another decision rejects the principle of emergency power on the basis of the equivocal or erroneous assertion that the powers of the national government have proved "adequate" "both in war and peace.'' Still another implies a theory of judicial autonomy in relation to legislative power which represents a *vast* departure from the views of the framers. Lastly, the American Liberty League, whose mission it is to spread the gospel of the Constitution as symbol of the "American way," informs us that the Constitution may be amended "in harmony with its fundamental principles"—that is, may *not* be amended in disharmony therewith. Perhaps it is to be regretted that the judicial history of the Prohibition Amendment contains small assurance of this doctrine ever receiving that acceptance which would round off most conclusively and artistically the triumph of the constitutional symbol over the constitutional instrument.[11]

Considered, in short, from the point of view of the national legislative power, especially in the important fields of taxation and interstate commerce regulation, the Constitution has passed through the following phases; from (1) an instrument of national government, a source of national power, to (2) an object of popular worship, finally valued chiefly for the obstacles it interposed to the national power, to (3) a protection of certain minority interests seeking escape from national power; or, in other words, from constitutional instrument to constitutional fetish, to constitutional tabu, to constitutional instrument again, albeit the *negative* instrument of certain special interests, not the *positive* instrument of a government of the people.[12]

And with what final result for national legislative power? The question is answered admirably by Mr. Irving Brant in his recent *Storm over the Constitution:* "During this later period the United States shifted from a Constitution of *implied powers* under the express powers [of Congress] to a Constitution of *implied limitations* on the express powers. It was virtually the same thing as writing a new, and infinitely narrower, Constitution"[13]—that is, the same thing as permitting the Court to do this.

It would be easy to ascribe this conversion, partial but immensely important, of the constitutional instrument of the many into the constitutional instrument of the few to a conspiracy of the latter; or, to use Sir Thomas More's words, to a "conspiracy of rich men, procuring their own commodities under the title of commonwealth.'' And the truth of the matter is that the effluvia of conspiracy are never altogether absent when authority joins itself to a mystery, such as the Constitution of the United States has to many intents and purposes become today. On the other hand, the propensity of the professional exalter of the constitutional symbol for modern propaganda technique hardly fits the charge, inasmuch as

11. It is doubtless with the Liberty League in mind that Professor Radin wrote recently: "The search for a new capitalist religion in the United States is rapidly taking the form of consecrating patriotic symbols and multiplying rituals which will inevitably be associated with the existing type of economic organization.'' 13 *N.Y.U. Law Quar. Rev.* 505 (1936).

12. In support of the immediately preceding paragraphs, see generally my *Commerce Power versus States' Rights*, published by the Princeton University Press on August 4 last {1936}.

13. Brant, *Storm over the Constitution* 129 (1936).

propaganda—or so we are assured—rarely builds *de novo,* but works upon *existing* beliefs. We may therefore concede that the propagandist against the expansion of national power *thinks* that there is that in the popular mind to which he can appeal successfully; and he may be right. For, as a colleague suggests, we are today in the presence of the reverse of the situation which elicited from Mr. Dooley his famous remark anent the Supreme Court's following the "election returns." The question at present is, Will the election returns follow the Supreme Court?

Certain of the characteristics of popular thinking which go to explain the rise of constitutional negativism, and thereby the implementation of certain minority interests by the Constitution, were adverted to early in this paper. One, however, I have reserved for more special mention in these closing paragraphs; and it is the fundamental premise of economic individualism. I mean the assumption that economic power is *natural* and political power *artificial,* from which the conclusion is drawn that *"arbitrary"* power is characteristically *governmental* power. The latter idea clearly underlies the more significant of the Court's recent decisions. Thus, in the A.A.A. Case the Court held that in requiring agriculturists to sign contracts as a condition of receiving certain payments from the Treasury, the government "coerced" the agriculturists, who "involuntarily" accepted its terms. Yet had Mr. Henry Ford stood in the place of the government in such a transaction, who would ever have thought of using such language about it? Moreover, there are still cases in good standing which hold that a laborer is not coerced when confronted by his employer with the alternative of giving up his job or quitting his union, although it *is* coercion for government to forbid the employers to do this! Likewise, in the Alton case {Alton Ry. Co. v. Illinois Comm., 305 U.S. 548 (1939)} the Court holds that for Congress to require a carrier to pension a superannuated employee is to deprive the carrier of liberty and property without due process of law, the "liberty" in question being the carrier's right to dismiss a superannuated employee without pensioning him.

The unreality of such thinking is hardly travestied in the following passage from Professor Arnold's witty little volume, *The Symbols of Government:* "If the American people were actually free from countless petty restrictions, it is not likely that they would build a mansion in the judicial heavens dedicated to the principle, before which we make such curious sacrifices, that there should be no such restrictions. If we were not so constantly subject to arbitrary and uncontrolled power over our very means of existence, we would not require the dramatization of the abstract ideal that no such power could exist in America, provided that the case could be properly presented to the Supreme Court of the United States. The only absolute essential of a heaven is that it be different from the everyday world."[14]

The American people are today moving rapidly toward a constitutional crisis

14. T. Arnold, *Symbols of Government* 224 (1935).

of unpredictable gravity, a crisis due chiefly to the Court's endeavor to put "big business" and its methods—the "American way"—out of reach of effective government. Thanks to the Court's excessive preoccupation with this problem, the question has even been raised whether the entire system of constitutional limitations, judicially implemented, is not incompatible with popular government. Personally, I am not convinced that this is so; but I do think that if the dilemma suggested is to be avoided, short of formal constitutional change, the Court will have to enlarge some of its conceptions, and especially will it have to enlarge its conception of public power *to include economic power*. For when this is done certain other important truths will also emerge. It will be seen that most people have to take orders from some source or other, and that therefore the problem of human liberty is not to be completely solved by the purely negative device of setting acts of Congress aside as contrary to the Constitution. Also recognition will dawn that there is no reason underlying the nature of things why acts or procedures which are regarded as unjust when they are resorted to by government are necessarily more defensible when resorted to by business management. Lastly, it will appear that unless we are to resign ourselves to economic autocracy, governmental power must be as little embarrassed by boundary lines as is economic power.

All this, however, I am conscious, is somewhat negative; and I would conclude on an affirmative note. I find it to hand in a passage from Señor Ortega's *Revolt of the Masses:* "The state is always, whatever be its form—primitive, ancient, medieval, modern—an invitation issued by one group of men to other human groups to carry out some enterprise in common. That enterprise, be its intermediate processes what they may, consists in the long run in the organization of a certain type of common life. State and plan of existence, program of human activity or conduct, these are inseparable terms." And he elsewhere adds: "When there is a stoppage of that impulse toward something further on, the state automatically succumbs . . . breaks up, is dispersed."[15]

Revision of the constitutional symbol there must be, I submit, to bring it into conformity with the constitutional instrument, regarded as the instrument of a people's government and of a unified nation which has not yet lost faith in its political destiny.

15. J. Ortega y Gasset, *Revolt of the Masses* 176, 183 (1932).

7. The Impact of the Idea of Evolution on the American Political and Constitutional Tradition

THE warp and woof of classical American political theory are seventeenth-century English political theory and the political thought of the eighteenth-century Enlightenment. The central motive of the resulting pattern, implicit even when not explicit, is supplied by the notion that man is a creature of reason, and that to this creature had been vouchsafed a revelation—by ratiocination, of course—of certain *final* political and social values. What these were is authoritatively stated in the famous second paragraph of the Declaration of Independence: "We hold these truths to be self-evident—that all men are *created* equal; that they are endowed by their Creator with certain *un*alienable rights; that among these are life, liberty, and the pursuit of happiness. That, to secure these rights, governments are instituted among men, deriving their just powers from the consent of the governed. . . ."

In the Constitution the word of the Declaration was made flesh—a too fleshly flesh, some have thought, inasmuch as the Constitution betrays considerable solicitude for the rights of property, which the Declaration does not mention. To compensate, on the other hand, for this concern for property, the quite negative conception of "consent of the governed" of the Declaration becomes in the Preamble of the Constitution positive and creative: "We, the people of the United States" not merely "consent" to a pre-established order, we "ordain and establish" one of our own devising.

Moreover, the Constitution of the United States was deemed by its framers to embody certain permanent principles of correct constitutional structure, a matter not touched upon by the Declaration. After invoking the eternal verities just recited in justification of the Revolution against Great Britain, the American

From "The Impact of the Idea of Evolution on the American Political and Constitutional Tradition," in S. Persons, ed., *Evolutionary Thought in America* (Yale University Press, 1950), 182–99. Reprinted by permission.

180

people next proceeded to erect a governmental system capable of giving permanent effect to these—an act of unexampled self-confidence, which sprang from the belief of that generation that it possessed a matured and perfected political science such as the world had never up to that time been blessed with.

Thus Alexander Hamilton wrote in the *Federalist, no.* 9:

> The science of politics, however, like most other sciences, has received great improvement. The efficacy of various principles is now well understood, which were either not known at all, or imperfectly known to the ancients. The regular distribution of power into distinct departments; the introduction of legislative balances and checks; the institution of courts composed of judges, holding their offices during good behaviour; the representation of the people in the legislature by deputies of their own election; these are wholly new discoveries, or have made their principal progress toward perfection in modern times. They are means, and powerful means, by which the excellencies of republican government may be retained and its imperfections lessened or avoided. To this catalogue of circumstances, that tend to the amelioration of popular systems of civil government, I shall . . . add one more . . . ; I mean the *enlargement of the orbit* within which such systems are to revolve.[1]

By its framers and by the generation which received it, the Constitution was regarded, and justly so, as marking the climax of a great, even though brief, period of original political creation. In the words of Lord Acton, the Constitution of 1787 "resembled no other Constitution, for it was contained in half a dozen intelligible articles"; indeed, outside of America, written constitutions did not yet exist. The idea of putting legal restraints upon government in the interest of private rights, while of respectable antiquity, had never before received embodiment in implementing institutions. Even in the early state constitutions the principle of the separation of powers was mere literary theory. Only in Massachusetts and New Hampshire did the executive veto exist even as late as 1787; and although judicial review had been asserted in a few dicta of state courts and in one or two decisions, it was still, when the Federal Convention assembled, the rawest sort of raw idea, unillumined by any practical experience in its operation. In the Constitution of 1789 the executive veto and judicial review are pivotal institutions.

Even more noteworthy was the work of the Convention in adjusting the relations of the states and the nation. There had been confederacies before—the past indeed was strewn with the wreckage of them—but no earlier confederacy had possessed a central government which operated directly upon *individuals* rather than indirectly through the governments of its corporate members and yet without sacrifice of the principle of local autonomy. Lastly, the method by which the Constitution was adopted employed the principle of popular sovereignty on a

---

1. George Washington listed in his will as one of the advantages to be anticipated from a national university the acquiring by those who studied there of "knowledge in the principles of politics and government." See also my *Court over Constitution* 220–25 (1938), for other similar statements of the period.

previously unparalleled scale. For the first time in history the right of revolution appeared as the more positive right of the citizens of a great national community, acting through bodies chosen for the specific purpose, to remodel their political institutions.

The final element of American political thinking is at core a fact rather than an idea—a physical presence rather than an intellectual conviction. I mean the frontier, a term which I use to symbolize those conditions of escape from ancient, inherited controls in which the American adventure was initially cast. The significant fact about these conditions was that they furnished a perpetual reminder and authentication of the possibility of environmental change not only without loss, but with positive betterment—in short, of the idea of *progress*. In the influence of the frontier and in the American talent for mechanical invention, which now and then spilled over into the political field, we encounter those factors of early American social life which most sharply challenged the static premises of classical American political thought and institutional devising, and which offered from the outset a handle to the dynamic presuppositions of the conception of evolution. Thus we come to our question: What has been, to date, the impact of evolutionary ideas on the American political and constitutional tradition?

A subordinate question at once arises; Whose conception of evolution are we talking about? Three lines of thought have to be taken account of in answering this question: (a) Spencerian evolutionism; (b) the Darwinian theory of biological descent; (c) modern "pragmatism" or "instrumentalism." But I propose to devote some passing attention also to a fourth line of thought, which, while not the product of evolutionism, has indubitably contributed to the latter's impact upon the American tradition—I mean the Marxian doctrine of *class struggle*— which, besides being a sort of specialized version of the general notion of the struggle for existence, has indirectly contributed to American reformism looking to the economic betterment of the masses.

The brand of the doctrine of evolution to which any considerable part of the American public first inclined a respectful ear was that of Herbert Spencer. This was owing in the first place to the *odium theologicum* which stigmatized the Darwinian doctrine of *biological evolution* on account of its challenge to the notion of special creation and especially its demotion of man from the kingdom of Heaven to the animal kingdom—from the status of fallen angel to the status of mere creature.[2] More than that, the early Darwinians, including Darwin himself, horrified many people by picturing nature as "red in tooth and claw." Even Darwin's great apostle to the Gentiles, Huxley, admitted this, and drew from it

---

2. Some of my readers may recall Tenniel's famous cartoon in *Punch* which was suggested by Disraeli's declaration when the controversy was at its height that he "took his stand with the angels." "Dizzy" as an angel was no very ingratiating spectacle. A later reminder of the same controversy occurred in connection with the late William Jennings Bryan's visit to Princeton in the early twenties. Seeing the eminent biologist Professor Edwin Grant Conklin in his audience, Mr. Bryan proclaimed with emphasis, "Professor Conklin can't make a monkey out of me," to which Professor Conklin replied *sotto voce* to a companion, "It's either monkey or mud!"

the conclusion that the course of biological evolution and that of social or ethical evolution were diametrically opposed, which meant, in effect, that Darwinism had no relevance to social purposes.

Spencer avoided both of these difficulties. His doctrine of the "Unknowable," by making the existence of Deity and its attributes and potencies articles purely of religious faith, gave leave and license to all and sundry to believe in evolution on weekdays and in the first chapter of Genesis on the Sabbath. Nor, in fact, was Spencer specially interested in biological evolution. He speaks, to be sure, of "the struggle for existence," but its outcome was preordained in "the survival of the fittest," whereas Darwin's fittest survivors were obviously fittest only for a particular environment, which might well be a very debased environment from the point of view of human values. While, therefore, evolution might with Darwin actually spell *retrogression*, with Spencer it was quite otherwise.

In short, Spencer's generalized theory of evolution explained *everything*—it was universal. Furthermore, it was a resolutely optimistic theory, whereas Darwin did not profess to pass on ethical or social issues. A great god called Evolution had the universe, at least the habitable part of it, in its grip and was hurrying it toward some far off divine event, willy-nilly. The idea appealed especially to the view that Americans took of their own destiny, and they were too generous a people to resent the discovery that other peoples might have destinies as well as they.

Again Spencer appealed to American individualism; indeed, for a time he virtually took over the American doctrine of rights *versus* the state. Just how Spencer contrived to reconcile the doctrine of evolution with that of natural rights and the utopianism which underlies the latter, would be much too long a story to set forth here. Professor Ernest Barker thinks Spencer failed in his attempt to square the circle, but I am not so sure. Concede Spencer his premises and he is generally fairly logical. Unfortunately, facts were always cropping up to disturb his logic. Hence Huxley's quip, that Spencer's "idea of a tragedy was a beautiful theory killed by an ugly fact."

But at the outset—in the late seventies and early eighties—Spencer seemed to have the facts on his side, and especially in the field in which he was keenest to see evolution get forward with its good work, the industrial field. For here his teaching seemed to be verified by the contemporary teachings of the Manchester school of political economy generally taught at this time in American universities. And the sum and substance of this teaching was that the state, a regrettable residue from feudal militarism, should carefully refrain from action which was calculated to interfere with the struggle for existence in the industrial field.

So Spencer became a sort of tutelary genius to rising big business in the United States and the accepted philosopher of the most influential class in the American community. Nor did his exponents—John Fiske and Professor William Graham Sumner of Yale pre-eminent among them—have long to wait before the Supreme Court at Washington, responding to the guidance of the foremost lawyers of the period, began translating the Manchester-Spencerian doctrine into terms of American constitutional law—the concept of "dual federalism," the doctrine of the separation of powers, the doctrine of due process of law, and others.[3]

Thus was the circle rounded out. The truths of evolution and the eternal verities of the American constitutional system were, it turned out, just different facets of the same thing—or in other words, the initial impact of evolution on the American ideological tradition was to *confirm* the notion of liberty *versus* government, and especially that phase of liberty in which men of property were most particularly interested, the liberty to drive advantageous bargains with labor— what the court of the day baptized "freedom of contract."

Finally, mention should be made of the missionary work for Spencer of John Fiske and Edward Youmans, editor of *Popular Science Monthly,* and especially of the former, who in his *Cosmic Philosophy* popularized the Spencerian sociology, with some improvements of his own, and gave it a decidedly theological cast, as in his little book, *Through Nature to God.* Evolution became a new religion, something for which the American people have always evinced a pronounced tenderness.[4]

Spencer's influence is today extinct. No intellectually respectable person would wish to be caught in the company of the "synthetic philosophy," or— since Professor Giddings and Professor Sumner, both men of great intellectual distinction, passed from the scene—in the company of the Spencerian sociology. It is true that there is still a social science which calls itself "sociology," but it is a very different affair from the Spencerian product. It is no longer greatly intrigued by the general notion of evolution. Indeed, it is often more than a little doubtful as to progress—at least, there is no progress without conscious and planned effort. It, therefore, studies specific situations, and is especially interested in questions of *environment,* "ecology," "demography," social statistics, and the like. This sociology owes little to Spencer except the idea that society, or "social groupings," are something of a definite, tangible nature enough to be made subjects of "scientific" investigation. In brief, sociology today owes most of its problems and procedures to Darwinian ideas rather than to Spencerian. Why is this?

For one thing, Spencer had given the idea of evolution favorable advertise-

3. The story is well told in Twiss's *Lawyers and the Constitution, How Laissez Faire Came to the Supreme Court* (1942). At about the time the Supreme Court was beginning its work of "translation," Sir Henry Maine was writing in his *Popular Government* 51 (1886): "There has hardly ever before been a community in which the weak have been pushed so pitilessly to the wall, in which those who have succeeded have so uniformly been the strong, and in which in so short a time there has arisen so great an inequality of private fortune and domestic luxury. And at the same time, there has never been a country in which, on the whole, the persons distanced in the race have suffered so little from their ill-success."

4. The theological tinge appears, for example, in Woodrow Wilson's Denver address of Sunday, May 7, 1911, where the idea that progress was inevitable and had the backing of God was proclaimed. 2 *Public Papers* 291–302 (1925–1927).

ment; at least, the expression no longer shocked religious sensibilities unduly. That much at least had Spencer done for Darwin. And meantime Darwin was winning out with the scientists, was becoming intellectually respectable. Eventually he was to be intellectual tops with those who knew, and that helped with the generality, even though the Darwinian thesis was, in its strictly scientific aspect, a comparatively narrow one.

And with the rise of Darwin's prestige in scientific circles, liberal-minded theologians began to cast favorable glances in his direction. Reinterpretations of the first chapter of Genesis began to pour from both pulpit and press, and sometimes the reinterpreters, as in the case of Professor Patrick Macloskie of Princeton, went on to show, at least to their own satisfaction, that the whale's exploit in swallowing Jonah and giving him shelter for three days and nights was feasible biologically and hence scientifically credible.[5]

Darwinism presently gave evidence, moreover, of being itself amenable to the evolutionary process; especially did the "red in tooth and claw" feature of the theory, which had caused Huxley to rule out the notion of Social Darwinism, undergo revision. Thus as early as 1872 Walter Bagehot advanced the notion in his brilliant volume *Physics and Politics* that the triumph of certain societies over others was to be accounted for in earliest times by their superior social coherence, i.e., by the suppression among their members of the struggle for existence; and thirty years later Peter Kropotkin brought out his *Mutual Aid as a Factor in Evolution,* which pointed out the importance of group cooperation as a factor of survival among certain of the lower species. At about the same time, Charles Horton Cooley, in his delightful volume *Human Nature and the Social Order,* which was published in 1902, reduced to absurdity the notion that self-reliant individualism was the fine fruit of evolution by pointing to the gorilla as the one perfect individualist. Human nature as distinct from animalism, Cooley proceeded to argue on the basis of observations he had made of his own children, was the product of social living, not of individual competition.

More important, however, for the purposes of this discussion was the suggestion presently put forth, that so far as civilized societies are concerned, the struggle for existence is not predominantly a struggle between individuals, as Spencer liked to imagine, *but a struggle with environment,* from which it followed that the prerequisite to social improvement was *improvement of social environment*—an idea which was confirmed for Americans in the history of the frontier.

But by what means, through what agencies, was environment to be improved? One means, obviously, was science, whose "conquest of nature," as it was termed, lay at the basis of the vast increase of social wealth since the Middle

---

5. President McCosh of Princeton, although he is said not to have relished Professor Macloskie's *tour de force,* contemporaneously revived in evolution's defense St. Thomas Aquinas' axiom that "truth is one." But whereas St. Thomas applied the axiom to subordinate reason to revelation, Dr. McCosh put revelation on the defensive vis-à-vis the truths of science.

Ages. Unfortunately, however, this increase in social wealth was not equitably distributed throughout society. So another agency, too, must be brought into operation, viz., government, which thanks to the spread of democratic ideas and institutions, had become adapted to precisely this task. *Darwinian evolutionism, translated into social terms, became reformism.*

One of the first voices to be raised in this behalf in the United States was, fittingly enough, that of the sociologist, government bureaucrat, and paleobotanist, Lester F. Ward, who in 1883 published his large two-volume work, *Dynamic Sociology.* This was at once a systematic attack on the negativism of Spencer's *Social Statics* and a positive demand for governmental intervention in the economic field. Asserting that, quite contrary to the assumptions of the Spencerian laissez-faire school, social control had been gradually expanding throughout the history of civilization, Ward continued:

> For more than a century the English school of negative economists has devoted itself to the task of checking this advance. The laissez-faire school has entrenched itself behind the fortifications of science, and while declaring with truth that social phenomena are, like physical phenomena, uniform and governed by laws, they have accompanied this by the false declaration and *non sequitur* that neither physical nor social phenomena are capable of human control; the fact being that all the practical benefits of science are the result of man's control of natural forces and phenomena which would otherwise have run to waste or operated as enemies to human progress. The opposing positive school of economists simply demands an opportunity to utilize the social forces for human advantage in precisely the same manner as the physical forces have been utilized. It is only through the artificial control of natural phenomena that science is made to minister to human needs; and if social laws are really analogous to physical laws, there is no reason why social science may not receive practical applications such as have been given to physical science.[6]

Ward, it turned out, had no monopoly of such ideas. In September 1885, the American Economic Association was founded at Saratoga, New York. Many of its outstanding members, most of whom were comparatively young men, had gone to Germany for their postgraduate work, and had been witnesses to Bismarck's experiments in state socialism, which constituted the German Reich's answer to Marxian socialism. In the new association's declaration of principles the following statement stood out as a challenge to Spencerian evolutionism and Manchester laissez faire-ism: "We regard the state as an agency whose positive assistance is one of the indispensable conditions of human progress."[7]

Four years later David G. Ritchie reiterated to the British public the same challenge to Spencerism in his *Darwinism and Politics;* and in 1907—to omit mention of others—Professor Simon N. Patten of the University of Pennsyl-

6. *Glimpses of the Cosmos* 352, quoted by Hofstadter, *Social Darwinism in American Thought* 57 (1944). It should be observed that Professor Hofstadter uses the expression Social Darwinism to cover Spencerian evolutionism, whereas I distinguish the two.

7. Hofstadter at 125. The notion that man's shortcomings are not grounded in his own nature but arise from external and remediable conditions stems, of course, from Rousseau.

vania, succeeded, in his *New Basis of Civilization,* in anticipating the "economy of abundance" theorists of the Coolidge era by more than two decades. Asserting that the world's food supply could easily be doubled, Patten went on to contend that among humans the prime factor of improvement was nurture, not nature. There is no inherent difference, he declared, between rich and poor; and "nature will care for progress if men will care for reform."[8]

Thus we are confronted with two interpretations of evolution for social application: the Spencerian, laissez-faire interpretation and the reformist interpretation. Which one was best warranted by the Darwinian doctrine of biological evolution? Inasmuch as Darwin centers his attention upon the struggle for existence among *creatures* and treats the environment in which this struggle takes place either as relatively inert or as changing in response to factors beyond human control, the answer must undoubtedly be in favor of the Spencerian interpretation.

Furthermore, as Darwin himself admits, his attention was originally drawn to the general problem of the struggle for existence by Thomas Malthus' famous *Essay on the Principle of Population,* which was conceived in part as an attack on the younger Pitt's effort through the Poor Law of 1796 to apply governmental relief to the poverty and distress resulting from the emergence of industrialism and the breakdown of feudal society in England. Malthus' contention was, briefly, that humans breed at a geometric ratio, while food supply increases merely at an arithmetical ratio—or more shortly, that population increases always outrun food supply. Nor were remedial measures ever long effective, since any measure of betterment was bound to operate as a stimulus to further breeding. Poverty, in short, was an ineradicable condition of society—a social fate. In a revision of his work Malthus admitted the possibility of moral checks on population increase, a position no more encouraging to the cause of economic reform through governmental action than his original position had been.

Taking, then, this doctrine as his point of departure, Darwin saw all creatures engaged in a struggle for existence, which only those individuals which were best adapted to a particular environment survived to establish new species. From these general premises the laissez-faire conclusion of "everyone for himself, and the devil take the hindmost" was perfectly logical if not inevitable. Yet since it was apparent that civilization had advanced, it also followed that the struggle for existence, severely as it bore on particular individuals, had in social terms proved beneficial. At least only a few aesthetes disputed this conclusion at the time.

The transmutation of Darwinism into a gospel of social reform required a complete reversal of the formula of adaptation of creature to environment. In the case of the human creature only the eugenists have ever thought to effect any radical improvements on Darwinian premises. So the formula had to be read backward—instead of the creature being adapted to the environment, *the envi-*

8. Curti, *The Growth of American Thought* 578 (1943).

ronment had to be adapted to the creature. But how adapted? By what methods? Science, of course, was one method, but, as was said before, its benefits had not been spread as they should have been. The *state* must, therefore, be brought into the business, that is to say, the democratically organized state, the state where politically each person counted as one, neither more nor less.

So we are brought to that chapter in the story of the transformation of the Darwinian hypothesis into a creed of social reform which is variously labeled "pragmatism," "instrumentalism," "experimentalism," "functionalism." Part of the argument, which centers chiefly about the names of William James and John Dewey, runs briefly as follows: in biological evolution the supreme problem is that of physical survival. In man's struggle for survival his principal weapon has been his mental superiority, that is, the ability to forecast events and to plan to meet them and divert them to his own advantage. Thus mind, or thought, directed originally to the problem of sheer existence, remains as an instrument of social improvement, and profitable thought to this end is *planning*. It follows that the most valid test of thought is its *planning* value—its anticipation of events and its usefulness in giving them an advantageous turn.

A paragraph from Mr. Hofstadter's excellent book, *Social Darwinism,* is much in point:

> While Dewey's interpretation of thinking is more than a simple extension of Darwinism, it is biological in its orientation. Thinking is not a series of transcendent states or acts interjected into a natural scene. Knowledge is a part of nature, and its end is not mere passive adjustment but the manipulation of the environment to provide "consummatory" satisfactions. An idea is a plan of action rooted in the natural impulses and responses of the organism. The "spectator theory of knowledge" is pre-Darwinian. "The biological point of view commits us to the conviction that mind, whatever else it may be, is at least an organ of service for the *control of environment* in relation to the ends of the life process." [9]

The questions arise: What ends are thought of; Whose "consummatory satisfactions"; and What is their nature? The answer is that in the process of becoming a gospel of reform, pragmatism has, like Darwinism itself, undergone a profound change. Permit me again to quote some words from Mr. Hofstadter's book, this time words of Professor Dewey himself:

> Long after "pragmatism" in any sense save as an application of his *Weltanschauung* shall have passed into a not unhappy oblivion, the fundamental idea of an open universe in which uncertainty, choice, hypotheses, novelties and possibilities are naturalized will remain associated with the name of James; the more he is studied in his historic setting the more original and daring will the idea appear. . . . Such an idea is removed as far as pole from pole from the temper of an age whose occupation is acquisition, whose concern is with security, and whose

9. Hofstadter at 115. My italics. Quoted with the approval of the publishers, the University of Pennsylvania Press.

creed is that the established economic regime is peculiarly "natural" and hence immutable in principle.[10]

These words express the pure spirit of Jamesian pragmatism, which regarded the universe as always "open" and centered its interest on the "open" mind. It is an aristocratic idea, and regards thought as primarily, or altogether, a personal adventure.

But this is not the attitude of present-day social reformers as it is set forth by one of the most eminent of them, Professor Charles E. Merriam, in his recent work *Systematic Politics*. In one respect Merriam is a thoroughgoing follower of James and Dewey, especially the latter. He rejects utterly the idea that inherited institutions have any necessary validity—they must daily prove their usefulness. But his test of usefulness is supplied by the very consideration which Dewey in the above quotation treats with scorn, "concern with security." To be sure, Dewey was talking about the security already attained of an "economic regime," a plutocracy, whereas Merriam is talking about the security still to be obtained of *the common man*. "Freedom," says Merriam, "is the great aim of the state," and this he defines in the words of the late President Roosevelt's message to Congress of January 11, 1944, and repeated in his campaign speech in Chicago that same autumn:

> We have come to a clear realization of the fact that true individual freedom cannot exist without economic security and independence. "Necessitous men are not free men." People who are hungry and out of a job are the stuff of which dictatorships are made.
>
> In our day these economic truths have become accepted as self-evident. We have accepted, so to speak, a second bill of rights, under which a new basis of security and prosperity can be established for all—regardless of station, race, or creed.
>
> Among these are:
>
> The right to a useful and remunerative job in the industries, or shops, or farms, or mines of the nation;
>
> The right to earn enough to provide adequate food and clothing and recreation;
>
> The right of every farmer to raise and sell his products at a return which will give him and his family a decent living;
>
> The right of every businessman, large and small, to trade in an atmosphere of freedom from unfair competition and domination by monopolies at home or abroad;
>
> The right of every family to a decent home;
>
> The right to adequate medical care and the opportunity to achieve and enjoy good health;
>
> The right to adequate protection from the economic fears of old age, sickness, accident, and unemployment;
>
> The right to a good education.
>
> All of these rights spell security. And after this war is won we must be prepared

---

10. Hofstadter at 103. On the origin of pragmatism, see Philip P. Wiener's excellent article, "Peirce's Metaphysical Club and the Genesis of Pragmatism," 7 *J. Hist. Ideas* 218–33 (April 1946). Professor Lovejoy is there cited for the statement that "pragmatism" had acquired thirteen or more meanings by 1908.

to move forward, in the implementation of these rights, to new goals of human happiness and well-being.

America's own rightful place in the world depends in large part upon how fully these and similar rights have been carried into practice for our citizens. For unless there is security here at home, there cannot be lasting peace in the world.[11]

In short, pragmatism, instrumentalism, experimentalism are merged with and go to swell the current of democratic reformism, in support of which the Darwinian hypothesis had begun to be invoked from the early eighties by Ward, Ritchie, Ely, Patten, and others.[12]

I wish now to turn for a moment to the Marxian doctrine of class struggle. The

---

11. *The New York Times,* Jan. 12, 1944. It ought to be added that Professor Merriam yielded no whit to the late President in optimistic outlook. The following passage from *Systematic Politics* 301 (1945) is in point in this connection: "The year 1945 may seem an unfortunately chosen moment to declare that violence is on the decline—in the midst of the world's greatest sweep of war. But war is likely to be curbed as a result of this titanic struggle. Internal violence is on its way out—as seen at many points. The father's power of life and death over his family, the master's right to brutality over his slaves, the officer's right to kick and beat his subordinates, the institution of the duel, private war and violent feuds, flogging in schools, disfigurements, torture—all tend to disappear as instruments of government or of society. In the broad field of criminology prevention tends to take the place of punishment in many instances.

"This does not mean, however, that there will not be an organization of violence for various purposes in future society. But war as an instrument of national policy and violence as the staple of internal order and justice are on the decline in modern civilization and, as far as the eye can see, will continue on their downward way. It is thinkable and possible that there may be yet more dreadful and destructive wars than the world has yet seen, raging over long periods of time and over the whole earth, and such an alternative must always be borne in mind. Yet, in dealing broadly, as here, with the tools of government and their trends, it is clear that we move in the direction of peaceful rather than violent methods of settling disputes between individuals and associations." It will be noticed how belief in a beneficent trend which has been operating for centuries colors this passage. Presumably the passage was written before Hiroshima. In the light of that event the notion of possibly bigger and better wars, leading ultimately to peace, somehow fails to appeal.

12. Important in this general connection is Professor Dewey's position on the question whether adjustment to environment can be effected through changes in environment. Dealing with this question Professor Sidney Ratner writes: ". . . Dewey laid down the doctrine that human thinking arises out of specific needs and frustrations. When it is successful, it leads to a control of the environment, which is achieved through acts based upon previous analysis or resolution of the original complex situation into its composite elements and upon a projection of a plan of action or experiment." "John Dewey and Charles Darwin, a Study in Some Unexplored Relationships" (MS.) citing John Dewey, *Essays in Experimental Logic* 1–74 (1916). Professor Ratner also brings to my attention the following pertinent statements in Dewey's own words: "The entire significance of the evolutionary method in biology and social history is that every distinct organ, structure, or formation, every grouping of cells or elements, has to be treated as an instrument of adjustment or adaptation to a particular environing situation. Its meaning, its character, its value, is known when, and only when, it is considered as an arrangement for meeting the conditions involved in some specific situation." *Studies in Logical Theory* 15 (1903). Idealistic logic "ignored the temporarily intermediate and instrumental place of reflection; and . . . overlooked its essential feature: control of the environment in behalf of human progress and well-being, the efforts at control being stimulated by the needs, the defects, the troubles which accrue when the environment coerces and suppresses man or when man endeavors in ignorance to override the environment." *Essays in Experimental Logic* 22. "Ideas that are plans of operations to be performed are integral factors in actions which change the face of the world." Dewey, *Quest for Certainty* 138 (1929). I wish to take this opportunity to acknowledge Professor Ratner's valuable counsel and aid on this phase of my paper.

historical connection between Marxism and Darwinism seems to have been very slight. The Marxian doctrine is the older, but there appears to be no evidence at all that Darwin owed anything to it, or was even aware of it. Indeed such indebtedness as existed appears to have been on the other side. For in 1860 we find Marx writing Engels regarding the *Origin of Species,* which had appeared the year before: It "is very important and serves me as a basis in natural science for the class struggle in history."[13] Darwin had furnished Marx a new propaganda weapon, but that was all.

That, nevertheless, certain logical affinities exist between Marxism on the one hand and each of the variants of evolutionism which we have been considering is apparent. Thus Spencerism, with its exaltation of a rigorously competitive society and the notion of the survival of the fittest, is a sort of inverted Marxism, in which the Marxian proletariate is replaced by the leaders of industry. Moreover, both Marx and Spencer looked forward to a time when the particular struggle which each depicted would *terminate in a more or less perfect society.* In the last analysis *they were utopians.* Between Marxism and Social Darwinism there is the affinity, first, of a common sympathy for the plight of the masses, but whereas Marx looked forward to violent revolution as the way out, Darwinism put its money at first on "the inevitability of gradualness," to use the graphic expression coined by those great exponents of social reform, the Webbs. Latterly, to be sure, the recognition that de Vries, Vernon Kellogg, and others have accorded the unheralded "sport" as a source of biological variation, tends to minimize this difference, while at the same time creating another. Chance mutations and quantum jumps are headed for no predictable destination; Marxism is very confident that it is.

But the principal affinity between Darwinism and Marxism appears when we turn to the philosophy of instrumentalism or experimentalism and its conception of thought as planning. Such a conception simply passes by as obsolete the idea of thought as the fine fruit of a cognitive, reasoning faculty which, just because of its detachment from the daily concerns of men, is able to arrive at abstract and permanent truths. Marxism, however, carries its rejection of the same idea even further. For according to Marx all institutions, all approved beliefs, even all the procedures of education and learning are conditioned by interest and situation and constitute "ideologies," the purpose of which is not the apprehension and the dissemination of truth but the defense of the established economic order, at least, its "mystification."[14] The autonomous reason of the eighteenth-century

13. *Marx-Engels Correspondence* 125–26 (1935). I am again indebted to Professor Ratner who writes: "The connection between the influence of Marxism in the United States and that of Darwinism is not close. Darwinism and Marxism, as you know, were both conceived and developed independently. I know of no scientist or philosopher or popular reader who was won over to Darwinism by first being converted to Marxism, or vice versa, at least in the United States."
14. "Upon the several forms of property, upon the social conditions of existence, a whole superstructure is reared of various and peculiarly shaped feelings, illusions, habits of thought, and conceptions of life. The whole class produces and shapes these out of its material foundation and out

Enlightenment, the power to see things *sub specie aeternitatis,* is demoted by instrumentalism to a planning device for meeting the shifting demands of an ever changing environment, and is then further reduced to the ignoble role of a tool of propagandists. The eternal verities become, first, relative truths, then half-truths, or less than half-truths, even deliberate falsehoods.

To sum up the argument to this point: the two principal efforts to give evolutionary concepts a social or political application are associated respectively with the names of Spencer and Darwin. Spencer emphasized the notion of the struggle for existence among individuals, and optimistically assuming that the survivors from the struggle were the "fittest" in a social sense, next proceeded to identify them with the economically successful, "the wise and the wealthy." His theory thus joined hands with other intellectual forces of contemporary laissez faire-ism, and in that company materially influenced the interpretation of the Constitution of the United States for more than a generation. Today its importance is negligible.

Darwinian social theory stands at the opposite pole to the theory just reviewed. *From the first it was an elaboration by advocates of economic reform in the interest of the masses.* Their initial step was to replace the idea of the struggle for existence among creatures with the idea of the struggle with environment, thus transforming the relatively inert, or only cataclysmically active environment of the Darwinian biology, into a *primary efficient agent of social improvement.* In the second place, the Darwinian social theorists laid down the proposition that the struggle with environment must take place under the active supervision of government if its beneficial results were to be equitably distributed throughout society. For Spencerian laissez faire-ism, the Darwinians substituted the gospel of governmental intervention in the economic sphere in the interest of the common man.

A derivative from Darwinian social theory via Jamesian pragmatism is the instrumentalism or experimentalism of John Dewey and his group. This too is democratic, reformist, socialistic. At the same time its extension of certain implications of evolutionary thought challenges some of the more fundamental elements of classical American political thought. The cornerstone of the latter at its inception was the notion of a natural law of final moral and political values which were the discovery of reason. The natural law of experimentalism, on the other hand, is the natural law of the sciences, which exists independent of and indifferent to moral values. So there are no final truths, and reason as such is left without any reason for being. In its place is that continuous mental activity which we term planning, man's capacity for which is the explanation of his survival in the struggle for existence, and his only ground for hope for the future. Truth, in

---

of the corresponding social conditions. The individual unit to whom they flow through tradition and education may fancy that they constitute the true reasons for the premises of his conduct." Quoted by Sabine, *A History of Political Theory* 693 (1937).

short, is a plan of action which is operationally successful. It is therefore relative and variable, the pliable instrument of an ever shifting problem of adjustment to "specific situations."[15]

And if instrumentalism demotes truth from the dignity of a discovery of the autonomous reason to the menial role of a tool in the struggle for satisfaction, Marxism carries the denigrating process still further, presenting "truth" (in quotation marks) as a weapon in the class struggle of a self-serving established economic order—as propaganda, in short.

One thing remains—to translate these results, or some of them, into the traditional categories of American political and constitutional thought. In view of what has been said already the subject does not require elaborate treatment. Social Darwinism—as I have redefined the term—has been a definite influence working with those who have within recent years sought to replace our original passive conception of governmental function with a positive, active conception. From the point of view of the former the *liberty* of the individual was the single most valuable asset of society, as on the frontier it undoubtedly was. In the activist conception, on the other hand, as illustrated in the late President's speech which was quoted a few pages back, the duty rests squarely on the shoulders of a democratic government to guarantee "the economic security and independence" of its constituents.

The efforts which have been made to date to realize the latter conception in terms of legislation have resulted in what is nothing less than a revolution in our constitutional law, one which has undone completely the work of Spencerian laissez faire-ism in that field. The principle of the "federal equilibrium," which was especially dear to lawyers and judges of the laissez-faire school, the doctrine of "freedom of contract," which was their own creation, and the doctrine of the separation of powers, have all today gone by the board as limitations on Congress' power. The Supreme Court's power to pass upon the constitutionality of legislation remains, to be sure, but bereft of the support once given it by the above-mentioned doctrines, is today, in the national theater, little more than a superfluous pageant, a fact which, nevertheless, has not sufficed to save it from heavy attack as still being incompatible with the majority's right to rule.[16]

The latter right, indeed, charged with the duty to spread the control of government over an ever widening circle of human relationships and activities in the interest of "the common man," promises to become, if it has not become already, the be-all and end-all of constitutional government in the United States.

---

15. "A distinctive feature of Dewey's *Ethics* was the Darwinian approach. He stressed the biological basis of human life and conduct: 'Moral conceptions and processes grow naturally out of the very conditions of human life.' He also broke new ground by demonstrating that moral principles, properly understood, were not commands to act or to forbear acting in a given way, but were 'tools or methods which enable each individual to make for himself an analysis of the elements of good and evil in the particular situation in which he finds himself.'" Ratner, article referred to in n. 12 {above}, citing Dewey and Tufts, *Ethics* 34 ff., 343–44 (revised ed. 1932).

16. See especially Commager, *Majority Rule and Minority Rights* (1943).

In the field of economic endeavor especially, "liberty," which once stood at the head of the column of constitutional values, has been supplanted by "equality." In terms of evolutionary theory, "survival of the fittest" has given way to the right of all to survive in comfort so far as this can be contrived by governmental action.

Finally, although the doctrine of evolution as a natural science construct is professedly indifferent to the quality of the changes which it purports to explain, yet when it has been brought into contact with the utopian presuppositions of the American political tradition it has strengthened these by lending to the naive faith of the frontier the vocabulary of philosophy. Also it has taught us to accept the fact that all improvement means change; and even if the further inference that all change means improvement is today regarded with increasing skepticism, the fault at any rate does not lie at the door of the doctrine of evolution.

8. The Debt of American Constitutional Law to Natural Law Concepts

ANCIENT Chinese philosophers were wont to distinguish the passive and active elements of Being, called respectively *Yin* and *Yang*. If I may be permitted to employ this locution for a moment, the "yang" element of American constitutional law is judicial review, the power, and corresponding duty of a court to pass upon the validity of legislative acts in relation to a higher law which is regarded as being binding on both the legislature and the court. By the same token the "yin" element is the aforesaid higher law. Today this role is ordinarily filled by a constitutional document, the Constitution of the United States being the supreme example; but earlier, natural law or some derivative concept took the part of "yin." Hence the purpose of this discourse—which is to demonstrate how very large a part of its content American constitutional law has always owed, and still owes, to its natural law genesis. As the matrix of American constitutional law, the documentary Constitution is still, in important measure, natural law under the skin.

Of natural law there is no end of definitions, as a casual examination of Sir Thomas Erskine Holland's *Elements of Jurisprudence* suffices to show. I venture to quote a few passages from the 13th edition:

Aristotle fully recognizes the existence of a natural as well as of a legal justice. He mentions as an ordinary device of rhetoric the distinction which may be drawn between the written law, and "the common law" which is in accordance with nature and immutable.

The Stoics were in the habit of identifying nature with law in the higher sense, and of opposing both of these terms to law which is such by mere human appointment. "Justice," they say, "is by nature and not by imposition." "It proceeds from Zeus and the common nature."

From 25 *Notre Dame Lawyer* 258 (1950). Reprinted with permission. © by the *Notre Dame Lawyer*, University of Notre Dame. The publisher is responsible for any errors that have occurred in reprinting or editing. Originally delivered as an address at the Third Annual Natural Law Institute, College of Law, University of Notre Dame, December 9, 1949.

The same view finds expression in the Roman lawyers. "Law," says Cicero, "is the highest reason, implanted in nature, which commands those things which ought to be done and prohibits the reverse." "The highest law was born in all the ages before any law was written or state was formed. . . . " "We are by nature inclined to love mankind, which is the foundation of law. . . . "

S. Thomas Aquinas: "Participatio legis aeternae in rationali creatura lex naturalis dicitur."

Grotius: "Jus naturale est dictatum rectae rationis. . . ."[1]

For our purposes it is not essential to choose nicely among these definitions of what Cicero and St. Thomas call *lex naturalis* and Grotius terms *jus naturale*. We are concerned only with certain juristic connotations of the concept: first, that natural law is entitled by its intrinsic excellence to prevail over any law which rests solely on human authority; second, that natural law may be appealed to by human beings against injustices sanctioned by human authority.

I. Natural Law into Natural Rights

In a famous passage in the *Rhetoric,* Aristotle advised advocates that when they had "no case according to the law of the land," they should "appeal to the law of nature," and, quoting the *Antigone* of Sophocles, argue that "an unjust law is not a law."[2] While this advice scarcely reveals any deep devotion on Aristotle's part to the natural law concept, it does evidence the short step, which even at that date existed in men's minds, between the concept and the idea of a *juridical* recourse to it. Three hundred years later we find Cicero in his *De Legibus* contrasting *summa lex* and *lex scripta; summum jus* and *jus civile; universum jus* and *jus civile;* and on one occasion appealing in the Senate to *recta ratio* against the *lex scripta*.[3]

It was during the Middle Ages, however, that the conception of natural law as a code of human rights first took on real substance and importance. This was so even on the Continent,[4] albeit institutions were lacking there through which such ideas could be rendered effective practically. In England, on the other hand, this lack was supplied by the royal courts, administering the common law. The impregnation of the common law with higher law concepts proceeded rapidly in the fourteenth century under Edward III. Of the thirty-two royal confirmations of the charter noted by Sir Edward Coke, fifteen occurred in this reign; and near the end of it, in 1368, to the normal form of confirmation the declaration was added by statute that any statute passed contrary to Magna Carta *soit tenuz p'nul,* words

---

1. Holland, *Elements of Jurisprudence* 32–34 (13th ed. 1924).

2. *Id.* at 32 n.4.

3. *Id.* at 33 n.6; see also the present writer's book, Corwin, *Liberty against Government* 15–17 (1948), and accompanying notes.

4. See Gierke, *Political Theories of the Middle Ages* 80–81 (Maitland tr. 1927).

which seem clearly to have been addressed to the royal officials, including the judges.[5]

Here, to be sure, Magna Carta fills the role of natural law, but it is a Magna Carta already infused with natural law content, as is shown by Bracton's earlier designation of chapter 29 as *constitutio libertatis;* and in the fifteenth century the *lex naturae* has completely replaced Magna Carta in the juristic equation. This is notably so, for example, in the pages of Fortescue's famous *In Praise of the Law of England (De Laudibus Legum Angliae),* which was but one of many similar encomia. As Father Figgis has written of this period:

> The common law is pictured invested with a halo of dignity peculiar to the embodiment of the deepest principles and to the highest expression of human reason and of the law of nature implanted by God in the heart of man. As yet men are not clear that an act of Parliament can do more than declare the common law. It is the common law which men set up as an object of worship. The common law is the perfect ideal of law; for it is natural reason developed and expounded by a collective wisdom of many generations. . . . Based on long usage and almost supernatural wisdom, its authority is above, rather than below that of acts of Parliament or royal ordinances, which owe their fleeting existence to the caprice of the king or to the pleasure of councillors, which have a merely material sanction and may be repealed at any moment.[6]

Thus the common law becomes higher law, without at all losing its quality as positive law, the law of the king's courts and of the rising Inns of Court. Nor does Fortescue fail to stress its dual character. Asserting the identity of "perfect justice" with "legal justice," and the subordination of the king to the law, that is, the law courts, he proceeds to counsel his prince as follows:

> There will be no occasion for you to search into the arcana of our laws with such tedious application and study. . . . It will not be convenient by severe study, or at the expense of the best of your time, to pry into nice points of law; such matters may be left to your judges and counsel . . . ; furthermore, you will pronounce judgment in the courts by others than in person, it being not customary for the kings of England to sit in court or pronounce judgment themselves (*proprio ore nullus regum Angliae judicium proferre uses est*). I know very well the quickness of your apprehension and the forwardness of your parts; but for that expertness in the laws which is requisite for judges the studies of twenty years (*viginti annorum lucubrationes*) barely suffice.[7]

In short, natural law has become a craft mystery—the mystery of bench and bar—what it has remained, now in greater, now in less measure ever since.

A century and a half later we find Lord Coke, Chief Justice of the Common Pleas, describing a scene[8] which reads like a re-enactment of that imagined by

---

5. The preceding sentence is taken from Corwin, *Liberty against Government* 26.
6. As quoted *id.* at 28.
7. *Id.* at 30.
8. 12 Rep. 63–65, 77 Eng. Rep. 1341–43 (1609).

Fortescue. But to his predecessor's work of edification, Coke adds official recognition that judicial custodianship of the common law signifies the power and duty of the law courts to apply its measure both to the royal prerogative and to the power of Parliament. The latter claim appears in his famous "dictum," so-called, in Dr. Bonham's Case,[9] which reads: "And it appears in our books, that in many cases, the common law will controul acts of Parliament, and sometimes adjudge them to be utterly void: for when an act of Parliament is against common right and reason, or repugnant, or impossible to be performed, the common law will controul it and adjudge such act to be void. . . ."[10] And this was said, it should be noted, at the end of a century in which the thesis of Parliament's absolute power to alter and abrogate any and all laws had been asserted again and again;[11] and not only asserted but demonstrated by its part in the Tudor ecclesiastical and religious revolution.

Eighty years after Dr. Bonham's Case, "the great Mr. Locke" produced his second *Treatise on Civil Government*, in which the dissolution of natural law into the natural rights of the individual—the rights of "life, liberty and estate"—is completed through the agency of the social compact. Of judicial review, to be sure, Locke appears to have no inkling. He relied for the protection of the individual's inherent and inalienable rights on: first, Parliament; second, the right of revolution. Even so, Locke's contribution to both the doctrinal justification of judicial review and to the theory of its proper scope is first and last a very considerable one.

Coke and Locke are the two great names in the common Anglo-American higher law tradition, and the contribution of each is enhanced by that of the other. Locke's version of natural law not only rescues Coke's version of the English constitution from a localized patois, restating it in the universal tongue of the eighteenth century, it also supplements it in important respects. Coke's endeavor was to put forward the historical *procedures* of the common law as a permanent restraint on power, and especially on the power of the English crown. Locke, in the limitations which he imposes on legislative power, is looking rather to the security of the *substantive* rights of the individual—those rights which are implied in the basic arrangements of society at all times and in all places. While Coke extricated the notion of fundamental law from what must sooner or later have proved a fatal nebulosity, he did so at the expense of archaism. Locke, on the other hand, in cutting loose in great measure from the historical method of reasoning, opened the way to the larger issues with which American constitutional law has been called upon to grapple in its latest maturity.[12]

9. 8 Rep. 113b, 77 Eng. Rep. 646 (1610).

10. *Id.*, 8 Rep. at 118a; see also Proclamations, 12 Rep. 74, 77 Eng. Rep. 1352 (1611).

11. See Corwin, *Liberty against Government* 32–33 and notes.

12. Parts of the above paragraph are taken from *id.* at 50–51; {*Contra*, Locke, *An Essay Concerning Human Understanding* bk. I, ch. 1, para. 2 at 44 (P. H. Nidditch ed. 1975) describes the "historical, plain method" of his "philosophical" or most authoritative work on "conduct." *Id.* para. 6 at 46; *id.* bk. III, ch. 9, para. 3 at 476}.

II. Natural Law and Judicial Review

The *fons et origo* of both the doctrine and the practice of judicial review in the United States is Coke's invocation in Dr. Bonham's Case of "common right and reason," which as explained by the sixteenth-century author of *Doctor and Student,* was the term used "by them that be learned in the laws of England" in place of the term "law of nature."[13] Commended by two Lord Chief Justices, Hobart and Holt, the dictum had won repeated recognition in various legal abridgments and digests before the outbreak of the American Revolution.[14] In the early 1700s it was relied on by a British colonial law officer as affixing the stigma of invalidity to an act of the Barbadoes assembly creating paper money.[15] In 1759, we encounter a casual reference by Governor Cadwallader Colden of the Province of New York to "a judicial power of declaring them [laws] void."[16]

But just as Coke had forged his celebrated dictum as a possible weapon for the struggle which he already foresaw against the divine rights pretensions of James I, so its definitive reception in this country was motivated by the rising agitation against the mother country. The creative first step was taken by James Otis in February 1761, in his argument for the Boston merchants against an application by a British customs official for a general warrant authorizing him to search their cellars and warehouses for smuggled goods. An act of Parliament "against natural equity," Otis asserted, was void. "If an act of Parliament," he continued, "should be made in the very words of this petition, it would be void," and it would be the duty of the executive courts to pass it "into disuse."[17] Four years later, according to Governor Hutchinson of Massachusetts, the prevailing argument against the Stamp Act was that it was "against Magna Carta and the natural rights of Englishmen, and therefore, according to Lord Coke, null and void," testimony which is borne out by a contemporaneous decision of a Virginia county court.[18] On the very eve of the Declaration of Independence, Judge William Cushing, later to become one of Washington's appointees to the original bench of the Supreme Court, charged a Massachusetts jury to ignore certain acts of Parliament as "void and inoperative" and was congratulated by John Adams for doing so.[19]

And meantime, in 1772, George Mason had developed a similar argument against an act of the Virginia assembly of 1682, under which certain Indian women had been sold into slavery. The act in question, he asserted, "was originally void of itself, because contrary to natural right."[20] And, he continued:

13. See Corwin, *Liberty against Government* 35; *id.* at n.40.
14. *Id.* at 39 n.43.
15. See 2 Chalmers, *Opinions of Eminent Lawyers* 27–38 (1814).
16. 2 New York Historical Society Collections 204; see also, Chalmers, *Political Annals* in 1 New York Historical Society Collections 81 (1868).
17. Adams' report of Otis' argument in Paxton's Case, Quincy (App. I) 474 (Mass. 1761).
18. Quincy (App. I) 519 n.18 (Mass. 1761).
19. 5 McMaster, *History of the People of the United States* 395 (1905).
20. Robin v. Hardaway, Jeff. 109 (Va. 1772).

> If natural right, independence, defect of representation, and disavowal of protection, are not sufficient to keep them from the coercion of our laws, on what other principles can we justify our opposition to some late acts of power exercised over us by the British legislature? Yet they only pretended to impose on us a paltry tax in money; we on our free neighbors, the yoke of perpetual slavery. Now all acts of legislature apparently contrary to natural right and justice, are, in our laws, and must be in the nature of things, considered as void. The laws of nature are the laws of God; whose authority can be superseded by no power on earth. . . . All human constitutions which contradict his laws, we are in conscience bound to disobey. Such have been the adjudications of our courts of justice.[21]

Mason concluded by citing Coke and Hobart. The court adjudged the act of 1682 repealed.[22]

Nor did the establishment of the first American constitution cause this course of reasoning to be abandoned. To the contrary, the most eminent judges of the first period of American constitutional law, which comes to an end approximately with the death of Marshall in 1835, appealed freely to natural rights and the social compact as limiting legislative power, and based decisions on this ground, and the same doctrine was urged by the greatest lawyers of the period without reproach. Typical in this connection is the case of Wilkinson v. Leland,[23] which was decided by the Supreme Court in 1829. Attorney for the defendants in error was Daniel Webster. "If," said he, "at this period there is not a general restraint on legislatures in favor of private rights, there is an end to private property. Though there may be no prohibition in the constitution, the legislature is restrained . . . from acts subverting the great principles of republican liberty and of the social compact. . . ."[24] To this contention his opponent William Wirt responded thus: "Who is the sovereign . . . ? Is it not the legislature of the state, and are not its acts effectual . . . unless they come in contact with the great principles of the social compact?"[25] The act of the Rhode Island legislature under review was upheld, but said Justice Story speaking for the Court: "That government can scarcely be deemed to be free where the rights of property are left solely dependent upon the will of a legislative body without any restraint. The fundamental maxims of a free government seem to require that the rights of personal liberty and private property should be held sacred."[26] Indeed, fourteen years before, this the same Court had unanimously held void, on the basis of these same principles, an act of the Virginia legislature which purported to revoke a grant of land.[27]

In short, *judicial review initially had nothing to do with a written constitution.* In point of fact, the first appearance of the idea of judicial review in this country

21. *Id.* at 114.
22. *Id.* at 114, 123.
23. 2 Pet. 627, 7 L. Ed. 542 (1829).
24. *Id.,* 2 Pet. at 646.
25. *Id.,* 2 Pet. at 652.
26. *Id.,* 2 Pet. at 657.
27. Terrett v. Taylor, 9 Cranch 43, 3 L. Ed. 650 (1815).

antedated the first written constitution by at least two decades. Judicial review continued, moreover, in a relationship of semi-independence of the written constitution on the basis of "common right and reason," natural law, natural rights, and kindred postulates throughout the first third of the nineteenth century. But meantime, a competing conception of judicial review as something anchored to the *written constitution* had been in the process of formulation in answer to Blackstone's doctrine that in every state there is a *supreme, absolute power*, and that this power is vested in the *legislature*. From this angle judicial review based on "common right and reason," or on natural law ideas, was an impertinence, as Blackstone took pains to point out in his *Commentaries*.[28] But suppose that the supreme will in the state was not embodied in the *legislature* and its *acts*, but in the *people at large* and their *constitution*—what conclusions would follow from this premise? In the *Federalist,* no. 78, Hamilton suggested an answer to this question, and in 1803, in Marbury v. Madison,[29] Chief Justice Marshall elaborated the answer: it is the duty of courts when confronted with a conflict between an act (that is, a *statute*) of "the mere agents of the people" (that is, of the ordinary legislature) and the act of the people themselves (to wit, the Constitution), to prefer the latter.

The inevitable clash between the two conceptions of judicial review was first unfolded in the case of Calder v. Bull,[30] decided by the Supreme Court in 1798. There it was held that the ex post facto clause of Article I, section 10, of the Constitution applied only to penal legislation and hence did not protect rights of property and contract from interference by a state legislature; but Justice Samuel Chase endeavored to soften this blow to proprietarian interests by citing the power of the state courts to enforce extraconstitutional limitations on legislative power, such as many of them were in fact already doing. Said he:

> I cannot subscribe to the *omnipotence* of a *state legislature*, or that it is *absolute and without controul;* although its authority should not be *expressly* restrained by the *constitution*, or *fundamental law*, of the state. . . . There are certain *vital* principles in our *free republican governments*, which will determine and overrule an *apparent and flagrant* abuse of *legislative* power. . . . The *genius*, the *nature*, and the *spirit* of our state governments, amount to a prohibition of *such acts of legislation;* and the *general principles of law and reason* forbid them.[31]

To hold otherwise, it was stated, would be "political heresy, altogether inadmissible."[32]

Chase belonged to the older generation of American lawyers and had been brought up on Coke-Littleton, having received much of his legal education in London in the Inns of Court. Alongside him on the Supreme bench, however, sat

---

28. 1 *W. Blackstone, Comm.* *46, 91.
29. 1 Cranch 137, 2 L. Ed. 60 (1803).
30. 3 Dall. 386, 1 L. Ed. 648 (1798).
31. *Id.*, 3 Dall. at 387–89.
32. *Id.*

a very different type of lawyer, one of "that brood of young lawyers," characterized by Jefferson as "ephemeral insects of the law," who had imbibed their law from Blackstone's *Commentaries*. This was James Iredell of North Carolina, who demurred strongly to Chase's natural rights doctrine. "True," said he, "some speculative jurists" had held "that a legislative act against natural justice must, in itself, be void"; but the correct view, he stated, was that

> if . . . a government, composed of legislative, executive and judicial departments, were established, by a Constitution, which imposed no limits on the legislative power . . . whatever the legislative power chose to enact, would be lawfully enacted, and the judicial power, could never interpose to pronounce it void. . . . Sir William Blackstone, having put the strong case of an act of Parliament, which should authorize a man to try his own cause, explicitly adds, that even in that case, "there is no court that has power to defeat the intent of the legislature when couched in such evident . . . words. . . ."[33]

The debate thus begun was frequently renewed in other jurisdictions; and long before the Civil War, Iredell had won the fight—but as we shall see, more in *appearance* than in *reality*. In 1868 Judge Cooley, in considering the circumstances in which a legislative enactment may be declared unconstitutional, wrote:

> The rule of law upon this subject appears to be, that, except where the constitution has imposed limits upon the legislative power, it must be considered as practically absolute, whether it operate according to natural justice or not in any particular case. The courts are not the guardians of the rights of the people of the state, except as those rights are secured by some constitutional provision which comes within the judicial cognizance.[34]

Yet, six years later we find the Supreme Court of the United States pronouncing a statute of the state of Kansas void on the very grounds that had been laid down in Chase's dictum. Speaking for an all-but-unanimous Court, Justice Miller said:

> It must be conceded that there are . . . rights in every free government beyond the control of the state. A government which recognized no such rights, which held the lives, the liberty, and the property of its citizens subject to {*sic;* at?} all times to the absolute disposition and unlimited control of even the most democratic depository of power, is after all but a despotism. It is true it is a despotism of the many, of the majority, if you choose to call it so, but it is nonetheless a despotism. It may well be doubted if a man is to hold all that he is accustomed to call his own, all in which he has placed his happiness, and the security of which is essential to that happiness, under the unlimited dominion of others, whether it is not wiser that this power should be exercised by one man than by many.[35]

One justice dissented, asserting that such views tended to " convert the government into a judicial despotism."[36]

33. *Id.* 3 Dall. at 398–99.
34. Cooley, *Constitutional Limitations* 168 (3d ed. 1874).
35. Citizens' Savings & Loan Ass'n. v. Topeka, 20 Wall. 655, 662, 22 L. Ed. 455 (1874).
36. *Id.,* 20 Wall. at 669.

But vastly more important is the fact that in the very process of discarding the doctrine of natural rights and adherent doctrines as the basis of judicial review, the courts have contrived to throw about those rights which originally owed their protection to these doctrines the folds of the documentary Constitution. In short, things are not always what they seem to be, even when they seem so most.[37] The indebtedness of the institution of judical review and of the rights protected by it to natural law ideas is by no means sufficiently summed up in the glib statement that nowadays judicial review is confined to the four corners of the written Constitution.

III. How Natural Law Doctrines Were Used to Fill a Gap, in the Written Constitution

It is a commonplace that the doctrine of natural rights was conveyed into the American written Constitution by bills of rights, the earliest example of which was the Virginia Declaration of Rights of June 12, 1776. This commonplace is, however, only a half of the truth, and indeed the lesser half. As has been indicated, the type of judicial review which stemmed from Coke's dictum supplied a second avenue for natural rights concepts into the constitutional document. In this section I shall first illustrate this proposition with the doctrine of vested rights.

Not all the early state constitutions were accompanied by bills of rights. Moreover, the availability of such bills of rights as existed as a basis for judicial inquiry into the validity of legislative measures was sharply challenged at times. Even more important was the fact that, as it came early to be appreciated, bill of rights or no bill of rights, the early state constitutions left proprietarian interests in a very exposed position vis-à-vis the new popular assemblies, for which the prerogatives of the British Parliament itself were sometimes claimed.[38]

The formidable character of legislative power in these early instruments of government as regards the property interest, was exhibited in more ways than one. In the first place, in the prevailing absence of courts of equity, legislative assemblies interfered almost at will with judicial decisions, and particularly those involving disputes over property. The case of Calder v. Bull,[39] mentioned earlier, affords an example of this sort of thing. The Connecticut courts, having refused to probate a certain will, were to all intents and purposes ordered to revise their decision, which they did, with the result that the heirs at law to an estate were ousted, after a year and a half of possession, by the beneficiaries of the will. A second and highly impressive proof of early state legislative power is

---

37. See, e.g., Cooley, *Constitutional Limitations* 174–76, where the principle of the separation of powers is made to do duty for natural law concepts.

38. See Coxe, *An Essay on Judicial Power and Unconstitutional Legislation* 223 *et seq.* (1893); 5 Hamilton, *Works* 116 (Lodge ed. 1904); 7 *id.* at 198.

39. Note 30 above.

afforded by the ferocious catalogue of legislation directed against the Tories, embracing acts of confiscation, bills of pains and penalties, even acts of attainder. One sample of such legislation came under the scrutiny of the United States Supreme Court in 1800, in the case of Cooper v. Telfair.[40] Said Justice Washington: "The constitution of Georgia does not expressly interdict the passing of an act of attainder and confiscation. . . . The presumption, indeed, must always be in favor of the validity of laws, if the contrary is not clearly demonstrated."[41] On this ground and one or two others, the Georgia act was sustained, although Justice Chase opined that with the Federal Constitution now in effect such an act would be clearly void; but this act was passed during the Revolution. Thirdly, with the general collapse of values early in 1780, every state legislature became a scene of vehement agitation on the part of the widespread farmer-debtor class in favor of paper-money laws and other measures of like intent. For the first time, the property interest was confronted with "the power of numbers," and, in the majority of cases, the power of numbers triumphed.

Could the state bills of rights withstand the flood? It soon transpired that they were an utterly ineffective bulwark of private rights against state legislative power. And so the movement was launched which led to the Philadelphia Convention of 1787. That abuse by the state legislatures of their powers had been the most important single cause leading to the Convention was asserted by Madison early in the course of its deliberations, and others agreed.[42] So far as we are concerned, the most important expression of the Convention's anxiety to clip the wings of the high-flying local sovereignties is to be found in the opening paragraph of section 10 of Article I, which reads:

> No state shall enter into any treaty, alliance, or confederation; grant letters of marque and reprisal; coin money, emit bills of credit; make any thing but gold and silver coin a tender in payment of debts; pass any bill of attainder, ex post facto law or law impairing the obligation of contracts, or grant any title of nobility.

The provision which here claims attention is the prohibition of ex post facto laws. What did those who urged their insertion in the Constitution think these words meant? Some of them, we know, thought the clause would rule out *all* "retrospective" legislation, meaning thereby legislation which operated detrimentally upon existing property rights.[43] But as we have seen in Calder v. Bull, the clause was confined to penal legislation, to statutes making criminal an act which was innocent when done. That the Court was thoroughly aware of the breach it was thus creating in the Constitution, the opinions of all the justices, except that of the Blackstonian Iredell, make amply apparent; and going beyond apology, Chase sought to show how the gap could be stopped by the local

40. 4 Dall. 14, 1 L. Ed. 721 (1800).
41. *Id.*, 4 Dall. at 18.
42. See 1 Farrand, *Records of the Federal Convention* 48, 133–34, 255, 424, 525, 533; 2 *id.* at 285 (1937).
43. On this point see Corwin, *Liberty against Government* at 60–61 n.4.

judiciaries by recourse to extraconstitutional limitations, "the spirit of our free republican governments," "the social compact," considerations of "natural justice," and the like. The local judiciaries responded to the suggestion with varying degrees of alacrity, and the sum total of their efforts was one of the most fertile doctrines of American constitutional law, the doctrine of vested rights, the practical purport of which was that the effect of legislation on existing property rights was a *primary* test of its validity, and that by this test legislation must stop short of curtailing existing rights of ownership, at least unduly or unreasonably.[44]

But in fact, Chase's dictum only stimulated a movement already begun. Three years prior to Calder v. Bull, we find Justice Paterson charging a federal jury in a case involving vested rights in these words:

> The right of acquiring and possessing property and having it protected, is one of the natural, inherent and unalienable rights of man. Men have a sense of property: property is necessary to their subsistence, and correspondent to their natural wants and desires; its security was one of the objects, that induced them to unite in society. . . . The preservation of property . . . is a primary object of the social compact, and, by the late constitution of Pennsylvania, was made a fundamental law.[45]

Indeed, a majority of the cases of judicial review after the Cokean model, referred to in section II of this paper, involved property rights. Nor should the great name of Chancellor Kent be overlooked in this connection. First as judge, then as chancellor in his home state, and finally as author of the famed *Commentaries*, Kent developed the doctrine's fullest possibilities and spread its influence fastest and farthest.

Yet even as Kent was vaunting private property as an instrument of God for realizing his plans for the advancement of the race, it was becoming less and less practicable to urge such considerations on American judges. The old-type Cokean judge had about disappeared—Blackstone was in the saddle in the law offices and in the court houses. What is more, with the accession of Jackson to the presidency there took place an immense resurgence of the doctrine of popular sovereignty. Of the numerous corollaries into which the doctrine proliferated, two are relevant to our interest: first, the Constitution was an ordinance of the people, and its supremacy sprang from the fact that it embodied their will; second, of the three departments of state government, the legislature stood nearest the people. It followed that the courts had better go slow in holding state legislative acts invalid; and that on no account must they do so except for a plain violation of the Constitution, that is, of the people's will as there expressed.

Bench and bar were confronted with a dilemma: either they must cast the doctrine of vested rights to the wolves or they must bring it within the sheepfold of the written Constitution. The second alternative was adopted in due course. Ultimately the doctrine found a home within the due process clause: "no person

---

44. *Id.* at 72 *et seq.*
45. Van Horne's Lessee v. Dorrance, 2 Dall. 304, 310, 1 L. Ed. 391 (1795).

shall be deprived of life, liberty, or property without due process of law.'' The original significance of the clause was purely procedural—nobody should be punished without a trial by jury or ''writ original of the common law.'' In the revamped clause the term ''due process of law'' simply fades out and the clause comes to read, in effect, ''no person shall be deprived of property,'' period. Thus was the narrow interpretation which was planted on the ex post facto clause in Calder v. Bull revenged in kind.[46]

This achievement was consummated in the famous case of Wynehamer v. People,[47] in which, in 1856, the New York Court of Appeals set aside a state-wide prohibition law as comprising, with regard to liquors in existence at the time of its going into effect, an act of destruction of property not within the power of government to perform ''even by the forms of due process of law.'' An interesting feature of Judge Comstock's opinion in the case is his repudiation of all arguments against the statute sounding in natural law concepts, like ''fundamental principles of liberty,'' ''common reason and natural rights,'' and so forth. Such theories said he—squinting, one suspects, at the antislavery agitation—were subversive of the necessary powers of government. Furthermore, there was ''no process of reasoning by which it could be demonstrated that the 'act for the prevention of intemperance, pauperism and crime' is void, upon principles and theories outside the Constitution, which will not also, and by an easier induction, bring it in direct conflict with the Constitution itself.'"[48]

The expansion of the obligation of contracts clause of Article I, section 10, by resort to natural law concepts follows a similar, though briefer course. The master craftsman was Chief Justice Marshall, and this time the infusion of the constitutional clause with natural law concepts was direct. The great leading case was Fletcher v. Peck,[49] in which, in 1810, Marshall, speaking for the Court, held that a state legislature was forbidden ''either by general principles, which are common to our free institutions, or by the particular provisions of the Constitution of the United States'"[50] to rescind a previous land grant; while Justice Johnson based his concurring opinion altogether ''on the reason and nature of things; a principle which will impose laws even on the Deity.'"[51] It is true that when, in 1819, the doctrine of Fletcher v. Peck was extended to the charters of eleemosynary corporations, the Court contented itself with invoking only the obligations clause.[52] The dependence, however, of the holding on natural law premises still remains. The constitutional clause presupposes a *pre-existent* obli-

---

46. See Corwin, *Liberty against Government* 84–115.
47. 13 N.Y. (3 Kern) 378 (1856).
48. *Id.* at 392.
49. 6 Cranch 87, 3 L. Ed. 162 (1810).
50. *Id.*, 6 Cranch at 139.
51. *Id.*, 6 Cranch at 143.
52. Dartmouth College v. Woodward, 4 Wheat. 518, 4 L. Ed. 629 (1819).

gation to be protected. Whence, if not from natural law, can such an obligation descend upon a public grant?

Of the four great doctrines of American constitutional law which the American judiciary developed prior to the Civil War, three (the doctrine of judicial review, the substantive doctrine of due process of law, and the doctrine that the obligation of contracts clause protects public contracts) are products of the infusion of the documentary Constitution with natural law, natural rights concepts. The fourth doctrine, that of dual federalism, was the creation of the Supreme Court at Washington under the presidency and guidance of Chief Justice Taney. It, of course, rests on different, highly political considerations. Yet even in this case, natural law may claim some credit if, as Thomas Hill Green argues in his *Principles of Political Obligation*,[53] the notion of sovereignty is also, in final analysis, rooted in the doctrine of natural law. Green, of course, was thinking of "sovereignty" as it is known to Western political thought, not the kind of sovereignty that is the offspring of Byzantine absolutism married to Marxian materialism.

IV. The Bench and Bar Present Us with an Up-to-Date Doctrine of Natural Law

In 1868, the Fourteenth Amendment was added to the Constitution. The first section of it reads as follows:

All persons born or naturalized in the United States, and subject to the jurisdiction thereof, are citizens of the United States and of the state wherein they reside. No state shall make or enforce any law which shall abridge the privileges or immunities of citizens of the United States; nor shall any state deprive any person of life, liberty or property, without due process of law; nor deny to any person within its jurisdiction the equal protection of the laws.

The fifth and final section gave Congress the power "to enforce, by appropriate legislation, the provisions of this Article."

In the understanding of most people at the time, the intended beneficiaries of the amendment were the recently emancipated freedmen, but in the very first cases to reach the Supreme Court under it, the famous Slaughter House Cases[54] of 1873, this assumption was sharply challenged by counsel, John Archibald Campbell of New Orleans, a former justice of the Court. No doubt, Campbell argued, the freedmen would and should derive benefit from the amendment, but their doing so would only be incidental to the realization of its much broader purpose, that of giving legal embodiment to the principle of "laissez-faire individualism which had been held by the colonists ever since they came to this

---

53. Green, *Principles of Political Obligation* (1901).
54. 16 Wall. 36, 21 L. Ed. 394 (1873).

soil."[55] "What," he asked, "did the colonists and their posterity seek for and obtain by their settlement of this continent . . . ? *Freedom, free action, free enterprise—free competition.* It was in freedom they expected to find the best auspices for every kind of human success."[56]

Campbell lost his suit, by the narrow margin of five justices to four; but he had sown an idea which, in the course of the next thirty years, imparted to judicial review a new and revolutionary extension. In 1878, the American Bar Association was founded from the *elite* of the American Bar. Organized as it was in the wake of the "barbarous" decision—as one member termed it—in Munn v. Illinois,[57] in which the Supreme Court had held that states were entitled by virtue of their police power to prescribe the charges of "businesses affected with a public interest," the Association, through its more eminent members, became the mouthpiece of a new constitutional philosophy which was compounded in about equal parts from the teachings of the British Manchester school of political economy and Herbert Spencer's highly sentimentalized version of the doctrine of evolution, just then becoming the intellectual vogue; plus a "booster"—in the chemical sense—from Sir Henry Maine's *Ancient Law,* first published in 1861. I refer to Maine's famous dictum that "the movement of the progressive societies has hitherto been a movement *from status to contract.*"[58] If hitherto, why not henceforth?

In short, the American people were presented *a new doctrine of natural law,* the content and purport of which appear—to take a specific example—in Professor William Graham Sumner's *What Social Classes Owe to Each Other,* which was published in 1883. I quote a passage or two:

> A society based on contract is a society of free and independent men, who form ties without favor or obligation, and cooperate without cringing or intrigues. A society based on contract, therefore, gives the utmost room and chance for individual development, and for all the self-reliance and dignity of a free man. . . . It follows that one man, in a free state, cannot claim help from, and cannot be charged to give help to, another.

And again:

> All institutions are to be tested by the degree to which they guarantee liberty. It is not to be admitted for a moment that liberty is a means to social ends, and that it may be impaired for major considerations. Any one who so argues has lost the bearing and relations of all the facts and factors in a free state. He is a center of powers to work, and of capacities to suffer. What his powers may be—whether they can carry him far or not; what his chances may be, whether wide or restricted; what his fortune may be, whether to suffer much or little—are questions of his personal destiny which he must work out and endure as he can; but for all that

55. These words are from Twiss, *Lawyers and the Constitution* 53 (1942).
56. *Id.* at 54, quoting Campbell's brief, pp. 42–44. Emphasis supplied.
57. 94 U.S. 113, 24 L. Ed. 77 (1876).
58. Maine, *Ancient Law* 165 (3d American ed. 1873).

concerns the bearing of the society and its institutions upon that man, and upon the sum of happiness to which he can attain during his life on earth, the product of all history and all philosophy up to this time is summed up in the doctrine, that he should be left free to do the most for himself that he can, and should be guaranteed the exclusive enjoyment of all that he does. . . . Social improvement is not to be won by direct effort. It is secondary and results from physical or economic improvement. . . . An improvement in surgical instruments or in anesthetics really does more for those who are not well off than all the declamations of the orators and pious wishes of the reformers. . . . The yearning after equality is the offspring of envy and covetousness, and there is no possible plan for satisfying that yearning which can do aught else than rob A to give to B; consequently all such plans nourish some of the meanest vices of human nature, waste capital, and overthrow civilization. . . .[59]

It is interesting to compare this new type of natural law, and its tremendous exaltation of individual effort, with the ancient type, which was set forth in the texts quoted in section I of this paper. There are two differences, the first of which approximates that between a *moral* code, addressed to the reason, and natural law in the sense in which that term is employed by the natural sciences. The former operates *through* men; the latter *upon* men, and altogether independently of their attitude toward it, or even of their awareness of its existence. The results of its operation would therefore be of no moral significance, except for one circumstance, the assumption, to wit, that *compliance with it—whether conscious or unconscious—forwarded progress.* Thus, according to Maine, it was *the progressive societies* which had heretofore moved from *status* to *contract;* while with Spencer *progressive societies* were destined to "evolve" from the *military state* into the *industrial society*—a process not yet completed, however, or the state would have vanished. In short, the laissez-faire version of natural law contrived, in the end, to combine the *moral* prestige of the older concept with the *scientific* prestige of the newer.[60]

The second difference can be put more briefly, although it is perhaps the more important one. The natural law of Cicero, of St. Thomas, Grotius—even of Locke—always conceives of man as *in* society. The natural law of Spencer, Sumner, et al., sets man, the supreme product of a highly competitive struggle for existence, *above* society—an impossible station in both logic and fact.

The chief constitutional-law precipitate from the new natural law, the doctrine of freedom of contract, confirms and illustrates this fatal characteristic of it. By this doctrine, persons *sui juris* engaged in the ordinary employments were entitled to contract regarding their services without interference from government; as reciprocally were those who sought their services. Endorsed by such writers as Cooley, Tiedeman, James Coolidge Carter, J. F. Dillon, and by a growing procession of state high courts headed by those of New York, Pennsylvania, Mas-

59. Extracted from Mason, *Free Government in the Making* 607–608 (1949).
60. Parts of this paragraph are taken from Corwin, *Liberty against Government* 198.

sachusetts, and Illinois, the doctrine attained culminating expression in 1905 in the famous Bakeshop Case.[61] There a New York statute which limited the hours of labor in bakeries to ten hours a day and sixty hours a week was set aside, five justices to four, as not "a fair, reasonable and appropriate exercise of the police power of the state" but "an unreasonable, unnecessary and arbitrary interference with the right of the individual to his personal liberty. . . ."[62]

How was this result reached? Very simply: it was the automatic result of the conception of an area of individual action *any* interference with which by the state put upon it a burden of justification not required in other cases. On this basis the Court came to operate a kind of "automatic" judicial review, the product of which was labelled by its critics "mechanical jurisprudence." Nor is this type of jurisprudence extinct today, as I shall now point out. Its application has merely been transferred to a different set of values and interests.

V. Natural Law and Constitutional Law Today

In 1925, in the now famous Gitlow Case,[63] which involved a conviction under the New York Anti-Syndicalist Act, the Supreme Court adopted tentatively the thesis, which it had rejected earlier, that the word "liberty" in the Fourteenth Amendment adopts and makes effective against state legislatures the limitations which the First Amendment imposes upon Congress in favor of "freedom of speech and press." Then in 1940 in the Cantwell Case,[64] the Court upset a conviction under Connecticut law of two Jehovah's Witnesses for breach of the peace on the ground that the proselyting activities of the said Witnesses did not under the circumstances constitute a "clear and present danger" to public order; and since then a majority of the Court has gone to the verge, at least, of making the "clear and present danger" formula a direct test of legislation, although in the Gitlow Case it had rejected the rule as spurious.

And what has all this to do with natural law? The answer is discovered when we note the rule by which the Court professes to be guided when interpreting the word "liberty" in the Fourteenth Amendment in the light of the Bill of Rights. Not all the provisions of the latter are regarded as having been converted by the Fourteenth Amendment into restrictions on the states, but only those that are protective of the "immutable principles of justice which inhere in the very idea of free government"; of the "fundamental principles of liberty and justice which lie at the base of all our civil and political institutions"; of the "immunities . . . implicit in the concept of ordered liberty"; of principles of justice "rooted

61. Lochner v. New York, 198 U.S. 45, 25 S. Ct. 539, 49 L. Ed. 937 (1905).
62. *Id.*, 198 U.S. at 56.
63. Gitlow v. New York, 268 U.S. 652, 45 S. Ct. 625, 69 L. Ed. 1138 (1925).
64. Cantwell v. Connecticut, 310 U.S. 296, 60 S. Ct. 900, 84 L. Ed. 1213 (1940).

in the traditions and conscience of our people''; principles, the violation of which would be "repugnant to the conscience of mankind.''[65]

This is entirely in line with the natural law tradition. But does it suffice to elevate the rights it deals with into a *superconstitution,* so that any law touching them is *ipso facto* "infected with presumptive invalidity''? As we have seen, this is precisely what happened in the case of "liberty of contract''; and today, "liberty of contract'' thus distended "is all,'' as they say in Pennsylvania; and may not a like fate overtake freedom of speech, press, and religion in time if the same slide-rule methods are applied to legislation touching them? I am thinking especially of such decisions as those in Saia v. New York,[66] McCollum v. Board of Education,[67] and Terminiello v. City of Chicago.[68] These were very ill-considered decisions to my way of thinking, and in fact the first of these has already been repudiated by the Court,[69] at least four of the five justices who were responsible for it lugubriously so assert. I contend, in short, that any patent formula or device which relieves the justices from considering relevant, however recalcitrant facts, or which exonerates them of the characteristic judical duty of adjusting the universal and eternal to the local and contingent, the here and the now, is to be deplored. I contend further that the "clear and present danger'' rule is just such a patent formula.

How are we to assess the importance of the natural law concept in the development of American constitutional law? What it all simmers down to is essentially this: while that distinctive American institution, judicial review, is regarded today as stemming from the principle of popular sovereignty, it sprang in the first instance from "common right and reason,'' the equivalent with men of law in the sixteenth-century England of natural law. What is more, popular sovereignty in the last analysis is itself a derivative from the natural law postulate, being neither more nor less than a sort of *ad hoc* consolidation of the natural right of human beings to choose their own governing institutions.

And the indebtedness of American constitutional law to natural law, natural rights concepts for its content in the field of private rights is vital and well-nigh all-comprehensive. It is, of course, true that not all of the corollaries that the courts have endeavored to attach to their premises have survived; and few have survived without modification. Yet it is a striking fact that while hundreds of constitutional provisions have been adopted since judicial review was estab-

65. Louisiana v. Resweber, 329 U.S. 459, 470–72, 67 S. Ct. 374, 91 L. Ed. 422 (1947), quoting from Holden v. Hardy, 169 U.S. 366, 389, 18 S. Ct. 383, 42 L. Ed. 780 (1898); Herbert v. Louisiana, 272 U.S. 312, 316, 47 S. Ct. 103, 71 L. Ed. 270 (1926); Palko v. Connecticut, 302 U.S. 319, 325, 58 S. Ct. 149, 82 L. Ed. 288 (1937); Snyder v. Massachusetts, 291 U.S. 97, 105, 54 S. Ct. 330, 78 L. Ed. 674 (1934).
66. 334 U.S. 558, 68 S. Ct. 1148, 92 L. Ed. 1574 (1948).
67. 333 U.S. 203, 68 S. Ct. 461, 92 L. Ed. 649 (1948).
68. {337} U.S. {1}, 69 S. Ct. 894 (1949).
69. The reference is to Kovacs v. Cooper, 336 U.S. 17, 69 S. Ct. 448 (1949).

lished, not one has ever proposed its abolition and only very few its modification. And meantime the American states have continued to incorporate in their successive constitutions, virtually without comment, the constitutional clauses—the due process clause, for example—that today incorporate the principal judicial doctrines which I have traced to natural law bases. It is true, as I just remarked, that some of these doctrines have become extinct and others have been qualified; but invariably these results have been achieved by judicial massage, as it were—sometimes a rather rugged massage—and not by legislative or constitutional surgery.

Not that the doctrine of natural law itself has escaped disturbing comment at times, even from American jurists. Frequently cited in this connection is the late Justice Holmes' discourse on "Natural Law." "It is not enough," said Justice Holmes in a characteristic passage, "for the knight of romance that you agree that his lady is a very nice girl—if you do not admit that she is the best that God ever made, you must fight"; and the same demand, he opines, "is at the bottom of the jurist's search for criteria of absolute validity."[70]

We can readily concede that such criteria may never be established in this far from perfect, and always changing world. Yet that admission does not necessarily discredit the search; perhaps, indeed, it makes it more necessary, as an alternative to despair. Holmes, in fact, exposes himself when he goes on to advance as an argument against natural law that the right to life "is sacrificed without a scruple whenever the interest of society, that is, of the predominant power of the community, is thought to demand it."[71] But the answer is plain: the right to life is more than the right to live—it is also the right to spend life for worthwhile ends; and so long as one is guaranteed a free man's part in determining what these ends are, natural law has *pro tanto* received institutional recognition and embodiment. But, of course, it is essential to this argument that the free man's part be kept a really vital one.

Our present interest, however, has been in natural law as a challenge to the notion of unlimited human authority. American constitutional law is the record of an attempt to implement that challenge. The record is a somewhat mixed one, but it is clear that in the judgment of the American people it has been on the whole a record of success. May it continue to be!

70. Holmes, *Collected Legal Papers* 310 (Laski ed. 1920).
71. *Id.* at 314.

9. James Madison: Layman, Publicist, and Exegete

I.

W E are told by Shakespeare that "some men are born great; some achieve greatness; and some have greatness thrust upon them." The classification is by no means exhaustive, since it takes no account of that vast company of heroes, saints, martyrs, and rogues who have had greatness thrust upon them posthumously. Indeed, one test of authentic historical greatness—or notoriety—may be said to be the ability of the great one to accumulate greatness *ex post facto* and *post mortem*.

That the deceased James Madison meets this test is unquestionable. Mr. Brant notes an indicative fact in the opening volume of his authoritative biography. Madison graduated from Princeton—I deliberately do *not* say "was graduated by Princeton"; the achievement was all his own—in September 1771. There were thirteen members of the class, all of whom participated in the exercises of the day except Madison, concerning which circumstance Mr. Hunt in his biography offers the following explanation: "The contemporary account of the commencement exercises when he graduated (*sic*) contains this note: 'Mr. James Madison was excused from taking any part in the exercises.' The reason probably was that he was ill at the time.''[1] In point of fact, as Mr. Brant shows, the contemporary account referred to, which was the *Pennsylvania Chronicle of September 30– October 30, 1771*, says not a word about Madison's being excused. "This," says Mr. Brant, "was probably an interpolation made over a century later" by

From 27 *New York University Law Review* 277 (1952). Reprinted by permission of the *New York University Law Review*. This article was originally delivered as an address at the James Madison Bicentennial Celebration, New York University Law Center, May 4, 1951.

The writer wishes to thank the *American Bar Association Journal* for permission to draw upon his article "The Posthumous Career of James Madison as Lawyer'' which appeared in the October 1939, issue of the *Journal*.

1. Hunt, *Life of James Madison* 16 (1902) {hereinafter *Life of Madison*}.

President McLean of Princeton in the said contemporary account, when he "reproduced" it in his *History of Princeton* (1777).[2]

But for a really egregious fable of these genre, consider the myth that Madison while a student at Princeton founded Whig Hall, one of the college's two erstwhile famous debating societies, that he wrote a constitution for it which was an outline and model of the Constitution of the United States, and that this constitution still governed Whig Hall's organization and procedures as late as 1890. As is shown by Professor Jacob Beam, the historian of Whig Hall, the one element of truth in this whole preposterous texture of baseless allegations, most of which was concocted by its pious author in 1869, is that Madison was one of the five founders of the Hall. As to the constitution referred to, which so remarkably anticipated by nearly two decades the document it took the Federal Convention four months to elaborate—it appears to have been a creation of the purest fantasy. The constitution of the Hall which was preserved from a disastrous fire in 1802 was modeled on that of the Presbyterian church. A later constitution did, it is true, resemble the Constitution of the United States to some extent. It was drawn up in 1840 by one Addison Alexander.[3]

The most remarkable of Madison's posthumous achievements, however, has still to be mentioned—I refer to his posthumous admission to the bar. This was no work of amateurs but a really *professional* job.

In his address marking the hundred and fiftieth anniversary of the signing of the Constitution President Franklin D. Roosevelt said: "The Constitution of the United States was a layman's document, not a lawyer's contract. That cannot be stressed too often. Madison, most responsible for it, was not a lawyer—nor was Washington or Franklin, whose sense of the given and take of life had kept the Convention together."[4]

The reaction of the bar, as might have been expected of those ever alert sentinels of our liberties and institutions, was both prompt and pronounced. As illustrative of its purport I quote the following communication of, I assume, a member of the profession, in the New York *Herald-Tribune:*

> Although the framers clothed its provisions in simple and direct language, using few technical or legal phrases, the Constitution was emphatically not a "layman's document" in the sense that it was made by laymen.
>
> First, James Madison was a lawyer. If the President had consulted the *World Almanac,* he would have found the statement that Madison was one of the twenty-two lawyer presidents out of a total of thirty-one. If he had looked in the government publication entitled *Biographical Dictionary of the American Congress, 1774–1927,* he would have found the statement that Madison "was graduated from Princeton College in 1771; studied law at Princeton College one year; returned to Virginia; continued the study of law, and was admitted to the bar." It is well known that Madison studied at Princeton one year after graduation, that he chose law as his

2. 1 Brant, *James Madison* 97 *(1941).*
3. Personal interview with Professor Beam.
4. *New York Herald Tribune,* Sept. 18, 1937, at 4, col. 4.

profession and studied it long and "assiduously." A person reading the debates in the Convention, or later in Congress, would hardly conclude that Madison's speeches were those of a layman because of any difference between them and those of his lawyer colleagues—James Wilson or Roger Sherman, for example.[5]

I must own that when the author of this statement kindly sent it to me, I read it with no little astonishment. First and last, I had gone over a great part of Madison's published writings and had never discovered anything in them which remotely indicated that he was ever a practicing lawyer or even a member of the bar. Also, I knew that William Pierce of Georgia, while describing Madison, in his sketches of his fellow members of the Philadelphia Convention, as the member who "evidently took the lead," and as blending "the profound politician with the scholar," did not mention his being a lawyer, although he notes that particular regarding several less conspicuous members. And other obvious sources of information conducted to substantially the same result. Rives, Madison's biographer, ever impressible regarding the achievements of his subject, credits Madison with vast legal attainments, but adds that he never made "any professional use" of them.[6] Warren, while meticulously listing in his *History of the American Bar* Madison's great contemporaries at the bar, omits Madison's name. Nor does the elaborate index to Madison's *Letters and Other Writings* (1867) afford the least clue to his having been of the profession further than a single reference to Blackstone, which is not to the *Commentaries*.[7]

That, on the other hand, Madison was interested from an early date in what Rives terms "the general principles of public law and politics" is apparent from a number of sources. Indeed, it appears that one of his reasons for preferring Princeton over the College of William and Mary was furnished by the fact that Dr. Witherspoon, the new President of Princeton, had extended the course of "moral philosophy" in that institution to embrace such subjects; and it has been plausibly suggested that it was through these lectures that he first made acquaintance with "the celebrated Montesquieu," to quote his characterization of the latter in the *Federalist*. And the index to *Letters and Other Writings* affords

---

5. Fourton, "The Constitution as It Is Not," *New York Herald Tribune,* Oct. 23, 1937, at 18, col. 5.

6. See also, Hunt's curt words dismissing the subject. Hunt, *Life of Madison* 17.

7. I have discovered just one statement by a contemporary which supports even faintly the idea that Madison was a "lawyer." I refer to an extract given in 6 Burnett, *Letters of Members of the Continental Congress* 20 (1921–1936), from the dairy of Thomas Podney, who was a delegate to the Congress from Delaware. The item, dated March 1781, reads: "I take notice of a Mr. Madison of Virginia . . . who, with some little reading in the law is just from college, and possesses all the self-conceit that is common to youth and inexperience in such cases, but it is unattended with that gracefulness and ease which sometimes makes even the impertinence of youth and inexperience agreeable or at least not offensive." We gather from this that Podney did not like the young man; also that the former's reasoning processes were far from impeccable; all young lawyers are "self-conceited"; young Madison is "self-conceited"; therefore, young Madison is a lawyer! It should be added in further proof of Podney's unreliability, that Madison was not at this date "just from college," but from college some nine years.

further evidence of like bearing. While Blackstone is here referred to but once and Coke not at all, Grotius is cited twelve times, Montesquieu seven times, Puffendorf six times, and Vattel twelve times. In short, Madison's interests, so far as they had a legalistic tinge, were those of a publicist rather than of a lawyer.

Where, then, did the compiler of the *Biographical Dictionary of the American Congress, 1774–1927*[8] learn that "Madison 'was graduated from Princeton College in 1771, studied law at Princeton College one year; returned to Virginia; continued the study of the law; and was admitted to the bar' "?[9] The answer is, that the *Biographical Dictionary* did not burst forth in all panoply—it had several antecedents. The nearest in point of time is a publication, also from the Government Printing Office, called *A Biographical Congressional Directory,* which first appeared in 1903. Here the item on Madison reads, so far as it is pertinent to our present purpose, as follows: "Graduated from Princeton College in 1771, studied law and was admitted to the bar"[10]—nothing, it will be observed, about his studying law at Princeton "one year," nothing about his returning to Virginia to "continue" the study of the law; merely that he "Graduated from Princeton College . . . , studied law and was admitted to the bar." However, the *Directory* went to a second edition in 1913, and when we turn to this later issue we find the sketch that was to appear in the *Biographical Dictionary* fifteen years later almost word for word, but without the slightest indication as to the source whence the additional "information" was obtained.

The source is, nevertheless, quite clear. It was Ben: (*sic*) Perley Poore's *Political Register,* which was first issued at Boston in 1878. Here the item in the first edition of the *Directory* appears word for word.[11] But where you may well ask, did Ben: Perley Poore get his information? It would appear that it was *revealed* to him in a dream—in short, that he dreamt it—although the dream was—perhaps—inspired by the fact that that same year, 1878, the American Bar Association was founded. For it is not at all improbable that there were those who on that auspicious occasion sought to invoke the hovering spirits of the departed great of the profession, and if so it is not at all improbable that the invoker descried the spirit of James Madison among them.

I turn now to an earlier and quite different account of Madison's postgraduate education. I refer to the one in Charles Lanman's *Dictionary of the American Congress,* the first issue of which appeared in Philadelphia in 1859, and so antedates Poore's performance by some 19 years. Here we learn that following his graduation from Princeton, Madison "remained at the College until 1772, for the purpose of studying Hebrew";[12] and this statement is repeated in the succeeding editions of the work in 1864, 1866, 1868, and 1869. It still occurs, indeed, in the

---

8. H.R. Doc. No. 783, 69th Cong., 2d Sess. (1928).

9. *Id.* at 1279.

10. *A Biographical Congressional Directory* 678 (1903).

11. Poore, *Political Register* 520 (1878).

12. Lanman, *Dictionary of the American Congress* 310 (1859) {hereinafter, *Dictionary*}.

enlarged and revised edition of the work which appeared under the editorship of Joseph J. Morrison, in New York, in 1887. There Madison's formal education is dealt with as follows: "After due preparation, entered Princeton College in 1769 and graduated in 1771, going through the junior and senior studies in one year; remained at the college until 1772, for the purpose of studying Hebrew."[13]

That Madison *returned* to Princeton for an additional year in the study of Hebrew with Dr. Witherspoon is asserted in Appleton's *Cyclopedia of American Biography,* (New York, 1898); in the *Twentieth Century Biographical Dictionary of Notable Americans* (Boston, 1904); in the *Dictionary of American Biography,* and in the biographies of Gay and Hunt. Rives alone is silent on the point. Certainly, as between the thesis that Madison returned to Princeton to study law and the thesis that he returned or remained there to study Hebrew there can be but one choice. Princeton, in the person of President Witherspoon, was prepared to teach him Hebrew; it was not prepared to teach him law.

But if Madison passed a graduate year in the study of Hebrew, what purpose did he have in view? Apparently theology, a conjecture which the account given by his biographer of his studies at this period reinforces. "Among his early manuscripts which have come down to us," says Rives, "are minute and elaborate notes made by him on the Gospels and Acts of the Apostles which evince a close and discriminating study of the sacred writings, as well as the whole field of theological literature. . . . He explored the whole history and evidences of Christianity on every side . . . from the Fathers and schoolmen down to the infidel philosophers of the eighteeneth century."[14] So vast, indeed, were his researches, so unwonted, continues Rives, that when Jefferson came to plan the library of the University of Virginia years later, he turned spontaneously to Madison for "a list of theological writers, ancient and modern," and the catalogue with which Madison complied "remains a memorial" to the latter's learning.

Let us, however, turn to Madison's own published letters, to see what light they shed on his studies after he left Princeton finally. There are four such letters worth considering in this connection, the first of which was to his friend William Bradford and bears the date of November 9, 1772. The relevant portions read as follows:

> A watchful eye must be kept on ourselves, lest while we are building ideal monuments of renown and bliss here, we neglect to have our names enrolled in the annals of Heaven. . . . As to myself, I am too dull and infirm now to look out for any extraordinary things in this world, for I think my sensations for many months past have intimated to me not to expect a long and healthy life; though it may be better with me after some time, but I hardly dare expect it, and therefore have little spirit or elasticity to set about anything that is difficult in acquiring, and useless in possessing after one has exchanged time for eternity.

13. Lanman, *Dictionary* 314 (Morrison ed. 1887).
14. As quoted in Gay, *James Madison* 12 (1884).

Madison thereupon recommends to his young friend that the latter add to his "judicious choice of history and the science of morals" for his winter's reading, "a little divinity now and then, which, like the philosopher's stone in the hands of a good man, will turn them and every lawful acquirement into the nature of itself and make them more precious than fine gold."[15]

Manifestly, the only bar that Madison had much in mind at this date was "the bar of Heaven." And that he did not consider himself a lawyer more than four years later is shown fairly convincingly by the following sentence from a letter which he wrote his father in March 1777, regarding the case of one Haley, a Loyalist: "I have stated the case thus particularly not only for your own satisfaction, but that you may, if an opportunity occurs, take the advice of some gentleman skilled in the law, on the most proper and legal proceeding against him."[16] If Madison was a lawyer at this date—and he was now twenty-six—he at least seems to have been unaware of the fact.

And meanwhile Madison had, {after?} his election to the Virginia Assembly in 1776, entered upon public life. In 1777 he became a member of the Governor's Council, and from 1780 to the end of 1783 he was one of Virginia's delegates to the Continental Congress. Then came a brief period of retirement in the course of which he began reading law. He wrote Edmund Randolph about the matter March 10, 1784, as follows:

> On my arrival here which happened early in December I entered as soon as the necessary attentions to my friends admitted, on the course of reading which I have long meditated. Co: Litt: in consequence & a few others from the same shelf have been my chief society during the Winter. My progress, which in so short a period could not have been great under the most favorable circumstances, has been much retarded by the want of some important books, and still more by that of some living oracle for occasional consultation. But what will be most noxious to my project, I am to incur the interruptions which will result from attendance in the legislature, if the suffrage of my county should destine me for that service, which I am made to expect will be the case.[17]

Madison was elected to the legislature, as he had anticipated, and July 26, 1785, he wrote Randolph again. The relevant portion of his letter reads:

> I keep up my attention as far as I can command my time, to the course of reading which I have of late pursued and shall continue to do so. I am however, far from being determined ever to make a professional use of it. My wish is if possible to provide a decent and independent subsistence, without encountering the difficulties which I foresee in that line. Another of my wishes is to depend as little as possible on the labor of slaves. The difficulty of reconciling these views, has brought into my thoughts several projects from which advantage seemed attainable. I have in concert with a friend here, one at present on the anvil which we think cannot fail to

15. 1 *Writings of James Madison* 9–13 (Hunt ed. 1900).
16. *Id.* at 51.
17. 2 *id.* at 30–31.

yield a decent reward for our trouble. Should we persist in it, it will cost me a ride to Philadelphia, after which it will go on without my being ostensibly concerned.[18]

What does this correspondence show? It shows that Madison had reached his thirty-fifth year without choosing a profession. It shows that for about a year and a half, in 1784–1785, he devoted such time as his increasing political activity and other interests permitted, to reading law by himself. It does not show, although some of his biographers, including Hunt, have carelessly so interpreted it, that even now he had any intention of making the law his profession—indeed, it is direct evidence to the exact contrary.

And the great epoch of Madison's life had now dawned—the period which witnessed his indispensable services, first at Richmond, then at Annapolis, then at Philadelphia, then at Richmond again, then at New York, then once more at Philadelphia, in the formation and establishment of the present national government. Between 1785 and 1817, except for the years 1797 to 1801, Madison was continuously in the public service and taking a constantly engrossing part in it. From 1785 we hear not another word of his reading law—let alone of his seeking admission to the bar. That is, we do not hear another word from Madison himself. But in 1878 Ben: Perley Poore decided to make him a member of the bar posthumously, by a sort of *nunc pro tunc* procedure of his own devising.

The charge that Madison in 1787 was a lawyer fails on all counts, certainly if due consideration be given the maxim that a man is innocent until proved guilty. He had read law subject to constant interruption two years previously, in the course of his thirty-fourth and thirty-fifth years, but had had the benefit of no instruction or direction in the subject. He had never practiced law a day, had given no legal advice, had not been admitted to the bar, and never appeared in court as advocate—at least so far as any evidence so far produced shows.

II.

We turn now to Madison the exegete—for who indeed was better entitled to interpret the Constitution, or whose interpretations were intrinsically better entitled to attention? Did Madison's constitutional exegesis owe anything to the fact that he was not a member of the bar? I think that perhaps it did. In the first place, he had no professional axe to grind; he did not have to consider the possible impact of his views on the interests of actual or potential clients. His thinking on problems of constitutional construction were, moreover, untrammelled by the principle of *stare decisis*. (Yet so too were those of John Marshall, who never cited a past decision, even his own; but always took off from the constitutional document itself.) Nor did Madison seem ever to consider it a matter of moment that somebody else, whether in authority or out of it, had committed himself to a particular view of the Constitution. Indeed, the fact that he had himself pre-

18. *Id.* at 154–55.

viously expressed a divergent or even a flatly contradictory view seems not to
have curtailed his intellectual freedom in exegesis at any particular moment. At
times, indeed, he indulged himself in what, on first consideration, seem to be the
wildest inconsistencies. At least consistency was no hobgoblin to him.

Yet on certain points he steadily, not to say obstinately, adhered to earlier
announced positions, even entrenched himself more deeply in them; for example,
in the conception of religious freedom which he fought for in his *Remonstrance*
of 1785; also his narrow conception of the national spending power as a power
simply to provision the government in the exercise of its other granted powers,
and not an independent power. This position he adumbrated in *Federalist,* no.
41, and it is the basis of his veto of the Bonus Bill thirty years later.

Are there, then, any clues to the course of Madison's performance as constitutional exegete? I find that there are two principal ones, and a third, rather minor
one. The first is, or was for a season, the overweening influence of Jefferson, his
surrender to which leaves the somewhat unpleasant impression of undue pliabil-
ity, not to say serviceability, and which, by way of retribution, involved him in a
nagging task of self-vindication all of his declining years. The second was a
natural preference for midway positions, which was certainly not to his discredit,
but which has resulted in his contribution to the course of constitutional interpretation being considerably less important, considerably less predictive of the
future, than that of the more positive and imaginative Hamilton. The third, minor
clue, was the temptation his somewhat oversubtle mind was always subject to, to
spin out refined distinctions, which one may sometimes admire without being
able to concede their practical feasibility.

By way of illustrating these points, I propose to deal, at not undue length, with
Madison's various and at times conflicting views on the two subjects: (1) the
nature and source of the Constitution; (2) interpretation of the commerce clause;
and when convenient I shall cite the urban Hamilton's contrasting views as a foil
to those of the rural Virginian.

In the prevailing opinion of its framers the Constitution represented an exercise
by the American people of their primitive inexhaustible right of determining their
own governmental institutions, unhindered by anything that had been done by
them in this respect previously. By this view, while its establishment was facilitated by both the Congress of the Confederation and the states, the Constitution
was in legal contemplation the act of the human beings upon whom the new
system was planned to operate, and derived its authority solely from them, as,
according to the Declaration of Independence, "all just governments" do. In the
words of Hamilton in *Federalist,* no. 22, "the fabric of American empire ought
to rest on the solid basis of the consent of the people. The streams of national
power ought to flow immediately from that pure, original fountain of all legitimate authority."[19]

19. *Federalist,* no. 22, at 141 (Earle ed. 1937).

Hence, in fact, stemmed the chief objection urged against the Constitution by opponents of its adoption. Said Patrick Henry in the Virginia convention, with reference to the first three words of the Preamble: "Have they said, 'We the states'—If they had, this would be a Confederation. It is otherwise, most clearly, a consolidated government. The question turns, sir, on a poor little thing—the expression, We the people, instead of states of America—Here is a revolution as radical as that which separated us from Great Britain.'"[20]

Henry was answered by Pendleton, a supporter of the Constitution, in the following words: "We the people, possessing all power, form a government, such as we think will secure happiness-but an objection is made of the form: The expression, We the people, is thought improper. Permit me to ask the gentleman who made this objection, who but the people can delegate powers? Who but the people have a right to form government?"[21]

Noteworthy too are the words of Wilson in the Pennsylvania ratifying convention: "In this Constitution all authority is derived from the people—The leading principle in politics and that which pervades the American Constitution is that the supreme power resides in the people."[22]

And again: "The Convention were forming compacts! With whom?—I am unable to conceive who the parties could be. The state governments were making a bargain with one another; that is the doctrine that is endeavored to be established by gentlemen in opposition; their state sovereignties wish to be represented. But far other were the ideas of this Convention, and far other are those conveyed in the system itself."[23]

Note, too, the words of Richard Henry Lee, an opponent of the Constitution: "It is to be observed," said he in the *Letters from the Federal Farmer*, "that when the people shall adopt the proposed Constitution it will be their last and supreme act; it will be adopted not by the people of New Hampshire, Massachusetts, &c., but by the people of the United States...."[24] Note, too, the words in which the Virginia convention ratified the Constitution: "We the delegates of the people of Virginia ... do in the name and in behalf of the people of Virginia declare and make known that the powers granted under the Constitution being derived from the people of the United States may be resumed by them whensoever the same shall be perverted to their injury or oppression and that every power not granted thereby remains with them and at their will."[25]

The view, nevertheless, that the Constitution was simply an act of consent by *human* beings endowed with the rights of men under the social compact represented the sophisticated outlook of a small group, well read in the Lockean

20. 3 *The Debates on the Constitution* 22–23 (Elliot ed. 1881).
21. *Id.* at 35.
22. 2 *id.* at 434–35.
23. *Id.* at 497.
24. *Pamphlets on the Constitution* 311 (P. L. Ford ed. 1888).
25. 3 *The Debates on the Constitution* 656 (Elliot ed. 1937).

political philosophy and having interests which transcended state lines. It was soon confronted with another theory which was much more accordant with the narrow social experience and localistic prejudices of a widely scattered agricultural population. This was the doctrine of the Virginia and Kentucky Resolutions of 1798 and 1799, that the Constitution was a compact of sovereign states, and that the ultimate voice in construing it lay with the state legislatures. I shall now sketch briefly Madison's part—a creative part—in bringing about this shift in fundamental constitutional doctrine.

That Madison shared the theory which found expression in the Virginia act of ratification is reasonably clear; but at the same time he must needs refine upon it. On the floor of the Virginia convention, where his divagations began, he said:

> Who are the parties to it? The people—but not the people as composing one great body; but the people as composing thirteen sovereignties. Were it, as the gentleman asserts, a consolidated government, the assent of a majority of the people would be sufficient for its establishment. . . . But, sir, no state is bound by it, as it is, without its own consent. Should all the states adopt it, it will be then a government established by the thirteen states of America, not through the intervention of the legislatures, but by the people at large. . . . The existing system has been derived from the dependent, derivative, authority of the legislatures of the states; whereas this is derived from the superior power of the people.[26]

Thus the source of the Constitution, once it was adopted, would be "the people at large."

But in *Federalist,* no. 39, his departure from the line taken by his fellow "Publius" is more manifest. Here, in the midst of an ingenious comparison of the "national" and the "federal" features of the proposed Constitution, he classifies its mode of ratification as "federal", in the following words:

> It appears on one hand that the Constitution is to be founded on the assent and ratification of the people of America, given by deputies elected for the special purpose; but on the other that this assent and ratification is to be given by the people, not as individuals composing one entire nation; but as composing the distinct and independent states to which they respectively belong. It is to be the assent and ratification of the several states, derived from the supreme authority in each state, the authority of the people themselves. The act therefore establishing the Constitution, will not be a national, but a federal act. . . .[27]

So far, so good; but at this point a new thought appears, or at any rate a new mode of expression: "Each state in ratifying the Constitution is considered as a sovereign body, independent of all others, and only to be bound by its own voluntary act. In this relation, then, the new Constitution will, if established, be a federal and not a national Constitution."[28] That is to say, the ratification of the Constitution will be, in the final analysis, an act of state *power*, not an exercise of human *rights*.

26. *Id.* at 94.
27. *Federalist,* no. 39, at 246 (Earle ed. 1937).
28. *Id.* at 247.

The next stage in the deterioration of Madison's nationalism is more evident, being marked by his authorship of the Virginia Resolutions of 1798, the third of which is the important one: I quote:

> That this assembly doth explicitly and peremptorily declare that it views the powers of the federal government as resulting from the compact to which the states are parties, as limited by the plain sense and intention of the instrument constituting that compact; as no further valid than they are authorized by the grants enumerated in that compact; and that, in case of a deliberate, palpable, and dangerous exercise of other powers not granted by the said compact, the states, who are parties thereto, have the right and are in duty bound to interpose for arresting the progress of the evil, and for maintaining within their respective limits the authorities, rights, and liberties appertaining to them.[29]

In short, the Constitution rests not on an act of the people, but on a *compact* of the states; and these in consequence possess the power and the duty of interposing between their citizens and the federal government in protection of the constitutional rights of the former. In other words, the relation between the states and their citizens is *primary;* that between the national government and these same citizens is *secondary.* Here, in brief is the whole Calhounist system, with the single exception that whereas Madison pointed to the state legislature (although he appears to have entertained doubts on that point) as the instrument of interposition, Calhoun held that the business must be performed by conventions in the individual states, inasmuch as it was by a convention that the Constitution was adopted in each state.

But Madison had still a few subtleties to cast: the Virginia and Kentucky Resolutions, having been transmitted to the legislatures of sister states, elicited from the seven northern of them unequivocal declarations of the power of the Supreme Court of the United States "ultimately" to decide "on the constitutionality . . . of any act of Congress."

In his famous Report to the Virginia legislature in 1800, Madison undertakes to answer the answers. He begins by reiterating his characterization of the Constitution as a *compact of states.* He writes:

> It is indeed true that the term "states" is sometimes used in a vague sense, and sometimes in different senses, according to the subject to which it is applied. Thus it sometimes means the separate sections of territory occupied by the political societies within each; sometimes the particular governments established by those societies; *sometimes those societies as organized into those* particular governments; and lastly, it means *the people composing those political societies in their highest political capacity.* . . . In the present instance, whatever different construction of the term "states" in the resolution may have been entertained, all will at least concur in that last mentioned; because in that sense the Constitution was submitted to the "states"; in that sense the "states" ratified it; and in that sense of the term "states" they are consequently parties to the compact from which the powers of the federal government result. . . . The Constitution of the United States was formed by

29. 6 *Writings of James Madison* 326 (Hunt ed. 1906).

the sanction of the states, given by each of *its* sovereign capacity. . . . The states then, being the parties to the constitutional compact, and in their sovereign capacity, it follows of necessity that there can be no tribunal above their authority to decide.[30]

Thus what is at the outset characterized as the highest political capacity of the *people* of the states is finally transmuted by verbal legerdemain into the highest political capacity of the *states* themselves. As to them, therefore, the Court's interpretations of the constitutional compact cannot be final. Later in the report occurs this sentiment: "The authority of constitutions over governments and of the sovereignty of the people over constitutions" are truths that cannot be enough emphasized. True enough. But if it was the purport of the Resolutions merely to assert the ultimate control of the people of the United States over the Constitution, why all the talk about "a compact of sovereign states"?

And the fact is that in the end, Madison abandons his entire case for state "interposition," writing:

A declaration that proceedings of the federal government are not warranted by the Constitution is a novelty neither among the citizens nor among the legislatures of the states, . . . nor can the declarations of either, whether affirming or denying the constitutionality of measures of the federal government, be deemed, in any point of view an assumption of the office of judge. The declarations in such cases are expressions of opinion, unaccompanied with any other effect than what they may produce on opinion by exciting reflection.[31]

Surely, a lame conclusion to so much fulmination! The boasted right of the "sovereign state" to insert itself between its citizens and the national government on such occasions as it deems the latter to be exceeding its powers comes down in the last analysis to a mere right on the part of its legislature to vote resolutions expressive of opinion, resolutions which are admitted to be no more authoritative than any ebullition of public opinion.

In his declining years Madison was greatly exercised over the use Calhoun was currently making of the Virginia and Kentucky Resolutions. He claimed that what the authors of those Resolutions had had in mind was merely to stir up a general protest by the states against the unconstitutional measures of the federal government. Unfortunately, the assertion that "the states have the right . . . to interpose for arresting the progress of the evil and for maintaining within their *respective* limits" their rights and powers somewhat blunts this defense.[32]

On another point Madison had, possibly, a better case against Calhoun; at least Professor McLaughlin thinks he had. In brief it is, that while Madison conceived of sovereignty as "divisible," Calhoun thought of it as "indivisible," and proceeded from the latter point of view to place an unwarranted construction on the resolutions of 1798 and 1799. And it was perhaps with Calhoun's alleged sophis-

---

30. *Id.* at 348 (italics added).
31. *Id.* at 402.
32. See note 28 above.

try in mind that Madison warned his countrymen late in life "against those errors which have their origin in the altered meaning of words and phrases."[33]

Lastly, though by no means least, is the fact that the Resolutions of 1798 and 1799 evoked from only *one* legislature, that of Vermont, a challenge to the theory that the Constitution was a compact of states. In this respect the Resolutions, as I indicated earlier, must be deemed to have crystallized what by that date had come to be a generally held view; and with the appearance of Tucker's *Blackstone* in 1803 the Resolutions became a gloss upon the Constitution that was ultimately as authentic as the original document. The impressive majority by which the Senate on December 27, 1837, voted the first of a series of resolutions moved by Calhoun, which asserted that the Constitution was adopted by "independent, sovereign states acting severally," showed that the compact theory, in its baldest form had become the creed, not of a section, but of a great part of the country.[34]

III.

I come now to consider Madison's influence on interpretation of the commerce clause—"the Congress shall have power to regulate commerce with foreign nations, among the several states and with the Indian tribes."[35] There came a time about the turn of the century when the proposition that Congress' power over interstate commerce was less than its power over foreign commerce comprised an important element of the system of constitutional interpretation which the Court was then in process of erecting in defense of laissez-faire conceptions of the proper role of government, and especially of the national government. What, if any, responsibility had Madison for this proposition?

In the debate early in the first Congress under the Constitution over a proposed revenue act which embodied mild protective features, Madison remarked: "I own myself the friend to a very free system of commerce, and hold it as a truth that commercial shackles are generally unjust, oppressive and impolitic; it is also a truth that if industry and labor are left to take their own course, they will generally be directed to those objects which are the most productive, and this in a more certain and direct manner than the wisdom of the most enlightened legislature could point out."[36]

Four years earlier Madison had requested Jefferson, who was then abroad, to procure for him a copy of Adam Smith's *Wealth of Nations*. Evidently Jefferson had done so, and Madison had been reading the book. But to contend on the basis of this evidence that Madison was responsible for the Supreme Court's decision in 1918 in the first Child Labor Case[37] or its decision in 1936 in Carter v. Carter

33. McLaughlin, *The Courts, the Constitution and Parties* 189–242 (1912).
34. *Cong. Globe*, 25th Cong., 2d Sess. 55 (1838).
35. *U.S. Const.* Art. I, sec. 8.
36. 5 *Writings of James Madison* 342 (Hunt ed. 1904).
37. Hammer v. Dagenhart, 247 U.S. 251 (1918).

Coal Co.,[38] holding that the national government was without power to govern labor-management relations in the industrial field, would no doubt be going rather far.

Much closer to the point, certainly, is the following passage from a letter which Madison wrote his friend, J. C. Cabell, in 1829, forty years after the debate on the first tariff.

> I always foresaw that difficulties might be started in relation to that power which could not be fully explained without recurring to views of it, which, however just, might give birth to specious though unsound objections. Being in the same terms with the power over foreign commerce, the same extent, if taken literally, would belong to it. Yet it is very certain that it grew out of the abuse of the power by the importing states in taxing the nonimporting, and was intended as a negative and preventive provision against injustice among the states themselves, rather than as a power to be used for the positive purposes of the general government, in which alone, however, the remedial power could be lodged. And it will be safer to leave the power with this key to it, than to extend to it all the qualities and incidental means belonging to the power over foreign commerce, as is unavoidable, according to the reasoning I see applied to the case.[39]

Now the first thing to note about this theory is its paradoxical nature. It is contended, in effect, that the grant of power to Congress to regulate commerce among the states merely took this power from the states without vesting the equivalent power in Congress. The net result of the transfer is therefore that both the states from which the power was taken and Congress to which it was in explicit terms given, have equal power to regulate commerce among the states "for positive purposes"—which is to say, *no power*. "The power perished as the result of the act by which it was conferred." But obviously if the framers intended such a result the logical way for them to achieve it would have been to impose a simple prohibition on the states; and at least they might reasonably be expected to have avoided the precise phrase which they would have employed had they sought the directly contrary result—which in fact, they did employ when they conferred on Congress the power to regulate foreign commerce "for the positive purposes of the general government"!

What we have here is another characteristic product of the ingenious hairsplitting mind of James Madison. Perhaps only this mind could have produced such a theory. At least we have negative evidence that nobody else had up to that time thought of it—even more that nobody else thought of it again for many years afterwards. Thus, if this theory had been generally available in 1841, Henry Clay would certainly have exploited it in his argument before the Court in the case of Groves v. Slaughter,[40] in which he sought to show that Congress had no power to ban the interstate slave trade. But no; the best Clay could do was to revive the

---

38. 298 U.S. 238 (1936).
39. 4 *Letters and Other Writings of James Madison* 14–15 (Lippincott ed. 1867).
40. 15 Pet. 448 (U.S. 1841).

argument which had been urged against Jefferson's Embargo years before, that the power to *regulate* commerce did not include the power to *prohibit* it. That there was any difference between its power over interstate commerce and its power over foreign commerce in this respect Clay does not so much as suggest.

The letter to Cabell became general property with Lippincott's publication in 1867 of Madison's *Letters and Other Writings*. Between that date and 1899 the Court took occasion to assert some ten times the identity in scope of the two branches of the commerce power (commerce "with the Indian tribes" may be ignored); and on the last three occasions it directly refuted counsel's countercontention. On two of these occasions Chief Justice Fuller spoke for the Court, and on the third Justice Peckham, who said:

> It is yet insisted by the appellants at the threshold of the inquiry that by the true construction of the Constitution, the power of Congress to regulate interstate commerce is limited to its protection from acts of interference by state legislation or by means of regulations made under the authority of the state by some political subdivision thereof. . . .
>
> The reasons which may have caused the framers of the Constitution to repose the power to regulate interstate commerce in Congress do not, however, affect or limit the extent of the power itself. . . .[41]

This was in 1899. That same year Mr. John Randolph Tucker's two-volume work titled *The Constitution of the United States*, appeared posthumously. Here is laid down the following extraordinary (at that date) proposition that "the Union is a *Staaten-bund,* not a *Bundestaat,*" that "each state is a republic of which the units are men," while "the United States is a confederate union, of which the units are not men but states.'"[42] This, of course, is but the Virginia and Kentucky Resolutions of 1798–1799, decked out with a couple of Germanic terms, borrowed, I surmise, from Professor John W. Burgess' currently famous work *Political Science and Constitutional Law*. At any rate, Tucker deduces from this alleged truth, the further theorem that "all powers vested in Congress" are "trust powers to be used for the states as beneficiaries." Turning then to the commerce clause, he writes:

> The power to regulate foreign and interstate commerce was given in the same terms *diverso intuitu*. In the first, to protect all against the machinations of foreign enemies; in the second, to protect and promote the free and unobstructed movement of men and things between the states in the family of the Union.
>
> These considerations conclusively show that the power to regulate interstate commerce is not commensurate with the power of Congress to regulate foreign

41. Addyston Pipe & Steel Co. v. United States, 175 U.S. 211, 226–28 (1899). See also License Cases, 5 How. 504, 578 (U.S. 1847); South Carolina v. Georgia, 93 U.S. 4, 16 (1876); Railroad Co. v. Husen, 95 U.S. 465, 469 (1877); Brown v. Houston, 114 U.S. 622, 630 (1885); Bowman v. Chicago & N.W.R. Co., 125 U.S. 465, 482, 483 (1888); Crutcher v. Kentucky, 141 U.S. 47, 57–58 (1891); Pittsburgh Coal Co. v. Bates, 156 U.S. 577, 587 (1895); *In re* Rahrer, 140 U.S. 548, 561 (1891) (C. J. Fuller speaking for the Court); United States v. E. C. Knight Co., 156 U.S. 1, 11–12 (1895) C. J. Fuller for the Court).

42. 1 Tucker, *The Constitution of the United States* 318 (1899).

commerce.... The whole Constitution, in all its parts, looks to the security of free trade in persons and goods between the states of the Union, and ... prohibits either Congress or the states to interfere with this freedom of intercourse and trade.[43]

The influence of Tucker's work with the Court first appears in two *dissenting opinions*, both by Chief Justice Fuller, who had previously, as has been noted, twice rejected the Madisonian thesis with emphasis. The second of these dissents occurred in the Lottery Case of 1903,[44] and is couched in the following terms:

It is argued that the power to regulate commerce among the several states is the same as the power to regulate commerce with foreign nations, and among the Indian tribes. But is its scope the same... ?

The power to regulate commerce with foreign nations and the power to regulate interstate commerce, are to be taken *diverso intuitu,* for the latter was intended to secure equality and freedom in commercial intercourse as between the states, not to permit the creation of impediments to such intercourse, while the former clothes Congress with that power over international commerce, pertaining to a sovereign nation in its intercourse with foreign nations, and subject, generally speaking, to no implied or reserved power in the states. The laws which would be necessary and proper in the one case would not be necessary or proper in the other....[45]

The Madison-Tucker-Fuller doctrine was pressed with increased insistence by Mr. Parmelee Prentice in his *The Federal Power over Carriers and Corporations,* which appeared in 1907, by way of reaction to President Theodore Roosevelt's proposals to Congress anent the further regulation of railroads and a national incorporation act for all companies engaged in interstate commerce; also by Mr. Carman F. Randolph, who wrote in his *Law and Policy of Annexation,* published in 1901, as follows:

The states did not transfer to Congress the sovereign power of restriction which each possessed. They renounced these powers, *left them in the air,* and authorized Congress to maintain the freedom of trade established by their renunciation. To regulate domestic commerce, then, is to *facilitate* an intercourse placed beyond reach of prohibition, and, while regulations may in fact involve some restraint upon the conduct of particular intercourse, they have their warrant and purpose in the facilitation of all intercourse.[46]

Meantime the torch of the new illumination had been taken over by Justice, later Chief Justice, White, who repeatedly seized the opportunity afforded by cases involving only *foreign* commerce to contrast Congress' power in respect thereto with its lesser power over interstate commerce.[47] But the Madisonian doctrine did not prove decisive till the first Child Labor Case, where it is not

---

43. 2 *id.* at 528–29, 533.
44. 188 U.S. 321 (1903).
45. *Id.* at 373.
46. Randolph, *Law and Policy of Annexation* 97, 98 (1901) (italics added).
47. See his opinions in Buttfield v. Stranahan, 192 U.S. 470, 492–93 (1904); The Abby Dodge, 223 U.S. 166, 176–77 (1912); Brolan v. United States, 236 U.S. 216, 222 (1915).

referred to by either counsel or Court. This was in 1918. Fourteen years later, in Atlantic Cleaners and Dyers v. United States,[48] Justice Sutherland, in sustaining the right of Congress to govern local trade in the District of Columbia, went straight back to the Madisonian thesis in a dictum which, of course, was entirely uncalled for by the case. He said:

> It is not unusual for the same word to be used with different meanings in the same act, and there is no rule of statutory construction which precludes the courts from giving the word the meaning which the legislatures intended it should have in each instance. Louisville & N.R. Co. v. Gaines (C.C.) 2 Flipp. 621, 3 Fed. 266, 277, 278. Thus, for example, the meaning of the word "legislature," used several times in the federal Constitution, differs according to the connection in which it is employed, depending upon the character of the function which that body in each instance is called upon to exercise. Smiley v. Holm, 285 U.S. 355, ante, 795, 52 S. Ct. 397, decided April 11, 1932. And, again in the Constitution, the power to regulate commerce is conferred by the same words of the commerce clause with respect both to foreign commerce and interstate commerce. Yet the power when exercised in respect of foreign commerce, may be broader than when exercised as to interstate commerce. In the regulation of foreign commerce an embargo is admissible; but it reasonably cannot be thought that, in respect of legitimate and unobjectionable articles, an embargo would be admissible as a regulation of interstate commerce, since the primary purpose of the clause in respect of the latter was to secure freedom of commercial intercourse among the states. See Groves v. Slaughter, 15 Pet. 449, 505; Southern S. S. Co. v. Portwardens, 6 Wall. 31, 32, 33; Buttfield v. Stranahan, 192 U.S. 470, 492. Compare Russell Motor Car Co. v. United States, 261 U.S. 514, 520, 521.[49]

This invocation by Justice Sutherland of "the rules of statutory construction" fittingly completes the record I have been tracing. As the Justice says, it is well recognized that a word which *recurs* in a document may not always sustain throughout the document the same meaning, although the legal *presumption* is that it does so. But that a word should have *two* quite different meanings in a single short sentence in which it occurs but *once,* is certainly a novelty to the science of hermeneutics and probably to that of linguistics as well. Yet it is this novelty precisely that James Madison fathered in 1829 in his letter to Cabell.

In Chief Justice Stone's opinion for the unanimous Court in United States v. Darby,[50] in which in 1941, the Fair Labor Standards Act of 1938[51] was sustained, the Madisonian thesis is consigned to the judicial scrap basket, not only without "the decent obsequies of a funeral oration," but even without mention. By the same token, Hamilton's conception of the scope of the power which is conferred on the national government by the commerce clause was, in effect, endorsed by the Court. Discussing in *Federalist,* no. 23, the principal purposes of the Union, Hamilton listed among them "the common defense of the members, the preser-

48. 286 U.S. 427 (1932).
49. *Id.* at 433–34.
50. 312 U.S. 100 (1941).
51. 52 Stat. 1060, 29 U.S.C. sec. 201 (1946).

vation of the public peace, . . . the regulation of commerce with other nations and between the states, . . ." As to all these purposes he continued, "government of the Union must be empowered to pass all laws, and to make all regulations which have relation to them. The same must be the case in respect to commerce, and to every other matter to which its jurisdiction is permitted to extend."[52]

Some years ago I received a letter from a Los Angeles gentleman, in which, among other things, he asked me whether I thought that Madison deserved to be called "the father of the Constitution" and whether I didn't think that Hamilton was better entitled to the designation. I answered him as follows:

> As to Madison's paternity of the Constitution—it has no doubt been considerably exaggerated, although I think that if there had to be a Father of the Constitution, in order to gratify the father complex of the American people, Madison was probably the most eligible candidate. I recommend that you read Pierce's sketch of him in the third volume of Farrand's *Records*. Hamilton, I should say, had only a minor influence on the Convention, which he attended rather discontinuously. Of course, his performance in the *Federalist* is superb. At least he was the Father of the interpreters of the Constitution; or, perhaps one should say, Father of the Constitution which interpretation has given us.

On the whole, I still think this estimate does justice to the relative claims of these two great men. Recent events have about erased the Madisonian gloss from the Constitutional Document, while the Hamiltonian gloss has about erased some of the most important features of that document, particularly those provisions which were intended to delineate the respective fields of legislative and executive power. And this truth is roughly symbolized by the import for our daily lives of New York City, Hamilton's abode, on the one hand, and the plantation life which nourished Madison's thinking, on the other. New York City awaits, by no means indifferently, its first atom bomb. The life and economy of the Virginia plantation has long since "gone with the wind"—"the eternally coursing winds of change." At the moment Hamilton appears to have won out.

52. *Federalist*, no. 23, at 142 (Earle ed. 1937).

II.

THE POWERS OF CONGRESS

10. The Treaty-making Power: A Rejoinder

IN his article in the April *North American Review*[1] Mr. Henry St. George Tucker argues that the reserved powers of the states limit the treaty-making power of the United States. In the following article the contrary view will be presented.

Mr. Tucker admits that it may be inconvenient "to permit the people of one state . . . by its independent and antagonistic action to defeat a treaty whose beneficent effects are intended to reach all the people of the United States," but he contends that "the argument *ab inconvenienti* . . . cannot be admitted in the consideration of constitutional rights." Unfortunately, he soon forgets this equally correct and sensible principle, for he contends with great urgency that if the view combated by him be correct, "the Negro from Haiti or the Congo may under a treaty be free to enter the schools of Texas and ride in any coach on a railroad that may suit his tastes, notwithstanding the law of Texas to the contrary"; and he inquires, with considerable indignation, whether American citizenship is "to be a badge of inferiority and the alien to be preferred to the native-born American." No doubt we incur grave risks in maintaining a national government at all. For with its powers to regulate commerce and to tax, Congress has trade, business, and private incomes pretty much at its mercy; with their powers of appointment the President and Senate can fill all of the offices with rogues; with his powers in the conduct of foreign relations the President can bring on that worst of calamities, a foreign war, for any sort of cause. But then we recall that the states themselves originally possessed some of these powers and used them to so little advantage that the people transferred them to the central government. Very likely they should have abolished them outright.

Reprinted from 199 *North American Review* 893 (1914) by permission of the University of Northern Iowa.

1. "The Treaty-making Power under the Constitution of the United States," 199 *North Am. Rev.* 560 (1914).

Turning, then, to the question at issue, we find that Mr. Tucker bases his argument upon some words from Story and Cooley, upon the admitted fact that the treaty-making power is a constitutionally limited power, upon one or two judicial utterances, and upon his reading of the Tenth Amendment and Article VI, paragraph 2, of the Constitution.

The words from Cooley sustain Mr. Tucker's position, but as Cooley cites in their support the same words of Story that Mr. Tucker does, the question before us is whether Story's words have been properly used. These are as follows: "But though the power [of making treaties] is thus general and unrestricted, it is not to be so construed as to destroy *the fundamental laws of the State.*" These words Mr. Tucker quotes four times, but on the last two occasions he introduces an interesting variation by making the word "State" plural! For this proceeding there is no warrant. Story in the passage quoted uses the word "State" in the generic sense and means by it the *United States.* This is shown, first, by his capitalization of it, whereas he always puts the states of the Union in the lower case. It is shown, secondly, by the words that immediately follow the ones quoted: "A power given by the Constitution cannot be construed to authorize a destruction of other powers *given* in the same instrument." If the powers of the states are *given* them by the Constitution, what becomes of their *reserved* rights? But it is shown finally by his words on the precise point under discussion: "The peace of the nation and its good faith and moral dignity indispensably require that *all* state laws shall be subject to the supremacy of treaties with foreign nations." (Section 1838.)

But the ultimate authority, that upon which commentators and courts must alike rest, is, of course, that of the Constitution. The Tenth Amendment to the Constitution reads: "The powers not delegated to the United States by this Constitution nor prohibited by it to the states are reserved to the states respectively or to the people."

These words, by Mr. Tucker's own presentation of the case, do not advance the discussion much, since the treaty-making power *is* delegated to the United States, wherefore the crucial question still demands answer, as to what happens when that power is so exercised as to conflict with the exercise by a state of one of its reserved powers. The really pertinent passage of the Constitution is therefore Article VI, paragraph 2, which reads thus: "This Constitution and the laws of the United States which shall be made in pursuance thereof and all treaties made or which shall be made under the authority of the United States shall be the supreme law of the land; and the judges in every state shall be bound thereby, *anything in the constitution or laws of any state to the contrary notwithstanding.*"

It would be tolerably difficult, I surmise, to select words conveying more clearly the idea that state power cannot limit national power. *For if the states possess a power, they may exercise it by enacting statutes or constitutions.* But it is here declared that *any* such statute or constitution, or part thereof, conflicting with a treaty made under the authority of the United States must fall to the ground; and how "the authority of the United States" is to be deemed limited by that over which it is pronounced invariably supreme is certainly more than the mind untutored in the dialectics of the state rights school can easily fathom.

But Mr. Tucker points out, what indeed is universally admitted, that the "authority of the United States" by virtue of which treaties are made is not an unlimited authority; that, for example, it does not constrain Congress to vote money to carry out a treaty; and he contends that "supremacy admits of no limitations, exceptions, or conditions." Very true, but the question still remains, supremacy of *what* over *what?* And the answer is, supremacy of treaties made by the authority of the United States, which is the authority established, created, and defined by the Constitution, over *all* conflicting state laws and constitutional provisions; and the similar supremacy of all acts of Congress made in pursuance of the Constitution.

However, not desiring to make Article VI mere empty verbiage, Mr. Tucker introduces a distinction. It is entirely apparent that Article VI owes its existence directly to the recognition by the framers of the Constitution that the states would continue to possess large and undefined powers of legislation which would probably be exercised in the future, as they had been in the past, to the derogation of national power. But Mr. Tucker would have us believe that the only kind of state laws against which the framers intended to safeguard national power were the laws which the states would pass by virtue of what he calls their "concurrent powers." Let us examine this contention.

Mr. Tucker defines "concurrent powers" as "powers which the federal and state governments each employ." The definition is imperfect. More accurately speaking, concurrent powers are those which the states may exercise within the field of power assigned by the Constitution to the national government *in the absence of conflicting national legislation*. Actually, the idea has been of little importance in constitutional law save in connection with state legislation *directly* regulating foreign or interstate commerce; and in this connection it did not obtain legal standing till 1851, in the famous case of Cooley v. The Board of Wardens, 12 How. 299, where, however, it is used, not in contradistinction to what Mr. Tucker calls "the reserved powers of the states," but to those branches of commercial regulation which are closed to the states by the mere grant of power to Congress. Moreover, the Court there declares explicitly that these powers belong to the states, not by virtue of any delegation of power from the national government, but of original right—that is, that they stand on the same footing with all other state powers. And today the term has substantially disappeared from the vocabulary of the Court, which regards all state legislation as enacted by virtue of the same power, to wit, "the police power." But suppose we admit what is apparently Mr. Tucker's view, that these powers are different from the states' reserved or police powers in that they owe their existence not to the states' autonomy, but to the allowance of the national government. Then indeed is

Article VI, paragraph 2, superfluous, since obviously this allowance may be withdrawn at any moment. Finally, Article VI knows nothing of this distinction: it says "*anything* in the constitution or laws of *any* state to the contrary notwithstanding."

But, lastly, Mr. Tucker makes his case concrete by citing a power which undoubtedly is one of the reserved powers of the states, in the strictest sense of the term, and which accordingly, if his contention is correct, cannot be invaded by the treaty power. Thus he quotes the language of Justice Field in United States v. Fox, 94 U.S. 315, 320 (1877): "The power of the state to regulate the tenure of real property within her limits, and the modes of its acquisition and transfer, and the rules of its descent, and the extent to which testamentary disposition of it may be exercised by its owner, is undoubted." And again the language of Justice Washington in McCormick v. Sullivant, 10 Wheat. 192, 202 (1825): "The title and modes of disposition of real property within the states, whether *inter vivos* or testamentary, are not matters placed under the control of federal authority."

At the close of his paper, furthermore, Mr. Tucker in a note "confidently asserts that no case has been decided by the Supreme Court involving the direct question herein discussed"—that is, the competence of the treaty-making power to invade the field of state rights. Let us see whether this confidence is well founded.

The same judges, with one exception, who decided the McCormick Case also decided Chirac v. Chirac, 2 Wheat. 259 (1817); the same judges, with one exception, who decided United States v. Fox also decided Hauenstein v. Lynham, 100 U.S. 483 (1880); and the judge who wrote the opinion in the United States v. Fox again spoke for the Court in Geofroy v. Riggs, 133 U.S. 258 (1890). In each of these three cases the issue was the same; it lay between claimants to real estate whose right to the property involved was admitted to be perfect under the local law and other claimants who asserted the right to claim the same property *as heirs* to it upon the basis of certain treaty provisions.[2] In each case the decision of the United States Supreme Court, given unanimously, was in favor of the latter claimants; and the basis of the decision was in each case announced to be Article VI, paragraph 2. Later, reviewing these and similar decisions, Attorney General Griggs stated the rule that they unmistakably establish: "*The fact that a treaty provision annuls and supersedes the law of a particular state upon the same subject is no objection to the validity of the treaty.*" (22 Opinions 214 [1900].)

Mr. Tucker's "confident assertion" just quoted is therefore plainly without merit; as is also his further assertion that "all of the cases have decided questions collateral with the real issue involved in this [his] paper."

Nor, had he turned from judicial decision to the practice of the treaty-making

---

2. The local law in Geofroy v. Riggs was that of the District of Columbia, but it was ruled that the term "state" of the treaty applied also to the District.

body, would he have found better support for his general thesis. The United States has since 1789 entered into dozens of treaties of amity and commerce, extradition treaties, and consular conventions, every one of which has to a greater or less extent invaded the field normally occupied by the states in the exercise of their reserved powers.[3] This subject naturally cannot be entered upon at length in a short article, but one treaty I will make specific reference to. This is the Convention of 1800 with France, which, in the language of the Supreme Court of the United States, gave citizens of France "the right to purchase and hold land in the United States"—in contravention of the common law rule, then prevalent in every state in the Union—"removed the incapacity of alienage, and placed them in precisely the same situation as if they had been citizens of this country." This indeed, to quote Attorney General Cushing, is "the most expressive of all precedents, it having passed through the hands and received the approbation of John Adams, John Marshall, Oliver Ellsworth, Thomas Jefferson, and James Madison, who, if anybody, should have understood the Constitution."

On the precise question, therefore, of the relation of the treaty-making power to the reserved rights of the states, our conclusion must be that the latter do not limit the former to any extent; that, in other words, *the United States has exactly the same range of power in making treaties that it would have if the states did not exist.* Further, it should be pointed out that the same rule of construction also applies to the powers of Congress, though those powers occupy only a portion of the field of legislative power.

The Convention of 1787 desired nothing so much as to get rid of that state intervention which had wrecked the Articles of Confederation. This is accomplished in three ways: by providing the national government with executive machinery of its own; by making the Supreme Court the final interpreter of the Constitution; by providing for the supremacy in all cases of the national authority, as defined by the Constitution, over conflicting state authority. The point of view of the Convention was voiced by Wilson thus: "With respect to the province and object of the general government they [the states] should be considered as having no existence."

Later a motion was offered in the Convention prohibiting the national government "to interfere with the government of the individual states in any matters of internal police which respects the government of such state only and wherein the general welfare of the United States is not concerned." Despite the careful language in which it was couched, the motion was voted down by eight states to two.[4]

The view that the reserved powers of the states comprised an independent limitation on national power probably first found expression in the debate on Hamilton's bank project of 1791. Opposed as he was to the bank, Madison

---

3. Corwin, *National Supremacy, Treaty Power v. State Power* (1913).

4. The scope and import of Article VI, paragraph 2, were well understood by the opponents of the Constitution. See *Federalist*, nos. 44 and 64.

pronounced the argument fallacious. *"Interference with the powers of the states,"* said he, *" was no constitutional criterion of the power of Congress.* If the power was not given, Congress could not exercise it; if given, they might exercise it, although it should interfere with the laws or even the constitutions of the states.*"*[5] Nevertheless, a generation later the same notion was again afoot, though now in a modified form. "It has been contended," recites Chief Justice Marshall in his opinion in Gibbons v. Ogden, 9 Wheat. 1 (1824), "that if a law passed by a state *in the exercise of its acknowledged sovereignty* comes into conflict with a law passed by Congress in pursuance of the Constitution, they affect the subject and each other like equal and opposing powers." In other words, it was not claimed on this occasion that the national government was under constitutional obligation not to invade the field occupied by the reserved powers of the states, but that whenever it did so the states could use their reserved powers to block it. "But," the chief justice answered, "the framers of our Constitution foresaw this state of things and provided for it." Whenever the federal government has acted in the exercise of powers entrusted to it, "in every such case the act of Congress or the treaty is supreme, and the laws of the state, *though enacted in the exercise of powers not controverted,* must yield to it."

The thing that really gave the doctrine urged by Mr. Tucker the slight standing that it has at isolated points obtained in our constitutional law was the spread of the dissolving theories of the "Great Nullifier," a circumstance which serves to bring out what had probably already become evident to the reader, that Mr. Tucker's doctrine is only a special form of the doctrine of nullification. The actual task of nullifying national authority is, so to speak, farmed out with the Supreme Court of the United States, but the supposed legal basis for doing this—namely, the vast, undefined, legislative powers of the states—remains the same. In the last analysis the doctrine is self-contradictory, since the right of the Supreme Court itself in taking appeals of constitutional cases originating in the state courts is a clear invasion of the reserved rights of the states.[6] Fortunately, therefore, not only for the treaty-making power and the powers of Congress, but for its own power as well, the Supreme Court has today returned to first principles. Of this such decisions as those in Henderson v. New York, 92 U.S. 279 (1875); Minnesota v. Barber, 136 U.S. 313 (1890); *in re* Rahrer, 142 U.S. 545 (1891); the recent Employer's Liability Cases, Mondou v. N.Y., N.H. & Hart. R.R. Co., 223 U.S. 1 (1912), the Minnesota Rate Cases, 230 U. S. 352 (1913), and Hoke v. United States, 227 U.S. 308 (1913) furnish proof positive, to say nothing of a host of dicta.

Thus in the Employer's Liability Cases, the Court was confronted with the now notorious decision of Chief Justice Baldwin of the Connecticut Supreme Court in the Hoxie Case, in which enforcement had been refused the act of

---

5. See 2 *Annals of Cong.* col. 1891, ff. (1791).
6. See Hunter v. Martin, 4 Munf. 1 (Va.).

Congress on the ground of its disharmony with "the policy of the state." Strangely unaware as the Connecticut court showed itself to be of the established canons of constitutional law, its view must, after all, be admitted to have been the inevitable one if the reserved powers of the states limit national power. But the Supreme Court of the United States no longer subscribes to this doctrine. The theory of the Connecticut court was accordingly swept aside, in the following language taken from the national Court's earlier opinion in Smith v. Alabama, 124 U.S. 465, 508 (1888):

> The grant of power to Congress to regulate commerce . . . is paramount over all legislative powers which, in consequence of not having been granted to Congress, are reserved to the states. It follows that any legislation of a state, *although in pursuance of an acknowledged power reserved to it,* which conflicts with the actual exercise of the power of Congress over the subject of commerce must give way before the supremacy of the national authority.

And not less significant is Hoke v. United States, in which the Court upheld the Mann Act forbidding the taking of women from one state to another for immoral purposes. The opponents of the act contended that, inasmuch as its obvious purpose was not to safeguard commerce, but the public morals, it represented an attempt by Congress to usurp the powers of the states. But the Court held unanimously that Congress, no less than the state legislatures, may exercise its constitutional powers for all the large recognized ends of government; that, in other words, though the *powers* of government are apportioned among us, *its objectives* are not. The decision expels the theory of indefeasible state rights from its last angle.

To conclude: The reserved powers of the states comprise, loosely speaking, the sum total of governmental powers after the powers granted the national government by the Constitution are counted out. The national government may use *only* the powers thus granted it and, as the Tenth Amendment makes clear, has no "inherent powers." But in using its granted powers, which it may do for all legitimate purposes of government, it often brings under its control subject matter that also falls to the control of the states in the exercise of their reserved powers. In *all* conflicts of authority thus resulting the states must give way because of the provisions of Article VI, paragraph 2, which, when it is not read "under the preposssession of some abstract theory of the relation between the state and the national governments" (Justice Bradley in *ex parte* Siebold, 100 U.S. 371 [1879]), is perfectly explicit. In short, though national power is limited power, the reserved powers of the states do not furnish one of the limitations.

11. The Power of Congress to Declare Peace

In the course of the discussion which has been aroused in Congress by the proposal to declare hostilities with Germany at an end by joint resolution, Senator Thomas of Colorado has brought forward evidence showing that on one occasion the Convention which framed the Constitution voted down unanimously a motion to vest Congress with the power to "make peace." This evidence is good so far as it goes, but it does not support all of Senator Thomas' deductions from it, nor indeed has he given an altogether complete account of it. The proposal in question was made and rejected by the Convention on August 17, 1787.[1] One ground for its rejection was that the making of peace would naturally fall, not to the executive, as Senator Thomas would have it, but to the treaty-making body, which was, by the plan at that date before the Convention, the Senate alone.[2] And the principal argument which was offered against the proposal Senator Thomas ignores altogether. It was the argument made by Ellsworth and repeated by Madison, that "it should be more easy to get out of war than into it"—the obvious deduction being that the making of peace ought therefore to be lodged with a less cumbersome body than Congress. The Convention were apparently unacquainted with the "single-track mind"!

There are certain facts, of course, which anybody who has ever read the Constitution would not think of denying in discussing Mr. Porter's resolution to declare war with Germany at an end.[3] One is that the Constitution does

---

From 18 *Michigan Law Review* 669 (1920). Reprinted by permission of the *Michigan Law Review*.

1. 2 Farrand, *Records of the Federal Convention* 318–19 (1911).

2. The President was not made a part of the treaty-making till Sept. 7th: 2 *id.* 538.

3. The text of the Parker {*sic;* Porter (referring to Stephen G. Porter, a Representative from Pennsylvania)} resolution is as follows: "Whereas the President of the United States in the performance of his constitutional duty to give to Congress information of the state of the Union had advised Congress that the war with the imperial German government has ended, resolved by the Senate and the House of Representatives of the United States of America in Congress assembled, that the state of

not specifically vest Congress with the right to make peace. Another is that peace in the international sense, and binding both parties to the war thus concluded, may be made by treaty, and therefore, on the part of the United

---

war declared to exist between the imperial German government and the people of the United States by a joint resolution of Congress, approved April 6, 1917, is hereby declared at an end.

"Section 2: That in the interpretation of any provision relating to the date of the termination of the present war, or of the present or existing emergency in any acts of Congress, joint resolutions or proclamations of the President containing provisions contingent upon the date of the termination of the war, or of the present or existing emergency, the date when this resolution becomes effective shall be construed and treated as the date of the termination of the war, or of the present or existing emergency, notwithstanding any provision in any act of Congress or joint resolution providing any other mode of determination of the date of the termination of the war, or of the present or existing emergency.

"Section 3: That, with a view to securing reciprocal trade with the German government and its nationals, and for this purpose, it is hereby provided that unless within forty-five days from the date when this resolution becomes effective the German government shall duly notify the President of the United States that it has declared a termination of the war with the United States and that it waives and renounces on behalf of itself and its nationals any claim, demand, right, or benefit against the United States, or its nationals, that it or they would not have the right to assert had the United States ratified the Treaty of Versailles, the President of the United States shall have the power, and it shall be his duty, to proclaim the fact that the German government has not given the notification hereinbefore mentioned and thereupon and until the President shall have proclaimed the receipt of such notification, commercial intercourse between the United States and Germany and the making of loans or credits, and the furnishing of financial assistance or supplies to the German government or the inhabitants of Germany, directly or indirectly, by the government or the inhabitants of the United States, shall, except with the license of the President, be prohibited.

"Section 4: That whoever shall willfully violate the foregoing prohibition, whenever the same shall be in force, shall upon conviction be fined not more than $10,000, or, if a natural person, imprisoned for not more than two years, or both; and the officer, director, or agent of any corporation who knowingly participates in such violation shall be punished by a like fine, imprisonment, or both, and any property, funds, securities, papers, or other articles or documents, or any vessel, together with her tackle, apparel, furniture, and equipment, concerned in such violation, shall be forfeited to the United States.

"Section 5: That nothing herein contained shall be construed as a waiver by the United States of its rights, privileges, indemnities, reparations, or advantages to which the United States has become entitled under the terms of the armistice signed November 11, 1918, or which were acquired by or are in the possession of the United States by reason of its participation in the war or otherwise; and all fines, forfeitures, penalties, and seizures imposed or made by the United States are hereby ratified, confirmed, and maintained."

Since the text of this article was written, the Parker {sic; Porter} resolution has passed the House and gone to the Senate, where it has been displaced by the Foreign Relations Committee with the Knox resolution. This latter document reads as follows:

"Joint resolution repealing the joint resolution of April 6, 1917, declaring a state of war to exist between the United States and Germany, and the joint resolution of December 7, 1917, declaring that a state of war exists between the United States and the Austro-Hungarian government.

"Resolved by the Senate and House of Representatives of the United States of America, in Congress assembled, that the joint resolution of Congress passed April 6, 1917, declaring a state of war to exist between the imperial German government and the government and people of the United States, and making provisions to prosecute the same, be, and the same is hereby repealed, and said state of war is hereby declared at an end:

"Provided, however, that all property of the imperial German government or its successor or successors, and of all German nationals which was on April 6, 1917, in or has since that date come into the possession or under control of the government of the United States or of any of its officers, agents, or employees, from any source or by any agency whatsoever, shall be retained by the United

States, by the President and Senate. Still another is that since treaties are "law of the land," a treaty of peace duly made and ratified would establish for the United States peace in the domestic sense as well as in the international sense; in other words, a status of which the courts, the executive, and all the agents of government would have henceforth to take due cognizance.

Yet these generally agreed facts do not take us very far. The mere fact that Congress is not specifically authorized to make peace does not prove that it does not possess powers in the exercise of which, on proper occasions, it may bring

---

States and no disposition thereof made, except as shall specifically be hereafter provided by Congress, until such time as the German government has by treaty with the United States, ratification whereof is to be made by and with the advice and consent of the Senate, made suitable provisions for the satisfaction of all claims against the German government of all persons wheresoever domiciled, who owe permanent allegiance to the United States, whether such persons have suffered through the acts of the German government or its agents since July 31, 1914, loss, damage, or injury to persons or property, directly or indirectly through the ownership of shares of stock in German, American, or other corporations, or otherwise, and until the German government has given further undertakings and made provisions by treaty, to be ratified by and with the advice and consent of the Senate, for granting to persons owing permanent allegiance to the United States; most-favored nation treatment whether the same be national or otherwise, in all matters affecting residence, business, profession, trade, navigation, commerce, and industrial property rights, and confirming to the United States all fines, forfeitures, penalties, and seizures imposed or made by the United States during the war, whether in respect to the property of the German government or German nationals, and waiving any pecuniary claim based on events which occurred at any time before the coming into force of such treaty, any existing treaty between the United States and Germany to the contrary notwithstanding.

"To these ends, and for the purpose of establishing fully friendly relations and commercial intercourse between the United States and Germany, the President is hereby requested immediately to open negotiations with the government of Germany.

"Section 2: That in the interpretation of any provisions relating to the date of the termination of the present war or of the present or existing emergency in any acts of Congress, joint resolutions or proclamations of the President containing provisions contingent upon the date of the termination of the war or of the present or existing emergency, the date when this resolution becomes effective shall be construed and treated as the date of the termination of the war or of the present war or existing emergency, notwithstanding any provision in any act of Congress or joint resolution providing any other mode of determining the date of the termination of the war or of the present or existing emergency.

"Section 3: That until by treaty or act or joint resolution of Congress it shall be determined otherwise, the United States, although it has not ratified the Treaty of Versailles, does not waive any of the rights, privileges, indemnities, reparations, or advantages to which it and its nationals have become entitled under the terms of the armistice signed November 11, 1918, or any extensions or modifications thereof or which under the Treaty of Versailles have been stipulated for its benefit as one of the principal allied and associated powers and to which it is entitled.

"Section 4: That the joint resolution of Congress, approved December 7, 1917, declaring that a state of war exists between the imperial and royal Austro-Hungarian government and the government and people of the United States and making provisions to prosecute the same, be and the same is hereby repealed and said state of war is hereby declared at an end, and the President is hereby requested immediately to open negotiations with the successor or successors of said government for the purpose of establishing fully friendly relations and commercial intercourse between the United States and the governments and peoples of Austria and Hungary."

It will be observed that the Senate substitute does not contain the provision of the House resolution declaring a trade embargo penalty unless Germany accepts the resolution within forty-five days. Instead, it requests the President to open negotiations with Germany. For the rest, the constitutional problems raised by the two resolutions seem to be identical.

peace about. Congress was also denied by the Convention of 1787 the power to charter corporations;[4] notwithstanding which it has repeatedly exercised this power, and has been sustained by the Supreme Court in so doing.[5] Nor, again, does the fact that peace, whether domestic or international, may be, and ordinarily is, attained by the treaty route prove that all other roads thereto are closed. To cite some parallel cases: certain businesses are subject to both the taxing power by Congress and to the police power of the states;[6] the penalties of offenses against the United States may be remitted either by presidential amnesty or congressional amnesty;[7] treaties may be abrogated, so far as the United States is concerned, both by act of Congress and by agreement between our government and the other parties thereto;[8] certain international conventions may be entered into by the President alone, upon authorization by Congress, or by the President and Senate without such authorization;[9] restrictions upon the entry of aliens into the United States,[10] may be imposed equally by treaty or by act of Congress, as may also certain regulations of foreign commerce.[11] In short, it frequently happens that the same legal result may be produced by very different powers of government; nor need this fact lead to confusion, since, as soon as any of the competent powers has acted, the result is produced.

The contention that war may be ended in a way to determine the question for our own people and government only by the ratification of a treaty of peace might conceivably produce very curious results. The President, who is commander-in-chief of the Army and Navy, and a majority of both branches of Congress, which declares war and maintains the forces necessary for its prosecution, might desire peace and yet be unable to obtain it because a third of the Senate plus one senator were contrary minded. Or our erstwhile antagonist might be the contrary-minded one. Or the war might have resulted in the extinction of said antagonist.[12] Such, in fact, was the situation at the close of the Civil War, which accordingly could not be brought to an end in the legal sense by a treaty of peace, albeit it was a public war in the fullest sense of the term.[13]

Neither general principles nor authority sanction any such anomaly. Congress may repeal or otherwise curtail the legal operation of any measure which it had the power to enact in the first place, though naturally it cannot repeal the acts

4. 2 Farrand, *Records* 615–16 (Sept. 14). See also comment of Bradley, J., in 12 Wall. 457, 460, 461.

5. McCulloch v. Maryland, 4 Wheat. 316 (1819), is of course the leading case. See also Luxton v. North River Bridge Co., 153 U.S. 525 (1894), and cases there cited.

6. See McCray v. United States, 195 U.S. 27 (1904), and cases there cited.

7. Brown v. Walker, 161 U.S. 591 (1896).

8. The Head Money Cases, 112 U.S. 580 (1884).

9. Field v. Clark, 143 U.S. 649 (1892).

10. Fong Yue Ting v. United States, 149 U.S. 698 (1893), and cases there cited.

11. Bartram v. Robertson, 122 U.S. 116 (1887), and Whitney v. Robertson, 124 U.S. 190 (1888).

12. Indeed Senator Knox makes the point that our antagonist, the German imperial government, has been extinguished.

13. The Prize Cases, 2 Black 635 (1863).

already done under the sanction of such measure while it was still operative. Congress cannot now invalidate, nor does it wish to, what was properly done by virtue of its declaration of war upon Germany; but it can withdraw its sanction from any further hostilities against our former foe, and this sanction is "war" in the legal sense. Likewise, it can require that in the future interpretation of any "provision relating to the termination of the present war or of the present or existing emergency in any" acts or resolutions of Congress or of any proclamations issued in pursuance thereof, the date when the now proposed resolution becomes effective "shall be construed and treated as the date of the termination of the war or of the present or existing emergency." All this upon the most obvious principles. As to authority, the following passage from Cooley's *Principles of Constitutional Law* is pertinent: "Over political questions the courts have no authority, but must accept the determination of the political departments of the government as conclusive. Such are the questions of the existence of war, the restoration of peace," etc.[14] By "political departments" Cooley means the President and Congress.

But the proposed Porter resolution has also a second purpose, namely, to force the German government, by the threat of cutting off all commercial relations with it—relations which are now going on in the midst of "war"!—to proclaim the cessation on its part of hostilities against this country and the renunciation of any claims against this country which the German government "would not have the right to assert had the United States ratified the Treaty of Versailles." This provision, at least, it will be contended, amounts to an attempt on the part of Congress to usurp the treaty-making power. In fact, however, the proposal is grounded on the securest of precedents, on Madison's Non-Intercourse Act,[15] on the "reciprocally unjust" clause of the McKinley Tariff Act, which was sustained by the Supreme Court in the case of Field v. Clark[16] against the objection just recited, on the "maximum and minimum" clause of the Dingley Act, on the Canadian Reciprocity Act passed during President Taft's administration and at his special instance.[17] In all these cases Congress did just what it is proposing to do at the present moment; it was using its power to regulate "commerce with foreign nations" to induce certain concessions from those nations. And the way it went about the business was the same as that taken in the Porter resolution; it enacted certain conditional restrictions or relaxations upon American trade with the nations designed to be reached, such restrictions or relaxations to go into effect upon the ascertainment by the President of the existence of a certain set of facts described in the congressional act itself. Such legislation is called "contingent legislation," and the right of Congress to pass it by virtue of its control over foreign commerce has been asserted far too long to admit of its being success-

14. At 157 [3d ed.].
15. Sustained in Brig Aurora v. United States, 7 Cranch 382 (1813).
16. See note 9 above.
17. See W. H. Taft, *Our Chief Magistrate* 111–12 (1916).

fully challenged today. Nor, again, is it any objection to such legislation that in carrying it out the President may be required to exercise his powers of diplomatic negotiation. Whatever powers the President is vested with are always available, within constitutional limits, the better to enable him to discharge his constitutional duty to "take care that the laws be faithfully executed."[18]

Congress has the right, then, simply by virtue of its power to repeal its previous enactments, to declare hostilities with Germany to be at an end, and its declaration to this effect, once duly enacted, will be binding upon the courts and the executive alike. Also, it has the right, by virtue of its power to regulate "commerce with foreign nations" and to "pass all laws necessary and proper" to that end, to curtail or even to prohibit American trade with Germany, and this it may do either forthwith, or conditionally upon the occurrence or nonoccurrence of certain events the ascertainment and proclamation of which may be left with the President. Both these propositions are sustained by analogy, principle, and authority, while the opposing view rests upon the fallacious supposition that since peace in a legal sense would undoubtedly ensue upon the ratification of a treaty of peace with Germany, a treaty of peace is the only way to obtain it. But there is more than one road leading to peace, as to Rome, and a sovereign government, which the United States undoubtedly is in the field of foreign relations,[19] has access to them all, unless it can be shown to be cut off therefrom by some definite constitutional prohibition, such as opponents of the Porter resolution have not yet produced. There is, in brief, no sound constitutional reason why Congress should not switch off the current which it turned on three years ago, and so permit Uncle Sam to let go at last a very troublesome and quite useless live wire.

18. *In re* Neagle, 135 U.S. 1 (1890).
19. Holmes v. Jennison, 14 Pet. 540 (1840); the Chinese Exclusion Cases, 130 U.S. 581 (1889).

12. The Spending Power of Congress apropos the Maternity Act

THE report that there is to be a concerted effort on the part of certain states[1] to challenge the constitutionality of the Sheppard-Towner Act of November 23, 1921, "for the promotion of the welfare and hygiene of maternity and infancy and for other purposes,"[2] revives a constitutional issue which once engrossed the attention of the country but of which little has been heard for a generation or more—the question of the scope of Congress' power of expenditure with respect to funds raised by national taxation. Briefly, the Act just referred to stipulates for the appropriation through a term of years of certain sums of money, to be expended under the direction of the Children's Bureau of the Department of Labor, in cooperation with certain state agencies, within— for the most part—states which, through their legislatures, accept the provisions of the act and duplicate their assigned portion of the national appropriation. So far as the constitutional questions raised by it are concerned, the act is not dissimilar in character to the still pending Towner-Sterling Education Bill, which in turn is the culmination of a series of measures whereby the national government has, since the year 1900, entered more and more upon a policy of subsidizing education within the states from the national revenues. These measures are treated below in their proper historical setting.

So far as I can gather from an opinion which was rendered by the attorney general of Massachusetts last May in response to inquiries from the Senate and House of Representatives of the Commonwealth, the constitutional objections levelled against the Maternity Act are four in number: (1) that is tends to defeat the general purposes of the Constitution to establish a federal government with limited and enumerated powers; (2) that it tends to invade the field of

From 36 *Harvard Law Review* 548 (1923). Copyright 1923 by the Harvard Law Review Association. Reprinted by permission.
1. Maine and Massachusetts have been mentioned in this relation.
2. 42 Stat. ch. 135 at 224.

powers reserved to the states by the Tenth Amendment[3]; (3) that it is in excess of the power granted Congress by Article I, section 8, clause 1, of the Constitution[4]; (4) that acceptance of the terms of the act by a state would be void as amounting to an abdication of the state's sovereignty.[5] The bulk of this paper will be devoted to the third objection; the fourth will be considered briefly at the close of it; the first and second objections may be disposed of in a paragraph.

It is an inaccurate terminology which characterizes the central government as "a federal government." The Constitution establishes a federal system with a *national government* at its center. However, there is no need to quarrel about words; the main point to be made clear is that not even the Supreme Court is entitled to set aside acts of Congress on some vague theory of the purpose or spirit of the Constitution, in the face of its specific terms. Thus, whatever else may be said about the federal system—and everybody no doubt has his notion of it—one feature of it is undeniable, namely, that the national government has been invested by the Constitution with certain powers. Where, therefore, any such investment of power has been effected in plain terms, other affirmations respecting the federal system must be made in deference thereto.[6] And similarly as to the Tenth Amendment; its very phraseology makes clear its inapplicability as a test of the scope of the delegated powers of the national government—a fact only reinforced by Article VI, paragraph 2. In words uttered by Madison early in the history of the Constitution: "Interference with the powers of the states is no constitutional criterion of the power of Congress. If the power is not

3. "The powers not delegated to the United States by the Constitution, nor prohibited by it to the states, are reserved to the states respectively, or to the people."

4. Quoted below, p. 248.

5. Attorney General Allen opines that it might be difficult for a state which had voluntarily accepted the act to raise the question, whereas a state which had not would not have surrendered any sovereignty. Whether a taxpayer's suit would stand on a better footing is also questionable. See Wilson v. Shaw, 204 U.S. 24 (1906). On the other hand, it would seem that the Court might permit a state to represent before it the consolidated interest of its citizens as taxpayers. See e.g. Georgia v. Tenn. Copper Co., 206 U.S. 230 (1907). And once the case was in court it is probable that the state might raise the question of the effect of the act, if accepted by it, on its sovereignty. See Missouri v. Holland, 252 U.S. 416 (1920), apparently overruling Georgia v. Stanton, 6 Wall. 50(U.S. 1867), as to the power of the Court to protect a state in its political rights.

6. The recent decisions of the Court in the Child Labor Cases, Hammer v. Dagenhart, 247 U.S. 251 (1918); Bailey v. Drexel Furniture Co., {259 U.S. 20} 42 Sup. Ct. Rep. 449 (1922), invite criticism on this very point. They seem to have been predicated on the theory that the national government may exercise its constitutional powers for relatively few purposes, not specified at present, but to be defined, as cases arise, by the Court. Any such notion is untenable for three reasons: first, because it invokes a vague "spirit of the Constitution" to the overthrow of its clear wording; secondly, because it deprives the national government of the best sovereignty which the best authority, e.g., Chief Justice Marshall in Gibbons v. Ogden, 9 Wheat. 1 (U.S. 1824) has always attributed to it within the range of its designated powers; thirdly, because, by the same sign, it claims for the Court a right of interposition within the acknowledged field of legislative discretion. *Why* a particular power of government should be exercised has hitherto usually been regarded as a question not of law but of policy, and such it must remain unless we wish to see the Supreme Court erected into a third house of Congress.

given, Congress cannot exercise it; if given, they may exercise it although it shall interfere with the laws or even the constitutions of the states."[17]

Let us turn, therefore, to the actual wording of the Constitution. The provision pertinent to our inquiry is Article I, section 8, clause 1, which reads as follows: "The Congress shall have power to lay and collect taxes, duties, imposts, and excises, to pay the debts and provide for the common defense and general welfare of the United States; but all duties, imposts, and excises shall be uniform throughout the United States." The phrase which demands special scrutiny is that which authorizes Congress to "provide," in some way or other, "for the general welfare." Our inquiry is therefore twofold: by what *means* precisely may Congress provide for the "general welfare"; and what *is* the "general welfare"? The first question may be dealt with rather briefly; but the second involves an extensive examination into congressional and presidential opinion, for thus far this is not a field in which the Court has interposed.

While the Constitution was before the country for ratification certain of its opponents charged that the phrase "to provide for the general welfare" was intended as a sort of legislative joker, which was designed, in conjunction with the "necessary and proper" clause, to vest Congress with power to provide for whatever it might regard as the "general welfare" by any means deemed by it to be "necessary and proper."[8] The suggestion was promptly repudiated by advocates of the Constitution,[9] and it is clearly unallowable. In the first place, the phrase stands between two other phrases, both dealing with the taxing power—an awkward syntax on the assumption under consideration. In the second place, the phrase is coordinate with the phrase "to pay the debts," which means the debts of "the United States" at the end of the clause, and which designates a purpose of money expenditure only. In the third place, the suggested reading, by endowing Congress with practically complete legislative power, makes useless the succeeding enumeration of specific powers. This last at least is a fatal objection, and we must therefore accept Jefferson's contention, in his Opinion on the Bank,[10] that the power to lay taxes to provide for the general welfare of the

7. 2 *Annals of Cong.* 1891 (1791).

8. See 1 Story, *Commentaries* secs. 907, 908, and references (5th ed. 1891). According to Gallatin, speaking in 1798, Gouverneur Morris attempted as a member of the Committee of Style, to throw the words "to provide" etc., "into a distinct paragraph, so as to create not a limitation, but a distinct power." 2 Farrand, *Records of the Federal Convention* 379 (1911) {hereinafter *Records*}. A similar accusation was brought against J. Q. Adams in 1819, because of the punctuation of the clause in the edition of the Journal of the Convention which was published by the government that year. 6 *Memoirs* 121–27 (1874–1877). For two diverse punctuations of the clause as it came from the Committee on Style, see 2 Farrand, *Records* 569 and 594. The history of the clause in Convention is related by Madison in his letter of Nov. 27, 1830, to Speaker Stevenson, 2 Farrand, *Records* 483 *et seq.;* 9 *Writings of James Madison* 411 *et seq.* (Hunt ed. 1900–1910). The accompanying "Memorandum" gives further data on the subject of punctuation. The idea that the "general welfare" clause effects a grant of general powers was reasserted only a few years ago by the editor of the *American Law Review.* See 30 *Am. L. Rev.* 787–90 (1896).

9. 1 Story, *Commentaries* sec. 908, and citations.

10. 1 Story, *Commentaries* sec. 926; 3 *Writings* {of Jefferson} 147–49. (Memorial ed. 1903). The

United States is the power "to lay taxes *for the purpose* of providing for the general welfare. For," as he continues, "the laying of taxes is the *power*, and the general welfare the *purpose*, for which the power is to be exercised. Congress are not to lay taxes *ad libitum*, for any purpose they please; but only to pay the debts, or provide for the welfare of the Union. In like manner they are not to do anything they please, to provide for the general welfare; but only to lay taxes for that purpose." The clause is, in short, not an independent grant of power, but a qualification of the taxing power.

But the question still remains: What is that "general welfare" which Congress may promote by the power of taxation and expenditure? It is obviously a case where words need to be given only their literal operation to produce the broadest effect, and as we have just seen, the opponents of the Constitution gave them this operation. The same, moreover, is true of Hamilton in *Federalist* nos. 30 and 34,[11] where, however, the "general welfare" clause is treated as qualifying the fiscal power. Madison, on the other hand, in answering the alarmist arguments of opponents of the Constitution, in *Federalist*, no. 41, not only confines Congress' power to promote the general welfare to its fiscal power, but also restricts the "general welfare" which Congress may thus promote to that welfare which it may further promote by its other delegated powers. In other words, the powers of taxation and appropriation are themselves but instrumental, and accordingly enlarge the field within which the national government may act, even when it is merely spending money, not at all.[12]

The difficulty in the way of this view, which, by its author's own admission, detracts from the literal meaning of words, has never been better pointed out than by Story in his *Commentaries:* "If there are no other cases which can concern the common defense and general welfare except those within the scope

---

date of the document is Feb. 15, 1791. Further along in the same paper Jefferson says: "It was intended to lace them [Congress] up strictly within the enumerated powers, and those without which, as means, those powers could not be carried into effect." These words seem to indicate that Jefferson at this date took the Madisonian view of the "general welfare" clause. See also 7 *Writings* {of Jefferson} 492 (Ford ed. 1892–1899).

11. Lodge's edition is followed. Hamilton's argument for the most part consists in urging the impossibility of foreseeing all the requirements of the *common defense*. His logic, however, is equally applicable to the *general welfare*.

12. Besides the *Federalist*, see Madison, "Report on the Resolutions" (1799–1800), 6 *Writings* {of James Madison} 354–56 (Hunt ed. 1900–1910); and the "Veto Message" of Mar. 3, 1817, 1 Richardson, *Messages and Papers of the Presidents* 584–85 (1896–1899) (hereafter cited as Richardson). It would seem that Madison originally formulated his peculiar view of the "general welfare" clause on rather short notice, for in setting forth the advantages to be expected from the proposed government in *Federalist*, no. 14, he had earlier written: "Let it be remarked, in the third place, that the intercourse throughout the Union will be daily facilitated by new improvements. Roads will everywhere be shortened, and kept in better order; accommodations for travellers will be multiplied and meliorated; and interiour [*sic*] navigation on our eastern side will be opened throughout, or nearly throughout, the whole extent of the thirteen states. The communication between the Western and Atlantic districts, and between different parts of each, will be rendered more and more easy by numerous canals...." The assumption seems to be that the new government will have an important hand in this work.

of the enumerated powers, the discussion is merely nominal and frivolous. If there are such cases, who is at liberty to say, that being for the common defense and general welfare, the Constitution did not intend to embrace them?"[13]

Nor has he greater difficulty in meeting Madison's contention that the literal view of the "general welfare" clause, even if invoked only in "cases which are to be provided for by the expenditure of money, would still leave within the legislative power of Congress all the great and important measures of government, money being the ordinary and necessary means of carrying them into effect." "The only question," Story rejoins, "is whether a power to lay taxes and appropriate money for . . . the general welfare does include all the other powers of government or even include the other powers (limited as they are) of the national government?"[14] And he justly opines that a negative answer must be returned to both branches of the inquiry. But Madison also urged in support of his theory the fact that the phrase "common defense and general welfare" was taken from the Articles of Confederation, the idea being that it could not have been the intention of an instrument which so carefully safeguarded the "sovereignty" of the states, to vest Congress with an indefinite power of appropriation. At the same time, however, he admits that even after the adoption of the Articles, "habit and a continued expediency, amounting often to a real or apparent necessity, prolonged the exercise of an undefined authority" in this as well as in other respects.[15] In other words, given simply their literal force, the phraseology of the Articles dealing with the power of expenditure did in fact only ratify the previous practice of Congress.

The classic statement of the literal view of the "general welfare" clause occurs in Hamilton's "Report on Manufactures," in 1791. The salient part of this document reads as follows:

> The phrase is as comprehensive as any that could have been used, because it was not fit that the constitutional authority of the Union to appropriate its revenues should have been restricted within narrower limits than the "general welfare," and because this necessarily embraces a vast variety of particulars which are susceptible neither of specification nor of definition. It is therefore of necessity left to the discretion of the national legislature to pronounce upon the objects which concern the general welfare, and for which, under that description, an appropriation of money is requisite and proper. And there seems to be no room for a doubt that whatever concerns the general interests of learning, of agriculture, of manufactures, and of commerce, are within the sphere of the national councils, *as far as regards an application of money.*
>
> The only qualification of the generality of the phrase in question which seems to be admissible is this: that the object to which an appropriation of money is to be made must be general, and not local; its operation extending in fact or by possibility, throughout the Union, and not being confined to a particular spot.

13. 1 Story, *Commentaries* sec. 924.
14. *Id*. sec. 923.
15. See the letter of Nov. 27, 1830, cited in note 8, above.

No objection ought to arise to this construction, from a supposition that it would imply a power to do whatever else should appear to Congress conducive to the general welfare. A power to appropriate money with this latitude, which is granted, too, in express terms, would not carry a power to do any other thing not authorized in the Constitution, either expressly or by fair implication.[16]

The practical nub of Hamilton's argument was a system of bounties for selected lines of manufacture; and though it otherwise bore no fruit, it may have furnished one reason why Congress voted, the following February, a subsidy to the cod fisheries—a proposal against which Madison vainly urged his narrow doctrine of the power of expenditure.[17] Nearly five years later, Washington, in his final message to Congress, brought forward a series of recommendations implying the possession by Congress of the broadest discretion in expenditure. The following passages from this document are especially noteworthy:

Congress have repeatedly, and not without success, directed their attention to the encouragement of manufactures. The object is of too much consequence not to insure a continuance of their efforts in every way which shall appear eligible. As a general rule, manufactures on public account are inexpedient: but where the state of things in a country leaves little hope that certain branches of manufacture will for a great length of time obtain, when these are of a nature essential to the furnishing and equipping of the public force in time of war, are not establishments for procuring them on public account to the extent of the ordinary demand for the public service recommended by strong considerations of national policy as an exception to the general rule?

It will not be doubted that with reference either to individual or national welfare agriculture is of primary importance. In proportion as nations advance in population and other circumstances of maturity this truth becomes more apparent, and renders the cultivation of the soil more and more an object of public patronage. Institutions for promoting it grow up, supported by the public purse; and to what object can it be dedicated with greater propriety? . . .

I have heretofore proposed to the consideration of Congress the expediency of establishing a national university. . . .

True it is that our country, much to its honor, contains many seminaries of learning highly respectable and useful; but the funds upon which they rest are too narrow to command the ablest professors in the different departments of liberal knowledge for the institution contemplated, though they would be excellent auxiliaries.

Amongst the motives to such an institution, the assimilation of the principles, opinions, and manners of our countrymen by the common education of a portion of our youth from every quarter well deserves attention. The more homogeneous our citizens can be made in these particulars the greater will be our prospect of permanent union; and a primary object of such a national institution should be the education of our youth in the science of *government*. In a republic what species of knowledge can be equally important and what duty more pressing on its legislature

16. 4 *Works* 70, 151 (Lodge ed. 1904).

17. See 1 Benton, *Abridgment* {*of the Debates of Congress, from 1789 to 1865*} 350 *et seq.* {1857–1861}.

than to patronize a plan for communicating it to those who are to be the future guardians of the liberties of the country?[18]

Here are three suggestions—manufactures on public account, encouragement to agriculture, a national university—none of which can be vindicated except by reference to the "general welfare" clause. It is worth noting Madison's complaint that a report of a committee of Congress, in January 1797, supporting the President's recommendations in behalf of agriculture, received not "the slightest mark of disapprobation from the authorities to which it was addressed."[19]

A few months later the Virginia and Kentucky Resolutions were promulgated, the theory of which was essentially that the Constitution, being a compact of sovereign states, reserved to the latter a mediating function between the people and the national government. It followed of course that the national government, before undertaking within the boundaries of the states any new or unaccustomed activity, must secure their consent. Indeed it was insisted that the "necessary and proper" clause implied this requirement, since no matter how *necessary* a measure might be as a means to a constitutional end, *propriety* required that the state or states most immediately concerned should be consulted;[20] and this doctrine was felt to be especially applicable to the construction by the national government of public works within the states, on account of the possibility— exaggerated by Madison, but evidently present—that national expenditures would carry with them jurisdictional consequences. Thus from the outset the question of "internal improvements"—which for the most part was the form assumed by the broader issue of Congress' spending power between the election of Jefferson and the Civil War—became involved with the doctrine of "state consent," and so it continued for nearly two decades.

The opening chapter in the history of internal improvements is the story of the compact, as it may be properly termed, under which Ohio was admitted to the Union in 1802.[21] In return for a grant of lands to each township for free schools and a pledge on the part of the national government to use five per cent of the money raised from the sale of lands within the state for the construction of roads between Ohio and the seaboard states, Ohio was required not to tax the public lands which should be sold within its borders for a term of five years after sale.

18. 1 Richardson 201–202. The fact that the proposed national university would have been established in the District of Columbia does not, of course, alter the constitutional question so far as Congress' power of expenditure is concerned; since the expenditure would have been, not for local governmental purposes, under sec. 8 clause 17 of Article I, but in furtherance of the "general welfare."

19. 6 *Writings* {of James Madison} 355–56 {Hunt ed.}.

20. 2 *American State Papers* (Miscel.) 443 {1809–1823}.

21. The early history of internal improvements is sufficiently sketched for our purposes in Monroe's "Views of the President of the United States," etc., of May 4, 1822, 2 Richardson 144 *et seq*. Special studies of important phases of the subject are the following: J. S. Young, *A Political and Constitutional Study of the Cumberland Road* (1904); David Walter Brown, *The Commercial Power of Congress* App. I (1910); and Lindsay Rogers, *The Postal Power of Congress* 61–96 (1916). See also notes 83 and 84, below.

The following year by an amendatory act Congress provided further that three per cent of the net proceeds from land sales in Ohio should be turned over "to such persons as might be authorized by the legislature of the state, to be applied to the laying out, opening, and making of roads within the state." Three years later the famous Cumberland road, which was to run from a point in Maryland to Ohio, was authorized by Congress. The act specified various features of the construction and stipulated that the consent of the states affected should be obtained. All these acts received Jefferson's approval; as also, presumably, did Gallatin's ambitious project, put forth in 1808, which called for a great canal from North to South along the Atlantic coast and a vast system of interior communications between the Atlantic on the one hand and the Great Lakes and Western rivers on the other. The scheme proved abortive; but notwithstanding, the national government opened, between the years 1806 and 1817, some eleven roads in various parts of the country—most of them log roads, to be sure, but good constitutional precedents for all that.[22]

Meantime, in December 1816, there had been introduced into Congress a measure which called for the segregation of the bonus from the recently chartered National Bank and of the government's share of the bank's dividends as a permanent fund pledged to internal improvements. This was the celebrated Bonus Bill, and its sponsor was John C. Calhoun, who at this stage was one of the most thoroughgoing nationalists in the country. Undertaking the defense of the measure in the House, Calhoun recited two objections of a constitutional nature: "First, that they were to cut a road or canal through a state without its consent; and next that the public moneys can only be appropriated to effect the particular powers enumerated in the Constitution." The first objection, he answered, did not apply, and at any rate was hardly worth discussing, "since the good sense of the states might be relied on. They will," he continued, "in all cases readily yield their consent." Indeed the thing to be feared was "in a different direction; in a too great solicitude to obtain an undue share to be expended within their respective limits." As to the second point, he cited both the tax clause and the postal clause. Granting the objection, did not the power to establish post roads comprehend more than the power merely to designate them? But his principal reliance was on the other clause. "He was no advocate for refined arguments on the Constitution. The instrument was not intended as a thesis for a logician to exercise his ingenuity on. It ought to be construed with plain good sense. . . . If the framers had intended to limit the use of money to the powers afterwards enumerated and defined, nothing could be more easy than to have expressed it plainly." Furthermore,

the habitual and uniform practice of the government coincided with his opinion. Our laws are full of instances of money appropriated without any reference to the

22. For most of the above data, see 2 Richardson 169–71; on Gallatin's scheme, see 4 Henry Adams, *History of the United States* 364–65 (1889–1891). For many features of Gallatin's plan, however, Jefferson thought a constitutional amendment necessary. See 1 Richardson 456.

enumerated powers. We granted, by a unanimous vote, or nearly so, fifty thousand dollars to the distressed inhabitants of Caraccas and a very large sum, at two different times, to the Saint Domingo refugees. If we are restricted in the use of our money to the enumerated powers, on what principle, said he, can the purchase of Louisiana be justified? To pass over many other instances, the identical power which is now the subject of discussion, has, in several instances, been exercised. To look no further back, at the last session a considerable sum was granted to complete the Cumberland road. In reply to this uniform course of legislation, Mr. C. expected it would be said, that our Constitution was founded on positive and written principles, and not on precedents. He did not deny the position; but he introduced these instances to prove the uniform sense of Congress, and the country (for they had not been objected to), as to our powers; and surely, said he, they furnish better evidence of the true interpretation of the Constitution, than the most refined and subtle arguments.[23]

In the course of his administration Madison had permitted repeated infractions by Congress of the strict constitutional doctrine which, as we have seen, he had developed at the outset with respect to Congress' spending power; but the far-reaching scheme of the Bonus Bill seems to have revived his original scruples in all their intensity. His veto of the bill was accompanied by a message in which he traversed the principal constitutional arguments in behalf of the measure.[24] Alluding to the commerce clause, which had been brought forward in the course of the debate for the first time as furnishing a constitutional warrant for internal improvements by the national government, he denied that it could "include a power to construct roads and canals, to improve the navigability of water courses in order to facilitate, promote, and secure . . . commerce"; the power granted by the clause, he contended, was merely "remedial." The "general welfare" clause he construed as he had a generation before in the *Federalist;* and he met the doctrine of state consent as follows: "If a general power to construct roads and canals and to improve the navigability of water courses, with the train of powers incident thereto, be not possessed by Congress, the assent of the states in the mode provided in the bill cannot confer the power. The only cases in which the consent and cession of particular states can extend the power of Congress are those specified and provided for in the Constitution."

On this point at least the message is unanswerable; for while a state may undoubtedly covenant as to how it will exercise its own powers, it cannot, generally speaking, surrender powers to the national government except through participation in the process of constitutional amendment. In point of fact, from this time forward the doctrine of state consent practically disappears from presidential discussions, though in other quarters it lingered on till it received its *coup de grâce* from the Civil War.

The Bonus Bill was vetoed March 3, 1817; the day following Monroe became President. In his first message to Congress the new executive took pains to give

23. 5 Benton, *Abridgment* 706–707.
24. 1 Richardson 584–85. See Rogers, *Postal Power* 82–88, and 91, n. *Cf.* Kohl v. United States, 91 U.S. 367 (1875), where the doctrine is decisively rejected.

notice that he shared the constitutional views of his predecessor with respect to internal improvements, and would govern himself accordingly, unless the difficulty were met by constitutional amendment, a course which he urged.[25] But others remained unconvinced. The passage in the message just alluded to was referred to a special committee of the House, which was headed by Tucker of Virginia; and on December 15th, this committee reported.[26] It rejected the presidential version of the Constitution on all points, and even appeared to scout the doctrine of state consent. Whether by virtue of the postal clause, or the commerce clause, or by virtue of its military powers, the national government, it was asserted, had the right to construct and improve roads and cut canals, "at least with the consent of the states" affected. Passing then to the "general welfare" clause, the report continued: "It would be difficult to reconcile either the generality of the expression or the course of administration under it with the idea that Congress has not a discretionary power over its expenditures, limited only by their application to the common defense and the general welfare." As instances of past expenditures outside the range of the enumerated powers of Congress, the report mentioned the purchase of a library by the national government, of paintings, of the services of a chaplain, "liberal donations to the wretched sufferers of Venezuela," the despatch of Lewis and Clarke's expedition to the Pacific, the granting of bounties for the encouragement of the fisheries, and "the virtual bounties" which a protective tariff affords manufactures. Nor was it to be apprehended that this power would be abused "while the vigor of representative responsibility remains unimpaired. It is on this principle," the report continues, "that the framers of the Constitution mainly relied for the protection of the public purse. It was a safe reliance. It was manifest that there was no other subject on which representative responsibility would be so great." Furthermore, it was a case in which legislative discretion was absolutely necessary, "since no human foresight could discern, nor human industry enumerate the infinite variety of purposes to which the public money might advantageously and legitimately be applied. The attempt would have been to *legislate,* not frame a Constitution; to foresee and provide specifically for the wants of future generations, not to frame a rule of conduct for the legislative body." At one point, however, the report does—inferentially at least—concede something to Madison's apprehensions. For it insists throughout that the states always "retain their jurisdictional rights," whatever operations the national government might undertake within their limits, and whether with or without state consent. Unfortunately, the basis on which this confident assertion was rested by the committee is not disclosed.[27]

Of the two most notable documents bearing on the question of Congress'

25. 2 Richardson 18.

26. 2 *American State Papers* (Miscel.) 443; 31 *Annals of Cong.* 451 *et seq.* {1817–1818}.

27. At the close of the debate, the House voted a resolution asserting the power of Congress "to appropriate money for the construction of postroads, military and other roads, and of canals and for the improvement of water courses." Other resolutions implying certain powers of jurisdiction were defeated by small majorities. 32 *Annals of Cong.* 1380 *et seq.* {1818}.

spending power, the report just cited is one, the other being the elaborate paper, *Views of the President of the United States on the Subject of Internal Improvements,* which Monroe transmitted to the House of Representatives on May 4, 1822, in connection with his veto of a bill "For the Preservation and Repair of the Cumberland Road."[28] The distinctive feature of this bill was a provision for turnpikes with gates and tolls; and because of this fact the presidential essay—it runs to approximately 30,000 words—is shaped throughout to meet the issue which the Tucker report deliberately scouted, that of jurisdiction.

On the simple question of the right of Congress to raise and spend money Monroe owns himself to have undergone a change of views.

> It was impossible to have created a power within the government or any other power distinct from Congress and the executive which should control the movement of the government in this respect and not destroy it. Had it been declared by a clause in the Constitution that the expenditures under this grant should be restricted to the construction which might be given of the other grants, such restraint, though the most innocent, could not have failed to have had injurious effect on the vital principles of the government and often on its most important measures.[29]

It follows that, while "each of the other grants is limited by the nature of the grant itself," this is limited "by the nature of the government only." Nor can there be any doubt that "good roads and canals will promote many very important national purposes."[30] Also, there was the plain verdict of the practice of the government from the beginning: "A practical construction, thus supported, shows that it has reason on its side and is called for by the interests of the Union. Hence, too, the presumption that it will be persevered in"[31] And,

> wherein consists the danger of a liberal construction to the right of Congress to raise and appropriate the public money? . . . Is not the responsibility of the representative to his constituents in every branch of the general government equally strong, and as sensibly felt as in the state governments, and is not the security against abuse as effective in the one as in the other government?" In short, "my idea is that Congress has an unlimited power to raise money, and that in its appropriation they have a discretionary power, restricted only by the duty to appropriate it to purposes of common defense and of general, not local, national, not state, benefit.[32]

But the power of appropriation is one thing, jurisdiction quite another, and the former, Monroe argues throughout, does not infer the latter. In his own words:

> The right of appropriation is nothing more than a right to apply the public money to this or that purpose. It has no incidental power, nor does it draw after it any consequence of that kind. All that Congress could do under it in the case of internal improvements would be to appropriate the money necessary to make them. For every act requiring legislative sanction or support the state authority must be relied

28. 2 Richardson 142–43; 144–83.
29. *Id.* 166.
30. *Id.* 167.
31. *Id.* 172.
32. *Id.* 173.

on. The condemnation of the land, if the proprietors should refuse to sell it, the establishment of turnpikes and tolls, and the protection of the work when finished must be done by the state. To these purposes the powers of the general government are believed to be utterly incompetent.[33]

Indeed in his veto, Monroe had put the same idea somewhat more positively:

A power to establish turnpikes with gates and tolls and to enforce the collection of tolls by penalties, implies a power to adopt and execute a complete system of internal improvement. A right to impose duties to be paid by all persons passing a certain road, and on horses and carriages, as is done by this bill, involves the right to take the land from the proprietor on a valuation and to pass laws for the protection of the road from injuries, and if it exist as to one road it exists as to any other, and to as many roads as Congress may think proper to establish. A right to legislate for one of these purposes is a right to legislate for the others. It is a complete right of jurisdiction and sovereignty for all the purposes of internal improvement, and not merely the right of applying money under the power vested in Congress to make appropriations, under which power, with the consent of the states through which this road passes, the work was originally commenced, and has been so far executed. I am of opinion that Congress do not possess this power; that the states individually cannot grant it, for although they may assent to the appropriation of money within their limits for such purposes, they can grant no power of jurisdiction or sovereignty by special compacts with the United States. This power can be granted only by an amendment to the Constitution and in the mode prescribed by it.[34]

Later Monroe illustrates his position by suggesting an analogy between the national government and a corporation. "There is not a corporation in the Union," he says, "which does not exercise great discretion in the application of the money raised by it to the purposes of its institution. It would be strange if the government of the United States, which was instituted for such important purposes and endowed with such extensive powers, should not be allowed at least equal discretion and authority."[35] But on the other hand, it is inferred, there would be also the same subordination to the law of the state. Yet this is all on the assumption that the expenditure does not take place within the field of jurisdiction which falls to the national government by virtue of its enumerated powers; for within that field, Monroe acknowledges, national power is, by Article VI, paragraph 2, of the Constitution, paramount over state power.

We are thus brought to the final turn of Monroe's argument. This consists in a careful examination of those clauses of the Constitution which, when read in conjunction with the "necessary and proper" clause, confer jurisdictional powers upon the national government within the limits of the states, for the purpose of demonstrating that none of these authorizes the national government to embark upon a system of internal improvements. Thus the power of Congress "to estab-

33. *Id.* 168.
34. *Id.* 142–43.
35. *Id.* 168–69.

lish postoffices and post roads" is, he argues, simply the power to designate such offices and roads. "The idea of a right to lay off the roads of the United States on a general scale of improvement, to take the soil from the proprietor by force, to establish turnpikes and tolls, and to punish" despoilers of the national property would never occur to an intelligent citizen.[36] Nor was the power "to declare war" a better foundation for such pretensions. "If it had been intended that the right to declare war should include all the powers necessary to maintain war," why the specific grant of power to raise and support armies and the navy, etc.?[37] Lastly, as to the commerce clause, the claims set up under this appeared to Monroe to have the least weight of all, the delegation of power effected by this clause having been dictated mainly by the "injuries resulting from the regulation of trade by the states respectively."[38]

Monroe's argument reduces itself to the following propositions: First, Congress' power to appropriate money is an independent power, unlimited in extent so long as the purpose of its exercise is national in character; but it carries with it no rights of jurisdiction within the states, nor may the states confer such rights by their individual action. Secondly, Congress may therefore contribute money *ad libitum* toward the construction and maintenance within the states of internal improvements planned on a national scale, but all jurisdictional rights in relation to the works thus brought into existence would remain with the states. Thirdly, none of the clauses of the Constitution which confer jurisdictional rights upon the national government authorize the construction by it of public works within the states, even when read in conjunction with the "necessary and proper" clause.[39]

Supplemented by "repeated, liberal, and candid discussions in the legislature," the *Views* "conciliated the sentiments and approximated the opinions of enlightened minds upon the question of constitutional power"[40] for fully two decades. On March 3, 1823, the first Rivers and Harbors Bill became law; in April of the following year $30,000 was appropriated for the survey of such roads and canals as the President should deem to be of national importance; by the Act of March 3, 1825, was authorized a subscription of $300,000 to the stock of the Delaware and Chesapeake Canal; at the same session $200,000, together with a grant of 24,000 acres of land, was voted General Lafayette, then the country's guest. In his inaugural the younger Adams sought to fire the imagination of Congress by citing "the magnificence and splendor" of the public works "of the ancient republics." In his first message[41] he announced that surveys had been completed "for ascertaining the practicability of a canal from the

36. *Id.* 157.
37. *Id.* 159.
38. *Id.* 161.
39. Congress, however, did not altogether agree with Monroe on the question of jurisdiction. See Rogers, *Postal Power* 84. In support of Monroe's position is Cleveland, P. & A. R. Co. v. Franklin Canal Co., 5 F. Cas. 1044 (C.C. W.D. Pa. 1853) (No. 2890).
40. The quoted words are from J. Q. Adams' Inaugural, 2 Richardson, 298-99.
41. *Id.* 299 *et seq.*

Chesapeake Bay to the Ohio River,'' for a road from Washington to New Orleans, and for the union of the "waters of Lake Memphremagog with Connecticut River''; also, that surveys for roads in the territories of Florida, Arkansas, and Michigan and from Missouri to Mexico, as well as for the continuance of the Cumberland Road, were under way or had been completed. Even so, "the great object of the institution of civil government,'' "the improvement of those who are parties to the social compact,'' was not to be accomplished exclusively by roads and canals; "moral, political, and intellectual improvements are duties assigned by the Author of Our Existence to social no less than to individual man,'' wherefore "governments are invested with power,'' the exercise of which for "the progressive improvement of the governed'' "is a duty as sacred and indispensable as the usurpation of powers not granted is criminal and odious.'' Specifically, Adams, recurring to Washington's suggestion, urged a national university; national patronage of voyages of discovery, the erection of an astronomical observatory. "There are,'' he noted, "one hundred and thirty of these lighthouses of the skies'' scattered through Europe, "while throughout the American hemisphere there is not one.'' He also pressed the execution of the resolution of December 24, 1799, providing for a monument in the city of Washington to the Father of his Country. Nor did he doubt that the various powers of Congress were adequate to these objects; and if they were, not to utilize them "would be treachery to the most sacred of trusts.'' "The spirit of improvement,'' he concluded, "is abroad upon the earth.'' "While foreign nations less blessed with that freedom which is power than ourselves are advancing with gigantic strides in the career of public improvement, were we to slumber in indolence or fold up our arms and proclaim to the world that we are palsied by the will of our constituents, would it not be to cast away the bounties of Providence and doom ourselves to perpetual inferiority?''[42]

Adams' vision outran the inclination of the country, perhaps its resources; certainly it made small appeal to the narrow imagination of the frontiersman who came after him. Nevertheless, it does not appear that Jackson rejected the broad doctrine which had been developed by Monroe as to Congress' power in the appropriation of money; on the contrary we find him attempting to foist this doctrine on Madison as well, whose veto of the Bonus Bill he interprets quite erroneously as "a concession that the right of appropriation is not limited by the power to carry into effect the measures for which money is asked.''[43] On the other hand, he is very explicit that no rights of jurisdiction accompany such appropriations; and furthermore they must be for "general not local, national not state'' purposes. His emphasis on this latter point, both in his celebrated veto of the Maysville Road Bill on May 27, 1830,[44] and in later communications constitutes in fact Jackson's distinctive contribution to the question of Congress' spend-

---

42. *Id.* 316.
43. See Madison's own words on the point, 9 *Writings* {of James Madison} 375–76 (Hunt ed.).
44. 2 Richardson, *et seq.* Other vetoes will be found *id.* 493, 508, 638.

ing power. Moreover, a series of vetoes which he based partly on this ground and partly on the ground that there ought to be no expenditures without attendant jurisdiction, by bringing to an abrupt close all general schemes of improvement by the national government, marks an epoch in the history of the subject. Pointing out in his message of December 1, 1834, that at the time of the veto of the Maysville Road Bill there had been reported to Congress bills calling for the appropriation of $106,000,000 for internal improvements, while memorials before Congress called for projects which would have involved an expenditure of another hundred million, Jackson thus congratulated himself and the country upon his decisive stand on that occasion:

> So far, at least, as it regards this branch of the subject, my best hopes have been realized. Nearly four years have elapsed, and several sessions of Congress have intervened, and no attempt within my recollection has been made to induce Congress to exercise this power. The applications for the construction of roads and canals which were formerly multiplied upon your files are no longer presented, and we have good reason to infer that the current of public sentiment has become so decided against the pretension as effectually to discourage its reassertion. So thinking, I derive the greatest satisfaction from the conviction that thus much at least has been secured upon this important and embarrassing subject.[45]

From 1830 until the Civil War the constitutional issue centers for the most part about rivers and harbors bills, the first one of which was, as noted above, signed by Monroe in 1823. The line of precedents for such measures, however, reaches back to the beginning of the government, specifically to the act of August 7, 1789, for the establishment and support of lighthouses, buoys, and other aids to navigation.[46] The narrow constructionist was thus presented with the problem either of distinguishing rivers and harbors bills from such measures, or if he admitted the validity of the former, of distinguishing them from internal improvements generally. Jackson, in an effort to apply his principle that appropriations must be for general not local purposes, wished to confine grants for rivers and harbors "to places below the ports of entry or delivery established by law,"[47] a test which resulted in the creation of many new ports of entry. Tyler fell back on the more general doctrine;[48] but Polk, confronted in 1846 with a bill which made provision for $1,378,450, to be applied "to more than forty distinct and separate objects of improvement," sought to erect Jackson's rule of thumb into one of constitutional obligation.[49] He also urged that such works should be accomplished by the states, which should then recoup themselves from tonnage dues;[50] and in general, it may be said, he sought to revive the doctrines of Madison's veto. Taylor and Fillmore, on the other hand, being disciples of Clay,

45. 3 *Id*. 120–21.
46. 5 *id*. 263.
47. 3 *id*. 122.
48. 4 *id*. 330.
49. *Id*. 460 *et seq*.
50. *Id*. 616–17.

instigated rivers and harbors appropriations;[51] while Pierce reverted once more to the Madisonian position, but with a significant difference. While he denied that Congress could make such appropriations by virtue of the "general welfare," the commerce, or postal clauses, he held them to be warrantable at times as measures of national defense and for facilitating the collection of the revenues; but the acquisition of jurisdiction should usually accompany appropriations, which it could do as to "needful buildings" in accordance with Article I, section 8, clause 17; for the rest, however, the national government must content itself with the jurisdiction conferred upon it by the "admiralty and maritime" clause of Article III.[52]

Thus as we approach the Civil War, we discover it to be the tendency of presidential doctrine to return to the grounds of Madison's veto of 1817, enlarged nevertheless by an invocation of the war power. Nor did the project of a railway to the Pacific, suggested by the outcome of the Mexican War, at first alter the status of the question.[53] Both Pierce and Buchanan recommended the enterprise by reference to military necessity,[54] an argument which the outbreak of the Civil War rendered conclusive. It was not until nearly a quarter of a century later that the Supreme Court had occasion to pass upon the acts of 1862 and 1864, which called the Union Pacific and Central Pacific lines into being, but when it did so, it invoked in their behalf not merely the war power but the commerce and postal powers as well.[55]

Nevertheless, it would be a mistake to suppose that Congress' broader power of appropriation, in however bad repute theoretically, was in fact defunct, even during that period when the doctrine of strict construction was most prevalent. In 1817 a committee of Congress had reported in favor of the establishment of a bureau of agriculture, but the suggestion had, like Washington's similar proposal, fallen by the wayside. Twenty-one years later an appropriation for the "collection of agricultural statistics and other . . . agricultural purposes" was voted, and fourteen years after that the purchase and distribution of seeds, which had in fact begun as early as 1836, was specifically provided for. Meantime, in 1850, an appropriation of one thousand dollars was made for the chemical analysis of vegetable substances, and eight years after that $3500 was voted for the publication of information concerning the consumption of cotton. The Department of Agriculture itself was established in 1862, and the year following

51. 5 *id.* 20 and 90.

52. *Id.* 218 *et seq.* and 259 *et seq.* Buchanan recurred to Madison's and Polk's views, *id.* 601 *et seq.* Later vetoes of rivers and harbors bills have not raised the general constitutional question, but have invoked the distinction between national and local improvements. See 7 Richardson 382; 8 *id.* 120; 9 *id.* 677. The last reference is to Mr. Cleveland's veto of May 29, 1896, of a bill carrying an appropriation of eighty millions. The measure was passed over the veto.

53. For the beginnings of the movement for a Pacific railway, see Lewis H. Haney, *A Congressional History of Railways in the United States to 1850* chs. 21–23 (1908).

54. 5 Richardson 220, 457, 526, 572, 650. Taylor and Fillmore had both recommended the enterprise earlier, but with little reference to the constitutional question. *Id.* 20 and 86.

55. The leading case is California v. Central Pacific Ry. Co., 127 U.S. 1 (1887).

$80,000 was voted to its use, for the study of plant and animal diseases and insect pests, the culture of tobacco, silk, and cotton, irrigation, the adulteration of foods, and the like.[56] The multifarious activities of this department today, involving the annual expenditure of nearly one hundred millions, are a matter of common knowledge. Yet this expansion seems to have stirred little if any protest on constitutional grounds, a remark which applies equally to the parallel development of the census, to the establishment of the geological and geodetic surveys, to the creation of the Fisheries Bureau, the Bureau of Mines, and the Labor Bureau (now the Department of Labor), and to the participation of the government in the business of irrigation, game preservation, etc., etc.

The entrance of the national government into the field of education, on the other hand, presents a somewhat different story, and an instructive one for our purposes. This began, as we have seen, with the provision in the act under which Ohio was admitted to the Union—a provision harking back, in turn, to the Ordinance of 1787[57]—whereby, in return for a grant of lands to each township in the state for public schools, and other concessions, the state pledged itself to withhold its hand in the matter of taxation for a term of years as regarded land sold by the national government to settlers. Later similar compacts were entered into with other states as they were admitted into the Union. Building upon these beginnings, and animated especially by its increasing interest in agricultural development, Congress in February 1859 passed a bill the purpose of which was stated to be "the endowment, support, and maintenance of at least one college [in each state] where the leading object shall be, without excluding other scientific or classical studies, to teach such branches of learning as are related to agriculture and the mechanic arts, as the legislatures of the states may respectively prescribe, in order to promote the liberal and practical education of the industrial classes in the several pursuits and professions of life."[58] The bill assigned to each state twenty thousand acres of land for each senator and representative in the existing Congress and an additional twenty thousand acres for each additional representative to which it might become entitled under the census of 1860. In return each state was required "to provide within five years at least not less than one college, or the grant to said state" was to cease forthwith, and the state was to pay over to the United States any amounts it had received from lands previously sold. Other conditions were also specified, and the consent of the state must be communicated to the national government within two years.

The bill was upset by a presidential veto. Speaking to the constitutional issue, Buchanan wrote: "I presume the general proposition is undeniable that Congress does not possess the power to appropriate money in the Treasury, raised by taxes out of the people of the United States, for the purpose of educating the people of

56. For the above and other details, see William L. Wanlass, *United States Department of Agriculture passim* (38 Johns Hopkins Univ. Studies 1920).
57. And back of that to the Ordinance of 1784, of which Jefferson was the principal author.
58. 5 Richardson 543.

the respective states."[59] Any other view would mean "an actual consolidation of the federal and state governments so far as the great taxing and money power is concerned, and constitute a government of partnership between the two in the Treasury of the United States, equally ruinous to both." But, he continued, this bill is justified as an exercise by Congress of its power "to dispose . . . of the territory and other property of the United States"; the argument was unacceptable:

> It would be a strange anomaly, indeed, to have created two funds—the one by taxation, confined to the execution of the enumerated powers delegated to Congress, and the other from the public lands, applicable to all subjects, foreign and domestic, which Congress might designate; that this fund should be 'disposed of,' not to pay the debts of the United States, not 'to raise and support armies,' not 'to provide and maintain a navy,' nor to accomplish any one of the other great objects enumerated in the Constitution, but he {sic; be?} diverted from them to pay the debts of the states, to educate their people, and to carry into effect any other measure of their domestic policy. This would be to confer upon Congress a vast and irresponsible authority, utterly at war with the well-known jealousy of federal power which prevailed at the formation of the Constitution. The natural intendment would be that as the Constitution confined Congress to well-defined specific powers, the funds placed at their command, whether in land or money, should be appropriated to the performance of the duties corresponding with these powers. If not, a government has been created with all its other powers carefully limited, but without any limitation in respect to the public lands.[60]

Nor was this all; for some of "these lands were paid for out of the Treasury from money raised by taxation. Now if Congress had no power to appropriate the money with which these lands were purchased, is it not clear that the power over the lands is equally limited? . . . If this were not the case, then by the purchase of a new territory from a foreign government out of the public Treasury, Congress could enlarge their own powers and appropriate the proceeds of the sales of the land thus purchased, at their own discretion, to other and far different objects from what they could have applied the purchase money which had been raised by taxation."[61]

Three years later the Morrill Act, embodying substantially the provisions which Buchanan had vetoed, but increasing the donation of lands for each representative in Congress from twenty to thirty thousand acres, became law.[62] An amendment in 1866 extended its benefits to newly admitted states, and today there is probably not a state in the Union which has not long since accepted it. The Bureau of Education was created in the Department of the Interior in 1867—in part, no doubt, as an outcome of the Freedmen's Bureau. In 1870 we find President Grant urging an appropriation of proceeds from the sale of public lands to educational purposes, a recommendation which was renewed by his

59. *Id.* 547.
60. *Id.* 548.
61. *Id.* 549.
62. Act of July 2, 1862, ch. 130, 12 Stat. 503.

immediate successors,[63] and led finally to the enactment of the act of 1890. By this statute donations amounting eventually to $25,000 per annum were to be made to each state and territory "for the more complete endowment and maintenance of colleges for the benefit of agriculture and the mechanic arts," already established or to be established in accordance with the Morrill Act. The grant was made subject to certain conditions designed to secure equitable participation by colored students in its benefits and to the legislative assent of the several states and territories.[64]

Thus was the transition effected from donations of land to donations of money, though the latter were still confined to proceeds from land sales. Meantime, in his message of 1882, President Arthur, asserting that "the census returns disclose an alarming state of illiteracy in certain portions of the country, where the provision for schools is grossly inadequate," had urged national aid on a much broader scale;[65] and in 1883 Senator Blair, chairman of the Senate Committee on Education, had introduced a bill providing for the distribution of some $77,000,000 among the states on the basis of illiteracy. The bill received strong support from Southern members and passed the Senate three times. Its final failure was due in part to the constitutional objection, but in greater measure to other considerations.[66] Not until 1900, did Congress make an appropriation from the general funds in aid of education within the states. By an act passed that year it was provided that whenever the receipts from the sale of public lands should be insufficient to meet the demands of the act of 1890, the deficit should be met out of "any funds in the national Treasury not otherwise appropriated."[67] Seven years later appropriations to supplement the grants which are forthcoming under the act of 1890 were authorized to the eventual amount of $50,000 per annum for each state and territory.[68]

And thus we are brought to the recent series of measures, which culminates in the Sheppard-Towner Act and the Towner-Sterling Bill. The first of these is the Smith-Lever Act of 1914,[69] which calls for the appropriation of increasing sums, to amount finally to more than four and one-half millions annually, for the promotion of agricultural extension work in the states and territories. The share of each state is determined by its proportion of the rural population of the country, and is conditioned on its appropriation each year of an equal sum for the same purpose. The next member of this series is the Smith-Hughes Act of 1917,[70] which authorizes on like terms appropriations to amount finally to seven millions per annum, which are to be turned over to the several states in varying

63. 7 Richardson 152, 203, 606, 626; 8 id. 58.
64. Act of Aug. 30, 1890, 26 Stat. 417.
65. 8 Richardson 143, 184, 253.
66. D. R. Dewey, *National Problems* 89–90 (1907).
67. Act of May 17, 1900, ch. 479, 31 Stat. 179.
68. Act of Mar. 4, 1907, ch. 2907, 34 Stat. 1281.
69. Act of May 8, 1914, ch. 79, 38 Stat. 372.
70. Act of Feb. 23, 1917, ch. 114, 39 Stat. 929.

proportions for the purpose of cooperating with them in the paying of salaries and the training of teachers of agricultural and industrial subjects and of home economics. A little later, the government began rehabilitation work with disabled soldiers, and this activity no doubt is what suggested the act of 1920, appropriating after 1921 one million dollars annually for cooperating with the states, on the now familiar fifty-fifty basis, in the vocational rehabilitation of persons disabled in industry.[71]

Meantime, in October 1918, the project originally known as the Smith-Towner Bill, but subsequently rechristened the Towner-Sterling Bill, had made its appearance. Besides providing for a national Department of Education, the measure would authorize an annual appropriation of approximately 100 million dollars, to be distributed among the states and territories in varying proportions, for the purpose of combating illiteracy, promoting Americanization, encouraging physical education, assisting the preparation of public school teachers, and most important of all, developing education in the public elementary and secondary schools. Fifty millions would be devoted to this last purpose alone; but in order to qualify for its share of this part of the appropriation, a state would be required to have a legal school term of twenty-four weeks each year, a compulsory school attendance law for children between the ages of seven and fourteen, and a law requiring that the English language should be the basic language of instruction in the common branches in all schools, both public and private. Furthermore, in order to qualify for any part of the appropriation, a state would be required to accept the terms of the act by legislative enactment and to match such sums as it received with like sums allocated to the same purposes.[72]

71. Act of June 2, 1920, ch. 219, 41 Stat. 715. Mention should also be made in this connection of the acts of Mar. 3, 1879, ch. 186, 20 Stat. 468; and June 25, 1906, ch. 3536, 34 Stat. 460. The former appropriated $250,000 "out of money in the United States Treasury not otherwise appropriated," as a perpetual fund for the purpose of aiding the education of the blind, through the American Printing House for the Blind, which is located at Louisville, Ky. The latter commutes the income from this fund with an annual appropriation of $10,000. See also the act of July 1, 1898, ch. 546, 30 Stat. 624, for an appropriation to Howard University with conditions attached.

72. For a copy of the bill and a survey of the discussion regarding it, both in Congress and out, see *The Reference Shelf* no. 5. The constitutional issue seems to have occupied small part in the discussion. A further precedent for the cooperative features of the Sheppard-Towner Act and the Towner-Sterling Bill is furnished by the Federal Highways Act of July 11, 1916, ch. 241, 39 Stat. 355, which is supplemented and extended by the acts of Feb. 28, 1919, ch. 69, 40 Stat. 1189, and Nov. 9, 1921, ch. 119, 42 Stat. 212. Though justified under the postal clause, the administration of these measures is assigned to the Department of Agriculture. As amended, the act authorized an appropriation of $75,000,000 for the fiscal year of 1921. Constructions under the act are to be done in each state under the highway department thereof, subject to the inspection and approval of the Secretary of Agriculture. Before a state can qualify for its share of the national appropriation, it must, through its legislature, accept the terms of the act, a compliance which, it is recognized, will sometimes involve constitutional amendment or a popular referendum, or both. No project may be entered upon which has not first received the approval of the Secretary of Agriculture, and of the funds required half must come from the state. A state may furthermore have its share of the national appropriation cut off if it does not provide for the proper maintenance of existing constructions. Only durable types of surface and materials may be adopted; all roads constructed under the act shall be free from tolls, etc.

All these measures, actual or prospective, obviously rest on the literal reading of the "general welfare" clause; whether some of them raise other questions we shall consider in a moment. But first let us turn for an instant to another class of evidence bearing on our principal topic—the views of writers.

Of all the numerous commentators on the Constitution before the Civil War, about the only one whose work has not long since found its way to the scrap heap is Joseph Story. His great work, the official prestige of its author, his nearness to Marshall, his wide scholarship, and modern point of view have rescued him from the common fate; and as we have seen, Story rejects absolutely the Madisonian version of the "general welfare" clause. Of commentators since the Civil War, Tucker comes to the defense of the Madisonian doctrine, but supplements it—as he is compelled both by practice and judicial precedent to do—by a greatly enlarged view of Congress' powers under the commerce and postal clauses, and of the war power.[73] Hare and Pomeroy, on the contrary, follow Monroe and Story. Both assert, moreover, that while in theory national expenditures must be for national purposes, the decision as to what purposes are national lies with Congress alone;[74] a proposition which more recent writers,[75] by their silence on the general issue, tend to confirm, since this silence reflects the silence of the Court.

Nevertheless, he could be a bold man who would assert dogmatically that legitimate occasion might never arise for judicial interposition within this field. For the Court to attempt to draw the line between general welfare on the one hand and local welfare on the other would no doubt land it into grave difficulties.[76] It

73. J. R. Tucker, *The Constitution of the United States* 478 *et seq.* (H. St. G. Tucker ed. 1899).

74. 1 J. I. C. Hare, *American Constitutional Law* 241 (1889); J. N. Pomeroy, *Constitutional Law* 228–29 (10th ed. 1888).

75. The reference is to the standard works of Willoughby, McClain, Cooley, and Hall. However, Professor Burdick's *The Law of the American Constitution* (1922), which has just appeared, deals specifically with the question and takes the literal view of the "general welfare" clause, which is stated in words borrowed from Monroe's "Views."

76. In Chief Justice Marshall's opinion in Gibbons v. Ogden, 9 Wheat. 1, 199 (1824), occurs the following sentence: "Congress is not empowered to tax for those purposes which are within the exclusive province of the states." These words have sometimes been cited in support of the idea that the Supreme Court might properly disallow an appropriation of Congress, in a case of which the Court had jurisdiction, on the ground that such appropriation represented an invasion by Congress of the field of state power. This seems, however, a rather hasty deduction. Quite aside from the fact that the words quoted were uttered *obiter*, it is apparent that they make no contribution toward a determination of what purposes are "within the exclusive province of the states." Elsewhere in the same opinion Marshall takes account of the occasional overlapping of national and state powers in the following words: "It is obvious that the government of the Union, in the exercise of its express powers . . . may use means that may also be employed by a state in the exercise of its acknowledged powers." Thus, to apply this proposition to the present case, the national government, being vested with the express power of providing by money for "the general welfare," may do so by means employed by the states in the promotion of their local welfare—for instance, the appropriation of money for education within the states. The only question to be determined is whether education within the states is a matter of national, that is, "general" welfare; and this question, which was answered affirmatively even at the outset of the government, has certainly been settled by the course of legislation since 1862. Story quotes the *dictum* with approval. 1 Story, *Commentaries* sec. 927

would next be asked to say whether the Boston Navy Yard was for the "common defense"—an embarrassing question. Indeed, the old-time distinction between "public" and "private" purpose—a distinction which has never been applied against the national Congress[77]—is none too clear nowadays.[78] On the other hand, some of the terms of the Towner-Sterling Bill—as for instance, that a state, in order to share the benefits of the measure, must have certain statutes on its books—suggest the theoretical possibility at least of conditions which would cut off a state from its fair share of an appropriation, ostensibly for the general welfare, on entirely arbitrary grounds. Thus, suppose an appropriation for the support of education in those states only which at the following election should choose Republican governors: Would the Court, assuming it to have obtained jurisdiction of a case raising the point, be obliged to presume such an appropriation to be for the "general welfare" of the United States? But Congress' power to stipulate conditions to its bounty which do not on their face contradict the notion of a national purpose but which are clearly relevant to the main object of an appropriation must, save for the political check, be nearly unlimited. Certainly, the mere fact that an appropriation holds out an inducement to states to do something which, perhaps, they would not otherwise do, is not enough to condemn it.

We turn now for a moment to the cases—not for the light which they shed on the main issue, for that is very little, but for what they have to say on the collateral subject of jurisdiction. As we have already noted, the Supreme Court in the Pacific Railroad Cases[79] attributed the right of the national government to construct interstate highways to the war power and to the powers of Congress under the commerce and postal clauses. But these cases also teach that, as auxiliary to the power to construct highways, Congress may vest a corporate agent with the power of eminent domain within the states and that the national franchises of such corporations may be exempt from state taxation.[80] This question therefore arises: Would the same jurisdictional rights and immunities be claimable in connection with an appropriation warranted only under the "general welfare" clause? United States v. The Gettysburg Railway Co.,[81] in which the Court, invoking this clause, unanimously sustained an exercise of the power of eminent domain in the laying out of a national park, seems to return an affirmative answer. The principle suggested by the decision is that Congress may take all

---

(5th ed.). And that his evaluation of it is correct seems to be proved by Marshall's own approval of Monroe's "Views." See letter from former to latter, of June 13, 1822, in Oster, *Political and Economic Doctrines of John Marshall* 179 (1914).

77. The broad language employed in United States v. Realty Co., 163 U.S. 427 (1896), suggests, moreover, that it never will be. See also Field v. Clark, 143 U.S. 649 (1891); and Allen v. Smith, 173 U.S. 389 (1899).

78. See e.g. Green v. Frazier, 253 U.S. 233 (1920).

79. 127 U.S. 1 (1887).

80. See also Luxton v. North River Bridge Co., 153 U.S. 525 (1894).

81. 160 U.S. 668 (1896).

measures which are "necessary and proper" to assure the application of an expenditure to its designated purpose. And of like implication is Van Brocklin v. Tennessee,[82] in which was asserted the immunity from taxation by a state of land acquired therein by the national government in the exercise of the latter's right "to lay and collect taxes to . . . provide for the common defense and general welfare of the United States." On the other hand, that general jurisdictional rights do not attend the right of appropriation—Madison's apprehensions to the contrary notwithstanding—seems clear. Thus suppose Congress should vote money for a school: it could under the cases just cited authorize the seizure by eminent domain of land for the building, and, as national property, both land and building could be exempted from local taxation; but if attendance at the school were to be compelled it would have to be by the state, not by the national government.[83]

And so much for the argument against the Maternity Act that it exceeds Congress' power of expenditure. The question really boils down to this: What weight should be given to the Madisonian doctrine that the national government's field of expenditure is precisely coextensive with the field of its other powers? The logical difficulties in the way of this proposition were pointed out by Story and his arguments need not be repeated. The historical difficulties are not less formidable. The only period when the doctrine was at all generally accepted was that between 1845 and 1860, when state's rights principles were dominant with all sections and parties. Of the earlier Presidents every one who put himself officially on record, Madison alone excepted, avowed the literal view of the "general welfare" clause, qualified to be sure after 1800, first by the doctrine of state consent and later by a general *caveat* against jurisdictional rights following in the wake of appropriations. But neither of these qualifications touches the Maternity Act in any way, nor does the logic of later decisions support them.

---

82. 117 U.S. 151 (1885).

83. In his brief on reargument in Smith v. Kansas City Title and Trust Co., 255 U.S. 180 (1921), in which the question of the validity of the Federal Farm Loan Act of July 17, 1916, ch. 245, 39 Stat. 360, was involved, Mr. Hughes based his case for the validity of the act on the following propositions (at 21): "I. Congress has power to use the public money, and to provide for the borrowing of money, to aid in agricultural development throughout the country in accordance with the systematic and general plan to promote the cultivation of the soil, involving the application of money through loans or otherwise, and that Congress, having this power, could exercise it by the adoption of appropriate means to that end and the creation of instrumentalities for that purpose;

"II. Congress has the power to judge for itself what fiscal agencies the government needs and that its decision of that question is not open to judicial review; that Congress may create in its discretion, as it has created in this instance, moneyed institutions equipped to serve as fiscal agents of the government and to provide a market, as stated in the act, for United States bonds."

Some of the data relied upon by Mr. Hughes in support of the first proposition are quoted in the note following. In support of the second proposition, he relied principally upon McCulloch v. Maryland, 4 Wheat. 316 (U.S. 1819), which he interpreted as permitting Congress to create corporate agencies for the purpose of applying funds appropriated by it to their designated uses, and to exempt such agencies from state taxation. The curiously narrow and illogical opinion of Mr. Justice Day for the Court, sustaining the act, avoided these issues.

And the verdict to be drawn from the practice of Congress is substantially the same. The validity of "internal improvements" was finally rested on views of the war, commercial, and postal powers which had not occurred to early champions of national expenditures for this purpose, or were repudiated by them; and probably rivers and harbors appropriations may be similarly justified. Not so, however, of the ever mounting sums which have been voted through more than eighty years for the encouragement of agriculture, and through more than sixty years—though only more recently from the general funds—for education within the states. Certain it is that any attempt to apply the Madisonian test to national expenditures today would call for a radical revision in the customary annual budget of the government and for a revolution in national administration.[84] Yet

84. At the risk of some repetition, I venture to quote in this connection the following passage from Mr. Hughes' brief (at 35): "Nothing could better illustrate the accepted principle than the appropriations to aid in agricultural development. Since the year 1839 there has been a constant disbursement of public moneys in the promotion and fostering of agriculture, in disseminating information, distributing seeds, and in aiding agricultural schools. For upwards of sixty years—since the act of 1857 (11 Stat. 226)—Congress has made provision for the distribution of cuttings and seeds. It was in that year also that provision was made for investigation as to the consumption of cotton (*id.*).

"The Department of Agriculture was established in 1862 (12 Stat. 387). The act provided as to this department: 'the general designs and duties of which shall be to acquire and diffuse among the people of the United States useful information on subjects connected with agriculture in the most general and comprehensive sense of that word, and to procure, propagate, and distribute among the people new and valuable seeds and plants.'

"The far-sighted policy of the Morrill Land-Grant Act of 1862 (12 Stat. 503) made possible through donations of public land the establishment of institutions for instruction in agriculture throughout the country. Funds have been provided to maintain bureaus of agricultural statistics, for the introduction and protection of insectivorous birds for laboratories to engage in experimentation in agricultural chemistry (12 Stat. 69). The great pests, or enemies of crops, have been the subject of constant consideration, and frequent appropriations have been made to aid in their elimination (21 Stat. 259; 40 Stat. 374).

"In 1884, the Bureau of Animal Industry was established to disseminate information as to domestic animals and their diseases (23 Stat. 277). In 1890, the Weather Bureau was put in charge of the Department of Agriculture (26 Stat. 653), to make readily available comprehensive information as to matters of special interest to those engaged in the cultivation of the soil.

"The Irrigation Survey was established in 1889 under the direction of the Secretary of the Interior (25 Stat. 960), and in 1913, the Bureau of Mines (37 Stat. 681).

"The scope of the activities of the Department of Agriculture now embraces those of the Weather Bureau; the Bureau of Animal Industry (including inspection and quarantine work, the eradication of scabies in sheep and cattle, tuberculin and mallein testing, experiments in animal feeding and breeding, including cooperation with state agricultural experiment stations, scientific investigations of hog cholera and other diseases of animals); the Bureau of Plant Industry (including investigations of diseases of plants, of orchard and other fruits, of forest and ornamental trees and shrubs, of soil bacteriology and plant nutrition, of soil fertility, of plants yielding drugs, poisons, and oils, of cereals and cereal disease, of sugar beets, and generally of crop production, and the purchase and distribution of valuable seeds, bulbs, shrubs, vines, cuttings, and plants); the Forest Service (including various investigations in forestry); the Bureau of Chemistry (embracing various chemical and physical tests and biological investigations of food products); the Bureau of Soils (including investigations of soil types and chemical properties, of productivity . . . etc.); the Bureau of Entomology (including investigations of insects affecting fruits, orchards, vineyards, and crops); the Bureau of Biological Survey (including the investigation of the food habits of birds and mammals in relation to agriculture); the Division of Publications; the Bureau of Crop Estimates (covering all important data relating to agriculture); the State Relations Service (including farmers' cooperative demonstration work in

with the Madisonian doctrine counted out, what other test is there with which, in any reasonably probable case, the Court could confront a congressional appropriation without palpably invading the field of legislative discretion? We must conclude that into the "dread field" of money expenditure the court may not "thrust its sickle"; that so far as this power goes, the "general welfare" is what Congress finds it to be.

But even if the Maternity Act is not to be attacked with much prospect of success from the side of national power, still the question of its validity from the side of state power remains; it may, however, be disposed of very briefly. On the one hand, the states may not surrender indefinite powers, nor any valuable power indefinitely;[85] on the other hand, they may enter into compacts respecting the exercise of their powers with each other—Congress consenting—and with the national government; nor is there any apparent reason why compacts of the latter sort should not have as broad scope as those of the former.[86] The arrangement proposed by the Maternity Act is subject to discontinuance by either party at any time, and curtails the freedom of action of states entering into it no more seriously than the compact of 1802 between Ohio and the national government, which was followed by a series of similar compacts with other states, did that of those states.[87] The kind of cooperation between the national and state governments which is provided for by the Sheppard-Towner Act and its antecedents is entirely wholesome, entirely in harmony with early ideas of the federal system,[88] and instead of deadening state policy, directly stimulates it. The scruples

---

connection with state organizations, and for the study of methods to combat the cotton boll weevil), the Office of Public Roads and Rural Engineering (including investigations as to farm irrigation and drainage and construction of farm buildings); the Office of Markets and Rural Organization (including investigations of marketing methods, studies of cooperation among farmers in rural credits and other forms of cooperation in rural communities); and the Federal Horticultural Board (see 39 Stat. 446–76; 1134–66; 40 Stat. 973–1008).

"The Federal appropriations in 1917, in support of agriculture amounted to upwards of $29,000,000, and in 1918 to upwards of $45,000,000.

"There can be no question as to the continuous practical construction of the powers of Congress to raise and appropriate money to the effect that this power is not limited to the objects enumerated in the subsequent provisions, but extends what may properly be deemed to be embraced within the general welfare as expressly provided in the clause which confers the taxing power itself.

"As Mr. Chief Justice Marshall said in McCulloch v. Maryland, 4 Wheat. 316, 401: 'An exposition of the Constitution, deliberately established by legislative acts, on the faith which an immense property has been advanced, ought not to be lightly disregarded.'"

85. See Home Telephone and Telegraph Co. v. Los Angeles, 211 U.S. 265 (1908).

86. According to an article in *The New York Times* of Jan. 21, last, "Congress soon will be asked to confirm a treaty between seven Western states, with the nation as an eighth partner, which is expected to clear the way for the greatest irrigation and power project ever undertaken in this country." To the compact of 1921 between New York and New Jersey, creating the Port Authority of the port of New York, the national government is also virtually a party. The compact involves a very extensive delegation of powers by the two states.

87. In Stearns v. Minnesota, 179 U.S. 223 (1900), a compact of this character is sustained.

88. Note, for example, the language of Hamilton in Federalist, no. 27: "The legislatures, courts, and magistrates of the respective members, will be incorporated into the operatives {sic; operations} of the national government, *as far as its just and constitutional authority extends*; and will be rendered auxiliary to the enforcement of its laws."

raised against such cooperation in the name of state autonomy tend rather to withdraw from the states what must often prove a most advantageous mode of exercising that autonomy. Reversing the scriptural text, they would save the ghost of state sovereignty by suspending its ineffectual body at the end of a chain of fine-spun legalism.

In a word, the powers which the national government is exercising in the Maternity Act are powers which indubitably belong to it, and the powers which the states accepting the act are called upon to exercise indubitably belong to them; that the two governments should elect to exercise their respective powers for a common purpose of legitimate interest to both is certainly no constitutional objection in any sound theory of our federal system.

13. The Anti-Trust Acts and the Constitution

CONGRESS' chief effort to regulate commerce in the primary sense of *traffic* is embodied in the Sherman Anti-Trust Act of 1890, the opening section of which declares "every contract, combination in the form of trust or otherwise, or conspiracy in restraint of trade and commerce among the several states, or with foreign nations" to be "illegal"; while the second section makes it a misdemeanor for anybody to "monopolize, or attempt to monopolize" any part of such commerce.[1]

The act was passed to curb the growing tendency to industrial combination, and the first case to reach the Court under it was the famous Sugar Trust Case,[2] United States v. Knight Company, in which the government asked for the cancellation of certain agreements, whereby, through purchase of stock in other companies, the American Sugar Refining Company had "acquired," it was conceded, "nearly complete control of the manufacture of refined sugar in the United States."

The question of the validity of the act was not discussed directly by the Court, but was subordinated to that of its proper construction. So proceeding, however, the Court, in pursuance of the doctrines of constitutional law which were then dominant with it, turned the act from its intended purpose and destroyed its effectiveness—as that of the Interstate Commerce Act was being contemporaneously destroyed—for some years.

In the following passage early in Chief Justice Fuller's opinion for the Court, we see the spirit of laissez faire seizing upon the dual theory of the federal system and turning it to account:

> It is vital that the independence of the commercial power and of the police power, and the delimitation between them, however sometimes perplexing, should always

From 18 *Virginia Law Review* 355 (1932). Reprinted by permission.
1. 26 Stat. 209 (1890) ch. 647, secs. 1 and 2; U.S.C.A. tit. 15, secs. 1 and 2.

be recognized and observed, for while the one furnishes the strongest bond of union, the other is essential to the preservation of the autonomy of the states as required by our dual form of government; and acknowledged evils, however grave and urgent they may appear to be, had better be borne, than the risk be run, in the effort to suppress them, of more serious consequences by resort to expedients of even doubtful constitutionality.[3]

From this, it followed that what was needed was a hard and fast line between the two spheres of power; and in the following series of propositions the Court endeavors to lay down just such a line: (1) Production is always local, and under the exclusive domain of the states. (2) Commerce among the states does not commence until goods "commence their final movement from their state of origin to that of their destination." This had been states in Coe v. Errol[4] as a rule delimiting the states' taxing power in relation to the commerce clause, and it is now reiterated as a principle restrictive of Congress' power under the same clause. (3) The sale of a product is merely an incident of production, and while capable of "bringing the operation of commerce into play," affects it only "incidentally." (4) Such restraints therefore as would reach commerce as above defined from combinations to control production "in all its forms," would be "indirect," "however, inevitable and whatever its extent";[5] and so beyond the purview of the act.

Applying, then, this reasoning to the case before it, the Court proceeds:

> The object was manifestly private gain in the manufacture of the commodity, but not through the control of interstate or foreign commerce. It is true that the bill alleged that the products of these refineries were sold and distributed among the several states, and that all the companies were engaged in trade or commerce with the several states and with foreign nations; but this was no more than to say that trade and commerce served manufacture to fulfill its function. Sugar was refined for sale, and sales were probably made at Philadelphia for consumption, and undoubtedly for resale by the first purchasers throughout Pennsylvania and other states, and refined sugar was also forwarded by the companies to other states for sale. Nevertheless it does not follow that an attempt to monopolize, or the actual monopoly of, the manufacture was an attempt, whether executory or consummated, to monopolize commerce, even though, in order to dispose of the product, the instrumentality of commerce was necessarily invoked. There was nothing in the proofs to indicate any intention to put a restraint upon trade or commerce, and the fact, as we have seen, that trade or commerce might be indirectly affected was not enough to entitle complainants to a decree. . . . [6]

In the earlier portion of his opinion the chief justice had stressed the idea that the *mere intention* of selling an article does not put it in commerce. In view of the concessions here made, such observations become altogether pointless. The

2. 156 U.S. 1 (1895).
3. *Id*. 13.
4. 116 U.S. 517 (1886).
5. United States v. E. C. Knight Co., above note 2 at 16.
6. *Id*. 17.

same concessions also make unconvincing, to say the least, the apology sometimes offered for this decision, that the government's pleadings were at fault, in
centering the Court's attention on defendant's monopoly of the *manufactory* of
sugar (as if, for that matter, monopoly of manufacturing did not mean monopoly
of selling power!). Finally, they clearly bring certain phases of the case, within
the principle which had been recognized by the Court some years earlier in the
first of the Drummer Cases—though then in the interest of *curbing* state
power—that a negotiation of sales to be followed by a shipment of goods is
commerce.[7]

What the doctrine of the case boils down to, as Justice Harlan points out in his
dissenting opinion, is that commerce is *transportation* and nothing more.[8] In its
professed anxiety to obtain a firm line of demarcation between the fields of state
and national power, the Court conceives of the entire industrial process as falling
simply into two operations, manufacturing and transportation, and merges commerce in the primary sense of traffic with the former as a mere incident thereof
necessary to enable it "to fulfill its function." In short, the very process which
the Anti-Trust Act was enacted to control is to all intents and purposes, held not
to exist!

To what extent is the law of this case good law today? Most immediately
pertinent in this connection is the case of Swift and Company v. United States,[9]
decided ten years after the Sugar Trust Case. The defendants were some thirty
firms engaged in Chicago and other cities in the business of buying livestock in
their stockyards, of converting it at their packing houses into fresh meat, and in
the sale and shipment of such fresh meat to purchasers in other states. The charge
against them was that they had entered into a combination to refrain from bidding
against each other in the local markets, to fix prices at which they would sell
there, to restrict shipments of meat, and to do other forbidden acts. The case was
appealed to the Supreme Court on defendant's contention that certain of the acts
enjoined were not acts of interstate commerce, and so did not fall within a valid
reading of the Sherman Act. The Court, however, sustained the government on
the ground that the "scheme as a whole" came within the act, and that the local
acts alleged were simply part and parcel of this scheme.

Referring to the purchases of livestock at the stockyards, the Court said:

> Commerce among the states is not a technical legal conception, but a practical one,
> drawn from the course of business. When cattle are sent for sale from a place in one
> state, with the expectation that they will end their transit, after purchase, in another,
> and when in effect they do so, with only the interruption necessary to find a
> purchaser at the stockyards, and when this is a typical, constantly recurring course,
> the current thus existing is a current of commerce among the states, and the
> purchase of the cattle is a part and incident of such commerce. . . . [10]

7. Robbins v. Shelby Taxing District, 120 U.S. 489 (1887).
8. Above note 2 at 21–22.
9. 196 U.S. 375 (1905).
10. *Id.* For this and the two ensuing quotations, see at 398–400 of Justice Holmes' opinion. An
attempt to distinguish the Knight case appears at 397.

Likewise the alleged sales of fresh meat at the slaughtering places fell within the general design. "Even if they import a technical passing of title to the slaughtering places, (they) also import that the sales are to persons in other states, and that shipments to other states are part of the transaction. . . . " Thus, the very type of sale which in the Sugar Trust Case was thrust to one side as immaterial from the point of view of the law, because it enabled manufacture "to fulfill its function," is here treated as merged in the interstate commerce stream.

Lastly, the Court added these significant words: "But we do not mean to imply that the rule which marks the point at which state taxation or regulation becomes permissible necessarily is beyond the scope of interference by Congress in cases where such interference is deemed necessary for the protection of commerce among the states. . . ." In other words, the line that confines state power from one side does not always confine national power from the other. For even though the line accurately divides the subject matter of the complementary spheres, still national power is always entitled to take on such additional extension as is requisite to guarantee its effective exercise, and is, furthermore, supreme. In this respect, the Swift Case only states what the Shreveport Case was later to declare more explicitly.

In 1921 Congress passed the Packers and Stockyards Act[11] whereby the business of commission men and livestock dealers in the chief stockyards of the country is brought under national supervision; and the year following it passed the Grain Futures Act,[12] whereby grain futures exchanges are subjected to a similar control. The decisions of the Court sustaining these measures both build directly upon the Swift Case.

In Stafford v. Wallace, which involved the former act, Chief Justice Taft, speaking for the Court, said:[13]

> The object to be secured by the act is the free and unburdened flow of livestock from the ranges and farms of the West and Southwest through the great stockyards and slaughtering centers on the borders of that region, and thence in the form of meat products to the consuming cities of the country in the Middle West and East, or, still as livestock, to the feeding places and fattening farms in the Middle West or East for further preparation for the market.

The stockyards, therefore, "are not a place of rest or final destination." They "are but a throat through which the current flows," and the sales there are not merely local transactions. "They do not stop the flow—but, on the contrary" are "indispensable to its continuity."

In Board of Trade of Chicago v. Olsen, involving the Grain Futures Act the same course of reasoning is repeated. Speaking of the Swift Case, the chief justice there remarks:[14]

11. 42 Stat. 159 (1921) ch. 64; U.S.C.A. tit. 7, sec. 181.
12. 42 Stat. 998 (1922) ch. 369; U.S.C.A. tit. 7, sec. 1.
13. 258 U.S. 495, 514 (1922).
14. 262 U.S. 1, 35 (1923).

That case was a milestone in the interpretation of the commerce clause of the Constitution. It recognized the great changes and development in the business of this vast country and drew again the dividing line between interstate and intrastate commerce where the Constitution intended it to be. It refused to permit local incidents of a great interstate movement, which taken alone were intrastate, to characterize the movement as such. . . .

Important too is the part of the opinion which is devoted to showing the relation between future sales and cash sales, and the effect of the former upon the interstate grain trade. The test, said the chief justice, was furnished by the question of price. "... The question of price dominates trade between the states. Sales of an article which affect the country-wide price of the article directly affect the country-wide commerce in it. . . . "[15] From this it was held to follow that a practice which undeniably affected prices also affected interstate trade, and so fell under the regulating power of Congress.

Finally, reference should be made at this point to the ruling that a sale of goods in one state for an established market in another is interstate commerce before shipment starts, and is beyond the power of the former state to regulate in an obstructive manner.[16]

These results, in summation, certainly leave little of the doctrine of the Knight Case standing. Probably if the government were called upon to argue that case over again today, it would make a good deal of the flow of raw sugar to the refinery, as well as of the flow of the finished product away from it. In this way the case would be fitted to the frame provided by the Swift and ensuing cases. Nevertheless, with the rule secure that sales for an established interstate market are already commerce among the states before any transportation in connection with them has taken place, this would not be strictly necessary. Indeed, in view of the Court's assertion that "price dominates trade among the states," even the proposition that manufacturing is "intrinsically" local, and so incapable when considered in isolation (if it ever can properly be so considered) of affecting interstate commerce "directly"[17] (whatever that may mean) becomes a mere superstition—one of those judicial "nevers" which seem to overlook how long a time *never* can be.

But acts of Congress have not only to square with the Court's theory of the nature of the federal system; they must also meet the tests imposed by its reading of the Fifth Amendment. For it was during the very period when the Sherman Act first came under judicial construction, that the term "liberty" as used in the amendment came to mean "*freedom of contract*," especially "*in the management of property,*" and the phrase "due process of law" came to mean "*reasonable law*"—that is, the Court's *view* of reasonable law.

---

15. *Id.* 40.
16. Lemke v. Farmers' Grain Go., 258 U.S. 50 (1922); Eureka Pipe Line Co. v. Hallanan, 257 U.S. 265 (1921); Dahnke-Walker Milling Co. v. Bondurant, 257 U.S. 282 (1921).
17. *Cf.* Oliver Iron Co. v. Lord, 262 U.S. 172 at 178–79 (1923).

The question whether the Anti-Trust Act imposed an "undue restraint on the liberties of the citizen" was first raised in the case of United States v. Trans-Missouri Freight Association,[18] decided in 1897, two years after the Sugar Trust Case. The association was a combination of previously competing railroad companies for the maintenance of a stipulated rate schedule. The application of the Anti-Trust Act to such an agreement was challenged on two grounds: first, that the act was not meant to apply to the activities of railroads, that subject having been dealt with earlier in the Interstate Commerce Act of 1887; secondly, that it was not meant to apply to "reasonable" restraints of trade.

The first proposition was easily disposed of. Justice Peckham, speaking for a closely divided Court, answered it by saying that in view of the result reached in the Knight Case its acceptance would leave so little for the act to govern that the "whole act might as well be held inoperative"—a conclusive answer, certainly, but not a convincing one. As shown by Justice White in his dissenting opinion, the act was undoubtedly intended for industrial combinations "so far as such combinations . . . are within reach of federal legislation," and was not thought to embrace railway transportation.[19]

Evaluation of the second proposition involves consideration of the possible meanings to be attached to the word "reasonable" as a qualification of the inhibitions of the Anti-Trust Act. Four such meanings have at various times been proffered in discussion of the act; three of them indeed appear in the opinions filed in the Trans-Missouri Case.

First, the word "reasonable" may mean simply that the reasoning faculty was employed by the Court to determine whether the case before it fell under the act. This self-evident sense of the term is, for instance, offered by Chief Justice White at one point in his opinion in the Standard Oil Case, which is discussed below.[20] It clearly adds nothing to the problem of construing the phraseology of the Anti-Trust Act itself; the application of any act by a judicial body must be *reasonable* in this sense, however unreasonable the result reached.

Second: The word may mean a *construction of the act that avoids palpably extreme and absurd consequences*—consequences which practically any informed person would say the legislature never intended. This, too, is a self-evident—or nearly self-evident—employment of the term and is recognized by all writers on legal interpretation. A familiar illustration of its utilization is the case given by Blackstone, on the authority of Puffendorf, of the Bolognian law which enacted, "that whoever shed blood in the streets should be punished severely," but which was held "not to extend to a surgeon who opened the vein of a person that fell down in the street with a fit.'"[21] In this sense, the "rule of

---

18. 166 U.S. 290 (1897).
19. *Id.* 313, 326, 358.
20. Standard Oil Co. of N.J. v. United States, 221 U.S. 1, 63–64 (1911).
21. 1 Bl. *Comm.* *61. See Church of the Holy Trinity v. United States, 143 U.S. 457 (1892) for an interesting application of the maxim.

reason" was adopted by the Court in interpretation of the Anti-Trust Act as early as 1898, where, in his opinion in the Joint Traffic Association Case, a close parallel with the Trans-Missouri Case, Justice Peckham, again speaking for the majority, stated *obiter*: "We are not aware that it has ever been claimed that a lease or purchase by a farmer, manufacturer or merchant of an additional farm, manufactory or shop, or the withdrawal from business of any farmer, merchant or manufacturer, restrained commerce or trade within any legal definition of that term. . . . "[22]

Third: The word may mean *valid at the common law*. This, indeed, was the meaning most strongly contended for by the minority of the Court in the case at bar. The purpose of the Anti-Trust Act, said Justice White, speaking for the dissenters, was not to ban "every contract in restraint of trade," but, as the title of the act itself proved, only "*unlawful* restraints," and the legal test thus invoked, he continued, was that of the common law, by which, at least in recent times, "if a contract was reasonable, it would not be held to be included with contracts in restraint of trade."[23]

The majority, however, held that the term "contracts in restraint of trade" as used at common law had no "such limited signification . . . a contract may be in restraint of trade and still be valid at common law," but not under the Anti-Trust Act, the opening section of which forbids "*every*" such contract.[24]

Fourth: "Reasonable" may mean *in accordance with sound policy*—a matter which, of course, would have ultimately to be determined by the Court. This was the meaning which in the case under review the attorneys of the Freight Association urged most strenuously. From its very nature, they contended, the railroad business could not be carried on advantageously under a regime of unlimited competition. The agreement before the Court was therefore for the benefit of the public itself in the long run; and furthermore, the rates stipulated in it were "reasonable" rates.

The Court "confessed" that these arguments bore "with much force upon the policy" of the act; but said that if the act was to be amended, it was for Congress to do the business, and not for the Court. Indeed, it is not impossible that in developing this fourth definition of "reasonable" the attorneys for the railways rather overreached themselves. They made the Court reflect that if it admitted the word even in the sense of *valid at common law* as qualifying the prohibitions of the act, this concession might only be the opening wedge for the fourth meaning of the word, which virtually substituted the Court's discretion for that of Congress as embodied in the act.[25]

22. United States v. Joint Traffic Association, 171 U.S. 505, 567 (1898).
23. United States v. Trans-Missouri Freight Association, 166 U.S. 290, 350 (1857 {*sic;* 1897}); and see the opinion generally.
24. *Id*. 328.
25. *Id*. 321–22, 329–31; see also United States v. Joint Traffic Association, above note 22 at 566.

Nor was the opinion of Justice White calculated to reassure his majority brethren on this point, involving, as it did, an apparent misunderstanding or distortion of the common law, although not without some foundation in then contemporary English decisions. The common law permits contracts which "reasonably" restrain trade if the restraint is ancillary to a main contract which is lawful. Hence a shopkeeper is permitted in disposing of his business to agree not to go into the same business for a limited time and within a limited area, the purpose of the stipulation being to enable him to realize on the "good will" he had built up in connection with his shop. Likewise, within similar limitations, a retiring partner may validly agree not to compete with the firm. But such seeming exceptions to the general rule which condemns contracts in restraint of trade are really only "in furtherance of it." Without them freedom of trade and competition would lose much of its value as a stimulation to individual enterprise.[26]

But Justice White, while recognizing all this and indeed stressing it, also uses language which is susceptible of much broader and very uncertain application. Thus he refers to the then recent decision of the British House of Lords in the Nordenfelt Case[27] as holding "that whether a contract was invalid because in restraint of trade must depend upon whether, on considering all the circumstances the contract was found to be reasonable or unreasonable. If reasonable, it was not a contract in restraint of trade, and if unreasonable it was." "Reasonable," however, in what sense? Reasonable, in the common law sense, of being really calculated, in the circumstances of the case, to preserve competition, or reasonable in the sense that sound public policy called in such a case for the abandonment of competition? Some of the expressions used by the law lords in deciding the Nordenfelt Case, as well as in Mogul S. S. Company v. McGregor[28] two years earlier, lend distinct countenance to the latter interpretation. Nor does Justice White, in adopting the broad language of the former case, or elsewhere, point out that the common law condemned without exception or qualification all contracts or combinations to restrain the trade of third parties, usually stigmatizing such agreements as "conspiracies." His opinion, in short, was at least ambiguous, and the ambiguity was dangerous for what the majority of the Court rightly felt to be the main purpose of the Sherman Act, namely, the preservation of competition.[29]

In the Joint Traffic Association Case, decided a year and a half later, the argument was renewed for recognizing the contracts banned by the opening section of the Anti-Trust Act as qualified by the word "unreasonable," with two considerations added: It was pointed out that whereas the common law only treats contracts in restraint of trade as "unlawful" (nothing was said about con-

---

26. See United States v. Addyston Pipe Co., 85 Fed. 271, 281–82 (1898): Rannie v. Irvine, 7 Man. & G. 969, 978, 135 Eng. Rep. 393 (C.P. 1844).
27. Nordenfelt v. Maxim Nordenfelt Guns Co. [1894] A. C. 535.
28. [1892] A.C. 25.
29. See United States v. Trans-Missouri Freight Association, above note 23 at 346–51.

spiracies), the Sherman Act *penalized* them, thus suggesting the justice of a mitigated construction of its terms. Also, the argument that the act as construed in the Trans-Missouri Case meant an "undue restraint on the liberties of the citizen" was now first definitely linked up with the doctrine of "freedom of contract," which as interpretative of the term "liberty" of the Fifth Amendment had hardly been formulated at the time of that decision.[30] Notwithstanding all this, the Court still maintained its earlier alignment.

A year later occurred the case of Addystone Pipe and Steel Company v. United States,[31] in which the Anti-Trust Act was successfully applied as against an industrial combination for the first time. The agreements in the case, though of manufacturing concerns, effected a division of territory among them, and so involved a "direct" restraint on the distribution and hence of the transportation of the products of the contracting firms. The case thus becomes a sort of half-way house between the Knight Case and the Swift Case.

At the same time, the objection to the act under the newly developed interpretation of the Fifth Amendment was aggressively pressed. It was even argued that the amendment forbade the national government to deal with rights of contract at all, this being a state function. The Court answered that private contracts which "directly and substantially, and not merely indirectly, remotely, incidentally, and collaterally, regulated commerce among the states" were subject to Congress' power to do the same thing. Even state laws, it pointed out, which regulate such commerce have to yield to acts of Congress within the same field; certainly, then, private contracts could not prevail against the national power.[32]

Now ensued a period, especially after the decision in the Swift Case during which the Anti-Trust Act underwent a perceptible recrudescence, largely in consequence of the stimulation applied by the Roosevelt administration. Meantime, however, since the Knight Case capitalistic agglomeration had increased vastly and was still advancing. Then in 1911 occurred the decisions of the Court in the Standard Oil[33] and American Tobacco Cases,[34] in which these diverse developments came to clash and found a *modus vivendi* in the famous "rule of reason" of those cases, which, it will be seen, derives very directly from the fourth of the above senses of the word "reasonable."

The author of the "rule of reason" was Chief Justice White. Fourteen years earlier he had been spokesman for the minority in the Trans-Missouri Case. Now the views then rejected were to become in an even more enlarged form, the accepted doctrine of an all but unanimous bench. This intellectual triumph, moreover, came on top of one more personal. For contrary to all precedent,

---

30. See United States v. Joint Traffic Association, above note 22 at 532 (argument of counsel); the way had been paved for the argument in Mr. Justice White's opinion in the Trans-Missouri case, above note 29 at 354–55.

31. 175 U.S. 211 (1899).

32. *Id.* 228–29.

33. 221 U.S. 1 (1911).

34. 221 U.S. 106 (1911).

which from the beginning of the Court has frowned on the idea of a justice being elevated to the chief justiceship, he had recently received this promotion, owing, it is said, to the strong insistence of his brother justices.

No more vigorous intellect, or one more dexterous in the art of legalistic casuistry, has ever adorned the Supreme Court. Also it may be fairly said that his opinion in the Standard Oil Case, if not his *chef d'oeuvre,* is at least one of his best pieces. His method on this occasion is, therefore, of interest for its own sake, as is that of any first-rate artist, even independently of results. With regard to one element of it, to be sure, owing to considerations of space, we shall have to be content with mere passing mention and that is its immense verbosity. Chief Justice White would seem at times to be deliberately creating a vast fog bank of words behind which the better to elaborate his predetermined result undisturbed till he was prepared to dazzle reason itself with the perfected product.[35] We must be much briefer.

Subjecting section 1 of the Sherman Act to "the rule of reason," "the light of reason," or the "standard of reason"—as one prefers—Chief Justice White translates its prohibition of "*every* contract in restraint of trade" into "every contract in *undue* restraint of trade." In justification of this procedure he invokes the common law, but scrutiny speedily shows that it is the common law with a considerable difference. The fundamental purpose of the common law in condemning restraints of trade is asserted to be avoidance of the results of monopoly or undue lessening of competition, such for instance as price enhancement. Ultimately, accordingly, it is further asserted, the common law came to regard contracts having "a monopolistic tendency" and contracts "in restraint of trade" as essentially synonymous. In short, "contracts in restraint of trade," in the sense of the common law, are contracts of "a monopolistic tendency," which is to say, "contracts in *undue* restraint of trade."[36]

And to the common law as thus sketched the opening sections of the Sherman Act are shown to present, when read "in the light of reason," a striking parallelism. The prohibitions of the opening section are paraphrased by the chief justice as forbidding "all contracts or acts which theoretically were attempts to monopolize, yet which in practice had come to be considered as in restraint of trade in a broad sense," while the second section is held to be merely supplemental, its purpose being to make sure that "by no possible guise could the public policy embodied in the first section be frustrated and evaded."[37] In other words, the two sections are held to be *in pari materia,* though strangely enough the controlling purpose of the two is more distinctly labelled in the supplemental than in the principal provision!

35. The chief justice's opinion in the Standard Oil Case occupies 52 pages, and that in the American Tobacco Case, 47 pages.

36. Above note 33 at 54–57.

37. *Id.* 59–62. This construction of the act was in part anticipated nearly twenty years earlier in United States v. Patterson, 55 Fed. 605 (1893).

Finally it is observed, with truly scholastic subtlety, that while the act forbids monopolization and attempts at monopolization, it nowhere contains a "direct prohibition against monopoly in the concrete," an omission which is held to evince the "consciousness" of the framers of the act that "the freedom of the individual right to contract when not unduly or improperly exercised was the most efficient means for the prevention of monopoly."[38] Thus the act read in the light of reason did not conflict with the Fifth Amendment, but supported it; for freedom of contract is freedom from "undue restraint" from whatever source proceeding.

In a separate opinion Justice Harlan warmly attacked the majority opinion as an invasion of the legislative field, and an attempt to amend the statute under the profession of construing it.[39] In view of all that had gone before, this would appear to be an assertion difficult to combat. As we have seen, the Court had for years rejected with emphasis every suggestion that the act was controlled by common law doctrines with regard to restraints on trade. Now, however, it had suddenly consented to something much more extreme. First subjecting the common law to a strong infusion of the then comparatively novel doctrine of "liberty of contract," it had next subjected the act to the common law thus "treated," with the result of weakening the common law and so the act in at least two particulars. Thus, while the proceedure of the common law is to evaluate each contract, combination, and *conspiracy* for its specific effect on competition, the "rule of reason" evaluates each "contract or act" simply as a possible implement of a monopolizing scheme. This obviously may amount to a considerable difference in any particular case. Again, it is significant that in all the chief justice's talk whether about the common law or the Sherman Act, the word "conspiracy"—a potent word at common law—is never mentioned except in one or two direct quotations in which it occurs. This silence was not unadvised. To have suggested that there might be *conspiracies* in restraint of trade which the act was not intended to reach because they were "reasonable" would have exposed the infant "rule of reason" to grave hazards. The word "combinations" was less embarrassing, having a colloquial as well as a legal connotation.

But not less important than the fact of "judicial legislation" on this occasion is the question of the Court's object in indulging in it. This has in a general way been indicated already, as the achievement of a *modus vivendi* between the status at which business had arrived under the encouragement lent by the Knight Case and the resuscitated vigor of the Sherman Act due to later decisions. For wishing to achieve such a *modus vivendi,* the Court had, it may be surmised, at least two good reasons: first, it must have felt some responsibility for the legal muddlement in which application of the Sherman Act had become involved, and the

38. Above note 33 at 62. See also at 69.

39. *Id.* 82 *et seq.* Justice Harlan also charged that the "rule of reason" part of the Court's opinion was *obiter dictum;* but it would seem clear that the defendants were entitled to know the meaning of the law under which they had been convicted.

uncertainties thence resulting to the business interests of the country; secondly, it had probably become convinced that, in consideration of the actual organization of business in the United States, there was a definite, although yet untraced limit, to what was legally possible or economically desirable in the way of "trust-busting." The difficulties which it encountered in devising even a theoretically workable remedy in the American Tobacco Case without seriously interrupting the entire tobacco industry could only have emphasized this conviction.[40]

So the Court laid down the "rule of reason"—"reason" being used in a cognate sense with the fourth meaning of the word "reasonable" given earlier. In other words, it decided to claim more elbowroom for itself in applying the Sherman Act; and the recently formulated doctrine of freedom of contract was at hand to lend constitutional color to an act of judicial legislation that would otherwise have been quite indefensible on constitutional grounds.

Many critics of the "rule of reason," friendly as well as hostile, were confident in 1911 that it spelled a sort of economic dictatorship of the country by the Supreme Court and the end of competition. Such anticipations seem largely to have been disappointed. The "rule of reason" itself recognizes that individual competition had already disappeared as a major economic factor—what it demands is that enough competition or possibility of competition remain to constitute a reasonable assurance against monopoly conditions in any given field; and the cases seem to show that the Court has really struggled to maintain this standard, though with what degree of success is another question.[41] Generally, indeed, its role has been commonplace enough, that of jury simply, struggling to sift the truth from a complex mass of facts. We find it already so engaged even in the Standard Oil and American Tobacco Cases, where, in face of the gospel of mercy which the "rule of reason" was supposed to radiate, both defendant companies were sent to the block for their crimes against "fair methods of competition" and "usual" and "normal" modes of business, whereby, it was held, they were shown to have attempted monopolization.[42] To be sure, cases occur in which the Court sharply divides, along the lines one suspects of the economic creeds of its members. Yet it has never been admitted that the issue was whether competition ought to be destroyed, but whether it was being destroyed. While of interest to the special student of the Sherman Act, such cases are without instruction in the present connection.[43]

Meantime, in 1914, Congress, distrustful of the "rule of reason"—or rather of the latitude which it gave judicial discretion—passed the Clayton Act[44] and the

40. See *id.* 184–88.
41. *Cf.* Fetter, *The Masquerade of Monopoly* (1931).
42. Above note 33 at 75–76.
43. For a brief review of the more outstanding cases, see chapters on "The Anti-Trust Acts" and "Unfair Competition," 2 Willoughby, *Constitution* {sic; *The Constitutional Law of the United States?*} secs. 537–558 (2d ed. 1929).
44. 38 Stat. 730 (1914) ch. 323; U.S.C.A. tit. 15, sec. 12.

Federal Trade Commission Act.[45] The former makes it unlawful, with certain qualifications, "for any person engaged in commerce" to discriminate in prices between different purchasers, to make sales or leases on the condition that the purchaser or lessee shall not use the goods of a competitor, or to acquire "directly or indirectly the whole or any part of the stock" of a competing corporation, where the result of any such acts would be "to substantially lessen competition or tend to create a monopoly in any line of commerce." The latter creates the Federal Trade Commission and vests it with authority "to prevent persons, partnerships, and corporations, except banks, and common carriers subject to the acts to regulate commerce, from using unfair methods of competition in commerce." The theory of the Court is that these acts harmonize with and enforce its own construction of the Sherman Act; and in fact the prohibitions of the Clayton Act are based in part on the detailed specification in the Chief Justice's opinion in the Standard Oil and American Tobacco Cases of the business delinquencies of these companies.

Only two questions of constitutional law of interest in the present connection have arisen under these acts. In Federal Trade Commission v. Gratz,[46] the Court, in setting aside any order of the Commission "to cease and desist," ruled that the term "unfair methods of competition," not being defined by the act, was subject to ultimate construction by the Court "as matter of law." "They are clearly inapplicable," the Court continued, "to practices never heretofore regarded as opposed to good morals because characterized by deception, bad faith, fraud or oppression, or as against public policy because of their dangerous tendency unduly to hinder competition or create monopoly." The powers of the Commission are, in other words, circumscribed by the Court's construction of the Sherman Act; that is circumscribed, as we have seen, by its interpretation of the Fifth Amendment.

More recently, in Federal Trade Commission v. Western Meat Company,[47] the Court strongly hints that section 7 of the Clayton Act gives the Commission "no power to prevent or annul the purchase of a competitor's plant and business, as distinguished from stock therein"—such a purchase being presumably a "normal method" of advancing the development of a business.

The Sherman Act has also been applied to combinations of laborers found by the Court to be "in restraint of trade or commerce among the several states." The question naturally arises whether it was intended by its authors to be so applied. The possibility of such application was pointed out in the Senate when the measure was first introduced, and an effort was made by Senator Sherman himself to have the bill so amended as to obviate the danger. The attempt failed, however, due largely to the opposition of Senator Edmunds, who urged that

45. 38 Stat. 717 (1914) ch. 311; U.S.C.A. tit. 15, sec. 41.
46. 253 U.S. 421 (1920).
47. 272 U.S. 554 (1926). See Eastman Kodak Co. v. Blackmore, 277 Fed. 694 (C.C.A. 2d, 1921).

combinations of laborers, by forcing up their wages, might often bring about an advancement in the price of their product which would materially affect trade among the states. What is more, it was following the debate just referred to, that, in the process of entirely recasting the bill, the Senate Judiciary Committee, with Senator Edmunds as chairman, first inserted in section one the phrase "conspiracies in restraint of trade," which was well understood to embrace some of the characteristic activities of labor combinations, especially those of a coercive or intimidating nature.[48]

Despite all which, the initial construction of the act by the courts might well have seemed to rule out the remotest likelihood of its ever reaching labor combinations. These exist primarily for the betterment—according to their own lights—of the condition of their members, chiefly through securing for them higher wages and shorter hours. Whatever they do therefore, in furtherance of these objectives would appear, in light of the Court's reasoning in the Sugar Trust Case, to be, from the point of view of trade among the states, "an indirect result, however inevitable and whatever its extent." Nor is this all, for it was ruled in the Trans-Missouri Case that the construction of the act was not to be controlled by the common law meaning of its terms, a holding which eliminated at one stroke the special significance in relation to labor, of the phrase "conspiracies in restraint of trade."

To be sure, the Trans-Missouri decision was later overruled in this respect in the Standard Oil and American Tobacco cases, yet hardly with the result of strengthening the argument for applying the Anti-Trust Act to the activities of labor combinations. The governing idea of the statute, according to Chief Justice White's opinion in those cases, is to prevent *monopolization* of trade among the states. But is there any sense in which it can be said that combinations of labor do aim at *monopolization?* Certainly they do not aim to monopolize the facilities of transportation among the states in order to secure the profits that would thus accrue to them; nor do they aim to monopolize the sale of commodities among the states, as does a great industrial combination—the Sugar Trust, for example. There is only one thing which labor combinations can ordinarily be said with the least logic or precision to attempt the monopolization of, and that is labor itself.

Was it, then, the intention of Congress, in enacting the Sherman Act, to prevent combinations of laborers from attempting to bring under dominant control the labor supply of the country? It is not improbable that some members of Congress—Senator Edmunds, for instance—had some such idea in mind; but it is not an idea which has ever found utterance or reflection in any decision of the Supreme Court. On the contrary, language employed by the Court on more than one occasion distinctly repels such an idea. Thus in Adair v. United States, it was asked,

---

48. See Mason, *Organized Labor and the Law* ch. 7 (1925) {hereinafter *Organized Labor*}; Loewe v. Lawler, 208 U.S. 274, 301–304 (1908).

> What possible legal or logical connection is there between an employee's membership in a labor organization and the carrying on of interstate commerce? . . . Labor associations . . . are organized for the general purpose of improving or bettering the conditions and conserving the interest of their members as wage earners—an object entirely legitimate and to be commended rather than condemned. . . . Surely those associations as labor organizations have nothing to do with interstate commerce as such. . . . "[49]

And to the same effect is the Court's language in Gompers v. Bucks Stove and Range Company, where its attention was specifically directed to a cognate question: "The law" including no doubt, the Sherman Act, ". . . recognizes the right of workingmen to unite and to invite others to join their ranks, thereby making available the strength, influence, and power that come from such association." To be sure, the Court adds, if such associations perform illegal acts, it is the business of government to intervene to see that justice is done; but that this declaration is not intended to weaken the force of the words quoted is apparent.[50]

Furthermore, if Congress ever did intend to prevent organized labor from engrossing the interstate labor market, it has since conclusively disavowed the intention. The reference is to section 6 of the Clayton Act, the salient language of which reads as follows:

> That the labor of a human being is not a commodity or article of commerce. . . . Nothing contained in the Anti-Trust laws shall be construed to forbid the existence and operation of labor . . . organizations, instituted for mutual help, . . . or to forbid or restrain individual members of such organizations from lawfully carrying out the legitimate objects thereof, nor shall such organizations, or the members thereof, be held or construed to be illegal combinations or conspiracies in restraint of trade under the Anti-Trust laws.[51]

Mr. {Samuel} Gompers, at the time head of the American Federation of Labor, hailed this declaration of the law as "the industrial Magna Carta, upon which the working people will rear their structure of industrial freedom"; but it is agreed by all authorities that the section added nothing to the law, at least as declared by the Supreme Court. In the words of an able writer, "this section was, in truth a 'Magna Carta'—that is, it was a recognition and affirmation of existing rights rather than an extension or enlargement of those rights; but it was never the 'Magna Carta' which Mr. Gompers conceived it to be. Nor did Congress intend that it should be."[52]

The first case in which the Sherman Act was held by the Supreme Court to be applicable to the activities of a labor combination was Loewe v. Lawlor,[53] decided in 1908. This was an action to recover treble damages under section 7 of

---

49. 208 U.S. 161, 178–79 (1908).
50. 221 U.S. 418, 439 (1911).
51. Above note 44.
52. Mason, *Organized Labor* ch. 10.
53. Above note 48.

the act, on the allegation that defendants, the United Hatters of North America and the American Federation of Labor, "for the direct purpose of destroying" the interstate trade of plaintiffs, hat manufacturers of Danbury, Connecticut, had combined "not merely to prevent plaintiffs from manufacturing articles then and there intended for transportation beyond the state, but also to prevent the vendees from reselling the hats which they had imported from Connecticut, or from further negotiating with plaintiffs for the purchase and interstate transportation of such hats from Connecticut to the various places of destination."

To defendants' answer that their design was to unionize plaintiffs' shops and so did not constitute a restraint of trade at the common law, the Court replied, citing the Trans-Missouri Case, that "the Anti-Trust Law has a broader application than the prohibition of restraints of trade unlawful at common law."[54] Defendants' further contention that their activities in support of their scheme, strikes at plaintiffs' factory and the circulation of an "unfair list" among patrons in other states, were purely local, and so by the authority of the Knight Case not within Congress' power, the Court met by quoting from the Swift Case: "The scheme as a whole seems to us to be within the reach of the law."[55]

Both these propositions are still good law as a reading of the Sherman Act in relation to labor activities. Although in "labor cases" falling under their jurisdiction solely because of the diverse citizenship of the parties, the federal courts are controlled by the common law as they interpret it regarding "conspiracies in restraint of trade," in similar cases arising under the Sherman Act they are not so limited.[56] Nor again, are they bound in the latter class of cases, as was pointed out above, by the doctrine of the Standard Oil and American Tobacco Cases, that the controlling purpose of the Sherman Act was to prevent "monopolization." As respects "labor cases," accordingly, what the phrase "combinations in restraint of trade among the states" of the Sherman Act means is any combination which by its activities is in fact *obstructive* of such trade, regardless of whether it would be a "conspiracy" at common law or not; and despite the self-evident fact that such activities can never be rationally described as being of "a monopolizing tendency."

Two questions which are frequently asked regarding the Sherman Act are thus brought sharply to mind. The first is, whether that statute is interpretable, as prohibiting railway strikes to the *interruption* of transportation among the states? In view of what has just been said, it would seem that a negative answer to this question must depend not upon the Court's reading of the Sherman Act but upon its reading of the Fifth Amendment. For most situations the Court would probably hold that the right to strike is an element of "liberty" beyond the reach of

54. *Id.* 297.
55. *Id.* 298.
56. Gompers v. Bucks Stove Co., above note 50, was such a case; also Hitchman Coal and Coke Co. v. Mitchell, 245 U.S. 229 (1917).

ordinary legislative power. Nevertheless in light of Wilson v. New,[57] it would probably refuse to say that this is always so.

The other question is, whether Congress could validly exempt labor combinations and activities from the operation of the act? Clearly it could. To all intents and purposes the Sherman Act constitutes at the present moment, in relation to combinations of workingmen, on the one hand, and in relation to combinations of capital, on the other hand, two entirely different statutes, and deals with two entirely different problems. Nor is there any constitutional reason requiring Congress to deal with both problems in the same statute, or to deal with both or neither.[58]

Of the cases which have arisen since the enactment of the Clayton Act, four demand brief mention in the present connection. In United Mine Workers of America v. Coronado Coal Company[59] it was held that trade unions are liable as entities under section 8 of the Sherman Act, and their funds are attachable in satisfaction of damages resulting from interference with interstate commerce. It was further found necessary in the same case, as well as in the later case of United Leather Workers v. Herkert,[60] to disavow an implication arising from the fact that the Court had appeared in Loewe v. Lawler to treat as a valid ground of complaint under the Sherman Act an allegation that the strike at plaintiffs' factory had prevented the making of hats for the filling of orders already accepted from other states. The Court, in the Leather Workers Case, said that curtailment of supply of an article to be shipped in interstate commerce, unless brought about for the purpose of monopolization or price control, does not fall within the act.

On the other hand, in both Duplex Printing Company v. Deering[61] and Bedford Cut Stone Company v. Journeymen Stone Cutters Association,[62] the Sherman Act appeared to undergo something of an extension in its application to "labor cases." Again asserting that common law doctrines do not limit the application of the act to combinations of workingmen whose activities are found

---

57. 243 U.S. 332 (1917).

58. Especially pertinent is International Harvester Co. v. Missouri, 234 U.S. 199 (1914), where the Court sustained a state statute prohibiting combinations of vendors of commodities and not vendors of labor and services. See Justice McKenna's opinion, 212-15.

An interesting case, however, in which we see labor conspiring with capital to bring about a monopolization from which both would profit, is United States v. Brims, 272 U.S. 549 (1926). It should be added, by way of caution, that the question just discussed and the question of the extent to which Congress may abolish the remedy of injunction in "labor cases" falling within the federal jurisdiction under the common law, are two entirely different questions. In point of fact, until the enactment of section 16 of the Clayton Act, private parties had no right to injunctive relief under the Sherman Act. Paine Lumber Co. v. Neal, 244 U.S. 459 (1917); with which compare Texas & N.O.R.R. v. Brotherhood, 281 U.S. 548 (1930). By the same token, the question of the proper construction of sec. 20 of the Clayton Act, limiting injunctive relief in "labor cases," has no bearing on constitutional aspects of the Sherman Act.

59. 259 U.S. 344 (1922).

60. 265 U.S. 457 (1924); see especially at 471.

61. 254 U.S. 443 (1921).

62. 274 U.S. 37 (1927).

in fact to "impede" interstate commerce, the Court held that activities of a national union to prevent the handling in one state of goods introduced from another state with a view to and the result of destroying the interstate market for such goods were violative of the act.

Whether such activities would have been held to fall under the ban of the act had they not been instigated by a national organization but had proceeded solely from the initiative of a local union, is a question not directly answered by these cases. Logically, nevertheless an affirmative answer is strongly suggested, inasmuch as the sole test of the application of the act is the factual one, whether commerce is impeded. Yet again, however, unpleasant consequences under the act and the commerce clause, while not avoidable by direct recourse to the common law, may possibly become avoidable by indirect resort thereto by way of the due process of law clause of the Fifth Amendment and the Court's theory of "liberty."

14. Congress' Power to Prohibit Commerce, a Crucial Constitutional Issue

THE striking failure to date of spontaneous recuperative forces to manifest themselves in the field of business and industry has produced a widespread and growing conviction that the national government must within the immediate future, and for some time to come, take a large hand in social and economic reconstruction. What is the constitutional basis upon which it may operate, whence is it to draw the authority for and the legal sanction of its enactments looking to this end? To an important extent these must be found in Congress' power "to regulate commerce among the states," and in the recognition that this power comprehends the power to prohibit such commerce when in the exercise of a fair legislative judgment Congress deems that prohibition would promote the national welfare.

The National Industrial Recovery Act is a case in point. By its provisions concerns engaging in interstate commerce are given the choice for two years between complying with regulations to be laid down by the President under authority delegated by the act and giving up their interstate business.[1] The Securities Act invokes the same idea; as does also the Farm Relief Act, for although in form a tax measure, the latter is actually a price-fixing measure, and its validity may well depend upon the principle that processors pay the fees exacted by the measure for the privilege of engaging in interstate commerce.[2] Proposals to stabilize oil production, whether by compact among the states with the approval of Congress, or more directly by national legislation, furnish still other illus-

From Edward S. Corwin, "Congress' Power to Prohibit Commerce, a Crucial Constitutional Issue," 18 *Cornell Law Quarterly* 477 (1933) © Copyright 1933 by Cornell University. Reprinted by permission. The material was prepared originally as a lecture delivered at the Cornell Law School, under the Frank Irvine Lectureship of the Phi Delta Phi Foundation, April 29, 1933.

1. *The New York Times*, May 11, 1933, at 3; *id*. May 12, at 1, 4. See also the discussion before the Senate of the now superseded "thirty-hour-a-week" bill, 77 *Cong. Rec.* 1105, 1171, 1241 and 1304 (1933).

2. 77 *Cong. Rec.* 944, 952, 1542, 1635, 1638 (1933).

trations of the same general principle, and hence of the immediate importance of the subject to be discussed in this paper.[3] It is furthermore a subject of theoretical and historical interest to students of constitutional law and history.

I.

That the power to regulate commerce which is vested in Congress by the Constitution *logically* comprises the power to prohibit it, appears to the point of demonstration from two considerations: First, that when prohibition is for any reason essential it is the regulatory body, in this instance Congress, which must supply it; secondly, that the right to determine when it is requisite to exercise any of its functions is the most fundamental attribute of legislative power. Indeed, a modicum of reflection must suffice to show that any regulation whatsoever of commerce necessarily infers some measure of power to prohibit it, since it is the very nature of regulation to lay down terms on which the activity regulated will be permitted and for noncompliance with which it will not be permitted.

What, then, are the outstanding differences between those prohibitions of commerce which "regulation" of it even in the most mitigated sense of the term necessarily imports and the type of prohibition which is the particular concern of this paper? In answer to this question we may first turn to the national statute book. Within the past forty years Congress has enacted many measures which fulfill the description of "prohibitions of commerce" as that term is here employed: the Wilson Act of 1890, subjecting intoxicants upon their "arrival" in a state to the laws thereof;[4] the Anti-Lottery Act of 1895,[5] closing the channels of interstate transportation to lottery tickets, an earlier act having already banned lottery tickets from the mails;[6] an act passed in 1900 excluding from interstate transportation game slaughtered in violation of state laws;[7] the Pure Food and Drug Act of 1906, barring from interstate transportation foods and drugs not inspected and labelled in accordance with the act;[8] the Commodity Clause of the Hepburn Act of the same year, forbidding interstate carriers to transport in interstate commerce commodities in which they had any interest "direct or

---

3. Reference should also be made to the series of proposals introduced in the last Congress by Senator Nye of North Dakota, for the purpose of fostering the trade practice conference. They may be summarized thus: (1) that the Federal Trade Commission be specifically authorized to hold such conferences with various industries; (2) that rules adopted at such conferences and approved by the Commission, be given the force of law; (3) that acts done under the sanction of such rules be not subject to prosecution under the Anti-Trust Acts; (4) that such rules be made binding on all members of an industry regardless of their participation in the conference, through Congress' power to prohibit interstate commerce. Equivalent proposals reappear in the Industry Recovery Act. On the question of oil production, see Marshall and Meyer, "Legal Planning of Petroleum Production: Two Years of Proration," 42 *Yale L. J.* 702 (1933).

4. 26 Stat. ch. 728 at 313.
5. 28 Stat. 963, 18 U.S.C.A. sec. 387 (1926).
6. 26 Stat. 465, 18 U.S.C.A. sec. 336 (1926).
7. 31 Stat. 188; amended by 35 Stat. 1137 (1909), 18 U.S.C.A. sec. 392 (1926).
8. 34 Stat. 768, 21 U.S.C.A. secs. 1–3 (1926).

indirect'';[9] the Mann Act of 1910, forbidding the transporting of women from one state to another for immoral purposes;[10] the Webb-Kenyon Act of 1913, prohibiting the shipment of intoxicants into a state there to be used in violation of its laws;[11] the Child Labor Act of 1916, banning from interstate transportation articles in the production of which child labor of a described type had entered;[12] the Federal Quarantine Act of 1917, forbidding the shipment from infected areas of diseased plants and shrubs;[13] the Read Bone-Dry Amendment of 1918 forbidding the transportation of intoxicants into any state which forbids the manufacture thereof;[14] the Federal Motor Vehicle Act of 1919, prohibiting the transportation of stolen motor vehicles from one state to another and the receiving, concealment, or sale of the same;[15] the Hawes-Cooper Act of 1929, which, upon going into effect January 1, 1934, will subject prison-made goods sent from one state to another, to the laws of the latter state.[16] It may be added that all these acts have been held, *under the construction given them by the Court,* to be within Congress' power under the "commerce" clause except the Federal Game Act of 1900, which has never been before the Court; the Hawes-Cooper Act, which is not yet operative; and the Child Labor Act, which was pronounced void in 1918 in Hammer v. Dagenhart.[17] We shall have occasion to consider this case at length later on.

The most evident feature common to these various measures is their exclusion, partial or complete, from the channels of interstate transportation of certain subjects thereof—usually *things,* but in one case *persons.* Such subjects, where their exclusion has been sustained by the Court, have been termed "illicit subjects of commerce." But *why* illicit? In some cases the "illicitness" is the outcome primarily of legislative history in the course of which the subjects affected have lost reputation—for instance, lottery tickets and intoxicants, the latter of which were "good articles of commerce" as late as 1890.[18] And in these cases, as well as others, a second source of "illicitness" is discoverable in certain results supposed to follow upon their *use* after the act of transportation is completed. However, the Commodity Clause is obviously not thus explicable, nor is the Federal Motor Vehicle Act—the "illicitness" justifying these measures is an infection from the *source* of the subjects of transportation.

But the aspect of these measures to which the cases invite attention most insistently, is their relation to the reserved powers of the states. Many re-

9. 34 Stat. 584, 49 U.S.C.A. sec. 1 (8) (1926).
10. 36 Stat. 825, 18 U.S.C.A. secs. 397–404 (1926).
11. 37 Stat. ch. 90 at 699.
12. 39 Stat. ch. 432 at 675.
13. 39 Stat. 1165, 7 U.S.C.A. sec. 161 (1926).
14. 39 Stat. 1069, 18 U.S.C.A. sec. 340 (1926).
15. 41 Stat. 324, 18 U.S.C.A. sec. 408 (1926).
16. 45 Stat. 1084, 49 U.S.C.A. sec. 65 (1929).
17. 247 U.S. 251, 38 Sup. Ct. 529 (1918).
18. Leisy v. Hardin, 135 U.S. 100, 10 Sup. Ct. 681 (1890).

gulations of commerce among the states not falling within the above category of acts have, to be sure, intruded upon the ordinary field of jurisdiction of the states, but this was because the transactions or relationships which they thus brought under national control were treated by the Court as "local incidents" of interstate commerce itself, or as so intimately related thereto that their control was essential to the effective control of such commerce. It is on this ground, for instance, that the Employers' Liability Act of 1908 was sustained;[19] and it is on this ground that the authority of the Interstate Commerce Commission, under the Transportation Act of 1920, to regulate intrastate rates of interstate carriers in certain circumstances rests ultimately.[20]

On the other hand, the relation of the type of act in which we are interested to the reserved powers of the states is precisely the inverse of this. The recognizable purpose of these acts is to reach and control matters ordinarily governed by the state police power, sometimes in order to make state policy more effective, sometimes in order to supply a corrective thereto from the point of view of a broader public interest. In other words, while the operation within the ordinary field of state power of the former class of acts is assumed to be *incidental* to the main purpose of those acts to "regulate" commerce, the similar operation of the measures here to be considered is itself held to be their *governing* purpose.

Even so, what of it; why should not Congress be entitled to exercise its power over commerce for any purpose that seems good to it? Prior to the Constitution the states exercised the equivalent power without let or hindrance, and foreign governments do the same today. It may be suggested possibly that the Tenth Amendment interposes a bar; but certainly this is not its literal or logical effect, for the powers which it recognizes as "reserved to the states respectively or to the people" are reserved conditionally on their not having been delegated to the United States. Furthermore, by the "supremacy" clause, if a state in the exercise of its "uncontroverted powers" and Congress in the exercise of any of its powers, come into conflict through an effort to control the same subject matter simultaneously, it is Congress whose will has the right of way.[21]

We are hence driven to the conclusion that the problem dealt with in this paper does not arise out of the *text* of the Constitution; that, on the contrary, if this *text* be interpreted simply with the aid of the dictionary and the ordinary rules of logical discourse, there can be no doubt whatsoever of the constitutional power of Congress to prohibit commerce among the states as it wills. Our problem arises indeed from a *doctrine*, one which has been deemed to be of such coercive authority and to safeguard such pre-eminent values as entitle it to control the interpretation of the text of the constitution even to the extent of superseding its logical import. We may term this doctrine "dual federalism."

19. Second Employers' Liability Cases, 223 U.S. 1, 32 Sup. Ct. 169 (1912).
20. R. R. Comm. of Wis. v. C. B. & Q. R. Co., 257 U.S. 563, 42 Sup. Ct. 232 (1922).
21. Gibbons v. Ogden, 9 Wheat. 1, 210, 211 (U.S. 1824).

II.

To James Madison has been assigned the paternity of the Constitution, possibly by a fiction akin to the one by which in polyandrous communities the first child born to the family group is credited to the eldest male. The attribution is honorific and intended in a somewhat Pickwickian sense. Madison's responsibility, however, in regard to the notion of dual federalism is clear. In this construction of his latter days the Madison of 1787 and the Madison of 1798 found at last a common roof over their heads.

Writing in 1819 in criticism of the decision in McCulloch v. Maryland,[22] Madison expressed a fear lest the Court had relinquished "all control on the legislative exercise of unconstitutional power." "In the great system of political economy," he urged, "having for its general object the national welfare, everything is related immediately or remotely to every other thing; and, consequently, a power over any one thing, if not limited by some obvious and precise affinity, may amount to a power over every other." The central vice of the Court's—that is, Marshall's—reasoning was to regard the powers of the general government as "sovereign powers," the tendency of which was "to convert a limited into an unlimited government. There is certainly," he continued, "a reasonable medium between expounding the Constitution with the strictness of a penal law or other ordinary statute and expounding it with a laxity which may vary its essential character, and encroach on the local sovereignities with which it was meant to be reconcilable. The very existence of these local sovereignties is a control on the pleas for a constructive amplification of the powers of the general government."[23]

In 1791, in the debate on Hamilton's bank measure, Madison had said: "Interference with the powers of the states was no constitutional criterion of the power of Congress. If the power was not given, Congress could not exercise it; if given, they might exercise it, although it should interfere with the laws or even the constitution of the states."[24] But in 1819 he offers a very different canon of constitutional interpretation: *the coexistence of the states and their powers is of itself a limitation upon national power.*

And all denial to Congress of the power to prohibit commerce among the states invokes this canon of 1819, pivots upon it.[25] The Constitution, the argument

22. 4 Wheat. 316 (U.S. 1819).
23. 8 *Writings of James Madison* 447-53 (Hunt ed. 1900-1910); 3 *Letters and Other Writings of James Madison* 143-47 (Phila., 1867). The latter collection is much fuller for Madison's later writings.
24. 6 *Writings of James Madison* 28 (Hunt ed.).
25. For the main sources of this and the following section see arguments of counsel and judicial opinions in Groves v. Slaughter, 15 Pet. 449 (1841); *In re* Rapier 143 U.S. 110, 12 Sup. Ct. 374 (1892); Champion v. Ames, 188 U.S. 321, 23 Sup. Ct. 321 (1903); Hoke v. United States, 227 U.S. 308, 33 Sup. Ct. 281 (1913); Hammer v. Dagenhart, above note 17. A document of much interest in this connection is the "Argument of Robert J. Walker, Esq. on the Mississippi Slave Question," in the case of Groves v. Slaughter. It does not appear in the official report of the case, but was separately

runs, clearly contemplates two spheres of governmental activity, that of the states and that of the United States; and while the latter government is supreme when the two collide with one another in the exercise of their respective powers, yet collision is not contemplated as the rule of life of the system, but the contrary. And since there are these two spheres, by what principle is the line to be drawn between them in a way to secure harmony instead of collision? The answer is, by recognizing that the purposes which the national government was established to promote are relatively few, while those which the states were retained to advance comprise the principal objectives of good government the world over, the public health, safety, morals, and general welfare. The power to promote these ends is, indeed, the very definition of the police power of the states, that power for which all their other powers exist. To impair seriously the police power of the states, or to diminish their authority in its employment, would be, in fact, to remove their reason for being, and so the reason for the federal system itself.

Among the powers granted to Congress is, to be sure, the argument proceeds, the power to regulate commerce among the states and with foreign nations; but it is promptly added that, while in terms this is a single power and is embraced textually in a single phrase, nevertheless, in the intention of the framers, it comprised two very different powers.[26] In the field of foreign relations the national government is completely sovereign, and the power to regulate commerce with foreign nations is but a branch of this sovereign power. The power to regulate commerce among the states is, on the other hand, not a sovereign power *except in the field of commercial motive;* in other respects it is confronted at every turn by the police powers of the states, and requires therefore to be defined in relation to the known and frequently reiterated objectives of those powers.

Furthermore, the federal grant, it is asserted, was designed for the *promotion* and *advancement* of commerce, not a power to strike commerce down in order to advance other purposes and programs. Admit, the advocates of dual federalism continue, that the power to regulate commerce among the states is the power to prohibit it at the discretion of Congress, and you at once endow Congress with a leverage whereby it may consolidate substantially all power into the hands of the national government. For if Congress may prohibit at discretion the carrying on of interstate commerce it may work deprivation of the right to engage in interstate commerce in any of its phases, even the right to move from one state to another. It may assert a sanction of ever increasing efficacy for whatever standards of conduct it may choose to lay down in any field of human action, and, since laws passed by Congress in pursuance of its powers are supreme over conflicting state laws, these standards would supersede

---

printed in Philadelphia, and runs to eighty-eight closely printed pages. Walker succeeds in anticipating almost every argument that has been made since on either side of the question here under discussion.

26. This idea seems to have originated with Madison; see 4 *Letters and Other Writings of James Madison* 14–15. *Cf.* notes 32, 34, 37, and 63 below.

the conflicting standards imposed under the police powers of the states. Henceforth, in effect, the police power would exist soley on "leave and license" of Congress; as "the power to govern men and things" it would be at an end.

The first effort at the elaboration of a restrictive argument somewhat along these lines was elicited by Jefferson's Embargo. Inasmuch, however, as the Embargo operated on foreign commerce, those who disputed its constitutionality found little occasion to emphasize the police power of the states as a limitation on the national commercial power; nor did they distinguish between the application of this power to foreign commerce on the one hand and to interstate commerce on the other. Their main reliance was on the proposition that the power to regulate commerce was the power "to protect and conserve" it, not the power to annihilate it. The same argument was later renewed by the proslavery interest in opposing the suggestion of antislavery radicals that Congress could strangulate slavery in the states by prohibiting the interstate slave trade, as it had already prohibited after 1808 the African slave trade. Yet this argument was evidently not regarded as entirely satisfactory, for it was supplemented by the contention that the commercial power reached only trade in *articles of property* and that the Constitution, in contradistinction to the laws of the slave states, looked upon slaves as *persons*.[27]

Finally, in recent years the argument that the power to regulate commerce is not the power to interdict it except for noncompliance with conditions designed for *its* greater prosperity and development has received aid and comfort from the Court's interpretation of the "due process" clause of the Fifth Amendment. The faculty of engaging in interstate commerce, it is urged, is not a mere revocable privilege but a constitutional *right*, and element of the liberty of the citizen, an adjunct of his rights of property; and it remains such even when exercised through the artificial agency of a corporation. This faculty Congress may protect and indeed control in a measure, but to abate it by the "arbitrary" assertion of unaccustomed powers is without constitutional warrant.

III.

Any rejoinder to the above argument must begin with Marshall's classic opinion in Gibbons v. Ogden,[28] the first case under the "commerce" clause to reach the Court. Characteristically Marshall selects for his point of departure an argument of counsel, in effect a reiteration of the Madisonian doctrine that national power should be construed in deference to the coexistence of the states and their powers. The contention rested, Marshall hinted, on "some theory not to be found in the Constitution," and its effect was to "deny to the government those powers which the words of the grant as usually understood, import." Turning accord-

27. Groves v. Slaughter, above note 25.
28. Above note 21.

ingly to the "commerce" clause itself, Marshall proceeded to annex to the word "commerce" the connotation of *intercourse,* a *tour de force* in exegesis which enabled him to add *navigation,* that is to say *transportation* to the usual signification of the term as *traffic*. He then put the question: "What is this power?" which he answered as follows:

> It is the power to regulate; that is, to prescribe the rule by which commerce is to be governed. This power, like all others vested in Congress, is complete in itself, may be exercised to its utmost extent, and acknowledges no limitations other than are prescribed in the Constitution. These are expressed in plain terms, and do not affect the questions which arise in this case, or which have been discussed at the bar. If, as has always been understood, the sovereignty of Congress, though limited to specified objects, is plenary as to those objects, the power over commerce with foreign nations, and among the several states, is vested in Congress as absolutely as it would be in a single government, having in its Constitution the same restrictions on the exercise of the power as are found in the Constitution of the United States. The wisdom and the discretion of Congress, their identity with the people, and the influence which their constituents possess at elections are, in this, as in many other instances, as that, for example, of declaring war, the sole restraints on which they have relied, to secure them from its abuse. They are the restraints on which the people must often rely solely, in all representative governments.[29]

The matter of controlling importance here, obviously, is the proposition that Congress' power over commerce, whether interstate or foreign, was that of a *"single,"* that is to say, a centralized government. It followed thence that the occasions for the exercise by Congress of this power were left as completely to Congress' own discretion as were the occasions for its exercise of its similarly unqualified power to declare war. Furthermore, it was a pivotal conception of Marshall's system of constitutional law that the degree to which any legislative power might be exercised was not a justiciable question. In his own words: "Questions of power do not depend upon the degree to which it may be exercised. If it may be exercised at all, it must be exercised at the will of those in whose hands it is placed."[30] So, whether commerce among the states should be prohibited, and for what reasons, were to Marshall's thinking, it seems clear, questions for Congress to determine, subject only to its political responsibility at the polls.

In more recent days the same general position has been elaborated in greater detail in response to the contrary argument.[31] That the national government is a government of limited powers the advocates of this view concede; but the powers which it uncontrovertibly possesses, they urge, it may utilize to promote all good causes, of which fact they assert the Preamble of the Constitution itself is proof. There the objectives of the Constitution and so, presumably, of the government created by it, are stated to be more a perfect union, justice, domestic tranquillity,

29. 9 Wheat. at 196, 197 (U.S. 1824).
30. Brown v. Maryland, 12 Wheat. 419, 439 (U.S. 1827).
31. Above note 25.

the common defense, the general welfare, and liberty. It was to forward these broad, general purposes, then, that the commercial power, like its other powers, was bestowed upon the national government. No doubt it was expected that the states, too, would use the powers still left to them to assist the same purposes, which indeed are those of good government the world over; yet that circumstance, surely, should not operate to withdraw the powers delegated to the national government from the service of these same ends. The fact, in other words, that the power to govern commerce among the states was bestowed by the Constitution on the national government should not imply that it thereby became utilizable merely for the purpose of fostering such commerce. It ought, on the contrary, to be applicable, as would be the equivalent power in England or France for instance, in aid and support of all enlightened social programs. As originally possessed by the several states the power to regulate commerce included the power to prohibit it at discretion; on what principle then, it is asked, can it be contended that the power delegated to Congress is not as exhaustive and complete as the power it was designed to supersede?[32]

The truth of the matter is, the protagonists of this view proceed, that if the public health, safety, morals, and general welfare—counting the commercial welfare of the country out of these for the moment—that if these objectives of good government must depend solely upon the police powers of the states, they must in modern conditions often fail of realization in this country; and this will be more and more the case as the interstate intercourse which the commercial power of Congress is putatively established to promote increases. With goods flowing over state lines in ever increasing quantities and people in ever increasing numbers, how is it possible to regard the states as watertight compartments? At least, then, when local legislative programs break down on account of the division of the country into states, it becomes the palpable duty of Congress to adopt supplementary legislation to remedy the situation. In doing so it is not undermining the federal system; it is supporting it, by making it viable in modern conditions. The assemblage of the states into one Union was never intended to put one state at the mercy of another. If, however, well-considered programs of social reform (prohibition for instance, or legislation against child labor, or against lotteries, and the like) are rendered abortive in any state in consequence of the

32. The argument in this and the preceding sentence is paralleled by Madison's argument in support of Congress' power under the "commerce" clause to enact a protective tariff for the purpose of encouraging manufactures. He denied that Congress' power to regulate foreign commerce was only the power to promote it or that such regulations must operate externally to the states. Answering then the question whether it was within Congress' discretion to impose duties upon commerce among the states "for the purpose of protecting the industry and productions of the states against the competition of each other," he said: "Waiving the constitutional obstacles presented by the communion of rights and privileges among citizens of different states, the difficulties, the inutility, and the odium of such a project would be a sufficient security against it." In other words, Madison did not contend that the power to regulate "commerce among the states" did not {sic}, considered by itself, extend so far. See 2 *Letters and Other Writings of James Madison* 571–73, 636 ff., 645 ff; and also 4, 232–66, especially at 236, 250, 253, 257.

flow of commerce into it from other states holding less advanced views, then it becomes the duty—certainly it is within the discretion of Congress, which alone can govern commerce among the states—to supply the required relief.

But notwithstanding that the advocates of this expansionist view stress modern conditions, they too, are able to cite discussion contemporaneous with Jefferson's Embargo, and indeed the Embargo itself, as sustaining their position. In the case of the Brigantine William,[33] the validity of the Embargo was assailed before the United States District Court of Massachusetts, on the ground that the power to regulate commerce did not embrace the power to prohibit it. Said Judge Davis in answer:

> It will be admitted that partial prohibitions are authorized by the expression; and how shall the degree or extent of the prohibition be adjusted but by the discretion of the national government, to whom the subject appears to have been committed? . . . . The power to regulate commerce is not to be confined to the adoption of measures exclusively beneficial to commerce itself, or tending to its advantage; but in our national system, as in all modern sovereignties, it is also to be considered as an instrument for other purposes of general policy and interest. . . . The situation of the United States, in ordinary times, might render legislative interferences relative to commerce less necessary; but the capacity and power of managing and directing it for the advancement of great national purposes seems an important ingredient of sovereignty.

And in confirmation of this argument Judge Davis cited the clause of Article I, section 9, of the Constitution interdicting a prohibition of the slave trade till 1808. This clause shows, he asserted, that those who framed the Constitution perceived that "under the power to regulate commerce, Congress would be authorized to abridge it in favor of the great principles of humanity and justice."

The Embargo, to be sure, operated on foreign commerce, but that there is any difference between Congress' power in relation to foreign and to interstate commerce the advocates of the doctrine now under consideration deny. The power "to regulate" is the power which belongs to Congress as to the one as well as to the other; and if this comprehends the power to prohibit in the one case, it must equally on acknowledged principles of statutory construction, comprehend it in the other case as well. Nor in fact, the argument continues, does it make any difference, by approved principles of statutory construction, what purposes the framers of the Constitution may have had immediately in mind when they gave Congress the power to regulate commerce among the states; the governing consideration is that they gave Congress the power, to be exercised in accordance with its judgment of what are proper occasions for its use.[34]

---

33. 28 Fed. Cas. 614 (No. 16,700) (D.C. Mass. 1808).

34. "The reasons which may have caused the framers to repose the power to regulate interstate commerce in Congress do not, however, affect or limit the extent of the power itself." Justice Peckham, speaking for the Court in Addyston Pipe and Steel Co. v. United States, 175 U.S. 211, 228, 20 Sup. Ct. 96, 102 (1899). "The legitimate meaning of the instrument must be derived from the text itself." 3 *Letters and Other Writings of James Madison* 228.

Finally, as to the Fifth Amendment, it is conceded that Congress may not make an "arbitrary," that is to say, what the Supreme Court finds to be an *arbitrary,* use of any of its powers. That does not signify, however, that an unaccustomed use of power is necessarily arbitrary. Congress is always making an unaccustomed use of its powers. Until 1887 it had never regulated railway rates; and until 1906, it had not attempted to regulate the legal liability of carriers to their employees in interstate commerce, and so on. In any but a static society, governmental power must constantly take on new aspects and undergo new uses; and it was never the intention of the Constitution to freeze things in the legal mould of 1789; and at any rate it has not succeeded in doing so.

So much for a debate that has proceeded with varying degrees of intensity throughout a great part of our constitutional history. It remains to discover the relative strength of the opposed positions in present-day constitutional law.

IV.

The earliest confrontation before the Court of the opposing arguments above set forth occurred in Champion v. Ames in 1903.[35] The case grew out of the Act of 1895 "for the Suppression of Lotteries," as it was frankly entitled. An earlier act excluding lottery tickets from the mails had been sustained in the case of *In re Rapier,*[36] on the proposition that Congress clearly had the power to see that the very facilities furnished by it were not converted to bad uses. But in the case of commerce the facilities are not, ordinarily, furnished by the national government, nor is the right to engage in it a gift of the government. With the preconceptions which it entertained at this period, the Court found the question produced by the act of 1895, forbidding any person "to bring within the United States or to cause to be carried from one state to another" any lottery ticket or an equivalent thereof, "for the purpose of disposing of the same," an extremely difficult one. This is shown by the fact that the case was thrice argued before it and that its decision finally sustaining the act was a five to four one. The opinion of the Court, nevertheless, presented by Justice Harlan, marked a wide swing away from dual federalism notions, and was an almost unqualified triumph at the time for the view that Congress' power to regulate commerce among the states includes the power to prohibit it, especially when it is thus exerted *in supplement and support of state legislation enacted under the police power.*

Early in the opinion extensive quotation is made from Chief Justice Marshall's opinion in Gibbons v. Ogden with special stress upon the definition there given of the phrase "to regulate." Justice Johnson's assertion on the same occasion is also given: "The power of a sovereign state over commerce, therefore, amounts

35. Above note 25.
36. *Id.*

to nothing more than a power to limit and restrain it at pleasure.'' Further along is quoted with evident approval Justice Bradley's statement in Brown v. Houston that ''the power to regulate commerce among the several states is granted to Congress in terms as absolute as is the power to regulate commerce with foreign nations.''[37] Nor did the Tenth Amendment oppose a constitutional barrier to the act. ''Congress,'' said Justice Harlan, ''does not assume to interfere with traffic or commerce in lottery tickets carried on exclusively within the limits of any state, but has only in view commerce of that kind among the several states. It has not assumed to interfere with the completely internal affairs of any state, and has only legislated in respect of a matter which concerns the people of the United States. As a state may, for the purpose of guarding the morals of its own people, forbid all sales of lottery tickets within its limits, so Congress, for the purpose of guarding the people of the United States against the 'widespread pestilence of lotteries' and to protect the commerce, which concerns all the states, may prohibit the carrying of lottery tickets from one state to another.''[38]

Broad, however, as are its possible implications, Champion v. Ames was decided by a Court whose thinking was much in the grip of laissez-faire concepts.[39] The consequence is that these implications were not fully accepted, even by justices who supported the actual decision. Especially was this true of Justice White, who was already thoroughly committed at this date to his great enterprise of watering down the Sherman Act with the ''rule of reason.'' Quite logically, he now enlarged his endeavor to include other aspects of the problem of Congress' power over interstate commerce.

The future chief justice was the very model of the constitutionalist. His youthful studies in the Jesuit schools of Louisiana included, one may confidently assume, mediaeval political thought, which is pervaded with the ecclesiastical conception of secular authority as subordinate and intrinsically limited. No justice ever sat on the Supreme bench who exercised a more bountiful hand in strewing dicta, queries, and arguendos with intent to garner fresh constitutional restraints; and he it is who more than any one else must be credited with having

37. 114 U.S. 622, 630, 5 Sup. Ct. 1091, 1095 (1885). So also J. Harlan in Crutcher v. Kentucky, 141 U.S. 47, 57 11 Sup. Ct. 851, 854 (1891). Cf. J. White in Buttfield v. Stranahan, 192 U.S. 470, 492, 24 Sup. Ct. 349, 359 (1904), which seems to be the first appearance of the contrary idea in an opinion for the Court.

38. The opinion recites the contention in opposition to the act, that if Congress may exclude lottery tickets from interstate commerce, it ''may arbitrarily exclude . . . any article, commodity, or thing of whatsoever kind or nature, or however useful or valuable, which it may choose, no matter with what motive, to declare shall not be carried from one state to another.'' The answer returned by Justice Harlan is ambiguous: If Congress should infringe rights secured by the Constitution or act in a way ''hostile to the objects for the accomplishment of which'' it was endowed with power over interstate commerce, it would be the duty of the Court to intervene; but the remedy for legislative *abuses* of power was resort to the polls not the courts.

39. On this point see my article, ''Social Planning under the Constitution,'' 26 *Am. Pol. Sci. Rev.*, 1, 7–16 (1932).

displaced Marshall's doctrine that questions of power do not depend on the extent of its exercise with an all-pervasive judicial review, in other words, with having transplanted Marshall's doctrine from the legislative to the judicial garden plot![40]

White's initial tilt against Marshall's conception of Congress' powers under the "commerce" clause was his opinion in the Trans-Missouri Freight Association Case in 1897.[41] Here he was in the minority, but the next year he spoke for a majority of the Court in Rhodes v. Iowa,[42] where, with the required amount of judicial face-pulling, the clear meaning of the earlier Rahrer Case[43] was disavowed and the Wilson Act of 1890 eviscerated, with the final result of adding the Eighteenth Amendment to the Constitution. But this rather ironic vindication of the mediaeval doctrine of conditional authority lay far in the future; and in 1904 White, speaking for four judges, protested against the decision in the Northern Securities Case as destructive in principle of the federal system, "of the great guaranty of life, liberty and property," and of "every other safeguard upon which organized society depends."[44]

In all these cases the greater constitutional issue was obscured by finesse in statutory construction. It was not until the first Employers' Liability Cases[45] of 1908 that Justice White obtained the opportunity to challenge squarely the doctrine that Congress' power under the "commerce" clause is unaffected by the coexistence of the states. Here the government had argued that though the act under review purported to govern the liability of "every" interstate carrier to "any" of its employees, whether engaged in interstate commerce or not when the liability fell, yet it was none the less valid, "because," in the words of Justice White's opinion, "one who engages in interstate commerce thereby submits all his business concerns to the regulating power of Congress." "To state the proposition," the opinion continued, in the characteristic White phraseology, "is to refute it. It assumes that, because one engages in interstate commerce, he thereby endows Congress with power not delegated to it by the Constitution; in other words, with the right to legislate concerning matters of purely state concern. . . . It is apparent that if the contention were well founded it would extend the power of Congress to every conceivable subject, however inherently local,

---

40. An excellent statement of White's general theory of political power and of the relation of judicial review thereto is that in the following passage from his opinion in the Intermountain Rate Cases ". . . doctrines which but express the elementary principle that an investiture of a public body with discretion does not imply the right to abuse but on the contrary carries with it as a necessary incident the command that the limits of a sound discretion be not transcended which by necessary implication carries with it the existence of judicial power to correct wrongs done by such excess." Intermountain Rate Cases, 234 U.S. 476, 491 34 Sup. Ct. 986, 993 (1914). His opinion in McCray v. United States, 195 U.S. 27, 24 Sup. Ct. 769 (1904), represents a half-way stage toward this doctrine from Marshall's point of view. On the "rule of reason," see my article, "The Anti-Trust Acts and the Constitution," 18 *Va. L. Rev.* 355–78 (1932) {reprinted in this volume}.

41. 166 U.S. 290, 17 Sup. Ct. 540 (1897).

42. 170 U.S. 412, 18 Sup. Ct. 664 (1898).

43. 140 U.S. 545, 11 Sup. Ct. 865 (1891).

44. 193 U.S. 197, 397, 24 Sup. Ct. 436, 486 (1904).

45. 207 U.S. 463, 28 Sup. Ct. 141 (1908).

would obliterate all the limitations of power imposed by the Constitution, and would destroy the authority of the states as to all conceivable matters which, from the beginning, have been, and must continue to be, under their control so long as the Constitution endures."[46]

And in the Commodity Clause Case[47] the year following, the same justice, once more the Court's mouthpiece, found the same issue involved. The act involved banned any shipment in interstate commerce by a carrier of any article in which it had any interest "direct or indirect." In order to avoid "a grave constitutional issue," the Court held, these words must be construed as not applying to articles produced or owned by a corporation in which the carrier owned stock. So by one and the same stroke the Court curtailed the act and gave its own power of judicial review a new extension, the power of avoiding "grave constitutional issues."[48]

Now, however, ensued a series of adjudications advantageous to Congress' pretensions. In the Hipolite Egg Case[49] the validity of the Pure Food and Drug Act was virtually taken for granted, and the authority of national officals under its provisions to pursue and confiscate adulterated articles being sent from one state to another so long as they remained in the original package was sustained. This was in 1911. Six years later, the validity of the Webb-Kenyon Act was likewise upheld, on the general proposition that with respect to the shipment of intoxicants, which the Court a generation before had labelled "good articles of commerce," Congress' power to regulate commerce among the states comprised the power to prohibit it outright, and so necessarily included the lesser power exercised in the act of adapting its regulations to such various local requirements and conditions as might be expressed from time to time in state laws.[50]

And meantime, in sustaining and applying the White Slave Traffic Act of 1910, the Court had been forced to much broader ground than is implied in either of the cases just mentioned. The act was assailed with the contention that it conflicted "with the reserved powers of the states individually to regulate or prohibit prostitution or other immoralities of their citizens." Justice McKenna speaking for the Court said: "Our dual form of government has its perplexities, state and nation having different fields of jurisdiction, . . . but it must be kept in mind that we are one people; and the powers reserved to the states and those conferred on the nation are adapted to be exercised, whether independently or concurrently, to promote the general welfare, material and moral."[51]

Indeed, the act was later held to apply to the case of a man who had purchased

46. Above note 45, at 499, 502, 503.
47. 213 U.S. 366, 29 Sup. Ct. 527 (1909).
48. See also Addy Co. v. United States, 264 U.S. 239, 44 Sup. Ct. 300 (1924); United States v. LaFrance, 282 U.S. 568, 51 Sup. Ct. 278 (1931).
49. 220 U.S. 45, 31 Sup. Ct. 364 (1911).
50. Clark Distilling Co. v. W. Md. Ry. Co., 242 U.S. 311, 37 Sup. Ct. 180 (1917).
51. Hoke v. United States, above note 25, especially at 322.

transportation for a woman and accompanied her to another state, not for illicit profit but illicit pleasure,[52] a result which suggests that the United States might punish any crime at all, provided only it followed passage by the criminal from one state to another fairly closely! Yet even in the Lottery Case we find Chief Justice Fuller, for the minority, saying with apparent, but it would now appear with misplaced confidence, "nobody would pretend that persons could be kept off trains because they were going from one state to another to engage in the lottery business."[53]

In short, despite the apparent success earlier of Justice White's missionary endeavor in behalf of the notion that Congress' power under the "commerce" clause is intrinsically limited, the outcome of the Child Labor Case when it reached the Court in 1918 was by no means a foregone conclusion.

V.

In the form in which it was finally passed the Child Labor Act of 1916 forbade the offering of products of child labor for transportation from one state to another. It operated therefore, not on the carrier, but the manufacturer or purchaser of the goods. Mr. Justice Day's opinion for the Court in Hammer v. Dagenhart,[54] holding the act void, boils down to three propositions: (1) that the act was *not* a regulation of commerce among the states; (2) that it *was* an invasion of powers reserved to the states; (3) that it was, therefore, inimical to the federal system which it was the design of the Constitution to set up and maintain.

One evident difficulty here is to determine whether the second proposition should be regarded as dependent on the first or as having independent force of its own sufficient to invalidate the act of Congress. Assuming the second possibility, Justice Holmes in his dissenting opinion asserted that a statute "within the power expressly given to Congress if considered only as to its immediate effects" was being held invalid for its collateral effects within the normal field of state power. "I should have thought," said he, "that the most conspicuous decisions of this Court had made it clear that the power to regulate commerce and other constitutional powers could not be cut down or qualified by the fact that it might interfere with the carrying out of the domestic policy of any state,"[55] a

52. Caminetti v. United States, 242 U.S. 470, 37 Sup. Ct. 192 (1917).
53. 188 U.S. 321, 374, 23 Sup. Ct. 321, 334 (1903). Could Congress keep people off the trains who are headed for Reno?
54. Above note 17, pp. 268-77.
55. Hammer v. Dagenhart, above note 17, pp. 278-80. In addition to the cases cited by J. Holmes, see the following cases of later date: Hamilton v. Ky. Distils. Co., 251 U.S. 146, 40 Sup. Ct. 106 (1919); Missouri v. Holland, 252 U.S. 416, 40 Sup. Ct. 382 (1920); Board of Trustees v. United States, 289 U.S. 48, 53 Sup. Ct. 509 (1933). In the last-mentioned case the doctrine of constitutional tax exemption as applied to state property and agencies received a fresh check. The original extension of the doctrine to such agencies in Collector v. Day, 11 Wall. 113 (1871), represents the most important recognition that the Court has given the concept of dual federalism as a judicially enforcible restriction on national power.

position which is clearly incontrovertible except on the assumption that Justice Day's third proposition states a transcendental value which rises above and nullifies the express phraseology of the Constitution itself where the two conflict.

Waiving this question for the moment, however, let us turn to Justice Day's first proposition. The ground of it is soon found to be the idea that a prohibition of commerce is not normally a regulation of it, because destructive of it. To be sure, Justice Day admits, there have been cases in which regulation legitimately took the form of prohibition, but, he contends, "in each of these instances the use of interstate transportation was necessary to the accomplishment of harmful results. . . . This element is wanting in the present case. . . . The goods shipped are in themselves harmless . . . when offered for shipment, and before transportation begins, the labor of production is over, and the mere fact that they were intended for interstate transportation does not make their production subject to federal control under the commerce clause."

Two quite distinct, and indeed conflicting, ideas are here intermingled, or confused: first, the idea that Congress may exclude from interstate transportation only things that are harmful *in themselves;* secondly, the idea that it may exclude objects the *transportation* of which is *followed* by harmful results. And not only are these ideas in conflict with each other, neither is valid as it is here applied.

To say that Congress may exclude from interstate commerce only objects that are harmful in themselves is to invoke the idea that any regulation of commerce must always be justified by an intention on the part of Congress to *protect* commerce itself, which, for reasons already made clear, cannot be admitted. Nor is this all; for the idea that Congress may exercise an express power given without qualification only for a certain purpose or certain purposes to be finally determined by the Court, is to endow the Court with the power to invalidate acts of Congress because of Congress' supposed purpose in passing them, something which Justice Day himself says may not be done—even in the act of doing it!

Moreover, Justice Day also admits that interstate transportation may be forbidden if it is followed by "harmful results," which means results *judged by the Court* to be harmful—which again is a palpable invasion of the field of legislative discretion. And it is an act of interstate *transportation* that must be followed by such results. That is to say, "commerce" is conceived of as primarily *transportation,* and Congress' power over it is envisaged as beginning only with an act of transportation from one state to another; and from this it follows that Congress must shut its eyes to all "harmful results" which precede such act of transportation.[56]

The first comment invited is, that granting this conception of commerce, still a "harmful result" that followed transportation from one state to another would be

---

56. In checking state power with the "commerce" clause, the Court has frequently regarded Congress' power as operative before any act of transportation has started. See Robbins v. Shelby Taxing Dist., 120 U.S. 489, 7 Sup. Ct. 592 (1886); Dahnke-Walker Milling Co. v. Bondurant, 257 U.S. 282, 42 Sup. Ct. 106 (1922).

just as much within the jurisdiction of the latter state as a harmful result which preceded the same act of transportation would be within the jurisdiction of the former state. Justice Day's argument therefore logically concedes that the fact that it reaches a subject matter which is within the normal jurisdiction of a state does not, of itself, suffice to invalidate an act of Congress.[57]

In the second place, the argument is directed to only one aspect of the Child Labor Act, which was intended not merely to repress child labor in certain states, but to prevent its spread through the operation of competition to other states. Justice Day himself recognizes this inadequacy of the argument, and proceeds to supplement it with the following contention: "The commerce clause," he asserts, "was not intended to give Congress a general authority to equalize conditions. In some of the states laws have been passed fixing minimum wage laws for women, in others the local law regulates the hours of labor of women in various employments. This fact does not give Congress the power to deny transportation in interstate commerce to those who carry on business where the hours of labor and the rate of compensation for women have not been fixed by a standard in use in other states and approved by Congress."

Not "a *general* authority" perhaps, but why not such authority as an otherwise valid exercise of its power to regulate commerce confers upon it? Certainly no words in the Constitution impose any such restriction upon its power over commerce. On the contrary, the "commerce" clause, altogether independently of Congressional legislation under it, has been held by the Court repeatedly to forbid state legislation designed to give the enacting state an advantage in competition with sister states.[58] Why then should not Congress exercise the power which, after all, the Constitution confers upon *it* and not upon the Court, with the same objective in mind, and thereby equalize, if it can, conditions of competition among the states according to *its* view of sound social policy? Justice Day's assertion in denial once again invokes the unallowable assumption that the Court may supervise the purposes of Congress. It is the *sic volo, sic jubeo* of final authority, no less—but also no more.

The whole opinion of Mr. Justice Day rests moreover on the assumption that "commerce" is primarily *transportation,* which, however, is not the case. As the etymology of the word reveals, it means primarily buying and selling, *traffic,* in brief. Indeed, in Gibbons v. Ogden, the first case to reach the Court under the

---

57. Levering and Garrigues Co. v. Morrin, 289 U.S. 103, 53 Sup. Ct. 549 (1933), is interesting in this connection. Here the Court held that petitioners were not entitled under the Anti-Trust Acts to an injunction against defendants forbidding the latter to conspire to halt local building operations in which materials fabricated or bought in other states were used. "Use (*sic*) of the materials," said Sutherland, J., for the Court, "was a purely local matter." The Court cited United Mine Workers v. Coronado Coal Co., 259 U.S. 344, 410, 411, 42 Sup. Ct. 587 (1921); United Leather Workers v. Herkert, 265 U.S. 457, 44 Sup. Ct. 623 (1923); Industrial Ass'n v. United States, 268 U.S. 64, 77-82, 45 Sup. Ct. 403 (1925).

58. See Minn. v. Barber, 136 U.S. 313, 10 Sup. Ct. 862 (1890); Oklahoma v. Kan. Nat. Gas Co., 221 U.S. 229, 31 Sup. Ct. 564 (1911).

clause, the crucial question was whether the term comprehended transportation at all. And indubitably the correct theory of the Child Labor Act is that it was designed to discourage a widespread and pernicious *traffic,* which both supported and was supported by child labor in certain states, and which furnished a constant inducement to its spread to other states. For without the interstate market for its products child labor could not long survive on any considerable scale. The act promised to be effective, in other words, not as a penalty *in terrorem,* as is the White Slave Act, but by *eliminating the substantial cause of the evil it struck at.* The Court's objection, therefore, that specific acts of production precede specific acts of transporting the product becomes frivolous; both these acts are but part and parcel of something much broader, and that something is interstate "commerce" in the original understanding of the term.

We are thus brought to Justice Day's exaltation of the Madisonian conception of dual federalism as a superconstitutional value to which even the express language of the Constitution must yield. He says:

> In interpreting the Constitution it must never be forgotten that the nation is made up of states to which are entrusted the powers of local government. And to them and to the people the powers not expressly (*sic*) delegated to the national government are reserved. Lane County v. Oregon, 7 Wall, 71, 76. The power of the states to regulate their purely internal affairs by such laws as seem wise to the local authority is inherent and has never been surrendered to the general government. New York v. Miln, 11 Pet. 102, 139,[59] Slaughter House Cases, 16 Wall. 36, 63; Kidd v. Pearson, above. . . . The far-reaching result of upholding the act cannot be more plainly indicated than by pointing out that if Congress can thus regulate matters entrusted to local authority by prohibition of the movement of commodities in interstate commerce, all freedom of commerce will be at an end, and the power of the states over local matters may be eliminated, and thus our system of government be practically destroyed. . . .

Thus Justice Day ventures to amend the Tenth Amendment by interpolating in it the word "expressly"! And since Congress admittedly is not vested *expressly* with the power to prohibit the transportation of the products of child labor from one state to another, its attempt to do so becomes an invasion of the reserved powers of the states over "their purely internal affairs." But though the premise were sound, the conclusion would not follow. As Justice Holmes points out in his dissenting opinion for himself and three brethren, admitting the right of the states to control their *purely internal affairs,* "when they seek to send their products across the state line they are no longer within their rights. If there were no Constitution and no Congress their power to cross the line would depend upon their neighbors. Under the Constitution such commerce belongs not to the states but to Congress to regulate. It may carry out its views of public policy whatever indirect effect they may have upon the activities of the states. Instead of being

---

59. This case, a relic of extreme states rights days, was substantially overruled in Henderson v. New York, 92 U.S. 259 (1875).

encountered by a prohibitive tariff at her boundaries the state encounters the public policy of the United States which it is for Congress to express. The public policy of the United States is shaped with a view to the benefit of the nation as a whole. . . . The national welfare as understood by Congress may require a different attitude within its sphere from that of some self-seeking state. It seems to be entirely constitutional for Congress to enforce its understanding by all the means at its command.''[60]

In other words, Hammer v. Dagenhart denies to Congress power over commerce which originally belonged to the individual states of the Union! As a matter of fact, when read along with certain decisions in which the "commerce" clause has been applied as a restraint on state power, it is found to do something even more remarkable. By the plain logic of the cases today neither Congress nor the states, nor both together, can stop interstate commerce in the products of child labor. Such products being "good articles of commerce," no state can prohibit their entry from another state nor their sale in the original package within its boundaries, since to do so would be to invade the field of Congress' power to regulate interstate commerce.[61] But Congress, nevertheless, we are now informed, may not exercise the power so solicitously guaranteed its exclusive control, since to do so would be to invade the field of power reserved to the states. So the states, which, without challenge, originally possessed this power, have now lost it by virtue of having delegated it to Congress, but Congress has never received it! Dual federalism thus becomes *triple* federalism—inserted between the realm of the national government and that of the states is one of "no government"—a governmental vacuum, a political "no man's land."

The subject is one that demands some further consideration. Since the Civil War the Court has decided scores of cases in which it has applied the "commerce" clause as a restriction on state power in relation to business interests of various sorts.[62] Such businesses have been thus enabled to spread out over state lines with a minimum of interference from state legislative policies, and to assume national proportions. Yet when the national government would fain take the same route into the states, it is confronted in the name of the federal principle with a sign of "road closed." The issue raised is spurious. So far as the great proportion of business is concerned the federal principle is today moribund, and the only question is whether the "commerce" clause is effective to supply a unified political control corresponding to the industrial and commercial unification of which it is the main legal prop. In returning in Hammer v. Dagenhart a negative answer to this question the Court assumes that a choice is still open to the people of this country which is in fact closed to them, and so, wittingly or unwittingly, converts the "commerce" clause into a charter of laissez faire-ism of the most

60. Hammer v. Dagenhart, above note 17, at 281.
61. Leisy v. Hardin, above note 18; Schollenberger v. Pa., 171 U.S. 1, 18 Sup. Ct. 757 (1898).
62. See 2 Willoughby, *Constitutional Law of the United States* 1004 ff. and 1061 ff. (2d ed. 1929).

extreme nature. At the same time it takes up a position which cannot by any possibility be harmonized with its own repeated assurance that "the Constitution, whilst distributing the pre-existing power, preserved it all."[63]

VI.

Hammer v. Dagenhart represents high tide in the more recent surges of Madisonian doctrine. What is the standing of this decision now, fifteen years later? Two subsequent holdings directly impair its logic, if indeed that were possible! In United States v. Hill,[64] decided within a twelve-month, the Court, speaking by the same justice, sustained the Read Bone-Dry Amendment to the Post Office Act of May 3, 1917, which prohibited the interstate transportation of intoxicants into states forbidding the manufacture and sale of the same. To the objection that if the provision was applied to liquors intended for personal use merely and not for sale, it conflicted with the laws of certain states, the Court answered: "Congress may exercise this authority over interstate commerce in aid of the policy of the state if it sees fit. It is equally clear that the policy of Congress acting independently of the states may induce legislation without reference to the particular policy or law of any given state. . . . The control of Congress over interstate commerce is not to be limited by state laws." That is to say, it is no objection to an otherwise valid exercise by Congress of its power to prohibit commerce, that its purpose is to correct state policy rather than to support it.

In 1925, in Brooks v. United States,[65] the Court upheld the Motor Vehicle Act of 1919, which makes it a penal offense against the United States to transport in interstate commerce a motor vehicle known to have been stolen, or to "conceal, barter, sell, or dispose" of the same. After what appears to be an entirely irrelevant review of previous cases, the chief justice notes "the radical change in transportation" brought about by the automobile, and the rise of "elaborately organized conspiracies for the theft of automobiles . . . and their sale or other deposition" in another police jurisdiction from the owner's. "This," the opinion declares, "is a gross misuse of interstate commerce. Congress may properly

---

63. White, J, in Northern Securities Co. v. United States, above note 44, at 399. See also to the same effect his opinion for the Court in United States v. Bennett, 232 U.S. 299, 305, 306, 34 Sup. Ct. 433, 437 (1914), and the Court's recent approval of this statement in Burnet v. Brooks, 282 U.S. 359, 53 Sup. Ct. 457 (1933). Note also White's sarcastic comment on the argument of the carriers in the Intermountain Rate Cases: "To uphold the proposition it would be necessary to say . . . that the power perished as the result of the act by which it was conferred." Intermountain Rate Cases, above note 38, at 493. "The powers [of the United States and states] taken together, ought to be equal to all of the objects of government, not specially excepted for special reasons, as in the case of duties on exports." 4 *Letters and Other Writings of James Madison* 250. "If Congress have not the power, it is annihilated for the nation; a policy without example in any other nation, and not within the reason of the solitary one in our own . . . the prohibition of a tax on exports." *Id.* 3, 640. See also *id.* 644 and 654.

64. 248 U.S. 420, 39 Sup. Ct. 143 (1919).

65. 267 U.S. 432, 45 Sup. Ct. 345 (1925).

punish such interstate transportation by any one with knowledge of the theft because of its harmful result and its defeat of the property rights of those whose machines against their will are taken into another jurisdiction." In short, the act is sustained chiefly as protective of owners of automobiles, that is to say, of *interests in "the state of origin,"* and this result is directly connected with the Court having taken notice of "elaborately organized conspiracies" for the theft and disposal of automobiles across state lines—that is, of a widespread *traffic* in such property.

Hammer v. Dagenhart is today elbowed into rather narrow quarters.[66] More-over, it may happen with a legal, as with a military position, which does not yield readily to assault, that it may be turned. Indeed, it has occurred more than once in recent years that the Court by a radical shift of position with reference to a vexed constitutional problem, has thrown the latter into an entirely new perspective, and with striking results in constitutional interpretation.[67] Why should not some-thing of the same nature take place in the present instance? The truth is that it has, although the transfer of position alluded to is not yet complete.

To continue our military mode of speech, the last-ditch position of the Court in Hammer v. Dagenhart undoubtedly consists in the proposition that "production is local."[68] The difficulty with this proposition is that in modern conditions it is not true in any important sense. Specific acts of production take place in specific places, but many such acts and at different places may be necessary to complete a marketable product. What, however, is more immediate relevance to our own problem is that, whether considered for the conditions surrounding them or for their possible effect upon future production, few acts of production are today purely local. Even before the World War the principal commercial countries of Europe had found it desirable to enter into agreements with one another with regard to labor conditions;[69] and as to the effect of present production on future,

---

66. In Bailey v. Drexel Furniture Co., 259 U.S. 20, the Court, in 1922, set aside a special tax by Congress upon the net profits of manufacturing concerns employing children under other than stated conditions. The opinion of Chief Justice Taft for the Court relies quite unequivocally on the canon of constitutional interpretation which is disavowed by Justice Day in Hammer v. Dagenhart that a measure otherwise within the power of Congress may be invalidated in defense of the federal system because of the supposed purpose of Congress to govern a matter within the normal control of the states. Indeed, the chief justice's explanation of the decision in Hammer v. Dagenhart, above note 17, puts it likewise upon the same ground. "When," he says, "Congress threatened to stop interstate commerce in ordinary and necessary commodities, *unobjectionable as subjects of transportation,* and to deny the same to the people of a state in order to coerce them into compliance with Congress' regulation of state concerns, the Court said that this was not in fact regulation of interstate commerce, but rather that of state concerns and was invalid." In short, Congress can prevent children from injuring commerce but cannot prevent commerce from injuring children!

67. By way of illustration, compare Burdick v. United States, 236 U.S. 79, 35 Sup. Ct. 267 (1914); and Biddle v. Perovich, 274 U.S. 480, 47 Sup. Ct. 664 (1926).

68. Kidd v. Pearson, 128 U.S. 1, 9 Sup. Ct. 6 (1888) is the leading case. Here it was held that the "commerce" clause did not prevent a state from prohibiting the manufacture of intoxicants for shipment in interstate commerce. All the other cases prior to Hammer v. Dagenhart assert the proposition in relation to the "commerce" clause as restrictive of state power in the *absence* of regulation by Congress.

69. See my *Doctrine of Judicial Review* 161 (1914).

one need only recall conditions in the oil fields. Furthermore, production is no more "local" in the sense of being within the normal jurisdiction of the police power of the states than is local transportation, which in 1914 was conceded by the Court to be within the power of Congress to regulate when in fact it affects interstate transportation.[70]

And meantime, since Swift and Co. v. United States,[71] which was decided early in 1905, the Court had come to recognize in cases arising under the Sherman Act, that commerce is something more than *transportation,* is in fact *traffic,* and that consequently the hard and fast line which it had drawn a decade earlier in the Sugar Trust Case[72] between commerce and production was no longer tenable.[73] Then in 1921 and 1922 Congress, building on these results, proceeded to enact the Packers and Stockyards Act and the Grain Futures Act, which were sustained respectively in Stafford v. Wallace and Board of Trade v. Olsen.[74]

There can be no question that, from the outlook provided by these cases, *production for the interstate market* has taken on an entirely altered aspect. From being something intrinsically local, it becomes merged in a steady-flowing continuum which knows no state lines; in the phrase of Chief Justice Taft, it is but an "eddy" in the interstate commerce stream; it is a recurrent episode in an established "course of business" essentially interstate; and an intention which is authenticated by such a course of business *can* put goods in interstate commerce.[75] The cases, in short, adumbrate an entirely new concept from the point of view of which "commerce" and "business" become interchangeable terms, and that is the concept of the interstate market. American business is today dominated by its national characteristics—buying and selling without regard to state lines, transportation without regard to state lines, communication without regard to state lines; but above all, it is dominated by the fact that it looks toward and culminates in, in short, exists for the interstate market.[76]

Interstate commerce, or rather interstate business, thus takes on the territorial aspect of a field over which national power must hold sway if its activities are not

---

70. The Shreveport Case, 234 U.S. 342, 34 Sup. Ct. 833 (1914).
71. 196 U.S. 375, 25 Sup. Ct. 276 (1905).
72. United States v. E. C. Knight, 156 U.S. 1, 15 Sup. Ct. 249 (1894).
73. See my article, above note 40.
74. 258 U.S. 495, 42 Sup. Ct. 397 (1921); 262 U.S. 1, 43 Sup. Ct. 470 (1922).
75. Dahnke-Walker Milling Co. v. Bondurant, note 54 above; So. Pac. Terminal Co. v. I.C.C., 219 U.S. 498 (1911). *Cf.* Kidd v. Pearson, above note 68.
76. This is not to say, of course, that the interstate market is *one* market, or yet the same market for different products; it is only to say that it overruns and ignores state lines. The interstate market for any particular product is likely, where competitive conditions obtain, to dissolve into a number of regional markets, in accordance with the law stated by Professor Fetter: "The boundary line between the territories tributary to two geographically competing real markets for like goods is a hyperbolic curve. At each point on this line the difference between freights from the two markets is just equal to the difference between the prevailing market prices, whereas on either side of this line the freight difference and the price difference are unequal. The relation of prices in the two markets determines the location of the boundary line: the lower the price in a market relative to that of a neighboring market, the larger the tributary territory." F. A. Fetter, *The Masquerade of Monopoly* 283 (1931).

to take place beyond the reach of a supervisory political judgment. Its articulated structure could indeed be restored to effective local control only to destroy it. As to it, state power is actually nonexistent—an empty fiction. If it is to be governed at all, it must be by the national government. Nor does this signify that Congress is entitled to use its power over commerce to bring within its control matters in no wise related to the interstate market, marriage and divorce, for instance. The determinative question is this: Does the interstate market serve to capitalize conditions which may reasonably be thought to be destructive of the national prosperity if persisted in, or does it afford the means of deriving private advantage from socially undesirable conditions? If so, Congress is entitled to take corrective action.

And the vital defect of Hammer v. Dagenhart against this background is seen at once to have been its sheer anachronism. With commerce among the states conceived as merely transportation from one state to another, any effort by Congress to prohibit it necessarily thrusts into prominence its aspect as an effort to reach subject matter normally within the power of the states, and this is so whether lottery tickets, intoxicants, stolen automobiles, or child labor products are the things involved.[77] But when "commerce" is properly defined as *traffic*, and the mental picture is formed, not of an isolated journey across a state boundary line, but of an onward coursing stream of business which knows no state lines, which is constantly fed by and as constantly feeds the streams of production, and which debouches into the interstate market, then regulation of it by Congress, whether taking the form of a prohibition of certain phases of transportation or some other form, ceases to be open to the charge of an ulterior intention to usurp power, because it operates upon the very subject-matter entrusted to Congress, or at most upon local incidents thereof, the fringe, so to speak, of a nation-spread fabric.

Within recent months the Supreme Court has taken pains on two occasions to assert: "Primitive conditions have passed; business is now transacted on a national scale."[78] This was said, it is true, in both instances, in support of decisions restrictive of the state taxing power. The burden of this paper is that the same fact must be given its proper weight in delimiting national power over business. The constitutional difficulty that stands in the way of the Court's doing so is the concept of dual federalism which has no support in the *text* of the Constitution, and which represents an entire inversion of Chief Justice Marshall's system of constitutional interpretation.[79] And whatever validity dual federalism may once

---

77. It is not meant of course to suggest that Congress' ulterior motives properly afford a ground of judicial review. Even if "commerce" be defined simply as *transportation*, the decision in Hammer v. Dagenhart, above note 17, still remains an act of unwarrantable intrusion by the Court upon Congress' legislative discretion.

78. Farmers' L. & T. Co., v. Minn., 280 U.S. 204, 211, 50 Sup. Ct. 98, 212 (1930); Burnet v. Brooks, above note 63.

79. Thus Marshall regarded *traffic* as "one of the most ordinary ingredients" of commerce; subsequently this most ordinary ingredient became entirely subordinated to "commerce" considered

have had as a canon of constitutional construction it has since lost, both because of its logical irreconcilability with a host of modern decisions and because of its actual unworkability in the presence of modern business conditions. The Constitution sets up as its foremost objective "a more perfect Union." Technologically, industrially, commercially, the perfect union has been achieved. As usually happens, legal and governmental development has lagged behind. But our present situation is a sharp reminder that there are times when law and government must quicken their pace if permanent disaster is to be avoided.[80]

Madison's and White's views are outmoded by times and conditions which vindicate Marshall's prophetic vision.[81]

---

as *transportation*—a purely derived concept. Again Marshall defined the power to "regulate" commerce as the power "to prescribe the rule by which commerce is to be governed," which in certain circumstances meant, naturally, the power to "foster and promote" it; and once more the enemies of the congressional power to "prohibit" commerce urge a purely secondary definition as the sole and exclusive one. Again, Marshall regarded the Constitution as having for its primary purpose the creation of a sovereign national authority with respect to a designated subject matter, while the concept of dual federalism makes state power, to some indefinite extent to be determined from time to time by judicial review, an independent limitation on national power.

80. Just how difficult it can be at times to distinguish production and commerce even verbally is illustrated by the recent case of Utah Power and Light Co. v. Pfost, 286 U.S. 165 (1932). The issue here was the validity of an Idaho statute imposing a license tax on the generation of electricity in the state. The company, which sent most of its power out of the state, contended that the process of generation was "simultaneous and interdependent with that of transmission and use," and that "because of their inseparability the whole" was interstate commerce. The state urged, to the contrary, that the process of conversion was "completed before the pulses of energy leave the generator in their flow to the transformer." Mr. Justice Sutherland for the Court: "*While conversion and transmission are substantially instantaneous, they are, we are convinced, essentially separable and distinct operations.*"

It would, of course, be quite unfair to assume that Justice Sutherland thought he was here making a contribution to scientific knowledge. Rather he was throwing verbal straws to a drowning theory of federalism—which he leaves balancing on the imaginary line that separates the imaginary final pulsation of an electric current in an induction coil from its imaginary first pulsation in a transmission wire! I am told, in fact, that if the separation suggested by Justice Sutherland were really attempted the result would be the disappearance of the generating plant in flames.

81. The debate in the Senate on Senator Black's "thirty-hour-a-week" bill (Apr. 3rd to 5th) elicited some interesting expressions of opinion concerning the obligation of a senator, under his oath to support the Constitution, toward decisions of the Supreme Court interpretative of the Constitution. Referring to Hammer v. Dagenhart, Senator Black himself said: "I assert the same right with reference to that opinion of the Court as has been asserted here with reference to other opinions, namely, that we are governed by the Constitution of the United States in the final analysis, and not by the prepossessions of a certain number of judges who may write an opinion on a particular matter." 77 *Cong. Rec.* 1112, above note 1. Senator Long reminded the Senate that "our Constitution simply provides for the 'creation' of the Supreme Court. It is possible for Congress to enlarge it, diminish it, or to make itself a part of the Court. The time might come in America when Congress itself would be in the same position in which the House of Parliament in England is, particularly if the Supreme Court were out of touch with what was necessary for the public at the time." *Id.* 1118. Senator Borah thought the fact that the decision in Hammer v. Dagenhart was a 5-to-4 decision made a difference, but Senator Barkley disagreed: "It is a perfectly legal and binding decision, just as a law passed by the Senate and the House by a majority of one is just as binding on the people as if it had been passed unanimously . . . ; and under our theory of the rule of the majority (*sic!*), I think the Court is just as much justified in having its decision by a majority of one respected as we would be justified in having the people respect our statutes which are passed by a majority of one." Senator Borah agreed in part:

"The senator from Kentucky . . . has very properly said that a 5-to-4 decision is binding upon the litigants [in fact the senator from Kentucky said nothing about "litigants"]. It is the law of the land; but we are here making laws, we are establishing policies. Therefore, following the example of Abraham Lincoln, I have always felt that it is a justifiable position to take that when a proposition seems unsettled, [Lincoln, however, was talking about the 7-to-2 decision in the Dred Scott Case], legislators, who make laws and establish policies, ought to have some freedom of judgment in the matter." *Id*. 1178–79. A little later the following interesting colloquy developed among the senators from Texas, Washington, and Idaho:

Mr. Connally: "Whenever we vote for these measures, does not each individual have to determine for himself whether they are constitutional or not?"

Mr. Dill: "Yes, I think that is true."

Mr. Connally: "The Senator from Idaho (Mr. Borah), a moment ago, was talking about the desirability of passing the bill so that the Supreme Court could pass on it. When I vote for the measure it will not be for that reason."

Mr. Dill: "I take the position that where a question is of doubtful constitutionality, because there are no cases that apply in all respects, I want to resolve the doubt in favor of the legislation which I believe is so highly desirable and leave it to the Court to decide the doubt in question."

Mr. Connally: "Senators will stand on this floor, and I dare say the senator from Idaho has done it repeatedly, and declaim against the encroachment of the courts on the legislative power. Yet senators stand on the floor from time to time and "pass the buck," as it were, over to the Supreme Court by saying, "Well, we will let the Court pass on it." We are encouraging the very encroachment against which senators declaim."

Mr. Borah: "Mr. President, will the senator from Washington yield to me?"

Mr. Dill: "I yield."

Mr. Borah: "May I say to the senator from Texas that I do think it is the duty of this body to pass upon the constitutionality of an act, and I am not willing to be bound in my view as to its constitutionality by a 5-to-4 decision."

Mr. Connally: "Mr. President, I congratulate the senator. I was sure that was his attitude; but there was some suggestion that the senator wanted the bill passed so that it could go up to the Court and the question be decided. . . ." *Id*. 1180.

The most conservative position developed was that of Senator Logan of Kentucky—unless he was indulging in irony: "It may be that my training throughout the years has caused me to think along lines from which I cannot easily depart. I cannot agree with the senator from Louisiana that we have the right to place our own construction on the Constitution when the Supreme Court of the United States, which is solely vested with the authority to tell us what the Constitution means, has determined a particular question. It may be that we could say that we disagree with its opinion, but however much we may disagree with the opinion of the Supreme Court, that opinion is right. It may not have been right five minutes before the opinion was delivered; it may not have been right during the entire history of the nation up to that time; but the very moment that that opinion is handed down and goes into the law books, when it becomes final, then the Constitution means and must mean exactly what the Supreme Court says it means. I can place no other construction on it." *Id*. 1257.

Most people will find it difficult to believe that the past decisions of the Court interpretive of the Constitution are entitled to greater respect from Congress than they are apt to receive from the Court itself. First and last the Court has overruled, in whole or in part, such decisions of its own on more than thirty occasions. See dissenting opinion of Justice Brandeis in Burnet v. Coronado Oil and Gas Co., 285 U.S. 393, 407–10, 52 Sup. Ct. 443, nn. 2 and 4 (1932). As is there pointed out, Blackstone v. Miller, 188 U.S. 189, 23 Sup. Ct. 277 (1903), which was overruled in the recent case of Farmers' L. & T. Co. v. Minn., above note 78, had been cited with approval by the Court some fifteen times in the twenty-seven years between the two cases. Shortly following the Burnet Case, the Court overruled another constitutional decision, that in Long v. Rockwood, 277 U.S. 142, 48 Sup. Ct. 463 (1928). This happened in Fox Film Co. v. Doyal, 286 U.S. 123, 131, 52 Sup. Ct. 546 (1932).

III.

THE PRESIDENT'S
REMOVAL POWER

15. The President's Removal Power under the Constitution

Preface

SEVERAL circumstances go to stamp the Supreme Court's decision in Myers v. United States a notable event in judicial and constitutional history. Not since 1899, when the Insular Cases were decided, had a Supreme Court decision on a constitutional question captured a prominent place—with headlines to match—on the front page of the morning paper. The case was before the Court for more than two years and was twice argued ere a majority could be obtained among the justices for a final disposition of it. On the occasion of the second argument the chief justice took the unusual step of inviting special argument by an *amicus curiae,* a role taken by Mr. George Wharton Pepper, then senator from Pennsylvania, who was enlisted to represent the peculiar interests of the Senate in the case. The quality of the argument before the Court, too, was extraordinarily high; the arguments of Mr. Pepper and Mr. Beck, then solicitor general of the United States, fully sustained the best traditions of the Court. Yet the labors of counsel seem to have done little to lessen those of the Court itself. In the matter of length the controlling opinion by the chief justice, as well as two of the dissenting opinions, find their nearest parallel again in the opinions which were filled in the Insular Cases, or at a remoter period in those of the Dred Scott Case.

Nor are these indications of the decision's claim upon public attention misleading. In sustaining the right of President Wilson in 1919 to remove from office the postmaster of Portland, Oregon, without consulting the Senate, as the act of Congress required, the Court laid down two propositions of constitutional law of first-rate importance. The first is that when an executive officer of the United States is appointed by the President by and with the advice and consent of the

From *The President's Removal Power under the Constitution* (New York: National Municipal League, 1927). Copyright 1927, by Edward S. Corwin.

Senate, the power to remove such officer belongs under the Constitution to the President alone, and that Congress may not grant the Senate a participation in the said power, a holding which, though decidedly vulnerable on both historical and logical grounds, is not improbably supported by practical considerations. At least it is a tenable position that the Senate's censorship over appointments affords that body all the opportunity to enforce its ideas of fitness for office that the best interests of the public service require it should have. But unfortunately the Court does not stop at this point. Because the President enjoys the constitutional power of removal in relation to executive officers of the United States, the conclusion is reached, in the second place, that therefore all such officers are *removable at his discretion*. The result of this ruling is to deny to Congress, which alone has power under the Constitution to create offices, any right to determine their tenure as against the removal power, and this notwithstanding the fact that its right to determine tenure as against the appointive power—that is, to limit the term for which an appointment to office may run—is freely conceded. The main purpose of the ensuing essay is, accordingly, to show that this more sweeping proposition of the decision in Myers v. United States is badly grounded in both history and logic, that it was unnecessary to the decision of the question actually before the Court, and that, furthermore, no such drastic cleaving of the Gordian knot with which the Court thought itself to be confronted was either required or desirable.

Why did the Court feel itself bound to establish the doctrine that all executive officers of the United States are subject at all times to removal by the President for any reason that may seem good to him? The Court's own language does not leave the answer far to seek. It is discovered in the chief justice's repeatedly expressed concern that the President should have unrestricted power of removal over the heads of the great executive departments, over those, in other words, who make up his official family. A head of department, says the chief justice, "is and must be the President's *alter ego* in the matters of that department where the President is required by law to exercise authority"; and again: in the political field "his Cabinet officers must do his will. He must place in each member of his official family, and his chief executive subordinates, implicit faith"; and yet again: "The imperative reasons requiring unrestrained power to remove the most important of his subordinates in their most important duties must, therefore, control interpretation of the Constitution as to all appointed by him." That is to say, because the President ought to be able to remove a member of his Cabinet at will, he must also be recognized as having the right to remove at will, for instance, a member of the Interstate Commerce Commission. The premise must be conceded; but it is hoped that the following study succeeds in demonstrating that the conclusion does not follow once the resources of our constitutional law and practice are sufficiently explored.

The central weakness of the Court's position is, in fact, very evident once it is pointed out. It consists in failing to recognize that the relation of the President's power of removal to Congress' power under the "necessary and proper" clause in the creation of offices may and should vary with the *nature of the office involved*. A head of department and a member of the Interstate Commerce Commission are, to be sure, both termed "executive officers"; but the similarity between them hardly proceeds beyond this extremely loose locution. A head of department may exist almost exclusively as an arm of presidential prerogative, as for example in the field of foreign relationship {*sic;* relations?}; always he is designated by the Constitution itself as a source to which the President may turn for advice; while nearly 140 years of constitutional practice have fastened upon him the further role of close political confidant of the President. In the chief justice's own words, he is apt to be, as to his principal duties, the President's *alter ego.''* So true is this indeed that the Senate itself has long since come, except in the most evident cases of unfitness, to forego its right to censor appointments to Cabinet offices.

Very different is it with an interstate commerce commissioner, who exercises no power within presidential authority, either constitutional or statutory, and is designated neither by the Constitution nor by custom to be an instrument of presidential policies or a recipient of presidential confidences. His powers are none of them a substraction from presidential prerogative, but are, on the contrary, derived from a delegation by Congress of its own express constitutional powers. That a President may sometimes be tempted to play politics with offices of this description has been made clear during the present administration by certain happenings in connection with the Shipping Board and the Tariff Commission. (See e.g., *Cong. Rec.*, January 13 and 16, 1926, at 1575 and 1819, respectively). On the other hand, the Court itself has said that the broad delegations of legislative power which bodies like the Interstate Commerce Commission commonly receive these days are constitutionally tolerable on the sole assumption that such bodies act upon careful and considerate inquiry and with a proper regard for the incidents of correct procedure. (See below, note 108.) Yet of what value is correct procedure except as it presupposes and is attended by independence of decision; and how is the latter to be reasonably predicated of an officer over whose head the Damocles sword of removal is ever suspended?

The positive thesis of the following essay is thus indicated. It is that *the essential nature of the office under consideration, as shown by its characteristic duties, determines the scope of the removal power in relation to the power of Congress, in creating an office, to fix its tenure*. At one end of the scale is such an office as Secretary of State, a mere instrument of presidential prerogative; at the other end are judicial offices which are recognized by the Constitution in terms as properly irremovable except for misbehavior and by process of impeachment. But there are also certain quasi-judicial bodies such as the Interstate Commerce Commission, as to which the idea of official good behavior equally exacts the *sine qua non* of official independence. To be sure, the decisions of the Interstate Commerce Commission may sometimes involve broad questions of policy. When they do, inasmuch as they lie within the field of legislative power, they are always subject to correction by that power, in which, it should not be forgotten, the President participates.

Nor are the possible repercussions of Myers v. United States necessarily to be confined to the field of national administration. What with the growth both in number and complexity of matters requiring governmental regulation and with the expansion of governmental services, the need for the administrative commission "informed by experience" as well as by the special training of its members is an ever increasing one in the field of state and municipal government alike; and the result is that the desirability of guaranteeing such bodies from political manipulation has long since come to be recognized in theory, even if not always in fact. In the measure that the broader propositions of Myers v. United States are calculated to interrupt the fixation of wholesome practice in this respect they are unquestionably to be regretted.

And in this connection, it is pertinent to recall that "scientific ideal" of a government in which questions of "principle" are resolvable into questions of fact, susceptible in turn of determination by the impartial processes of scientific research. The truth is that, in a government such as ours, operating upon the basis of the democratic principle as a fixed and unchallengeable axiom, this ideal is not so far fetched as it is sometimes thought to be; and particularly is it true that the main objectives of government and the main tests of "good government" are generally agreed upon today within the sphere of local government. It is not impossible even that the vexed problem of legal reform may someday owe its solution in part to this ideal and to the type of administrative machinery which today comes nearest to embodying it. More than 300 years ago Bacon properly stigmatized the notion that the truth can be best got at by the species of contest that characterized our courts of law—a contest neither party to which ordinarily desires that the whole truth be brought out, and which is waged under rules of evidence that more often than not cut off the most obvious sources of truth; while, as if to heap absurdity upon absurdity, the final assessment of such evidence as is forthcoming under this procedure is generally left to a body constituted *ad hoc* out of individuals the very grounds of whose *legal* availability are frequently conclusive proof of their *actual* unfitness. Nor is it irrelevant to mention in this same general connection the question of international peace. Disputes among nations more often than not involve issues of concrete fact which, could they be torn from their envelopes of emotion, would prove readily determinable upon agreed principles. In other words, the question of providing peaceable methods of settling controversies among nations is to no slight extent simply the question of providing agencies of investigation which, once they are set up, will be free from all kinds of political pressure.

But indeed the issue of "official independence," as it may be termed, is of far greater reach than is indicated by its reference to the quasi-judicial tribunal, important as that is. To return to the national government, we are faced by this dilemma: on the one hand, the complexity of the administrative tasks put upon it and the consequent difficulty of obtaining that mastery of them which is requisite to successful administration are all the time increasing; on the other hand, as has been pointed out, the heads of departments, upon whom still rests nominally the primary responsibility for discharging the greater part of this growing burden, have become political chiefs and as such are generally chosen less for administrative experience or capacity than for the larger views they represent of governmental policy, or even merely for their fidelity to the political fortunes of their chief. What is the remedy? One is the curtailment of the tasks of government; but if we are to judge the future by the past, it is one on which small dependence should be placed. Another is reorganization of the national departmental administration on the principle which has long been recognized in the British and other governments, that it is not the business of the minister to administer but to direct policy. Concretely, this would mean the creation of permanent under-secretaries, men, who being reasonably assured of a life career in their offices, would become masters of the administrative details of the several departments, and so would be in position at each change of administration to put their accumulated knowledge at the disposal of their new political heads. The benefits of such a reform would ramify in all directions. Changes in administrative policy would not be entered upon in ignorance, nor when entered upon be handicapped by it. The disposition shown by Congress in recent years to create administrative agencies outside of the departmental organization, in the interest of securing their independence from a purely political control, would be abated. The lower grades of the civil service would be toned up immensely by the knowledge that the lowest clerk in it might become a permanent secretary. The civil service would become a career for talent rather than a shelter for mediocrity. (See Ex-Governor Lowden's article {"Permanent Officials in the National Administration of the United States"} in 21 *Am. Pol. Sci. Rev.* 529–36 [August 1927].)

Of course, the ever ready answer to all this is the old cry of "Bureaucracy!" It has some validity without question, but less today than previously, when the example—and competition—of "big business" is a stimulus to efficiency in government as never before. Besides, some of the most serious evils laid at the door of bureaucracy can often be shown rather to be the characteristics of an inexpert administration, ignorant of its own tasks and of the interrelation of its constituent parts—evils such as duplication, overlapping, and the like. Yet again, it must be frankly recognized that when the issue is put today of "bureaucracy" versus "political responsibility," the verdict of thoughtful students of government will by no means be given unqualifiedly in favor of the latter alternative. Which, however, is not to say that political responsibility either can or should be entirely eliminated even in the case of the permanent secretary.

We hear much nowadays about the "breakdown of democracy." What does this phrase signify? Partly it reflects the discontent of certain groups which think that under a regime based upon counting heads they have less weight than they deserve. But a more definite and pause-worthy interpretation of the phrase is furnished by the actual breakdown of political responsibility as a guarantee of good administration. To refer again to the question of legal reform, would any student of it seriously deny either that the crux of this issue is to be found in the unsatisfactory quality of our judges, or that this fact, in turn, is to a great extent explicable by our having transformed the judiciary years ago from a body responsible primarily to itself into a body responsible primarily to the electorate? And if this is so, is there not here a lesson capable of wider application?

In this connection the following passages from Robert MacGregor Dawson's volume on *The Principle of Official Independence* (1922) seem extremely well worth quotation:

> Independence is not a mystical formula that will solve all the problems which confront a modern government; but it does give scope for the development of the positive side of the official's character. Instead of the physical threat of loss of office, independence supplies the moral inducement to do well; in place of distrust, it gives confidence; it calls forth a host of qualities that otherwise might have remained dormant—the official's vanity, his conscience, his desire for applause, his zeal for the public good, his feeling of special fitness for his post, his craftsman's delight in his skill—any one or all of these are given freer play.

He then quotes Faguet's words:

> There is a moral as well as a technical efficiency, and in limiting the independence that is essential to moral efficiency, democracy neutralizes the technical efficiency of its servants. . . . Formerly the magistracy . . . enjoyed an absolute independence. This gave, or rather preserved intact, its moral efficiency. For moral efficiency consists in an ability to act according to the dictates of conscience, and is equivalent to a sort of moral independence.

Elsewhere, referring to certain remarks of Carlyle, Mr. Dawson adds:

> Carlyle thought that he was pointing out the absurdity of democracy; instead of that he was merely showing, what modern experience has confirmed, that the use of skilled officials is an essential condition of a democracy's existence. It is clear that to ascertain the will of the people is not sufficient; there must also be the means to ensure that what they desire will be carried out in the best possible manner. The real democracy demands a subtle combination of election and appointment, of nonexpert minds and expert minds, of control and trust, of responsibility and independence. The size of the modern state and the complexity of our civilization may make it extremely difficult to attain this combination; but the survival of democratic government nevertheless depends on its attainment.

The exclusive emphasis, therefore, which Myers v. United States lays upon political responsibility and its corollary, unqualified removability from office, is, as regards all offices below the strictly political ones, as unfortunate as it was unnecessary.

Again quoting Mr. Dawson: "Removal may vary from a mere formality and simple dismissal in some cases to a long and weary procedure in others, as necessitated by statute, constitutional custom, or both. Its effect on independence is obvious and may be expressed almost algebraically: the more involved and numerous are the formalities of removal, the greater are the opportunities for independence, and in proportion as the process becomes more simple the independence tends to diminish.''

The very simplicity of the Court's solution of an extremely complex question is what above all else condemns it.

One criticism, it must be owned, Myers v. United States does not incur. It at least puts no *legal* obstacles in the way of development by the removal power itself of self-restraining principles favoring official independence. And unquestionably there are cases in which such principles must always be the main reliance—the case of the permanent secretary being an instance. Yet even in such cases, as to which the applicability of the principle of official independence is in general admitted, it would seem unwise to exclude the possibility of the legislature's laying down a procedure of removal calculated to guarantee fair play and publicity. Such degree of legislative intervention would seem to be the minimum that is desirable, for while Congress may create offices, it is happily without the power to appoint to or remove therefrom. It is indeed extravagant to suppose that the tradition of unrestrained political discretion which Myers v. United States endeavors to elevate into constitutional law—a discretion which, as a source of largess, is incessantly the object of solicitation and pressure by selfish interests—can go either so far or so fast without the support of statute as with it.

And so much for the primary issue raised by this notable case. There is, however, a second—and scarcely secondary—reason why a critical study of this decision should be worth while which can be stated very briefly. In Myers v. United States we find the Court discharging its constitutional function with much more than its customary conscientiousness and thoroughness. Examination of the technique displayed by it on this occasion ought therefore to throw unusually instructive light on the institution of judicial review as it operates in the complex conditions of today. The subject is one of the highest interest to all students of our constitutional system.

In closing, a word should be given to the deep concern manifested by Mr. Beck in his oral argument before the Court regarding "the traitor in office." It must be conceded that office is no fit place for a full-blown traitor; but why leave it to the President to do the necessary removing—why not call in the police? I am reminded of the story of an experience of Mr. Morgan Shuster's when he was running things in Persia some years ago. After receiving many complaints that a certain Teheran official was both incompetent and corrupt, he ordered the man removed. He was presently somewhat startled to learn that the official in question had been indeed *removed*—and his head as well!

For leave to reprint the following study, most of which appeared in the April issue of the *Columbia Law Review,* I am indebted to the editors of that publication. I have taken the opportunity, with the kind permission of the Editor of the *National Municipal Review,* to recast the argument at points and to add some

items of new material. The work of revision was materially aided by courtesies
extended by the staff of Williams College library.

                                                                            E. S. C.

I.

In the recently decided case of Myers v. United States[1] a divided Court
pronounced void an act of Congress, which had been on the statute books for
more than fifty years. The provision in question read: "Postmaster of the first,
second, and third classes shall be appointed and may be removed by the President
with the advice and consent of the Senate, and shall hold their offices for four
years unless sooner removed or suspended according to law. . . ."[2] Standing by
itself the disallowance of this measure does not necessarily imply more than that,
so long as Congress chooses to leave the appointment of an inferior executive
officer with the President, acting with the consent of the Senate, it may not make
the officer's removal also dependent on such consent—a rule which, in turn, may
be, and in fact is by the Court, rested on a strict reading of the provision of the
Constitution regarding the vesting of the appointment of "inferior officers" by
act of Congress. But with this comparatively narrow, albeit entirely adequate,
basis for its decision the Court is not content, and in an elaborate opinion by the
chief justice, speaking for the majority of the bench, the broad doctrine is
advanced in further support of the decision, that the President is endowed by
Article II with a power of removal which, so far as executive officers of the

---

1. 47 Sup. Ct. 21, decided Oct. 25, 1926 {272 U.S. 52 (1926)}. I have read the case in the
original printing furnished by the clerk of the Court, in which each opinion is separately paged. Three
of these are quite lengthy. That of the chief justice for the Court runs to fifty-five pages, while the
dissenting opinions of Justices McReynolds and Brandeis attain respectively fifty and forty-four
pages. The latter, however, with its voluminous footnotes in fine type, really contains the greater
amount of matter. Justice Holmes' pithy dissent occupies less than a page.
    The facts of Myers v. United States are stated at the beginning of the chief justice's opinion (47
Sup. Ct. at 22) {272 U.S. 52, at 106}: "Myers, appellant's intestate, was on July 21, 1917, appointed
by the President, by and with the advice and consent of the Senate, to be a postmaster of the first class
at Portland, Oregon, for a term of four years. On January 20, 1920, Myers' resignation was demanded. He refused the demand. On February 2, 1920, he was removed from office by order of the
postmaster general, acting by direction of the President. {On} February 10th, Myers sent a petition to
the President and another to the Senate Committee on Post Offices, asking to be heard, if any charges
were filed. He protested to the department against his removal, and continued to do so until the end of
his term. He pursued no other occupation and drew compensation for no other service during the
interval. On April 21, 1921, he brought suit in the Court of Claims for his salary from the date of his
removal, which, as claimed by supplemental petition filed after July 1, 1921, the end of his term,
amounted to $8,838.71. In August 1920 the President made a recess appointment of one Jones, who
took office September 19, 1920."
    The Court of Claims gave judgment against Myers on the ground that he had delayed unduly in
suing. The case having been twice argued before it, the Supreme Court held that Meyers (sic; Myers)
and his representatives had acted with sufficient promptitude, but affirmed the judgment of the Court
of Claims on the constitutional ground.
    The opinions, as well as briefs and arguments of counsel, have recently been brought together in a
pamphlet, which is published by the government as S. Doc. No. 174, 69th Cong., 2d Sess. (1926).
    2. 19 Stat. 80, 81 (1876), U.S. Comp. Stat. (1916) sec. 7190.

United States are concerned, is not constitutionally susceptible of restraint by Congress. This, as will be seen in an instant, is a very formidable proposition indeed, and to the question of its soundness the present study is directed.

The practical scope of the decision in Myers v. United States when it is viewed in the light of the general reasoning of the Court could not be better set forth than in the following passage from the chief justice's opinion:

> The duties of the heads of departments and bureaus in which the discretion of the President is exercised and which we have described are the most important in the whole field of executive action of the government. There is nothing in the Constitution which permits a distinction between the removal of the head of a department or a bureau, when he discharges a political duty of the President or exercises his discretion, and the removal of executive officers engaged in the discharge of their other normal duties. The imperative reasons requiring an unrestricted power to remove the most important of his subordinates in their most important duties must, therefore, control the interpretation of the Constitution as to all appointed by him.
>
> But this is not to say that there are not strong reasons why the President should have a like power to remove his appointees charged with other duties than those above described. The ordinary duties of officers prescribed by statute come under the general administrative control of the President by virtue of the general grant to him of the executive power, and he may properly supervise and guide their construction of the statutes under which they act in order to secure that unitary and uniform execution of the laws which Article II of the Constitution evidently contemplated in vesting general executive power in the President alone. Laws are often passed with specific provision for the adoption of regulations by a department or bureau head to make the law workable and effective. The ability and judgment manifested by the official thus empowered, as well as his energy and stimulation of his subordinates, are subjects which the President must consider and supervise in his administrative control. Finding such officers to be negligent and inefficient, the President should have the power to remove them. Of course there may be duties so peculiarly and specifically committed to the discretion of a particular officer as to raise a question whether the President may overrule or revise the officer's interpretation of his statutory duty in a particular instance. Then there may be duties of a quasi-judicial character imposed on executive officers and members of executive tribunals whose decisions after hearing affect interests of individuals, the discharge of which the President cannot in a particular case properly influence or control. But even in such a case he may consider the decision after its rendition as a reason for removing the officer, on the ground that the discretion regularly entrusted to that officer by statute has not been on the whole intelligently or wisely exercised. Otherwise he does not discharge his own constitutional duty of seeing that the laws be faithfully executed.[3]

In short, the Constitution permits Congress to vest duties in executive officers in the performance of which they are to exercise their own independent judgment; then it permits the President to guillotine such officers for exercising the very discretion which Congress has the right to require of them![4] Or in still

---

3. 47 Sup. Ct. at 31 {272 U.S. 52 at 134–35}.

4. In both Billings v. United States, 232 U.S. 261 (1914), and Brushaber v. Union Pacific R.R. Co., 240 U.S. 1 (1916), we are assured that the Constitution does not grant power in one clause to withdraw it in another.

different phraseology, whatever measure of discretion Congress may at any time choose to vest in an executive officer or an administrative body in connection with the enforcement of its acts belongs in the last analysis to the President; and even if this is not true as a matter of law, still it is true as a matter of fact.[5]

Still another way of elucidating the practical purport of the Court's doctrine is by confronting it with certain legislation of Congress of the last forty years. Thus by the act of August 24, 1912, "... no person in the classified civil service of the United States shall be removed therefrom except for such cause as will promote the efficiency of said service and for reasons given in writing, and the person whose removal is sought shall have notice of the same and of any charges preferred against him," and shall "be allowed a reasonable time" for answering same. Furthermore, no postal employee shall be reduced in rank or dismissed for joining an organization not imposing the obligation to strike which has for its purpose the improvement of "the condition of labor of its members"; nor may "the right of persons employed in the civil service of the United States, either individually or collectively, to petition Congress or any member thereof, or to furnish information to either house of Congress, or any committee or member thereof ... be denied or interfered with." The general purpose of the act is, obviously, to furnish the rank and file of the national civil service an assurance of security of tenure in addition to that resting on presidential mandate, while the more specific provisos in terms disallow grounds for dismissal which had been previously announced in executive orders.[6]

From somewhat different considerations Congress had much earlier provided that members of the Interstate Commerce Commission should be removable by the President "for inefficiency, neglect of duty, or malfeasance in office."[7] Here the controlling idea was to secure "a tribunal informed by experience" and capable of passing impartially upon issues arising out of the act to regulate commerce between the railroads and the public on the one hand, and between the railroads and shippers on the other—a tribunal whose members would become experts in the vast variety of problems growing out of the intricate relationship of the railways to the social and industrial structure of the nation; and it was rightly felt that neither the impartial outlook not the breadth of knowledge demanded of such a tribunal, if it was to function properly, could be obtained on other terms than comparative security in office. It is true that in the Shurtleff Case[8] the Court found the language employed in this instance to be less effective in curbing the President's power of removal than at first had been supposed; but the case did not

---

5. That is to say, the theory of the law may be that the officer must exercise his own individual discretion (see Butterworth v. United States, 112 U.S. 50 [1884]); but the fact is that under the Court's doctrine in the instant case he invites his official destruction if he does so.

6. 37 Stat. 555 sec. 6 (1912), U.S. Comp. Stat. (1916) sec. 3287. The executive orders referred to were those of Jan. 31, 1902, and Jan. 25, 1906, of President Roosevelt, and those of Nov. 26, 1909, and Apr. 8, 1912, of President Taft. See J. Brandeis' opinion in the instant case, note 34.

7. 24 Stat. 383 sec. 11 (1887), U.S. Comp. Stat. (1916) sec. 8575.

8. Shurtleff v. United States, 189 U.S. 311 (1903).

challenge the power of Congress, by the use of more explicit language, to cure the defect of the act; and in fact, the dignity and authority of the office of interstate commerce commissioner has grown steadily. That this is so is in no way better attested than by the Supreme Court's own altered attitude toward the Commission's finding in recent years.[9]

The need of the administrative expert is, moreover, in modern conditions, an ever increasing one, a situation to which Congress has not been blind. In 1914 Congress created the Federal Trade Commission, in 1916 the Federal Tariff Commission, in 1919 the United States Shipping Board, and in all these cases the members of the commissions hold their posts on the same terms as interstate commerce commissioners.[10] Then, in 1920, in the act creating the Railroad Labor Board, Congress took a further step. In an endeavor to confer upon the members of this body a quasi-judicial status, it provided that they should be removable by the President "for neglect of duty or malfeasance in office, but for no other cause."[11] A similar tenure is bestowed upon the members of the Board of General Appraisers and the Board of Tax Appeals by the acts of 1922 and 1924 respectively.[12]

Meanwhile, in 1921, with the enactment of the Budget and Accounting Act, Congress had inaugurated an almost revolutionary reform in methods of national financial legislation. The act pivots to a considerable extent upon the office of comptroller general of the United States, and the success of the reform unquestionably hinges upon the independence of this functionary from executive pressure. The act accordingly provides that the comptroller general shall hold office for fifteen years, and save upon impeachment shall be removable only by joint resolution of Congress and then only after a hearing which shall establish to Congress' satisfaction his incapacity, inefficiency, neglect of duty or malfeasance, or "conduct involving moral turpitude."[13] Although in its original form, in which it provided for the removal of the comptroller general by "concurrent resolution," the bill was vetoed by President Wilson on the ground that it unconstitutionally limited the presidential power of removal, in the form just given it received the assent of President Harding.[14] It should be added that none of the other measures above mentioned were at any time confronted with either presidential veto or protest.

---

9. See the Court's reference to "a tribunal informed by experience" in Illinois Cent. R. Co. v. Interstate Commerce Commission, 206 U.S. 441, 454 (1907); also in Virginian R. Co. v. United States, 47 Sup. Ct. 110.

10. See 38 Stat. 717–18 sec. 1 (1914), U.S. Comp. Stat. (1916) sec. 8836a; 39 Stat. 795 sec. 700 (1916), U.S. Comp. Stat. (Supp. 1923) sec. 5326a; 41 Stat. 989 sec. 3 (1920), U.S. Comp. Stat. (Supp. 1923) sec. 8146b.

11. 41 Stat. 470 secs. 306–307 (1920), U.S. Comp. Stat (Supp. 1923) secs. 10071 1/4gg, 10071 1/4ggg.

12. 43 Stat. 336–37 sec. 900 (1924), U.S. Comp. Stat. (Supp. 1925) sec. 6371 5/6b.

13. 42 Stat. 23 sec. 303 (1921), U.S. Comp. Stat. (Supp. 1925) sec. 400 4/5aa.

14. 59 *Cong. Rec.* 8609–10 (1920). For an acute criticism of the Wilson veto see Powell, "The President's Veto of the Budget Bill," 9 *National Municipal Rev.* 538 (1920).

But it may possibly be urged that there is a partial escape from the consequences of the Court's reasoning in Myers v. United States in the power of Congress to vest the appointment of "such inferior officers, as they think proper, in the President alone, in the courts of law, or in the heads of departments." The idea is, apparently, illusory. Answering the suggestion that it would be possible for Congress, under this clause, by enlarging the President's power of appointment, to diminish his power of removal the chief justice writes:

> Whether the action of Congress in removing the necessity for the advice and consent of the Senate and putting the power of appointment in the President alone, would make his power of removal in such case any more subject to congressional legislation than before is a question this Court did not decide in the Perkins Case. Under the reasoning upon which the legislative decision of 1789 was put, it might be difficult to avoid a negative answer, but it is not before us and we do not decide it.[15]

The same logic is equally cogent to forbid the notion that by transferring the power of appointment to a head of department the President could be deprived of the power of removal. Such power of removal as was incident to the power of appointment would, of course, go to the head of department exercising the latter power, but the power of removal attributable to the President as an incident of his "executive power" could not be controlled by Congress in the one case any more than in the other.

So our final conclusion must be that the decision in the Myers Case, considered in the light of the reasoning supporting it, endows the President with a power of removal over all executive officers of the United States however appointed, which power Congress cannot control either by transferring it in whole or in part to other organs of government, nor yet by confining its exercise to stated causes. In a word, *the logic of the case renders all executive or administrative officers of the United States removable by the President at will*. It follows that the statutes reviewed above are void, and furthermore, that it would be beyond the power of Congress to attain their general purpose by treating the offices involved as "inferior offices," assuming them to all within that category.

II.

The remainder of this essay will be devoted, first, to examining the reasoning by which the chief justice arrives at his sweeping, not to say destructive, conclusions; and secondly, to setting forth a series of propositions which, in the writer's opinion, come much nearer to doing justice to the subject on the score both of history and of logic.

The only provisions of the Constitution which deal directly with the question of removal as it affects civil officers of the United States are the following:

15. 47 Sup. Ct. at 40 {272 U.S. 52 at 161–62; reference in this paragraph is to United States v. Perkins, 116 U.S. 483 [1886]}.

Article II, section 4, reads, "the President, Vice-President and all civil officers of the United States, shall be removed from office on impeachment for, and conviction of, treason, bribery, or other high crimes and misdemeanors," while section 2 of Article III provides that ". . . the judges, both of the Supreme and inferior Courts, shall hold their offices during good behaviour. . . ." This reticence of the Constitution need not, however, disturb us, for that document is silent on many points as to which we know from the Court's decisions that its intentions are crystal clear, requiring only the projection of the judicial searchlight to discover them.

In the present case the lines of the Constitution between which the majority of the Court found the answer to the question before them lurking were the following: "The executive power shall be vested in a President of the United States of America. . . . he shall nominate, and by and with the advice and consent of the Senate, shall appoint ambassadors, other public ministers and consuls, judges of the Supreme Court, and all other officers of the United States, whose appointments are not herein otherwise provided for, and which shall be established by law: but the Congress may by law vest the appointment of such inferior officers, as they think proper, in the President alone, in the courts of law, or in the heads of departments. . . . he shall take care that the laws be faithfully executed, and shall commission all the officers of the United States."[16]

The dissenting justices assent to the pertinence of these provisions, though not to the majority's application of them; but they also insist upon the relevancy of the following clause which the chief justice's opinion elbows aside almost entirely: "The Congress shall have power . . . to make all laws which shall be necessary and proper for carrying into execution the foregoing powers, and all other powers vested by this Constitution in the government of the United States, or in any department or officer thereof."[17]

The confrontation of the "executive power" of the President with the "necessary and proper" powers of Congress supplies, indeed, the grand issue of the case.[18]

---

16. U.S. Constitution, Art. II, sec. 1(1); sec. 2(2); sec. 3.

17. U.S. Constitution, Art. I, sec. 8(18).

18. It is especially with the necessary and proper clause in mind that Justice Holmes writes (47 Sup. Ct. at 85) {272 U.S. 52 at 177}: "The arguments drawn from the executive power of the President, and from his duty to appoint officers of the United States (when Congress does not vest the appointment elsewhere), to take care that the laws be faithfully executed, and to commission all officers of the United States, seem to me spiders' webs inadequate to control the dominant facts.

"We have to deal with an office that owes it existence to Congress and that Congress may abolish tomorrow. Its duration and the pay attached to it while it lasts depends on Congress alone. Congress alone confers on the President the power to appoint to it and at any time may transfer the power to other hands. With such power over its own creation, I have no more trouble in believing that Congress has power to describe a term of life for it free from any interference than I have in accepting the undoubted power of Congress to decree its end. I have equally little trouble in accepting its power to prolong the tenure of an incumbent until Congress or the Senate shall have assented to his removal. The duty of the President to see that the laws be executed is a duty that does not go beyond the laws or require him to achieve more than Congress sees fit to leave within his power."

III.

The main citadel of the chief justice's argument is his interpretation of what took place in Congress in 1789 in connection with the establishment of the Department of State. As related by him:

> On June 16, 1789, the House resolved itself into a committee of the whole on a bill proposed by Mr. Madison for establishing an executive department to be denominated the Department of Foreign Affairs in which the first clause, after stating the title of the officer and describing his duties, had these words "to be removable from office by the President of the United States." After a very full discussion the question was put: Shall the words 'to be removable by the President' be struck out? It was determined in the negative—yeas 20, nays 34.

Later the objection was raised to the clause "to be removable by the President" that it appeared to represent an attempt by Congress to confer power on the President which perhaps did not otherwise belong to him. In order to meet this objection, the clause was stricken out, and in its place was inserted the clause "whenever the said principal officer shall be removed from office by the President of the United States."[19] Subsequently similar action was taken in reference to the Secretary of the Treasury and the Secretary of War.[20]

From this history the chief justice deduces the following conclusions: first, that

---

With these words should be compared the following passage in which the chief justice (47 Sup. Ct. at 41) {272 U.S. 52 at 163–64} sums up the position of the majority: "Our conclusion on the merits sustained by the arguments before stated is that Article II grants to the President the executive power of the government, i.e., the general administrative control of those executing the laws, including the power of appointment and removal of executive officers, a conclusion confirmed by his obligation to take care that the laws be faithfully executed; that Article II excludes the exercise of legislative power by Congress to provide for appointments and removals except only as granted therein to Congress in the matter of inferior offices; that Congress is only given power to provide for appointments and removals of inferior officers after it has vested and on condition that it does vest their appointment in other authority than the President with the Senate's consent; that the provisions of the second section of Article II, which blend action by the legislative branch, or by part of it, in the work of the executive are limitations to be strictly construed and not to be extended by implication; that the President's power of removal is further established as an incident to his specifically enumerated function of appointment by and with the advice of the Senate, but that such incident does not by implication extend to removals the Senate's power of checking appointments; and finally that to hold otherwise would make it impossible for the President in case of political or other differences with the Senate or Congress to take care that the laws be faithfully executed."

19. 47 Sup. Ct. at 23, 24 {272 U.S. 52 at 112} making various citations to 1 *Annals of Cong.* (Gales & Seaton eds. 1789). There were two printings of the first two volumes of the *Annals*. In the one used by the chief justice the debates and votes bearing upon the removal question will be found in the following columns of the first volume: 368–83, 396, 455–585, 611–14. In the printing which I have used, the same debates and votes are given in the following columns: 383–99, 412, 473–608, 635–38. The discrepancy in columning increases, it will be noted, from fifteen to twenty-four. This clue should enable the reader, without too great difficulty, to trace the references given in the ensuing notes to the corresponding passages in the other printing.

20. Act of Aug. 7, 1789, 1 Stat. 50 sec. 2; act of Sept. 2, 1789, 1 Stat. 65 sec. 7. The act of 1798, establishing the Department of the Navy, on the other hand, omits the clause indicating the President as having the power to remove the Secretary. 1 Stat. 553 (1798). This was probably because of the hostility in Congress to President Adams.

this action of Congress recognized the power both of appointment and of removal as belonging to the President by virtue of the "executive power," except as specifically provided to the contrary in later clauses of Article II; secondly, that it also recognized the power of removal as belonging to the President in virtue of the doctrine that the power of removal is incident to the power of appointment; thirdly, that it established that the Senate cannot claim on constitutional grounds the right to participate in the removal of officers appointed by the President by and with the advice and consent of the Senate; fourthly, that it also established that Congress has no power to diminish the President's power of removal over executive officers of the United States, either by transferring it elsewhere, or by qualifying the removability of such officers. Furthermore the chief justice insists that the action of Congress above described was treated until the passage of the Tenure of Office Act in 1867 by all branches of the government as well as by the overwhelming weight of authority as settling the construction of the Constitution on the points just mentioned, and that it was regarded as doing so not only with reference to superior officers, but also with reference to inferior officers, so long as their appointment was left with the President acting with the consent of the Senate. Are these contentions sound—that is to say, are they sound *historically?* For it is as assertions of historical fact that the chief justice offers them. As such, therefore, they will be examined.[21]

Madison's proposal to vest the President with the power to remove the Secretary of State without concurrence of the Senate produced several shades of opinion in the House which it is necessary to distinguish if we are to obtain an accurate idea of the scope and meaning of "the decision of 1789"—to employ the chief justice's term. Three fairly equal parties eventually disclosed themselves: first, those who believed that the power of removal was the President's alone by the intention of the Constitution; secondly, those who believed, on like grounds, that it belonged to the President acting by and with the advice and consent of the Senate; thirdly, those who held that the Constitution had not settled the question, and that, therefore, it remained for Congress to settle it, by virtue of its powers under the "necessary and proper" clause. A fourth group, comprising apparently only two or three members, were of opinion that impeachment was the only constitutional method of removal.[22]

---

21. The bulk of the opinion is devoted to these propositions; 47 Sup. Ct. at 25–41 {272 U.S. 52 at 114–64}.

22. The three principal groups may be labelled respectively the presidential, the senatorial, and the congressional. Of the presidential party ten spoke, but six others voted, as the ten did, in favor of Benson's two motions. See 1 *Annals of Cong.* cols. 603, 608. The outstanding spokesmen of this group were Madison, Ames, Vining, and Boudinot. The senatorial party furnished seven speakers, the chief of whom were Gerry, Page, Sherman, White, and Stone. Eight others are assignable to this party on the ground just indicated, that they voted as the seven did on Benson's two motions, that is to say, against the first one and in favor of the second one. Of the congressional party seven also were vocal, while nine others followed their lead for the most part in voting for Benson's first motion and against his second motion. As exception was Tucker of Virginia, whose position, however, is revealed by his speech in explanation, *id.* cols. 607–608. The principal speakers of the congressional

Thus less than a third of the membership of the House was at any time of the opinion that the Constitution vested the President alone with the power of removal; while even this fraction were by no means in agreement as to the constitutional basis of the power of removal. Madison, who started out with the idea that the question lay with Congress, Ames of Massachusetts, and Clymer of Pennsylvania, and they alone, argued unambiguously for the proposition that the power was incident to "executive power."[23] But Ames also, as well as Vining of Delaware and Boudinot of New Jersey assigned the power of removal to the President as a part of the appointing power, under section 2 of Article II, the argument being that whereas the Senate is given a *check* on the appointing power, it does not *share* that power.[24] The others who spoke for this party, as indeed some of those just mentioned, relied largely or altogether on the argument from convenience, the implication being that removal by the President would be so obviously expedient at least as to the office under consideration that the Constitution must have intended that he should have the power, certainly in this instance.[25]

In brief, a mere fraction of a fraction, a minority of a minority, of the House, can be shown to have attributed the removal power to the President on the grounds of executive prerogative. And even less secure is the chief justice's second proposition which, stated in his own words, is as follows: "The view of Mr. Madison and his associates was that not only did the grant of executive power to the President in the first section of Article II carry with it the power of removal, but the express recognition of the power of appointment in the second section enforced this view on the well-approved principle of constitutional and statutory construction that the power of removal of executive officers was incident to the power of appointment."[26]

---

party were Hartley, Lawrence, Sedgwick, and Sylvester; but their contention that it was within the power of Congress to determine the location of the removal power was voiced also by Boudinot and Vining of the presidential party, as well as by Madison originally, though he later recanted; and by Sherman of the senatorial party. This is a point of some significance and is dealt with later. Those who expressed themselves as confining the power of removal to the process of impeachment were Smith of South Carolina, Huntington, and Jackson, but the last mentioned seems finally to have lined up with the senatorialists. The speeches of the debates are easily traceable through the index to 1 *Annals of Cong.*

23. *Id.* cols. 397, 479–84, 492–93, 508, 516–17, 561. Clymer was apparently the discoverer of the "executive power" theory. For Madison's original position see *id.* cols. 389, 393–95. It should perhaps be noted that some of those who believed that it was within the power of Congress to determine the location of the removal power, also hold that in the absence of positive action by Congress or otherwise, the power lay with the President. See note 30 below.

24. *Id.* cols. 484, 548, 561. The theory in question is criticized at a later period in this study. The originator in this case was Vining, who, however, states the theory only *arguendo*. Madison too may have availed himself *arguendo* of the theory on one occasion; but his words are cryptic, perhaps due to faulty reporting, col. 569. For his real position see col. 516.

25. See, e.g., Vining, *id.* col. 483; Benson, cols. 525–27; and Goodhue, cols. 554–55.

26. 47 Sup. Ct. at 26 {272 U.S. 52, at 119}. The passage continues thus: "It was *agreed* [my italics] by the opponents of the bill, with only one or two exceptions that as a constitutional principle

It is truly unfortunate that in every inference which it reasonably suggests the passage just quoted is totally misleading. As we have just seen, only three members of the presidential group argued that the appointment clause of section 2 vested the President alone with the power of appointment, while of these only one appealed to the "executive power" clause of section 1. Contrariwise, of those who traced the power of removal to the power of appointment the overwhelming number assigned the latter power, and consequently the former, to the President and Senate jointly.[27] But even more essential is it to note the chief justice's practical objective in this passage. It is made plain in his own words: "The well-approved principle of constitutional and statutory construction that the power of removal of executive officers was incident to the power of appointment." The support of this principle, the chief justice correctly discerns, would enable him to eliminate at one stroke what, as we shall see presently, is the most formidable difficulty in the way of his contention that the decision of 1789 was regarded all but universally, until the unhappy events of Johnson's administration, as fixing the meaning of the Constitution. On purely historical grounds, nevertheless, this advantage must be denied him. Not only in 1789 but ever since, down to October 25, 1926, the idea that the power of removal is an incident of executive power and the idea that it is an incident of the appointing power have generally been regarded as flatly antagonistic propositions, and especially is this true as regards the issue between the President and the Senate.[28]

We come now to the chief justice's third and fourth contentions which together yield the rule of the present case. But however sound this rule may be in other respects, as an historical verdict it is clearly unsound. As we have seen, the act of 1789 received its final shape regarding the matter of removals from majorities in which the champions of presidential prerogative found themselves ranged alternately with those who held that the Constitution was silent on the subject and those who held that it made the Senate participant in the power of removal.[29] Moreover, it is essential that we be on our guard against an assumption, quite natural today and obviously indulged by the chief justice, that a member who believed the Constitution, unaffected by congressional action, to indicate the repository of the power of removal, necessarily concluded that Congress had consequently no power in the premises. Sherman of Connecticut, Boudinot of New Jersey, Vining of Delaware, and Sylvester of New York, the first two of whom had been members of the Philadelphia Convention, certainly took exactly

the power of appointment carried with it the power of removal." The fact is, of course, that the principle just stated was the main point of *disagreement* between the supporters and the opponents of the bill.

27. See references in note 21 above. Ellsworth in the Senate brackets both arguments in support of presidential removal. 3 *Works of John Adams* 409 (C. F. Adams ed. 1850–1856).

28. The principle in question is, of course, serviceable also in enabling the chief justice to recruit votes for his position in the Congress of 1789 itself. {Reference in this paragraph is to Andrew Johnson, seventeenth President of the United States [1865–1869].}

29. 1 *Annals of Cong.* cols. 603, 609.

the opposite view, and there may very well have been others.[30] If, then, the question is, what significance the majority of Congress attributed to the bill in its final form as a reading of the Constitution, the answer must be that at least they did not regard it as settling the question against the Senate in such a sense that Congress could not again unsettle it in the Senate's favor. [31]

But not only does the chief justice deny Congress authority to vest elsewhere the power of removal which he finds lodged in the President by the Constitution, or to give other organs of government a participation therein; what is of much greater importance, he denies that Congress in creating an office may fix its tenure as against this same power. "To Congress," he writes, "under its legislative power is given the establishment of offices, the determination of their functions and jurisdiction, the prescribing of reasonable and relevant qualifications and rules of eligibility of appointees, and the fixing of the term for which they are to be appointed and their compensation—all except as otherwise prevented by the Constitution."[32] By "fixing of the term" the chief justice means, as his language elsewhere makes amply clear, the fixing of the term *beyond* which the appointee may not remain in office, not the term *during* which he shall be entitled to remain in office. As we have seen earlier, the chief justice regards all executive officers of the United States as holding {office?} at the pleasure of the President; and this notwithstanding that Congress may determine the period beyond which an appointee shall *not* hold office, although in so doing it would seem clearly to be limiting the power of appointment, also vested in the President acting with the approval of the Senate, and by specific constitutional grant.[33]

The sins of commission of the chief justice's argument as to this feature of his interpretation of the decision of 1789 are, however, less vital than its sins of

---

30. *Id*. cols. 547–48 (Boudinot), 595 (Vining). In one place Sherman expressed doubt on the point, *id*. col. 559. At the end, however, he wished to see a "general law" made, "declaring the proper mode of removal," *id*. col. 599. For Sylvester's position see cols. 583–84.

31. In *Ex parte* Hennen, 13 Pet. 230, 259 (1839), we find the Court asserting of the debate of 1789, that "no one denied the power of the President and Senate, jointly, to remove." This statement logically implies that all members were in agreement on the proposition that but for the action of Congress, the power of removal as to the Secretary of State would have belonged to the President and Senate jointly. This, however, is clearly erroneous. Madison, Benson, Ames, Boudinot, Vining, and Clymer at least were agreed that if Congress took *no action,* the removal power would in this instance belong to the President alone, though this fact did not put it beyond the power of Congress, to Boudinot and Vining's way of thinking, apparently, to determine the question otherwise.

32. 47 Sup. Ct. at 29 {272 U.S. 52 at 129; it should be noted that the chief justice wrote "provided" where E.S.C. has used "prevented."}.

33. 47 Sup. Ct. at 28–32 {272 U.S. 128–35}. Answering the argument that "the power of appointment and removal cannot arise until Congress creates the office and its duties and powers, and must accordingly be exercised and limited only as Congress shall in the creation of the office prescribe," the chief justice says: "The moment an office and its powers and duties are created, the power of appointment and removal, as limited by the Constitution, vests in the executive." This passage indicates again the confrontation of "executive power" with the "necessary and proper" powers of Congress, at the same time that it also illustrates the Court's confusion of power to *vest* the power of appointment and removal with a power to determine the *tenure* of an office at the time of creating it.

omission. I refer to its almost total neglect of a consideration which unquestionably had with many members the greatest weight in causing them to support the cause of presidential removal, whether on constitutional or other grounds. What this consideration was the following passages from the debate make plain.

Said Benson: "I will instance the officer to which the bill relates. To him will necessarily be committed negotiations with the ministers of foreign courts. This is a very delicate trust. The supreme executive officer, in superintending this department, may be entangled with suspicions of a very delicate nature, relative to the transactions of the officer, and such as from circumstances would be injurious to name. . . ."[34]

Said Vining: "The argument of convenience is strong in favor of the President; for this man is an arm or an eye to him; he sees and writes his secret despatches, he is an instrument over which the President ought to have a complete command. . . . The Departments of Foreign Affairs and War are peculiarly within the powers of the President, and he must be responsible for them; but take away his controlling power, and upon what principle do you require his responsibility?"[35]

Said Sedgwick:

> If expediency is at all to be considered, gentlemen will perceive that this man is as much an instrument in the hands of the President, as the pen is the instrument of the Secretary in corresponding with foreign courts. If, then, the Secretary of Foreign Affairs is the mere instrument of the President, one would suppose, on the principle of expediency, this officer should be dependent upon him. It would seem incongruous and absurd that an officer who, in the reason and nature of things, is dependent on his principal, and appointed merely to execute such business as is committed to the charge of his superior (for this business, I contend, is committed solely to his charge); I say it would be absurd, in the highest degree, to continue such a person in office contrary to the will of the President, who is responsible that the business be conducted with propriety, and for the general interest of the nation.[36]

Said Boudinot:

> If we were not at liberty to modify the principles of the Constitution, I do not see how we could erect an office of foreign affairs. If we establish an office avowedly to aid the President, we leave the conduct of it to his discretion. Hence the whole executive is to be left with him. Agreeably to this maxim, all executive power shall be vested in a President. But how does this comport with the true interest of the United States? Let me ask gentlemen where they suspect danger? Is it not made expressly the duty of the Secretary of Foreign Affairs to obey such orders as shall be given to him by the President? And would you keep in office a man who should refuse or neglect to do the duties assigned him? Is not the President responsible for the administration? He certainly is. How then can the public interest suffer?[37]

34. 1 *Annals of Cong.* col. 525.
35. *Id.* cols. 531–32.
36. *Id.* col. 542.
37. *Id.* cols. 548–49. A similar argument was made for the participation of the Senate. *Id.* cols. 512, 589.

In brief it is *the essential character of the office involved* which stands forth in these passages as constituting the reason for claiming the power of removal for the President, and the President alone, in relation to it. The Secretary of State, it is pointed out, is primarily the instrument of the President, his personal representative, in the diplomatic sphere. For Congress, then, to qualify this officer's removability in any way would mark an intrusion upon an unquestioned field of executive prerogative—the direction of our foreign relations. Of this principal power the power of removal is auxiliary, and for *that* reason, if no other, beyond the reach of Congress.

But "it is a poor rule that won't work both ways." If the character of the office, as determined by its primary duties and functions, suffices to mark certain officers as inherently removable in the view of the Constitution, then the character of other offices ought to mark their incumbents as within the protective power of Congress in creating such offices. Fortunately, we have testimony from the highest source that even those who—a minority of a minority—put the President's power of removal on the loftiest constitutional grounds in 1789, nevertheless recognized that it might be curtailed in certain cases. Precisely one week from the passage of the bill to establish the Department of State, while the bills establishing the treasury and war departments were still pending, we find Madison speaking on the former of these measures as follows:

> The committee has gone through the bill without making any provision respecting the tenure by which the comptroller is to hold his office. I think it is a point worthy of consideration, and shall, therefore, submit a few observations upon it.
>
> It will be necessary to consider the nature of this office, to enable us to come to a right decision on the subject; in analyzing its properties, we shall easily discover they are not purely of an executive nature. It seems to me that they partake of a judiciary quality as well as executive; perhaps the latter obtains in the greatest degree. The principal duty seems to be deciding upon the lawfulness and justice of the claims and accounts subsisting between the United States and particular citizens: this partakes strongly of the judicial character, and there may be strong reasons why an officer of this kind should not hold his office at the pleasure of the executive branch of the government. I am inclined to think that we ought to consider him something in the light of an arbitrator between the public and individuals, and that he ought to hold his office by such a tenure as will make him responsible to the public generally....
>
> Whatever, Mr. Chairman, may be my opinion with respect to the tenure by which an executive officer may hold his office according to the meaning of the Constitution, I am very well satisfied, that a modification by the legislature may take place in such as partake of the judicial qualities, and that the legislative power is sufficient to establish this office on such a footing as to answer the purposes for which it is prescribed.[38]

38. *Id*. cols. 635–36. Later he added: "I question very much whether he [the President] can or ought to have any interference in the settling and adjusting the legal claims of individuals against the United States." And again: "Surely the legislature have the right to limit the salary of any officer; if they have this, and the power of establishing offices at discretion, it can never be said that, by limiting the tenure of an office, we devise schemes for the overthrow of the executive department." *Id*. col. 638.

It is true that Madison followed this argument with a motion to limit the term of the comptroller, while still leaving him removable by the President. His object, he explained, was to make the comptroller responsible all around, rather than to the President exclusively, which could be done by requiring his periodic reappointment. Why, then, did he make the argument just quoted? The answer seems to be that he regarded the decision which had just been made with reference to the Secretary of State as preventing Congress from fixing the tenure of that officer as against *either* the power of appointment or that of removal—assuming them to be distinct powers.[39] This decision, however, he did not consider applicable to the case of the comptroller. That the reasons which he urged against its applicability reached the power of removal no less than the power of appointment was perceived by all his hearers, one of whom raised objection to his motion on that account.[40] It should be added that in a letter written just before the final vote on the removal clause of the bill establishing the state department, Madison had characterized the House debate as dealing with the "question as to the power of removal from offices held during pleasure."[41] Why speak of offices "held during pleasure" if there could be no others?[42]

Madison was moreover, after all, but one member of the House, albeit an important one. Of others whose utterances bore—often obliquely—on the question of the power of Congress to fix the tenure of offices as against the removal power, the great majority clearly recognized such a power.[43] Most of them, to be sure, belonged to the party which also attributed to Congress the right to vest the power of removal where it saw fit, yet not all. Thus we find Sherman, an outstanding member of the senatorial party, using these words: "As the office is the mere creature of the legislature, we may form it under such regulations as we

39. This was still his position in 1820. Writing of the Tenure of Office Act of that year, to Jefferson, under date of Dec. 10, 1820, he said: "The law terminating appointments at periods of four years ... overlooks the important distinction between repealing or modifying the office and displacing the officer. The former is a legislative, the latter an executive function. ... If the principle of the late statute be a sound one, nothing is necessary but to limit appointments held during pleasure to a single year, or the next meeting of Congress, in order to make the pleasure of the Senate a tenure of office instead of that of the President alone." 3 *Letters and Other Writings of James Madison* 196 (1867).

40. "Mr. Benson did not like the object of the motion, because it was, in some measure, setting afloat the question which had already been carried." 1 *Annals of Cong.* col. 638. See also remarks of Stone, Smith, and Sedgwick, *id.* col. 637.

41. Letter to Samuel Johnston (June 21, 1789), 5 *Letters* 409–410n. The letter continues: "Four constructive doctrines have been maintained: 1. that the power is subject to the disposal of the legislature; 2. that no removal can take place otherwise than by impeachment; 3. that the power is incident to that of appointment and therefore belongs to the President and Senate; 4. that the executive power being generally vested in the President every power of an executive nature, not expressly excepted is to be referred thither, and consequently the power of removal, the power of appointment only being taken away."

42. As the words quoted in the text show, Madison's position was considerably less rigid than that of Benson. Said the latter: "The judges hold theirs [offices] during good behavior, as established by the Constitution; all others, during pleasure"—(1 *Annals of Cong.* col. 638)—which is substantially the position of the majority in the case at bar.

43. 1 *Annals of Cong.* cols. 392, 500, 503, 511, 532, 541, 545–46, 584, 596.

please, with such powers and duration as we think good policy requires. We may say that he shall hold his office during good behavior, or that he shall be annually elected. We may say he shall be displaced for neglect of duty, and point out how he shall be convicted of it; without calling upon the President or Senate.''[44] Utterances of opposite tenor are generally interpretable either as relating to the precise officer under discussion, whose removability at pleasure was obviously counseled by the same practical considerations as was the President's having the power to remove him independently of the Senate, or else were by members who held that the Constitution regarded all civil offices as tenable during good behavior.

Summing up the decision of 1789, certain points seem worthy of reiteration and emphasis. This decision related to a high political office, to an office created to be the organ of the President in the principal field of executive prerogative, to an office whose tenure was left indeterminate. Such was the scope of the decision as originally given, though it was immediately afterward extended to the heads of other departments whose powers and duties are of mixed character, being partly instrumental of executive, partly of legislative powers. The precise problem dealt with by the decision was that of the residence of the power of removal of such an officer. In form the decision avoided a direct implication of the exercise by Congress of a discretionary power to *vest* the power of removal in the case being dealt with. On the other hand, the practical result of the decision, to designate the President alone as the custodian of the power of removal in this case, was brought about by a combination in which those who attributed the broadest discretion to Congress outnumbered those who attributed the removal power to the President exclusively on constitutional grounds. Nor did the decision touch the question of the power of Congress in creating an office to determine the tenure thereof, whether by limiting its duration as against the appointing power, or by making it secure as against the removal power, while the trend of the discussion was decidedly favorable to congressional pretensions in this respect, even Madison conceding it as to officers having quasi-judicial duties. Lastly, it should be recalled once more that the theory that the power of removal is an incident of "executive power" was generally regarded as flatly opposed to the theory that it is an incident of the appointing power; that those who held the latter theory generally regarded the President and Senate as sharing the power in the case of officers appointed with the Senate's consent; and that those who held the former theory were a fraction of a fraction, a minority of a minority.

IV.

It was remarked of Dr. Samuel Johnson's controversial methods that "if his pistol missed fire, he knocked you down with the butt of it." So it is apt to be

44. *Id.* col. 511; see also col. 596.

with judges, for what a judge cannot *prove* he can still *decide*. Viewed purely as history, the chief justice's interpretation of the decision of 1789 is without validity. It is not that he has *no* facts on his side; but the "over-plus" from their addition is rather excessive. Nor is it otherwise with his endeavor to show that this interpretation was generally accepted down to the Civil War—that, in other words, the decision of 1789 was generally treated as settling the construction of the Constitution on the points and *in the way* he asserts it to have done. Let us in this connection examine, first, some expressions of opinion which the chief justice reviews in order to show that either they do not controvert his theory or else confirm it; and then, more briefly, some congressional legislation. But to begin with, we must dispose of a preliminary although related question.

The question of the proper *interpretation* of the decision of 1789 is conceivably one thing—that of its *finality* another. To what extent did the Congress that produced it regard this decision—all questions of interpretation aside—as *final?* As we have noted before, of those who wished to see the President in possession of the power of removal, more than half did so on grounds purely of expediency. But a decision resting on considerations of expediency may certainly be modified or reversed on the like ground; nor may a legislature curtail the purely legislative freedom of its successors. On the other hand, spokesmen of all contingents conceded that whatever reading Congress gave the Constitution would be subject to judicial review and correction.[45] Madison, however, contended for the view "that the meaning of the Constitution" on the point in issue might "as well be ascertained by the legislature as by judicial authority," that is, ascertained in a way to bind the other organs of government. The ground of his contention was that the question concerned marked out "the limits of the powers of the several departments"; and he asserted: "If the constitutional boundary of either be brought into question, I do not see that any one of these independent departments has more right than another to declare their sentiments on that point."[46] This opinion may be sound or unsound. If it is sound, it leaves the present intervention of the Court in a field in which Congress has at least an equal right to construe the Constitution without justification.[47] If it is unsound, then the authority of the decision of 1789 was always, in theory, contingent on its being the true reading of the Constitution, a question obviously demanding to be determined on other grounds than the mere fact of the decision having been made.

The first witness whom the chief justice summons in his behalf is Alexander Hamilton. In *Federalist,* no. 77, we find Hamilton declaring without qualifica-

45. Most of those who urged the claims of judicial review belonged to the senatorial group. *Id.* cols. 477, 485, 489, 492, 524, 529, 539, 557–58, 572, 596. But some of the congressionalist group also admitted the revisionary power of the judiciary, *id.* cols. 496, 585, as did also Baldwin of the presidential group, *id.* col. 582.

46. *Id* col. 568; also cols. 514 and 520–21. Boudinot and Stone agreed with Madison, as also apparently did Benson. *Id.* cols. 488, 511, 525. Hartley was of opinion that the judges would sustain what Congress did, *id.* col. 505.

47. This question is considered briefly at the close of this article.

tion that the consent of the Senate "would be necessary to displace as well as to appoint" officers, and commending this feature of the Constitution as contributing to the stability of the administration. Naturally the chief justice is concerned to break the force of such eminent testimony, which he attempts to do by bringing forward Hamilton's argument in 1793 that "the Constitution by vesting the 'executive power' in the President gave him the right, as the organ of intercourse between the nation and foreign nations, to interpret national treaties and to declare neutrality." The chief justice then proceeds: "He [Hamilton] deduced this from Article II of the Constitution on the executive power, and followed exactly the reasoning of Madison and his associates as to the executive power upon which the legislative decision of the first Congress as to presidential removals depends, and he cites it as authority."

In short, the contention is that Hamilton "changed his view of this matter," that is, of the residence of the power of removal. But did he? In this connection, the following words, quoted by the chief justice himself, from Hamilton's *Letters of Pacificus* of 1793, are of critical importance:

> The general doctrine of our Constitution then is, that the executive power of the nation is vested in the President; subject only to the exceptions and qualifications, which are expressed in the instrument.
>
> Two of these have already been noticed; the participation of the Senate in the appointment of officers, and in the making of treaties. A third remains to be mentioned; the right of the legislature to "declare war and grant letters of marque and reprisal."
>
> With these exceptions, the executive power of the United States is completely lodged in the President.[48]

So far, therefore, was Hamilton from holding in 1793 that the appointing power was an exclusive prerogative of the President, that he held exactly the contrary. Thus he speaks of "the *participation* of the Senate in the appointment of officers," and of its "*cooperation*" therein—the latter being, indeed, his very expression in the *Federalist*. If, then, he still held, as he did in 1789—and the chief justice adduces no evidence to the contrary—that the power of removal is incident to the power of appointment, which the chief justice himself characterizes as a "well-approved principle of constitutional and statutory construction," then his position in 1793 was exactly identical with his position in 1789. His alleged change of mind remains highly doubtful, to say the least.

What, on the other hand, of Madison? Madison, as we have already learned, is the chief justice's chief reliance. Did he, then, stick by his guns? If he had, it would have marked a unique chapter in a history which abounds in feats of right-about-face. But in fact he did not. Implored by Jefferson to enter the lists

---

48. 7 *Works of Alexander Hamilton* 76 *et seq*. (J. C. Hamilton ed. 1850–1851) quoted by the chief justice in 47 Sup. Ct. at 32–33 {272 U.S. 52 at 138–39; A. Hamilton, *The Letters of Pacificus and Helvidius (1845) with the Letters of Americanus* 10–11 (1976); In the Epilogue below, the editor of this volume discusses Corwin on Alexander Hamilton and the President's removal power}.

with Pacificus on the question of the right of the President to declare neutrality and "to cut him to pieces in the face of the public," he promptly complied with the *Letters of Helvidius,*[49] in which the entire argument significantly ignores the general grant of "executive power" in the opening clause of Article II. While the chief justice is aware of the *Letters of Pacificus,* he makes no reference to the answering *Letters of Helvidius.*[50]

But perhaps the most formidable difficulty in the way of the chief justice's thesis that the decision of 1789 was deemed to have the scope he claims for it is to be found in the case of Marbury v. Madison.[51] Marbury had been appointed, with the consent of the Senate, to be justice of the peace in the District of Columbia under a statute which defined the term of the office as five years and made no provision concerning removal. Sustaining Marbury's contention that he was entitled to the delivery of his commission, which had been signed by the President and sealed by the Secretary of State, Chief Justice Marshall said: "Where an officer is removable at the will of the executive, the circumstance which completes his appointment is of no concern; because the act is at any time revocable; and the commission may be arrested, if still in the office. But when the officer is not removable at the will of the executive, the appointment is not revocable, and cannot be annulled. It has conferred legal rights which cannot be resumed."

Chief Justice Taft spends some three pages in an endeavor to show that Marbury v. Madison is not "authority" on the point covered by this quotation.[52] No doubt he is right, but of what avail is that to him? The important question is whether the decision of 1789 was interpreted by so great a constitutional authority as Chief Justice Marshall as preventing Congress from fixing the tenure of inferior offices appointed with the consent of the Senate, with the result of rendering them irremovable, and it is obvious from the above quotation that he did not so interpret it. Nor does the extract which the chief justice reproduces from the fifth volume of Marshall's *Life of Washington,* giving an account of the debate of 1789, prove that the great chief justice later changed his mind on that

49. 6 *Writings of James Madison* 138 *et seq.* (Hunt ed. 1900–1910).

50. Referring to "the power of removal from office, which appears to have been ajudged to the President by the laws establishing the executive departments," Madison says further: "No analogy, or shade of analogy, can be traced between a power in the supreme officer responsible for the faithful execution of the laws, to displace a subaltern officer employed in the execution of the laws; and a power to make treaties and to declare war." He then charges Hamilton with borrowing his idea of "executive power" from British commentators on royal prerogative. In the case at bar the chief justice refers without apology to the prerogative of the British crown, 47 Sup. Ct. at 25, 26 {272 U.S. 52 at 118?}. See below p. 353.

It must, of course, be conceded the chief justice, in light of the utterance quoted in note 39, above, that Madison in 1820 was of opinion that the decision of 1789 applied to all purely executive officers appointed with the consent of the Senate; but it should also be recalled that he interpreted that decision to forbid Congress to fix the term beyond which an officer should not hold as well as the term during which he should be secure in office.

51. 1 Cranch 137 (1803).

52. 47 Sup. Ct. at 33–34 {272 U.S. 52 at 139–43}.

point. The extract concludes with the words: "As the bill passed into a law, it has ever been considered as a full expression of the sense of the legislature on this important part of the American Constitution."[53] Chief Justice Taft evidently deems these words as voicing strong approval of the decision of 1789. To me they seem wholly colorless of either approval or censure, as Marshall's account of the entire debate was evidently intended to be. And whether they are so or not, they certainly shed no light on their author's interpretation of that decision, while the dictum in Marbury v. Madison does exactly that. Besides, Marshall was not the whole Court which rendered the decision of Marbury v. Madison. Another member was Justice William Patterson (sic; Paterson), first a member of the Philadelphia Convention, and then one of the ten senators who voted in favor of the President's having the power of removal, when the bill to establish the state department came up to the Senate from the House.[54] Obviously these positions were irreconcilable if the chief justice's interpretation of the decision of 1789 is correct.

Nor should one overlook in connection with Marbury v. Madison the support which Marshall's opinion lends to the principle that it is the character of the office which determines whether the officer is removable at will by the President. The passage alluded to reads as follows:

> By the Constitution of the United States, the President is invested with certain important political powers, in the exercise of which he is to use his own discretion, and is accountable only to his country in his political character and to his own conscience. To aid him in the performance of these duties, he is authorized to appoint certain officers, who act by his authority, and in conformity with his orders. In such cases their acts are his acts; and whatever discretion may be used, still there exists and can exist no power to control that discretion. The subjects are political. They respect the nation, not individual rights, and, being entrusted to the executive, the decision of the executive is conclusive. The application of this remark will be perceived by adverting to the act of Congress for establishing the Department of Foreign Affairs. This officer as his duties were prescribed by that act, is to conform precisely to the will of the President. He is the mere organ by whom that will is to be communicated. The acts of such an officer can never be examined by the courts.[55]

The office of justice of the peace in the District of Columbia, on the other hand, was a very different sort of office; and the consequence of the difference was that an incumbent, though appointed by the President with the advice and consent of the Senate, could be validly clothed with security of tenure.

The other principal authorities quoted by Chief Justice Taft are Kent, Story, and Webster. None of them sustains him in his theory either of the irreversibility or of the scope of the decision of 1789. Kent says that the decision "amounted to a legislative construction of the Constitution" and says that it has been so long

53. 5 Marshall, *Life of Washington* 200 (2d ed. 1850).
54. 3 *Works of John Adams* 412, n.3 (C. F. Adams ed. 1850–1856).
55. 1 Cranch 165–66.

acquiesced in that "it may now be considered as firmly and definitely settled." He also praises "the good sense and practical utility in the construction." At the same time he points out that it rests on a "loose incidental declaratory opinion of Congress" and the practice of government since then, and that "the question has never been made the subject of judicial discussion." Also, "it applies equally to every other officer of government appointed by the President and Senate *whose term of duration is not specially declared.*"[56]

One of the passages quoted by the chief justice from Story's *Commentaries* is the following:

> If there has been any aberration from the true constitutional exposition of the power of removal (which the reader must decide for himself), it will be difficult, and perhaps impracticable, after forty years' experience, to recall the practice to correct theory. But, at all events, it will be a consolation to those who love the Union, and honor a devotion to the patriotic discharge of duty, that in regard to "inferior officers" (which appellation probably includes ninety-nine out of a hundred of the lucrative offices in the government), the remedy for any permanent abuse is still within the power of Congress, by the simple expedient of requiring the consent of the Senate to removals in such cases.[57]

Another section of the *Commentaries* makes it fairly clear that Story himself regarded the "true constitutional exposition of the power of removal" to be that which treats it as incident to the power of appointment,[58] while he leaves no room for doubt that in his view this theory of the power of removal is absolutely antagonistic to the theory that it is an attribute of the "executive power." Nor, as the words above quoted show, did he question the constitutional right of Congress to review the decision of 1789, though to do so would be "difficult," "perhaps impracticable." Yet even with this decision standing, Congress might still require the consent of the Senate to removals in the case of inferior offices. That is to say, Story did not interpret the decision in question as extending to such offices.[59]

With regard to Webster the chief justice's opinion reads in part, as follows:

> In a speech, May 7, 1834, on the President's protest, Mr. Webster asserted that the power of removal, without the consent of the Senate, was in the President alone, according to the established construction of the Constitution, and that Duane's dismissal could not be justly said to be a usurpation. A year later, in February 1835, Mr. Webster seems to have changed his views somewhat, and in support of a bill requiring the President in making his removals from office to send to the Senate his reasons therefor, made an extended argument against the correctness of the decision of 1789. He closed his speech thus: "But I think the decision of 1789 has been established by practice, and recognized by subsequent laws, as the settled construction of the Constitution, and that it is our duty to act upon the case accordingly for

56. 1 Kent, *Comm.* *310; italics mine. See also 47 Sup. Ct. at 35, 36 {272 U.S. 52 at 150}.
57. 2 Story, *Comm.* sec. 1544, quoted in 47 Sup. Ct. at 36.
58. *Id.* sec. 1539. See also sec. 405 and accompanying note.
59. It should be noted that Story wrote with the Tenure of Office Act of 1820 in mind, which made important categories of inferior offices, offices with fixed terms.

the present; without admitting that Congress may not, hereafter, if necessity shall require it, reverse the decision of 1789.''

In short, Webster's position on the question of the *finality* of the decision of 1789 was that, so long as this decision stood, the President should not be charged with usurpation for having acted under it, but he refused to concede that Congress could not reverse the said decision.[60]

But it is also worth while inquiring what *scope* Webster gave the decision of 1789. As the chief justice notes, Webster delivered his speech on the appointing and removing power in support of a bill requiring the President in making removals to send the Senate his reasons therefor. What he overlooks is Webster's contention that the bill was entirely harmonious with the decision of 1789 as a reasonable regulation by Congress of the tenure of offices. That is to say, Webster did not regard the decision of 1789 as in any wise affecting Congress' power to legislate upon this subject. A salient passage from his speech dealing with the point is the following:

> The regulation of the tenure of office is a common exercise of legislative authority, and the power of Congress in this particular is not at all restrained or limited by anything in the Constitution, except in regard to judicial officers. All the rest is left to the ordinary discretion of the legislature. Congress may give to offices which it creates (except those of judges) what duration it pleases. When the office is created and is to be filled, the President is to nominate the candidate to fill it; but when he comes into the office, he comes into it upon the conditions and restrictions which the law may have attached to it.

"If Congress," he continued, "were to declare by law that the attorney general, or the Secretary of State should hold office during good behavior," its action might be unwise, but it would not be unconstitutional.[61] On the question of the

---

60. 47 Sup. Ct. at 37 {272 U.S. 52 at 151}; 7 *Writings and Speeches of Daniel Webster* 103, 198 (1903). In the later speech, which was devoted to the appointing and removing power, Webster also used this language: "I must still express my own conviction that the decision of Congress in 1789, which separated the power of removal from the power of appointment, was founded on an erroneous construction of the Constitution, and that it has led to great inconsistencies, as well as to great abuses . . ." (at 194); and again "I believe it to be within the just power of Congress to reverse the decision of 1789" (at 196). Chief Justice Taft also notes Webster's denial "that the vesting of the executive power in the President was a grant of power. It amounted, he said, to no more than merely naming the department." (Cf. Webster, *Writings and Speeches* 186–88.) Such a construction, the chief justice argues, is not in accord with that canon of interpretation "which requires that real effect should be given to all the words it uses," citing Hurtado v. California, 110 U.S. 513, 534, and other cases. Mr. Webster's view, however, does not seem to be widely different from that which was formerly expressed by Mr. Taft himself in his *Our Chief Magistrate and His Powers* (see *id.* at 139–40), and which is noted above. The history of the "executive power" clause in the Convention certainly does not support the idea that it was intended as a grant of power. See {Author's} Note at end of this essay; also note 92 below. Recurring for a moment to Webster's speech, we find him meeting the much stressed argument from convenience in support of executive prerogative with the query, "Why, then, did they (the framers) leave their intent in doubt? *Why did they not confer the power in express terms?* Why were they thus totally silent on a point of so much importance?" 7 Webster, *Writings and Speeches* 195.

61. There is more to the same effect. Webster, 7 *Writings and Speeches* 196–99.

meaning of the decision of 1789, no less than on the question of its *finality*, the testimony of Webster is directly against the chief justice's position.

Next, in his review of opinion anterior to the Civil War and of legislation giving rise to the case at bar, the chief justice appeals to the case of *Ex parte Hennen,*[62] which was decided in 1839, and in which he says, "the prevailing effect of the legislative decision of 1789 was fully recognized." The question at issue was the right of a district judge of the United States to remove at his own mere pleasure a clerk appointed by him under the Judiciary Act of 1789 for no stated term. Counsel for the displaced incumbent urged that the latter, having been appointed to an inferior office for an *indefinite* term, must be recognized, in accordance with principles of the common law, to have a vested right to his office, from which accordingly he was removable only for good cause and by judicial process. The Supreme Court rejected the argument for the proposition that "all offices the tenure of which is not fixed by the Constitution or limited by law" must be regarded as "subject to removal at pleasure," which meant in this case removal at the pleasure of the judge, it being, "in the absence of all constitutional provision or statutory regulation, a sound and necessary rule to consider the power of removal as incident to the power of appointment." The justice then alludes to the decision of 1789 in the following words:

> The great question was whether the removal was to be by the President alone, or with the concurrence of the Senate, both constituting the appointing power. No one denied the power of the President and Senate jointly to remove when the tenure was not fixed by the Constitution, which was a full recognition of the principle that the power of removal was incident to the power of appointment. But it was early adopted as the practical construction of the Constitution that this power was vested in the President alone. And such would appear to have been the legislative construction of the Constitution.

Later the opinion characterizes this as "the settled and well-understood construction of the Constitution."

As in Story's *Commentaries,* so here it is strongly implied that the correct theory of the power of removal is that which assimilates it to the appointing power; also that this theory would deny the power to the President alone in the case of officers appointed with the consent of the Senate. Nor is there any implication that Congress might not reverse the decision of 1789 in favor of the correct theory, though it is inferred that the Court itself would not venture to disturb that decision. Also, while the common law doctrine of estate in office is rejected, it is nevertheless assumed that, as Webster had contended, the power to remove an officer is always contingent on legislation defining the tenure of the office involved.

Of acts of Congress having interpretative value as regards the decision of 1789, we may first note the Tenure of Office Act of May 15, 1820. This provided

62. 13 Pet. 225 (1839). See also note 31 above.

that "district attorneys, collectors of the customs," etc., should be "appointed for the term of four years," but should "be removable from office at pleasure."[63] The act thus implies either that the decision of 1789 did not prevent Congress from fixing the terms of inferior officers appointed by the President with the advice of the Senate as against the power of appointment and so, in the contemporary view of Madison at least, as against the power of removal; or else that it was reversible by Congress. Also the act implies that where the term of an officer was fixed by Congress the power of removal must be provided for specifically or did not exist. The phrase "shall be removable from office at pleasure," when considered in light of the debate of 1789, must be regarded as language of direct delegation of power.

Even more to the point is a series of acts regarding the tenure of officers, and especially of judges, in the territories and the District of Columbia. The first such act was that of August 7, 1789, providing for the government of the Northwest Territory.[64] This statute directed that the appointment of all territorial officers should be by the President acting with the advice and consent of the Senate, but specifically vested the President with the power of removal of such officers except the three judges provided for in the act, whose commissions were to "continue in force during good behavior." Subsequent acts providing for the government of the territory south of the Ohio River (1790) and for the organization of the territories of Indiana (1800), of Michigan (1805), and of Illinois (1809) all endowed the judges of those territories with the same tenure. As late as 1836 Congress provided in the act establishing the territorial government of Wisconsin that the judges of that territory should "hold their offices during good behavior," although in the meantime by the act of 1804 it had provided that the judges of the Louisiana territory should hold for only four years.[65]

The earliest courts in the District of Columbia were established under the act of February 27, 1801, which authorized three judges to be appointed by the President with the consent of the Senate "to hold their respective offices during good behavior." The same act also provided for a marshall to serve for a term of four years but to be subject to removal at pleasure; a district attorney without definite term, and "such number of discreet persons to be justices of the peace as the President of the United States shall from time to time consider expedient to serve for a term of five years."[66] It was under this clause that the case of Marbury v.

---

63. 3 Stat. 582 (1820).

64. 1 Stat. 50, 53 (1789).

65. Justice McReynolds' opinion, 47 Sup. Ct. at 57–58 {272 U.S. 52 at 213}: The chief justice makes the statement, 47 Sup. Ct. at 38 {272 U.S. 52 at 155}, that in the face of this legislation there were "between 1804 and 1867 . . . ten removals of such judges in Minnesota, Utah, Washington, Oregon, and Nebraska." As a matter of fact, none of these territories was organized before 1848. See United States v. Guthrie, 17 How. 284, 303 (1854) in which the Court evaded the issue presented by such a removal.

66. 2 Stat. 103.

Madison[67] arose. It should be added that good behavior has always remained the tenure of all superior District of Columbia judges.

It is not impossible that, as Chief Justice Taft conjectures, Congress at first assimilated judges appointed for the territories and for the District of Columbia to those appointed under Article III. Even so, this theory will not account for the claim of Congress to place territorial and District of Columbia judges beyond the power of removal after that date. As a matter of fact the chief justice in the end declines to decide whether Congress may provide for the removal of such a judge in some other way than by the President alone.[68] The question thus arises whether the reasoning of the opinion logically extends to such a case.

If the chief justice had been content to attribute the power of removal to the President on the score of his executive power alone, then it would have been logical to hold that such power of removal existed only as to executive officers, although even then a difficulty would have existed from the fact that early territorial judges exercised executive and legislative as well as judicial functions. But in claiming the power of removal for the President as incident to the power of appointment the chief justice has closed this door of escape from the logic of his argument. If the power of appointment belongs to the President alone in the case of officers appointed with the consent of the Senate, and if the power of removal is an incident of this power, then it follows that the President is vested by the Constitution with the power of removal of all officers appointed by him with the consent of the Senate, whether they be executive officers or judicial officers. Nor is there any reason for holding that this power of removal should stand in a different relation to the power of Congress to fix the tenure of an office than does that power of removal which is attributable to the President as an incident of his "executive power." The long course of legislation, therefore, fixing the terms of territorial and District of Columbia judges is, on the chief justice's own premises, available to prove that the decision of 1789 was not regarded, and indeed never has been regarded by Congress itself, as inhibiting it from fixing the tenure of an office as against the power of removal.

Summing up, then, opinion anterior to the Civil War regarding the decision of 1789, the following contentions seem fairly secure. The decision was not regarded either as embracing officers with fixed term, or as affecting Congress' right to fix official terms, except perhaps those of certain principal offices standing in a peculiarly close relation to the "political powers" of the President. And while it *was* regarded as determining the question of the residence of the power of removal *when such power existed* in favor of the President as against the Senate, yet even in this respect it was held to rest on grounds of expediency and to be at the expense of correct theory. And being at the expense of correct theory,

67. See note 51 above.
68. 47 Sup. Ct. 39 {272 U.S. 52 at 157–58}.

it was not beyond the power of Congress to reverse, although reversal might for various reasons be "impracticable."

V.

What were the literary sources of the chief justice's interpretation of the decision of 1789? The principal elements of it were brought together for the first time in the following passage from Jackson's famous Protest of April 15, 1834:

> By the Constitution "the executive power is vested in a President of the United States." Among the duties imposed upon him . . . is that of "taking care that the laws be faithfully executed." Being thus responsible for the entire action of the executive department, it was but reasonable that the power of appointing, overseeing, and controlling those who execute the laws . . . should remain in his hands. . . . The executive power vested in the Senate is neither that of "nominating," nor "appointing." It is merely a check upon the executive power of appointment. . . . The whole executive power being vested in the President . . . it is a necessary consequence that he should have a right to employ agents of his own choice . . . and to discharge them when he is no longer willing to be responsible for their acts. In strict accordance with this principle, the power of removal, which like that of appointment, is an original executive power, is left unchecked by the Constitution in relation to all executive officers, for whose conduct the President is responsible, while it is taken from him in relation to judicial officers, for whose acts he is not responsible. In the government from which many of the fundamental principles of our system are derived the head of the executive department originally had power to appoint and remove at will all officers, executive and judicial.[69]

The indebtedness of the Chief Justice's opinion to this document appears at every turn. Bridging the temporal gap between the two, however, are various opinions of attorneys general. It is not the kind of source to be taken too seriously. The attorney general is the family lawyer of the administration in power, and it is his business to make out as good a legal case as possible for what the head of the family wants to do. Nor, in fact, does it appear on careful examination that the real preponderance of opinion from this source supports the chief justice's case, but rather the contrary.[70]

---

69. 3 Richardson, *Messages and Papers of the Presidents* 79–80 (1903–1905).

70. The chief justice cites 4 *Op. Att'y Gen.* 1, 603 (1852); 5 *id.* 288 (1852); 6 *id.* 4 (1871). The following comment in a note to Justice Brandeis' dissenting opinion, 47 Sup. Ct. at 84, n. 81 {272 U.S. 52 at n. 81}, surveys this field of doctrine quite adequately: "Attorneys General Legaré, Clifford, and Crittenden seem to have been of the opinion that the President possessed an absolute power of removal. 4 *Op. Att'y Gen.* 1, 603 (1852); 5 *Op. Att'y Gen.* 288 (1852). Legaré, however, having occasion to consider Story's contention that the power of removal might be restricted by legislation with respect to inferior officers, said that he was 'not prepared to dissent from any part of this sweeping proposition.' 4 *Op. Att'y Gen.* 165, 166 (1852). In 1818 Attorney General Wirt in holding that where an act of Congress gave the President power to appoint an officer, whose tenure of office was not defined, that officer was subject to removal by the President, said: 'Whenever Congress intend a more permanent tenure (during good behavior, for example,) they take care to express that intention clearly and explicitly. . . .' 1 *Op. Att'y Gen.* 212, 213 (1852). Following the

New vitality was imparted to the "presidential theory" of the removal power by the debate which was stirred by the Tenure of Office Act of 1867, a measure which endeavored to transfer the power of removal with respect to the President's Cabinet from the President alone to the President and Senate.[71] Nor should the arguments developed by President Johnson's counsel at the time of his impeachment trial be overlooked in this connection. Yet even these gentlemen for the most part contented themselves with asserting that Johnson, assuming that he had violated the Tenure of Office Act, had acted in good faith and with a view to bringing the question into court, not that he had, beyond peradventure, acted constitutionally.[72] Lastly, efforts extending through nearly a decade to obtain the complete repeal of the Tenure of Office Act also doubtless served to advertise the presidential point of view.[73]

Notwithstanding all which, the chief justice's opinion in the case at bar finds surprisingly little support in anything that the Court itself has previously said with regard to the power of removal. The chief justice cites the following cases subsequent to the Civil War: United States v. Perkins, 116 U.S. 483 (1886); McAllister v. United States, 141 U.S. 174 (1891); Parsons v. United States, 167 U.S. 324 (1897); Shurtleff v. United States, 189 U.S. 311 (1903). While in all these cases the Court manifests some reluctance to come to grips with the direct question of the scope of Congress' power in relation to the removal of officers appointed with the advice and consent of the Senate, their further implication is decidedly against the extreme propositions of the case at bar.

---

passage of the Tenure of Office Act the subject was considered by Attorney General Evarts, who disposed of the problem 'within the premises of the existing legislation.' 12 *Op. Att'y Gen.* 443, 449 (1870). In 1873 Attorney General Akerman refused to concede the President a power of removal in that under that act he was limited to a power of suspension. 13 *Op. Att'y Gen.* 300 (1873). In 1877 Attorney General Devens concurred in the provisions of the Tenure of Office Act restoring a suspended officer to his office upon the failure of the Senate to act upon the confirmation of his successor. 15 *Op. Att'y Gen.* 375 (1880)."

For censure by Mr. Taft himself of a too complaisant opinion of an attorney general in support of the policy of his presidential master, see *Our Chief Magistrate and His Powers* 127–28 (1916).

71. While Johnson's veto message strongly asserted the irreversibility of the decision of 1789 as respects the *location of the removal power,* it is worth while noting that he expressed no opinion regarding the power of Congress *in fixing the tenure of office,* except what is implied in his observation at the outset that the bill related to "officers whose terms of service are not limited by law," and his quotation with apparent approval of Kent's statement that the decision of 1789 applied to all officers appointed by the President "whose term of duration is not specially declared." It cannot, therefore, be asserted that Johnson himself held executive officers to be inherently removable; and this is significant since he had excellent legal advice and unquestionably chose what seemed at the time the strongest position open to him. 6 Richardson, *Messages and Papers* 492 *et seq.* (1903–1905).

72. See the arguments of Curtis, Groesbeck, and Evarts. 1 *Trial of Andrew Johnson* 387–92; 2 *id.* 202, 206–207, 217, 320–21, 341 *et seq.,* 347 *et seq.* (1868). For a more extreme claim, approximating the doctrine of Jackson's Protest, as well as that of the Court in the instant case, see Senator Fowler's opinion, 2 *id.* 199, wherewith compare Senator Trumbull's terse but accurate statement, *id.* 320.

73. 47 Sup. Ct. at 43 {272 U.S. 52 at 168?}.

In the Perkins Case, Congress' power by law to "limit and restrict the power of removal as it deems best for the public interest" is sustained in the case of inferior officers appointed by the heads of departments, while the power of removal is clearly assumed always to be an incident to the power of appointment. The case thus directly negatives the idea of an outstanding "executive" power of removal in the President in relation to inferior officers whose appointment has been vested elsewhere by act of Congress. In the McAllister Case, as Justice McReynolds' opinion in the case at bar points out, a line of argument is pursued which "would have been wholly unnecessary if the theory now advanced, that the President has illimitable power to remove, had been approved." In the Parsons Case, the decision of 1789 is again characterized as a "practical construction" of the Constitution. Furthermore, the whole difficulty of the case arose from the assumption that when an office is created with a definite term, the power of removal is nonexistent. From a close construction, however, of the statute before the Court considered as a whole this assumption was held not to apply as to the provision of it which was immediately involved in the case. "We are satisfied," said the Court, "that its [Congress'] intention in the repeal of the Tenure of Office sections of the Revised Statutes was again to concede to the President the power of removal which was taken from him by the original Tenure of Office Act, and by reason of the repeal to thereby enable him to remove an officer when in his discretion he regards it for the public good, although the term of office may have been limited by the words of the statute creating the office." Congress' intention, not constitutional considerations, determined the case.

Finally, in the Shurtleff Case, it was held that an act which provided that an officer without fixed term might "be removed from office at any time by the President for inefficiency, neglect of duty, or malfeasance in office" should be interpreted not as confining the President's power of removal to the causes stated but only as providing that if removal was sought for one of such causes, "the officer is entitled to notice and a hearing." The contrary contention, said the Court, is based on the maxim *expressio unius est exclusio alterius;* but it answered as follows: "We are of opinion that as thus used the maxim does not justify the contention of the appellant. We regard it as inapplicable to the facts herein. The right of removal would exist if the statute had not contained a word upon this subject. It does not exist by virtue of the grant, but it inheres in the right of appointment unless limited by Constitution or statute. It requires plain language to take it away."

Also should be noted the implication here, that the power of appointment belongs to the President alone even in the case of officers appointed with the consent of the Senate. For the rest, Justice McReynolds' comment upon the language just quoted seems entirely just: "The distinct recognition of the right of Congress to require notice and hearing if removal were made for any specific cause is, of course, incompatible with the notion that the President has illimitable power to remove. And it is well to note the affirmation that the right of removal inheres in the right to appoint.''[74]

The chief justice also relies on the venerability of the decision of 1789. But just how venerable is the chief justice's version of this decision regarded as authoritative, rather than merely casual or partisan, view of the Constitution? Even as recently as 1916 we find Mr. Taft himself writing, anent Mr. Roosevelt's ''stewardship theory'' of the presidency, as follows: ''The true view of the executive functions is, as I conceive it, that the President can exercise no power which cannot be fairly and reasonably traced to some specific grant of power or justly implied and included within such express grant as proper and necessary in its exercise. Such specific grant must be either in the federal Constitution or in an act of Congress passed in pursuance thereof. There is no undefined residuum of power which he can exercise because it seems to him to be in the public interest. . . .''[75] It is difficult to see how, given their ordinary meaning, these words are to be harmonized with the chief justice's present invocation of the opening clause of Article II as a grant of power.

''*Stare super antiquas vias,* '' says the chief justice. But the retort of Sergeant Maynard, once aptly quoted by Mr. Evarts, is surely pertinent: ''It is not a question of standing upon the ancient ways, for we are not on them.''

---

74. 47 Sup. Ct. at 62 {272 U.S. 52 at 228}. This opinion also contains, *id.,* a reference to Reagan v. United States, 182 U.S. 419 (1901), which is ignored by the chief justice. Reagan, Commissioner of the United States court in Indian Territory, was dismissed by the judge, and sued to recover salary. He claimed that the judge's action was invalid because the cause assigned therefor was not one of those prescribed by law. Chief Justice Fuller said (182 U.S. at 425–27): ''The inquiry is, therefore, whether there were any causes of removal prescribed by law, March 1, 1895, or at the time of removal. If there were, then the rule would apply that where causes of removal are specified by Constitution or statute, as also where the term of office is for a fixed period, notice and hearing are essential. If there were not, the appointing power could remove at pleasure or for such cause as it deemed sufficient. . . . The commissioners hold office neither for life, nor for any specified time, and are within the rule which treats the power of removal as incident to the power of appointment, unless otherwise provided. By chapters forty-five and forty-six, justices of the peace on conviction of the offenses enumerated are removable from office, but these necessarily do not include all causes which might render the removal of commissioners necessary or advisable. Congress did not provide for the removal of commissioners for the causes for which justices of the peace might be removed, and if this were to be ruled otherwise by construction, the effect would be to hold the commissioners in office for life unless some of those specially enumerated causes became applicable to them. We agree with the Court of Claims that this would be a most unreasonable construction and would restrict the power of removal in a manner which there is nothing in the case to indicate could have been contemplated by Congress.''

To be sure, these words relate to an inferior officer whose appointment had been vested by Congress in a court of law. But as is pointed out later, the principles which determine Congress' general legislative power in relation to such officers are the same as those which determine in relation to officers appointed with the consent of the Senate. See below at 366.

75. *Our Chief Magistrate and His Powers* 139–40.

VI.

While, as remarked earlier, the chief justice's main citadel is his historical argument, there are certain of his supporting outposts which must not be overlooked. First and foremost is his interpretation of the doctrine of the separation of powers. Second are his deductions from the President's responsibility in connection with the enforcement of the laws. (These two will be considered together.) Third is his construction of Article II, section 2, in relation to the power of Congress to vest the appointment of "inferior officers" elsewhere than in the President and Senate.

The purport of the chief justice's doctrine of the separation of powers, which is derived from Madison, is that each department possesses certain inherent powers which the other departments may not limit the exercise of.[76] Conceding the proposition, what ground is there for contending that the power of removal is an inherent element of the "executive power" of the President? First and last the chief justice suggests two grounds, that of history and that of necessity. The former is indicated in the following passage from his opinion:

> It is quite true that in state and colonial governments at the time of the constitutional convention, power to make appointments and removals had sometimes lodged in the legislatures or in the courts, but such a disposition of it was really vesting part of the executive power in another branch of the government. In the British system, the crown, which was the executive, had the power of appointment and removal of executive officers, and it was natural, therefore, for those who framed our Constitution to regard the words "executive power" as including both. *Ex parte* Grossman, 267 U.S. 87, 110. Unlike the power of conquest of the British crown, considered and rejected as a precedent for us in Fleming v. Page, 9 How. 603, 618, the association of removal with appointment of executive officers is not incompatible with our republican form of government.[77]

76. Speakers who referred to the doctrine of the separation of powers in the debate of 1789 in the House were Madison, 1 *Annals of Cong.* cols. 481–82, 515; Vining, col. 531; Boudinot, cols. 547–48; Scott, col. 555. No others seem to have regarded it as an essential factor of the constitutional problem under discussion. Stone denied that there was any "such principle as a separation of powers brought into the Constitution at present," col. 587. Madison's version of the principle represents a characteristically enthusiastic reaction on his part against the overwhelming domination of the legislative power in the state constitutions. See *Federalist*, nos. 47–51; 2 Farrand, *Records of the Federal Convention* 35 (1911). His remarks, however, should be read with the fact in mind that he was discussing the question of Congress' power to vest the power of removal, not the question of its power to fix the tenure of offices.

The self-defensive power of courts of the United States to punish for contempt is of ancient lineage. Congress has inherited a similar power from Parliament, which in early times was regarded as a court. In neither instance is the power beyond the reach of reasonable regulation by Congress, although there is in theory an ultimate residuum of it of which the department enjoying it may not be deprived. See Gompers v. Buck's Stove and Range Co., 221 U.S. 418 (1911); Michaelson v. United States, 266 U.S. 42 (1924); *In re* Chapman, 166 U.S. 661 (1897); Marshall v. Gordon, 243 U.S. 521 (1917).

77. 47 Sup. Ct. at 25–26 {272 U.S. 52 at 118}. The chief justice's indebtedness to Jackson's Protest is again apparent. See at 348, above. For a good argument against defining the "executive

The argument proves too much. The power of the British crown in the appointment and removal of officers is an historical outgrowth of and is still intimately involved with a much wider prerogative in the creation of offices. Far down into the last century the judicial system of England was substantially altogether of royal creation, while even today the king may if he chooses erect new common law courts, though apparently no new court to administer any other law.[78] As to executive offices, the general situation would seem to be the same. The five great secretaryships of state all sprang originally from royal fiat, all being in fact but offshoots of a single office which traces back to early feudal times. Furthermore, the only restriction recognized by authoritative writers even today upon royal creation of offices is that the king shall not create new offices with fees attached, inasmuch as this would amount to laying a tax, which can be done only by act of Parliament.[79] But in the United States the rule is, of course, exactly contrary. The only offices known to the Constitution of the United States are those "which shall be established by law." Any comparison between "executive power" as known to the Constitution of the United States and the prerogative of the British monarch, as regards the power of removal, is consequently not only valueless to the chief justice's argument, it is positively detrimental, in that it draws attention to the fact that the Constitution itself assigns the germinal element of prerogative in connection with offices, to wit, their creation, to Congress.

The ground of necessity is suggested by the chief justice's repeated appeal to the President's duty "to take care that the laws be faithfully executed." The argument is not a novel one; many years ago it was answered by Calhoun in the following words:

> Congress shall have power to make all laws, not only to carry into effect the powers expressly delegated to itself, but those delegated to the government, or any department or officer thereof; and of course comprehends the power to pass laws necessary and proper to carry into effect the powers expressly granted to the executive department. It follows, of course, to whatever express grant of power to the executive the power of dismissal may be supposed to attach, whether to that of seeing the law faithfully executed, or to the still more comprehensive grant, as contended for

---

power" of the President by the prerogative of the British crown, see 1 *Annals of Cong.* col. 566. See also note 50, above.

78. Maitland, *Constitutional History* 419–20 (1908); 2 Anson, *Law and Custom of the Constitution* 405–406, 449–50 (1892). Both writers cite *In re* The Bishop of Natal, 3 Moore, P.C., N.S., 115 (1864) which in turn relies for the distinction between courts proceeding according to the common law and other kinds of courts on a passage from 4 Coke, *Institutes* 200. Coke was jealous of the Star Chamber; but notwithstanding his statement the subsequent abolition of that body required a statute. As Anson remarks, "the limitations on the part of the crown laid down by Coke and Comyns and adopted by Lord Westbury, were not always in force." *Law and Custom* 450.

79. 1 Todd, *Parliamentary Government in England* 609 (2d ed. 1887); 22 *Encyclopaedia Britannica* 280 (11th ed. 1913), article on *Prerogative*. See also 1 Bl. *Comm.* *272. For some of these references I am indebted to my friend, Dr. John Dickinson.

by some, vesting executive powers in the President, the mere fact that it is a power appurtenant to another power, and necessary to carry it into effect, transfers it, by the provisions of the Constitution cited, from the executive to Congress, and places it under the control of Congress, to be regulated in the manner which it may judge best.[80]

Certainly a duty to see that the laws be faithfully executed cannot by ordinary principles of construction afford an independent restriction on the power by virtue of which the laws needing to be executed are enacted. The language of duty rather than of power was employed advisedly in this clause of the Constitution; since by other clauses powers which are obviously essential to successful enforcement of the law are assigned to Congress. No one would contend that the President could appropriate money, or erect courts, or create offices, or enlarge the military forces, on the justification that such action was necessary in order to assure the enforcement of the laws. Yet Congress' power to create offices is itself mere matter of inference from the "necessary and proper" clause, an inference, albeit, which is directly and significantly confirmed by the express language of the Constitution. Nor should it be overlooked in this connection that the clause requiring the President to "take care that the laws be faithfully executed" was taken almost verbatim from the New York Constitution of 1777, which nonetheless accorded the executive of that state very little voice in either appointments or removals.

But, the chief justice rejoins, just "as his [the President's] selection of administrative officers is essential to the execution of the laws by him, so must be his power of removing those for whom he cannot continue to be responsible."[81] The answer is twofold: first the *duty* which devolves upon the President from the Constitution is not to *execute* the laws, but to *take care* that they be executed by those upon whom *Congress* has conferred the *power* of execution; secondly, for that reason, as was just pointed out, neither the one duty nor the other can possibly override a constitutional act of Congress calling it into play. So the issue comes down to this: May Congress ever validly confer power upon an official or body to be exercised by such official or body upon his or its own independent judgment of the requirements of the situation? As we saw earlier, the chief justice himself concedes that Congress may do this; and certainly such has always been the doctrine of the Court heretofore.[82] With the chief justice's further contention

---

80. 11 *Cong. Deb.* 553 (1835). This passage is thrust at the chief justice by both Justice McReynolds and Justice Brandeis, but he ignores the challenge.

81. 47 Sup. Ct. at 25 {272 U.S. 52, 117}.

82. *Id.* 31. As to the theoretical relation of the President to his subordinates in the execution of the law, the following from the opinion of Justice Thompson, in Kendall v. United States, is pertinent: "It by no means follows [from the President's duty to "take care," etc.] that every officer in every branch of that [executive] department is under the exclusive direction of the President. . . . It would be an alarming doctrine that Congress cannot impose upon any executive officer any duty they may think proper, which is not repugnant to any right secured and protected by the Constitution; and in such cases the duty and responsibility grow out of and are subject to the control of the law, and not to the direction of the President." 12 Pet. 524, 610, (1838). Note also the following from an opinion of

that the President should have "an unrestricted power to remove his most important subordinates as to their most important duties" it is unnecessary to quarrel;
but his conclusion therefrom that this fact "must control the interpretation of the
Constitution as to all appointed by him" is much too drastic. The dilemma which
he imagines does not exist, once the resources of our constitutional law and
practice are adequately explored.

Returning for a moment to the doctrine of the separation of powers, there is
still another aspect of the principle as it is sometimes expounded, and while the
extent to which the chief justice intended to sanction it is somewhat uncertain, it
should receive consideration. This consists in the notion—or superstition—that
the Constitution effects such a nice apportionment of the total field of governmental activity among the three departments, that no department can constitutionally lay claim to powers in the exercise of which it would be brought into
collision with another department in the exercise of the powers thereof.[83] Strictly
adhered to, the theory leads to an impasse reminiscent of the Nebraska statute
which decreed that when two trains met at a crossing, neither should start until
the other had moved on. But practically, since a beginning of construction must
be made somewhere, the advantage—the right to move on—falls to that department whose powers happen to be construed first. Thus, in consequence of the
accidental circumstance that the location of the power of removal came up for a
decision at the very beginning of our constitutional system—a power on all hands
admitted not to belong to Congress, albeit Congress might, possibly, determine
its location—this power then and there became by the theory under discussion an

---

an attorney general of the United States, written when Mr. Taft was solicitor general: "The President
has, under the Constitution and laws, certain duties to perform, among those being to take care that
the laws be faithfully executed; that is, that the other executive and administrative officers of the
government faithfully perform their duties; but the statutes regulate and prescribe these duties, and he
has no more power to add to, or subtract from, the duties imposed upon subordinate executive and
administrative officers by the law, than those officers have to add or subtract from his duties." 19
Op. Att'y Gen. 686–87 (1890). In his *Our Chief Magistrate,* Mr. Taft writes: "In theory, all the
executive officers appointed by the President directly or indirectly are his subordinates, and yet
Congress can undoubtedly pass laws definitely limiting their discretion and commanding a certain
course by them which it is not within the power of the executive to vary. Fixing the method in which
executive power shall be exercised is perhaps one of the chief functions of Congress. Indeed, by its
legislation, it often creates a duty in the executive which did not before exist. Then in prescribing how
that duty is to be carried out, it imposes restrictions that the executive is bound to observe." *Our
Chief Magistrate* 125. Actually, of course, the bulk of the executive duties flow from statutes passed
by Congress in the exercise of its granted powers. Such discretion as Congress accords the executive
agent to which it entrusts the carrying out of its will is obviously in theory at the disposal of Congress
and subject to its direction. On the related question of limitations surrounding the right of the
President to take appeals from his subordinates, see 15 *Op. Att'y Gen.* 94 (1880), and opinions there
cited. See also note 5, above, and note 92, below.

83. For an approximation to this view, see the present writer's *President's Control of Foreign
Relations* 36–37 (1917). A similar view has often been expressed as to the relation of national and
state power. It is sufficiently refuted by such a case as Houston, E. & W. Texas Ry. Co. v. United
States, 234 U.S. 342 (1914).

independent limitation on Congress' power under the "necessary and proper" clause in the creation of offices.

The theory cannot pass muster. If each department were to retire sufficiently far from its own frontiers to avoid all results taking effect beyond them, governmental power would be totally disabled. The obvious fact is that the subject matter upon which governmental power may operate is not for the most part parcelled out at all among the three departments, but on the contrary underlies all three, and is often operated upon in succession by all three in exercise of their diverse powers, with the result not unfrequently that the action of one curtails, modifies, or even nullifies that of another. Thus the President may proclaim neutrality, but Congress may still declare war; the President and Senate may make a treaty, but Congress may repeal the treaty as "law of the land"; the Court may sentence for contempt of Court, but the President may pardon the offender; and so on.[84] But still anarchy does not ensue, and that because of another principle which exponents of the principle of the separation of powers are much too prone to forget, the principle, to wit, of the natural primacy both in point of time and of authority of legislative action.[85] In "a government of laws and not of men," such as ours is supposed to be, not only is there ordinarily no occasion for executive or judicial action *until* the legislature has acted, but the conditions of their action, the channels in which it may proceed, and the scope which it may take, are predetermined by the legislature. Clearly it is so as to the matter at hand. Until Congress has acted there is no office to which there may be appointment or from which there may be removal. Everybody concedes, moreover, that Congress may stipulate the qualifications of appointees, short of designating a specific eligible, although the power of appointment is thereby curtailed. What, then, is to prevent Congress from fixing the tenure of an office created by it with resultant curtailment of the removal power? So far as the principle of the separation of powers is concerned the two things stand on precisely the same footing, while in practice they may be but different phases of the same thing, since security in office may be the *sine qua non* of the kind of behavior which an office requires for the successful discharge of its characteristic duties.

The third incidental feature of the opinion may be dismissed in a few words. Reiterating at one point of his opinion the proposition that "in the absence of any specific provision to the contrary, the power of appointment to executive offices carries with it, as a necessary incident, the power of removal," the chief justice proceeds to contend that the clause of Article II which authorizes Congress to

84. *President's Control of Foreign Relations* 109–11; *Ex parte* Grossman, 267 U.S. 87 (1925).

85. Both Locke and Montesquieu, whence comes the doctrine of the separation of powers, recognize always the supremacy of legislative power. "The legislative is the only creative element in our government, and precedes in logical succession as well as in actual experience the action of the other departments, inasmuch as they only act upon that which the legislative power has brought into existence." Argument of counsel, United States v. Guthrie, 17 How. 284, 296 (1854). See also note 82 above.

vest the appointment of inferior officers "in the President alone, in the courts of law, or in the heads of departments," should be treated as "words of exception," and that it, therefore, "by the plainest implication excludes congressional dealing with appointments and removals of executive officers not falling within the exception."[86] But if by this it is meant that the "necessary and proper" clause vests Congress with no power whereby it may practically curtail the power of appointment and the power of removal, the conclusion is a plain *non sequitur*. For even granting—as indeed one should—the chief justice's argument as to the proper construction of the clause regarding *the vesting of appointment of inferior officers*, yet this clause deals only with that precise subject. It has nothing whatever to do with the power to create offices or the power to determine the qualifications of officers and fix their tenure.[87]

To sum up: Granting that there are certain inherent "executive" powers, the proof offered by the chief justice that the removal power is one of these is unacceptable; while, in view of the fact that the appointive power is specifically provided for, the presumption must be to the contrary. Granting, on the other hand, that the removal power is an inherent executive power, the proof offered by the chief justice that it can override powers otherwise claimable for Congress under the "necessary and proper" clause is also unconvincing, although in this case too the normal relationship of the law-making to the law-enforcing function establishes the contrary presumption. Nor is there anything about the language in which the Constitution enjoins upon the President the duty to "take care that the laws be faithfully executed" which reverses this relationship—rather it confirms it. Lastly, there is nothing whatever to show that the limitation implied in the terms in which power is conferred upon Congress to vest the appointment of inferior officers was intended to reach any other power than the one thus conferred.

VII.

Chief Justice Taft was once President himself, and this fact, it may be surmised, accounts in no small measure for the trend of his opinion in the case at bar. Nor is this conjecture weakened when one compares the actual basis of the opinion with the much broader foundation of fact and law upon which an opinion might have been grounded. So, even if the chief justice's interpretation of the decision of 1789 were all that he claims for it, still his argument would invite the serious criticism that in attempting to settle a constitutional problem of the year of grace 1926 by predominant reference to what had taken place nearly a hundred

---

86. 47 Sup. Ct. at 28–29 {272 U.S. 52 at 127}. United States v. Germaine, 99 U.S. 508 (1879), unquestionably supports a strict construction of this clause.

87. I have no doubt that the intention of the argument as {*sic;* is?} to vindicate the President's power of removal, on whatever ground resting, as against a power in Congress to determine tenure. See above, pp. 324–26, 328, 330–31, 334.

and forty years earlier, he had ignored intervening material of greater pertinence and validity. In the following paragraphs accordingly an effort has been made to supply this deficiency of the opinion, and to correct its consequent bias. The propositions offered are submitted with a view to doing something like justice not only to the history of the subject under discussion anterior to the Myers Case but also to existing necessities as these are reflected in congressional legislation of recent years. They have also the advantage that they are largely supported by what has already been said by way of negative criticism.

1. *The power of appointment is not an inherent executive power but a specific power.* This has always been the controlling principle in the state constitutions;[88] and by accepted canons of construction it is likewise the view of the United States Constitution. The Constitution provides specifically that the President ". . . shall nominate, and by and with the advice and consent of the Senate, shall appoint ambassadors, other public ministers and consuls, judges of the Supreme Court, and all other officers of the United States, whose appointments are not herein otherwise provided for, and which shall be established by law."

By the recognized maxim that the Constitution contains no superfluous language,[89] this clause is the sole source of the appointing power as it is known to the Constitution of the United States, and so it was regarded by Madison, Hamilton, and the overwhelming number of those who participated in the debate of 1789, by Marshall, by Story, by Kent, by Webster, and, indeed, by the vast consensus of opinion anterior to the decision in Myers v. United States. And how does the chief justice seek to obviate this maxim? He suggests that it is the purpose of the clause just quoted from Article II simply to supply emphasis "where emphasis is

---

88. For the appointing power in the early state constitutions, see Thorpe, *Federal and State Constitutions, Colonial Charters* (1909). The appointing power rested largely with the legislature in the following states: Connecticut (until 1818), *id.* 531; Delaware (constitution of 1776), *id.* 563–65; New Hampshire (constitution of 1776), *id.* 2452; New Jersey (constitution of 1776), *id.* 2596; North Carolina (constitution of 1776), *id.* 2797; Rhode Island (until 1842), *id.* 3215; Virginia (constitution of 1776), *id.* 3817. The same power was early assigned to the governor (or President) and council, or governor and Senate in the following states; Georgia (constitution of 1777), *id.* 781; Maryland (constitution of 1776), *id.* 1699; Massachusetts (constitution of 1780), *id.* 1902; New Hampshire (constitution of 1784), *id.* 2464; Pennsylvania (constitution of 1776), *id.* 3085, 3087, Vermont (constitution of 1777 and 1793), *id.* 3745, 3766. South Carolina divided appointments between the Assembly, and the governor and council, or governor and Senate, in both the constitution of 1776 and in that of 1778, *id.* 3246, 3254. New York had a council of appointment over which the governor presided and in which he had a casting vote, *id.* 2633–34.

One or two special provisions for the appointment of officials standing in a special relation to the legislature are of significance. In Maryland, under the constitution of 1776, the treasurer was appointed by the House of Delegates, *id.* 1693. In Massachusetts, under the constitution of 1780, the secretary, treasurer, receiver general, naval officers, and some others, were appointed by joint ballot of Senate and House, *id.* 1905.

By its constitution of 1790, Pennsylvania gave the power to the governor alone to "appoint all officers, whose offices shall be established by this constitution, or shall be established by law, and whose appointments are not herein otherwise provided for," *id.* 3095.

89. Calder v. Bull, 3 Dall. 386 (1798); Hurtado v. California, 110 U.S. 516 (1884).

appropriate.'"[90] At least this is a new principle in constitutional construction. But in point of fact the clause in question does much more than lend emphasis "where emphasis is appropriate." For without it, by the chief justice's own argument, the President would have no power to appoint other than executive officers; he would have no power at all to appoint to judicial offices. It follows that unless there are two kinds of power of appointment vested by the express language of the Constitution, the purpose of the clause in regard to appointments is to confer a power otherwise withheld.

2. *The power of removal when it exists is an incident solely of the power of appointment.* Not only was this the decided verdict of opinion in 1789, but it has remained so ever since when the question has been discussed on the basis of correct principle.[91] In the constitutional law of the states especially has the doctrine that the power of removal inheres in "executive power" found slight lodgment.[92] And even in the national government, as was pointed out by Webster many years ago, the power of removal has in actual practice been usually exercised, notwithstanding the decision of 1789, in direct connection with the power

90. 47 Sup. Ct. at 26, 29 {272 U.S. 52 at 118, 128}. The chief justice's new canon might have an entirely revolutionary effect on the "general welfare" clause of Art. I, sec. 8. See J. F. Lawson, *The General Welfare Clause* (1926). The salient points in the history of the appointment clause in {the} Convention of 1787 are given in the {Author's} Note at the end of this essay.

91. Said Smith of South Carolina, in the debate of 1789: "The gentleman from Virginia has said that the power of removal is executive in its nature. I do not believe this to be the case. I have turned over the constitutions of most of the states, and I do not find that any of them have granted this power to the governor. In some instances, I find the executive magistrate suspends, but none of them have the right to remove officers; and I take it that the Constitution of the United States has distributed the powers of government on the same principles which most of the state constitutions have adopted. For it will not be contended that the state governments did not furnish the members of the late Convention with the skeleton of this Constitution." 1 *Annals of Cong.* col. 490.

The prevailing doctrine today is stated by Mechem, *On Public Officers* sec. 445 (1890), as follows: "Where . . . the tenure of the office is not fixed by law and no other provision is made for removals, either by the Constitution or by statute, it is said to be a 'sound and necessary rule to consider the power of removal as incident to the power of appointment.' " citing *Ex parte Hennen*, above, note 62, and state cases. To the same effect is Goodnow, *Principles of Administrative Law of the United States* 311–12 (1905). See also Fox v. MacDonald, 101 Ala. 51, and cases there cited. Many state constitutions nowadays, however, vest the governor with the power of removal as to certain specified offices, while the state legislature often has broad powers in providing for the removal of inferior, statutory, or nonimpeachable officers. Stimson, *Federal and State Constitutions* secs. 265, 268 (1908) and citations.

92. A leading, and oft-cited case, is Field v. People, 2 Scam. 79 (Ill. 1839). Alluding to the duty of the governor to "see that the laws are faithfully executed," the court says in this case (at 91): "This clause of the constitution, like those dividing the powers of government, and declaring the attributes of each, is the declaration of a general principle, which is 'not to be regarded as a rule to fetter and control, but as matter merely declaratory and directory.' It confers no specific powers 'nor does it enjoin any specific duty.' 'This power of general supervision,' says an able commentator on American law, 'is a duty enjoined on the federal and state executives.' 'It would be dangerous, however, to treat this clause as conferring any specific power which they would not otherwise possess. It is to be regarded as a comprehensive description of the duty of the executive to watch with vigilance over all the public interests,' " citing T. Walker, *Introduction to American Law* 103 {1837?}.

of appointment, presidential removals having ordinarily taken place in consequence of and coincidently with the appointment of a new incumbent.[93]

The main purpose in attributing to the President an "executive power" of removal in 1789, moreover, no longer exists. This was to secure for him an unrestricted power of removal in relation to the heads of certain departments. Owing to the notion that the Senate *shared* the power of appointment in relation to such officers, it was obviously essential if the purpose just stated was to be realized to trace the power of removal to some other source, one enjoyed by the President alone. So the opening clause of Article II was resorted to. But this recourse is no longer necessary. The Myers Case itself establishes that the President may today claim exclusive control of all legal power of removal in relation to officers appointed by him without any reference to his "executive power."

3. *The power of removal affecting officers appointed by and with the advice and consent of the Senate is exercised by the President under the Constitution without such advice and consent.* The indicated premise of this proposition is that in such cases the power of appointment belongs in the contemplation of the Constitution to the President alone. The conception is only to be defended as an interpretative device, for to the common understanding a power requiring to be exercised conditionally on the consent of another is shared by that other.[94] Indeed, that this is so is virtually recognized by the holding of the Court itself in the case at bar, which is to the effect that in requiring the Senate's *consent* to certain removals, Congress was endeavoring to *vest* the power of removal in a quarter not permitted by the Constitution. Nor should the precise language in which the Constitution authorizes Congress to vest the appointment of inferior officers "in the President alone" be overlooked. It clearly implies that until Congress acts the power is not his *alone*.

The theory that the power to appoint, although its exercise is conditioned upon the consent of the Senate, is nevertheless the President's exclusive power was

93. "In all the removals which have been made," said Webster, in his speech of Feb. 16, 1835, "they have generally been effected simply by making other appointments. I cannot find a case to the contrary. There is no such thing as any distinct official act of removal." Webster, 7 *Writings and Speeches* 189 (1903). As Butler put it, in introducing the case of the managers against President Johnson: "This [Webster's contention] would seem to reconcile all the provisions of the Constitution, the right of removal being in the President, to be executed, *sub modo,* as is the power of appointment, the appointment, when consumated, making the removal." 1 *Trial of Andrew Johnson* 98. The fact that the Myers Case was so long in arising goes to confirm Webster's rather too sweeping statement. Also, see Wallace v. United States, 257 U.S. 541 (1922).

94. Gerry made an interesting observation on this point in the debate of 1789: "If we observe the enacting style of the statutes of Great Britain we shall find pretty nearly the same words as those used in the Constitution, with respect to appointments—Be it enacted by the King's most Excellent Majesty, by and with the advice and consent of Parliament. Here it might be said that the king enacts all laws; but I believe the truth of the fact will be disputed in that country. I believe no one will pretend that the king is the three branches of Parliament; and, unless my colleague will do all this, I never can admit that the President in himself has the power of appointment." And see 1 Bl. *Comm.* *85; also 1 McElroy, *Life of Grover Cleveland* {*sic; Grover Cleveland: The Man and Statesman?*} 166–168 (1923).

first advanced *arguendo* in the debate of 1789.[95] Far more important is the countenance which the same theory receives from certain expressions of Chief Justice Marshall in Marbury v. Madison: "The appointment. This is also the act of the President . . . though it can only be performed by and with the advice and consent of the Senate"; and again, "The appointment, being the sole act of the President. . . ."[96] While in Jackson's Protest the theory is reasserted with vigor, the attention which it receives, a generation later, from Johnson's counsel in his impeachment trial is hardly more than casual.[97] Casual, too, is its implied approval by the Court in the Shurtleff Case. Then in 1920 it is seized upon by President Wilson and made the pivotal proposition of his veto message of the first Budget Bill.[98] Finally, in the Myers Case the stone which was rejected of the builders has become the head of the column.

So it is settled that the Senate's function of advice and consent does not make it participant in the appointive power. A difficulty nevertheless remains; for the necessity of obtaining this consent as a condition of exercising the said power is stated in the Constitution in terms too plain to be obliterated by verbal legerdemain. Why, then, does not the same necessity exist as to the removal power, *incident* as it is said to be of the appointive power? In other words, by what warrant may the power of removal be claimed for the President on the ground of its being *included* in the power of appointment, and then straightway *separated off* from the same power in order to relieve it from the restrictions resting thereon? A partial justification for this procedure is perhaps furnished by the *usus loquendi* of the Constitution itself. Thus in one clause it is said that "The President shall *nominate,* and by and with the advice and consent of the Senate, shall *appoint*" officers; while the next clause reads that "Congress may vest the *appointment* of inferior officers," meaning thereby *both* their nomination *and* appointment. Thus the Constitution itself at one moment distinguishes the incidents of appointment and in the next blends them; while the chief justice does the converse when he says in the instant case: "The power of removal is incident to the power of appointment, not to the power of advising and consenting to appointment." Once again what may be lacking on the score of logic is supplied by the voice of authority.[99]

95. See p. 332 above.

96. 1 Cranch 137, 155, 157 (1803).

97. Referring to the contention of the senatorial party in the debate of 1789, "that the same power that appointed should have the removal," Mr. Evarts rejoined: "That was a little begging of the question—speaking it with all respect—as to who the appointing power was really, under the terms and intent of the Constitution. But conceding that the connection of the Senate with the matter really made them a part of the appointing power, the answer to the argument," etc. 2 *Trial of Andrew Johnson* 313–14 (1886).

98. See note 14, above.

99. 47 Sup. Ct. at 27 {272 U.S. 52 at 122}. Unquestionably the only self-consistent view to take of the constitutional provision regarding appointment is that the Senate participates in both the appointive and removal power, the two constituting one power. The weight of the argument from expediency may favor the view stated in the text, which is now "law of the land."

4. *Both the power of appointment and the power of removal are conditioned by what Congress may constitutionally do, under the "necessary and proper" clause, in the way of imposing qualifications for the officer and defining the tenure of the office.* From the first, Congress has exercised its power under the "necessary and proper" clause to fix the qualifications of officers, not only in respect to inferior offices but also in respect to superior offices, and this notwithstanding that in so doing it has obviously restricted the President's power of nomination.[100] The fact is, of course, that there is no power of nomination until there is an office to nominate to, and then nomination must be made from those qualified to meet the legal requirements of the office. So also, Congress has often restricted the efficacy of the power of appointment by stipulating the terms beyond which appointments to certain offices might not run. Why, then, should it not have the analogous power in relation to the power of removal, whether this be an incident of the power of appointment or an independent power? The fact is that its possession of such power has been repeatedly demonstrated in practice.[101]

---

100. On this point, examine the vast mass of data brought together in Justice Brandeis' dissenting opinion, and accompanying notes. 47 Sup. Ct. 75-78 {272 U.S. 52 at 265-74}. Hundreds of statutory provisions are cited. "Thus," the opinion summarizes, "Congress has, from time to time, restricted the President's selection by the requirement of citizenship [some thirty distinct acts of Congress]. It has limited the power of nomination by providing that the office may be held only by a resident of the United States [act of Mar. 1, 1855, ch. 133, dealing with ministers and their subordinates]; of a state [one act]; of a particular state [five acts]; of a particular district [two acts]; of a particular territory [three acts]; of the District of Columbia [Act of May 3, 1802, and four other acts]; of a particular foreign country [one act]. It has limited the power of nomination further by prescribing professional attainments [some fifty-six acts and joint resolutions], or occupational experience [eighteen acts and joint resolutions]. It has, in other cases, prescribed the test of examinations [seven acts, including the Civil Service Act of Jan. 16, 1883, ch. 27, sec. 2, and the Foreign Service Act of May 24, 1924, ch. 182, sec.5]. It has imposed the requirement of age [three acts]; of sex [two acts]; of race [one act]; of property [act of Mar. 26, 1804, ch. 38, sec. 4, legislative council of Louisiana, to be selected from holders of realty]; and of habitual temperance in the use of intoxicating liquors [one act—obsolete, no doubt, under the Eighteenth Amendment]. Congress has imposed like restrictions on the power of nomination by requiring political respresentation [eighteen acts, including those organizing the Interstate Commerce and Federal Trade Commissions]; or that the selection be made on a nonpartisan basis [twenty-three acts]. It has required, in some cases, that the representation be industrial [six acts]; in others, that it be geographic [seventeen acts and joint resolutions]. It has at times required that the President's nominees be taken from, or include representatives from, particular branches or departments of the government [twenty-six acts and joint resolutions]. By still other statutes, Congress has confirmed the President's selection to a small number of persons to be named by others [five acts, including act of Feb. 23, 1920, ch. 91, sec. 304, requiring that the Railroad Labor Board consist of three to be appointed from six nominees by employees, and three to be appointed from six nominees by carriers]." This last mentioned act is especially interesting in view of one of the grounds of the recent veto of the McNary-Haugen Bill.

101. See the mass of data given above on pp. 326-27, 340-42, 344-47, above, and in the accompanying notes; Justice Brandeis's opinion, 47 Sup. Ct. at 74-75 {272 U.S. 52 at 262-64}; Senator Pepper's brief in S. Doc. No. 174, 69th Cong., 2d Sess. 145-149; 1 *Trial of Andrew Johnson* 100; 2 *id.* 44 *et seq.*, 85 *et seq.*, 242 *et seq.*

"Certainly if, when the Constitution is silent, the legislative power may declare that whoever is appointed to a particular office shall *cease* to hold it at the end of four years, it may also declare that the appointee shall enjoy it during that time. The two things are complementary to each other, and logically inseparable." Senator Edmund's Opinion, 3 *id.* 84. See also note 39, above.

It is not claimed, however, that Congress' power is in this respect an unlimited one. If the office is one which, from its nature, reasonably requires that the officer be secure or that his removal be for good cause only, then Congress may so decree, with the result that the removal power is correspondingly curtailed; while, contrariwise, there are also offices security of tenure in which is not a necessary and proper requirement and with reference to which the power of removal may not be restricted. Nor may Congress at any time *transfer* the power of removal except in the case of inferior officers, and then only in consequence of vesting their appointment in the President alone, in the courts of law, or in the heads of departments.

5. *Heads of departments composing the President's Cabinet, regardless of their statutory duties, today occupy an advisory capacity in relation to the President which is political in nature and which renders these officers inherently subject to an unqualified power of removal in the President.* As we have seen, the decision of 1789 concerned primarily an officer whose principal importance was that of an instrument of presidential power in the field of foreign relations. It was properly felt that the President's power to remove such an officer must remain unrestricted. Subsequently, the decision was applied also to the case of the Secretary of the Treasury and the Secretary of War, although in the former case the powers of the officer were largely of statutory origin. Yet, from the first all heads of departments were by specific provision of the Constitution subject to consultation by the President in writing.[102] From the outset, therefore, all heads of departments stood in a quasi-political relation to the President, and today this relationship has become the dominant characteristic of the offices concerned.[103]

The most important episode in the history of this transformation was Jackson's removal of Duane and his ensuing appointment of Taney in order that he, Jackson, might control the discretion vested by statute in the Secretary of the Treasury concerning the removal of deposits from the Bank of the United States. By writers on constitutional and administrative law this incident is almost universally interpreted as establishing the proposition that whenever a head of department is vested with discretionary powers, the President is authorized to control

---

102. Art. II, sec. 2(1): "... he may require the opinion, in writing, of the principal officer in each of the executive departments, upon any subjects relating to the duties of their respective offices." The opinion was to be (1) in writing; (2) confined to the field of officer's official duties. Why, to employ the chief justice's newly discovered canon of construction, did the framers of the Constitution feel that "emphasis was appropriate" on this matter of advice-taking? It would appear that they conceived that some of the heads of departments would normally occupy a very independent position in relation to the President.

103. As early as Marbury v. Madison, we find the Court referring to "the intimate political relation, subsisting between the President of the United States and the heads of departments." Marbury v. Madison, 1 Cranch 137, 169 (1803). Marshall had been Secretary of State and President Adams' chief advisor. "The Cabinet Council of the President should be of his bosom confidence." Jefferson to Dexter, Feb., 1801. 7 *Writings* {of Jefferson} 498 (Ford ed. 1892–1899). This intimacy of political relationship is further testified to be general understanding that the Senate will ordinarily ratify all presidential nominations to "cabinet posts." See also note 106, below.

and direct his discretion.[104] Nor does this conclusion follow from the duty of the President to take care that the laws be faithfully executed. In the analogous situation a court may only require that the officer *exercise* his discretion—it may not assume to control such discretion.[105] The President's right is solely a deduction from the facts of history, but these facts are today of so conclusive a nature as to infer {*sic;* imply?} a positive principle of constitutional practice.

But an officer whose discretion he may legitimately control the President should be able to remove at will. That is to say, in relation to the heads of departments who compose his Cabinet, the President should today be regarded as having power of removal at pleasure, a power which, therefore, Congress may not constitutionally limit. And this is so not because the power of removal is an inherent executive power—it is because of the relationship in which the heads of departments stand to other powers and rights which either always have been or in the course of time have become recognized attributes of the presidential office, and especially the President's right to surround himself with a board of confidential advisors of a political character.[106]

6. *The same principle which forbids Congress to qualify the removability of political advisors of the President, namely, the essential character of the office, fairly requires Congress in other instances to render officers reasonably secure from removal.* In providing for territorial judgeships Congress from the first was accustomed to fix their tenure, and legitimately so, since it is clearly the understanding of the Constitution that a judge ought to be secure in office. Hence, too, the statutory provision under which Marbury v. Madison arose. The Court in that case, though operating in full light of the decision of 1789, had no difficulty in holding that the President was without the power of removal although the officer concerned had been appointed with the advice and consent of the Senate. If Congress chooses, in other words, it may entirely eliminate removability as to

104. See Goodnow, *Principles of Administrative Law of the United States* 80–81 citing 7 *Op. Att'y Gen.* 453, 470; Wyman, *Administrative Law* sec. 69 (1903). Said Attorney General Cushing in the opinion just referred to: "I think . . . the general rule to be . . . that the head of department is subject to the direction of the President. I hold that no head of department can lawfully perform an official act against the will of the President and that will is, by the Constitution, to govern the performance of all such acts." Wyman phrases the same doctrine thus: "The President it appears has the power in all matters whatsoever to force any officer to do any act which the officer has power to do. He can dictate in all matters, because he has the power of instant dismissal without giving reasons therefor, and thereupon the right of immediate appointment without limitation therein." Wyman, *Administrative Law* 233. *Cf.* pp. 353–55 above and notes 82 and 92.

105. United States v. Black, 128 U.S. 40 (1888).

106. Notwithstanding his general language, what Chief Justice Taft has foremost in mind all the time is the relationship of President and Cabinet. "Each head of a department," he writes, "is and must be the President's *alter ego* in the matters of that department where the President is required by law to exercise authority." 47 Sup. Ct. at 30 {272 U.S. 52 at 133}. "In this [the political] field his Cabinet officers must do his will. He must place in each member of his official family, and his chief executive subordinates, implicit faith." *Id.* at 31 {272 U.S. 52 at 134}. "The imperative reasons requiring an unrestricted power to remove the most important of his subordinates in their most important duties must, therefore, control the interpretation of the Constitution as to all appointed by him." *Id.*

judicial officers except only such removability as results from the provision made by the Constitution itself that all civil officers shall be liable to impeachment.[107]

Nor is there anything to prevent Congress from assimilating membership in the Interstate Commerce Commission, the Federal Trade Commission, and the like, more or less completely to those of judicial officers—on the contrary, there are considerations which exact it. Such bodies are termed "administrative" rather than "executive," and the designation has come to denote a distinct type of governmental agency. While the authority of such an agency is apt to be *legislative* in scope, its method of procedure is modelled in greater or less measure on *judicial* practice, and indeed must be, the Court informs us, if the constitutional principle against delegations of legislative power is to be obviated.[108] And even when the determinations of such bodies do not affect private interests primarily, they are supposed to rest, nevertheless, upon careful and unbiased findings of fact which often require for their proper evaluation and application a highly expert and technical knowledge. The very idea of official good behavior when extended to such a body connotes independence of judgment as an essential ingredient, and therefore the conditions in which this may be reasonably expected to obtain.

This, moreover, is only a part of the story. For the rest of it let us consider by way of illustration the specific case of Interstate Commerce Commission. The powers of the body arise altogether out of a delegation by Congress of its own expressly granted power to regulate commerce among states, and are in nowise subtracted from any constitutional prerogative of the President. Yet if all "executive" officers be removable at the President's will, the commission's powers must frequently be at his disposal to greater or less extent. It follows that the possession by Congress of the power to determine tenure may be "necessary and proper" not only in the sense of being essential to confer independence of judgment upon an office of its creation, but also in the sense of being essential to protect Congress itself in the full control of its express legislative powers.[109]

107. See pp. 345–47 above.
108. Wichita R. and Light Co. v. Pub. Utils. Com's'n, 260 U.S. 48 (1922). Note also the language of the court in State Pub. Utils. Com's'n v. Springfield Gas and Electric Co., 291 Ill. 209, as quoted in Dickinson's *Administrative Justice* 76n. (1927): "It is clear from the salary fixed for the commissioners and the great power vested in the commission that the legislature intended to create an office of dignity and great responsibility.... The commission sits to administer justice.... The notion that commissions of this kind should be closely restrained by the courts, and that justice in our day can only be had in courts is not conducive to the best results. There is no reason why the members of the Public Utilities Commission... should not develop and establish a system of rules and precedents as wise and beneficial within their sphere of action, as those established by the early common law judges."
109. Whatever general policies a national administrative commission formulates are, it must be remembered, subject to alteration or repeal by the national legislative power, which the President shares. And, as we have seen, if Congress chooses to delegate its powers to one of the President's "*alter egos,*" it thereby delegates them to the President, practically if not theoretically; but it does so, presumably, with its eyes open. Indeed, the multiplication in recent years of administrative bodies outside any department is to be explained in part by Congress' recognition of the fact just stated.

7. *Congress' power to vest the appointment of inferior officers gives it no peculiar or added power to restrict the removability of such officers.* Unless the Constitution contemplates in one and the same sentence two different kinds of appointive power, the power of appointment which, with the incident power of removal, may be vested by Congress as to inferior officers is of the same scope in relation to such officers as is the power of appointment which is exercised by the President with the consent of the Senate in relation to officers thus appointed; nor does Congress enjoy any peculiar power in relation to inferior officers save precisely this power to vest their appointment together with the attendant power of removal. It follows that Congress' power to stipulate the qualifications and tenure of inferior officers rests on precisely the same basis as its power to stipulate the qualifications and tenure of superior officers.[110] It rests upon the "necessary and proper" clause, and is measured, accordingly, by the consideration of what qualifications and tenure are reasonably necessary and proper to guarantee the successful functioning of the office involved.

On the other hand, one consequence of the dismissal of the theory that the President has an "executive" power of removal is to enable Congress, in vesting the appointment of inferior officers elsewhere than in the President, also to vest the entire power of removal in relation to such officers elsewhere.[111] No doubt the President might often indirectly procure the removal of an inferior officer by bringing pressure to bear upon the head of department making the appointment, but even in such a case the head of department could not remove the appointee contrary to the provisions of a necessary and proper law.

8. *When Congress has the right to limit the removability of an officer to causes touching his competency and good behavior in office, it has also the right to provide a proper procedure for passing on the question of fact which arises when exercise is attempted of the power to remove such officer.* This proposition is of chief importance today in relation to the office of comptroller general as established by the Budget Act of 1921. As was mentioned early in this article, the comptroller general, who holds office for fifteen years, is removable, except upon impeachment, only by joint resolution of Congress, and then only after a hearing which establishes to Congress' satisfaction his incompetency, neglect of duty, malfeasance in office, or "conduct involving moral turpitude."[112] No doubt as to most offices legislative provision of this sort would amount to an attempt by Congress to vest the power of removal in a way not authorized by the Constitution. The important question is again that of the essential nature of the office involved. That the comptroller general is appointed by the President with the advice and consent of the Senate throws no light on this question, inasmuch as that is the only method of appointment which the Constitution recognizes for

110. See 2 *Trial of Andrew Johnson* 45–46, 242.
111. *Cf.* above pp. 327–28.
112. Above, p. 327.

any kind of officer except where the power of appointment has been constitutionally vested by act of Congress in the President alone, in the courts of law, or in the heads of departments. Considered in the light of its characteristic functions, which is the true test, the office is an organ of the legislature; or to speak more exactly, it is an organ of the national revenue power which is vested by the Constitution in Congress. Historically the office is a lineal descendant of the British comptroller and auditor general, "who holds his office during good behavior, with a salary paid by statute directly out of the Consolidated Fund and who considers himself in no sense a servant of the Treasury but an officer responsible to the House of Commons."[113] In light of these considerations it would seem to have been well within the power of Congress to endow itself with jurisdiction of the question of the comptroller general's liability at any time to removal for one or other of the causes stated in the act creating his office. An actual removal, of course, would have to be attributed to the President signing the resolution of ouster, he or a predecessor having made the appointment.

But, it may be asked, do the eight propositions stated above conflict with the *actual decision* in the Myers Case in any way? It seems clear that they do not. This decision disposes once and for all time of the proposition that the Senate has a constitutional right to participate in the power of removal. It also puts a bar in the way of Congress conferring upon the Senate the power to participate in the removal of officers in whose appointments it had already taken a hand. It does not, on the other hand, determine to any extent the power of Congress to regulate official tenure as incident to its power to create offices and fix the qualifications of officers. No doubt the reasoning of the Court attempts to do this, but this reasoning is not essential to the decision, which has ample basis in the following propositions: first, that the power of appointment is vested by specific grant of the Constitution in the President alone although it may be exercised even in the case of inferior officers, until Congress otherwise provides, only conditionally upon obtaining the consent of the Senate; secondly, that the power of removal which is incident to this power of appointment is not qualified by the necessity of senatorial assent; thirdly, that Congress can vest the power of removal in the case of inferior officers only in consequence of a specifically granted power to vest their power of appointment, and so may vest the power to remove in such cases only in "the President *alone,*" in the courts of law, or in the heads of departments. Everything that the opinion of the Court says or implies which tends to call into question the power of Congress, creating an office, to determine its tenure is unneccessary, and as has been amply shown, without adequate basis in either history or logic.

It all comes down, then, to this: *the power of removal* is not a constitutional absolute, but *is a conditional power,* being subject to what Congress may con-

113. 1 Lowell, *Government of England* 289 (1908). See also Dicey, *Introduction to the Law of the Constitution* 315 (7th ed. 1908).

stitutionally do under the "necessary and proper" clause in the way of defining
the tenure of offices created by it under that clause. But Congress' power is not
absolute either, being conditioned in each case by the nature of the office being
dealt with as shown particularly by the source and nature of its powers. The
question remains whether the Court is entitled, by the principles governing
judicial review, to censor Congress' decisions in this matter, and this may be
disposed of very briefly.

VIII.

Madison's contention that the Court would have no right to review the decision
of 1789, the issue being one between departments, was mentioned earlier. More
accurately stated, the reason for denying judicial intervention in this instance is
that the issue raised is one concerning title to governmental authority, that is to
say, is political in nature.[114] It is true that the Court often decides what from one
point of view are "political questions" in this sense. Every case which involves
the familiar issue of national versus state power is of that character. But the
justification for judicial review in such cases is that the powers in issue are
powers which are capable of reaching ordinary private rights, which do in fact in
the case actually before the Court directly affect such rights. Myers v. United
States, on the other hand, was not that kind of case except for the accidental
circumstance that the government permits itself to be sued for official salaries, a
permission which could be retracted at any moment by adding three words to the
Tucker Act. In substance, this case involved simply constitutional title to a power
which has its operation exclusively within the internal organization of the national government, a power which, therefore, does not touch the liberty or
property of the citizen.

Besides, the concept of political questions is a cautionary as well as a logical
one.[115] The Court has found it discreet to withhold its hand in instances in which
it might not be able to put its views across with complete success, a calculation
which makes its incline in controversies between the executive and Congress to
favor the former. An act of Congress is disposed of by the mere pronouncement
of its nullity; an act of the executive is not always so readily dealt with. It may
have produced an effect on the external world not easy to cancel out, and at any
rate, executive power means obvious physical power. Furthermore, courses of
reasoning which favor the expansion of "executive power" can often be turned
to good account in aggrandizing "judicial power."[116]

And yet can the Court be sure that this time it has put its money on the right

---

114. Luther v. Borden, 7 How. 1 (1849); Georgia v. Stanton, 6 Wall. 50 (1867).

115. See the present writer's "Judicial Review in Action," 74 *U. of Pa. L. Rev.* 639–71 (1926).

116. Note the parallel between the Court's argument in Kansas v. Colorado, 206 U.S. 46, 80–84
(1907), in favor of its own jurisdiction and its argument in favor of "executive power" in the instant
case. The latter, in turn, is derived from the debate of 1789.

horse? In his dissenting opinion Justice Holmes expresses skepticism. The arguments drawn from Article II of the Constitution seem to him "spiders' webs inadequate to control the dominant facts." Certainly the power which creates the office, which can at any time abolish it; which determines its powers, which can at any time transfer, modify, or abolish these; which fixes the term beyond which the officer cannot hold without reappointment, which fixes the officer's pay, and which votes that pay, or may refuse to do so—to say nothing of the power which vests the right of appointment in the case of inferior offices—this power is not without the weapons of retaliation of its views be disregarded concerning matters on which under the present decision it has perhaps no right to views.

For a hundred and thirty-five years the Court was dexterous to avoid a decisive expression of opinion on the issue presented in Myers v. United States. Its present departure from this wise policy of circumspection, involving as it does an effort to arrest constitutional practice in middevelopment, is unfortunate. In the form in which it today stands, Myers v. United States is not only a menacing challenge to an administrative organization which represents years of planning and experimentation in meeting modern conditions—it is a positive instigation to strife between the President and Congress.[117]

{Author's} Note

Early in his opinion the chief justice makes the following reference to the proceedings in the Convention of 1787:

> Consideration of the executive power was initiated in the Constitutional Convention by the seventh resolution in the Virginia plan, introduced by Edmund Randolph. (1 Farrand, *Records of the Federal Convention* 21) It gave to the executive "all the executive powers of the Congress under the confederation," which would seem therefore to have intended to include the power of removal, which had been exercised by that body as incident to the power of appointment. As modified by the Committee of the whole, this resolution declared for a national executive of one person, to be elected by the legislature, with power to carry into execution the national laws and to appoint to offices in cases not otherwise provided for. It was referred to the Committee on Detail (1 Farrand 230), which recommended that the executive power should be vested in a single person to be styled the President of the United States; that he should take care that the laws of the United States be duly and

---

117. One remaining feature of this case should be adverted to. It is touched upon by Justice McReynolds in his dissenting opinion in the following words: "A certain repugnance must attend the suggestion that the President may ignore any provision of an act of Congress under which he has proceeded." 47 Sup. Ct. at 46 {272 U.S. 52 at 179}. The doubt thus expressed receives strong support from Chief Justice Taney's opinion for the Court in United States v. Ferreira, 13 How. 40, 46 (1852). With reference to a statutory tribunal for the adjustment of certain international claims, it is there said: "The tribunal created to adjust the claims cannot change the mode of proceeding or the character in which the law authorizes it to act, under any opinion it may entertain, that a different mode of proceeding, or a tribunal of a different character, would better comport with the provisions of the treaty. If it acts at all, it acts under the authority of the law and must obey the law." The subject of waiver in constitutional law is one that still awaits satisfactory treatment.

faithfully executed; and that he should commission all the officers of the United
States and appoint officers in all cases not otherwise provided by the Constitution.
The committee further recommended that the Senate be given power to make
treaties and to appoint ambassadors and judges of the Supreme Court.

"After the great compromises of the Convention—the one giving the states
equality of representation in the Senate and the other placing the election of the
President, not in Congress as once voted, but in an Electoral College, in which the
influence of larger states in the selection would be more nearly in proportion to their
population—the smaller states, led by Roger Sherman, fearing that under the second compromise the President would constantly be chosen from one of the larger
states, secured a change by which the appointment of all officers, which theretofore
had been left to the President without restriction, was made subject to the Senate's
advice and consent, and the making of treaties and the appointment of ambassadors, public ministers, consuls, and judges of the Supreme Court were transferred
to the President but made subject to the advice and consent of the Senate. This third
compromise was effected in a special committee in which Gouverneur Morris, of
Pennsylvania, represented the larger states and Roger Sherman, the smaller states.
Although adopted finally without objection by any state in the last days of the
Convention, members of the larger states, like Wilson and others, criticized this
limitation of the President's power of appointment of executive officers and the
resulting increase of the power of the Senate. (2 Farrand, *Records* 537–39)"

This account of matter, supplemented at points, yields, when analyzed, results
that militate decidedly against important propositions in the chief justice's argument. In the first place, it should be noted that the Convention found it necessary,
when conferring the power of executing the laws upon the executive, to make
further specific provision giving him also the power of appointment. The power
of appointment involved, moreover, was that affecting executive officers alone,
since at this date the Supreme Court was to be appointed by the Senate and the
judges of the inferior courts by Congress. 1 Farrand, *Records* 127, 233. Nor is
the provision to be explained on the theory that it was necessary in order to
qualify the power, as it is qualified in the final Constitution, by participation of
the Senate—this came later. In short, the appointive power, even as it affects
executive officers, was not deemed an incident of executive power, but as a
specific power; and a suggestion to the contrary effect by Madison was ignored.
Secondly, in providing for the appointive power the Convention doubtless
thought that it was also providing for the removal power. This would have been
harmonious with the theory of the early state constitutions, as we have seen; and
also with practice under the Articles of Confederation, as Chief Justice Taft
himself suggests. It is, indeed, difficult to believe that a body which thought it
necessary to make specific provision for conferring the appointive power upon
the executive, could have regarded the removal power to be an incident of
executive power. On this point Hamilton in the *Federalist* was expressing no
merely individual view. But, thirdly, it is about as clear as such things can be that
the Convention did not regard the opening clause of Article II as constituting a
grant of powers. The issue which this clause was designed to settle was whether

there was to be a plural or single executive; and as it came from the Convention in the first place, and afterwards from the Committee of Detail, it read as follows: "The executive power of the United States shall be vested in a single person. His style shall be 'the President of the United States of America'; his title shall be 'His Excellency.' " 2 *id.* 171, 185, 398. The final form of the clause came from the Committee of Style, and was never separately acted upon by the Convention. There is evidence, on the other hand, of strong feeling in the Convention that the President should have a free hand in the selection of the heads of departments. In Hamilton's plan it was provided that "the Governor" should have "the sole appointment of the heads or chief officers of the Departments of Finance, War, and Foreign Affairs, and the nomination of all other officers (ambassadors to foreign nations included) subject to the approbation or rejection of the Senate." *Id.* 292. Also, it was proposed by Gouverneur Morris and seconded by Charles Pinckney that there should be a Council of State to consist, with the chief justice, of the following: a Secretary of Domestic Affairs, a Secretary of Commerce and Finance, a Secretary of Foreign Affairs, a Secretary of War, a Secretary of Marine, and a Secretary of State, all to be "appointed by the President during pleasure." The proposition was referred to the Committee of Detail without debate. *Id.* 342. Inasmuch as Morris and Pinckney were the two foremost champions of a strong executive, their belief that it was essential to provide specifically for the unlimited removability of the heads of departments may be fairly thought to be of some significance.

Epilogue, by Richard Loss

Corwin on Alexander Hamilton
and the President's Removal Power

CORWIN'S essay on the President's removal power concludes that in *Federalist,* no. 77, Hamilton makes the advice and consent of the Senate necessary for removals, and so the President and the Senate share the power of removal. Corwin objects that Chief Justice Taft's opinion in Myers v. United States "adduces no evidence" to support the conclusion that Hamilton later changed his opinion. More important, Corwin implies that no such evidence is available. Contrary to Corwin, the chief justice did adduce evidence in quoting from Hamilton's Pacificus letters. Hence, Corwin was incorrect in his removal power essay. By 1939 Corwin retreated to the position that "in the *Federalist* Hamilton had stated explicitly that the Senate would be associated with the President in the removal of officers, although he *seems* later to have retracted this opinion."[1] Curiously, Corwin's evidence is a quotation from Madison: "In the *Federalist,* he {Hamilton} had so explained the removal from office as to deny the power to the President. In an edition of the work at New York, there was a marginal note that 'Mr. Hamilton had changed his view of the Constitution on that point.' "[2]

It is perplexing that Corwin neither went beyond Madison's letter nor mentioned Hamilton's writings, which Corwin knew well. Madison's reference to an "edition" of the *Federalist* "at New York" is perhaps to the *Federalist, on the New Constitution . . . to which Is Added Pacificus, on the Proclamation of Neutrality . . .* (2 vols.; revised and corrected; New York: printed and sold by George F. Hopkins at Washington's Head, 1802). Madison's reference to a "marginal note" to the passage of *Federalist,* no. 77, on the removal power may be to a

1. Corwin, "The President as Administrative Chief," 1 *Journal of Politics* 17 (February 1939), reprinted in *Presidential Power and the Constitution: Essays, by Edward S. Corwin* 100 (R. Loss ed. 1976), italics added.
2. Madison, Letter to Rives, Jan. 10, 1829, 4 Madison, *Letters and Other Writings of James Madison* 5 (1865).

note in Volume 2 at 202: "This construction has since been rejected by the legislature; and it is now settled in practice, that the power of displacing belongs exclusively to the President." This note in the 1802 edition of the *Federalist,* of course, contains nothing of Madison's quotation from "an edition" of the *Federalist* "at New York," that " 'Mr. Hamilton had changed his view of the Constitution on that point.' " The authority for the note in the 1802 edition of the *Federalist,* other than the debate leading up to the "decision of 1789," is unclear and the note itself is anonymous.

The editor of the 1802 edition was evidently partial to Hamilton. The editor wrote that the *Federalist* "is principally the production of a man, whose talents and integrity render him the ornament and boast of this country: the name of Hamilton will be held in sacred respect, long after the malignant attempts which have been made to slander his fame shall have sunk, with their authors, into oblivion."[3] Whether the note on page 202 of the 1802 edition of the *Federalist* was added on the editor's own authority or whether Hamilton wrote or approved of the note is impossible to decide from the printed text. Hamilton's Pacificus I, however, puts it beyond doubt that he placed the removal power in the President. Pacificus I cites the "debate on the power of removal from office" as an "important instance" of Congress having recognized "in formal acts upon full consideration and debate," the correct understanding of Article II, namely, that with limited exceptions, which do not include the power of removal, "the executive power of the United States is completely lodged in the President."[4] Madison, writing as Helvidius, charged that Pacificus was inconsistent with *Federalist,* no. 77, on the removal power. In sum, Corwin's essay on the removal power overlooks the evidence presented by Chief Justice Taft, Pacificus I, to show that Hamilton changed his mind on the removal power. Pacificus I, rather than Madison's letter or alleged statements in "an edition" of the *Federalist* at New York, is the source that shows Hamilton's matured conclusion on the removal power. Accordingly, neither Corwin's essay on the removal power nor his 1939 correction cite the proper evidence and draw the appropriate conclusion.

The relationship of *Federalist,* no. 77, and Pacificus I raises the more important question of the relationship between *Federalist,* nos. 67–77, on executive power and the Pacificus letters. What is the comparative excellence, rank, and authority of *Federalist,* nos. 67–77, and the Pacificus letters? Tradition ranks the *Federalist* with the Declaration of Independence, the Articles of Confederation, and the Constitution itself as one of the seminal works defining the principles and practices of American politics. Tradition assigns the Pacificus letters a secondary rank, presumably because they are inferior to the *Federalist* in excellence and

---

3. 1 *Federalist* "Preface" iii (1802 ed.).

4. A. Hamilton, J. Madison, *The Letters of Pacificus and Helvidius on the Proclamation of Neutrality of 1793 (1845) with the Letters of Americanus* 11 (1976); 15 A. Hamilton, *The Papers of Alexander Hamilton* 40 (H. Syrett ed. 1969); on the difference between the manuscript and published versions of Pacificus, see R. Loss, "Introduction," *The Letters of Pacificus and Helvidius* vi (1976).

authority. Consequently, tradition decides the comparison of the *Federalist* and the Pacificus letters in all respects in favor of the *Federalist*.

The difficulties with the traditional understanding of the *Federalist* are hinted at in Justice Joseph Story's description of the *Federalist's* character and limits: "the *Federalist* could do little more than state the objects and general bearing of these powers and functions."[5] Moreover, the *Federalist* was written in important measure to influence the ratification of the Constitution. Although Hamilton wrote both *Federalist,* nos. 67-77, and the Pacificus letters, *Federalist,* nos. 67-77, are of necessity lacking in complete candor on divisive issues such as the extent of executive power. The traditional understanding overlooks the possibility that in *Federalist,* nos. 67-77, Hamilton accommodated the expression of his ideas on presidential power to the necessity of winning votes for the ratification of the Constitution. For example, the *Federalist* introduces the term "energy," one of Hamilton's favorite terms for a well-conducted executive, but then proceeds to equate energy with what one may call the minimum understanding of presidential power. The *Federalist* interprets section 1 of Article II ("The executive power shall be vested in a President of the United States of America") to settle the number or unity of the presidency and repudiates by implication the thesis that this provision is a positive grant of power. Without discussing the alternative, of which he was certainly aware, as is shown by his great speech in the Philadelphia Convention, Hamilton's *Federalist* ingeniously insinuates that presidential power is enumerated and therefore safe.

Hamilton was under no such prudential constraints when writing as Pacificus. Pacificus I, for example amends the *Federalist's* restrained idea of presidential energy, which is qualified by considerations of responsibility and safety, through the contention that with limited exceptions the entire executive power of the nation is completely lodged in the President. Pacificus discloses, contrary to the *Federalist,* that section 1 of Article II is a general grant of executive power, to be "interpreted in conformity with other parts of the Constitution, and with the principles of free government."[6] Clearly, then, Pacificus is not simply embroidery or repetition of the teaching on presidential energy in *Federalist,* nos. 67-77. Pacificus is a corrective to the *Federalist's* understandable yet distorting exaggeration of republican principles of limitation. Since Washington's Proclamation of Impartiality in 1793 (the occasion of the Pacificus letters) was not intended to be submitted to a vote, Pacificus deals soberly with the President's prerogative, understood in Locke's sense as the power to act for the public good without a law or against the letter of a law. Pacificus also treats the President's role in foreign relations and, by implication, his role in the foreign intelligence field.[7]

5. 1 J. Story, "Preface," *Commentaries* vii-viii (T. Cooley ed. (1873).
6. Washington understood the theme of the *Federalist* to be "the principles of freedom and the topics of government." 5 A. Hamilton, *The Papers of Alexander Hamilton* 207 (H. Syrett ed. 1962).
7. Can the thought of Alexander Hamilton be conscripted into the service of the modern presidency? According to Edward S. Corwin, "the modern theory of presidential power" is "the con-

Nor did Hamilton dismiss the Pacificus letters as an occasional writing of no permanent importance in comparison to the *Federalist*. Douglass Adair reminds us that "Hamilton insisted on the republication of his 'Letters of Pacificus' in the 1802 edition of the *Federalist*" itself.[8] Indeed, Hopkins, the publisher of the 1802 edition of the *Federalist*, told Hamilton's son that "the letters of Pacificus were added at your father's suggestion; and corrected with his own hand. He remarked to me at the time; that 'some of his friends had pronounced them to be his best performance.' "[9] Were the Pacificus letters perhaps a better performance

---

tribution primarily of Alexander Hamilton." E. S. Corwin, ed., *The Constitution of the United States of America: Analysis and Interpretation*, Sen. Doc. 170, 82nd Cong., 2nd Sess., at 381 (1953). Let us turn briefly to Hamilton's understanding of government before comparing it to an authoritative exposition of the modern theory of presidential power. On the subject of prerogative, Hamilton opposed the thesis that a king and by implication an executive must not give up his authority: "A false sentiment; it would often be praiseworthy in a prince to relinquish part of an excessive prerogative to establish a more moderate government better adapted to the happiness or temper of his people!" 1 A. Hamilton, *The Papers of Alexander Hamilton* 396 (H. Syrett ed. 1961). According to Hamilton's son, who had an unrivalled understanding of his father's writings, Hamilton stood for "free, vigorous, yet moderate government." John C. Hamilton, "Historical Notice," *Federalist* cxxxvii (J. C. Hamilton ed. 1864). "To him nothing was more distasteful than an irregular and unnecessary exercise of power. Order working by its proper means to secure and enlarge the sphere of order, was all his favorite thought—moderation in the selection and use of means, his favorite practice." *Id.* xxix. An example of Hamilton's moderation is his advice to George Washington: ". . . the members of the Senate should also have a right of *individual* access [to the President] on matters relative to the *public administration.*" The Senate's relationship to the President in treaties and nominations makes the Senators the President's "constitutional counsellors and gives them a *peculiar* claim to the right of access." Hamilton to Washington, May 5, 1789, 5 A. Hamilton, *The Papers of Alexander Hamilton* 337 (H. Syrett ed. 1962), italics in the original. Hamilton's classical search for balance and moderation disappears with, for example, Woodrow Wilson's injection of romanticism and sentiment into the idea of government and the presidency. Wilson teaches that the "personal force of the President is perfectly constitutional to *any* extent to which he chooses to exercise it." W. Wilson, *Constitutional Government in the United States* 71 (1921; 1908), italics added. "The President is at liberty, both in law and in conscience, to be as big a man as he can. His capacity will set the limit." Wilson, *Constitutional Government* 70.

An authoritative exposition makes it clear that the modern theory of presidential power pays little attention to freedom and moderation and is therefore of a piece with Wilson's but essentially opposed to Hamilton's understanding of government and the presidency: "Our constitutional law and theory today ascribes to the President an indefinite range of 'inherent' powers, places these beyond the reach of congressional curtailment, enables the President to receive and exercise delegated legislative powers of indefinite range, and attributes to him alone all nonjudicial discretion which either the Constitution or the laws of Congress permit." E. S. Corwin, *The Twilight of the Supreme Court* 147 (1934). The modern theory of presidential power is based on an inflation of Theodore Roosevelt's stewardship theory, according to which presidential power "was limited only by specific restrictions and prohibitions appearing in the Constitution or imposed by Congress under its constitutional powers." T. Roosevelt, *An Autobiography* 388–89 (1913), quoted in Corwin, *Twilight of the Supreme Court* 139. "It would follow," continues the exposition of the modern theory of presidential power, "that if and when Congress lacked the constitutional power to do something in the public interest, its deficiency would become a mandate to the 'executive power' to do it; nor, obviously, would executive action taken on this premise be subject to congressional control." The modern theory of presidential power, which I have elsewhere called the idea of the dominant presidency, is a drastic and dangerous oversimplification when measured against Hamilton's complex trinity of "free, vigorous, yet moderate government."

8. D. Adair, *Fame and the Founding Fathers* 73 (1964).

9. "Historical Notice," *Federalist* xcii (John C. Hamilton ed. 1892); on the relationship of

than Hamilton's papers in the *Federalist?* Hopkins related that Hamilton "did not regard" the *Federalist* "with much partiality." "He seemed indeed to doubt" whether a revised edition of the *Federalist* was "desirable."[10] Hamilton's opinion of the *Federalist* is reflected in Hopkins' report that "when Hamilton hesitated his consent [to a revised edition of the *Federalist*], that he remarked to him, *'Heretofore* I have given the people *milk;* hereafter I will give them *meat;'* words indicating his formed purpose—to write a treatise upon government."

Douglass Adair concludes that "Hamilton was intensely proud of Pacificus, not because it was better written than Publius [the *Federalist*], but because, pragmatically speaking, it had worked to keep the United States neutral in 1793 and could still be used for the same purpose in 1802.'"[11] An alternative conclusion, supported by the above considerations, is that Hamilton was intensely proud of the Pacificus letters because they were better and more deeply reasoned than the *Federalist*. That is, Hamilton understood the Pacificus letters to be superior in excellence and authority to *Federalist,* nos. 67–77, on executive power. The Pacificus letters are a midpoint between the *Federalist* and the unwritten treatise on government that Hamilton saw with his mind's eye. If *Federalist,* nos. 67–77, are the antechamber, the Pacificus letters are the interior of Hamilton's teaching on presidential power.

---

printings of the *Federalist* and the Pacificus and Helvidius letters, see R. Loss, "Introduction," *The Letters of Pacificus and Helvidius* xiv (1976).

10. "Historical Notice," *Federalist* ciii (John C. Hamilton ed. 1892).

11. D. Adair, *Fame and the Founding Fathers* 73.

Table of Cases

379

Index

Corwin on the
Constitution

Designed by G. T. Whipple, Jr.
Composed by The Composing Room of Michigan, Inc.
in 10 point VIP Times Roman, 2 points leaded,
with display lines in Times Roman.
Printed offset by Thomson-Shore, Inc.
on Warren's Number 66 Text, 50 pound basis.
Bound by John H. Dekker & Sons
in Holliston book cloth
and stamped in Kurz-Hastings foil.

Library of Congress Cataloging in Publication Data

CORWIN, EDWARD SAMUEL, 1878–1963.
    The foundations of American constitutional
and political thought, the powers of Congress, and
the President's power of removal.

    (His Corwin on the Constitution; v. 1)
    Includes index.
    1. United States—Constitutional history.
2. United States. Congress—Powers and duties.
3. Political science—United States—History.
I. Loss, Richard. II. Title.
JA38.C67 1981, vol. 1 [JK31] 342.73s 81-450
ISBN 0-8014-1381-8 [342.73′029] AACR1